GOD'S FINAL EPISTLE
TO THE
CHRISTIAN CHURCH

GOD'S FINAL EPISTLE

TO THE

CHRISTIAN CHURCH

*"What the assemblies fail
to teach you out of the Bible"*

STEVEN B RIDDLEY

"Your story is our priority"

LitPrime Solutions
East Brunswick Office Evolution
1 Tower Center Boulevard, Ste 1510
East Brunswick, NJ 08816
www.litprime.com
Phone: 1-800-981-9893

Published by LitPrime Solutions: 12/11/2024

ISBN: 979-8-88703-446-1(sc)
ISBN: 979-8-88703-445-4(hc)
ISBN: 979-8-88703-447-8(e)

Library of Congress Control Number: 2024922053

CONTENTS

OPENING INTRODUCTION

As a proper opening to these chronicles, containing the four stages of growth to spiritual maturity; Our origin **History,** The **Doctrine of law & Grace,** and **Prophecies,** and the **Hidden Mysteries** to the last generations, held to be revealed at the end of man's time to rule on Earth. This book is a simple walk through the bible for all who want to know the truth that will deliver you and set you free. This is to inform you of what Satan never wanted you to know. This topic-to-topic walk through the bible is what I was removed from the present church assembly to be taught by the Holy Spirit to see what we all have been ever learning but have not come to the knowledge of what God will require of all whose hope is to live with him for eternity with him. God has now appointed this time to get our attention through worldwide chaos that no man can change, the beginning of a new time continuum.

The repeat of history

Now under grace and truth we will repeat history at the end of another age. The Christian assemblies in their divisions, are far removed from the doctrine of Jesus Christ where they can't recognize his voice of warning them to repent. They have been told God does not raise up prophets like those in the Old Testament in this age. Therefore, without the vision of their times, only those given ears to hear will be saved while the others will be judged along with the world they refuse to leave behind. As I have found under this anointing, there's nothing new under the sun; history is just being repeated in another time, another age, and another dispensation as we come to the end of another stage of a new time continuum as the world is being prepared to enter the seventh millennium. This is a walk through the bible to see what it is to be ever learning and never come to the knowledge of the truth.

OBSERVATIONS OF A MESSENGER

God's Final Epistle to The Christian Church

"What the assemblies fail to teach you out of the Bible"

A short introductory version of God's Final Epistle observed and revealed through one of His messenger

These two short publications are introductions to this book which is a final end time epistle to all given ears to hear what the Holy Spirit has to say as man's final warning.

These seventeen edicts of our state are what will cause history to be repeated throughout times, ages, and dispensations, showing how we have forgotten what we confess to represent. If God did not let his chosen people into the promise land by their disobedience who lived in slavery for four hundred years, enter the promise land for forgetting all he had done to show he is the God that delivers you from oppression and supplies all your needs has not changed, we have. We are about to repeat history in this great apostacy where he will have mercy on some of our children and save them to take your place at the marriage supper when we are raptured this time, heaven is our promise land.

1. Because of this fact, there's only **"one lord, one faith and one baptism"**. (Ephesians 4 verse 5) This book is an inside view of what God see is our state as a confessing body that name his name but don't know their state of apostasy nor what spirit they are of by the fruit.

2. This is another fact; many identify themselves with some form of religion they believe in. Those that have been educated under mostly seminary trained pastors will say what denomination they believe in. This tells you what doctrine you were influence by as having more than one form of religions.

3. Under the 501c-3 government mark of the beast system, the third six of the natural order, without your knowledge, you are a state-run religious corporation that will be overseen and control by your own willing ignorance to submit to government oversite of what God gave you the power to oversee, will keep you carnal under their rule while confessing to be spiritual.

4. In our present state of apostasy, the church assembly is a place of formal practical logical theology teaching sessions whose doctrine centers around denominational or non-denominational practical bible beliefs as an application of what the bible means to them.

5. Each denomination represents another twisted form of the apostle's doctrine, teaching in part truth and principals but not the whole council of the five-fold ministry that brings deliverance and fruit that remain as in the early church assembly.

6. These errors in the application of the doctrine of Christ, caused these great divisions in the interpretation of the bible. Most seminary trained leaders, are trained to work for God instead of working with him. (Mark 16:20) They without knowing put the Holy Ghost in the pew to build their mega earthly kingdoms as leaders, presenting a structured order where-in they speak for him.

7. These new doctrinal teachings, introduced by seminary trained ministers, does not require a deep conviction, nor standard of holiness in the application of these bible principals that does not require salvation to cause you to prosper in your own way.

8. This doctrine, under Christianity, teach faith principals as to be godly is to gain. This also is the sign that we have become a Nicolaitan type operation under the influence of these renown noble academic theologians that now is seen as the Laodicean church body in these end times.

9. The 501c-3 mark has created family-owned religious run corporations in the name of God in America, taking advantage of your lack of knowledge by obligating you to pay a tithe to them that was only applicable under the Jewish nation system as a separate nation unto God. This was their tax as a nation to support the sovereignty of its existence. Under the new covenant, Christ in you is the gift that's more precious than silver, or gold. Therefore, to have him in you, you are a joint air to all he has created, by restoring you back to your Adamite state as a new creature. All your needs are met in him as was Adam's. You will not have to beg. Satan in the crossover from law to grace, cause us to error by using the Jewish tithes system. There's no deliverance that last as seen in the early church when we come together. Therefore, it has become a corporate religious assembly, run by this renown seminarian trained theologians that rob you in the name of God to support their family kingdom building legacies here on earth.

10. What the church has fail to see, under the new covenant, Christ gave the Earth back to every believer when he became a new creature. That is a faith statement that is proved by working with him. Satan has the title deed, but you own the land. The introduction of new doctrines, many are being taught to live for this world and not the world to come. That's why we see by their actions what type of faith they have been taught.

11. The true message has been lost in religious confusion by having more than one interpretation of who is the right God. Therefore, tribulation is the only way we will see the only God of creation, come to the rescue of those that know him.

12. The God that met Abraham, Moses and all the others we read about in the bible, is the only God that shows his witness as in the fruit of his spirit as being one, when there's divisions; God has departed. The

bible is his road map of instructions for our learning to be taught the interpretation, meaning and context by the Holy Spirit who wrote it.

13. To be educated by the Holy Spirit from above, you must be born from above. The Holy Spirit is God's mind that lives in heaven; therefore, your mind will be in heavenly places in Christ Jesus that opened the portal to be born from above.

14. The influence of the Catholic seminary system kept the church carnal by introducing pagan gods and traditions that made the church unacceptable among those who keep these practices while confessing to be a Christian assembly. This also is a sign you don't know the God you serve.

15. In the book of Galatians 5:19-21, we see seventeen sins as outlined in the KJV that will be what will cause 98 percent of the confessing Christian church to miss heaven by presenting a hypocritical view as parents and be replace by their children by being guilty of these unconfessed sins in their lives. Satan has a black book to write these sins in against you if you don't confess them before you die. He will justify taking your soul with him to hell. Most of us were taught about the fruit of the spirit while not being delivered from some of these sins of our old ways, has kept you defiled before God by lack of knowledge of these sins of omission. Ninety-eight percent of the confessing Christian community are guilty of many of these sins as I was being taught a once save always saved doctrine. Many will be guilty in the judgment by not knowing what spirit you are of.

16. The reason why many will be rejected as those that left Egypt that did not survive the wilderness experience is because of this fact; we all have fallen into Apostacy. We can no longer recognize the voice of the God in the name of Christianity you say you serve. Jesus stood before his own who had to study the Torah for thirty years before they could touch it. They forgot what the scriptures said about him and his works and therefore, killed him in the name of God by not recognizing him as their Messiah, standing in their presence.

Finally

17. This book is written as a last warning before we see a repeat of history.

I have had theologians to tell me, God does not talk to men like he did to Enoch anymore, if he had not given me that experience, I probably would believe that too. As a messenger raised up by God, I also have experienced rejections of what it is, not to know God's voice when he is speaking through these messengers. God has not changed the way he operates. Too much education from carnal minded teachers caused seminary trained theologians to be taught in error of the doctrine he is to represent. That was the plan of the Catholic seminary system they instituted to penetrate Christianity from the pulpits of these religious assemblies they brought under the 501c-3 system. The endgame will cause Christianity to become the great whore, as these men become Popes in the pulpits of their assemblies seduced with the spirit of sodomy from the Catholic church and caused us as a declared Christian nation to legalize it. Therefore, ensuring our destruction as never to be found again as the Babylon of old fate. (Rev. 18:21) Without any holiness among them, seduce their followers into a form of godliness as they will embrace all forms of seducing spirits by lowering God's standard of holiness. (Hebrews 12:14) Satan has become its spiritual leader by not knowing what spirit they have become by the fruit. This is what it is to be educated in religions without being called by God. When I was called in question about my credentials for speaking these truths, I was put out from among them for trying to be like Christ. In my deep convictions as called to speak the unadulterated truth, I have experience what those I read about in the bible before me, not as though I have arrived … *John 15:20 "(KJV)* [20] *Remember the word that I said unto you, the servant is not greater than his lord. If they have persecuted me, they will also persecute you; if they have kept my saying, they will keep yours also."* Now may the God of the descendants of Abraham and all the others that died to bring us these words only God can speak, be with you and grant you his peace and understanding. AMEN

The Author

INTRODUCTION TO
THE SPIRIT WORLD

(The Enoch type observations of an
end time messenger of our times)

Biblical background:

Hebrews 13:2 "(KJV) [2] **Be not forgetful to entertain strangers: for thereby some have entertained angels unawares."** The purpose of this book is to bring us all to the knowledge of the truth. This is a walk through the bible, made simple to all with ears to hear and understand.

In the year 2004, I had what I would be determine in my mind, the beginning of a Pauline revelation or a burning bush experience in what would become an Amos type messenger to the last generation. I did not fully comprehend the full scope of what I was about to undergo in receiving a revelation that was withheld to be revealed to this last generation. What I was experiencing in my mind was a transformation to understand what I could never comprehend until I was driven into the word for God to reveal himself to me as **"THE GREAT I AM"** over time.

The brothers I was associated with at that time, I knew I could not tell them what I was being made to see. It was like I was being held back from revealing or sharing what I was being made to see. This in time led to my being separated by God from all that would interfere with what he was about to reveal to me. He would become the source of all I need to know. Since I could not share it with anyone that would understand these deeper revelations at that level. What I was hearing from the Holy Spirit was not being taught in the pulpits across this nation.

What I gathered; this is what the church world fails to see by rejecting the God sent messengers with the vision of our future. My first experience was when I was sent all over the state of Arizona to warn pastors, I saw the state of the present church that represents their rejection of these unknown messengers. Out of 153 churches, only four received us as messengers from God; that was my wake-up call. After this, for the next seven years in my private prayer time, I would sit in a state of meditation for hours and hear the Holy Spirit speaking to me in a clear voice in my mind, things that no man was speaking about to this degree. I began writing them down and after seven years, the topical subjects are things we need to know to complete our understanding and spiritual stability in our walk with Christ. He did not send anyone to edit these writings, he was going to be my teacher because this is not from man but God. He just said, *"This is for those I have given ears to hear it."*

I have self-published the first layer in several books; however, this final layers of the twos and threes are what you will read in this final legacy edition, I have combined and rewritten in this third edition in the form of chronicles under the title; **"Times Ages and Dispensations,"** *(A world in Chaos)"* What Confessing Christian's need to know. My inspiration is from the leading of the Holy Spirit to those that have been given ears to hear what the spirit has to say to this end time generation as one of its messengers.

This introduction to you, the reader, is a present-day revelation of what I now see as our future. This is what has been so difficult to get the church to see as to what the prophets foretold of this time now being revealed to this generation. **Amos 3:7 "(KJV)** [7] **Surely the Lord GOD will do nothing, but he revealeth his secret unto his servants the prophets. Ephesians 3:5 (KJV)** [5] **Which in other ages was not made known unto the sons of men, as it is now revealed unto his holy apostles and prophets by the Spirit.'** This shall be a repeat of history as in the days of Noah. Our message to those in America, raised up to be the protector of Israel. We have turned against that covenant that kept us from foreign invasion. Now we will now be invaded by a foreign country that will lead us into captivity and then

God will rain down the curse of fire as in Sodom and Gomorrah on us to where we will never exist again as the Modern-day Babylon. This is what will bring in the new time continuum, the seventh and final millennium of God's timeline.

Now the mystery begins

When I watch the news, I see what you don't see. You are being controlled by an AI medium that has already taken us over through mind controlling algorisms introduced through the **internet** and the **Apple smart phone** technologies. Eight out of ten phones are Apple's by products. The chronicle that explains the details in the book; **"The Mystery of the Mark of the Beast."** As I have said, these messages are on-going.

I watch my news from a world-wide point of view and other noteworthy outlets. Since my view of things is in, interpreting just enough to keep those with ears to hear and eyes to see with a vision of things on the horizon to watch for that you might save yourself from the wickedness of these times that would eventually destroy us all if God was not in charge. Biblically, we have reached the point of no return, as in time for us is no more, that … **Matthew 24:19-21 (KJV)** [19] **And woe unto them that are with child, and to them that give suck in those days!** [20] **But pray ye that your flight be not in the winter, <u>neither on the sabbath day:</u>** [21] **For then shall be great tribulation, such as was not since the beginning of the world to this time, no, nor ever shall be."** Read the chronicle: **"During the Tribulation Siege."** Tribulation is God having to rise out of his sabbath rest to judge the world.

Mankind has entered the forbidden zone of knowledge that caused the flood. He can now replace himself with an AI body that is controlled by an extension of his own mind. He without the ability to control the temptations of the spirits that is within him, in the form of angelic beings, using our bodies, will enter the forbidden zone of knowledge. He will make himself a prisoner of his own mind that will bring about his own extinction as a human being if God did not intervene. This is due to the return of the two factions of angels at war in the spirit world, manifested as angels among us, disguised as human beings. Nephilim DNA, converging to develop these technologically advanced off springs of their DNA in what is now concentrated in three areas of the world, Russia, China and the United States.

The spirits controlling this are what is attempting to reduce the human footprint in the world as attempting to create an earthly version of a heavenly utopia through these carrying the geek technology strands, illuminated with heavenly DNA. This is what's happening in the spirit world among these unseen angels at war for the control of the world. This is what Daniel could not describe in **Daniel 12:4,** and John could not reveal in **Rev. 10:4.** This is where this verse in the bible that reads ... **Matthew 24:22 (KJV)** [22] **And except those days should be shortened, there should no flesh be saved: but for the elect's sake those days shall be shortened.** "**The Mystery of the Seven Thunders.**" What is happening among these illuminated ones or illuminati's as they are called; they are assembling their linage of geek hackers and techno nerd residues together in this war for superior technological advances that will create chaos through cyber war first, then begin to eliminate the use of certain sectors of this society, by robotic human replacements, no longer needed by creating conditions that lead to population reduction. This period will be noted by the signs.

These are they being used in this window of opportunity, is that short time period, God is in charge, to allow them this time to fulfill all these things that is now a mystery to those in the dark that are being led to their own destruction. Those with residues of their DNA, will use hi-tech-biological warfare targeted to reduce the human population. This can be traced back to those German scientists we were told to destroy. They are the **deep state** operatives whose fundings, can be traced back to our CIA government's covert secret Opps divisions.

Now you see why there is so much activity going on in the world that has kept the masses in the dark until one morning you will wake up to a total change here in America, you are not prepared to accept. This patriot movement consisting of blind confessing Christians, led into their entrapment as was Barabbas in his days that were exposed in the insurrection on Jan. 6, 2020, that took place in the capital. That was the repeat of the return of the Barabbas patriot spirit released by Pilate. You can see History being repeated in these hidden mysteries. Read the chronicle titled: "**The Return of the Barabbas Patriot.**" All is spiritual under grace and truth.

The level of this generation's darkness is due to being controlled by your AI devices that have succeeded in reducing your attention span to bring you under control by lack of knowledge until that day. These media algorisms are designed to link your mind to the AI seduction apps, linked to your smart phone that will have you … **2 Timothy 3:7 (KJV)** [7] **Ever learning, and never able to come to the knowledge of the truth.** The evidence of your seduction is the time you spend on it feeding your mind to a state of confusion through information overload. Many of you have started ministries of information that have the tail end of the activities, have become confused by not being led by the Holy Spirit in your search. **Many of you are also been ever learning but have not come to the knowledge of the truth.** Your ministry for some of you is your means of entanglement that takes God's place in your life. Many Christian parents in their unbelief, practiced hypocrisy before their children, God will have mercy on your children for misrepresenting what you confess to be. His mercy will cause many of them to be saved to take your place if you do not repent from the error of your ways. Read the chronicle; **"Who are the Children of Disobedience."**

These hi-tech spiritual strongholds are primarily located in China and America. This is what we gave them in our corporate greed to take advantage of their cheap labor force. God could have given the world an extension if we as the lead nation had not given this technology to China out of greed for more wealth to an enemy that will use it to develop their infrastructure and then turn and destroy you with your own technology with the warring faction of angels in the Gog ruled nations. Here in America, known as the silicon district, where all these algorisms are written that will bring about this sudden change is converging, they will confront the Gog sect in a hacking contest. They don't want to destroy America; they are trying to gain control through this technology first before they resort to out-rite world war.

Now both sects of these angelic beings in the form of humans, are using this technology against each other. The **Me' Gog** sector of angels described in Ezekiel 38, is preparing for war that will start in Europe is controlled by Satan. They are the angelic faction whose stronghold is in the communist sisters, Russia and China. God describes their end in chapter 39. They are getting ready for the final assault we come to know as World War

Three.   This is the revelation message to the modern-day prophets and messengers, raised up by God as in the days of old, to reveal this vision to those with ears to hear and eyes to see, your eminent future to save yourself from. Now if you are one of these mockers, heartened by rejecting these messengers, this is the biblical truth that cannot be changed.

These conspiracy theorists have the tail end of some of these mysteries without the whole vision, will cause many of them to parish along with the rest of the world, being caught up in the circumstances that will lead to this tragic end. Just remember, this is the same spirit of the mockers in Noah's time when they were being warned it was going to rain. Our message to America in our time, you are about to be invaded by another nation and ultimately destroyed by fire. **Ecclesiastes 1:9 (KJV)** [9] **The thing that hath been, it** *is that* **which shall be; and that which is done** *is* **that which shall be done: and** *there is* **no new** *thing* **under the sun. AMEN**

THE COMING NEW TIME CONTINUUM

Hebrews 13:2 (ASV) [2] **Forget not to show love unto strangers: for thereby some have entertained angels unawares. Matthew 24:22 "(NKJV)** [22] **And unless those days were shortened, no flesh would be saved; but for the elect's sake those days will be shortened."** This will be the second stage of earth's tribulation.

I dedicated a day to meditation and prayer and fasting just to keep my mind in a ready channel to receive the thoughts of the Great "I AM." Since I have learned to see God in all things, is where I saw the revelation of his ways are past our level of comprehension. This is a whole new dimension that opens the portal of heaven that cause you to receive heavenly thoughts in the spirit world that explains why we must walk by faith. Those who receive these thoughts will be distinguished by the fruit. It is hard for me not to lament at the level of deception by an enemy many have never come to know that only God can restrain the activity of. Now he is in every soul at birth. Satan assigns a spirit being to operate in your temple at your birth. As I have been told by some who have read some of my chronicles, it's like having an Enoch experience in these modern times before the end comes; telling those given ears to hear what they need to know to save themselves from as in the days of Noah.

There's no escape until God calls you or you cry out to him for deliverance of your soul from the torment of living in sin. **John 6:44 (NKJV)** [44] **No one can come to Me unless the Father who sent Me draws him; and I will raise him up at the last day.** Now what I am about to tell you, represent some of my Enoch moments in meditation. The warfare for souls in the spirit world is between God and Satan, because of the law of sin and death. Cain was Satan's child and Abel God's child. This is where the war will begin in the natural world in man in his fallen state. This is who you are between the two spiritual powers manifested in this natural world in the battle for your soul. In your sin state, Satan will cause you to believe you are your own God; that is to say, you don't believe in God while he believes and tremble because he knows that the lake of fire is his ultimate destiny. Your thoughts are either from God or the devil because your body came from the natural earth, but your soul and life came from God, he cannot be killed. Hell was created for Satan and his angels and when Adam and Eve acted on the words of a condemned angel, we are all now born his children.

You are a piece of clay God spit on and molded out of that clay his image. He put within this mass of clay his spirit, his soul and his life. Adam represents what God look like in heaven. Now, he can be seen in the natural world as Adam in the earth. This will give you some insight into His image as to why the New Testament's message is death to the flesh for God to be seen in your body as a spirit man that has been restored to a new version of Adam. Whether you believe in him or not, he created you from Adam.

His son Jesus Christ paid the price to free us from the curse of the law of sin and death, under which, we all were born. Jesus became the slain lamb predestined in God's master plan to recover the earth through man after his fall. It will take three-time continuums to completely restore the state of Eden.

That's the message of the New Testament to instruct us through his elects, how to conform to his image, as being restored examples back to Adam's state of dominion to walk in this short span of life in the natural with your creator as he is for eternity. **1 John 3:2 "(NKJV)** [2] **Beloved, now we are children of God; and it has not yet been revealed what we shall be, but we know that when He is revealed, we shall be like Him, for we shall see Him as He is."**

You were created to live for eternity with God and his host of angels. God gave Adam a free will to choose without knowing the reality of a hell that was created for those fallen angels that rebelled with Satan. All he had to do was listen to the voice of God and live by every word that came from his mouth that keep him in union as one with his creator. **Matthew 4:4 "(NKJV) ⁴ But He answered and said, "It is written, *'Man shall not live by bread alone, but by every word that proceeds from the mouth of God.'* " John 17:22 (NKJV) ²² And the glory which You gave Me I have given them, that they may be one just as We are one:"**

When Eve acted on the voice of Satan as a condemned angel; she, at that moment became his child. He entered her soul by her own free will when she was told not to go near or to touch that tree of forbidden fruit. The fruit of that tree was curse and was set there as a test of their free will to remain loyal to their creator by hearing his voice only. That was a test of their free will they were unaware of until they sinned. That's why our mind will have to be renewed to get back to that state. **Romans 12:2 "(NKJV) ² And do not be conformed to this world, but be transformed by the renewing of your mind, that you may prove what *is* that good and acceptable and perfect will of God." 1 Corinthians 2:16 (NKJV) ¹⁶ For "who has known the mind of the LORD that he may instruct Him?" But we have the mind of Christ. Romans 8:9 (NKJV) ⁹ But you are not in the flesh but in the Spirit, if indeed the Spirit of God dwells in you. Now if anyone does not have the Spirit of Christ, he is not His."**

When Adam yield to Eve's suggestion to partake, Satan used her voice to talk through her to get him to partake, her disobedience by eating the forbidden fruit, likewise, he became a willing partaker to her sin and likewise received the same curse. At that time, they became co-conspirators with Satan that turned them against God. This is what they will discover in their fallen state. **Genesis 3:9-15 "(NKJV) ⁹ Then the LORD God called to Adam and said to him, "Where *are* you?" ¹⁰ So he said, "I heard Your voice in the garden, and <u>I was afraid because I was naked</u>; and I hid myself." ¹¹ And He said, "<u>who told you that you *were* naked?</u> Have you eaten from the tree of which I commanded you that you should not eat?" ¹² Then the man said, <u>"The woman whom You gave *to be* with me, she gave me of the tree, and I ate."</u> ¹³ And the LORD God said to the woman, "What *is* this you have done?" The woman said, "The serpent deceived** me, and I ate." ¹⁴ So the LORD God said to the serpent: "Because you have done this, you *are* cursed more than all cattle, and more than every beast of the field; On your belly you shall go, And you shall eat dust All the days of your life. ¹⁵ And I will put enmity Between you and the woman, and between your seed and her Seed; (Interpretation) There will be a difference in your seeds and my seeds.

My seeds will have the power to keep your seeds under their feet through my son whom I will send to save them from you by his power when he has taken the keys to life and death from you and give to my children. **He shall bruise your head, and you shall bruise His heel."** Birthing children will become a traumatic experience as he enters a world of sin. "*Man, born in his sins state, will have six-thousand years to regain his rule over you. Because of the evils unleased into the world, this war for souls will continue in stages of times, ages and dispensations until he reaches the sixth millennium. I will send prophets and messengers during this time to keep my people I have given ears to hear, the vision to follow for their time. Those that hear them will make their calling and election sure and be added to my kingdom in heaven. The earth is about to go through another travail of epic proportions at a time when many are caught up among those in the great fall away, unaware of their time. Though I will give them many signs, that 98% in that delusion, will perish as in the days of Noah by rejecting my messengers.*" (The above is one of my Enoch moments, therefore you be the judge of what's being said.)

There were things illuminated in my mind that I cannot put in print because your hearts will lose hope, seeing the other side of God in your present state of not being fully spiritually aware of. These are some of the horrors of the **Seven Thunders** John was told not to write down in Rev. 10:4 that the wicked will face in the cross-over of the new time continuum. This book is a chronicled volume of the things God wanted to share with his children throughout the times until the end of days. The battle in the spirit world against the doctrine of the New Testament, prevented on a large scale, by doctrines that brought divisions and traditions of men, contributed to the great fall away of the church. We are now at the end of days and about to face these scenarios leading up to the end of man's time to rule on earth. One thing the seminary institutions did, removed holiness from the assemblies. Therefore, **Hebrews 12:14 (KJV)** ¹⁴ **Follow peace with all *men*, and holiness, without which no man shall see the**

Lord: This is what we have come to see on a worldwide scale because of many divisions.

1. The threshold of forbidden knowledge in the hands of evil men, if God did not intervene, we are now on the brink of extinction.

2. In the past decade, we have seen increases in natural disasters as a direct result of climate change, contributing to diverse weather patterns all over the world. The original latitudes from Noah's time are being restored in the earth. That's contributing to climate changes that have now become the signs of this time.

3. The mass migration is a result of wars and rumor of wars, famine and overpopulation in some arears of the world where conditions of extreme poverty and the will to survive.

4. Hi tech mind controlling AI devices have caused the love of many to wax cold, contributing to a rapid increase in crimes against humanity.

5. There will be new disease strains with no known cure readily available. This forbidden technology in the hands of a powerful few will be used to reduce the world's population by being exposed to newly created biotechnology virus strains, linked to your DNA of which we have no immunity or cure, over time will cause multisystem failure. That's the new type warfare funded by the elites.

6. Foreign Governments will begin to collapse after the fall of America. There will be no monetary resources available to change these conditions. These are the biblical prophecies being fulfilled at the hand of God to save the world from extinction at the hands of men possessed with this strain of Nephilim DNA that has returned in man that caused the flood. Russia and China are the most powerful military threat to the world that God will use to bring the tribulation conditions of World War Three to end mankind's rule on earth.

7. God's mission at this time is to prepare his people that will be used to glorify himself as the only God of this world by cutting short time to extract or rapture his glorified saints, purified in the fires of tribulation, cleanse the earth of all mankind that has polluted it through evil running its course that brought us to this end. Time is no more. America's judgment cannot be changed.

Thus is a fitting introduction to what you are about to read from one of his end time messengers. This book details the revelations of history, doctrine and prophecy of the horrible end to those that have been given over to the devil to punish those without ears to hear and eyes to see **"What the Church has Fail to reveal to them.**

These chronicles are not to be read as a sequential book story. Each Chronicle stands alone as an answer to questions about bible truth over a seven-year period. Search among these chronicles to find the biblical answer to a question relevant to the revelation of mysteries to these truths, locked in the Holy Bible for those who seek, ask and knock through a surrendered mind. AMEN

All scriptures are taken from KJV, NKJV, NTL 2nd edition, ASV, NASB77 and ESV are used by permission within the guidelines as permitted by the publishers.

The Author's background:

After graduating from high school, I was trained and educated at **Sloan Kettering Institute** (NYC) where I became a Bord certified Medical Technologist, specializing in diagnostic Histology. (M.T. H.T. PA., (ASCP) from 1962-1972. I later trained in forensic autopsy science where I found God had gifted me with the knowledge of the working functions of the human body where I spent the later part of my career assisting in training resident pathologist in the art of medical and forensic autopsy procedures until God retired me from **Barrow Neurological Institute** in Phoenix, Arizona in December of 2004.

The foundation for deep thought:

Throughout time and history, we, as human beings created in the image of

God have been walking blind men as children of the devil. The enemies of our souls have by deceit, cause us to think of ourselves more than what we really are. Our ignorance comes from not seeking the real meaning of this life we have been given a privilege to live.

Why is it with all our good intensions, many of us end up in bondage to each other and things that cannot speak or hear? Could it be that in our thinking, our deception is from an unknown enemy from within, destroying us by lack of knowledge? I really cannot fully comprehend the full scope of what I have been given ears to hear straight from our creator's mind. Mankind from the day Adam sinned against his creator; has become an accident waiting to happen at some point in his life so God can get his attention.

We are born with a desire to pursue knowledge; the trouble is, our choices in the pursuit. Our world is flooded with an unlimited number of books on subjects of whatever comes to the mind of a man. Now you know the meaning of the term **"Authors of confusion."** Therefore, I have chosen not to use my own thoughts. You see, I have found the source of all truth and knowledge as to the answer to why I do not have to rely on my thoughts anymore.

The mystery of life has us all defeated at birth; being born in sin, we just choose not to believe it. What I am attempting to share with you in these chronicles is what we all have failed to see except for a few, born as elects to preserve God's presents in the earth.

God is the only source of truth that leads to living for eternity because he is the giver of life. Many have been entrusted to ministers as vessels to communicate this truth to mankind created in his image as to the reason why we were born.

Have you ever pondered the question, what's beyond the end of my life? Many theologians are teaching in division, principles, and part truth without a clear understanding of who they represent, it's not about you, but the God in you that can speak for himself.

As vessels of honor and dishonor, we are just temples waiting to be used by him or the devil. I will let him communicate what we all fail to see. The reality of what we were born to be, do and serve during this short life span of our life. The authors of confusion are about to see the source of their inspiration be tested as to truth or a lie from a biblical standpoint.

I am the first to admit that we are the dumbest creatures on the face of the earth as being born in sin and die in that state. Even our pets get to rule over us as lesser creatures. This I came to see after having my "I AM" experience. What you are about to read is his last communication to man in this dispensation before he comes to reap the harvest worthy of his Son' sacrifice.

These mysteries have been hidden from us by the enemy of our souls by our willing ignorance. This is not going to be a pleasant revelation but if heeded, will become your ticket to escape into eternity with your creator in heaven or spend it with Satan and his angels in hell. The choice will be yours after you hear the truth.

What you are about to be told represent the full scope of what its' like to be tutored under blind guides that in division, taught you in part. We all are going to meet our creator in the judgment; that's when we will come face to face with our creator.

This final revelation will reveal the horrific consequences of our choices after we have been told and shown our destiny and given a choice where you want to spend your eternity. Hell is real and heaven is real; we all will be given this choice while here in the flesh and will be without excuse in the final judgment. All the prophets that brought this message before me were killed including Dr. Martin Luther King in our time and as a reminder of his sacrifice in his God given love, warned this nation of its corruption and oppression of its citizens in this nation that were also equally entitled to these freedoms.

Dr King represented the forefathers in slavery speaking from the grave, the last plea for equal justice guaranteed in the constitution they were inspired to write; to remind us that, every soul that set foot on this soil was guaranteed by God in that constitution, would be free to serve the one true God of Abraham, Isaac, and Jacob without oppression. Now we have been … **Daniel 5:27 "(NKJV)** [27] **TEKEL: You have been weighed in the balances and found wanting." AMEN**

THE AUTHOR

My Calling:

Jeremiah 33:3 (KJV) "**3** *Call unto me, and I will answer thee, and shew thee great and mighty things, which thou knowest not." Ephesians 3:5 (KJV) Which in other ages was not made known unto the sons of men, as it is now revealed unto his holy apostles and prophets by the Spirit;"*

The overview

During the seven years of 2004 to 2011, these chronicles contain the mysteries revealed to me during that time. From the beginning of time after the fall of Adam, man has not understood His purpose in life on this Earth. The unknown mysteries of life, put man on a pursuit to find answers that are already before him; not knowing his creator who has all the answers, it will be the enemy of our souls that has kept us from knowing the age-old question, what is truth?

Born in sin, many will be ever learning but never come to the knowledge of the truth until we have an encounter with God. The universal mysteries have put man in pursuit of the infinity to his own short life span and dies never to find the answer to his purpose in this natural life. Have you, the reader, ever looked upon the wonders that are in this world and asked the question? Where did it all get its origin? Is there someone out there greater than I? I have found that there are some people who believe that there is no higher intelligence than themselves. We call them atheist and men with megalomania personalities. Well, this book is about to introduce you to the reality of there is a God and at some point, in this life, you will meet Him here or in the hereafter. The fear of the unknown has caused us all without this revelation to create an imaginary world, especially in America where prosperity has become a way of life that exists in our thoughts that leads us to pursue these dreams created in our thoughts to live a life of willing ignorance. This reality block in our minds creates a false sense of reality and security that is base in material things of this world that cannot speak or hear but will control our actions by our pursuit of them. These are the idols we in the western world, that have become the cymbals of our earthly achievements that we value as a reason for living. Have you ever thought to yourself, where all these gifts to create these natural phenomena came from? Well, for seven years the God I serve has given me answers to some of these questions about man, the cosmos and planet Earth; all of which He created.

I am sure that when you read this book, the obvious signs will convince you of these realities. We all have been willing victims as participants to follow evil men as buffoons of Satan to think that we can change time against the spoken word of God in our disobedient state as a nation under a covenant with God. *Mark 8:36 (KJV)*[36] *For what shall it profit a man, if he shall gain the whole world, and lose his own soul.*

Introduction to these chronicled mysteries of the bible

One of the greatest mysteries the church has fail to see spiritually, is our state of division. The true message of the **Holy Spirit** is only seen in parts of truth and principles of faith. The real scope of the fullness of God has been sidelined in these divisions. The body must be brought back to one before Christ can return. Being in division, these mysteries were kept hidden from an apostate church to be revealed at the time of its time of judgment.

What Daniel was told not to reveal in the seals in **Daniel 12:** and John was told not to write down about the thunders in **Rev. 10:4** … what the atheist refused to believe and what the church has fail to see; the truth about our state at the time God chooses to open our eyes to the reality of why there must be a tribulation. This is the time of the end God has chosen to reveal these mysteries of why there will be no rapture before the tribulation begins. How the church has failed to see how Satan has seduced it into splinters of truth, taught in part, has led to this prophesied present-day apostasy that has a great majority in a state of not knowing what spirit they are of. Tribulation will open all eyes to see the other side of God's wrath that the devil has kept from them by all these new doctrines that only show God's love as in their compromised teaching of biblical principles, voided of holiness and suffering that will give you a true sense of the presence of Christ in your vessel that will not compromise truth. *2 Timothy 3:12 (ASV)* [12] *Yea, and all that would live godly in Christ Jesus shall suffer persecution.*

What has been kept from man by his own willing ignorance has cursed him as a sinner to join his father the devil for eternity in hell. The history of Israel's siege and fall as a nation from God's grace under a covenant is about to be repeated in America as this gentile nation that was blessed to be their protector under the new covenant until she is restored as a nation in the 1967 war. Forty years after will come the signs in Matthew 24, of the coming tribulation this last generation will see the inherent beastly nature of man as human beings created in the image of God begin to turn on each other as nations, as the unknown spiritual forces in the spirit world begin to show up in man's activities. All tribes, kindreds and tongues. He will do what he could never imagine he would ever become in today's western society, a bruit beast bent on self-survival that will turn on his own kind and as a last resort to survive, turn to cannibalism.

Just as there are those that believe there's no God and confessing Christians by lack of knowledge, limit the world's ability to see him in the fullness of his power as one body in the resurrected Christ ... we are now at the point where Christ himself must return to set his house back in order. History will be repeated in another Pentecost known as the latter rain. What is about to be revealed between these pages are some of my Enoch moments that in our time, represent the other side of God, in his wrath. Noted theologians will take issue with many statements within these pages. At our best academically, we are either led by God or the devil, the difference is the fruit. The academia of theology has taken the holiness out of the gospel many preach and teach which have men ... **2 Timothy 3:7 (KJV)** [7] **Ever learning, and never able to come to the knowledge of the truth.**

THE THRONE ROOM COURT OF JUDGEMENT

The beginning warfare for your mind during the Natural Man's Time on Earth.

The   Son and the Father

The Mercy Seat

1Timothy 2:5 (KJV) *⁵ For there is one God, and one mediator between God and men, the man Christ Jesus; Psalm 89:14 (KJV) ¹⁴ Justice and judgment are the habitation of thy throne: mercy and truth shall go before thy face.*

Satan's Bench

Revelation 12:10 (KJV*) ¹⁰ And I heard a loud voice saying in heaven, Now is come salvation, and strength, and the kingdom of our God, and the power of his Christ: <u>for the accuser of our brethren is cast down, which accused them before our God day and night.</u>* Satan stands before God as the prosecutor to justify his accusations based on our sins of omissions.

The Accused on the Mercy Seat

Psalm 90:8 (KJV) *⁸ Thou hast set our iniquities before thee, our secret sins in the light of thy countenance. Proverbs 10:12 (KJV) ¹² Hatred stirreth up strifes: but love covereth all sins. Psalm 103:10 (KJV) ¹⁰ He hath not dealt with us after our sins; nor rewarded us according to our iniquities.* (This is the seat of mercy for the accused on Earth.) **Revelation 8:3-4 (KJV)** *³ And* *another angel came and stood at the altar, having a golden censer; and there was given unto him much incense, that he should offer it with the prayers of all saints upon the golden altar which was before the throne.* ⁴ *And the smoke of the incense, which came with the prayers of the saints, ascended up before God out of the angel's hand.* (The intercessors prayers coming to the defense of the accused.) *John 8:7 (KJV)* ⁷ *So when they continued asking him, he lifted up himself, and said unto them, He that is without sin among you, let him first cast a stone at her. Matthew 7:5 (KJV)* ⁵ *Thou hypocrite, first cast out the beam out of thine own eye; and then shalt thou see clearly to cast out the mote out of thy brother's eye.*

How soon so many of us with well intensions neglect these simple truths. I have learned through the teachings of the Holy Spirit why none of us are able to judge; we all came from sin, cursed from our birth. God created Satan, the accuser of the brethren to perfect all whom he has chosen to live for eternity with him; therefore, *Zechariah 4:6 (KJV)* ⁶ *Then he answered and spake unto me, saying, This is the word of the LORD unto Zerubbabel, saying, Not by might, nor by power, but by my spirit, saith the LORD of hosts. Romans 8:28 (KJV)* ²⁸ *And we know that all things work together for good to them that love God, to them who are the called according to his purpose.* All scriptures are written for our learning; where we all have fallen short is seeking the teacher... *John 16:13 (KJV)* ¹³ *Howbeit when he, the Spirit of truth, is come, he will guide you into all truth: for he shall not speak of himself; but whatsoever he shall hear, that shall he speak: and he will shew you things to come.*

What God allow and permit does not have anything to do with whether you are born again because of the two wills, yours or his. God does his own choosing; therefore, it is He that seeks to save the lost not you.

John 3:5 (KJV) ⁵ *Jesus answered, Verily, verily, I say unto thee, Except a man be born of water and of the Spirit, he cannot enter into the kingdom of God. John 4:23 (KJV)* ²³ *But the hour cometh, and now is, when <u>the true worshippers</u> shall worship the Father in spirit and in truth: for <u>the Father seeketh such to worship him.</u> John 6:44 (KJV)* ⁴⁴ *No man can come to me, except the Father which hath sent me draw him: and I will raise him up at the last day. John 15:16 (KJV)* ¹⁶ *Ye have not chosen me, but I have chosen you, and ordained you, that ye should go and bring forth fruit, and that your fruit should remain: that whatsoever ye shall ask of the Father in my name,* *he may give it you.* He saves you for himself. At that time, he overturns the decision of the accuser and grants you mercy and from that time on, you are to live and walk by every word to keep the devil under your feet so... *Isaiah 54:17 (KJV)* [17] *No weapon that is formed against thee shall prosper; and every tongue that shall rise against thee in judgment thou shalt condemn. This is the heritage of the servants of the LORD, and their righteousness is of me, saith the LORD.* **1 John 4:4 (KJV)** [4] *Ye are of God, little children, and have overcome them: because greater is he that is in you, than he that is in the world.*

The devil, now become his instrument to bring you into perfection during times, ages and dispensations as God is selecting souls for his kingdom. God use him to perfect you for his use, just by keeping God's word, he cannot overtake you. Now where's our boast as though we can cast stones while we are on the mercy seat, God has Christ and someone praying in your defense, grants you mercy, reverses the devil's decision and you are kept in right standing with God to be used according to the purpose he has chosen you. The only reason we all fall short is because of false teachings coming from blind guides and hypocrites.

Matthew 23:13-16 (KJV) [13] *But woe unto you, scribes and Pharisees, hypocrites! for ye shut up the kingdom of heaven against men: for ye neither go in yourselves, neither suffer ye them that are entering to go in.* [14] *Woe unto you, scribes and Pharisees, hypocrites! for ye devour widows' houses, and for a pretence make long prayer: therefore, ye shall receive the greater damnation.* [15] *Woe unto you, scribes and Pharisees, hypocrites! for ye compass sea and land to make one proselyte, and when he is made, ye make him twofold more the child of hell than yourselves.* [16] *Woe unto you, ye blind guides, which say, whosoever shall swear by the temple, it is nothing; but whosoever shall swear by the gold of the temple, he is a debtor!*

 God cannot get any glory out of us until you are fully converted; then he uses your temple to convert and strengthen others. That's why He told Peter ... *Luke 22:32 (KJV)* [32] *But I have prayed for thee, that thy faith fail not: and <u>when thou art converted, strengthen thy brethren.</u> Matthew 18:3 (KJV)* [3] <u>*And said, Verily I say unto you, except ye be converted, and become as little children, ye shall not enter into the kingdom of heaven.*</u>

This can only happen when ...*Isaiah 55:7-8 (KJV)* [7] *Let the wicked forsake his way, and the unrighteous man his thoughts: and let him return unto the LORD, and he will have mercy upon him; and to our God, for he will abundantly pardon. ⁸ For my thoughts are not your thoughts, neither are your ways my ways, saith the LORD.* Under the new covenant, you become the sacrifice as in … *Romans 12:1-2 (KJV) ¹ I beseech you therefore, brethren, by the mercies of God, that ye present your bodies a living sacrifice, holy, acceptable unto God, which is your reasonable service. ² And be not conformed to this world: but be ye transformed by the renewing of your mind, that ye may prove what is that good, and acceptable, and perfect, will of God.*

This is what will happen when the real gospel is preached as God restores the church by walking in the fullness in you. How do we know who is born of God? *Matthew 7:16-18 (KJV) ¹⁶ Ye shall know them by their fruits. Do men gather grapes of thorns, or figs of thistles? ¹⁷ Even so every good tree bringeth forth good fruit; but a corrupt tree bringeth forth evil fruit. Matthew 7:20 (KJV) ²⁰ Wherefore by their fruits ye shall know them. Galatians 5:22-23 (KJV) ²² But the fruit of the Spirit is love, joy, peace, longsuffering, gentleness, goodness, faith, ²³ Meekness, temperance: against such there is no law.* This is the devil' fruit … *Galatians 5:19-21 (KJV) ¹⁹ Now the works of the flesh are manifest, which are these; Adultery, fornication, uncleanness, lasciviousness, ²⁰ Idolatry, witchcraft, hatred, variance, emulations, wrath, strife, seditions, heresies, ²¹ envyings, murders, drunkenness, revellings, and such like: of the which I tell you before, as I have also told you in time past, that they which do such things shall not inherit the kingdom of God."* These are the sins of omission that will keep you out of heaven that are found in confessing Christians.

If Christ is not seen in you to this degree by the world, then we are vessels being made into the image of the son. While this process is taking place, we are to rest and … *Hebrews (KJV) 4:9 therefore a rest to the people of God. Psalm 46:10 (KJV) ¹⁰ Be still and know that I am God: I will be exalted among the heathen, I will be exalted in the earth.* Therefore, we must be sent into the wilderness to meet the devil; he will be used to kill our flesh and break our will by God allowing him to put you into circumstances that he and he alone can deliver you from.

This is the teaching you will receive from the Holy Ghost when he causes you to be still and rest. This is known as the wilderness experience. Only Christ will come out when he completes your death. All of God's elect will have a wilderness experience. This is where his hidden elects are now being perfected. These are the few that are led to their death in the flesh that find him. The flesh of the old man is defiled and therefore must be destroyed by death. Read the chronicle **"Preparation for Glory."** Most of us was sent out by organized religions; therefore, the fruit will not remain when tried. That's why we cannot preach in their assemblies because you must have formal accredited credentials. That's being born from below under Satan's seduced religions. They will all operate the same way.

No sins in the flesh will be tolerated in the elects when they come out of the wilderness, so make your calling and election sure. If God is showing you the hidden things that will keep you from coming out, be ready to confess them and ask for deliverance or else you may be turned over to the devil for the destruction of the flesh because of the prayers of the saints have come to your defense. (1 Corinthians 5:5) Contrary to false teachings, the only way you will go to heaven is by God's choice not yours. *John 6:44 (KJV)* ⁴⁴ *No man can come to me, except the Father which hath sent me draw him: and I will raise him up at the last day.* We are not born with a desire to serve the lord. We are born children of the devil. (John 8:44) God in his sovereign will has chosen all who are going to heaven before the foundation of the world. *Isaiah 46:10 (KJV)* ¹⁰ *Declaring the end from the beginning, and from ancient times the things that are not yet done, saying, my counsel shall stand, and I will do all my pleasure:*

This mystery is now being revealed to his elects that were hidden from those that are lost. *2 Corinthians 4:3 (KJV)* ³ *But if our gospel be hid, it is hid to them that are lost: Matthew 22:14 (KJV)* ¹⁴ *For many are called, but few are chosen. Matthew 7:21 (KJV)* ²¹ *Not everyone that saith unto me, Lord, Lord, shall enter into the kingdom of heaven; but he that doeth the will of my Father which is in heaven.*

As one coming into the mind of God as seeing through his eyes, hearing through his ears discerning in his mind, I am not empress with any man, only the words of God. All who are born of God lives by every word that proceeds out of his mouth. He and he alone know his voice in the spirit. This is the unction John spoke about as to how we will know each other. If we are born again, we live move and have our being as surrendered vessels being made meat for the master's consumption. He is purifying our bodies to become his temple and the sweet smell of our flesh savoring in the cooker as gold be purified in the fires of tribulation, gives him great pleasure to consume when he, the master chef, has finished the meal we sacrificed to him (our bodies) willingly without hesitation will be with him for eternity.

When the word said, **"he that hath an ear let him hear,"** the spirit of the lord knows who has been given ears to hear, and eyes to see; therefore, don't go ahead of God when the word is rejected, it then become a witness against them; remember, we are just vessels to be led by the Holy Spirit. If we lose sight of who is at work, our zeal will transfer us without knowing it into the permissive will of God by being tempted to help him by not obeying.

The only one that came from heaven and can return is Jesus; therefore, he is coming back for himself, this time in you. You are an extension of him to continue his work. We are living in a time when the hidden mysteries being revealed are now for those given ears to hear and eyes to see because of the great fall away, we cannot recognize his voice of warning. *Hebrews 1:1-2 (KJV)* [1] *God, who at sundry times and in divers manners spake in time past unto the fathers by the prophets,* [2] *Hath in these last days spoken unto us by his Son, whom he hath appointed heir of all things, by whom also he made the worlds;* Many of us need a revelation of grace and mercy to prevent us from judging each other under the Nicolaitan's doctrines that have caused many splits and divisions among us. *Jeremiah 13:23 (KJV)* [23] *Can the Ethiopian change his skin, or the leopard his spots? then may ye also do good, that are accustomed to do evil. Amos 3:3 (KJV)* [3] *Can two walk together, except they be agreed?* God see man as his creations as tribes' kindred and tongues. Our fleshly minds operating outside of the will of God, have by evil, allowed these prejudices to be accepted among confessing Christians are superiority complex spirits, based on race.

When we understand the revelation of the above verse, we will see why none of us can cast stones when we all are of one man and one woman. Race, creed and color have no merit in the operation of the Holy Spirit. Grace is the time when God is walking in man to fulfill his word; that is why you will live above the law in perfect love and righteousness. *Matthew 5:17 (KJV)* [17] *Think not that I am come to destroy the law, or the prophets: I am not come to destroy, but to fulfil.*

This is the marriage of law and grace to show the world the perfect man.

Only God can produce his perfect image by affecting your death in the flesh; now the new creature can be seen that comes out of the volume of his book. God is a majority in himself, that is why he only need a few of whom he has chosen from the foundation of the world. In the great high court of heaven, Satan has justified a claim on our souls for lack of knowledge as predestined before the foundation of the world. (Jn.6:44, Jn. 8:44)

Hosea 4:6 (KJV) [6] *My people are destroyed for lack of knowledge: because thou hast rejected knowledge, I will also reject thee, that thou shalt be no priest to me: seeing thou hast forgotten the law of thy God, I will also forget thy children.* All of us are guilty before God standing at the mercy seat. This is the end time when God will once again bring back the spirit of Elijah to show the world who is the real God. *Matthew 24:24 (KJV)* [24] *For there shall arise false Christs, and false prophets, and shall shew great signs and wonders;* Today's apostate church world represents generations of false teachings in division and signs not to be compared to the early church.

These new doctrines have them thinking that they have arrived.) *"insomuch that, if it were possible, they shall deceive the very elect."* This last part is in reference to the tribulation time when the elect (God in the fullness) will confront the devil in the fullness. This warfare has already begun in heaven and now being manifested in the activity of men in the earth both good and evil. *Mark 13:20 (KJV)* [20] *And except that the Lord had shortened those days, no flesh should be saved: but for the elect's sake, whom he hath chosen, he hath shortened the days.*

Finally, all those under the mercy seat outside of the perfect will of God as unwise virgins will be reaped when they repent in the second sickle of (Rev. 14:18-19); they will be saved by the prayers of the righteous who came to their defense in Revelation 8 and God will give them mercy and sacrifice their bodies to Satan. Their bodies are being sacrificed to the world they refused to leave on the first call. They will have to suffer the destruction of their flesh to be saved. **(1 Cor.5:5)** When all who are going to heaven have been chosen in this last generation, Satan's work will be finished. Then tribulation will become full circle in the earth.

The final reaping in the tribulation is the remnant in this last generation when time as we know shall be no more in America and the world. **(Rev. 18:21)** The books were closed when the devil, the accuser, was cast out of heaven by Michael. This war in heaven will last seven years. Satan and all his evil demons will be bound, and the earth will be cleansed for the new time continuum of the last millennium. The New Jerusalem will be brought down from heaven, Christ will return in his glory to sit on his throne. AMEN (Completed 5/2005)

THE RESILIENCE OF A PIONEERING SOLDIER

After ten years serving in my profession at **Sloan Kettering Institute**; in 1972, I came back to my hometown as the first person of color to serve as a hospital lab supervisor in that part of the south in my home state for eight months; under great pressure of racial tension where God will used me to set an example to break the color barrier and pave the way for other people of color to be hired in hospital labs in the newly integrated hospitals in the south. After eight months holding a position in a supervisory capacity in my hometown hospital, I took another position in another city in a new hospital as Histology Lab Supervisor and forensic autopsy assistant with a group of certified forensic Pathologist.

I served fifth teen years there until I moved to Arizona in 1988 after being banished from my hometown as a controversial preacher that caused the loss of my marriage by my uncompromising biblical views. When I arrived in Arizona, having been left behind by the evangelistic group I traveled with, I had no one around me I knew; all alone in the city of Phoenix, Arizona. I lived in my VW van for a few days. I had only a suit, two pairs of pants and a change of underwear, no credentials of my past accomplishments such as my certified degrees to my background as a professional lab technician.

I took a job at a bakery, working for minimum wage; I could only afford a cheap motel room in an area I did not know at the time was the red-light district. Later, I discovered that God was still with me because in my state, I never gave into the prostitutes in that area. I was so depressed to the point that it took all my energy just to go to work and back to that motel room. This is when I had an encounter with Satan. The state of my mind at the time, I learned he knows when to come to you. I could not lie straight in a bed; my position was fetal at best.

My encounter with Satan

One evening, while lying in this position soaking in self-pity, I felt an evil presence like none I had ever felt before, it came over and sat on me and I instinctively knew that it was Satan. I felt life going out of me as he began to speak to me and tell me what everyone was saying about me back in my hometown. This went on for two weeks and just when I felt life going out of me, he would leave. I would curl up in a tight fetal position trying to hold on to my sanity, not knowing when he would return.

Finally, he would begin to tell me I was better off committing suicide. I was seriously considering it but did not have the nerve to follow through. All this is in retrospect; I did not know then what I have come to know now, God oversaw it all … giving me a unique experience to know the reality of Satan for later in my life. When Satan could not get me to kill myself, he left for a season. That gave me a chance to think of what I was going to do with my life in this state. One morning I got up the nerve to ask God about my state and how am I ever going to recover from all that had happened to me. This is what was spoken to me in my spirit, *"concerning what I have for you; you will walk into everything."* Instantly after that word, I was restored in my spirit and mind.

My Restored state

The only ID I had was a social security card and a NC driver's license. Every day I would go to a hospital in the area and put in an application. When I had covered the ones I knew around the area, one day on my way back I saw this hospital name **St. Joseph's Hospital & Burrow Neurological Institute,** I immediately turned, went in and found the personnel department, sat down, filled out the application, listed all my credentials gave it back to the lady at the desk and sat down. A few moments later, the personnel director called me into her office and said to me, we have been looking for someone like you. She called the director of Neuropathology research, set up an immediate appointment; during the interview, I was never asked to show my credentials. I was hired on the spot, became his special assistant to the point that he depended on me for everything, often calling me his right arm. God gave me a special gift that distinguished me from others throughout my career as a Medical Technologist and forensic autopsy assistant. As a skilled Lab Technician, I could perform a quick procedure on fresh frozen tissue for microscopic diagnosis while the patient was under in an operating room. In the autopsy room, I could dissect the body like a surgeon without destroying the organs to get to the area in question to find the cause of death with precision. I knew where to find every organ in the body and how it functioned.

Now that God had restored me back to what he gave me the ability to do, I moved up town in a nice one room suite apartment. What God allowed the devil to do, told me about the people and what they were saying. I was out of communication with my past, during the first seven years of my second marriage, I had to fight a secret battle with a spirit of oppression and depression. My grandparents died and I did not get to go to their funerals. This was the grandmother that helped raise and taught me. This was how God made me see about forsaking all and breaking ties with the past that included my immediate family that would give me a testimony out of the volumes of his book of forsaking all. Now I can say to him be the glory because I got out of these experiences, what I was supposed to learn. AMEN

HE THAT HATH AN
EAR LET HIM HEAR

Background Scriptures:

John 12:24 (KJV) "²⁴ *Verily, verily, I say unto you, Except a corn of wheat fall into the ground and die, it abideth alone: but if it die, it bringeth forth much fruit. 1 Corinthians 15:30-33 (KJV)* ³⁰ *And why stand we in jeopardy every hour?* ³¹ *I protest by your rejoicing which I have in Christ Jesus our Lord, I die daily.* ³² *If after the manner of men I have fought with beasts at Ephesus, what advantageth it me, if the dead rise not? let us eat and drink; for tomorrow we die.* ³³ *Be not deceived: evil communications corrupt good manners. 1 Corinthians 11:26-28 (KJV)* ²⁶ *For as often as ye eat this bread, and drink this cup, ye do shew the Lord's death till he come.* ²⁷ *Wherefore whosoever shall eat this bread, and drink this cup of the Lord, unworthily, shall be guilty of the body and blood of the Lord.* ²⁸ *But let a man examine himself, and so let him eat of that bread, and drink of that cup.*"

When the Lord began to open my mind about many things these doctrinal traditions have taken for granted or has become a ritual in most assemblies, it is this premise that the many corrections the Lord made in me as being taught this more excellent way by the Holy Spirit. I speak of what the Holy Spirit has revealed to me as being led to my own death in my flesh. It has been my experience to see many well-meaning brethren seeking the return of God's acts are failing to see that for what we are about to experience will be in those who give place to His ways. I was on the field preaching and teaching until God had to give me a stiff rebuke to get my attention to bring me into His rest. I would have never known what rest is if God had not caused it.

What does it mean to REST? What I am about to tell you now is what every elect will have to experience in order to begin the process of dying daily, rest from your labor. *Hebrews 4:9 (KJV) "⁹ There remaineth therefore a rest to the people of God."* This was the process I experienced in God bringing me to rest. I was put out of the assemblies because what I taught was contrary to building a mega church. I conducted home meetings for anyone who wanted to hear the word for five years. It was during the first week in December of 04, God led me to leave my job. December 29, 2004, was my last day at work. Like the apostles, I did not question God. This experience gave me an understanding of why the apostles walked away when He said come. On January 4ᵗʰ, 2005, I, with two brothers were told to take our funds and go all over the state of Arizona for forty days to a total of 153 assemblies to take this message. *1 Peter 4:17 (KJV) "¹⁷ For the time is come that judgment must begin at the house of God: and if it first begin at us, what shall the end be of them that obey not the gospel of God?"* We were told not to ask for an offering but take what you are given and bless that house. I was sixty-one with a mortgage, and bills. I took a cash settlement of my retirement funds, paid off my bills, we pooled our funds together, bought an RV, paid our expenses until it all ran out in September of 2008.

The last of it was spent for thirty-eight weeks feeding the homeless and preaching the gospel on the street. Now, if you got a little money, you do not need faith until it all runs out, well now is the test to prove I really trusted God to meet my needs. The very next month I qualified at sixty-two for Social Security. That paid my mortgage expenses, I had no other steady income to depend on; my wife continued working which was in God's plan. The coming months after would prove to be a trial that only God could get me through.

I was removed from participating in any part of an assembly. When I tried to continue a home church, He gave me a hard rebuke to the point that I never wanted to preach or teach again. This was the REST that he brought me to and for eighteen months, walked by faith seeing my needs met every month. During this period, I was led on a forty day fast to bring my flesh under subjection to focus on him alone learning His ways and dying to my own self. I have not had to go back to work to supplement my income. What I experienced is his miraculous provisions that gave me an experience by becoming content in him how all my needs are met in him. He has been pouring parts of Himself into me until I began to see into the deep spiritual things, made known he wanted to reveal to me as in … *Jeremiah 33:3 (KJV) "³ Call unto me, and I will answer thee, and shew thee great and mighty things, which thou knowest not."*

I began to see and discern things that only His mind can show you. These are some of the things He told me while in preparation of the day of full occupancy; the reason we have so many denominations, each have a part of Him that appeals to our comfort zone, but none have enough that we see the beauty of holiness. The purposes of the elects are to return the church back to the apostle's doctrine established in…. *Ephesians 4:12-13 (KJV) ¹² For the perfecting of the saints, for the work of the ministry, for the edifying of the body of Christ: ¹³ Till we all come in the unity of the faith, and of the knowledge of the Son of God, unto a perfect man, unto the measure of the stature of the fulness of Christ:"* Till we all return back to Pentecost where we had our first experience as believing in … *Ephesians 4:5 (KJV) "⁵ One Lord, one faith, one baptism,"*

Many assemblies train you to go to work for God; that is his permissive will. Those of us called from above to His Sovereign will are waiting in the wilderness, resting from our labor, preparing to work with him to perform his perfect sovereign will, separated from all as John the Baptist was in his day to be taught this more perfect way that He only can accomplished through our death. We will only see Him in the fullness when we die to self. *John 14:30 Hereafter I will not talk much with you: for the prince of this world cometh, and hath nothing in me.* This is where we will be when he takes full possession of us. He directs our footsteps to … *Matthew 7:13-14 (KJV) "¹³ Enter ye in at the strait gate: for wide is the gate, and broad is the way, that leadeth to destruction, and many there be which go in thereat: ¹⁴ Because strait is the gate, and narrow is the way, which leadeth unto life, and few there be that find it."*

This strait way separates you from all man's traditions, works, and forms in this religious worldly church. Just as John the Baptist was separated so will all that are called to this place will be separated unto God as His sons elected from the foundation of the world. That will be the only distinction the world will see in these chosen vessels that will manifest the MAN CHILD calling that will do the exploits during the tribulation. This is by His choice not ours. If you think you know something about deliverance, then examine yourself, just notice how many did not endure these gifts in the deliverance movements and fell along the wayside. None of us are experts at anything or to even think you know all there is to know about a thing. You see, we have only known Him in part, there is nothing to compare to the full but Christ. This is our shortcomings.

Those who think you know all about deliverance by your past experiences, be careful not to become a judge. None of us know what we think we know because we are still thinking; outside of God, your thoughts are evil. *Isaiah 55:7 (KJV) "7 Let the wicked forsake his way, and the unrighteous man his thoughts: and let him return unto the LORD, and he will have mercy upon him; and to our God, for he will abundantly pardon."* Let's have a reality check here; not one of us can justify our actions outside the perfect will of God. We are in the process of being made meat for the master's use. It's not about what we use to be but what we are about to become as His elects. We have not lived our lives to the glory of God. This is what you will see when he reveals your heart. *Romans 3:24 (KJV) "24 Being justified freely by his grace through the redemption that is in Christ Jesus: Romans 3:28 (KJV) 28 Therefore we conclude that a man is justified by faith without the deeds of the law. Romans 5:1 (KJV) 1 Therefore being justified by faith, we have peace with God through our Lord Jesus Christ:"*

The death of our flesh is the only way we will be able to walk as humble as our lord in our temples. This is what is required? *Romans 12:1 (KJV) "I beseech you therefore, brethren, by the mercies of God, that ye present your bodies a living sacrifice, holy, acceptable unto God, which is your reasonable service."* I have come to see that many lack the love that followed the prophet's message because of what we have been made to see have made some of us turn to judging in the flesh instead of loving in Christ. This is a temptation we all will deal with daily in this calling. It is Christ who will seek to save the lost. This is the fruit that will remain because God is doing the choosing where His house is concern. How soon we forget where we came from, DUST. Dust is a formless element of the ground until He formed it in His image and blew his life in the image of his likeness. He sent His Holy Spirit to represent Him in our flesh to affect our death and the rebirth as a man child. This now will be the new creation to remain with Him forever as the expressed image of His person. When His seed is replanted in His elects, then and only then will we see who is made into a new creature. If you are called to this election, the spirit of Christ is making your calling and election sure, resting from your labor, separated and taught by Him as he taught his disciples. We are being restored to our first love with the former rain; preparing for the fires of tribulation that will usher in the latter rain. If you have not ceased from your own works, it is evident that you are not called to this rest.

To be more specific, pastors will have to repent when they hear this message to their congregations for hindering the works of Christ to the fullness by producing fruit that is corrupt with a mixture of the world in the traditions of religious men Christ condemned. Because of the zeal of most pastors, they will reject this message because of their pride. *Mark 7:9 (KJV) "⁹ And he said unto them, Full well ye reject the commandment of God, that ye may keep your own tradition."* As carrying this message, the sad part is to see that they know not what spirit they are of, and neither would I If Christ had not opened my eyes.

Many will reject Christ in the vessels that will carry this message because they will not be well known as those established in the traditional assemblies. As an intercessor, just as Jeremiah weep for the souls of men. When Christ began to reveal himself to me, He also had to contain me. If you think you know what it is to weep for souls, wait until He lets you feel just a little of what he feels. I have never had dreams or visions as some have had but when He ask me what I wanted from Him, there was only one reply, **your mind**. He put it in me to ask, I am now beginning to experience his thoughts that only cause me to love Him more and more as striving to be perfected in his love.

I am now experiencing the word being made flesh in me. Once you have been given the vision by the prophets, there is no need to constantly chase event after event unless that's your calling. Now we must walk in that vision. All the promises that come with this vision are to protect you during the hard times by the faith of His spoken word. From that time on, you were to cease from your labor, rest so he can prepare our vessel through total surrender for the groom to receive. There is no need to dwell on the negatives, I have learned to stand on the sure foundation of His word. Many of you moving to places you have been told of safety, storing up food and making preparation for survival.

Remember, when you mix law with grace you will be in error and miss God's deep revelation. What I have been made to see in the spirit, boarders on comparing natural things to spiritual things. The Type and Shadow with a revelation of what they mean in the spirit. We are going through the wilderness to be proved as did the Israelites. They entered in with the provision they plundered from the Egyptians as back pay. The debts of God's people are about to be cancelled. The plunder you will receive will not be in houses or land but the power of the spoken word that will cause men to give unto those in need as did the early apostles. (Acts 4:37) Some of you have received your back pay in advance and are making your own provision. Have we forgotten the lessons that were written for our learning in the past of how God provided for His people while they were in the wilderness? Now I am not telling you what to do. This is what I have been taught by God that assures me that he is not going to starve His temple in us to death or allow Himself to be killed before that appointed time of his departure in your temple. That's the faith he seeks to find in every believer. That what will make you see him as the greater one now in you. (1 John 4:4)

I am learning that for me to live for eternity, allow Him to complete my death in the flesh. This is the faith that shows you believe He is who He says He is by acting on His spoken word; therefore, I am not responsible for my preservation, He is. I take no thought of these things as I now become the living sacrifice; the brunt offering of my flesh. Therefore, I am hiding my life in Him because the work is His and not mine. This is a *"Thus Say the Lord, all who have made your own preparation will not see His provisions until you have nothing to depend on but Him as the Israelites did. There will be no glory until the provisions of Egypt (the world) are gone."*

If God has not given you the task of preparing for His people, how are you going to know that where you are is a place of safety? I live in the heart of a city, until God tells me to move, I will not live-in fear, and I am in the process of perfecting my love in Him. *1 John 4:18 (KJV) "18 There is no fear in love; but perfect love casteth out fear: because fear hath torment. He that feareth is not made perfect in love. Hebrews 13:6 (KJV) 6 So that we may boldly say, The Lord is my helper, and I will not fear what man shall do unto me. Hebrews 4:1 (KJV)* [1] *Let us therefore fear, lest, <u>a promise being left us of entering into his rest</u>, any of you should seem to come short of it. Revelation 2:10 (KJV)* [10] *Fear none of those things which thou shalt suffer: behold, the devil shall cast some of you into prison, that ye may be tried; and ye shall have tribulation ten days: be thou faithful unto death, and I will give thee a crown of life".* These are the words of promise He gave me which is the reason why I am at rest.

Finally, *Luke 18:17 (KJV) "17 Verily I say unto you, whosoever shall not receive the kingdom of God as a little child shall in no wise enter therein. Matthew 18:4 (KJV) 4 Whosoever therefore shall humble himself as this little child, the same is greatest in the kingdom of heaven." Matthew 23:12 (KJV)* [12] *And whosoever shall exalt himself shall be abased; and he that shall humble himself shall be exalted."* (Updated 8/2019)

LIVING IN THE REALITY
OF THE NEW BIRTH

In this chronicle, I will share some more of the revelations given to me by the Holy Spirit. Now not to shock you, if you ask the average confessing Christian are you born again, they will say without a doubt, yes. While at rest from my labor, the Holy Spirit, having my attention, brought to light the sum of my shortcomings as to why I did not see any notable signs and wonders during the time of my ministering.

Like most ministers who have been preaching and teaching for many years in God's permissive will, we have acquired a zeal that only God can stop us. To get my attention, He rebuked me with a word so hard that made me not want to speak again. I knew it was the voice of God speaking; he used the least person to speak through.

Now that he had my attention, he activated his Holy Spirit to correct me in the errors of the past, open my eyes to see and my ears to hear and now the transformation has begun in me being made meat for the master's use. I had nothing to do with this. He took over my will and now I speak what I hear him say because I now have nothing to tell anyone.

I am in the process of dying; this is his sovereign will at work with-in me now. Now that the Holy Ghost is released in me, I am being taught the more excellent way in the perfect will of God. This is what rest is. When it was his time, he sat me down and took me over, there was nothing I could do but rest, though it was not easy, under the hand of God, his will be done. Questions some of us have had after finding myself in the state of rest, I am receiving answers for those that have ears to hear as to why we are at rest.

These one hundred chronicles are some of the answers given to me that I now am sharing with you. These seven characteristics of The Holy Spirit are bringing us into this most excellent way of total submission in preparation of the fullness of time, the end of our will and ways. He himself will use these vessels to glorify himself in showing the world that he is the only God and there's no other.

#1

WHERE DOES IT ALL BEGIN?

Ephes. 1:13 "In whom ye also trusted, after that ye heard the word of truth, the gospel of your salvation: in whom also after that ye believed, ye were sealed with that Holy Spirit of promise," Only the pure gospel can bring the presence of the Holy Spirit because God does not share his glory in half truths. In our shortcomings, he still works according to his own will to bring about his purpose.

While we are operating in his permissive will, which in the end will bring about the salvation that produce the fruits of the spirit in his perfect will. *Romans 8:16 "The Spirit itself beareth witness with our spirit, that we are the children of God: Romans 8:28 (KJV)* [28] *And we know that all things work together for good to them that love God, to them who are the called according to his purpose."* Rest is how we are brought into the reality of the inward dwelling of His spirit when he said be still so the hidden man of the heart can be reunited with the Holy Spirit that created him with the spoken word from dust; now we are one with Christ. *1 John 5:13 "These things have I written unto you that believe on the name of the Son of God; that ye may know that ye have eternal life, and that ye may believe on the name of the Son of God."*

Now, hold on to your hats, in this verse, with-out a revelation, you will be deceived. **First** is the name. You can believe on the name and not know God and perform lying signs and wonders by faith in his name. (Matthew 7:22-23) Now you see it is more than just the name. It is only when we receive the Son that he will magnify his own name and the word will come out of the volume of his books. His character is manifested in true holiness as Sons of God. The faith works done in his name through a vessel living in part truth usually does not remain. His mercy will be extended on whom He will and that's according to your faith. (John 1:12)

#2 WHAT PEOPLE WILL SEE IN YOU

Matthew 7:16 "Ye shall know them by their fruits. Do men gather grapes of thorns, or figs of thistles?" Only through an ensample can this fruit remain be seen. This Parable speaks of the natural branch producing after its own kind. Whatever spirit is in the person representing God will be in you. Their shortcomings will be your shortcomings if the fullness is not there. Note the red letters who's speaking. *Acts 4:20 "For we cannot but speak the things which we have seen and heard."* This is the true testimony of Jesus Christ that comes through a surrendered vessel that will produce the whole man as in ... *(Eph. 4:12) Ephes. 3:17 "That Christ may dwell in your hearts by faith; that ye, being rooted and grounded in love,"*

This is the kind of love that he and he alone can produce that will draw all men to him not flesh and blood. If men glorify themselves, they are deceived of their father the devil. The spirit of truth only points you to the father as the source of all help. *John 14:23 "Jesus answered and said unto him, If a man love me, he will keep my words: and my Father will love him, and we will come unto him, and make our abode with him."* This is the true religion undefiled before God that worships him in spirit and truth and is where we will be perfected in tribulation. **(John 16:13***) John 1:12 "But as many as received him, to them gave he power to become the sons of God, even to them that believe on his name:"* Now we know that to receive Christ is to believe in the one that sent him in his name which makes you completely whole. AMEN

#3

THE POWER OF PRAYER

Romans 8:26_"Likewise the Spirit also helpeth our infirmities: for we know not what we should pray for as we ought: but the Spirit itself maketh intercession for us with groanings which cannot be uttered." The prayer language is not a sign of being born again or else he would have said **by the tongues ye shall know them**.

The fruit must follow the prayer language of the Holy Spirit as a sign of what spirit you are of; those that are of the same spirit will know who's at work in the vessel. This is that unction that keeps us from being deceived. (1 John 2:20) Praying in the spirit brings you into this reality of who's at work with-in you which builds your faith in him by performing his word as a sign that you were heard. *Ephesians. 2:1 "And you hath he quickened, who were dead in trespasses and sins";* (This is the new creature, quicken in the spirit by receiving Christ. He now is the Adam restored.) **(2 Cor. 5:17, 1 cor. 15:45)** *Acts 1:14 "These all continued with one accord in prayer and supplication, with the women, and Mary the mother of Jesus, and with his brethren."*

Those that have been begotten in the spirit will only seek to know the things of the spirit in this prayer language. Often as they come together and activate the Holy Spirit in prayer with a hunger and thirst for righteousness; this is what keeps the accord. God puts this in you by his spirit. This is the body he joins that no man can put asunder. *Acts 4:24 "And when they heard that, they lifted up their voice to God with one accord, and said, Lord, thou art God, which hast made heaven, and earth, and the sea, and all that in them is:"* When one is introduced to the heavenly host, you see him as THE GREAT I AM; therefore, you see him in all the universe. This is where you will begin to seek those things in heavenly places with a mind on things above as dying to this world and seeking the one to come.

Jeremiah 33:3 "Call unto me, and I will answer thee, and shew thee great and mighty things, which thou knowest not.") *Rev. 3:2 "Be watchful, and strengthen the things which remain, that are ready to die: for I have not found thy works perfect before God."* When we receive the true gospel, we will seek to strengthen ourselves in the Holy Spirit in prayer that he will remain strong and in the forefront of our lives and as we are dying to self, he becomes our guide and teacher, bringing us into perfection as one with Christ and the Father.

#4

WHEN IS THE REALITY OF THE NEW BIRTH SEEN?

James 4:4 "Ye adulterers and adulteresses, know ye not that the friendship of the world is enmity with God? whosoever therefore will be a friend of the world is the enemy of God." What the world has been made to see is what we as confessing Christian fail to see; there is a difference in the natural man and the spiritual man. The two cannot walk together unless they agree. (Amos 3:3) The natural man stays the same. The spiritual man separates himself from the carnal environment as coming out of the world as a sign of salvation that he or she has received the report of Jesus Christ; therefore, have been delivered from the sins of the past. False teaching will not produce this type of fruit that remains.

#5

THEIR SUFFERING AND SUBMISSION

1 Peter 4:1 (KJV) Forasmuch then as Christ hath suffered for us in the flesh, arm yourselves likewise with the same mind: for he that hath suffered in the flesh hath ceased from sin;" Now the world, who does not know Christ, will hate you but get ready for the unexpected, unregenerate confessing Christians will murder you with their mouth by saying all manner of evil against you because they are not in the right spirit. Their works in tradition and yours in truth will cause them to be offended with you because their deeds are evil. You are now a doer of the word. Their lives demonstrate this...**Isaiah 29:13 (KJV)** *"Wherefore the Lord said, forasmuch as this people draw near me with their mouth, and with their lips do honour me, but have removed their heart far from me, and their fear toward me is taught by the precept of men:"* Seduced though modern theology and false teachings, this is what you are being separated from. *2 Corinthians 6:17 (KJV)* [17] *Wherefore come out from among them, and be ye separate, saith the Lord, and touch not the unclean thing; and I will receive you, 2 Tim. 3:12 "Yea, and all that will live godly in Christ Jesus shall suffer persecution."* It is not the nature of man to suffer in his own will; therefore, ever present seducing spirits will cause many to stumble at this truth in false teaching. Satan will wrest the scriptures to get around this passage and you will enter the way of the broad road that seems right.

This was demonstrated in ... *Matthew 4:8-9 (KJV) "8 Again, the devil taketh him up into an exceeding high mountain, and sheweth him all the kingdoms of the world, and the glory of them; 9 And saith unto him, All these things will I give thee, if thou wilt fall down and worship me."* This is where many will be seduced into a false sense of reality and security to go after prosperity to escape the suffering. *John 16:33 "These things I have spoken unto you, that in me ye might have peace. In the world ye shall have tribulation: but be of good cheer; I have overcome the world.* This lifestyle can only be accomplished through the pure gospel, demonstrated by example to produce fruit that will be remaining during great tribulation that shall be inflicted on those that lift the name of Jesus very soon.

6

THE POWER OVER TEMPTATION

Romans 7:25 "I thank God through Jesus Christ our Lord. So then with the mind I myself serve the law of God, but with the flesh the law of sin. 1 Cor. 10:13 There hath no temptation taken you but such as is common to man: but God is faithful, who will not suffer you to be tempted above that ye are able; but will with the temptation also make a way to escape, that ye may be able to bear it'. **Romans 7:25 (NLT) 25 Thank God! The answer is in Jesus Christ our Lord. So you see how it is: In my mind I really want to obey God's law, but because of my sinful nature I am a slave to sin.** *Romans 8:10" And if Christ be in you, the body is dead because of sin; but the Spirit is life because of righteousness." 1 John 5:18 (KJV) 18 We know that whosoever is born of God sinneth not; but he that is begotten of God keepeth himself, and that wicked one toucheth him not.* Now we are at rest, you cannot boast of that you do not have the power to perform, we are to be in this mind set... *1 Cor. 15:31 "I protest by your rejoicing which I have in Christ Jesus our Lord, I die daily."* As a chosen vessel, Jesus will bring you into his fullness at his appointed time not before. *John 10:28 "And I give unto them eternal life; and they shall never perish, neither shall any man pluck them out of my hand."*

We have seen men fall from grace in our time by lack of endurance in his permissive will; therefore, this statement is to the elects of Christ. The eleven apostles are the proof that none will fall and them that come thereafter by election. The permissive will does not give you the power to this degree because their convictions lack the pure love where we see the fall. Remember… *Matthew 10:22 (KJV) "²² And ye shall be hated of all men for my name's sake: but he that endureth to the end shall be saved.*

Only those elected will have this distinction and guarantee because they have been called from the foundation of the world by the Father. Those that receive the word of the elects are receiving Christ; therefore, they will enter in the kingdom though his grace and mercy by the blood of the lamb. *1 Cor. 15:57 "But thanks be to God, which giveth us the victory through our Lord Jesus Christ."*

#7

THE FULLNESS OF THE GODHEAD

Luke 21:28 "And when these things begin to come to pass, then look up, and lift up your heads; for your redemption draweth nigh". This is the mystery to our translation from death to life, when Christ who is our perfection has completed His work in every called-out believer, we will be offered up as a sacrifice in glory to the Father as his bride. *Rev. 22:20 "He which testifieth these things saith, Surely I come quickly. Amen. Even so, come, Lord Jesus."* All our life is for this moment in time. We are to live in the hope of our calling with great expectation for that moment of our appointment with death. The last enemy in the world that Christ delivered us from is the death. Death now is swallowed up in victory in him who had power over us until Christ came; took the power from him and liberated us to the place where we now have pass from the death to life. We now live, move, and have our being in eternity. *Romans 8:3 For what the law could not do, in that it was weak through the flesh, God sending his own Son in the likeness of sinful flesh, and for sin, condemned sin in the flesh:* We who are converted look forward to the day to be absent from this body and be present with the lord for eternity.

Only Christ can live the life in us that keeps us free from sin. That's the revelation of who it is that enable you to inter into eternity by your death to self and the resurrected Christ in you will walk you into eternity with him and the father. He will produce the faith needed to endure to the end that He will find when he returns.

Luke 18:8 (KJV) "⁸ I tell you that he will avenge them speedily. Nevertheles, when the Son of man cometh, shall he find faith on the earth?" John 3:16 For God so loved the world, that he gave his only begotten Son, that whosoever believeth in him should not perish, but have everlasting life. Galatians 3:13 Christ hath redeemed us from the curse of the law, being made a curse for us: for it is written, Cursed is every one that hangeth on a tree: Matthew 27:51 And, behold, the veil of the temple was rent in twain from the top to the bottom; and the earth did quake, and the rocks rent; John 19:30 When Jesus therefore had received the vinegar, he said, It is finished: and he bowed his head, and gave up the ghost. A who receive him … **Romans 8:1 (KJV)** [1]**There *is* therefore now no condemnation to them which are in Christ Jesus, who walk not after the flesh, but after the Spirit.** All who are called have a course to run. When you are delivered up to your cross, his course in you will be finished. That is when you will pass from death to eternal life. *Ezekiel 33:11 Say unto them, As I live, saith the Lord GOD, I have no pleasure in the death of the wicked; but that the wicked turn from his way and live: turn ye, turn ye from your evil ways; for why will ye die, O house of Israel? Matthew 18:3 And said, Verily I say unto you, Except ye be converted, and become as little children, ye shall not enter into the kingdom of heaven.* (Updated 05/2019)

AS A MAN THINKS, SO IS HE

My beloved sisters and brothers, I am putting this message together for the benefit of those who's mind is set on things above given the present situation in the world. Many of you in waiting are under attack. The devil is going to send many things your way to divert your attention to cause you to miss our day of visitation as the Manifested Sons of God. Satan knows he has but a short time, therefore, all those who are marked in the spirit will be singled out to be persecuted. I am interceding that our faith fails us not in our hour of trials. Please join me in prayer. God has let me know that this is our only weapon to deliver us into His glory. All our lives have been for this moment.

Seeing that we are coming to the end of man's rule on earth, to get a good perspective of where we came from and what is now being perfected in us throughout the years, I will let the Holy Spirit talk to you out of the scriptures as to the work that is being done in all whose death is being effected in the flesh in preparation to come out of the wilderness in fullness as Christ did.

Our Origin

Genesis 1:26-27 (KJV) "**²⁶ And God said, Let us make man in our image, after our likeness: and let them <u>have dominion over the fish of the sea, and over the fowl of the air, and over the cattle, and over all the earth, and over every creeping thing that creepeth upon the earth.</u> ²⁷ So God**

created man in his own image, in the image of God created he him; male and female created he them."

Our fall

Read the account in Genesis 3:1-17

<u>Our Warfare With The Two Natures</u> Deuteronomy 11:26-28 (KJV) [26] Behold, I set before you this day a blessing and a curse; [27] A blessing, if ye obey the commandments of the LORD your God, which I command you this day: [28] And a curse, if ye will not obey the commandments of the LORD your God, but turn aside out of the way which I command you this day, to <u>go after other gods,</u> which ye have not known. 1 Samuel 15:22 (KJV) [22] And Samuel said, Hath the LORD as great delight in burnt offerings and sacrifices, as in obeying the voice of the LORD? Behold, to obey <u>is better than sacrifice,</u> and to hearken than the fat of rams. Jeremiah 7:23 (KJV) [23] But this thing commanded I them, saying, Obey my voice, and I will be your God, and ye shall be my people: and walk ye in all the ways that I have commanded you, that it may be well unto you. John 14:21 (KJV) [21] He that hath my commandments, and keepeth them, he it is that loveth me: and he that loveth me shall be loved of my Father, and I will love him, and will manifest myself to him. 1 John 2:3-6 (KJV) [3] And hereby we do know that we know him, if we keep his commandments. [4] He that saith, I know him, and keepeth not his commandments, is a liar, and the truth is not in him. [5] But whoso keepeth his word, in him verily is the love of God perfected: hereby know we that we are in him. [6] He that saith he abideth in him ought himself also so to walk, even as he walked. Psalms 143:10 (KJV) [10] Teach me to do thy will; for thou art my God: thy spirit is good; lead me into the land of uprightness.

Our Fallen State

Proverbs 23:7 For <u>as he thinketh in his heart</u>, so is he: Eat and drink, saith he to thee; but his heart is not with thee. Jeremiah 17:9 (KJV) [9] The heart is deceitful above all things, and desperately wicked: who can know it? Matthew 19:17 (KJV) [17] And he said unto him, Why callest thou me good? there is none good but one, that is, God: but if thou wilt enter into life, keep the commandments. James 4:14 (KJV) [14] Whereas ye know not what shall be on the morrow. For what is your life? It is even a vapour, that appeareth for a little time, and then vanisheth away. Psalms 94:11 (KJV) [11] The LORD knoweth the thoughts of man, that they are vanity. Psalms 8:4 (KJV) [4] What is man, that thou art mindful of him? and the son of man, that thou visitest him? Isaiah 55:8 For my thoughts are not your thoughts, neither are your ways my ways, saith the Lord. Proverbs 16:3 (KJV) [3] Commit thy works unto the LORD, and thy thoughts shall be established. Romans 8:5 For they that are after the flesh do mind the things of the flesh; but they that are after the Spirit the things of the Spirit. Genesis 6:5 And God saw that the wickedness of man was great in the earth, and that every imagination of the thoughts of his heart was only evil continually.

Job 7:17 (KJV) [17] What is man, that thou shouldest magnify him? And that thou shouldest set thine heart upon him? Hebrews 2:6 (KJV) [6] But one in a certain place testified, saying, what is man, that thou art mindful of him? or the son of man, that thou visitest him? Ecclesiastes 6:11 (KJV) [11] Seeing there be many things that increase vanity, what is man the better? Psalms 39:5 (KJV) [5] Behold, thou hast made my days as an handbreadth; and mine age is as nothing before thee: verily every man at his best state is altogether vanity.

Romans 3:4 (KJV) [4] God forbid: yea, let God be true, but every man a liar; as it is written, that thou mightest be justified in thy sayings, and mightest overcome when thou art judged. Job 35:2 (KJV) [2] Thinkest thou this to be right, that thou saidst, my righteousness is more than God's? Amos 3:3 Can two walk together, except they be agreed? Romans 8:6 -7(ASV) [6] For the mind of the flesh is death; but the mind of the Spirit is life and peace: [7] because the mind of the flesh is enmity against God; for it is not subject to the law of God, neither indeed can it be: Ecclesiastes 1:14 (KJV) [14] I have seen all the works that are done under the sun; and, behold, all is vanity and vexation of spirit ... We are but the dust of the earth in God's sight. It is his life in us we will have to give an account of in this world.

Christianity, Law and Grace

Romans 8:2 (KJV) [2] For the law of the Spirit of life in Christ Jesus hath made me free from the law of sin and death. Romans 8:3 (KJV) [3] For what the law could not do, in that it was weak through the flesh,

God sending his own Son in the likeness of sinful flesh, and for sin, condemned sin in the flesh, Romans 8:14 (KJV) [14] For as many as are led by the Spirit of God, they are the sons of God. 1 Timothy 1:7(KJV) [7] Desiring to be teachers of the law; understanding neither what they say, nor whereof they affirm. Psalms 1:1-2 (ASV) [1] Blessed is the man that walketh not in the counsel of the wicked, Nor standeth in the way of sinners, Nor sitteth in the seat of scoffers: [2] But his delight is in the law of the LORD; and in his law doth he meditate day and night.

Matthew 7:1-5 (ASV) [1] Judge not, that ye be not judged. [2] For with what judgment ye judge, ye shall be judged: and with what measure ye mete, it shall be measured unto you. [3] And why beholdest thou the mote hat is in thy brother's eye, but considerest not the beam that is in thine own eye? [4] Or how wilt thou say to thy brother, let me cast out the mote out of thine eye; and lo, the beam is in thine own eye? [5] Thou hypocrite, cast out first the beam out of thine own eye; and then shalt thou see clearly to cast out the mote out of thy brother's eye.

Romans 2:1 (ASV) [1] Wherefore thou art without excuse, O man, whosoever thou art that judgest: for wherein thou judges another, thou condemnest thyself; for thou that judgest dost practise the same things. Ephesians 4:17-18 (ASV) [17] This I say therefore, and testify in the Lord, that ye no longer walk as the Gentiles also walk, in the vanity of their mind, [18] being darkened in their understanding, alienated from the life of God, because of the ignorance that is in them, because of the hardening of their heart;

Romans 6:4-6 (ASV) [4] We were buried therefore with him through baptism unto death: that like as Christ was raised from the dead through the glory of the Father, so we also might walk in newness of life. [5] For if we have become united with him in the likeness of his death, we shall be also in the likeness of his resurrection; [6] knowing this, that our old man was crucified with him, that the body of sin might be done away, that so we should no longer be in bondage to sin; Ephesians 4:21-25 (ASV) [21] if so be that ye heard him, and were taught in him, even as truth is in Jesus: [22] that ye put away, as concerning your former manner of life, the old man, that waxeth corrupt after the lusts of deceit; [23] and that ye be renewed in the spirit of your mind, [24] and put on the new man, that after God hath been created in righteousness and holiness of truth. [25]

Wherefore, putting away falsehood, speak ye truth each one with his neighbor: for we are members one of another.

2 Corinthians 3:17 (ASV) [17] Now the Lord is the Spirit: and where the Spirit of the Lord is, there is liberty. Jeremiah 13:23 (ASV) [23] Can the Ethiopian change his skin, or the leopard his spots? then may ye also do good, that are accustomed to do evil. Romans 12:1-2 (ASV) [1] I beseech you therefore, brethren, by the mercies of God, to present your bodies a living sacrifice, holy, acceptable to God, which is your spiritual service. [2] And be not fashioned according to this world: but be ye transformed by the renewing of your mind, and ye may prove what is the good and acceptable and perfect will of God. John 3:16 (KJV) [16] For God so loved the world, that he gave his only begotten Son, that whosoever believeth in him should not perish, but have everlasting life.

We are coming out of the volume of the books

John 3:3-6 (KJV) [3] Jesus answered and said unto him, Verily, verily, I say unto thee, except a man be born again, he cannot see the kingdom of God. [4] Nicodemus saith unto him, how can a man be born when he is old? can he enter the second time into his mother's womb, and be born? [5] Jesus answered, Verily, verily, I say unto thee, except a man be born of water and of the Spirit, he cannot enter into the kingdom of God. [6] That which is born of the flesh is flesh; and that which is born of the Spirit is spirit.

2 Corinthians 5:17 (KJV) [17] Therefore if any man be in Christ, he is a new creature: old things are passed away; behold, all things are become new. Ephesians 2:3 (KJV) [3] Among whom also we all had our conversation in times past in the lusts of our flesh, fulfilling the desires of the flesh and of the mind; and were by nature the children of wrath, even as others. Romans 12:2 (KJV) [2] And be not conformed to this world: but be ye transformed by the renewing of your mind, that ye may prove what is that good, and acceptable, and perfect, will of God.

1 Corinthians 14:33 (KJV) [33] For God is not the author of confusion, but of peace, as in all churches of the saints. 2 Timothy 1:7 (KJV) [7] For God hath not given us the spirit of fear; but of power, and of love, and of a sound mind. Romans 8:9 (KJV) [9] But ye are not in the flesh, but in the Spirit, if so be that the Spirit of God dwell in you. Now if

any man have not the Spirit of Christ, he is none of his. 1 Corinthians 2:16 (KJV) [16] For who hath known the mind of the Lord, that he may instruct him? But we have the mind of Christ. Ephesians 5:8 (KJV) [8] For ye were sometimes darkness, but now are ye light in the Lord: walk as children of light:

1 John 1:7 (KJV) [7] But if we walk in the light, as he is in the light, we have fellowship one with another, and the blood of Jesus Christ his Son cleanseth us from all sin. Romans 7:6 (KJV) [6] But now we are delivered from the law, that being dead wherein we were held; that we should serve in newness of spirit, and not in the oldness of the letter. Galatians 5:16 (KJV) [16] This I say then, walk in the Spirit, and ye shall not fulfil the lust of the flesh. Galatians 5:25 (KJV) [25] If we live in the Spirit, let us also walk in the Spirit. Romans 6:1-2 (KJV) [1] What shall we say then? Shall we continue in sin, that grace may abound? [2] God forbid. How shall we, that are dead to sin, live any longer therein? Romans 8:2 (KJV) [2] For the law of the Spirit of life in Christ Jesus hath made me free from the law of sin and death.

Romans 8:36 (KJV) [36] As it is written, for thy sake we are killed all the day long; we are accounted as sheep for the slaughter. 2 Timothy 2:12 (KJV) [12] If we suffer, we shall also reign with him: if we deny him, he also will deny us: 2 Timothy 3:12 (KJV) [12] Yea, and all that will live godly in Christ Jesus shall suffer persecution. Hebrews 11:13 (KJV) [13] These all died in faith, not having received the promises, but having seen them afar off, and were persuaded of them, and embraced them, and confessed that they were strangers and pilgrims on the earth. James 4:14 (KJV) [14] Whereas ye know not what shall be on the morrow. For what is your life? It is even a vapour that appeareth for a little time, and then vanisheth away. Ephesians 2:19 (KJV) [19] Now therefore ye are no more strangers and foreigners, but fellow citizens with the saints, and of the household of God.

1 John 2:15 (KJV) [15] Love not the world, neither the things that are in the world. If any man love the world, the love of the Father is not in him. Colossians 3:1-2 (KJV) [1] If ye then be risen with Christ, seek those things which are above, where Christ sitteth on the right hand of God. [2] Set your affection on things above, not on things on the earth. 1 Corinthians 4:10 (KJV) [10] We are fools for Christ's sake, but ye are wise

in Christ; we are weak, but ye are strong; ye are honourable, but we are despised. Ephesians 1:12 (KJV) ¹² That we should be to the praise of his glory, who first trusted in Christ. Philippians 2:5 (KJV) ⁵ Let this mind be in you, which was also in Christ Jesus: 2 Timothy 2:10 (KJV) ¹⁰ Therefore I endure all things for the elect's sakes, that they may also obtain the salvation which is in Christ Jesus with eternal glory.

The finished Works of Jesus Christ in You as You Come Out of the Wilderness

Romans 6:6-8 (KJV) ⁶ Knowing this, that our old man is crucified with him, that the body of sin might be destroyed, that henceforth we should not serve sin. ⁷ For he that is dead is freed from sin. ⁸ Now if we be dead with Christ, we believe that we shall also live with him. Peter 1:23 (KJV) ²³ Being born again, not of corruptible seed, but of incorruptible, by the word of God, which liveth and abideth forever. 1 John 3:14 (KJV) ¹⁴ We know that we have passed from death unto life, because we love the brethren. He that loveth not his brother abideth in death. Galatians 2:20 (KJV) ²⁰ I am crucified with Christ: nevertheless, I live; yet not I, but Christ liveth in me: and the life which I now live in the flesh I live by the faith of the Son of God, who loved me, and gave himself for me. Ezekiel 36:26-27 (KJV) ²⁶ A new heart also will I give you, and a new spirit will I put within you: and I will take away the stony heart out of your flesh, and I will give you an heart of flesh. ²⁷ And I will put my spirit within you, and cause you to walk in my statutes, and ye shall keep my judgments, and do them. 1 John 4:4 (KJV) ⁴ Ye are of God, little children, and have overcome them: because greater is he that is in you, than he that is in the world. This is the work being done while we are in this wilderness that's in God's timing; you will come out as He did in the fullness as the restored Adam the new creature to live forever, and Satan will find nothing in you but Christ. This is where I have been in waiting since 2011 after I printed my first book. AMEN

WHAT IS SALVATION?

"The Real Romans Road"

Background scripture:

Romans 10:9-10 (KJV) [9] "That if thou shalt confess with thy mouth the Lord Jesus, and shalt believe in thine heart that God hath raised him from the dead, thou shalt be saved. [10] For with the heart man believeth unto righteousness; and with the mouth confession is made unto salvation."** In all my learning, I have found that no man is an authority on this matter but God who is the one that extends the invitation to those who he has given ears to hear and receive him. When one comes to the knowledge of the truth, that is the mind of Christ, then and only then are you aware of who it is at work with-in you. The depth of that conviction and knowledge can only come from God who is doing the choosing because of this fact as stated by God himself … **John 6:44 (KJV)** [44] "**No man can come to me, except the Father which hath sent me draw him: and I will raise him up at the last day.**"

This verse has been the central focus of many things revealed to me by the spirit. It is all about what God is doing and never about you. You see, God does not need you to do anything for him but realize who is taking the time to talk with you; what he has to say has such an impact, you will never be the same and that's just his presence.

Here is one of the mysteries of the calling. When he put it in your heart to come to him, all he has to say is come, and you will come. When Jesus called his disciples, is not that what he said; come. You do not see where none of them resisted his words. There is only one that has this kind of power over your mind to cause you to drop everything in your past and follow him is God where eternal life is concern. Now on the other hand, there is a counter fit Christ. This is the antichrist that comes through being carnally minded. This is where you meet Satan the deceiver. Although he is a spirit being, He can only manifest himself in natural things. Therefore, those in his kingdom will be born from below and by their fruit you will know them. Their corporate body will operate under a worldly government charter that will have them ever learning but not coming to the knowledge of the truth.

Our most vulnerable point in our life is when we come to realize at a crossroad in our life to ponder this question, is there a God and can he help me. **Revelation 3:20 (KJV)** [20] **"Behold, I stand at the door, and knock: if any man hears my voice, and open the door, I will come into him, and will sup with him, and he with me."** Now the next question is, who extended the invitation?

Colossians 2:8 (KJV) [8] **"Beware lest any man spoil you through philosophy and vain deceit, after the tradition of men, after the rudiments of the world, and not after Christ. 2 Peter 2:1 (KJV)** [1] **But there were false prophets also among the people, even as there shall be false teachers among you, who privily shall bring in damnable heresies, even denying the Lord that bought them, and bring upon themselves swift destruction. Matthew 7:15 (KJV)** [15] **Beware of false prophets, which come to you in sheep's clothing, but inwardly they are ravening wolves."** Now let me show you what I learn that's beyond my comprehension in an environment such as the above scriptures describe, God can pluck you out for himself and separate you unto himself, being under a false prophet. This is known as election.

No matter what you see as far as the circumstances are concern, God oversees it all because of this fact … **Isaiah 45:7-9 (KJV)** [7] **"I form the light, and create darkness: I make peace, <u>and create evil:</u> I the LORD do all these** *things.* [8] **Drop down, ye heavens, from above, and let the skies pour down righteousness: let the earth open, and <u>let them bring forth salvation,</u> and let righteousness spring up together; I the LORD have created it.** [9] **Woe unto him that striveth with his Maker!** *Let* **the** potsherd *strive* with the potsherds of the earth. Shall the clay say to him that fashioneth it, What makest thou? or thy work, He hath no hands?"

This is who we are dealing with when it comes to salvation; that's why Jesus said it like this, those my father plucked out will be known by their fruit and they will live as sons that will never turn back. Now not to leave you on a cliff hanger, those that God did not pick out as his own will become victims of these false teachers and their fruit will not be of God. If those that led them to Christ are corrupt in the doctrines of man, then they will suffer by lack of knowledge and become victims of false teachers by not searching the scriptures behind them to make their calling and election sure. Now let's examine the background scriptures.

Romans 10:9-10 (KJV) [9] **"That if thou shalt confess with thy mouth the Lord Jesus, and shalt believe in thine <u>heart</u> that God hath raised him from the dead, thou shalt be saved."** The reason why you must do this, you are renouncing your former father the devil in public, to tell the world I am leaving you behind. The word **heart** in the above verse is where God steps in and deals with the sin matter that will produce the fruit that remain. [10] **For<u>with the heart man believeth</u> unto righteousness; and with the mouth confession is made unto salvation.**

I relate this to falling in love with God through his son Jesus Christ. You now have been introduced to him and that love has covered your sins and made you righteous. You will be tested when those you love, do you wrong, and you remain the same because you were born under the influence of the Holy Spirit not man and his traditions. You will no longer ... **Ephesians 5:11 (NASB77)** [11] **And do not participate in the unfruitful deeds of darkness, but instead even expose them.** Have you ever wondered why the scripture said ... **Matthew 7:14-16 (KJV)** [14] **"Because strait *is* the gate, and narrow *is* the way, which leadeth unto life, and few there be that find it?"** Out of this experience, I question everyone's spirit that stands in the office of one of these five ministerial graces to instruct God's people, not as a judge but in keeping with what John teaches in his epistles ... **1 John 4:1 (KJV)** [1] **"Beloved, believe not every spirit, but try the spirits whether they are of God: because many false prophets are gone out into the world."** That includes me as a messenger of God if I stand not on this truth.

To declare the whole council of the doctrine of Jesus Christ is to be fully converted beyond fears, doubts, and unbelief where you seek … **1 Corinthians 2:2 (KJV)** [2] **"For I determined not to know anything among you, save Jesus Christ, and him crucified."** What I found out through my salvation experience, it is all about what God desires to do in your body and if you would be obedient unto death, you get to go back with him because he is coming back for himself this time in you. Now I see why our obedience is far more profitable than our sacrifices. All our wealth and influences cannot buy this. When I read the parable of the rich man, I got the revelation of the spirit of riches as to why Jesus told him he had to let go all his personal gains in his own strength to gain the strength to endure other temptations that Satan will offer in this world that will bound you to it.

What he could not see, he was being offered what only God can give, that is heavenly riches that will last for eternity; instead, without knowing, choose what he sees as the meagerly beggarly elements of this world which carries the spirit of bondage or being bound to this world. Jesus do not go against your conscious but let you make your own choice; then he turned and said … **Mark 10:25 (KJV)** [25] **"It is easier for a camel to go through the eye of a needle, than for a rich man to enter into the kingdom of God. John 16:15 (KJV)** [15] **All things that the Father hath are mine: therefore, said I, that he shall take of mine, and shall shew *it* unto you. Deuteronomy 8:18 (KJV)** [18] **But thou shalt remember the LORD thy God: for *it is* he that giveth thee power to get wealth, that he may establish his covenant which he sware unto thy fathers, as *it is* this day."**

Although I have dealt with various aspects of this topic in previous writings, I was prompted to add another layer to this subject because of the revelation of the 98 percent figure that God gave me about the present church. I wanted to know why such a large number as this. This I found is a repeat of what happen to his chosen people: they fail into their own ways and forgot about God until worship became a ritual where God did no longer except their sacrifices. We as the New Testament church have done the same as a repeat of history and now, we are in the same state as Jesus found his own people, only we now cannot recognize his voice. All I can say after seven years of being tutored by the Holy Spirit; I, like Solomon have concluded the matter, the only thing that is important to God is seeking to save those he has chosen to show his presence while on earth in the body created in his image. Besides this, all is vanity in the sight of God since your life is just a bubble that may burst at any time and that's the only time we have to save our soul.

Being delivered from this world renders transparency of confessions because of God's acts in you becomes your testimony, not man. During those seven years from 2004 until January of 2011, I did not walk perfect before God. I struggled with many revelations about my own short comings before my conversion into these truths; I had to accept on his terms as to enter his kingdom and that has been my personal wake up calling.

When I was persuaded to let myself die, it became a daily process. It was not until I was converted that I felt led to release these truths in the form of an informal book which is a testament to my personal conversion into this relationship with the lord as to how he walked me into this place.

Finally, the teachings in the New Testament made known the revelation of the new creature in Christ finished works that put as many as receive him back in the dominion as the restored Adam over the earth. If we miss out in the judgment, it is because we took this life and God for granted and assumed that God would not let this happen to us because we named his name and lived as though we could not be like him. **1 John 3:2 "(NASB77)** [2] Beloved, now we are children of God, and it has not appeared as yet what we shall be. We know that, when He appears, **we shall be like Him, because we shall see Him just as He is".** Life is a terrible thing to waste if you neglect such a privilege.

All things are yours but all you need as a temporary dweller is what it takes to get through each day before your bubble burst as in … **James 4:14 (NASB77)** [14] Yet you do not know what your life will be like tomorrow. You are *just* **a vapor that appears for a little while and then vanishes away. 1 John 3:2 (NASB77)** [2] **"Beloved, now we are children of God, and it has not appeared as yet what we shall be. We know that, when He appears, we shall be like Him, because we shall see Him just as He is.** That's because we have been made through Christ to be like him at his return. **Hebrews 9:27 (KJV)** [27] **And as it is appointed unto men once to die, but after this the judgment:"** (Completed for release 8/ 2015)

REVELATION OF SELF DELIVERANCE

"God's last day works in man"

Background scriptures:

Matthew 11:28 (KJV) [28] **Come unto me, all ye that labour and are heavy laden, and I will give you rest. Isaiah 55:7 (KJV)** [7] **Let the wicked forsake his way, and the unrighteous man his thoughts: and let him return unto the LORD, and he will have mercy upon him; and to our God, for he will abundantly pardon. Hebrews 4:9 (KJV)** [9] **There remaineth therefore a rest to the people of God. Romans 12:1 (KJV)** [1] **I beseech you therefore, brethren, by the mercies of God, that ye present your bodies a living sacrifice, holy, acceptable unto God, which is your reasonable service.**

One thing the above scriptures reveals, to be delivered, self must die. Now as I have found, there's a great difference in studying and reading. Studying is to grasp and in-depth understanding of what is being revealed in what you are reading. One must receive the Holy Spirit for the scriptures to be rightly divided in the right context for understanding so one can act on it for revelation. This faith in the spoken word is where Jesus shows himself as real and with you through his word.

Proverbs 4:1" Hear, ye children, the instruction of a father, and attend to know understanding. Proverbs 3:13 Happy is the man that findeth wisdom, and the man that getteth understanding". When I realized what the Holy Spirit was given to me to do through studying the scriptures, He alone has the key to understanding the revelations of the scriptures. My next step now was to learn how to activate Him. It is quite common in the Pentecostal assemblies to acknowledge they have received the Holy Spirit by speaking in tongues; however, what I have come to see through him, the Holy Spirit, the reason we do not see the works of the Holy Spirit, we are thinking and speaking for him. **Isaiah 55:7-8 "Let the wicked forsake his way, and the unrighteous man his thoughts: and let him return unto the LORD, and he will have mercy upon him; and to our God, for he will abundantly pardon. 8For my thoughts are not your thoughts, neither are your ways my ways, saith the LORD."**

Now when I instructed people not to think, the response was to be expected; how is that possible? The answer to this question is where we learn how to activate the Holy Spirit. As born children of the devil through Adam's sin, we all are by-products of a sin nature. Now this brings us back to why we must be born again. Now read the scriptures above in **Isaiah 55:7** again. For this to become a reality, we must be taught by example to produce this kind of fruit that only comes by receiving the Holy Spirit and releasing Him to do what he did in Jesus; that is, quicken our mortal into becoming an instrument of immortality; the restored Adam.

Matthew 11:28 (KJV) "28 Come unto me, all ye that labour and are heavy laden, and I will give you rest." This can be demonstrated in dying daily to self by forsaking our will so He can perform His. When Paul spoke through the inspiration of the Holy Spirit in... **Romans 12:1 (KJV) "1 I beseech you therefore, brethren, by the mercies of God, that ye present your bodies a living sacrifice, holy, acceptable unto God, which is your reasonable service." Revelation 12:10 (KJV) "10 And I heard a loud voice saying in heaven, Now is come salvation, and strength, and the kingdom of our God, and the power of his Christ: for the accuser of our brethren is cast down, which accused them before our God day and night."**

Satan has been defeated by Christ. Now, we walk as new creatures, only when we sin Satan has a right to afflict us. Our knowledge of this revelation will be tested until the day we are called home. **Hebrews 12:1 (KJV) "1 Wherefore seeing we also are compassed about with so great a cloud of witnesses, let us lay aside every weight, and the sin which doth so easily beset us, and let us run with patience the race that is set before us," Matthew 10:22 (KJV) "22 And ye shall be hated of all men for my** name's sake: but he that endureth to the end shall be saved." Self does not like rejection; therefore, the only way you will be able is through the draw of the spirit. **John 6:44 (KJV) "⁴⁴No man can come to me, except the Father which hath sent me draw him: and I will raise him up at the last day."** God chooses you to come into His presents and put you under His divine care. We see in Job this hedge of protection that is around us when we are obedient. **Job 1:10 (KJV) "¹⁰Hast not thou made an hedge about him, and about his house, and about all that he hath on every side? thou hast blessed the work of his hands, and his substance is increased in the land."**

If this was true under the law; how much more now that Christ's spirit is in us to keep Satan at bay. That's the faith he seeks to find in all of us. Perfect obedience can only be accomplished when we rest from our labor. You see, many leaders have never learned that the work is the Lords not ours. Pastors, meaning well, as part of their seminary training, those who are pastors and leaders, send you out to gather souls to help build their kingdoms without consulting with God. They are not converted so what you are doing is opening your sanctuary to bring in evil spirits. The work of the Holy Spirit seeks out those the father has called to the house he builds. This is what is required to achieve this level of perfection… **Romans 12:1 (KJV) "¹I beseech you therefore, brethren, by the mercies of God, that ye present your bodies a living sacrifice, holy, acceptable unto God, which is your reasonable service."** Christ in you the hope of glory is Him in total possession of the vessel. He and He alone can deal with Satan. **1 Corinthians 6:19 (KJV) "¹⁹What? know ye not that your body is the temple of the Holy Ghost which is in you, which ye have of God, and ye are not your own?" 2 Corinthians 5:17 (KJV) "¹⁷Therefore if any man be in Christ, he is a new creature: old things are passed away; behold, all things are become new." Romans 12:2 (KJV) "²And be not conformed to this world: but be ye transformed by the renewing of your mind, that ye may prove what is that good, and acceptable, and perfect, will of God."**

Now we must ask ourselves, what is the perfect will of God for all of us? **Romans 4:20 (KJV) "²⁰He staggered not at the promise of God through unbelief; but was strong in faith, giving glory to God;"** God gives us all a measure of faith as he gave Abraham. He put in those whom He will to come into His presents and surrender all in total trust as ... **1 Peter 5:7 (KJV) "⁷ Casting all your care upon him; for he careth for you."** He will give us the ability to "walk by faith and not by sight" when you are brought to the place to see that it is ... **Zechariah 4:6 (KJV) ⁶ Not by might, nor by power, but by my spirit, saith the LORD of hosts."**

When Jesus takes full possession of these elect vessels, then we will know what He means when He said be perfect which means be totally possessed by Him, the perfect one. **Matthew 22:44 "The LORD said unto my Lord, Sit thou on my right hand, till I make thine enemies thy footstool."** Jesus's prayers are to bring us into this revelation and understanding so He can begin to occupy His temple in you to continue His work through the acts of the Holy Spirit. By dying to self, the flesh is being consumed as we are becoming meat for the master's use. God never told us to save others; He is the only one that can seek to save that which was lost. We must give up our will so His will can be done; therefore, it is finished with Satan once again under His feet. We cannot speak for God. When you become possessed by Him, He will speak for Himself.

John 16:13 (KJV) "¹³ Howbeit when he, the Spirit of truth, is come, he will guide you into all truth: for he shall not speak of himself; but whatsoever he shall hear, that shall he speak: and he will shew you things to come." Mankind has taught us that we must work for God, that's law, not grace. The mixture of the two is the sum of all our shortcomings. If He did not have an elect there will be no flesh to save. **Isaiah 53:6 (KJV) "⁶ All we like sheep have gone astray; we have turned everyone to his own way; and the LORD hath laid on him the iniquity of us all."** Law is the type and shadow while grace is another dimension that is only seen in the spirit. Our bodies are now the holy of holies, the temple of God. **1 Corinthians 6:19 (KJV) "¹⁹ What? know ye not that your body is the temple of the Holy Ghost which is in you, which ye have of God, and ye are not your own?"**

What we have never understood, we must offer up our bodies as a living sacrifice as Christ did to walk in the perfect will of God to be acceptable unto Christ and the Father. He is our example; we are to follow Him in man as we see Him walking in man. His works follow Him as in the four gospels but even greater in our time of the end. We lie by saying we love Him, but by not keeping His word, we show Him that we do not love

Him. It is easy to lie before the lord when you know not what spirit you are of. **Proverbs 16:25 (KJV) "²⁵ There is a way that seemeth right unto a man, but the end thereof are the ways of death."**

God's elects are on the shelf in preparation to become the **manifested sons of God** at the appointed time in the tribulation that will arrest the attention of the world; just mere men made perfect, walking in the fullness of the godhead bodily putting the devil under His feet. He reveals Himself in the glorified body of believers, as His bride. Our thoughts are either good or evil, there is no in between. The in between is where we are seduced by false doctrine when it comes to Christianity. This doctrine justifies willful sinning by lack of convictions, we can't live perfect. **Matthew 5:48 (KJV) "⁴⁸ Be ye therefore perfect, even as your Father which is in heaven is perfect."** For years, like many of us who were brought up under false teaching, Satan used our ignorance to wrest the scriptures to our own destruction. If God did not choose us to walk in His perfect will, we would still be in the dark today, but by election, God in His own time, brought us into his light. Now we are to follow men as they follow Christ.

Now you may ask this question, how will I know who is following Christ? The answer is, when your mind has been renewed into the mind of Christ, you will know them by their fruit. If you don't have his mind, you will not know him when He speaks. **1 Corinthians 2:16 (KJV) "¹⁶ For who hath known the mind of the Lord, that he may instruct him? But we have the mind of Christ." Romans 8:9 (KJV) "⁹ But ye are not in the flesh, but in the Spirit, if so be that the Spirit of God dwell in you. Now if any man have not the Spirit of Christ, he is none of his."**

The revelation of the cross is where the flesh was consumed in death under the law as the slain lamb. Now in the spirit under grace, our flesh is consumed and sanctified in the spirit through your dying to self so you now can become meat for the master's use. When you can say… **Galatians 2:20 (KJV) "²⁰ I am crucified with Christ: nevertheless, I live; yet not I, but Christ liveth in me: and the life which I now live in the flesh I live by the faith of the Son of God, who loved me, and gave himself for me."** I must say that none of this can be accomplished unless the spirit of God draws you into this way. Man cannot do good when there's none in him. **John 6:44 (KJV) "⁴⁴ No man can come to me, except the Father which hath sent me draw him: and I will raise him up at the last day."** When

He say, **"I will raise him up at the last day,"** He is raising himself up in you. This time, He is in your body and you now get to live in eternity with him again after the sixth day. When Christ said … **Luke 18:8 (KJV) "⁸ I tell you that he will avenge them speedily. Nevertheless, when the Son of man cometh, shall he find faith on the earth?"**

What is he saying? Will I see the fullness of my spirit operating in you because he is coming back for Himself. Up until now, those received in heaven are there by election and mercy. The fullness of God has only been reserved for the last days to be manifested in man. We have only managed to become apostate as evident that Satan has deceived the whole world.

Revelation 12:9 (KJV) "⁹ And the great dragon was cast out, that old serpent, called the Devil, and Satan, <u>which deceiveth the whole world:</u> he was cast out into the earth, and his angels were cast out with him." **Mark 13:20 (KJV) "²⁰ And except that the Lord had shortened those days, no flesh should be saved: but for the elect's sake, whom he hath chosen, he hath shortened the days."** God takes you from fear to love. **1 John 4:18 (KJV) "¹⁸ There is no fear in love; but perfect love casteth out fear: because fear hath torment. He that feareth is not made perfect in love."** These are some of the teachings I have received from the Holy Spirit concerning the perfect and sovereign will of God, these are chosen and drawn in by His spirit. God does not reveal this to everyone although it is available to all but only a selected few will walk in this revelation. **Matthew 7:13-15 (KJV) "¹³ Enter ye in at the strait gate: for wide is the gate, and broad is the way, that leadeth to destruction, and many there be which go in thereat: ¹⁴ Because strait is the gate, and narrow is the way, which leadeth unto life, <u>and few there be that find it</u>. ¹⁵ Beware of false prophets, which come to you in sheep's clothing, but inwardly they are ravening wolves."**

There is nothing we can do to empress God. God is only impressed by what he can do in us. This was also revealed to me by the Holy Spirit, many are trying to compare the latter rain to the former rain, now get this, up until now, we have only operated in part with gifts in a separated environment as knowing in part but not in full. The present church world is divided into separate kingdoms. The Pentecostal experience began in one body, and it will end in one body. There is nothing we have seen or done in the past to compare with a latter rain experience.

Your knowledge you learn in deliverance was in part but not in full. Christ has called his elect to rest in preparation for the fullness of perfection that only he can bring as stated in Ephesians 4:11-12. Down through the years, the church failed from this place in Christ. The reason we all must repent, that is what we fail short of, the fullness of his glory. We all have been deceived to a certain point. The reason for election is to restore God's presents in the body as his head is now being placed on his finished body which he has put together in this valley of dry bones as stated in Ezekiel 37 to show that he is God and beside him there is none other. I was reminded of this prophecy that will be apparent in the end time.... **Isaiah 53:6 (KJV)** **"⁶ All we like sheep have gone astray; we have turned everyone to his own way; and the LORD hath laid on him the iniquity of us all."** Remember we were just dust in the beginning. (Updated for Released 12/2019)

EVENTS TIMELINE OF
THE TRIBULATION

Signs that precede the tribulation:

1. Fighting undeclared wars beginning with Korea to Afghanistan; these undeclared wars will lead to the downfall of our economy in our vein attempts to police the world.

2. Terrorist attacks will become common. After 911, seven years of calm is the grace period. Natural disasters will begin to increase at the end of the seven years of grace.

3. Very wet seasons, there will be floods across the nation. Climate change will show signs of diverse weather patterns, abnormal high temperatures and dry crop failures.

4. Stock Market will spike up and down before the final fall. The economy will show signs of weakening.

5. Major change in the economy will contribute to Job losses that will not return. Food shortages and job losses will lead to a rapid increase in crime as neighbors' resort to survival.

6. Marshall Law will be declared in many of the major cities; many prisoners will be released because of the loss of state operating funds.

7. A new world money system in America.

All these projections point to begin after 2010

1. Earthquakes and volcanic eruptions will be diverse around the world. Major cities will see   eruptions in the mid-west and West Coast.

2. A very cold winter will sweep parts of the nations with temperatures reaching -40 below.

3. North Korea invades South Korea.

4. China attacks Taiwan.

5. 98% of the rebellious patriotic Christian will die when World War Three is declared.

6. A Biological pandemic will start in New York, California and will spread to many other states.

7. China and Japan will become economic partners.

8. An earthquake will become diverse as the weather patterns will take out a major northern city.

9. Earthquakes will begin to occur all over US.

10. Major events will shake this nation's foundation. A major earthquake hits Chicago.

11. All the elects will begin to operate in the fullness of Christ who are chosen will have the power to stand in the fullness of the two witnesses in the spirit.

12. After the earthquake in Chicago, all out nuclear attack on USA.

13. Florida - (from Orlando southward) will be under water; destroyed. A third portion of California will be under water.

14. Russia and China will invade the US.

15. California - Chinese are ordered to kill all Americans.

16. Russia takes Alaska and everyone in this state are killed.

17. Hawaii - surrenders to Japan.

18. Washington D.C. is blown up with a nuclear device.

19. 70% of all Americans will be killed before a fragmented asteroid take out the western hemisphere. We will no longer exist. That will be the fulfillment of the Sodomy curse.

What we as American's never realized, our state of internal divisions gave our enemies the opportunity to dismantle our infrastructure through cyber warfare before the invasion begin. *Revelation 10:4 (KJV) "4 And when the seven thunders had uttered their voices, I was about to write: and I heard a voice from heaven saying unto me, Seal up those things which the seven thunders uttered, and write them not."* Read the chronicle on "**What Will Happen during the Tribulation Siege**".

These things will befall the CHILDREN OF DISPBEDIENCE as Christians that will meet their fate as unwise virgins. They will be reaped in the second sickle, Rev.14:17-19. They will be the residue saved by the prayers of the righteous that shall cut short the time before the wrath of God is poured out that will change the geography of the Earth.

This is when the rapture will take place ... *Revelation 14:15-18 (KJV)* *"15 And another angel came out of the temple, crying with a loud voice to him that sat on the cloud, thrust in thy sickle, and reap: for the time is come for thee to reap; for the harvest of the earth is ripe. 16 And he that sat on the cloud thrust in his sickle on the earth; and the <u>earth was reaped</u>.* (This is the rapture) *17 And <u>another angel</u> came out of the temple which is in heaven, he also having a sharp sickle. 18 And another angel came out from the altar, which had power over fire; and cried with a loud cry to him that had the sharp sickle, saying, thrust in thy sharp sickle, and <u>gather the clusters</u> of the vine of the earth; for her grapes are fully ripe.* These are the children of disobedience prayed for by the righteous.

During these seven years, the elect's time will be shortened and removed before the wrath is poured out without mixture. This is the other side of God that could not be revealed but experienced by all the ungodly. The **six remaining thunders along with the vials** are for the wicked. The reason this need not be revealed; the church will be gone. These writings described seven years of events. These messages have been timed because of the content of the revelations. In time past, I revealed bits and pieces of this summery in other self-publications; all have pointed us to this end.

The timelines were collected from other major prophecies and are to be judged according to their appearance. *"Father, I thank you for this privilege you have given me to be a vessel chosen for your use, and now for the benefit of those who hunger and thirst for truth, in the name of Jesus, I employ the Holy Spirit the dictate this summary to those that have ears to hear." AMEN*

The great mystery of the seven thunders in Rev. 10:4 could not be revealed until the time was right as God has ordained, not before. All that have been written about the book of Revelation has been in part and somewhat imaginary; however, the most significant part of this book is hidden as the third and final layer to be revealed to this last generation. The other side of God experienced by Israel is a type and shadow of the end time judgment of the Church in America. God has no regard for people who are given over to the devil for eternal separation.

They will suffer at the hand of their father the devil without mercy. (John 8:44) This is the mystery of iniquity. **2 Timothy 2:7 (KJV) "⁷ Consider what I say, and the Lord give thee understanding in all things. 2 Thessalonians 2:7 (KJV) ⁷ For the mystery of iniquity doth already work: only he who now letteth will let, until he be taken out of the way."** The general view of the first half of the tribulation are signs to watch by those that have been given eyes to see and ears to hear. The dates of these events are in the timing of the Father which no man knows. I have always been skeptical when a person gives a specific date; however, the signs will reveal the times in which these things will take place. Whenever His people are in harm's way, if their course has not been completed, they will be warned or miraculously transported as Phillip to safety. The angels assigned to you will guard over you as airs of salvation. That's why we are told …. *2 Corinthians 5:7 (KJV) "⁷ For we walk by faith, not by sight:"* Christ demonstrated in himself what those who come after him will do when you have had a wilderness experience.

You will come out perfect as Christ and all will see. The sign of conversion is the death of you. That fruit is manifested when you have … *Isaiah 55:7 (KJV) "⁷ Let the wicked forsake his way, and the unrighteous man his thoughts: and let him return unto the LORD, and he will have mercy upon him; and to our God, for he will abundantly pardon. Romans 12:1 (KJV) ¹ I beseech you therefore, brethren, by the mercies of God, that ye present your bodies a living sacrifice, holy, acceptable unto God, which is your reasonable service.* This is where you will see the Sons of God come out of the volume of the book. These scriptures are some of the mysteries of Godliness where we see Christ working with the father in the type and shadow of the old covenant. This shows us that God is in control of all things not the devil. When God brought me to rest, it was to get my attention; when I got still, this is what He said; what do you desire of Me? Now I could have never come up with an answer to such a question unless He had put it in me to ask with this reply, **I want your mind** because you said if I do not have your mind, I don't have you. Now some of you know the date you were born again and time you were born again, as for me, I have only been interested in what He said to me and from that time on, act on it by faith; That was just the beginning, he gave you his power and you let Satan take it from you by fear of things God told you would come that he gave you the victory in Christ over.

He has made me see Him as the GREAT I AM, that experience alone is enough for me that I do not have to ask Him much of anything anymore. He has given me a knowing at the time I need to know and that is good enough for me as to walk by faith not by sight. My beloved brothers and sisters, this is deliverance. As he establishes His work in me, let us examine the topic in question. **Daniel 12:11-13 (KJV) "**[11]** And from the time that the daily sacrifice shall be taken away, and the abomination that maketh desolate set up, there shall be a thousand two hundred and ninety days."** Hold on to your hearts, he is describing the end of the works the law that will take seventy years for the destruction of that natural temple. The crossover into the spirit is where the new temple **in you** will take on a spiritual meaning. Now Christian martyrs will become the sacrifices.

This will be the change of the system we know as the N.W.O. which in the spirit means NOW is the time Satan will be seen as Santa, (the god of materialistic bondage) to set up his earthly kingdom of deception and persecute the saints during the tribulation.[12] **Blessed is he that waiteth, and cometh to the thousand three hundred and five and thirty days.** [13] **But go thou thy way till the end be: for thou shalt rest and stand in thy lot at the <u>end of the days</u>.**" At the end of days, the mystery will be revealed. **Daniel 12:4 (KJV) "**[4]** But thou, O Daniel, shut up the words, and seal the book, even to the time of the end: many shall run to and fro, and knowledge shall be increased."**

Now we can fast forward to the present and see what God has kept being revealed at this time. Man's knowledge has not profited him; the presents of evil has made him a captive. What God has meant for good in the hands of evil men, Satan has encapsulated him into a prison of self-bondage and destruction. Sense Adam sinned, man has retrogressed with knowledge not progressed; with all the knowledge we have gained, it has only managed to guarantee the end of all things with mutual assured destruction. What have we accomplished if it can all be destroyed in one hour of time? **Revelation 18:17 (ASV)** [17] **for in an hour so great riches is made desolate. And every shipmaster, and everyone that saileth any wither, and mariners, and as many as gain their living by sea, stood afar off.** (They are looking at the destruction of America.) **Revelation 18:8 (ASV)** [8] **Therefore in one day shall her plagues come, death, and mourning, and famine; and she shall be utterly burned with fire; for strong is the Lord God who judged her. Revelation 10:4 (KJV)** "[4] **And when the seven thunders had uttered their voices, I was about to write: and I heard a voice from heaven saying unto me, Seal up those things which the seven thunders uttered, and write them not.**" This is the thunder judgment being carried out on America after the church is removed.

As with Daniel and so as with John. These mysteries were sealed until the time of the end. The state of the church world at that time, in apostasy could not believe this hard saying before the time; therefore, for 98 percent of them, if revealed in that state before time, many would faint for lack of hope through fear. God knowing the evils of sin as children of the devil would take its toll on mankind until the end. They will be in a state of delusion being seduced in the fallaway that will lead up to God having to reveal their fate after rejecting the call, kept these revelations sealed from his creations so they could receive hope to be saved.

What Daniel and John were told not to write are the events that reveal the other side of God, who at that time, will destroy all that is not elected or by mercy and grace, to be added to his kingdom. Keep this in mind, what happen to Israel for their rebellion will happen to us in the dispensation of grace, twofold. **Revelation 18:6 (KJV)** [6] *Reward her even as she rewarded you, and* **double unto her double** *according to her works: in the cup which* **she hath filled fill to her double. Ecclesiastes 1:9 (KJV)** "[9] **The thing** that hath been, it is that which shall be; and that which is done is that which shall be done: and there is no new thing under the sun."

The world has a saying ... **"What goes around comes around"** although not scriptural, it describes the teachings of the laws of good and evil as in Deut. Chapter twenty-eight. To get an understanding of what this statement means, let us examine the type and shadow in the old covenant. **Lamentations 1:7 (KJV)** [7] **Jerusalem remembered in the days of her affliction and of her miseries all her pleasant things that she had in the days of old, when her people fell into the hand of the enemy, and none did help her: the adversaries saw her and did mock at her sabbaths.** (Unholy ways) **Now** our day of reckoning in the gentiles age, God will remind us of the covenant we neglected to keep "IN GOD WE TRUST" before we are handed over to our enemies. This is history being repeated.

We will be shaken to see how our so-called allies turn against us also. **Ezekiel 9:8 (KJV)** [8] **And it came to pass, while they were slaying them, and I was left, that I fell upon my face, and cried, and said, Ah Lord GOD! wilt thou destroy all the residue of Israel in thy pouring out of thy fury upon Jerusalem?** The prophets of this time will cry and lament at the destruction of the people and lukewarm Christians who will die in the siege that will have horrific consequences. **Isaiah 13:6 (KJV)** [6] **Howl ye; for the day of the LORD is at hand; <u>it shall come as a destruction from the Almighty</u>.**

Just as Israel so as the church. God has predestined evil to run its course to fulfill all things. **Isaiah 51:19 (KJV)** [19] **These two things are come unto thee; who shall be sorry for thee? Desolation, and destruction, and the famine, and the sword: by whom shall I comfort thee? Matthew 24:7 (KJV).** [7] **For nation shall rise against nation, and kingdom against kingdom: and there shall be famines, and pestilences, and earthquakes, in divers** [8] **All these are the beginning of sorrows. Revelation 6:4-8 (KJV)** [4] **And there went out another <u>horse that was red</u>: and power was given to him that sat thereon to take peace from the earth, and that they should kill one another: and there was given unto him a great sword.**

This is where we are before the great tribulation for the saints that will usher in the latter rain. Many will be martyred for the glory of God. Wars will cause much bloodshed. [5] **And when he had opened the third seal, I** heard the third beast say, Come and see. And I beheld, and lo a <u>black horse</u>; and he that sat on him had a pair of balances in his hand. ⁶ And I heard a voice in the midst of the four beasts say, A measure of wheat for a penny, and three measures of barley for a penny; and see thou hurt not the oil and the wine. This will be the hope of the saints; those elected with the anointing (oil) and covered in the blood of the lamb (wine) will not be harmed. ⁷ And when he had opened the <u>fourth seal</u>, I heard the voice of the fourth beast say, Come and see. ⁸ And I looked and behold a <u>pale horse:</u> and his name that sat on him was Death, and Hell followed with him. And power was given unto them over the fourth part of the earth, to kill with sword, and with hunger, and with death, and with the beasts of the earth. This is what Daniel and John were told not to write as in Dan.12:4 and Rev. 10:4. as previously described.

This is the first and only revelation I received that will befall the children of disobedience…. **Ephesians 5:6 (KJV) ⁶ Let no man deceive you with vain words: for because of these things cometh the wrath of God upon the children of disobedience. Romans 1:18 (KJV) ¹⁸ For the wrath of God is revealed from heaven against all ungodliness and unrighteousness of men, who hold the truth in unrighteousness; Matthew 24:19 (KJV) ¹⁹ And woe unto them that are with child, and to them that give suck in those days! Deuteronomy 28:57 (KJV) ⁵⁷ And toward her young one that cometh out from between her feet, and toward her children which she shall bear: for she shall eat them for want of all things secretly in the siege and straitness, wherewith thine enemy shall distress thee in thy gates.**

The demon principality, (the beast) that ruled the N.W.O. will have no mercy and take no prisoners. Those with the mark that are willing servants will be given rewards for turning in Christians including members of their own families for temporary comforts. All the patriots will be sought out and killed first. This is the return of the Barabbas patriot spirit as deceived evangelicals that must be destroyed for taking up arms in the name of God against the authorities, they will die by the same means. In the meantime, this distraction will prepare the true saints to be glorified and received.

Romans 8:23 (KJV) "²³ And not only they, but ourselves also, which have the first fruits of the Spirit, even we ourselves groan within ourselves, waiting for the adoption, to wit, the redemption of our body. Joel 3:14

(KJV) [14] Multitudes, multitudes in the valley of decision: for the day of the LORD is near in the valley of decision. **1 Thessalonians 5:9 (KJV)** [9] **For God hath not appointed us to wrath, but to obtain salvation by our Lord Jesus Christ, Ephesians 3:5 (KJV)** [5] **Which in other ages was not made known unto the sons of men, as it is now revealed unto his holy apostles and prophets by the Spirit; Matthew 24:21 (KJV)** [21] **For then shall be great tribulation, such as was not since the beginning of the world to this time, no, nor ever shall be."**

This is the punishment of the children of disobedience of whom the prayers of the righteous shall avail on their behalf. These are the rewards of those who gave up their lives for the sake of others. God has given space to receive their prayers … **Revelation 8:4 (KJV) "**[4]**And the smoke of the incense, which came with the prayers of the saints, ascended up before God out of the angel's hand. James 5:16 (KJV)** [16] **Confess your faults one to another, and pray one for another, that ye may be healed. The effectual fervent prayer of a righteous man availeth much.** God gave us his love so we could lay down our life for those we love who did not love us back. He is now giving you the desires of your heart as He promised. As Jesus was led as a sheep to the slaughter, these children will be literally slaughtered for food. **(Micah 3:3) 2 Peter 2:12 (KJV) "**[12] **But these, as natural brute beasts, made to be taken and destroyed, speak evil of the things that they understand not; and shall utterly perish in their own corruption;"**

These are the people that will be given over to cannibalism, having no hope of salvation will result to a survival mentality, by their conscious being seared, therefore, they will resort to… **Isaiah 36:12 (KJV)"12 that they may eat their own dung, and drink their own piss with you? Jeremiah 19:9 (NLT)** [9] **I will see to it that your enemies lay siege to the city until all the food is gone. Then those trapped inside will have to eat their own sons and daughters and friends. They will be driven to utter despair.**

Ezekiel 5:10 (KJV) "[10] **Therefore the fathers shall eat the sons in the midst of thee, and the sons shall eat their fathers; and I will execute judgments in thee, and the whole** remnant of thee will I scatter into all the winds. **(Zechariah 14:2 (NLT)** [2] **On that day I will gather all the nations to fight against Jerusalem. The city will be taken, the houses**

plundered, and the women raped. Half the population will be taken away into captivity, and half will be left among the ruins of the city.) ... half of the city, shall go forth into captivity, and <u>the residue of the people shall not be cut off from the city</u>.

This will be that remnant saved to repopulate the millennium. Chuck Youngbrandt, a Prophet saw a vision of green bubbles that represented the people encapsulated to survive the tribulation for this purpose. **Isaiah 26:20 (ASV)** **20 Come, my people, enter thou into thy chambers, and shut thy doors about thee: hide thyself for a little moment, until the indignation be overpast.**

 It is very apparent as revealed today via internet, concentration camps FEMA has constructed around this nation on sites outside the cites for mass burials. This has been well documented on the internet. You will be taken to one of these camps during the siege when martial law is declared; you will have no power to resist. Your young wives and daughters will be rape by the invading army and loose criminals. **Lamentations 5:11 (KJV/ NLT) "11 Our enemies rape the women in Jerusalem and the young girls in all the towns of Judah. Hosea 13:16 (KJV/NLT) 16 They will be killed by an invading army, their little ones dashed to death against the ground, their pregnant women ripped open by swords."** Bruit beast cannibalism will cause you to eat your children. These are the zombielike people that have lost their minds and control by flesh eating demons.

Their unborn child will become a delicacy as a young sheep led to the slaughter. I asked the Holy Spirit why this will be allowed. The reply, China has raised up a demonic army of young men by the blood sacrifice of baby girls that has never known a woman; they will be turned loose in the cities on the west coast to destroy all Americans. Your young wives and daughters will become the spoils as their rewards for our aborted unborn.

We will see this curse returned upon us for allowing the legalization of abortions. Our young virgin daughters will be sacrificed to them. They will not feed you because you have been brought to these camps to die as in the days of Hitler, but our punishment will be double as describe here, and to survive, you will feed on each other. The spirits within those rejected will become like bruit beast, wild dogs zombie like creatures, ready to literally eat each other. As punishment, those lukewarm Christians that would not listen to you when you tried to warn them will have to give up their bodies for food. **Micah 3:3** To get a perspective by not having dreams or vision, God gave me the liberty to watch practically every disaster movie I could find. This was difficult to hear and write.

Micah 3:3 (KJV) "³ Who also eat the flesh of my people and flay their skin from off them; and they break their bones, and chop them in pieces, as for the pot, and as flesh within the <u>caldron</u>." This is a large pot that will be used for cooking human flesh. My dear friends, God has repeated this several time in these writings. This is a very grievous thing for him to allow a second time now to be repeated among us as gentiles as a double curse. Now you see why these revelations were held back for this time to be revealed as a final warning to those that have ears to hear. In the second half of the tribulation for the sake of the elects; time will be cut short. This is the time that no man knows as in the type and shadow before the new moon on the Jewish calendar, no one will know the minute or the hour until the moon appears; likewise, so shall it be when Jesus returns.

Ephesians 5:6 (KJV) ⁶ Let no man deceive you with vain words: for because of these things cometh the wrath of God upon the children of disobedience. They will be raptured in that second sickle reaping of the cluster in Rev. 14:17-19 ... **Matthew 24:29-30 (KJV) ²⁹ Immediately after the tribulation of those days shall the sun be darkened, and the moon shall not give her light, and the stars shall fall from heaven,** (A fragmented asteroids and meteorites, raining down the sodomy curse that will hit the western hemisphere.) **and the powers of the heavens shall be shaken: ³⁰ And then shall appear the sign of the Son of man in heaven:** (Christ himself will appear) **and then shall all the tribes of the earth mourn, and they shall see the Son of man coming in the clouds of heaven with power and great glory.**

These are the remnants that will see this wonder. **John 6:39 (KJV) ³⁹ And this is the Father's will which hath sent me, that of all which he hath given me I should lose nothing, but should raise it up again <u>at the last day</u>. 1 Corinthians 15:52 (KJV) ⁵² In a moment, in the twinkling of an eye, <u>at the last trump</u>: for the trumpet shall sound, and the dead shall be raised incorruptible, and we shall be changed. 1 Thessalonians 4:16-17 (KJV) ¹⁶ For the Lord himself shall descend from heaven with** a shout, with the voice of the archangel, and with the trump of God: and the dead in Christ shall rise first: Revelation 14:15 (KJV) "¹⁵ And another angel came out of the temple, crying with a loud voice to him that sat on the cloud, Thrust in thy sickle, and reap: <u>for the time is come for thee to reap;</u> for the harvest of the earth is ripe." Ezekiel 37:12 (NKJV) ¹² Therefore prophesy and say to them, 'Thus says the Lord GOD: "Behold, O My people, I will open your graves and cause you to come up from your graves, and bring you into the land of Israel. 1 Thessalonians. 4: <u>vs</u> ¹⁷ Then we which are alive and remain shall be caught up together with them in the clouds, to meet the Lord in the air: and so shall we ever be with the Lord.

Revelation 14:18 (KJV) ¹⁸ And another angel came out from the altar, which had power over fire; and cried with a loud cry to him that had the sharp sickle, saying, Thrust in thy sharp sickle, and <u>gather the clusters of the vine</u> of the earth; for her grapes are fully ripe." This cluster being received are the souls of the children of disobedience prayed for who suffered the destruction of their bodies … 1 Corinthians 5:5 (KJV) ⁵ To deliver such an one unto Satan for the destruction of the flesh, that the spirit may be saved <u>in the day of the Lord Jesus</u>.

This is the revelation given for those who suffered the first of the seven thunders. After that the wrath will be poured out without mixture on the condemned. The following six thunders and vials will end all things. Matthew 24:37 (KJV) ³⁷ But as the days of Noe were, so shall also the coming of the Son of man be. Acts 2:20 (KJV) ²⁰ The sun shall be turned into darkness, and the moon into blood, before that great and notable day of the Lord come: 2 Peter 3:12 (KJV) ¹² Looking for and hasting unto the coming of the day of God, wherein the heavens being on fire shall be dissolved, and the elements shall melt with fervent heat?

The Earth will be renovated and purified by an asteroid to complete the second stage of the Earth's restoration for the seventh millennium. This is stage two of the **Thunder judgment;** no flesh would have survived. A remnant will be preserved in all parts of the world for repopulation during the millennium. Read Zachariah 13: 8-9, 14:2. This is the final Judgment of the wrath. (Zach. 14: 12. Rev. 1:7)

In final summation:

1. The last Generation of Matthew twenty-four began after the 1967 war when Israel captured Jerusalem, now the Messiah can return to the city of David as recaptured by Israel to reign during the millennium.

2. Sept. 11, 2001, began the seven years of grace that ended on Sept.11, 2008. This completed the forty years of the last generation of gentiles. The year 2008, a new beginning when God said… **Isaiah 43:19 (KJV)** [19] **Behold, I will do a new thing; now it shall spring forth; shall ye not know it? I will even make a way in the wilderness, and rivers in the desert.**

3. There will be places of safety for those people during the tribulation; He will cause to survive for the millennium.

4. All things are now preparing for His return. The end of man's time is up. We are now in the period of transition which will be in two parts comprising a total of seven years. These two parts will produce the former and latter rain in the glory of his coming.

Finally, the world as it was shall be no more. We are in the beginning stages of a **New Time Continuum** that will take us through a seven-year period of change. When all is completed, only a remnant will be left for repopulation of the earth in all parts of the world. **Zechariah14:16 (KJV)** [16] **And it shall come to pass, that every one that is left of all the nations which came against Jerusalem shall even go up from year to year to worship the King, the LORD of hosts, and to keep the feast of Tabernacles.** The reason why Satan had to be bound was to fulfil this prophecy of every tongue must come and bow down before the throne of Christ from every tribe, tongue and kindred. Satan, being bound will not be here to temp those that were allowed to be in that number. The reason why he will be loosed is to claim the souls that were never meant to go to heaven but were there to fulfill that prophecy. These revelations were given to me for release at this time. They were not meant to be known until just before the tribulation began. God separated me from all else to complete this writing of this revelation. Some of those close to me could not receive this revelation as being from God.

All God's people will be sealed to become meat for the master's consumption in the fires of tribulation to His glory. (Rev.3:18) Vary soon; our lives will never be the same. The world will now get to see what Israel saw in their tribulation siege when they were given over to their enemies for destruction. THIS IS OUR LAST WARNING. REPENT! REPENT! REPENT! The Kingdom of Heaven is at hand, THE MYSTERY IS ABOUT TO BE FINISHED.

"Father, lay not this charge to the innocent victims of false teaching, have mercy on these who cry out for forgiveness. It is for this reason that you cause your elects to lay down their lives that these might be saved. Father, please have mercy on our loved ones who hated us, forgive them for they knew not what they were doing. It is for this cause that we laid our lives down in intercessory prayer that they might be saved. Father, let my life be the ransom for the salvation of their souls in their hour of judgment, put my tears in a bottle; remember them and my sacrifice of love for them. You laid down your life for me, so I now lay down my life for them. Let not the enemies steal your heritage for I know it is not your will for them to perish, please bring them to repentance. You said you were going to and fro looking for someone to stand the gap, please Father, let not my tears be wasted, hear my plea for the innocent souls whose hearts were right but became victims of blind guides. Even I plead as Abraham did; Have mercy on them in the name of our Lord Jesus Christ." AMEN

Having been given these revelations, it became apparent to me that a great many of us confessing Christians are so religious to the point that God can no longer teach them and so holy that they act like what God said is not enough to the point that we add more to his word in our own strength to make us look more like him. How pitiful we are in his sight not knowing what spirit we are of. I too was one of them until he opened my eyes. As a messenger, therefore, I have been rejected most of my life by having to reveal what was held back by Daniel and John in a time of spiritual darkness to a generation unprepared to hear it. (Updated 5/2021)

THE FINAL BATTLE
FOR SOULS

Whether we believe it or not? The final battle for souls has begun; the scale of which the world is about to see the manifestation of the spirit world embodied in the souls of evil men. The NATURAL MAN against the SPIRITUAL MAN, the SONS of PERDITION against the SONS of GOD. THE BODY of the ANTICHRIST against THE BODY of THE CHURCH of CHRIST, GOOD against EVIL and EVIL against GOOD. All will come to a head as manifested in the chaos that will be seen in this last generation.

Revelation 12:12 (KJV) "¹²Therefore rejoice, ye heavens, and ye that dwell in them. Woe to the inhabiters of the earth and of the sea! for the devil is come down unto you, having great wrath, because he knoweth that he hath but a short time. 2 Thessalonians 2:3 (KJV) ³Let no man deceive you by any means: for that day shall not come, except there come a falling away first, and that man of sin be revealed, the son of perdition; John 17:12 (KJV) ¹²While I was with them in the world, I kept them in thy name: those that thou gavest me I have kept, and none of them is lost, but the son of perdition; that the scripture might be fulfilled." Now I am going to reveal to you what was told to me about what we are about to see in the sons of perdition? Where they get their source of power. The world as we know it is about to go through a radical change naturally and spiritually and God overseeing it all.

First: Who is the Son of Perdition? **(Satan)** 2 Corinthians 4:4 (KJV) **"⁴In whom the god of this world hath blinded the minds of them which believe not, lest the light of the glorious gospel of Christ, who is the image of God, should shine unto them.** Luke 9:55 (KJV) ⁵⁵ **But he turned, and rebuked them, and said, <u>Ye know not what manner of spirit ye are of</u>."** The Holy Spirit was sent to establish the church body of Christ. This is the body we will see Christ operating in. This body will be put together by Christ.

John 10:27 (KJV) "²⁷My sheep hear my voice, and I know them, and they follow me: Acts 2:47 (KJV) ⁴⁷ Praising God and having favour with all the people. <u>And the Lord added to the church daily such as should be saved.</u>" This is the true body of Christ that the world saw birth in the apostle's doctrine where the world will see Christ. The fruit of this church will be manifested as in Gal. 5:22, having all things in common.

Satan over the past two thousand years has pressed this body into his spirit where this present church does not know what spirit they are of ... **Daniel 7:25 (KJV) "25 And he shall speak great words against the most High, and shall <u>wear out the saints of the most High</u>, and think to change times and laws: and they shall be given into his hand until a time and times and the dividing of time."**

Now let's examine the context of this scripture because it speaks of past, present and future. ²⁵ **<u>And he shall speak great words against the most high</u>** ... When he penetrated the church body, he defiled it with a new doctrine; this seduction was so smooth that when God open our eyes, this revelation will be apparent ...**Revelation 12:9 (KJV) "⁹ And the great dragon was cast out, that old serpent, called the Devil, and Satan, <u>which deceiveth the whole world</u>: he was cast out into the earth, and his angels were cast out with him."** ... and shall wear out the saints of the most High,

Through generations of teaching this compromised doctrine, he will succeed... **and think to change times and laws:** This will give rise in the last days to a new world religion that will be manifested in the Laodicea church... **Revelation 3:14-17 (KJV "¹⁵ I know thy works, that thou art neither cold nor hot: I would thou wert cold or hot. ¹⁶ So then because thou art lukewarm, and neither cold nor hot, I will spue thee out of my mouth. ¹⁷ Because thou sayest, I am rich, and increased with goods,** and have need of nothing; and knowest not that thou art wretched, and miserable, and poor, and blind, and naked:" <u>and they shall be given into his hand until a time and times and the dividing of time</u>.

This is where we are today in that last generation of **Matthew 24. "1 John 5:19 (KJV) "**[19]**And we know that we are of God,** these are the elects that kept God's presents in the world, now are about to become glorified with the latter rain. **and the world lieth in wickedness.**" This is our state when God visit us. When the prophets bring this message, all who repent, will enter his rest, those that reject will be given over to a spirit to continue in their deceived state as a child of the devil, not knowing what spirit they are of, they will persecute you in the name of God as sons of perdition, the antichrist body.

As I have already experienced, this present-day church world cannot receive this report of their state because of two thousand years of deception. This will be the natural man at war with the spiritual man. **Revelation 12:7-9(KJV) "**[7]**And there was war in heaven: Michael and his angels fought against the dragon; and the dragon fought and his angels,** [8]**And prevailed not; neither was their place found any more in heaven.** [9]**And the great dragon was cast out, that old serpent, called the <u>Devil, and Satan, which deceiveth the whole world</u>: he was cast out into the earth, and his angels were cast out with him.**" At that time wicked men... 2 **Timothy 3:13 (KJV) "**[13]**But evil men and seducers shall wax worse and worse, deceiving, and being deceived.**"

God, at this time will begin the judgment of all who name His name in the earth. **"The great Separation"** will commence; the eyes of the elected prophets will be opened to see and discern the times and warn all those who have ears to hear. I discovered this was my calling to deliver these revelations. **"The Holy Spirit, God inside of you,"** the body of elects, shall make war in the earth with the devil. All that has been spoken by the prophets will began to happen at an accelerated pace in the earth as seen in the year 2008 the year that ended the last gentile generation forty years after the 1967 war of Israel's final deliverance to recapture the capital city of Jerusalem.

Sept.11 of that year ended the seven-year grace period of "911". All is set now for Christ return which will now come through a transition of seven years of tribulation. These seven years of spiritual warfare in heaven and earth will be seen in the evil that God will allow Satan to run his course to fulfill all that have been spoken by the prophets, then Satan's rule on earth will come to an end. The Sons of Elijah will once again go up against the renowned religious leaders in the spirit. The spirit of Moses will return against the sons of Perdition in government, masquerading as the beast and the false prophet will be taken down in these two witnesses in the spirit for the last time. The war in the spirit world manifested in the natural will be in the form of natural as well as man-made disasters as the hidden third layer of the book of Revelation is revealed. This is the tribulation that will renovate the earth for Christ to reign in the millennium.

All the scriptures regarding this warfare will be fulfilled through demon possessed men ruled by these two principalities, The **Beast** and The **False Prophet** headed by the son of perdition, Satan. All at this time **"Living in The Reality of The New Birth"** will see the glory of God manifested in their bodies during the tribulation. **Matthew 16:3 (ASV) "³ And in the morning, It will be foul weather to-day: for the heaven is red and lowering. Ye know how to discern the face of the heaven; but ye cannot discern the signs of the times."**

1 Thessalonians 5:2-3 (ASV) "2 For yourselves know perfectly that the day of the Lord so cometh as a thief in the night.³ When they are saying, Peace and safety, then sudde destruction cometh upon them, as travail upon a woman with child; and they shall in no wise escape. 2 Peter 3:10 (ASV) ¹⁰ But the day of the Lord will come as a thief; in the which the heavens shall pass away with a great noise, and the elements shall be dissolved with fervent heat, and the earth and the works that are therein shall be burned up." This is our destiny during the tribulation period with only a few remnants of Israel and Gentile nations, preserved to repopulate the millennium.

While in meditation the past few days, studying over some notes dictated to me by the Holy Spirit, on the eve of the death of **Michael Jackson,** this message came to me about the sons of the devil? Who are they and how are they manifested in time past to this present day? Satan's idols of the entertainment industry. **Jimmy Hendrix, Marilyn Monroe, Elvis Presley, Anna Nicole Smith and Michael Jackson and many more that will come out of the entertainment industry to become the idols of**

this last generation to sell their soul to the devil. When the Holy Spirit brought this to my mind about the sons of the devil, I was taken back with what he revealed to me. **Matthew 4:9 (ASV) "⁹ and he said unto him, All these things will I give thee, if thou wilt fall down and worship me."**

Now let's examine this passage of layered scripture with a deeper revelation. When you read the context of this chapter, you will see that Jesus is being tempted of the devil. The fact that he was not of this earth but from above is a lesson to us as confessing Christians. When we receive Christ, we will have this same power to resist this temptation of worldly fame over heavenly gain. **Romans 3:23 (ASV) "²³ for all have sinned and fall short of the glory of God; Hebrews 4:1-2 (ASV) ¹ Let us fear therefore, lest haply, a promise being left of entering into his rest, any one of you should seem to have come short of it. ² For indeed we have had good tidings preached unto us, even as also they: but the word of hearing did not profit them, because it was not united by faith with them that heard."**

What cause us to come short of this glory was prophesied in **Dan. 7:25** by no longer having the apostle's doctrine preached in the assemblies. Our spiritual leaders, seduced through the seminary system, birth the Laodicea church, never got to see Christ because they entered by way of the broad road without knowing they were seduced by a father that will blind them of the reality of who they represent. All who are confessing to be of Christ will be given a chance to repent when the warning of our state is revealed by the prophets. This blind church will not see how they have led this generation of off springs to sell their souls to the devil. Talents given to edify the church assembly will be enticed to sale their talents for worldly fame.

This youthful generation has not seen a Godly view of Christ to arrest their attention; therefore, they will be set up to sell their God given talents to the highest bitter; Satan, having robbed the church of the gospel, took those with these talents and made them idols. Satan made them an offer they could not refuse, a transforming spirit that will make them the idols of glitter, fame and wealth. This curse is reserved to be manifested in the last generation in our children for being hypocritical Christian parents. Satan claimed their children by having no ensample, rule their parents. Satan will change the laws to protect them. (Isaiah. 3:12) As I examine the lives of all the above-mentioned names, they all had one thing in common? They all sold their souls in exchange to become worldly idols.

When Satan made this offer at the crossroad of their lives, it's on one condition? You must give your soul in exchange for this position. The human body is limited to certain physical feats; however, to be crowned an icon idol which carries a worldly title as king of this or that, in exchange, Satan will give you what you ask for by calling the demon from the pit with the ability to perform these feats physically until you reach that status to captivate these young souls. This church, under Satan's influence as 501c-3, will not see how your natural God given talent is taken to another level that will captivate the innocent souls who see these demons perform at that level, and become mesmerized and seduced into captivity by these powerful demons until they can mimic the physical abilities of that person who is under the influence of this demon. This is that thin line of deception that will be seen in this last generation.

The church, being part of this worldly seduction, many confessing Christians under the influence of this doctrine will sacrifice their children to these idols and even become sympathetically influence themselves. What Satan blinds you too, is what these church assemblies are failing to see … the effect this evil will have on this generation will become a curse that only God can reverse through repentance.

Religious celebrity preachers will produce religious celebrity Christians that demonstrate a double minded man, very unstable, bordering on self-destruction. These are some of the victims of idol preachers, hirelings for the sake of filthy lucre, (money and fame) behind the pulpit, tithe robbing in the name of God, taking advantage of your ignorance. On the worldly level, **Jimmy Hendrix** demonstrated a supernatural ability to play a guitar that only one with that level of a demonically influenced talent can match. **Marylyn Monroe's** beauty and sex appeal cause men to lust after her body until she became a non-person as an idol object of desire.

Elvis Presley mesmerized his followers with his body moves and singing talent while under the same demonic anointing that sold his soul to the devil; his crown; King of Rock & Roll. **Prince** received the same anointing and suffered the same fate when his time came to an end. Their being idols of worship led them to a state of deep depression brought on by the drugs they used to keep them under Satan's control until their bodies were used up and the sickle angels come to claim them. **Michael Jackson** was given the crown and glory by Satan to exceed all others, in this time, as a confessing Jehovah's witness, he thrilled souls to spiritual death. His reward crowned the king to this pop culture of this last generation. He also received the **Elvis & Hendrix** anointing to suffer the same fate. Pharmacia (drugs) given to sustain the body until all the life and will to live is gone, Satan fills them with legions of demons before he comes to collect the soul.

The pain they feel comes from burning out mentally, physically and emotionally. That's the power of the presence of that demon, using their body to perform those feats physically. That's the price their body pays to perform at that level. This opens the door to suicidal demons which are among those legions they receive. Multiple personalities will manifest in their behavior before they are taken out. This is what we see as a result when the end of their life comes. This familiar pattern is so predictable, there's no need to guess any more. It was also revealed that **Anna Nichol Smith** and **Marylyn Monroe** were being sexually molested in their dreams by a demon of lust and sensuality. These kinds of demons cause you not to have lasting relationships with males because natural men cannot perform sexually at that level. This is what caused them to die young. Their bodies can no longer stand the physical strain given by this demon of pleasure. **Marylin Monroe** was always late for her movie sets.

Ecclesiastes 2:17 (KJV) "**¹⁷ Therefore I hated life; because the work that is wrought under the sun is grievous unto me: for all is vanity and vexation of spirit.**" When one takes Satan's offer in exchange for fame, you also become the world's prisoner. As I watched the world morn its own, the sad and most grievous thing to me is the residue of sin sick followers who, with-out the gospel, are about to receive the same fate in the end. *"Father, send and restore this gospel of the kingdom less we all perish."* I know that some of you who's hearts have been hardened against truth will find this observation unacceptable as the world and the church are seemingly one in the same in their sympathies' and hopes that all will remain and recover so they can continue in their comfort zone. We as well as the world shall very soon see the end of all things.

Ecclesiastes 3:19 (ASV) "[19] **For that which befalleth the sons of men befalleth beasts; even one thing befalleth them: as the one dieth, so dieth the other; yea, they have all one breath; and man hath no preeminence above the beasts: for all is vanity.**" (Updated for Released (6/2021)

THE STATE OF THE UNION & STATE OF THE CHURCH

As a preface to this chronicle, please read Ezekiel Chapter seven. This prophecy from Ezekiel 16: is the type and shadow of America, Israel, and the Church's state at the time this is revealed. This chapter for clarity in the English language will be parallel from The New living Translation (second edition)), however, I suggest you use the KJV to compare verses.

The State of the Union

As you begin to read this chronicle, remember, Israel and America are joined as one union in the spirit as the two becomes one (11). This in part is due to the rejection of Christ as the Messiah. We became the off springs of the Jewish nation, the gentiles. As a nation, chosen out of due time, would be instrumental in the resurrection of Israel's reinstatement as a nation before America is judged. On May 15, 1948, in the United Nations, God fulfilled the first part of this prophecy...**Isaiah 66:8 (KJV) "⁸Who hath heard such a thing? who hath seen such things? Shall the earth be made to bring forth in one day? or shall a nation be born at once? for as soon as Zion travailed, she brought forth her children."**

Its **first** stage was the state of Israel; the **second** was completed in the 1967 war where they recaptured the Abraham land grant which included the city of David, Jerusalem. This is where full national status was achieved as a nation. The **third** tribulation is when Jesus returns to reign. **Ezekiel 16:1-**

56 (KJV/NLT) [1] **Then another message came to me from the LORD:** [2] **"Son of man, confront Jerusalem with her loathsome sins.** [3] **Give her this message from the Sovereign LORD: You are nothing but a Canaanite! Your father was an Amorite and your mother a Hittite!** [4] **When you were born, no one cared about you. Your umbilical cord was left uncut, and you were never washed, rubbed with salt, and dressed in warm clothing.**

This is a parallel prophecy of the rebirth of Israel in 1948, her state in the sight of God. [5] **No one had the slightest interest in you; no one pitied you or cared for you. On the day you were born, you were dumped in a field and left to die, unwanted.** [6] **"But I came by and saw you there, helplessly kicking about in your own blood. As you lay there, I said, 'Live!'** In 1967 when God came to their rescue in that famous war that they could not win without divine intervention; God delivered them from the hands of the Assyrians. Here again, Zion's travail was a cry for help, God returned in the tribe of Judah to rescue his people. Israel is now in control of the capital city, Jerusalem. The Abraham land grant was now complete. This now would mark that generation (Matthew 24:34) that would end after forty years.) [7] **And I helped you to thrive like a plant in the field. You grew up and became a beautiful jewel. Your breasts became full, and your hair grew, though you were still naked.** This is where we see the present-day Israel & America. [8] **And when I passed by and saw you again, you were old enough to be married. So I wrapped my cloak around you to cover your nakedness and declared my marriage vows. I made a covenant with you, says the Sovereign LORD, and you became mine.** [9] **"Then I bathed you and washed off your blood, and I rubbed fragrant oils into your skin.** [10] **I gave you expensive clothing of linen and silk, beautifully embroidered, and sandals made of fine leather.** [11] **I gave you lovely jewelry, bracelets, and beautiful necklaces,** [12] **a ring for your nose and earrings for your ears, and a lovely crown for your head.** [13] **And so you were made beautiful with gold and silver. Your clothes were made of fine linen and were beautifully embroidered. You ate the finest foods—fine flour, honey, and olive oil—and became more beautiful than ever. You looked like a queen, and so you were!** [14] **Your fame soon spread throughout the world on account of your beauty, because the splendor I bestowed on you perfected your beauty, says the Sovereign LORD.**

Israel and America will flourish for a season during that last half of the forty years. [15] "But you thought you could get along without me, so you trusted instead in your fame and beauty. You gave yourself as a prostitute to every man who came along. Your beauty was theirs for the asking! [16] You used the lovely things I gave you to make shrines for idols, where you carried out your acts of prostitution. Unbelievable! How could such a thing ever happen? Two nations chosen to serve the one God; "Hear O Israel the lord our God is one". [17] You took the very jewels and gold and silver ornaments I had given you and made statues of men and worshiped them, which is adultery against me.

The riches that were for the care of the poor went to build shrines to themselves. **Isaiah 3:12 (KJV)** The last part of this verse will be fulfilled...." **O my people, they which lead thee cause thee to err, and destroy the way of thy paths." (KJV)** [18] You used the beautifully embroidered clothes I gave you to cover your idols. Then you used my oil and incense to worship them. [19] Imagine it! You set before them as a lovely sacrifice the fine flour and oil and honey I had given you, says the Sovereign LORD. [20] "Then you took your sons and daughters—the children you had borne to me—and sacrificed them to your gods. Was it not enough that you should be a prostitute?

This is also a judgment against the church who now has been seduced by temptations as in all these riches God gave the church have now become our source of motivation that gave our children a false sense of reality and security, now our children in return will be protected by law and will rule over you. Israel has now chosen to follow the same path and acquire the wealth of the world, with all its idols in their pursuit of prosperity. [21] **Must you also slaughter my children by sacrificing them to idols?** These idols will produce a false sense of reality and security in our children, many will be sacrificed through abortion. [22] **In all your years of adultery and loathsome sin, you have not once thought of the days long ago when you lay naked in a field, kicking about in your own blood.** [23] **"Your destruction is certain, says the Sovereign LORD. In addition to all your other wickedness,** (As a church and a nation) ... [24] **you built a pagan shrine and put altars to idols in every town square.**

Under the 501C-3 nonprofit government charter, pastors will build large edifice assemblies to themselves that will be their family-owned religious business. Many will even ware their doctrinal names to show the degree of divisions from corner to corner in their cities that will give people a choice of the manner of worship in these buildings as monument shrines of their own accomplishments. They will lose sight of the real temple as themselves and enter a traditional form of worship. The Holy Spirit will depart from them without their ever knowing it. ²⁵ **On every street corner you defiled your beauty, offering your body to every passerby in an endless stream of prostitution.** Enticing innocent souls into bondage as pimps in the pulpits to come in and sale their talents to the devil. ²⁶ **Then you added lustful Egypt to your lovers, fanning the flames of my anger with your increasing promiscuity.** A church full of sodomy spirits. We brought the world into the sanctuary. ²⁷ **That is why I struck you with my fist and reduced your boundaries. I handed you over to your enemies, the Philistines, and even they were shocked by your lewd conduct!**

As we embraced other religions after knowing the real God, they were offended by our worldly ways. Now they will bring you under the bondage to their ways. ²⁸ **You have prostituted yourselves with the Assyrians, too. It seems you can never find enough new lovers! And after your prostitution there, you still were not satisfied.** The very people you knew as your enemies by your giving place to them, will cause you to be overtaken without a fight. ²⁹ **You added to your lovers by embracing that great merchant land of Babylonia—but you still weren't satisfied!** We as Americans, The Modern Babylon became their protectors, cause the to compromise their sovereignty for greed and ill-gotten gain. ³⁰ **"What a sick heart you have, says the Soverign LORD, to do such things as these, acting like a shameless prostitute ³¹ You build your pagan shrines on every street corner and your altars to idols in every square. You have been worse than a prostitute, so eager for sin that you have not even demanded payment for your love!** As a nation, we sacrifice our young men to enemy nations as the world's policemen and demanded no retribution. ³² **Yes, you are an adulterous wife who takes in strangers instead of her own husband.** We make more provisions for our so-called allies than we do our own. ³³ **Prostitutes charge for their services—but not you! You give gifts to your lovers, bribing them to come to you.** We offer them our best and receive no benefits from them. ³⁴ **So you are the opposite of other prostitutes. No one pays you; instead, you pay them!** ³⁵ **"Therefore, you prostitute, listen to this message from the LORD!** ³⁶ **This is what the Sovereign LORD says: Because you have** exposed yourself in prostitution to all your lovers, and because you have worshiped detestable idols, and because you have slaughtered your children as sacrifices to your gods, [37] this is what I am going to do. <u>I will gather together all your allies—these lovers of yours with whom you have sinned, both those you loved and those you hated—and I will strip you naked in front of them so they can stare at you.</u> (Rev. 18:17) [38] I will punish you for your murder and adultery. I will cover you with blood in my jealous fury. [39] Then I will give you to your lovers—these many nations—and they will destroy you. They will knock down your pagan shrines and the altar (church buildings) to your idols. They will strip you and take your beautiful jewels, leaving you completely naked and ashamed. [40] They will band together in a mob to stone you and run you through with swords.

God will open the eyes of the nations you have deceived with your false prophets with the doctrine of democracy as a nation and the doctrine of rapture and prosperity as your religion. **They will burn your homes and punish you in front of many women. I will see to it that you stop your prostitution and end your payments to your many lovers.** As a nation, seduced by the **Deep State** will now be used to police the world. Under Christianity, their pastors, taught by Jesuit professors, will rule the church as popes in the pulpit; all will be brought down. [42] **"Then at last my fury against you will be spent, and my jealous anger will subside. I will be calm and will not be angry with you anymore.** [43] **But first, because you have not remembered your youth but have angered me by doing all these evil things, I will fully repay you for all of your sins, says the Sovereign LORD. For to all your disgusting sins, you have added these lewd acts.** [44] **Everyone who makes up proverbs will say of you, `**<u>**Like mother, like daughter.**</u>**'** Great Britain is the mother of America. We have become as godless as she. [45] **For your mother loathed her husband and her children, and so do you. And you are exactly like your sisters, for they despised their husbands and their children. Truly your mother must have been a Hittite and your father an Amorite.** [46] **Your older sister was Samaria,** People departing from God's ways to mixed with those who worship idols. ... **who lived with her daughters in the north.** (Russia and China) **Your younger sister was Sodom,** (This is the sister they hate, America.) **who lived with her daughters in the south.** [47] **But you have not merely**

sinned as they did—no, that was nothing to you. In a very short time, you far surpassed them!

America 237+ years and 60+ at the time of this revelation for Israel as a nation.[48] **As surely as I live, says the Sovereign LORD, Sodom and her daughters were never as wicked as you and your daughters. [49] Sodom's sins were pride, laziness, and gluttony, while the poor and needy suffered outside her door.** In the last days, Satan cause America to change the laws of gender nature to legalize sodomy. They will cause your doors to be closed as a famine of the word begins that will birth the greatest spiritual revival that will lead to the rapture of the saints.

We will be as Rome had become in their last days. [50] **She was proud and did loathsome things, so I wiped her out, as you have seen. 51 Even Samaria did not commit half your sins. You have done far more loathsome things than your sisters ever did. They seem righteous compared to you!** Even our enemies were not as immoral in their state as we have become. [52] **You should be deeply ashamed because your sins are so terrible. In comparison, you make your sisters seem innocent! [53] "But someday I will restore the fortunes of Sodom and Samaria, and I will restore you, too.** *Isaiah 26:20 "(KJV) [20] Come, my people, enter thou into thy chambers, and shut thy doors about thee: hide thyself as it were for a little moment, until the indignation be over past."* These will be the remnant that God will bring through the tribulation to repopulate the earth of all nations. [54] **Then you will be truly ashamed of everything you have done, for your sins make them feel good in comparison. [55] Yes, your sisters, Sodom and Samaria, and all their people will be restored, and at that time you also will be restored.**

This time represents the last days leading into the signs that will precede the tribulation, beginning in the year of transition, 2008. [56] **In your proud days you held Sodom in contempt. 57 But now your greater wickedness has been exposed to all the world, and you are the one who is scorned— by Edom and all her neighbors and by Philistia.** Their sins were as Sodom and, their mixture as Samaria, America The Mystery Babylon of the Gentile age, will become a legalized state of Sodom and Gomorrah in the last days. **58 This is your punishment for all your disgusting sins, says the LORD. 59 "Now this is what the Sovereign LORD says: I will give you what you deserve, for you have taken your solemn vows**

lightly by breaking your covenant. "In God We Trust", **saith the Lord GOD. 60 Yet I will keep the covenant I made with you when you were young, and I will establish an everlasting covenant with you. 61Then you will remember with shame all the evil you have done. I will make your sisters, Samaria and Sodom, to be your daughters, even though they are not part of our covenant. 62And I will reaffirm my covenant with you, and you will know that I am the LORD. 63You will remember your sins and cover your mouth in silence and shame when I forgive you of all that you have done, says the Sovereign LORD."**

The remnant that is left will be in other countries after we are destroyed in the tribulation will live in the millennium reign of Christ where the devil is bound from tempting people to disobey God. In summary, Israel is the natural branch, America represents the grafted branch of the Gentiles, the spiritual body. To understand the context of this prophecy; you must think spiritual because all this relates to past, present and future. The ending: Israel existence is still in a state of the past as being ruled by the seeds that killed their Messiah.

These seeds of the present-day Israel are the Pharisee's and Sadducee's that rejected Jesus and is still awaiting their Messiah. America represents the Gentiles that received what the Jews rejected. In the end, became the false prophet, spreading the doctrine of democracy all over the world and in the end, God opened the eyes of her enemies to see her deceptive practices of hypocrisy, will use them to bring her down. This is the hour of the great crash of America's Beast system that empowered the false prophets. (Rev. 20:20) The church gave up its position as prayer warriors to uphold the constitution as the conscious of the state, thus the enemies of the state moved their sleeper cells into this nation raised up leaders and put them in high places of government, financed institutions of higher learning to change the doctrine, fulfill the prophecy in … **Daniel 7:25 (NLT) "He will defy the Most High and wear down the holy people of the Most High. He will try to change their sacred festivals and laws, <u>and they will be placed under his control for a time, times, and half a time."</u>**

President #44 will fulfill this prophecy. These things can only happen in a nation of a dead church, America, willingly crippled by the enemy of the state, the church, divided by religious foes, willingly seduced; in her wilderness, gave in to the temptations of the meagerly idols of this world.

The grandeur in the natural, thus the church thinking herself spiritual, became blinded by the enemy of her soul, false teaching. <u>This Is The state of the church and Israel when God will separate out a</u> people to re-populate the millennium. **Isaiah 26:20 (KJV) 20 Come, my people, enter thou into thy chambers, and shut thy doors about thee: hide thyself as it were for a little moment, until the indignation be over past.** AMEN (Released: 1/2015)

IT IS WRITTEN

Background scripture:

Matthew 4:4 (KJV) "But he answered and said, It is written, Man shall not live by bread alone, but by every word that proceedeth out of the mouth of God."

Most confessing Christians are unaware of the spirit world where our warfare as Christians begins when we confess our salvation. Our whole life from that time on is spent learning how to resist the devil to live the privilege Jesus died to give every believer … to be totally delivered from the devil. You have been given the keys to life and death to enter the kingdom of God by the authority given to every born-again believer. God is now inside of you as the greater one to prove his word in you as … **1 John 4:4 (KJV) "Ye are of God, little children, and have overcome them: because greater is he that is in you, than he that is in the world."** We are to walk in faith as we study his word as in … **2 Timothy 2:15 (KJV) "Study to shew thyself approved unto God, a workman that needeth not to be ashamed, rightly dividing the word of truth."**

Now the weapon we have been given to use as prayer worriers in the word by speaking in faith to the devil as Christ did. **Mt 4:4 (KJV) "But he answered and said, <u>It is written</u>, Man shall not live by bread alone, but by <u>every word that proceedeth out of the mouth of God.</u>"** Make sure you have renounced every generational curse in your family bloodline as a seed from past generations.

This is how you do that, all in faith. *"Father, in the name of Jesus, I renounce all generational curses in my family bloodline from four generations past that are against what you have given me deliverance from; name those you know and call them out before the devil for the angels to witness to give them authority over his spirits when you speak the word in faith."*

This is your hedge of protection that he cannot penetrate. Remember Job's hedge was his obedience to the word. God will allow the devil to try you to perfect his fruit in you. The faith you must have, is to know that … **1 Cor. 10:13 (KJV) There hath no temptation taken you but such as is common to man: but God is faithful, who will not suffer you to be tempted above that ye are able; but will with the temptation also make a way to escape, that ye may be able to bear it.**

This is where you are to put your total trust in the lord, he is not going to kill himself in you or cause you to suffer longer than needed to accomplish his purpose in you. Every confessing Christian will have a wilderness trial in their lifetime to perfect their faith to produce the right fruit. It is the devil's place to try to cause you to fear or doubt what God said is already yours in his word.

Your actions will determine whose report you believe, the one who created the body and restored you back to Adam as a new creature in Christ **or** the devil whose desire is to kill you or prolong your suffering because of your unbelief … you decide because Jesus said … **Mt 9:29 (KJV) "Then touched he their eyes, saying, <u>according to your faith be it unto you;</u>"** Now, it's according to your faith! Everything Jesus died for was completed when he said … **John 19:30 (KJV) "When Jesus therefore had received the vinegar, he said<u>, it is finished:</u> and he bowed his head, and gave up the ghost."** Now all we must do is … **2 Timothy 2:15 (KJV) "Study to shew <u>thyself approved unto God,</u> a workman that needeth not to be ashamed,** (and the Holy Spirit will teach you by …) **rightly dividing the word of truth."** From that time on, your walk with God is between **You, God** and the **devil.**

The circumstances are what the devil use to generate fear, doubt and unbelief because his source of power is in what you see, taste, touch, smell and feel that will lead you to obey what the circumstance suggest by lack of faith to believe what God said. What God has said supersedes the circumstances because he is in control of all things.

This is the faith he seeks to find in you that will keep you delivered from the power of the devil. **Hebrews 11:6 (KJV) But without faith it is impossible to please him: for he that cometh to God <u>must believe that he is</u>, and that he is a rewarder of them that diligently seek him. John 17:13 (KJV) "And now come I to thee; and these things I speak in the world, that they might have my joy fulfilled in themselves." John 17:13 (NLT) "And now I am coming to you. I have told them many things while I was with them so they would be filled with my joy. Romans 10:8 (KJV) "But what saith it? The word is nigh thee, even in thy mouth, and in thy heart: that is, the word of faith, which we preach;" Isaiah 55:11 (KJV) So shall my word be that goeth forth out of my mouth: it shall not return unto me void, but it shall accomplish that which I please, and it shall prosper in the thing whereto I sent it. Isaiah 55:11 (NLT) It is the same with my word. I send it out, and it always produces fruit. It will accomplish all I want it to, and it will prosper everywhere I send it. Titus 1:2 (KJV) "In hope of eternal life, which God, that <u>cannot lie</u>, promised before the world began;"** The suffering we undergo as a believer is to be identified as being a follower of Jesus Christ who said … **2 Timothy 3:12 (KJV) "Yea, and all that will live godly in Christ Jesus shall suffer persecution." … 1 Peter 4:1 (KJV) "Forasmuch then as Christ hath suffered for us in the flesh, arm yourselves likewise with the same mind: for he that hath suffered in the flesh hath ceased from sin; 1 John 3:13 (KJV) Marvel not, my brethren, if the world hate you. John 15:21 (KJV) But all these things will they do unto you for my name's sake, because they know not him that sent me. John 15:25 (KJV) But this cometh to pass, that the word might be fulfilled that is written in their law, they hated me without a cause. Luke 9:23 (KJV) And he said to them all, If any man will come after me, let him deny himself, and take up his cross daily, and follow me. Matthew 5:12 (KJV) Rejoice and be exceeding glad: for great is your reward in heaven: for so persecuted they the prophets which were before you.** This is our guarantee that he will never leave you or forsake you …. **Isa 54:17 (KJV) "No weapon that is formed against thee shall prosper; and every tongue that shall rise against thee in judgment thou shalt condemn. This is the heritage of the servants of the LORD, and their righteousness is of me, saith the LORD." Isa 54:17 (NLT) But**

in that coming day, no weapon turned against you will succeed. And everyone who tells lies in court will be brought to justice. These benefits are enjoyed by the servants of the LORD; their vindication will come from me. I, the LORD, have spoken! Luke 18:8 (KJV) "I tell you that he will avenge them speedily. Nevertheless, when the Son of man cometh, shall he find faith on the earth?"

This is what the Holy Spirit taught me that built my faith in him to make a blood covenant to lay my life down as the apostles did for those I love. This is what God has given us through the resurrection of Christ; the ability to walk as a new creature in the Earth as the new Adam in the world but no longer of this world. The devil has seduced the church world to the point of teaching all the knowledge and principles from the bible that is truth but left out the cross that will identify you as one of his by not knowing what spirit you are of.

We all have been taught and schooled in parts of the truth that have created these comfort zones of division that tickle our ears and have us living in a state of a false sense of reality and security. What I have been made to see about those of which I was once a follower, this is where that 98 percent fall into that will cause many to choose to remain in an antichrist assembly when this country's economy crashes very soon, great fear which have most of us following the world's system of prosperity which has brought this nation to this current state of moral decay.

The fruit of deliverance will be demonstrated in those who have given their lives for others. These are they that have overcome the fear of death. **Proverb 14:27 (KJV) The fear of the LORD is a fountain of life, to depart from the snares of death. 1JohJn 3:14 (KJV) We know that we have passed from death unto life, because we love the brethren. He that loveth not his brother abideth in death. 1John 3:16 (KJV) Hereby perceive we the love of God, because he laid down his life for us: and we ought to lay down our lives for the brethren. John 15:13 (KJV) Greater love hath no man than this that a man lay down his life for his friends.** Finally; **2 Corinthian 5:17 (KJV) Therefore if any man be in Christ, he is a new creature: old things are passed away; behold, all things are become new.** (Updated for release 1/2019)

BIPOLAR, THE DOUBLEMINDED CHRISTIAN

Background scripture:

James 1:8 (KJV) A double minded man is unstable in all his ways. Luke 9:55 (KJV) But he turned, and rebuked them, and said, Ye know not what manner of spirit ye are of.

During this time in the wilderness, the Holy Spirit has been re-educating me in this more excellent way in the perfect will of God. I now understood the many different character flaws I encountered over the course of these experiences among fellow confessing Christians and my own.

These things I question how one could be a confessing Christian that when provoked, changed into a completely different person. It became apparent to me when God revealed the revelation of the spirit world. The difference is the lack of knowledge when the spirit of the devil is camouflaged as an angel in disguise, when provoked, the real fruit show a different personality.

Being brought up in a traditional environment of carnality by man interpreting for God, is those born from below in Satan's sanctuaries   not knowing what spirit you are of, gives place to being deceived by these spirits manifested in blind leadership, are well-meaning, but lack of knowledge of who is in possession of their soul.

This spirit can masquerade as a good person. **1Thessalonians 1:5 (KJV) For our gospel came not unto you in word only, but also in power, and in the Holy Ghost, and in much assurance as ye know what manner of men we were among you for your sake. 2 John 1:10 (KJV) If there come any unto you, and bring not this doctrine, receive him not into your house, neither bid him God speed:**

The gospel as preached by the Holy Ghost is the only means by which these spirits are exposed in the assembly that must be cast out of the people they possess. This is a result of being convicted in a carnal church environment by your leader not having the right spirit by giving place to compromise to please those in their assemblies. This character flaw shows a blatant disregard for truth. Now you know how we are destroyed just by lack of knowledge. Only those born from above will recognize these false spirits. In a large assembly they often can masquerade as being very spiritual in an environment of familiar spirits. **Amos 3:3 (KJV) "Can two walk together, except they be agreed?"** Often divorced couples are victims of this hidden spirit past through by a generational curse. While I was ministering on the street for thirty-eight weeks, I met many religious people on medication after having been abandoned by churches who sent them to programs possessed with this spirit that put them on drugs. This represent that our gospel of deliverance has been lost in the assemblies, led by unbelieving leaders. I found that those who were not delivered became homeless where I met them on the street. My experience with them, they would sit and witness with you in the bible and when you come to a major disagreement with some of them, some would turn violet if they have not had their medication. I only cast out one demon while preaching on the street. God put me there to see what I would face later that only he will be able to perform in me.

This is where I gained knowledge of where the church had failed by not having the Holy Spirit liberated in the assembly. I was later told that the person had been diagnosed with Bipolar by the county health department who supplied them with the drugs. What has happened to the churches in America represent the present state of apostasy as in organized theological religions with no power to cast out devils. I am a witness, if you do not humble yourself as a child and trust God to lead you, you may become a victim of one of these spirits operating in your pulpit. That's why the word said ... **1 Timothy 5:22 (NASB77)** [22] *Do not lay hands upon anyone too hastily and thus share responsibility for the sins of others; keep yourself free from sin ...* Or do not let anyone who do not believe and operate in the doctrine of Jesus Christ, lay hands on you. Therefore, you must be born again.

James 1:23 (KJV) For if any be a hearer of the word, and not a doer, he is like unto a man beholding his natural face in a glass: 24 For he beholdeth himself, and goeth his way, and straightway forgetteth what manner of man he was. Let me be clear! Being diagnosed as Bipolar, you have more than one personality in your body. **Jeremiah 7:19 (KJV) Do they provoke me to anger? saith the LORD: do they not provoke themselves to the confusion of their own faces?**

This is a major offence to the world that cause them to stumble when they have had an encounter with this type of character while confessing to be a Christian. In today's church environment as carnal confessing Christians, pastors in following peace, tolerate them in the midst that will eventually infect the whole assembly because they will attract likeminded spirits. These spirits like to talk a lot by being purveyors of gossip will likewise dominate the conversation. They tend to see others' fault rather than their own problem. When God separated me from the assembly environment and away from those who would interfere with what he alone wanted to teach and show me. **1 Peter 1:23 (KJV)** [23] *Being born again, not of corruptible seed, but of incorruptible, by the word of God, which liveth and abideth* **forever.** This is the calling that gets you into God's presents by election for this reason ... **John 6:44 (KJV)** [44] **No man can come to me, except the Father which hath sent me draw him: and I will raise him up at the last day.**

God can use anything or anybody because he is God; but they that hear the elect of God will receive the real gospel and lead you by example. This is the gospel of the kingdom that those who receive make their calling and election sure. God and the devil do not dwell in the same temple because they cannot agree so when a person chooses to live in sin, The Holy Spirit is in grief, and if you over-stay your day of grace, he will leave. That person at that point becomes a religious child of the devil without ever knowing what spirit he or she is of. This! Is where you will see the character of the two spirits emerge where we get the diagnosis of Bipolar. A confessing

Christian living in a state of two mind sets will show as a dual personality or mental instability. They are not to the point of being a candidate for institutionalization because they can perform as normal human beings until provoked. A great many of them are not violet but have personality clashes that leads to difficulty getting along in normal setting because of this confusion of mind, causes them to become sensitive. I know now how we can be a hearer of the word and become a reproach of the word by not being a doer. Those that know God will be doers of the word and produce fruit that remain because they are born from above and being led by the Holy Spirit. There are some scriptures that leaves a mystery as to why we must seek ask and knock for the deep layered revelation that only the Holy Ghost can reveal to you. These are some of them.

John 6:44 (KJV) [44] *No man can come to me, except the Father which hath sent me draw him: and I will raise him up at the last day. Matthew 7:22 (KJV)* [22] *Many will say to me in that day, Lord, Lord, have we not prophesied in thy name? and in thy name have cast out devils? and in thy name done many wonderful works? Luke 6:46 (KJV)* [46] *And why call ye me, Lord, Lord, and do not the things which I say? Matthew 5:20 (KJV)* [20] *For I say unto you, that except your righteousness shall exceed the righteousness of the scribes and Pharisees, ye shall in no case enter into the kingdom of heaven. Matthew 7:21 (NASB77)* [21] *"Not everyone who says to Me, 'Lord, Lord,' will enter the kingdom of heaven; but he who does the will of My Father who is in heaven. Matthew 18:3(KJV)* [3] *And said, Verily I say unto you, Except ye be converted, and become as little children, ye shall not enter into the kingdom of heaven. Mark 10:25 (KJV)* [25] *It is easier for a camel to go through the eye of a needle, than for a rich man to enter into the kingdom of God. John 3:5 (KJV)* [5] *Jesus answered, Verily, verily, I say unto thee, Except a man be born of water and of the Spirit, he cannot enter into the kingdom of God. Matthew 5:8 (KJV)* [8] *Blessed are the pure in heart: for they shall see God. Acts 14:22* [22] *Confirming the souls of the disciples, and exhorting them to continue in the faith, and that we must through much tribulation enter into the kingdom of God. 1 Peter 1:22 (KJV)* [22] *Seeing ye have purified your souls in obeying the truth through the Spirit unto unfeigned love of the brethren, see that ye love one another with a pure heart fervently:1 Corinthians 8:2 (KJV)* [2] *And if any man think that he knoweth anything, he knoweth nothing yet as he ought to know. 1 Corinthians 2:2 (KJV)* [2] *For I determined not to know anything among you, save Jesus Christ, and him crucified. 1 Corinthians*

11:28 (KJV) [28] *But let a man examine himself, and so let him eat of that bread, and drink of that cup.* [29] *For he that eateth and drinketh unworthily, eateth and drinketh damnation to himself, not discerning the Lord's body.* [30] *For this cause many are weak and sickly among you, and many sleep.* (Or died before your time.) (Updated for release 10/2017)

THE GREAT SEPARATION

Background scripture:

(KJV) [40] **Then shall two be in the field; the one shall be taken, and the other left. Luke 17:35 (KJV)** [35] **Two women shall be grinding together; the one shall be taken, and the other left." Matthew 13:30 (KJV)** [30] **Let both grow together until the harvest: and in the time of harvest I will say to the reapers, Gather ye together first the tares, and bind them in bundles to burn them: but gather the wheat into my barn.**

We are at the time when God is judging the hearts of all who name His name. There are two separations taking place currently in our generation. **First,** the elects as his last day apostles to himself to receive the fullness in the final preparation for His Eminent Domain; the elect of God that will arrest the attention of the world and the sons of perdition, the antichrist body.

Their persecution will usher in the latter rain of the Holy Spirit. **Second,** the tares and children of disobedience turned over to the devil. He will put the devil under his feet in the final victory before they are martyred or if alive, translated. I know that this may come as a shock to some of you as now being revealed the mysteries of this time. This message is to encourage those who are now being persecuted by their loved ones and well-meaning confessing Christians for your stand as a chosen vessel of honor. Your first trial is in your home or among your own.

Hold on, your moment to glorify Christ is about to begin. I know most of you have been misunderstood, criticized, call everything but a child of God, even by some of your spouses. **Matthew 5:11-12 (KJV) "11 Blessed are ye, when men shall revile you, and persecute you, and shall say all manner of evil against you falsely, for my sake. 12 Rejoice and be exceeding glad: for great is your reward in heaven: for so persecuted they the prophets which were before you."**

In the spirit of the loving father and his loving son will vindicate himself and all the words spoken in faith through you that caused you to be in this predicament. What we are now experiencing is the power that has brought you to the reality that has prevailed in you by faith ... **1 John 4:4 (KJV) "4 Ye are of God, little children, and have overcome them: because greater is he that is in you, than he that is in the world.** You now are about to become.) **Matthew 5:13-15 (KJV) 13 Ye are the salt of the earth: but if the salt have lost his savour, wherewith shall it be salted? it is thenceforth good for nothing, but to be cast out, and to be trodden under foot of men. 14 Ye are the light of the world. A city that is set on an hill cannot be hid. 15 Neither do men light a candle, and put it under a bushel, but on a candlestick; and it giveth light unto all that are in the house."**

All those tears you have shad for those who were persecuting you by not knowing what spirit they were of, confessing their Christianity as you. Now our father has opened your eyes and put more love in your hearts, you will understand this separation was all for this moment of His glory. He through you, will seek to save all those you laid down your life for in prayer to be saved.

My beloved sisters and brothers, this is one of my great comforts in the lord as to know that He honored my sacrifice He enabled me to make for those I loved despite what they did to me. After all, it was Christ that was being persecuted all over, this time in my body. Contrary to the current false teachings of rapture, we are going through a part of the tribulation. Some of us have become so willingly ignorant to believe that God is going to take a divided church world and translate it into heaven. It's the last warning to this Laodicea church... **Revelation 3:18 (KJV) "18 I counsel thee to buy of me gold tried in the fire, that thou mayest be rich; and white raiment, that thou mayest be clothed, and that the shame of thy nakedness do not appear; and anoint thine eyes with eyesalve, that thou**

mayest see." One church body birth on the day of Pentecost believed in **...Ephesians 4:5 (KJV) "⁵ One Lord, one faith, one baptism,"** Until` God remove all that we have gained through this false teaching, then and only then is when we will see who really knows God. This separation will produce the saints that will be the body that will be glorified and translated. That is the great mystery Satan has kept from this generation through false prophets in sheep clothing.

God is now drawing these elects and faithful servants to His secret place as His friends that.... **1 John 2:28 (KJV) "²⁸ And now, little children, abide in him; that, when he shall appear, we may have confidence, and not be ashamed before him at his coming. Proverbs 8:17 (KJV) ¹⁷ I love them that love me; and those that seek me early shall find me."**

While we are at rest, this is what the spirit of Christ will teach his chosen ones ... **Colossians 3:16 (KJV) "⁶ Let the word of Christ dwell in you richly in all wisdom; teaching and admonishing one another in psalms and hymns and spiritual songs, singing with grace in your hearts to the Lord. Acts 17:28 (KJV) ²⁸ For in him we live, and move, and have our being; as certain also of your own poets have said, For we are also his offspring. 1 John 2:3-6 (KJV) ³ And hereby we do know that we know him, if we keep his commandments. ⁴ He that saith, I know him, and keepeth not his commandments, is a liar, and the truth is not in him. ⁵ But whoso keepeth his word, in him verily is the love of God perfected: hereby know we that we are in him. ⁶ He that saith he abideth in him ought himself also so to walk, even as he walked. Proverbs 8:34 (KJV) ³⁴ Blessed is the man that heareth me, watching daily at my gates, waiting at the posts of my doors. Romans 11:28 (KJV) ²⁸ As concerning the gospel, they are enemies for your sakes: but as touching the election, they are beloved for the fathers' sakes. 1 Peter 4:12-13 (KJV) ¹² Beloved, think it not strange concerning the fiery trial which is to try you, as though some strange thing happened unto you: ¹³ But rejoice, inasmuch as ye are partakers of Christ's sufferings; that, when his glory shall be revealed, ye may be glad also with exceeding joy. 1 Peter 4:1 (KJV) ¹ Forasmuch then as Christ hath suffered for us in the flesh, arm yourselves likewise with the same mind: for he that hath suffered in the flesh hath ceased from sin; John 15:18-21 (KJV) ¹⁸ If the world hate you, ye know that it hated me before it hated you. ¹⁹ If ye were of the world, the world would** love his own: but because ye are notof the world, but I have chosen you out of the world, therefore the world hateth you. [20] Remember the word that I said unto you, the servant is not greater than his lord. If they have persecuted me, they will also persecute you; if they have kept my saying, they will keep yours also. [21] But all these things will they do unto you for my name's sake, because they know not him that sent me. Matthew 7:21-23 (KJV) [21] <u>Not everyone that saith unto me, Lord, Lord, shall enter into the kingdom of heaven</u>; but he that doeth the will of my Father which is in heaven. [22] Many will say to me in that day, Lord, Lord, have we not prophesied in thy name? and in thy name have cast out devils? and in thy name done many wonderful works? [23] And then will I profess unto them, I never knew you: depart from me, ye that work iniquity. Matthew 7:13-14 (KJV) [13] <u>Enter ye in at the strait gate</u>: for wide is the gate, and broad is the way, that leadeth to destruction, and many there be which go in thereat: [14] Because strait is the gate, and narrow is the way, which leadeth unto life, and <u>few there be that find it.</u> Luke 14:26 (KJV) [26] If any man come to me, and hate not his father, and mother, and wife, and children, and brethren, and sisters, yea, and his own life also, he cannot be my disciple.

I, like many others, never really understood the depth of these scriptures until the Holy Spirit open my mind to the revelation that I was going to have to die to self so Christ can be birth in me to save them with fruit that will remain under any circumstances. This is true discipleship. If God did not join you both in the spirit by marriage, this is the price we must pay to correct our mistake.

Luke 14:33 (KJV) [33] So likewise, whosoever he be of you that forsaketh not all that he hath, he cannot be my disciple." What we are about to see take place in this country is... Proverbs 13:22 (KJV) [22] A good man leaveth an inheritance to his children's children: Christ is the good Sheppard, and he is about to correct all the injustices of ill-gotten gain of the wicked and return it to His children. and the wealth of the sinner is laid up for the just." This heritage will be the word you planted in the spirit in those who heard you while you suffered to keep that word alive is now about to be rewarded. This rest we have been placed is for this moment for his glory to become His adopted sons where-in ... 1 John 3:2 (KJV) "[2] Beloved, now are we the sons of God, and it doth not yet appear what we shall be: but we know that, when he shall appear, we shall be like him; for we shall see him as he is. Isaiah 55:8 (KJV) ⁸ For my thoughts are not your thoughts, neither are your ways my ways, saith the LORD. Proverbs 14:18 (KJV) ¹⁸ The simple inherit folly: but the prudent are crowned with <u>knowledge.</u>

<u>Warning: This message is to confessing husband and wives</u>

Matthew 10:34-42 (KJV) "³⁴ Think not that I am come to send peace on earth: I came not to send peace, but a sword. ³⁵ For I am come to set a man at variance against his father, and the daughter against her mother, and the daughter in law against her mother-in-law. ³⁶ And a man's foes shall be they of his own household. ³⁷ He that loveth father or mother more than me is not worthy of me: and he that loveth son or daughter more than me is not worthy of me. ³⁸ And he that taketh not his cross, and followeth after me, is not worthy of me. ³⁹ He that findeth his life shall lose it: and he that loseth his life for my sake shall find it. ⁴⁰ He that receiveth you receiveth me, and he that receiveth me receiveth him that sent me. ⁴¹ He that receiveth a prophet in the name of a prophet shall receive a prophet's reward; and he that receiveth a righteous man in the name of a righteous man shall receive a righteous man's reward. ⁴² And whosoever shall give to drink unto one of these little ones a cup of cold water only in the name of a disciple, verily I say unto you, he shall in no wise lose his reward."

All of you who read these chronicles will see that I do not hold back the truth; after all, it's what we missed in the gospels by the word being taught in part as a divided body. **Mark 10:9 (KJV) "⁹ What therefore God hath joined together, let not man put asunder.** Your life belongs to God, He has provided everything we need in his sovereign will including a perfect mate, as a believer, seek God for that person and wait and he or she will walk into your life with many confirming signs, this is the one. These are the blessings He send that add no sorrow, only joy. The new creature is the restoration of Adam and Eve in the earth. This is what God joins when you wait. **Matthew 19:6 (KJV) ⁶ Wherefore they are no more twain, but one flesh. What therefore God hath joined together, let not man put asunder."** We are all victims of our five senses, therefore when we look at some of our current circumstances, as the lord revealed the truth about our choices, repentance is in order. Unlike the type of gospel, we were exposed to in this present church world based in compromise, you will never know true deliverance until you surrender totally.

This is where you are made whole as Jesus spoke to the many that came believing in Him. No matter what predicament you find yourself, unless the word is preached and demonstrated in the purity and power of holiness with a demonstration of faith, you will be put on the wrong path to the solution to your problems. The power of the spoken word is in the faith to those that act on it with an understanding that God cannot lie, your reward is a test of your endurance to produce the fruit of patience in you.

Isaiah 55:11 (KJV) "[11] So shall my word be that goeth forth out of my mouth: it shall not return unto me void, but it shall accomplish that which I please, and it shall prosper in the thing whereto I sent it. Romans 10:8 (KJV) 8 But what saith it? The word is nigh thee, even in thy mouth, and in thy heart: that is, the word of faith, which we preach; Mark 10:27 (KJV) [27] And Jesus looking upon them saith, with men it is impossible, but not with God: for with God all things are possible."

These scriptures set the basis for which the context can be understood to act on it in faith. When you surrender your will, you must be willing to accept His will be done on His time that will bring a resolve that will be acceptable to Him, done in your following peace under what will look like hopeless circumstances. When one chooses to serve God out of a heart conviction or the draw of the spirit; these two conditions are where you will find the **few**. The heart of one's convictions will be tested first among his or her own biological off springs. The husband under conviction is now going to have to let God restore him as priest of his house. The process of becoming a Christian is ... **1 Timothy 3:5 (KJV) "[5] For if a man know not how to rule his own house, how shall he take care of the church of God."**

The only way you will see Him prove His word is when you act in faith as a surrendered vessel. **That is why we are few.** The wife under the conviction to become a godly woman, surrenders her will and is to be.... **Titus 2:5 (KJV) "[5] To be discreet, chaste, keepers at home, good, obedient to their own husbands, that the word of God be not blasphemed."** When we are joined to mates of our own choosing, having to come from sin to salvation is where all the above must apply. Only God can do the impossible not you. You must walk in total obedience to avoid the pitfalls of Satan in his efforts to steal your faith by looking at the circumstances.

As the scripture say...**1 Corinthians 7:16-17 (KJV) "16 For what knowest thou, O wife, whether thou shalt save thy husband? or how knowest thou, O man, whether thou shalt save thy wife? 17 But as God hath distributed to every man, as the Lord hath called everyone, so let him walk. And so ordain I in all churches. Matthew 11:12 (KJV) 12 And from the days of John the Baptist until now the kingdom of heaven suffereth violence, and the violent take it by force." 2Th 3:2 (KJV) And that we may be delivered from unreasonable and wicked men: <u>for all men have not faith.</u>** Don't think that just because you said I am saved, all is going to be well as you think; that's where most pastors leave you at the Romans road of confession. If that's the case, we would not have been warned of the troubles we are going to face to prove to the world that we are saved from willfully sinning. You are no match for Satan, only God can handle him and that is through your obedience. Remember Job's hedge...**Job 1:10 (KJV) "10 Hast not thou made an hedge about him, and about his house, and about all that he hath on every side? thou hast blessed the work of his hands, and his substance is increased in the land."**

When Satan goes before God to accuse you, the only justification he has are your un-confessed sins. When you surrender your will, God knows what to allow him to do to make you perfect, in the end, you will be better able to trust God in all things as you are led to walk with Him. 1 Peter **3:7-11 (KJV) "7 Likewise, ye husbands, dwell with them <u>according to knowledge</u>, giving honour unto the wife, as unto the weaker vessel, and as being heirs together of the grace of life; that your prayers be not hindered. 8 Finally; be ye all of one mind, having compassion one of another, love as brethren, be pitiful, be courteous: 9 Not rendering evil for evil, or railing for railing: but contrariwise blessing; knowing that ye are thereunto called, that ye should inherit a blessing. 10 For he that will love life, and see good days, let him refrain his tongue from evil, and his lips that they speak no guile: 11 Let him eschew evil, and do good; let him seek peace, and ensue it."** All this can only be accomplished by dying daily and being taught by the Holy Spirit. That's why God must do the joining. When you both are one, you will know your place in God. Case in point, Adam did not refuse to eat because they were of one spirit.

Colossians 3:19-20 (KJV) "¹⁹ Husbands, love your wives, and be not bitter against them. ²⁰ Children, obey your parents in all things: for this is well pleasing unto the Lord." This is where, as the priest of your house, you are to be single minded.

We must yield to God's ways so He will be lifted in our presented vessels that the unbelieving partner may be persuaded by love in action. Only Christ can do this as you die. That's how I brought my wife and three daughters to a saving knowledge of God by the way I treated their mother.**1 Peter 3:1-2 (KJV) "¹ Likewise, ye wives, be in subjection to your own husbands; that, if any obey not the word, they also may without the word be won by the conversation of the wives; ² While they behold your chaste conversation coupled with fear. 1 Peter 3:6 (KJV) ⁶ Even as Sara obeyed Abraham, calling him lord: whose daughters ye are, as long as ye do well, and are not afraid with any amazement."** The proof of a woman that knows God, she will line up to the order of the word as in the apostle's doctrine or else she will become a jezebel. **1 Corinthians 7:14 (KJV) ¹⁴ For the unbelieving husband is sanctified by the wife, and the unbelieving wife is sanctified by the husband: else were your children unclean; but now are they holy.** This is an area I wanted to know more about, and this is what I was told.

The Bible teaches principles of how to be a wise servant. When one truly receives Christ, you will ... **Matthew 6:33 (KJV) "³ But seek ye first the kingdom of God, and his righteousness; and all these things shall be added unto you.** What will be added to you? All you give unto the lord will be returned to you as a blessing that will add no sorrow. Be prepared for what God will add which may surprise you when you see His ways are not like yours and he will do whatever it takes to bring peace so you can continue to rest in His perfect will for you. Just die. Some of us have buried our children who die under the influence of the devil. What makes our children go astray and bring us much sorrow? When we are not obedient to God, Our Children will not be obedient to us. Satan knows the word and takes advantage of what you do not know. Here again we see were Christ in you as leading by example will produce this fruit in your seed, in your children that remain. This is where you must have a prayer altar in your home like Job to cover your children. **Proverbs 22:6 (KJV) "⁶ Train up a child in the way he should go: and when he is old, he will not depart**

from it" When we are exposed to false teachings, this leads to error in our applying the word; therefore, it comes back in the form of a curse instead of a blessing, Isaiah 3:12 (KJV) ¹² **As for my people, <u>children are their oppressors, and women rule over them</u>. O my people, <u>they which lead thee cause thee to err, and destroy the way of thy paths.</u>** Do your children tell you what to do?

In all my teachings by the Holy Spirit, He will always end up here... **Deuteronomy 6:5 (KJV) "⁵And thou shalt love the LORD thy God with all thine heart, and with all thy soul, and with all thy might. Matthew 22:37-39 (KJV) ³⁷ Jesus said unto him, thou shalt love the Lord thy God with all thy heart, and with all thy soul, and with all thy mind. ³⁸ This is the first and great commandment. ³⁹ And the second is like unto it, thou shalt love thy neighbour as thyself."** Beloved, I hope you have been enlightened as I was to be taught by the Holy Spirit. This is the rest those elected to this last day call, being brought into this more excellent way of being made perfect. When God sent my second wife into my life, little did I know that he would use her to perfect me in the application of his word. We both were to become a work in progress.

I had to do all the above by demonstration to win her so we could become one. That took thirty years. She held me to a higher standard because of my convictions to let her see Christ in me. I had one request before the lord, that when she became fully persuaded, I would hear her say that I am her Abraham. That took twenty-five years to come to pass. That to me confirmed her complete conversion by my life as a priest to her as a husband. I became her Adam, and she became my Eve. We learn to look beyond each other's faults. You see my beloved, all this I had to prove to her that made her a believer. You see my belove, charity begins first at home before you can be used to save others. Both wives passed from this life two years apart, diagnosed with the same condition; one was taken and the other left. I had to do as a husband in my second marriage is what I did not have the knowledge to do in my first. That is **... Colossians 3:14 (KJV) ¹⁴ And above all these things *put on* charity, (love) which is the bond of perfectness.** Little did I know that God would use her in my wilderness training to keep me in that straight and narrow way that led us both to that oneness when her time to serve was finished. God used her to help me become a man of convictions. Beloved, He has proved all this in the above word to be true to me when it all came to pass. Now, I belong to him completely. I could not be at more peace and rest, knowing that God rewarded her with eternal life for all she was to me. Now may God bless you and keep you in perfect peace. AMEN (Updated for Released 12/2020)

FAITH THAT PLEASES GOD

What kind of faith is this?

This in-depth study of the kind of faith Jesus will be looking for when he returns. These scriptures are the key to the hidden revelations of the faith in God that will get you into heaven.

The foundation to the God like faith

Hebrews 11:6 (KJV) **6 But without faith it is impossible to please him: for he that cometh to God must believe that he is, and that he is a rewarder of them that diligently seek him.** You will not believe in someone you doubt can do what he said. **James 2:23 (KJV)** **23 And the scripture was fulfilled which saith, Abraham believed God, and it was imputed unto him for righteousness: and he was called the Friend of God. Luke 18:8 (KJV)** **8 I tell you that he will avenge them speedily. Nevertheless, when the Son of man cometh, shall he find faith on the earth?** One of the layered revelations of Abraham's faith; we will all be given the same ability by faith to please God under grace and truth. It will be up to you to believe God to bring his presence to the forefront of your life.

That's why he is called the father of the faithful. **Hebrews 11:1(KJV)** **1 Now faith is the substance of things hoped for, the evidence of things not seen.** The ability to take God at his word is a revelation of the testimonies left of those in the hall of faith. This is where our faith has failed to produce the right fruit as being of God. Without a Godly example of the word being manifested when it is spoken in faith as often as we assemble, without the five ministerial graces in our presence; Christ cannot manifest himself in the fullness. **"Ephesians 4:11-12 (KJV)** [11] **And he gave some, apostles; and some, prophets; and some, evangelists; and some, pastors and teachers;** 12 **For the perfecting of the saints, for the work of the ministry,** **for the edifying of the body of Christ: Galatians 5:22-23 (KJV)** [22] **But the fruit of the Spirit is** love, joy, peace, longsuffering, gentleness, goodness, faith, [23] meekness, temperance: **against such there is no law."** Our shortcomings are based in like of knowledge by only having one of these graces in our midst, the pastor. If God wanted the pastor to do everything, we would have seen it clearly written in the Scriptures. Instead, they have use faith to build their mega ministries preaching salvation without deliverance. That's what they were taught in many Jesuits staff seminaries.

This error in the assembly has caused men to result to the principles of faith which work without salvation in the permissive will of God. It has an open show of God but denies the power thereof. **Mark 11:22 (KJV)** [22] **And Jesus answering saith unto them, Have faith in God.** The only faith that moves God is his word, not man's ways and ambitions. **Luke 18:8 (KJV)** [8] **I tell you that he will avenge them speedily. Nevertheless, when the Son of man cometh, shall he find faith on the earth?** Now to have this kind of faith is only by acting on God's word without question by believing he is. **John 14:12 (KJV)** [12] **Verily, verily, I say unto you, He that believeth on me, the works that I do shall he do also; and greater works than these shall he do; because I go unto my Father.** When Christ returns, he will be only looking to see himself in you exercising the kind of faith he had in the father that got people healed delivered and set free. The perfect will of God was performed in those in the earth he has chosen to run this course in your vessel. He is the one that caused you to surrender the vessel when he called you. **Hebrews 11:2 (KJV)** [2] **For by it the elders obtained a good report.** Those who exercise lordship over God's flock are duty bound to let Christ be seen and not flesh.

This faith points you to the father because you live in the reality of knowing you are a chosen vessel for that purpose. **Romans 1:17 (KJV)** [17] **For therein is the righteousness of God revealed from faith to faith: as it is written, the just shall live by faith.** Herein is the understanding of what being converted really is; living by faith in the spoken word as led by the Holy

Spirit. What the church has failed to see is the revelation of Jesus Christ and his finished work that has restored you to walk as a new creation, having dominion over all things as Adam. This reality of Christ in you has quickened all who have received him to become a new creature. In him there is no condemnation because he is in possession of the vessel walking out his word by faith as being one with the father; therefore, your mind is being transformed and renewed daily as you are led by the Holy Spirit. The following Scripture is where we see an error in its interpretation.

3 John 1:2 (KJV) [2] **Beloved, I wish above all things that thou mayest prosper and be in health, even as thy soul prospereth.** This verse taken out of context will cause you to prosper in the permissive will of God and have an open show of opulence and pride in acquiring the things of this world that cause you to fall short of his glory and perish with the using. The reality is Christ in you, seeking to save all those the father has chosen to be with him for eternity. When you look at the present faith ministries, there is a discernible error in its presentation of faith. It shows a manifestation with a void of producing the right fruit. I see false humility and hidden pride in those who live in this principle of the word. In Galatians 5:22, demonstrates nine manners of fruit that are produced in the completely converted Christian. The key association with deity is love; now faith works by love.

God has given man the power to get wealth without being saved.

Deuteronomy 8:18 (KJV) [18] **But thou shalt remember the LORD thy God: for it is he that giveth thee power to get wealth, that he may establish his covenant which he sware unto thy fathers, as it is this day. Matthew 5:45 (KJV)** [45] **That ye may be the children of your Father which is in heaven: for he maketh his sun to rise on the evil and on the good, and sendeth rain on the just and on the unjust.** In this observation, I see a religious corporation being like worldly businesses. That's the 501c-3 curse where the pastor is elected as the CEO, the Deacons are the board of directors and the Members are the contributor's in the bible products which are the principal of truth that does not require salvation to work. When we surrender our vessel to the Lord, we are surrendering our will to lift himself in all who come after him. This is the faith that is given to everyone who is drawn in by his spirit. This is the faith he will see that is in Luke 18:8. Now let's go back to ... **Hebrews 11:6 (KJV)** [6] **But without**

faith it is impossible to please him: for he that cometh to God must believe that he is, and that he is a rewarder of them that diligently seek him. This is what I have been taught by the Holy Spirit to be the true riches. The diligence is when you approach God as a willing and obedient servant, dying daily as surrendering all that will hinder God from using your vessel.

Christ at that time, takes over the vessel and begin to walk out your salvation as according to your obedience in his perfect and sovereign will for you, conforming you to his image by the renewing of your mind into his mind through self-denial. Now you are seeking those things above as in dying to the world. The Holy Spirit brings you into the reality of the source of all riches in glory by Christ Jesus. It is not necessarily the wealth of this world but in knowing the revelation that you are the new Adam, restored to dominion, power, and all things available to you daily, as a new creature in Christ. All your needs are met in him, he in you seeks after those the father has called to receive salvation. The reason you are asked to cast all your cares upon him because they become his cares and his desires by reasons of you surrendering your will that his will now be done in the earth as he would have in heaven.

This is a revelation, all things in the world are yours because of this fact stated in ... **1 John 4:4 (ASV)** [4] **Ye are of God, my little children, and have overcome them: because greater is he that is in you than he that is in the world. Isaiah 54:17 (KJV)** [17] **No weapon that is formed against thee shall prosper; and every tongue that shall rise against thee in judgment thou shalt condemn. This is the heritage of the servants of the LORD, and their righteousness is of me, saith the LORD. Ecclesiastes 5:8 (KJV)** [8] **If thou seest the oppression of the poor, and violent perverting of judgment and justice in a province, marvel not at the matter: for he that is higher than the highest regardeth; and there be higher than they.** Regardless of what you see in this world and in your circumstances, the only one that can change anything in his creation including the hearts of men is God inside of you, working all things for his good in the earth.

Christ walking as the second Adam is walking in dominion of the first Adam; therefore, needed not to take anything with him because all things are his and now in you all things are yours with one exception, your mind is now on heavenly things and not worldly things. You only need what it takes to get through each day because of this reality… **Luke 19:10 "KJV)** **¹⁰ For the Son of man is come to seek and to save that which was lost.** His work of love is in … **1 John 3:17 (KJV) ¹⁷ But whoso hath this world's good, and seeth his brother have need, and shutteth up his bowels of compassion from him, how dwelleth the love of God in him? Matthew 19:24 (KJV) ²⁴ And again I say unto you, It is easier for a camel to go through the eye of a needle, than for a rich man to enter into the kingdom of God."** Our days are numbered here on earth. **Job 14:1 (KJV) ¹ Man that is born of a woman is of few days, and full of trouble. James 4:14 (KJV) ¹⁴ Whereas ye know not what shall be on the morrow. For what is your life? It is even a vapour, that appeareth for a little time, and then vanisheth away. Luke 12:22 (KJV) ²² And he said unto his disciples, Therefore I say unto you, take no thought for your life, what ye shall eat; neither for the body, what ye shall put on.**

Matthew 6:34 (KJV) ³⁴ Take therefore no thought for the morrow: for the morrow shall take thought for the things of itself. Sufficient unto the day is the evil thereof. John 3:13 (KJV) ¹³ And no man hath ascended up to heaven, but he that came down from heaven, even the Son of man which is in heaven. 1 John 3:13 (KJV) ¹³ Marvel not, my brethren, if the world hate you. Jesus's prayers are for you to come into agreement with him and the father so his will can be done in earth as in heaven. Every vessel, chosen by God **"walks by faith and not by sight."** This is the faith he seeks to find when he returned for his chosen vessels walking in the image of his person. The faith of the father performing those things predestined in your vessel of which he has given you his strength … **Zechariah 4:6 (KJV) …. ⁶ Not by might, nor by power, but by my spirit, saith the LORD of hosts. Now the bible says that all men do not have faith;** your *elections* is made sure by walking in faith as directed by the Holy Spirit.

All who are chosen by God will have what they need when they need it because you are living in the reality that all things are yours, including perfect health, perfect peace, perfect wealth and perfect knowledge of who is in possession of the vessel; as you see, he is coming back for himself in you. Until you are brought into this place, you will not operate as a son. **Matthew 26:42 (KJV) ⁴² He went away again the second time, and prayed, saying, O my Father, if this cup may not pass away from me, except I drink it, thy will be done.**

All who have received his report will drink of this cup of suffering. **1 Peter 4:1 (KJV)** [1] **Forasmuch then as Christ hath suffered for us in the flesh, arm yourselves likewise with the same mind: for he that hath suffered in the flesh hath ceased from sin;** The Holy Spirit, when released will bring all who have been chosen to this reality to obtain eternal life. **Luke 14:33 (KJV)** [33] **So likewise, whosoever he be of you that forsaketh not all that he hath, he cannot be my disciple.** This is where I learned that surrendering your will is the difference between eternal separation or eternal life. Outside of his perfect and sovereign will, is only mercy for the children of disobedience. When you see God as lord of the universe and all creation, then you will be able to say ... **Acts 3:6 (KJV)** [6] **Then Peter said, Silver and gold have I none; but such as I have give I thee: In the name of Jesus Christ of Nazareth rise up and walk.**

When our minds are in heavenly places in Christ, he speaks the word, and it is done. What are the meagerly beggarly elements of this time compared to heaven when all will pass away very soon? When Christ said **"it is finished"** another understanding is to rest from your labor and let the father be about his business in you as the new Adam, doing the things he said he would do when you receive him. You won't need to carry anything with you but him because all things are yours in him. That's why he told his disciples not to take anything with them, and nowhere in the New Testament did they teach paying tithes where they went. The word of faith came from the father, spoken through Christ and they acted on what Christ told then to do. The whole reason for us to come to rest in him is so He can be seen, not you. That's why we are told to wait for the endowment of the Holy Spirit's anointing which is the power when the word is spoken to confirm God's presence by demonstrating signs, wonders, and miracles. Now if we are operating in one of these ministerial graces and these signs does not follow your words; our hard speeches based in knowledge alone is what seminary train hirelings do. It is my experience that seminary theology will not produce this in our midst. Most of us being brought to this knowledge will have to build others faith to see these miracles as when the apostles walked among the people. I see God in Paul performing a miracle when he needed to get the attention of the people.

When God open my eyes to these revelations, I realize I had gone ahead of him without the anointing. Sadly, I ministered like this for many years until God call me in and sat me down to complete rest away from all in preparation to take possession of the vessel by walking me into his perfect will. I was given this revelation to complete my rest as in total surrender that he now can do these greater works that HE said HE would do when He bid you to come into the secret place of the most high (the throne room) to receive his mind for the work whereunto we were called to present our vessel. When we come out of this wilderness as John the Baptist was separated to God, we have been separated to Jesus and he will return from the wilderness and Satan will find nothing in you but Him. All who are call to this place are being perfected in the wilderness.

Finally, this is where all elects are at this time, God has brought his elects to rest from their labor as the John the Baptist of the latter day, announcing his return. All of God's elects are separated to himself being prepared to come out of their wilderness in the fullness of God. None of us have reached this level of the manifestation of the sons of God yet. *"The world is not worthy of their presents until they begin to travail in their tribulation of Zion, then, I will rise up in them when the great tribulation begins and put all principalities under my feet."* I am often asked, where do you attend church. That's why your assemblies are being closed by this pandemic. We see that 98% that does not have the faith in the God they have been presented to keep them from fear. Now, God is trying to get your attention to see He dwells in you not that assembly of false teaching.

This is a foot note to this message when I inquired about when we will see the sign of this reality? **Revelation 18:17 (KJV) "17 For in one hour so great riches is come to nought. And every shipmaster, and all the company in ships, and sailors, and as many as trade by sea, stood afar off, Revelation 18:21 (KJV) [21] And a mighty angel took up a stone like a great millstone, and cast it into the sea, saying, Thus with violence shall that great city Babylon be thrown down, and shall be found no more at all."** America's prosperity is ending to bring the great revival. All who are not chosen, great fears will come upon them, they will follow the beast system because they were marked in the spirit for rejecting God. God sees all and have selected all his saints to be saved and his elects will be used for his glory. The children of disobedience did not act on the word in faith; therefore, the prayers of the righteous will come to their rescue. They will suffer with the wicked as their punishment.

This is what came in my spirit after meditation on this message? *"All will lose everything they have including my people. Those chosen, will live in no continual city and will go where I send them under divine protection …. No one will be able to harm them …. They will be offered up for my glory. Many things I have kept hidden from my people because they are not where they think they are …Your only safety is in me … your homes will be ravaged by those looking for food. I will divinely supply all your need as I did for my children in the wilderness…those who complain will be cut off from among my people … There is nothing to compare with what I am about to do in my chosen elect that are at rest, chosen and predestined for my glory before the foundation of the world."* **Isaiah 55:7-8 (KJV)** [7] **Let the wicked forsake his way, and the unrighteous man his thoughts: and let him return unto the LORD, and he will have mercy upon him; and to our God, for he will abundantly pardon.** [8] **For my thoughts are not your thoughts, neither are your ways my ways, saith the LORD. Proverbs 3:5 (KJV)** [5] **Trust in the LORD with all thine heart; and lean not unto thine own understanding. Proverbs 4:26 (KJV)** [26] **Ponder the path of thy feet and let all thy ways be established.** (Updated Released 8/2020)

WOE TO THE AHAB'S AND THE JEZEBEL'S OF TODAY

The present-day state of the church is ... **Mark 13:20 (KJV) "²⁰ And except that the Lord had shortened those days, no flesh should be saved: but for the elect's sake, whom he hath chosen, he hath shortened the days. Isaiah 53:6 (KJV) ⁶ All we like sheep have gone astray; we have turned everyone to his own way; and the LORD hath laid on him the iniquity of us all."**

The following revelation may be very offending to many religious organizations; false teachings have changed the order of the body of Christ. **1 Corinthians 11:3 (KJV) "3 But I would have you know, that the head of every man is Christ; and the head of the woman is the man; and the head of Christ is God. Ephesians 5:23 (KJV) ²³ For the husband is the head of the wife, even as Christ is the head of the church: and he is the savior of the body. 1 Corinthians 11:8 (KJV) ⁸ For the man is not of the woman; but the woman of the man.** (I have heard ministers say that was Paul's interpretation.) **Galatians 3:28 (KJV) ²⁸ There is neither Jew nor Greek, there is neither bond nor free, there is neither male nor female: for ye are all one in Christ Jesus.** (Some have based it on the above scripture.) **1 Timothy 2:12 (KJV) ¹² But I suffer not a woman to teach, nor to usurp authority over the man, but to be in silence.** (The Holy Spirit does not work against the words of God because he is the interpreter.) **Daniel 7:25 (KJV) ²⁵ And he shall speak great words against the most High and shall** wear out the saints of the most High, <u>and think to change times and laws</u>: and they shall be given into his hand until a time and times and the dividing of time."

Christ told Peter on one occasion… **Luke 22:32 (KJV) "³²But I have prayed for thee, that thy faith fail not: and when thou art converted, strengthen thy brethren."** Now we need to know what we are to be converted too. Conversion is when you come to the reality of … **1 John 4:4 (KJV) ⁴Ye are of God, little children, and have overcome them: because greater is he that is in you, than he that is in the world."** Now we are to … **Mark 11:22 (KJV) "²²Have faith in God.** (Now the Holy Spirit oversees the administration of the ministerial offices to keep the doctrine from being compromised.) **1 Timothy 4:6 (KJV) ⁶If thou put the brethren in remembrance of these things, thou shalt be a good minister of Jesus Christ, nourished up in the words of faith and of good doctrine, whereunto thou hast attained. 1 Timothy 6:3 (KJV) ³If any man teach otherwise, and consent not to wholesome words, even the words of our Lord Jesus Christ, and to the doctrine which is according to godliness. ⁴ He is proud, knowing nothing, but doting about questions and strifes of words, whereof cometh envy, strife, railings, evil surmisings, ⁵Perverse disputings of men of corrupt minds, and destitute of the truth, <u>supposing that gain is godliness</u>: from such <u>withdraw thyself</u>. ⁶But godliness with contentment is great gain.** (You will never be content until you are totally surrendered to the Holy Spirit.)

Isaiah 5:20 (KJV) ²⁰Woe unto them that call evil good, and good evil; that put darkness for light, and light for darkness; that put bitter for sweet, and sweet for bitter! The Bible is written to all. The reality is, only a few will walk in the glory out of the volumes of his book. **Matthew 7:14 (KJV) ¹⁴Because strait is the gate, and narrow is the way, which leadeth unto life, and few there be that find it. John 6:65 (KJV) ⁶⁵And he said, Therefore, said I unto you, that no man can come unto me, except it were given unto him of my Father. Malachi 3:6 (KJV) <u>6 For I am the LORD, I change not</u>. Revelation 22:18 (KJV) ¹⁸For I testify unto every man that heareth the words of the prophecy of this book, If any man shall add unto these things, God shall add unto him the plagues that are written in this book:**

The Jezebel spirit is in both male and female

Isaiah 3:12-26 (KJV) "¹²As for my people, children are their oppressors, and women rule over them. O my people, <u>they which lead thee cause thee to err, and destroy the way of thy paths.</u> 3:12 (KJV/NLT) ¹² Childish leaders oppress my people, and women rule over them. O my people, your leaders mislead you; they send you down the wrong road. (KJV) ¹³ The LORD standeth up to plead, and standeth to judge the people. 3:13 (NLT) ¹³ The Lord takes his place in court and presents his case against his people! (God is judging his people for changing the order of his house before the accuser.) 1 (Peter 4:17 (KJV) "¹⁷ For the time is come that judgment must begin at the house of God: and if it first begin at us, what shall the end be of them that obey not the gospel of God?") ... 14 The LORD will enter into judgment with the ancients of his people, and the princes thereof: for ye have eaten up the vineyard; the spoil of the poor is in your houses. 3:14 (NLT) ¹⁴ The Lord comes forward to pronounce judgment on the elders and rulers of his people: "**You have ruined Israel,** (Under grace and truth Israel is in the spiritual church which includes the gentiles.) ... **my vineyard. Your houses are filled with things stolen from the poor.** (Modern day faith preachers)

They, being blind by keeping the people under the law by taking this scripture out of context. **Malachi 3:10-12 (KJV) "¹⁰ Bring ye all the tithes into the storehouse, that there may be meat in mine house, and prove me now herewith, saith the LORD of hosts, if I will not open you the windows of heaven, and pour you out a blessing, that there shall not be room enough to receive it. Malachi 3:9 (KJV) ⁹ Ye are cursed with a curse: for ye have robbed me, even this whole nation."** The same scripture, used out of context is what led to this prosperity doctrine. In the New Testament, Freedom from debt is the as taught in the NT is freely you were given all things that money cannot buy. That's why you can't charge for something you get by faith you were given freely. If people are not being healed, delivered and set free as in the days of the apostles, you are pilfering the innocent with a woe used against them in the judgment for robbing the poor and enriching your own pocket as false Sheppard's. Nowhere in the New Testament does it say pay tithes. That's why we need a revelation of the new creature. When Paul spoke of Melchizedek, that what was required in the dispensation of the law.

When we learn who is at work with-in us and that he already owns everything, you will learn why Peter and James said to the beggar, **"silver and gold have I none but such as I have give I unto thee, Rise up and walk."** They had just come out of a meeting where people sold their excess possession and gave it all to the poor. They kept nothing for themselves, or they would have had some money to give the poor beggar. Now you see why they knew what they had was more precious than silver and gold. In this better covenant in Christ, we live beyond the meagerly beggarly elements in this world. That's why he told us not to be entangled with its affairs. Christ in you has made you content by having all your needs met daily while seeking the welfare of others. What's in you, money can't buy. That is what so hard for us to believe.

If Christ be in you to that degree, the rich cannot buy healing and deliverance that last so they will be bringing the silver and gold to Christ in you, he will give to those in need as he did in the early apostles because he owns everything, his purpose is to seek to save the lost. That's why you will not need to carry any of the meagerly things of this world because they are all God's possessions in the hands of the people, entrusted to be used at the appointed time he requires them.

This is what you have been freely given in him ... **1 John 3:17 (KJV)** **"¹⁷ But whoso hath this world's good, and seeth his brother have need, and shutteth up his bowels of compassion from him, how dwelleth the love of God in him?" Isaiah 3:15 ¹⁵ What mean ye that ye beat my people to pieces and grind the faces of the poor? saith the Lord GOD of hosts. Isaiah 3:15-16 (NLT) ¹⁵ How dare you crush my people, grinding the faces of the poor into the dust?" demands the Lord, the Lord of Heaven's Armies. ¹⁶ Moreover the LORD saith, Because the daughters of Zion are haughty, and walk with stretched forth necks and wanton eyes, walking and mincing as they go, and making a tinkling with their feet: Revelation 2:20 (KJV/NLT) ²⁰ But I have this complaint against you. You are permitting that woman—that Jezebel who calls herself a prophet—to lead my servants astray. She is encouraging them to worship idols, eat food offered to idols, and commit sexual sin.**

This spirit in the form of a women, is dressed to bring down the priest of God's house. **Isaiah 3:16-17 (KJV/NLT) ¹⁶ The Lord says, "Beautiful Zion is haughty: craning her elegant neck, flirting with her eyes, walking** with dainty steps, tinkling her ankle bracelets. [17] Therefore the Lord will smite with a scab the crown of the head of the daughters of Zion, and the LORD will discover <u>their secret parts.</u> They will seduce their men from the bedroom through lust and sensuality. **(KJV)** <u>[18] In that day the Lord</u> will take away the bravery of their tinkling ornaments about their feet, and their cauls, and their round tires like the moon, Because they use of their charm, physical beautify and Causley array. **(NLT)** [18] On that day of judgment the Lord will strip away everything that makes her beautiful: ornaments, headbands, crescent necklaces. They became vain and indecent and use their physical apparel to seduce the opposite sex.

This inherent vanity was received in Eve when she ate from the forbitten tree and discovered her body for the first time. Satan will use this to war for gender supremacy the flesh. **Isaiah 3:19 (KJV)** [19] **The chains, and the bracelets, and the mufflers,** Isaiah 3:19 (NLT) [19] **earrings, bracelets, and veils; (KJV)** [20] **The bonnets, and the ornaments of the legs, and the headbands, and the tablets, and the earrings, 3:20 (NLT)** [20] **scarves, ankle bracelets, sashes, perfumes, and charms; (KJV)** [21] **The rings, and nose jewels, 3:21 (NLT)** [21] **rings, jewels, (KJV)** [22] **The changeable suits of apparel, and the mantles, and the wimples, and the crisping pins, 3:22 (NLT)** [22] **party clothes, gowns, capes, and purses;** [23] **The glasses, and the fine linen, and the hoods, and the vails. 3:23 (NLT)** [23] **mirrors, fine linen garments, head ornaments, and shawls. (KJV)** [24] <u>**And it shall come to pass,**</u> **that instead of sweet smell there shall be stink; and instead of a girdle a rent; and instead of well-set hair baldness; and instead of a stomacher a girding of sackcloth; and burning instead of beauty. 3:24 (NLT)** [24] **Instead of smelling of sweet perfume, she will stink. She will wear a rope for a sash, and her elegant hair will fall out. She will wear rough burlap instead of rich robes. Shame will replace her beauty."** This is what will become a reality when all is gone in the coming downfall of America.

This specific warning to the women in the church will become a woe in this Day of Judgment. The doctrine of rapture and prosperity will be the downfall of many well-meaning Christians. At the advent of these great calamities, many will faint in fear for lack of knowledge as victims of false teachings. Many will discover, they have received the mark of the beast and be interned in concentration camps where <u>you will wear your same stinking</u>

garments until you die. Dogs will eat the flesh of those killed during the siege in the streets as did Jezebel's fate. Read the chronicle; **"Tithes and Offering" and "What will Happen During the Tribulation siege"**

This is the fate of the jezebel spirit as women host. The wrath of the first of the seven thunders of **Revelation 10:4** on the children of disobedience. The women who were disobedience to their husbands while confessing to be a Christian, put themselves as the head of man and did not repent will be turned over to the devil and destroyed like lots wife without remedy as Jezebels; their flesh will feed the dogs. **(KJV) 25 Thy men shall fall by the sword, and thy mighty in the war. Isaiah 3:25 (KJV/NLT) "25 The men of the city will be killed with the sword, and her warriors will die in battle." Likewise the Ahab's will suffer the same fate of eternal separation if they do not repent when the country is seized in tribulation."** This is the church being judged for forsaking the doctrine of Jesus Christ. **(KJV) 26 And her gates shall lament and mourn; and she being desolate shall sit upon the ground."**

This will be a wartime environment. **In that day** many so call Christian's will weep and mourn as wondering sheep outside the fold, gathered by the authorities and destroyed. Young wives and girls will be raped. They will eat their newborn babies at birth. **(Matt.24:19, Deut. 28: 57)** As brute beast; they will become food for the masses. **(Mal. 3:3) (KJV/ NLT) 26 The gates of Zion will weep and mourn. The city will be like a ravaged woman, huddled on the ground."** In Rev. 10:4, God revealed to me what he told John not to write because, if this were known during the fall away, the people would lose hope if revealed before time. People would have lost hope to see that God would allow such a thing to happen to his peoples. Though He revealed the whole of his wrath of the seven thunders to me later, only the children of disobedience will experience the first as their punishment and be translated as the cluster in (Rev. 14:17-18) as they are martyred ... **Isaiah 4:1 (KJV/NLT) 1 In that day so few men will be left that seven women will all marry you! We will provide our own food and clothing. Only let us take your name so we won't be mocked as old maids."**

War will deplete the male population drastically and many that are in the patriot movements will be killed. Women in this state will be accommodating to be with a man as with multiple companions. We see this spirit manifested in some cult religions today as a polygamist relationship. **Warning!** This tea party movement is a branch of the **Barabbas patriot** spirit, spearheading civil unrest at the wrong time in history; they think they can save America. This is the same spirit that emerged in Daniel Webster; like Christian patriots, their actions will single them out for destruction, blinded at the wrong time in history to be the reason to enact martial law.

My beloved sisters and brothers, these words of warning to repent to the present-day church will fall on many deft ears. The devil, having deceived this church by presenting only the good side of God. Israel experienced his wrath, the other side of God for their hard-hearted stiff-necked ways. We, like them, will suffer the same fate twofold. (Matt.23:15, Rev. 18:6)

God would have to repent to Israel if we were to escape after having done the same thing. We are at the end of the time of man's rule on earth. The judgment has begun. **1 Corinthians 11:23-28 (KJV) "23 <u>For I have received of the Lord that which also I delivered unto you</u>, That the Lord Jesus the same night in which he was betrayed took bread: ²⁴ And when he had given thanks, he brake it, and said, Take, eat: this is my body, which is broken for you: this do in remembrance of me. ²⁵ After the same manner also he took the cup, when he had supped, saying, This cup is the new testament in my blood: this do ye, as oft as ye drink it, in remembrance of me. ²⁶ <u>For as often as ye eat this bread, and drink this cup, ye do shew the Lord's death till he come.</u> ²⁷ Wherefore whosoever shall eat this bread, and drink this cup of the Lord, unworthily, shall be <u>guilty of the body and blood of the Lord.</u> ²⁸ <u>But let a man examine himself</u>, and so let him eat of that bread, and drink of that cup."**

The sacrament is not to be administered with-out knowing what you are doing spiritually. It is self-explanatory; you are either blessing yourself or cursing yourself. Do not perform this sacred act unless you are committed to surrendering daily as being led by the Holy Spirit. The fact that most assemblies have made this a ritual, is the reason why there's so much sickness and disease among Christians. Many are being led to take this vaccine that's designed to de-populate the world by their pastors. The most grievous part about carrying this message is to see it fall on deft ears. I plead to you all who are confessing Christians in the exercising of your faith to examine yourself. When God showed me my heart, it was out of his love for me to give me a second chance to get right. I had been a confessing Christian for many years and what I saw in my heart is what man had put there. God is giving everyone that is called by his spirit a chance to repent for the kingdom of heaven is now at hand. REPENT! REPENT! REPENT! (Updated for Released 8/2021)

EXPOSING THE JEZEBEL SPIRITS

Background Scripture:

1 Kings Chapters 18-22

In the last article I wrote entitled **"Woe to the Ahab' and Jezebels of Today",** I felt led to expand on this subject in more detail as to its origin for the benefit of those who may not recognize this spirit and how it operates in the church body that has contributed to this present-day apostasy.

"Father, In the name of Jesus, I employ the Holy Spirit to dictate the revelations in this message that we may be completely delivered from this spirit." Amen

In the book of first Kings, chapters eighteen thru twenty- two, we get a good picture of the operation of this spirit in kingdoms and how governments are brought down. This demon got its fame in the use of Jezebel and Ahab. Its origin is of a fallen angel, Satan. Eve received this spirit in the Garden. Since this spirit can only manifest in a host body, it's one of choice is a female. Now to clarify this, let's go back to the Garden of Eden. Why did Satan approach Eve? **First,** she was created as a helpmate who, being the weaker vessel of Adam, made her subject to the male gender as an equal in spirit as one. Her physical make up will prove to be the ideal host for his most diabolical schemes to gain the dominance over the male which is created in the image of God.

This will reverse the order of creation, causing mankind under this demonic seducing spirit to reverse the role of male and female; therefore, causing the female to become an object of worship and desire after the fall. The nature of a female's physical features after the fall will enable this demon to use the woman's physical attributes of sex, manipulation and sensuality to gain power and control. By use of the female, it can cover its masquerade in this host.

The natural man is no match for this dominate spirit in a female. Given her natural beauty, charm, and sex appeal, in a carnal environment, she will rewrite history in all the wrong ways unacceptable in the site of God. All a man must do is loose his fear of God and becomes an Ahab, trapped in the charms of his bedroom lover.

This spirit has caused many kingdoms to fall at the hand of this evil companions in the bedroom mimicking the relationship of Ahab and Jezebel where she is in control reversing the priesthood of God, the male image. This spirit contributed to the fall of Israel. **Galatians 3:28 (NLT) "28 There is no longer Jew or Gentile, slave or free, male or female. For you are all Christians—you are one in Christ Jesus."** (Compare KJV) This scripture, used out of context has contributed to the present-day apostasy. God has never changed the order of His creation, man wresting the scriptures by using his own thoughts without the leading of the Holy Spirit will be as a blind man leading the blind. **Matthew 15:14 (KJV) "14 Let them alone: they be blind leaders of the blind. And if the blind lead the blind, both shall fall into the ditch."**

This also explains why we have so many forms of religions identified as denominations. This spirit does not like to be subject to authority, it is the authority. They like to be in renowned circles as a preeminent equal to its peers in males. The rebellious nature of this spirit is more identified in women. It likes to be in control. As male and female, it exercises a matriarchal control over societies, religions, and governments. It creates idols to worship that have attachments of these spirits that cause you to seek after the things in the natural without knowing these things can become a point of your possession. We have a record mentioned in the account in 1 Kings 11:5-7, Solomon having too many wives, got seduced by one of his wives to serve the god of Ashtoreth. This idol represented sex and sensuality of which he gave place and defiled the temple of God with this abomination. Solomon as the king, setting in Christ stead; defiled himself and the temple of God. God had him to write about this in the **"Song of Solomon."** This is another form of Baal worship.

There again initiated through women. Many cult teachings are derived from Greek and mythical Babylonian teachings regarding the female dominance. Today, we see a resurgence of new age mythical medieval spirits further capturing the minds of ignorant Christians. In the Bible reference to Ahab and Jezebel, we see all these in operation in the kingdom including murder. Biblical history teaches us that there is nothing new under the sun and these things were written for our learning. (Eccl. 1:9)

How does one become a host be it male or female?

These are some of the facilitators that open the doors to women. Past sexual abuse instills fear that leads to self-protection and control of the circumstances. It becomes generational when he or she suffers as a child, as victims of incest or physical abuse. Woman, being the weaker vessel, has no way of dealing with this psychological trauma and as a result will think that she is the cause of what has happen to her as a child due to her physical make up.

These predator spirits in the males or females form have made them the objects of desire. Therefore, she will enter adolescence sexually withdrawn or sexually promiscuous. This will become the medium of a generational curse as a victim in the family; if he or she never gets delivered, will turn to manipulation of the opposite sex. Now this brings us to how generational curses are perpetuated through the blood line. Usually this is a pattern that has started generations ago.

As I examine the source of this seducing spirit through the leading of the Holy Spirit; the deep cover of this spirit can only be detected in the spirit of a delivered believer. Therefore, confessing Christian's born from below are the seduce. These spirits blind them to not know what spirit they are of. **Luke 9:55 (KJV) "55 But he turned, and rebuked them, and said, Ye know not what manner of spirit ye are of."**

When it comes to salvation, man has refined it down to a science as a blind guide in the pulpit. Not knowing what manner of spirit is operating in him, not being converted in Christ. This is their character ... **1 Timothy 6:4-6**

(KJV) "⁴ He is proud, knowing nothing, but doting about questions and strifes of words, whereof cometh envy, strife, railings, evil surmisings, ⁵ Perverse disputings of men of corrupt minds, and destitute of the truth, supposing that gain is godliness: from such withdraw thyself." These that are in leadership will manifest the above character.

Whatever is in the teacher or pastor from his or her past are hidden manifestation that can only be detected by the Holy Spirit. Jesus encountered this spirit in the religious leaders of His time on earth. What did He say to them… **John 8:44 (KJV) "⁴⁴ Ye are of your father the devil, and the lusts of your father ye will do. He was a murderer from the beginning, and abode not in the truth, because there is no truth in him. When he speaketh a lie, he speaketh of his own: for he is a liar, and the father of it. Luke 9:55 (KJV) ⁵⁵ But he turned, and rebuked them, and said, Ye know not what manner of spirit ye are of."**

This same spirit is what Jesus will put down again through His elects when He visits these pastors to give them a chance to repent again. This is the time when … **Psalm 95:8 (KJV) ⁸ Harden not your heart, as in the provocation, and as in the day of temptation in the wilderness.** None of them came out of the wilderness alive that did not hear Moses, all died except their children for rejecting Moses in the wilderness. This is a type and shadow of things to come. This will be repeated in the spirit in our time when 98 percent of this end-time church world, rejects these prophets and messengers by not knowing the voice of God. Their children will replace them.

Many will choose to reject God in His chosen servants and suffer the same fate of eternal separation. Read the Chronicle … **"Preparation for Glory." Joshua 24:15 (KJV) "¹⁵ And if it seem evil unto you to serve the LORD, <u>choose you this day whom ye will serve;</u> whether the gods which your fathers served that were on the other side of the flood, or the gods of the Amorites, in whose land ye dwell: <u>but as for me and my house, we will serve the LORD.</u>"**

My beloved brothers and sisters, I have suffered much at the hands of well-meaning Christians who, not knowing what spirit they were of as I too erred in my flesh in this area without knowing it. My devotion to truth got me put out of the assemblies for teaching truth just by saying I have no bible evidence to prove that women have been elevated to usurp authority over men in the assembly. We know that in the spirit, there is neither male of female; therefore, in the Holy Spirit, all things will be done according to the doctrine of Jesus Christ as laid down in the scriptures as decent and in order.

This is the work of the Jezebel spirit. I have born much grief, loss a wife and all things in my past to get here and presently contending with the enemy daily to stay here. It has cost me all this to find God. I live daily knowing that in the end, I will probably come out of this alone to keep him. I tell you like Satan found out with Job, my only protection has been the fact that God has chosen me and put the hedge of the word, grace and mercy upon me. All my issues of rejection have been resolved in Christ. He and He alone has giving me this ability to suffer with Him, not that I have reach that place of perfection. If you have these past issues mentioned in the jezebel spirits, ask God to deliver you. It would be a shame to devote your life to a false representation of Christ a Christian and be cast into to hell for all you thought was right in your own sight.

I remember when I exposed these spirits in Christians, many years ago, I to, like Elijah, had to escape the city I grew up in as having no honor among my own. It took me seven years to get over that degree of rejection and the loss of all things. I later learned; God was giving me an experience that comes with forsaking all things including the loss of my family. In that state, it took me seven years before I could return home again. I can only say, through it all, God had a purpose for me being born. The only reason I escape to be where I am today is to be used for His glory. Most Christians, not delivered, will oppress those who are doers of the word.

Christ will suffer long with these as tares among us to perfect his servants under these conditions. These oppressors show signs of being double minded which make then easily provoked when they are exposed. James described this in... **James 1:8 (KJV) "⁸A double minded man is unstable in all his ways."** In the assembly where there is no deliverance, the pastor under this spirit will oppress the people while meaning well, thinking he is doing the right thing, taking scriptures out of context without the spirit of God. This spirit hidden in a pastor is no more than a demon angel; disguise in religion, it's leading the people that follow, down the path of destruction. **Isaiah 3:12 (KJV) "¹²As for my people, children are their** oppressors, and women rule over them. O my people, <u>they which lead thee cause thee to err, and destroy the way of thy paths</u>." I am glad to be on the latter end of God's grace. As I look back at pass movements, not many have endured who received the former thing that guided some of us into this place of rest awaiting the latter rain.

<u>This is what it looks like in assemblies where this spirit rule:</u>

This has been my experience in the past to have suffered at the hands of people used by these spirits.

1. Some may appear humble until provoked and then become arrogant, haughty, disdainful and full of pride. These are mostly identified with males.

2. Seductive: Male or female. The male has the tendency to ... **2 Timothy 3:6 (KJV) 6 For of this sort are they which creep into houses, and lead captive silly women laden with sins, led away with divers lusts,"** The women usually will marry the man she seduces and later divorce him for another if she can't be in control; being deprived of love at some point in their life that left them with a spirit of insecurity, is hard for them to trust for fear of losing.

3. They are very persuasive as leaders, both male and female. They will exploit the leadership for positions and seek to find a place of power. Weak pastors will see their congregation become splintered, self interest groups ruling and causing division.

4. They will find fault with leadership and conduct their activity covertly. Women are more commonly used in this activity. They will try to get to the pastor through their wives or husbands' faults to fill a void in their lives.

5. They will appear to be super spiritual and may even have a gift to produce signs, but further examination will show corrupt fruit.

6. They will question authority, having an agenda will calculate their moves through others to do their bidding, casting dispersions and doubt on leadership decisions.

7. They may be stealthy as to not be accountable to leadership.

8. They are active in assembly affairs but answerable to no one.

9. They can have bisexual tendencies, when they encounter likeminded spirits, they may even encourage co-habitation with the same sex.

10. In marriage, the wife will take the lead and the husband will be very accommodating; vice-versa the husband will be overbearing, authoritative and will not listen to reasoning.

11. **Finally,** in the worst-case scenario, an assembly operating under this spirit of darkness can cause any one of these above condition in a carnal environment, literally to commit murder in the sanctuary.

Point one; all demons are fallen angelic beings. The extent of their manifestation is not limited to the gender host. In their perverted state, they can have female tendencies in a male's body and vice versa which is where we see manifested in homosexuality. The use of the female is to weaken the male, created in the image of God. This is where Satan's accusations are against him before God. **Revelation 12:10 (KJV) "which accused them before our God day and night."** What is he accusing us of day and night? 1 **Timothy 4:2 (KJV) "2 Speaking lies in hypocrisy; having their conscience seared with a hot iron;"** This is what they do as perverting the gospel.

I have shared this with you for self-examination. Now do not become a judge or a demon hunter by now being opened to discern this activity. Do not try to cast out this demon unless directed by God in the spirit. Given the present state of the church, without knowing what you are dealing with, could give you a <u>Sons of Sceva</u> experience. **Acts 19:14-16 (KJV) "14 And there were seven sons of one Sceva, a Jew, and chief of the priests, which did so. 15 And the evil spirit answered and said, Jesus I know, and Paul I know; but who are ye? 16 And the man in whom the evil spirit was leaped on them, and overcame them, and prevailed against them, so that they fled out of that house naked and wounded.** None of us can cast stones at each other in our present state while on the mercy seat before God.

This type of exorcism can only be done by mature Christians walking in the spirit of truth led by the Holy Spirit. One I went to council a troubled confessing Christian; unaware this person was possessed with a demon. When I arrived in the room, I saw bloody handprints on the wall.

I instinctively knew she was possessed. I look her in the eye and asked if she wanted to get delivered, she said nothing, I got up and left. This spirits ability to manipulate feeling and emotions, do not be alone at any time as Eve. I was divinely protected by God in her presence. These demons have succeeded in deceiving the whole world. **Revelation 12:9 (KJV) "⁹ And the great dragon was cast out, that old serpent, called the <u>Devil, and Satan, which deceiveth the whole world:</u> he was cast out into the earth, and his angels were cast out with him."** This is a word for right now, follow peace, God is about to do the separating of these tares. This is the spirit that wrecks marriages, divide churches and bring down leaders in governments.

The carnal Christian is no match for its repertoire of seducing spirits. Continue to rest and be still and you will see the salvation of the lord bring this spirit down not many days from now.

<u>Observations from a Spiritual Standpoint</u>:

This I have observed; men with Jezebel wives envy another brother whose wife appears submissive in public but, behind closed doors is an oppressor. Women with an overbearing and authoritative husband will tend to react the same way to a nice brother, whom she wishes her husband was like. In the real world of Christianity, we are a mess in God's sight and we had better repent of these envies that gender strife among ourselves. God sees all our faults and is judging our hearts, who do we think we are fooling. In the epistles is the doctrine that governs what God expects of the husband and of the wife in His sight as confessing to be of Him. I suggest we all study these again and you will see where we fall short.

The Root Characteristics of This Spirit in The Laodicean Church Time

Psalms 51:5 (KJV) "⁵ Behold, I was shapen in iniquity; and in sin did my mother conceive me." If we never encounter the truth demonstrated in the purity, power, and beauty of holiness as ministered by the Holy Ghost, we are no more than confessing Christian's needing deliverance.

Unless God build the house, all your work is in vain; therefore, pastors are no more than a hireling after the teachings of man. I started out that way and God intervene and corrected me.

What we have heard and seen preached and taught in the pulpits across this nation, in reality is mostly man' teachings; manifested in structured order bible principles of theology and his traditions. That's what Jesus found when He went to the physical temple. In our time, He will cause your assembly doors to be closed before he returns. What he was doing literally is a type and shadow of what he will be doing in the spiritual temple when the Holy Ghost returns. He drove out Lust, lying, cheating, graft, stealing, corruption, deception, robbers, greed, false teachings, and the world with man's traditions.

The abominations in most assemblies as carnal Christians, is thinking we are spiritual, and all this is acceptable by God. Your early life experiences as a sinner may still be in you as hidden spirits waiting to be exposed if you have never been delivered. Satan has only suppressed these spirits by joining one of his false assemblies. Many have followed family traditions, passing down what was in the father to the son which becomes more watered down to compromised standards of religious opportunities in established institution of false teachings with generations of followers. These are the family church corporations.

If your mother dominated the household over the father, more than likely, your wife will be the dominate one in your home and behind the pulpit. Jesus led by example by showing us what the father will do in you to please Himself as Jesus did; these spirits are passed on whether good or bad. Early life traumas and teachings are where we without ever knowing, manifest these hidden demonic spirits. Remember, only when one is converted can God use him to convert others.

That's why He told Peter in… **Luke 22:32 (KJV) "[32] But I have prayed for thee, that thy faith fail not: and when thou art converted, strengthen thy brethren."** When you come to the place that … **Galatians 2:20 (KJV) "[20] I am crucified with Christ: nevertheless, I live; yet not I, but Christ liveth in me: and the life which I now live in the flesh I live by the faith of the Son of God, who loved me, and gave himself for me."** Therefore, you will … **1 Corinthians 2:2 (KJV) [2] For I determined not to know**

anything among you, save Jesus Christ, and him crucified. These are chosen by God of whom He will use to carry His message.

Where Christ is the head of the house, all things are in order operating in His body. There's nowhere in the scriptures to justify that God put Eve's head on Adam's body when he sinned. Christ as the head will build you up in the most holy faith that produces fruit that remains. This fruit will remain till he comes. This fruit is not evident in the present church because we fail to receive the fullness, that's why we all must repent of our unbelief on our day of visitation. I have also observed that when God uses us, some are tempted, have a tendency not to be open to others who God is using also. This is a form of hidden pride and envy.

I also see the body God is putting together consist of broken vessels which have been put back in the fire to be molded into a perfect vessel. **2 Corinthians 4:3 (KJV) "3 But if our gospel be hid, it is hid to them that are lost: Romans 9:11 (KJV) 11 (For the children being not yet born, neither having done any good or evil, that the purpose of God according to election might stand, not of works, but of him that calleth; 1 Peter 1:10 (KJV) 10 Of which salvation the prophets have enquired and searched diligently, who prophesied of the grace that should come unto you: 2 Peter 1:10 (KJV) 10 Wherefore the rather, brethren, give diligence to make your calling and election sure: for if ye do these things, ye shall never fall:"**

"Father, in the name of Jesus, I pray these words fall on good ground that you have prepared; I command the quickening power of the Holy Ghost to come upon them for the work where unto you have called them began, revealed yourself unto them as you have to me, it is my desire that none stumble at your truth. Father open their eyes, ears, hearts and minds, let them see the hour is late and time is no more. I thank you for their deliverance in Jesus Name. Father, open their eyes all around them to see the need to repent and totally surrender their vessels. Father, forgive us of our unbelief, restore to us the joy of our salvation, return us to our first love, deliver us from the evils of this world, help us to never look back and to see that you are our only hope. Father, I thank you in faith for this fruit in Jesus name." AMEN (Updated for Released 10/2019)

DEALING WITH EVIL THOUGHTS

Question: How do you deal with evil thoughts as a Christian?

Answer: Until we understand how to get the power to control our thoughts, the enemy of our old man will constantly bombard our mind with the past and the present to prevent you from entering the realm of right thinking. The fact that we will have to give an account of our sins of omission … how are we to overcome these thoughts of evil? Learning to reject them requires a conscious level of right and wrong. I learned by speaking the word back to the enemy of our mind. Often, I must tell him to get behind me like Jesus did in the wilderness. **Matthew 4:4 (KJV) ⁴ But he answered and said, It is written, Man shall not live by bread alone, but by every word that proceedeth out of the mouth of God.** This is how you do it … **2 Corinthians 10:5 (ASV) ⁵ "casting down imaginations, and every high thing that is exalted against the knowledge of God and bringing every thought into captivity to the obedience of Christ;"** We learn this by reading the account of Jesus in the wilderness temptation; what did he say to the devil in the above scripture. This is where this scripture must be applied … **2 Timothy 2:15 (NASB) ¹⁵ Be diligent to present yourself approved to God as a workman who does not need to be ashamed, accurately handling the word of truth.** You must take time to study the word to feed your spirit man so he can bring it to your remembrance at the time you need to hear so you can act on it. That's how you see all these

143

scripture reference in the chronicles to support the comments; That's him in me.

This is where we must live in the reality of the new birth to activate our teacher, the Holy Spirit. The only weapon we must have to defend ourselves is the word of God spoken in faith. Brother, I know what you are saying but some of these thoughts are so evil, they make me feel like I am not saved. When God saved you, he did not do a partial forgiveness. He gave you the ability to have the power to control your actions not to give in to them once you were forgiven. This is what he did ... **Hebrews 10:17 (NASB77)** [17]**"AND THEIR SINS AND THEIR LAWLESS DEEDS I WILL REMEMBER NO MORE."** Now if God is your final judge and he does not remember your past sins, why can't you believe you are forgiven? Now every time the devil reminds you of your past sins, there is no sin that God will not forgive you for as coming from sin to salvation, no matter how bad; you could not help yourself as a sinner. Now tell him to get behind you. As often as I have said, these unconfessed sins of omission are what will keep many well-meaning confessing Christians out of heaven. AMEN

THE SINS OF OMISSION

In the book of Galatians chapter five are seventeen sins in this category that are often overlooked that has contributed to the present-day apostasy. Through-out my early life as a confessing Christian, I never heard any minister teach on these passages other that what followed in verses 22-23, the fruits of the spirit. Knowledge and understanding has a lot to do with how you develop spiritually. Lack of it can cause you to be rejected as a religious child of the devil and not even know it. What caught my attention are these sayings ... **Luke 6:46 "(KJV) ⁴⁶ And why call ye me, Lord, Lord, and do not the things which I say? Matthew 7:21-22 (KJV) ²¹ Not everyone that saith unto me, Lord, Lord, shall enter into the kingdom of heaven; but he that doeth the will of my Father which is in heaven. ²² Many will say to me in that day, Lord, Lord, have we not prophesied in thy name? and in thy name have cast out devils? and in thy name done many wonderful works? Matthew 22:14 (KJV) ¹⁴ For many are called, but few *are* chosen. 1 Corinthians 1:26 (KJV) ²⁶ For ye see your calling, brethren, how that not many wise men after the flesh, not many mighty, not many noble, *are called*: Matthew 24:38 (KJV) ³⁸ For as in the days that were before the flood they were eating and drinking, marrying and giving in marriage, until the day that Noe entered into the ark,"**

When the lord separated me unto himself to teach me what was going to judge man in the last days, these scriptures became very apparent to me that the error of our ways will be what we will have to give an account of in the judgement. This is what I found that will cause many of us to miss the mark. Now let's examine these sins of omission as found in ... **Galatians 5:19-21 (KJV)** [v19] *Now the works of the flesh are manifest, which are these;*

Adultery- (Having two or more living wives or husbands.)

Fornication- (Sexual relations as being a confessing Christian outside of marriage.)

Uncleanness- (Habits that defile the body of cause death with the using.)

Lasciviousness- (immoral behavior, wearing garments that demonstrate and promote sexual sensuality by exposing your flesh. [v20] **Idolatry-** (Loving anything more than you love God)

Witchcraft- (Consulting with Satan' mediums for advice.)

Hatred – Holding malice in your heart for another person or unforgiveness.)

Variance-(Not knowing who you worship.) Luke-warm Christians

Emulations- (Seeking to follow or be like men of renown statue in the world.)

Wrath- (Anger that leads to murder or death.)

Strife- (Always have something evil to say about a person you don't like.)

Seditions- (Acting contrary to the law, offensive language.)

Heresies- (Repeating gossip and talking too much about people or what you see.) [21] **Envying's-** (Desiring what others have.)

Murders- (Baring false witness that leads to a person's death of literally killing another human being.)

Drunkenness- (Consuming anything that takes control of your mind that brings you under its control and out of God's will.)

Revellings- (Like to see people fall when they are trying to do good or self-idling.) **and such like: of the which I tell you before, as I have also told *you* in time past, that <u>they which do such things shall not inherit the kingdom of God.</u>**

This is what God hates the most?

Proverbs 6:16-19 (KJV) [16] *"These six things doth the LORD hate: yea, seven are an abomination unto him:* [17] <u>*A proud look, a lying tongue, and hands that shed innocent blood,*</u> [18] <u>*An heart that deviseth wicked imaginations, feet that be swift in running to mischief,*</u> [19] <u>*A false witness that speaketh lies, and he that soweth discord among brethren.*</u>*"*

This was the answer to my question as to what will keep many confessing Christians out of heaven. The reason the above sins will justify Satan's claim on your soul; these sins are what we were delivered from in our past life as a sinner that carry a sentence of death. If you are still guilty of partaking in such sinful ways as a confessing Christian, you have judge yourself unworthy to enter heaven.

Your leaders must be an example of the truth they teach, searching the scriptures behind them to keep yourself on the straight path to avoid becoming a victim of lack of knowledge or false teachings. **Hebrews 9:27 (NASB77)** [27] **"And inasmuch as it is appointed for men to die once and after this comes judgment," 2 Corinthians 5:10 (NASB77)** [10] *"For we must all appear before the judgment seat of Christ, that* **each one may be recompensed** (Give an account of your words that God did not say that you did not repent of.) **for his deeds in the body, according to what he has done, whether good or bad."** This is the judgment where we will be ... **Daniel 5:27 (NASB77)** [27] **"you have been weighed on the scales and found deficient."**

This is where Satan gets to justify his claim on your soul by having too many un-confessed sins that out weighted your good. Now this dilemma will cause you to end up at the great white throne judgment because God knew what state you were in at death. This statement may shock you; going to heaven is not based on your confession but whether you are a doer of the word. Some will be given mercy as the thief that repented on the cross. Those of us who confess him will be without excuse because we had time to get right before we passed from this life.

John 14:15 (NASB77) [15] **"If you love Me, you will keep My commandments. John 15:10 (NASB77)** [10] **"If you keep My commandments, you will abide in My love; just as I have kept My Father's commandments and abide in His love. Hebrews 11:6 (NASB77)** [6] **And without faith it is impossible to**

please Him, for he who comes to God must believe that He is, and that He is a rewarder of those who seek Him." Avoid this form of delusion … 2 Timothy 3:7 (NASB77) [7] "always learning and never able to come to the knowledge of the truth. Luke 6:46 (NASB77) [46] "And why do you call Me, 'Lord, Lord,' and do not do what I say?" The sin that deceives us is not being aware of a man-made traditional standard of living that God does not accept.

There are two wills we may be operating in; one is **the permissive** will as in serving God through feeling and emotions. This is where we reach a comfort zone by not knowing what spirit has possessed us, we begin to serve God by doing good deeds on the bases of how we feel about what the scripture says. This is where most of us are by not knowing what spirit we are of as by-products of hireling pastors that tell us what we want to hear. Now we did not get like this overnight, most of us came through generations of divisions under these false teachings. We have been hearing parts of the truth instead of the whole council of the truth. Once you are indoctrinated under your denomination's teachings, we will automatically reject anything new because we did not hear it from our leader. **1 Corinthians 1:12 (NASB77)** [12] **Now I mean this, that each one of you is saying, "I am of Paul," and "I of Apollos," and "I of Cephas," and "I of Christ." 1 Corinthians 3:4 (NASB77)** [4] *For when one says, «I am of Paul,» and another, «I am of Apollos,» are you not mere men?*

This is what we are saying when we associate what traditional men in the flesh, we honored more than God in the flesh. Living in this Christian comfort zone, we tend to reject anything new as a carnal Christian. This is a result of not studying after your leader under the guidance of the Holy Spirit. This type of wrong teaching result in wrong thinking that has led to our stunted spiritual growth because it carries an element of judging others on the bassist of false teaching. The will that gets you into heaven and gives you mercy is his **perfect and sovereign will** that serves God out of a pure heart as a child. **Matthew 18:4 (NASB77)** [4] **"Whoever then humbles himself as this child, he is the greatest in the kingdom of heaven.**

What traditions of men will do as members of the doctrine of the Nicolaitans', (man's ways) will cause you to fall short of God's glory in your life by only being taught principles of truth in part? That's why we tend to cater to men of renown, we look to as having the credentials worthy of our attention to the point that we consider what they as the authorities in religious circles. Now that's a seducing spirit. How do you know you are not in the right doctrine; when you hear a pastor say, these are my members. The reason why so many confessing Christians are so easily wounded, we have been kept drinking milk toast gospel, by being kept from hearing the whole council of the word so Satan can rob you in the name of God.

God, through the Holy Spirit is manifested in these five ministerial graces in his body ... **Ephesians 4:11-13 (NASB77)** [11] *"And He gave some as* **apostles,** and some as **prophets,** and some as **evangelists,** and some as **pastors** and **teachers,** [12] *for the equipping of the saints for the work of service, to the building up of the body of Christ;* 13 *until we all attain to the unity of the faith, and of the knowledge of the Son of God, to a mature man, to the measure of the stature which belongs to the fulness of Christ.* **Galatians 5:22-24 (NASB77)** [22] **But the fruit of the Spirit is love, joy, peace, patience, kindness, goodness, faithfulness,** [23] **gentleness, self-control; against such things there is no law.** [24] **Now those who belong to Christ Jesus have crucified the flesh with its passions and desires.**

When we encounter convictions through an elect servant, the Holy Spirit will set you on ... **Matthew 7:13-23 (NASB77)** [13] **Enter by the narrow gate; for the gate is wide, and the way is broad that leads to destruction, and many are those who enter by it.** [14] **"For the gate is small, and the way is narrow that leads to life, and few are those who find it.** [15] **"Beware of the false prophets, who come to you in sheep's clothing, but inwardly are ravenous wolves.** [16] **"You will know them by their fruits. Grapes are not gathered from thorn bushes, nor figs from thistles, are they?** [17] **"Even so, every good tree bears good fruit; but the bad tree bears bad fruit.** [18] **"A good tree cannot produce bad fruit, nor can a bad tree produce good fruit.** [19] **"Every tree that does not bear good fruit is cut down and thrown into the fire.** [20] **"So then, you will know them by their fruits.** [21] **" Not everyone who says to Me, 'Lord, Lord,' will enter the kingdom of heaven; but he who does the will of My Father who is in heaven.** [22] **" Many will say to Me on that day, 'Lord, Lord, did we not prophesy in Your name, and in Your name cast out demons, and in Your name perform**

many miracles?' [23] **"And then I will declare to them, 'I never knew you; DEPART FROM ME, YOU WHO PRACTICE LAWLESSNESS.'**

This shows you that the doctrine once save is always save is not the truth. Many will be caught in that state of lack of knowledge and be lost in the judgment by being weighed in the balance and found wanting. I find this among many King James only bible readers; by not having a full understanding revelation of scripture to discern when God is speaking, they will judge you. A word from the Lord … *"My dearly beloved children, don't take my words for granted, I warn you in this way so you may examine yourself by my words and judge for yourself where you are before your appointed time of departure."* (Updated for Release 8/2015)

THE WORD OF GOD VS
THE WORD OF MAN

NIV vs JKV

Background scripture:

Rev. 22:19 (KJV "And if any man shall take away from the words of the book of this prophecy, God shall take away his part out of the book of life, and out of the holy city, and from the things which are written in this book."

I have examined a few of these new bible versions; however, as I examined these editions, it became apparent to me the confusion in knowledge of the word. I have always used the KJV (Thompson Chain Edition) as my primary study Bible; I am not a K J only bible reader. Now let me be clear! The Holy Spirit wrote the Bible and the early history of how we got the English translation was a direct act of God, moved on King James to authorize this version that bears his name.

The original version had a strong Anglo-Saxon delivery hard to be read by today's English standards. Although there were others, the second edition published in 1679, prove to be the widely accepted version as well as the first edition of the American Standard Bible (ASV). These two versions are the standard use among well-read scholars today. When it comes to these more recent translations, here is where I see the problem of confusion in the assemblies. I was once setting in a large assembly and nearly every other Sunday, the pastor would read out of different version of these parallel easy reading English versions. What caught my attention, there were far more versions among the congregation. While sitting as the scripture was being read, many in my row would ask? Where is he reading from, what bible? If he did not mention it, I would not know myself. What I found that most Christians do not have a foundational relationship in the Lord not to be influenced by these parallel easy reading versions. I have not found many of the versions I examined to be scripturally accurate or sound. When it comes to modern day English, it's like a forest with all these versions. Without the leading of the Holy Spirit, deception is the order of the day.

I will not name these versions; I have never viewed them as bibles. These easy readers to people who do not want to search the scriptures, out of the KJV or ASV are why we need to be taught by submission or else deception is inevitable. In my chronicles, you will see references to KJV, ASV and NLT (second edition), NASB77 and ESV. Without the Holy Spirit as your guide, even K J only Christians will also miss the mark without the leading of the Holy Spirit.

This is what I have found that is most noteworthy, the New Living Translation (second edition) is the most agreeable with the spirit of interpretation; however, it is not a bible, just a help. I am not endorsing it as a primary word, as a help when you understand the KJV as all quote from. You be led by the spirit in all things where the word is concern. This I would recommend as a parallel help; the 2005 edition of the KJV/NLT put out by Tyndale Publishers, Inc. This is one of the most significant discoveries in my research in one of the most widely use easy reading translations. **"The New International Version" (NIV).** Let me remind you that none of these are authorized by God. He does not need to improve on what he gave the Holy Spirit to as many as received Him to guide us into all truth. These are some of the comparisons in the NIV that not only change the doctrine but twist the truth into a lie. In many instances, many passages of scripture are omitted that are vital to your deliverance. This is a master work in false doctrine. It is not only the author of confusion but is the culprit. I see many renowned pastors and leaders using this as their primary bible. These are some of the passages below I found to be troublesome to me.

1. Luke 9:56 (KJV) "For the Son of man is not come to destroy men's lives, but to save them. And they went to another village."

2. Luke 9:56(NIV) and they went to another village. (The first part omitted)

3. Matthew 18:11(KJV) "For the Son of man is come to save that which   was lost."

4. Matthew 18:11 (NIV) OMITTED

    Mark 2:17 (KJV) "When Jesus heard it, he saith unto them, They that are whole have no need of the physician, but they that are sick: I came not to call the righteous, but sinners to <u>repentance.</u>"

5. Mark 2:17 (NIV) On hearing this, Jesus said to them, "It is not the healthy who need a doctor, but the sick. I have not come to call the righteous, but sinners."(Repentance omitted)

6. Acts 8:37 (KJV) "And Philip said, If thou believest with all thine heart, thou mayest. And he answered and said, I believe that Jesus Christ is the Son of God."

7. Acts 8:37 (NIV) OMITTED

8. Col. 1:14 (KJV) "In whom we have redemption through <u>his blood</u>, even the   forgiveness of sins:"

9. Col. 1:14 (NIV) " in whom we have redemption, the forgiveness of sins. (Blood omitted)

Isaiah 14:12-15 (KJV) "[12]How art thou fallen from heaven, O Lucifer, son of the morning! how art thou cut down to the ground, which didst weaken the nations! [13] For thou hast said in thine heart, I will ascend into heaven, I will exalt my throne above the stars of God: I will sit also upon the mount of the congregation, in the sides of the north: [14] I will ascend above the heights of the clouds; I will be like the most High. [15] Yet thou shalt be brought down to hell, to the sides of shoal.

Isaiah 14:12-15 (NIV) How you have fallen from heaven O morning star, son of the dawn! You have been cast down to the earth, you who once laid low the nations![13] You said in your heart, I will ascend to heaven; I will raise my throne above the stars of God; I will sit enthroned on the mount of assembly on the utmost heights of the sacred mountain.[14] I will ascend above the tops of the clouds; I will make myself like the Most High.[15] But you are brought <u>down to the grave</u>, to the depths of the pit. (Hell omitted) (This reads as if there is no hell)

This is just a short view of what I found to be a major problem throughout the whole NIV version. The International Bible Society has roots to the Jesuit's, introduce this as a bible counterpart to the reading of the KJV in modern English and promoted it to where it is the most widely used version on the market of the easy reading versions. This version has contributed to the apostasy of the present-day Laodicea church. The **"Deep State'"** religious division has succeeded in taking the holy sayings out of the context by removing whole passages of scriptures that in teaching bring no deliverance to the church world. Now what you see in most assemblies are a compromised view of the gospel, taught in part. Need I say more; if you have a copy of the NIV, compare it with the KJV or ASV which are the most accurate translations of the Hebrew and Greek scrolls.

The New Living Translation 2nd edition is a translation based on the modern English words from these scrolls. I suggest you get rid of the NIV version or face a stiff rebuke or even rejection to continue using this version after you have been warned. This version will be the reason that 98 percent of the church will be given over to a strong delusion. If you want to read the modern text, then, I recommend the KJV and ASV and for a good parallel side by side English translation, the NASB 1977 & NKJV were translated from the (ASV) & KJV are good translations. When you read these modern English interpretations, without the anointing of the Holy Spirit, you may miss the understanding of a passage in its right context. The versions I use in my daily studies as parallel help to the ASV and KJV is the NLT (second edition) and the NASB 1977 edition.

One of the observations I notice about well-meaning Christians, many are bound by long standing traditions that make them resistant to change. The pre-imminence of well-established authorities who endorse these books containing gross doctrinal errors are too steeped in pride to renounce their errors in judgment when brought in question. **2 John 1:10 (KJV) "If there come any unto you, and bring not this doctrine, receive him not into your house, neither bid him God speed: Revelation 22:18 (KJV) For I testify unto every man that heareth the words of the prophecy of this book, If any man shall add unto these things, God shall add unto him the plagues that are written in this book."** (Released 3/2009)

THE RETURN OF THE BARABBAS PATRIOT

Question; Are you a modern-day Christian Barabbas Patriot?

Background scriptures:

Mark 15:7 And there was one named Barabbas, which lay bound with them that had made insurrection with him, who had committed murder in the insurrection. Matthew 27:21-22 The governor answered and said unto them, whether of the twain will ye that I release unto you? They said, Barabbas. 22Pilate saith unto them, what shall I do then with Jesus which is called Christ? They all say unto him, Let him be crucified. Mark 15:15 And so Pilate, willing to content the people, released Barabbas unto them, and delivered Jesus, when he had scourged him, to be crucified."

"Holy Spirit, reveal the mystery surrounding Barabbas and why he was released. Amen."

To begin with the history of the sacrificial customs of the Jews, a pure lamb had to be selected for the atonement of the sins of the people at the Feast of the Passover, at the same time the scapegoat had to be selected to represent their sins were removed when the scapegoat was released into the dessert to wander. That's why it is call the scapegoat. To show the divine wisdom of God that surpasses our understanding, this time we have two subjects, Jesus and Barabbas. One (Jesus) represents the pure lamb readied for the slaughter, the other, (Barabbas) is now about to become the scapegoat. Let's see this type and shadow that will become spiritual in the cross over from law to grace.

Barabbas represents a Christian that takes matters into his own hands as to help God when he thinks God is not doing what he interprets as righteous. The zeal part of him acts in the name of God to do evil, thinking he is right. At that point, he becomes a Christian patriot, by lack of knowledge of the perfect will of God. He thinks he is right in the sight of God. In Barabbas, his patriotic zeal led him to attempt to overthrow the Roman Government in defense of the Jewish law. Zeal without knowledge in your insurrections will get you killed because you underestimate the capabilities of the enemy by confronting evil with evil as a Christian, you will lose as a victim of the enemy on his turf God warned you not to go.

The Roman's knew who Barabbas was and his activities were known to them to be <u>covertly watched</u> by the authorities to be put down when an insurrection is attempted. That's what happened to Barabbas. This whole scene is a type and shadow of the end-time scenario that will be repeated by patriot Christian when they take up arms against the government. This is what we fail to see that was not explained in the church from a biblical perspective. The constitutional right to bear arms is not for insurrection against the government, that's where the church has failed as to be the influence over our leaders in government. They were to pray over their leaders they send to represent them. It was the intent of the founding fathers that the church would be the conscious of the state to avoid this kind of internal civil disobedience.

<u>This is a warning to those in the patriot movement</u>

Matthew 26:52 (KJV) "⁵² Then said Jesus unto him, Put up again thy sword into his place: for <u>all they that take the sword shall perish with the sword.</u> Peter, vexed with that same patriot spirit sought to defend Jesus that caused Christ to make the above statement, operating in the perfect will of God, not the zeal of man. He will now become a prisoner in Pilot's court to join Barabbas in preparation to become the purified sacrificial Lamb of God that shall take away the sins of the world, by whose stripes, we that believe on him shall be healed, delivered and set free from the power of sin and death over the devil. He is now ready to become the Passover Lamb. This applies to Christian patriots who will seek to defend themselves during the siege of this nation very soon. Daniel prophesied that knowledge would increase; (Dan.12:4) given the technology surveillance of today, there will be no escape this time; as patriot Christians taking up arms, you will die and go to hell in your ignorance for attempting to take back this country after it has been curse by legalizing sodomy.

The Barabbas spirit was allowed to escape for history to repeat itself, this time in Christian patriots who will die the death of eternal separation for their acts of insurrection against the state which says ... **Amos 9:10-11 (KJV) "All the sinners of my people shall die by the sword, which ... say, The evil shall not overtake nor prevent us."** (This is the motivation behind the patriot spirit that will cause many to die in the tribulation.) **[11] In that day will I raise up the tabernacle of David that is fallen, and close up the breaches thereof; and I will raise up his ruins, and I will build it as in the days of old:"** The seeds of the modern day Pharisees and Sadducees that kill Jesus will take this scripture out of context to think is to rebuild the temple before their Messiah return.

At the end of these insurrections that will judge the people of God and the nations during the tribulation, Jesus will return to rebuild the city of David at the end. We do not need a lot of words to explain the circumstances around the crucifixion of Jesus. Many are of the belief that the natural temple will be rebuild before Christ return; that's why he had the Ishmaelite descendants to build the Temple Mount over that site to cease the oblation (sacrifices) by destroying Solomon's temple in seventy A. D. and prevent them from attempting this abomination in the sight of God. When the veil was destroyed and the Ark removed, from that time, the only way man would be excepted will be through the son.

He represented the last sacrifice acceptable under the law until Christ himself return. In the millennium, there will be no sacrifices made under the perfect law. Only the feast of the tabernacle will become an annual vigil to the temple of Christ. There will be no temptation to sin. Christ will rule with the rod of iron with zero tolerance for disobedience.

All will come to worship the feast of tabernacles. Since the resurrection, under the new covenant, **we are the temple** to keep a continual **feast of**

the tabernacles as our bodies become his temple during the time of grace. God at this time is selecting souls to be resurrected **at the feast of the last trumpet.** I hope this revelation of history will help as many as received Christ to prepare to die the death in obedience to the word to the glory of God. (Released 10/2009)

WARNING TO ALL
WEB MINISTRIES

Background scripture:

John 12:24 (KJV) ²⁴ *Verily, verily, I say unto you, except a corn of wheat fall into the ground and die, it abideth alone: but if it die, it bringeth forth much fruit."*

"Holy Spirit dictate this message to all those that have ears to hear." Amen

Genesis 6:3-6 (KJV) *"3 And the LORD said, my spirit shall not always strive with man, for that he also is flesh: yet his days shall be an hundred and twenty years.* ⁴ *There were giants in the earth in those days; and also after that, when the sons of God came in unto the daughters of men, and they bare children to them, the same became mighty men which were of old, men of <u>renown</u>.* ⁵ <u>*And GOD saw that the wickedness of man was great in the earth*</u>, *and that every imagination of the thoughts of his heart was only evil continually.* ⁶ *And it repented the LORD that he had made man on the earth, and it grieved him at his heart.*

Hebrews 12:23 (KJV) ²³ *To the general assembly and church of the firstborn, which are written in heaven, and to God the Judge of all, and to the spirits of just men made perfect, 2 Corinthians 6:14 (KJV)* ¹⁴ *Be ye not unequally yoked together with unbelievers: for what fellowship hath righteousness with unrighteousness? and what communion hath light with darkness? 1 Peter*

3:20 (KJV) [20] *Which sometime were disobedient, when once the longsuffering of God waitedt days of Noah, <u>while the ark was a preparing</u>, wherein <u>few, that is, eight souls were saved by water</u>.*

Ecclesiastes 1:9 (KJV) [9] *The thing that hath been, it is that which shall be; and that which is done is that which shall be done: and there is no new thing under the sun. 2 Thessalonians 2:3 (KJV)* [3] *Let no man deceive you by any means: for that day shall not come, except there come a falling away first, and that <u>man of sin be revealed, the son of perdi</u>tion; Matthew 7:15 (KJV)* [15] *Beware of false prophets, which come to you in sheep's clothing, but inwardly they are ravening wolves. Psalms 82:6 (KJV)* [6] *I have said, Ye are (gods); and all of you are children of the most High. 2 Thessalonians 2:4 (KJV)* [4] *Who opposeth and exalteth himself above all that is called God, or that is worshipped; so that he as God sitteth in the temple of God, shewing himself that he is God. (False Sheppard's) 2 Peter 2:2 (KJV)* [2] *And many shall follow their pernicious ways; by reason of whom the way of truth shall be evil spoken of. Ezekiel 16:35-36 (KJV)* [35] *Wherefore, O harlot, hear the word of the LORD:* [36] *Thus saith the Lord GOD; Because thy filthiness was poured out, and thy nakedness discovered through thy whoredoms with thy lovers, and with all <u>the idols of thy abominations</u>, <u>and by the blood of thy children, which thou didst give unto them.</u>* (Abortions and Generational curses.) **Ezekiel 16:45 (KJV/NLT)** [45] **For your mother loathed her husband and her children,** (unequally yoked) **and so do you. And you are exactly like your sisters,** (worldly) **for they despised their husbands and their children. Truly your mother must have been a Hittite** (a non-descendant) **and your father an Amorite.** (Rightful descendant) **John 14:23 (KJV/NLT)** [23] **Jesus replied, "All those who love me will do what I say. My Father will love them, and we will come to them and live with them.**

Matthew 13:24-30 (KJV) [24] *Another parable put he forth unto them, saying, the kingdom of heaven is likened unto a man which sowed good seed in his field:* [25] *But while men slept, his enemy came and sowed tares among the wheat, and went his way.* [26] *But when the blade was sprung up, and brought forth fruit, then appeared the tares also.* [27] *So the servants of the householder came and said unto him, Sir, didst not thou sow good seed in thy field? from whence then hath it tears?* [28] *He said unto them, an enemy hath done this. The servants said unto him, wilt thou then that we go and gather them up? (The obedient servants)* [29] *But he said, Nay; lest while ye gather up the tares, ye root up also the wheat with them.* [30] *Let both grow together until the harvest: and in the time of harvest, I will say to the reapers, gather ye together first the tares, and bind them in bundles to burn them: but gather the wheat into my barn.*

Rev. 14:15-18 explains the final reaping of the harvest at the end time by God himself separating the wheat from the tares; He alone knows the hearts of all men. This will be the great homecoming. *Matthew 25:1-13 (KJV)* [1] *Then shall the kingdom of heaven be likened unto ten virgins, which took their lamps, and went forth to meet the bridegroom.* [2] *And five of them were wise, and five were foolish.* [3] *They that were foolish took their lamps and took no oil with them:* [4] *But the wise took oil in their vessels with their lamps.* [5] *While the bridegroom tarried, they all slumbered and slept.* [6] *And at midnight there was a cry made, Behold, the bridegroom cometh;* (The elects that remain will see the glory of His coming) *go ye out to meet him.* [7] *Then all those virgins arose and trimmed their lamps.* [8] *And the foolish said unto the wise, Give us of your oil; for our lamps are gone out.* These are the children of disobedience, dressed in worldly garments. [9] *But the wise answered, saying, not so; lest there be not enough for us and you: but go ye rather to them that sell, and buy for yourselves.* (These are the righteous that obeyed the call and are ready at the call.)*1 Peter 4:18 (KJV) "And if the righteous scarcely be saved, where shall the ungodly and the sinner appear?"*

NOW THESE UNWISE VIRGINS are they that were seduced into false teachings that told you had to buy the Holy Ghost, by giving an offering in the prayer lines. They are gleamed after the first harvest. Rev.14:18) [10] *And while they went to buy, the bridegroom came; and they that were ready went in with him to the marriage: and the door was shut.* [11] *Afterward came also the other virgins, saying, Lord, Lord, open to us.* [12] *But he answered and said, Verily I say unto you, I know you not.* They will incur God's wrath for their disobedience that was prayed for. The other 98% will perish. Read the chronicle of *"What will happen during the siege."* [13] *Watch therefore, for ye know neither the day nor the hour wherein the Son of man cometh. 1 Peter 4:17 (KJV)* [17] *For the time is come that judgment must begin at the house of God: and if it first begin at us, what shall the end be of them that obey not the gospel of God? Matthew 7:14 (KJV)* [14] *Because strait is the gate, and narrow is the way, which leadeth unto life, and few there be that find it: Amos 3:7 (KJV) Surely the Lord GOD will do nothing, but he revealeth his secret unto his servants the prophets. Ephesians 3:5 (KJV) Which in other ages was not made known unto the sons of men, as it is now revealed unto his holy apostles and prophets by the Spirit; Romans 12:1 (KJV) [1] I beseech you therefore, brethren, by the mercies of God, that ye present your bodies a living sacrifice, holy, acceptable unto God, which is your reasonable service. 2 Corinthians 12:9 (KJV) [9] And he said unto me, My grace is sufficient for thee: for my strength is made perfect in weakness. Most gladly therefore will I rather glory in my infirmities, that the power of Christ may rest upon me.*

Isaiah 55:7-8 (KJV) [7] Let the wicked forsake his way, and the unrighteous man his thoughts: and let him return unto the LORD, and he will have mercy upon him; and to our God, for he will abundantly pardon. [8] For my thoughts are not your thoughts, neither are your ways my ways, saith the LORD. Mark 7:8-9 (KJV/NLT) [8] For you ignore God's specific laws and substitute your own traditions." [9] Then he said, "You reject God's laws in order to hold on to your own traditions. Hebrews 4:1 (KJV/NLT) [1] God's promise of entering his place of rest still stands, so we ought to tremble with fear that some of you might fail to get there. Matthew 5:11-12 (KJV/NLT) [11] "God blesses you when you are mocked and persecuted and lied about because you are my followers. [12] Be happy about it! Be very glad! For a great reward awaits you in heaven. And remember, the ancient prophets were persecuted, too.

Romans 11:5 (KJV) [5] Even so then at this present time also there is <u>a remnant</u> according to the election of grace. Revelation 3:18 (KJV) [18] I counsel thee to buy of me gold tried in the fire, that thou mayest be rich; and white raiment, that thou mayest be clothed, and that the shame of thy nakedness do not appear; and anoint thine eyes with eyesalve, that thou mayest see. Amos 3:3 (KJV) [3] Can two walk together, except they be agreed? Ephesians 4:5 (KJV) [5] One Lord, one faith, one baptism, Romans 11:28 (KJV) [28] As concerning the gospel, they are enemies for your sakes: but as touching the election, they are beloved for the fathers' sakes. 1 Peter 4:12-13 (KJV) [12] Beloved, think it not strange concerning the fiery trial which is to try you, as though some strange thing happened unto you: [13] But rejoice, inasmuch as ye are partakers of Christ's sufferings; that, when his glory shall be revealed, ye may be glad also with exceeding joy. John 15:19-21 (KJV) [19] If ye were of the world, the world would love his own: but because ye are not of the world, but I have chosen you out of the world, therefore the world hateth you. [20] Remember the word that I said unto you, The servant is not greater than his lord. If they *have persecuted me, they will also persecute you; if they have kept my saying, they will keep yours also. ²¹ But all these things will they do unto you for my name's sake, because they know not him that sent me. Matthew 7:21 (KJV) ²¹ Not everyone that saith unto me, Lord, Lord, shall enter into the kingdom of heaven; but he that doeth the will of my Father which is in heaven. Luke 14:33 (KJV) ³³ So likewise, whosoever he be of you that forsaketh not all that he hath, he cannot be my disciple. Matthew 10:34-39 (KJV) ³⁴ Think not that I am come to send peace on earth: I came not to send peace, but a sword. ³⁵ For I am come to set a man at variance against his father, and the daughter against her mother, and the daughter in law against her mother in law. ³⁶ And a man's foes shall be they of his own household. ³⁷ He that loveth father or mother more than me is not worthy of me: and he that loveth son or daughter more than me is not worthy of me. ³⁸ And he that taketh not his cross, and followeth after me, is not worthy of me. ³⁹ He that findeth his life shall lose it: and he that loseth his life for my sake shall find it.*

Matthew 4:4 (KJV) ⁴ But he answered and said, It is written, Man shall not live by bread alone, but by every word that proceedeth <u>out of the mouth of God</u>. Ephesians 6:17-19 (KJV) ¹⁷ And take the helmet of salvation, and the sword of the Spirit, which is the word of God: ¹⁸ Praying always with all prayer and supplication in the Spirit, and watching thereunto with all perseverance and supplication for all saints; Isaiah 55:11 (KJV) ¹¹ So shall my word be that goeth forth out of my mouth: it shall not return unto me void, but it shall accomplish that which I please, and it shall prosper in the thing whereto I sent it.

Deuteronomy 11:26-28 (KJV) ²⁶ Behold, I set before you this day a blessing and a curse; ²⁷ A blessing, if ye obey the commandments of the LORD your God, which I command you this day: ²⁸ And a curse, if ye will not obey the commandments of the LORD your God, but turn aside out of the way which I command you this day, to go after <u>other gods</u>, which ye have not known. Jeremiah 7:23 (KJV) ²³ But this thing commanded I them, saying, obey my voice, and I will be your God, and ye shall be my people: and walk ye in all the ways that I have commanded you, that it may be well unto you.

Romans 8:6-7 (KJV) ⁶ For to be carnally minded is death; but to be spiritually minded is life and peace. ⁷ Because the carnal mind is enmity against God: for it is not subject to the law of God, neither indeed can be. Matthew 12:34 (KJV) ³⁴ O generation of vipers, how can ye, being evil, speak good things?

for out of the abundance of the heart the mouth speaketh. Proverbs 23:7 (KJV) <u>*7 For as he thinketh in his heart, so is he:*</u> *Eat and drink, saith he to thee; but his heart is not with thee. Matthew 7:1 (KJV)* [1] *Judge not, that ye be not judged.1 Peter 4:8 (KJV/NLT)* [8] *Most important of all, continue to show deep love for each other, for love covers a multitude of sins. 1 John 3:2 (NLT)* [2] *Yes, dear friends, we are already God's children, and we can't even imagine what we will be like when Christ returns. But we do know that when he comes, we will be like him, for we will see him as he really is.*

Ephesians 4:21-25 (KJV/NLT) [21] *Since you have heard all about him and have learned the truth that is in Jesus,* [22] *throw off your old evil nature and your former way of life, which is rotten through and through, full of lust and deception.* [23] *Instead, there must be a spiritual renew your thoughts and attitudes.* [24] *You must display a new nature because you are a new person, created in God's likeness—righteous, holy, and true.* [25] *So put away all falsehood and "tell your neighbor the truth" because we belong to each other.*

1 John 1:7 (KJV) [7] *But if we walk in the light, as he is in the light, we have fellowship one with another, and the blood of Jesus Christ his Son cleanseth us from all sin. 1 John 4:1 (KJV)* [1] *Beloved, believe not every spirit, but try the spirits whether they are of God: because many false prophets are gone out into the world. Ephesians 2:3 (KJV)* [3] *Among whom also we all had our conversation in times past in the lusts of our flesh, fulfilling the desires of the flesh and of the mind; and were by nature the children of wrath, even as others.*

1 Corinthians 14:33 (KJV) [33] *For God is not the author of confusion, but of peace, as in all churches of the saints. 2 Corinthians 5:17 (KJV)* [17] *Therefore if any man be in Christ, he is a new creature: old things are passed away; behold, all things are become new. 1 Corinthians 6:20 (KJV)* [20] *For ye are bought with a price: therefore glorify God in your body, and in your spirit, which are God's.*

James 4:14 (KJV) [14] *Whereas ye know not what shall be on the morrow. For what is your life? It is even a vapour, that appeareth for a little time, and then vanisheth away. Colossians 3:1-2 (KJV)* [1] *If ye then be risen with Christ, seek those things which are above, where Christ sitteth on the right hand of God.* [2] *Set your affection on things above, not on things on the earth.*

1 Corinthians 4:10 (KJV) [10] *We are fools for Christ's sake, but ye are wise in Christ; we are weak, but ye are strong; ye are honourable, but we are despised.*

2 Timothy 2:10 (KJV) [10] *Therefore I endure all things for the elect's sakes, that they may also obtain the salvation which is in Christ Jesus with eternal glory. Romans 6:6-8 (KJV)* [6] *Knowing this, that our old man is crucified with him, that the body of sin might be destroyed, that henceforth we should not serve sin.* [7] *For he that is dead is freed from sin.* [8] *Now if we be dead with Christ, we believe that we shall also live with him:"*

This is the last message to the Generation

1 Peter 4:17 (KJV) [17] *For the time is come that judgment must begin at the house of God: and if it first begin at us, what shall the end be of them that obey not the gospel of God? 2 Timothy 4:3-4 (KJV)* [3] *For the time will come when they will not endure sound doctrine; but after their own lusts shall they heap to themselves teachers, having itching ears;* [4] *And they shall turn away their ears from the truth, and shall be turned unto fables.*

Matthew 7:15 (NLT) [15] *"Beware of false prophets who come disguised as harmless sheep but are really wolves that will tear you apart. 2 Peter 2:2 (KJV)* [2] *And many shall follow their pernicious ways; by reason of whom the way of truth shall be evil spoken of. (KJV) 2 Timothy 3:1-5 (KJV)* [1] *This know also, that in the last days perilous times shall come.* [2] *For men shall be lovers of their own selves, covetous, boasters, proud, blasphemers, disobedient to parents, unthankful, unholy,* [3] *Without natural affection, trucebreakers, false accusers, incontinent, fierce, despisers of those that are good,* [4] *Traitors, heady, highminded, lovers of pleasures more than lovers of God;* [5] *Having a form of godliness, but denying the power thereof: from such turn away .*

1 John 4:1 (KJV) [1] *Beloved, believe not every spirit, but try the spirits whether they are of God: because many false prophets are gone out into the world. 1 John 2:20 (KJV)* [20] *But ye have an unction from the Holy One, and ye know all things. 1 John 4:4 (KJV)* [4] *Ye are of God, little children, and have overcome them: because greater is he that is in you, than he that is in the world. Isaiah 54:17 (KJV)* [17] *No weapon that is formed against thee shall prosper; and every tongue that shall rise against thee in judgment thou shalt condemn. This is the heritage of the servants of the LORD, and their righteousness is of me, saith the LORD.*

Daniel 11:32 (KJV) [32] *And such as do wickedly against the covenant shall he corrupt by flatteries: but the people that do know their God shall be strong and do exploits. Hebrews 4:1 (KJV)* [1] *Let us therefore fear, lest, a promise being left us of entering into his rest, any of you should seem to come short of it. Hebrews 4:9 (KJV)* [9] *There remaineth therefore a rest to the people of God." AMEN*

My beloved brothers and sisters, the Holy Spirit has summarized the teachings in this chronicle out of the volumes of the Holy Scriptures. This testimony of Jesus I received through the Holy Spirit has brought me off the field to rest from my labor. All his elects are separated unto himself in preparation in the wilderness for the fullness. We are the hidden that shall arrest the attention of the world when we come out of this wilderness in the fullness of God in Christ as the manifested Sons of God that will do great exploits. We are the end time messengers, the John the Baptist of today. We know who we are and our place in the body of which Christ is our head. There is no division in our ranks. We operate as a unit of one body in Christ that shall do great exploits during the tribulation. Every eye shall see Christ in his elected saints that shall glorify God as only He can. *1 Corinthians 2:9 (KJV)* "[9] *But as it is written, Eye hath not seen, nor ear heard, neither have entered into the heart of man, the things which God hath prepared for them that love him.*" Remember the parable of the wise Virgins; their only desire was to be ready when the groom showed up.

This is the true love we have for Christ that caused us to die so he could live move and have his being with-in us that produced his image to the world. This is the bride that shall be presented in glory. (Amen)

This I speak by spiritual observation; Many of you as well as I myself have followed prophets and messengers throughout the years; however, I am beginning to discern some inconsistencies in the visions as to what God is doing in his elects among some well-respected ministers operating in the office as prophets. This was a disturbing revelation to see in the spirit.

Not that they are not well meaning but it appears their time is coming to an end. This I speak by permission; these ministers have served their purpose to get us to this point. Their vision during their course has come to an end. God is doing a new thing through his elects that has never been seen or done and is reserved for the tribulation saints elected to bring in the latter rain. I would not make this statement if I had not witnessed a few others with this same last day vision of the elects calling of which we all have received the same word to rest from our labor.

Not many ministers have this vision of the wilderness experience to birth the Man Child through those elected for this time. God's mercy is on them for their service. They will be taken out early or else would be confounded in the days ahead without this vision. God will suffer them to...*1 Corinthians 5:5 (KJV)* "⁵ *To deliver such an one unto Satan for the destruction of the flesh, that the spirit may be saved <u>in the day of the Lord Jesus</u>.*" This is what will happen to the true prophet that has led us to this present day. If you have been called to this secret place in the most high for a time such as this, you are blessed indeed. Praise God. AMEN (Released January 2010)

THE SONS OF GOD AND GIANTS TODAY

<u>Jeremiah 33:3</u> **"Call unto me, and I will answer thee, and shew thee great and mighty things, which thou knowest not."** This is not for the shallow believer. I share this reluctantly because some of my close brethren departed from me when I spoke of these mysteries hidden in the scriptures as though I was teaching a new doctrine while only revealing a mystery.

<u>Background scripture: Gen. 6:1-9</u>

The Type and Shadow of Things to Come:

Genesis 6:1-4 (KJV) "And it came to pass, when men began to multiply on the face of the earth, and daughters were born unto them, [2] That the sons of God saw the daughters of men that they were fair; and they took them wives of all which they chose. [3] And the Lord said, My spirit shall not always strive with man, for that he also is flesh: yet his days shall be an hundred and twenty years. [4] There were <u>giants</u> (Nephilim) (ASV) in the earth in those days; and also after that, when the sons of God came in unto the daughters of men, and they bare children to them, the same became mighty men which were of <u>old, men of renown</u>." Webster's meaning to this word Renown is "A state of being <u>widely acclaimed, Honor, Fame and celebrity status</u>." **(RENOWN)**, (keep this word in mind). The influence of these seeds can be seen in the spirit of the electronic church media today. Men of renown, looked up too by their preeminence in the church world.

The foundation on which this mystery has now been revealed

Rev. 22:18-19 "For I testify unto every man that heareth the words of the prophecy of this book, If any man shall add unto these things, God shall add unto him the plagues that are written in this book: [19] <u>And if any man shall take away from the words of the book of this prophecy, God shall take away his part out of the book of life,</u> and out of the holy city, and from the things which are written in this book." There have been books written at the time the bible was being written, however, God did not let them become part of the 66 books He authored strictly at the hands of the Holy Spirit's anointing with mysteries that go beyond today's biblical theology.

Although these books contain some truth, yet God did not set His approval on any of these writings. Many of these teachings can be attributed to some of these books. What I have found; most are describing the historical significance at the time of the biblical writings. With the Holy Ghost as our teacher and guide, His teachings are to take over our thought process and keep us within the confines of the Holy Scriptures, the only basis of sound doctrine given under the law after the flood. We are to teach what we know, not what we think. Our inspiration must only come from the Holy Scripture, not flesh and blood.

Some of the early movements that made history like Martin Luther, Calvin and John Wesley, and Spurgeon were great reformers and left their mark in church history. *Deut. 29:29 "The secret things belong unto the Lord our God: but those things which are revealed belong unto us and to our children forever, that we may do all the words of this law. and to the testimony: if they speak not according to this word, it is because there is no light in them."*

The Scripture is very plain about not being seduced by spirits that lead to error. Therefore, we are to... *2 Timothy 2:15 (KJV) "15 Study to shew thyself approved unto God, a workman that needeth not to be ashamed, rightly dividing the word of truth." 1 Tim. 4:7 "But refuse profane and old wives' fables and exercise thyself rather unto godliness. 1 Tim. 6:20-21 "O Timothy, keep that which is committed to thy trust, avoiding profane and vain babblings, and oppositions of science falsely so called: [21] Which some professing have erred concerning the faith. Grace be with thee. 1 Tim. 6:3 If any man teach otherwise, and consent not to wholesome words, even the words of our Lord Jesus Christ, and to the doctrine which is according to godliness; 2 Tim. 1:13 Hold fast the form of sound words, which thou hast heard of me, in faith and love which is in Christ Jesus. 4 He is proud, knowing nothing, but doting about questions and strifes of words, whereof cometh envy, strife, railings, evil surmisings, 2 Tim. 2:1-2 Thou therefore, my son, be strong in the grace that is in Christ Jesus. [2] And the things that thou hast heard of me among many witnesses, the same commit thou to faithful men, who shall be able to teach others also. 2 Tim. 3:10 But thou hast fully known my doctrine, manner of life, purpose, longsuffering, charity, patience, 2 Tim. 4:3 For the time will come when they will not endure sound doctrine; but after their own lusts shall they heap to themselves teachers, having itching ears; 4 And they shall turn away their ears from the truth, and shall be turned unto fables. 2 Tim. 3:14-17 But continue thou in the things which thou hast learned and hast been assured of, knowing of whom thou hast learned them; [15] And that from a child thou hast known the holy scriptures, which are able to make thee wise unto salvation through faith which is in Christ Jesus. [16] All scripture is given by inspiration of God, and is profitable for doctrine, for reproof, for correction, for instruction in righteousness: [17] That the man of God may be perfect, thoroughly furnished unto all good works." Ephesians 4:11-12 (KJV) "[11] And he gave some, apostles; and some, prophets; and some, evangelists; and some, pastors and teachers; [12] For the perfecting of the saints, for the work of the ministry, for the edifying of the body of Christ:"* These scriptures are the basis on which we are to adhere to sound doctrine.

The Origin of Sin

Genesis 6:1 "And it came to pass, when men began to multiply on the face of the earth, and daughters were born unto them, Psalm 82:6 I have said, Ye are gods; and all of you are children of the most High." (These are the seeds of Adam as the first created in the Earth. These are seeds of Seth which God gave Adam to replace Abel, God's DNA from heaven the righteous seed that God showed His favor as His chosen. (Gen.4:4) Angels called the sons of God, they are not born but created sexless ministering spirits beings that cannot procreate.

Adam was created natural but spiritual in his existence. *Hebrews 1:5 "For unto which of the angels said he at any time, Thou art my Son, this day have I begotten thee?* (In Greek means born) *and again, I will be to him a Father, and he shall be to me a Son? v. [7] And of the angels he saith, Who maketh his angels spirits, and his ministers a flame of fire.*" Adam, being created as a natural human being, had all the natural parts in the flesh until sin revived the natural part of him, God foreknew he would need them to populate the earth.

Now let's study these passage Genesis 6:1-6

Genesis 6:1-2 And it came to pass, when men began to multiply on the face of theearth, and daughters were born unto them, 2That the <u>Sons of God</u> saw the <u>daughters of men</u> that they were fair; and they took them wives of all which they chose. These are a special class of angels created and assign to record the activity and deeds of man after the fall in the book of life in heaven for the final judgment. They stood around the throne of God and knew all things.

All this begin in the **"Antediluvian Dispensation"** where man was ruled by his conscience. These angels took on the form of men in the Earth to record the deeds of men as reported in the book of Enoch. When the Holy Spirit gave me this revelation, I had to wait for a witness. The phenomenal thing about this, I asked God in my early studies why there was no books of Enoch's writings in the bible? One day, a dear fellow brother of mine, purchased a book containing the writing of Enoch and ask me to have a look at it to get my opinion of its content.

To my surprise, I saw passages that were quoted in the bible such as ... *Jude 1:6 "And the angels which kept not their first estate, but left their own habitation, he hath reserved in everlasting chains under darkness unto the judgment of the great day."* I discovered that the Sanhedrin often read passages from Enoch's writing. This prophecy was written as recorded in... *Jude 1:14 "And Enoch also, the seventh from Adam, prophesied of these, saying, Behold, the Lord cometh with ten thousands of his saints,"* The book of Enoch gives graphic details of what took place; however, I cannot elaborate in this area because God chose not to let this become part of the written scripture. Therefore, I can only reference these two scriptures.

This is the way He chose to answer my question. I also found that when God puts his trust in you, he will reveal his long-kept secrets to your heart. *Genesis 6:3-6 "And the LORD said, my spirit shall not always strive with man, for that he also is flesh: yet his days shall be an hundred and twenty years.* This statement points to the flood; after, the Earth will go through a major change in atmospheric pressure and a latitude shift where in the time of the end of days, a man's life will reduced to one hundred and twenty years, the time it took to build the Ark.

Throughout time this will be reduced to three score and ten, due to the earth being defiled by the sins of men. (Ps. 90:10) *4There were giants in the earth in those days; and also after that, when the sons of God came in unto the daughters of men, and they bare children to them, the same became mighty men which were of old, men of renown. 5And GOD saw that the wickedness of man was great in the earth, and that every imagination of the thoughts of his heart was only evil continually. 6And it repented the LORD that he had made man on the earth, and it grieved him at his heart."* After reading a few passages, I now knew why this book was not included in the original sixty-six books of the bible.

The full scope of what happen ... these angels referred to as **"Sons of God"**, left their first estate because they were not born of men, they then became **Sons of God.** This act caused them to be reserved in a special place for a separate judgment in the underworld called **Tartarus.** In our time, under grace, the church is a spiritual body, Satan, the adversary, is constantly making accusation and justifying his actions on the bases of our willing ignorance and disobedience not to study under the leading of the Holy Spirit.

As you study behind this chronicle, the revelation will become apparent, these are seeds of fallen angels as described in...*Jude 1:6 "And the angels which kept not their first estate, but left their own habitation, he hath reserved in everlasting chains under darkness unto the judgment of the great day.* This is what caused them to leave their first estate as angels; Cain seed produced daughters not only were beautiful but as perfect in appearance as a woman in the natural as an angel with the ability to procreate. It was this appearance the cause them to transform themselves into human form to marry them. This mixing transformed what was forbidden unequal yoking with beings not of this earth. thus, became co-conspirators with Satan that will manifest a fruit contrary to the Holy Spirit that shows signs of not of this earth. Therefore, Jesus said ... *"a tree is known by its fruit" (Mat.12:33) John 3:6 "That which is born of the flesh is flesh; and that which is born of the Spirit is spirit."* Now we have two seeds growing together wherein, there is no oneness in mind but two separate unseen angelic beings, which throughout times and ages will bring the world to another END OF DAYS as the <u>Laodicea</u> church spirit. The instability of mankind, in his sinful state, will penetrate every aspect of human society and change the world as now we see as evident in the activity of these beings DNA in man on earth as they confront each other as evident in the final days of this last generation.

These seeds were transferred through Ham's linage; his wife was of that blood line that facilitated their DNA to pass through the flood, now using human bodies, with accessed through Adam's sin. When they possess a male body and procreate, this seed will produce after its own kind down through the ages. Just one strand of their DNA can produce what we will come to see in this last generation as megalomaniacs.

Modern technology has now decoded your DNA or life's footprint origin. In our dispensation of time, men do not produce literal giants in human stature, but a spiritual half-breed, **part Son of God and part child of the devil;** the double-minded man. To the church, **he will become a religious child of the devil**. Medical science will diagnose them as Bipolar. Now, I know this may seem very controversial to the average bible reader because we don't study to this depth of revelation in the Holy Spirit about the spirit world. Some of these DNA strands may show up in children with autism which represent an incomplete state of mind. How did Jesus deal with these hybrid seed while he walked on earth as God's Son, he reverses that when he encountered them. They will take advantage of the Roman collapse to use their plundered wealth to come back as a religious form of godliness to penetrate all the nations of the world and form ne religions and seek to change laws according to the times. (Daniel 7:25)

 This is how they penetrated the church, not only by persecution, but build a seminary system to transform the church into a form also as will be the sign that we have fallen away from the apostle's doctrine. *Matthew 13:25 "But while men slept, his enemy came and sowed tares* (hybrid seed of genetically altered DNA) *among them and went his way. verse [38] The field is the world;* This hybrid seed, part world and part son of God will now come to spoil, using bodies of men, as angels in disguise. They will pass through generations to produce what we see today as renowned religious spirits in Christianity and worldly renown megalomaniacs ... *the good seed* *are the children of the kingdom; but the tares are the children of the wicked one." <u>Matthew 7:15</u> Beware of false prophets, which come to you in sheep's clothing, but inwardly they are ravening wolves.* (False brethren) *Mark <u>7:23</u> All these evil things come from within and defile the man. <u>Matthew 13:30</u> Let both grow together until the harvest: and in the time of harvest I will say to the reapers, gather ye together first the tares, and bind them in bundles to burn them: but gather the wheat into my barn."* (Rev.14:15-16)

Now get this, the worldly part of this seed, seeks the pre-eminence of the world or man, acclaim, honor, notoriety, fame and celebrity status. These seeds will always seek to become **renowned** among its peers and some will have a cult like following. Here we see where the transformation in our time, as a **Spiritual Giant** in the world. I hope now you are beginning to get the revelation of the Laodicea church. These seeds are the residue DNA of the sons of (fallen angels) which was passed through Ham after the flood which became the Canaanites where the spies Moses sent out, saw them again as literal giants. Ham's wife was a descendant of these seeds, mixed with this DNA and pass through the flood.

Now I want to show you an interesting parallel I discovered in this study that will explain who built the Pyramids. Cain's first son was named Enoch the fourth from Adam; (4th means worldliness) that's because his seeds will be earthy with a beastly nature. God is now going to use these seeds to perfect his chosen that will be used throughout times, ages and dispensations to perfect his chosen until this present day. All that man has fallen from will be restored in those elected in this final time during the tribulation period that will glorify God as God and restore the world back to the first millennium With Christ as king.

Side Note:

Today in our generation, man has discovered the secrets of mixing human DNA with other species to produce what he thinks is an improvement of what God has created. This is what caused the flood. The genetic code of the human DNA came from God. When it is altered, man without knowing, will alter his mind set that will cause the evil in him to wax worse and worse until he destroys himself. Hollywood shows us this in the many **Science Fiction** and paranormal movies they have produced.

This is what will ultimately cause the destruction of mankind as we know him. The science fiction movies have produced this scenario with a twist, in the end man win. Remember the devil can only produce more evil humans, cursed with this knowledge. *Genesis 4:17 "And Cain knew his wife; and she conceived, and bare Enoch: and he builded a city, and called the name of the city, after the name of his son, Enoch."*

When you read the linage of Cain's seed, many are hidden in the seeds of the Canaanites and the Amorites you will see that they were great builders and inventers. Keep this in mind and you will begin to get a revelation. Cain's knowledge was from Adam and Adam's was from God. They had superior knowledge and intellect at that time which as mathematicians could construct buildings as precise as the PYRAMID, whose stones were so perfectly cut, they did not need any mortar. We still do not know how it was done. Archaeologists have found human remains as tall as eighteen feet. Where did that knowledge come from? The Pyramids were built to survive the floods; look at the water marks on the side of the Sphinx. This knowledge is divine and represents the powers that were heavenly with the knowledge of the cosmos. That's why they aligned their structures with the position of the stars. Remember, as the first set of offsprings, they had the knowledge to move things with their minds. That's why they were duplicating in the Earth things in heaven in this natural world that when we discovered them, would be beyond our level of comprehension. They came from standing around the throne with the knowledge of God. That's why civilization had to be destroyed when that happened.

Seth's linage produced the righteous seed fifth from Adam carrying God's DNA of grace that will be extended to a remnant that will be saved throughout times, ages and dispensations. Seth's seed produced Enos (Enoch the fifth from Adam, grace). Cain had an evil seed named Enoch and Seth seed produced the righteous one. This is where you see Satan begin to duplicate what God is doing in man, but this will become the evil seeds. They both had the same names. (Gen. 5:18) He would live to record the events of these angels that co-habited with the seeds of Cain's linage that would cause the flood. *Luke 3:38 "Which was the son of Enos, which was the son of Seth, which was the son of Adam, which was the son of God.* (This is the linage that will carry the DNA that will link man to God through-out the ages.) *Genesis 5:3 "And Adam lived an hundred and thirty years, and begat a son in his own likeness, after his image; and called his name Seth:"* (Adam was in God's image and likeness, Seth was after Adam's image and likeness; being born in sin, he will inherit the curse that's on his father as now having to die in the flesh but God's grace will be upon him.)

The foundation of these two seeds are evidenced in Adam's sin, Cain who was of that wicked one. (I John 3:12) Christ could only come through the pure seed Seth. After his birth men begin to call on the name of the Lord. (Gen. 4:26). This scripture should bring some light to those who are prayerfully studying behind this chronicle essay in the form of a revelation taken from Gen. 6:1-4, expanded to the understanding of the baby Christian to let you know the importance of in-depth bible study and meditation under the guidance of the Holy Spirit, what redeeming the time means. **_Eccles. 1:9_** *"The thing that hath been, it is that which shall be; and that which is done is that which shall be done: and there is no new thing under the sun."*

The origin of giants in the earth.

This implies that history repeats itself in the cycles every time, age and dispensation. Beloved, I am making every effort to make this as plainly understood to you, the reader, to greatly enhance your understanding of what the Holy Spirit was given to do in all that receive and activate Him; He will guide you into all truth. Gen. 6:1-4 refers to them as giants, in that day, men were bigger, stronger and more intelligent having the best of both worlds; their offspring, mixed with those beautiful daughters of the Cain linage. Now sons of God, cursed never to enter heaven. It stands to reason that he, Satan through Cain, was going to birth some of the most beautiful women on the face of the earth that got the attention of those angels that fell for them. They were angel like in their appearance with the ability to procreate. Remember, Satan was the most beautiful angel in heaven. Now on earth he will defile this special class of angels through Cain's daughters.

This fallen angelic DNA, now in man, will manifest a form of **megalomania**. Webster's dictionary described this character as: (Disorder of mind, feelings of omnipotence, grandeur and superiority.) These demon spirits are so dominating in the people they possess to the point, they will seek to defy God. Some Kings and Pharaoh's have believed themselves to be gods.

Cain's seeds, the daughters of men, seduced these angels of God who by this act, became the fallen angelic beings to leave their first estate and transform themselves into human beings to marry them. This Special class of angels had powers that make ordinary men into extra-ordinary human beings. This is an especially important fact to understand, these two principalities will be manifested in the ages after the fall will become … *Ephesians. 6:12 "For we wrestle not against flesh and blood, but against principalities, against powers, against the rulers of the darkness of this world, against spiritual wickedness in high places."* Satan and all the angels that rebelled with him are disembodied spirits living in all un-regenerated souls of man, doomed for hell if they are not saved.

These seeds of the **fallen angels,** now with bodies as sons of God because they were created and left their first estate, can transform themselves into human beings with a megalomania personality. This linage after the flood will be seen in Dynasties, Kingdoms and people with high intellect with powers to control and create governments. They penetrated David's house by marrying his daughters to produce a false blood line of future kingdoms to associate themselves with a kingly origin of their blood line. Men are seed carriers; women are the means by which their off springs enter the world. That's why kings and monarch dynasties keep a close watch on the bloodline not to defile it to keep their royal status intact.

That is the time the two DNA' becomes one. They are often the hidden powers in governments, manipulating the course of their agenda. Because their personalities are so dominating, when they assemble in their secret places, it becomes a think tank with one single agenda; to rule the world; therefore, controlling the people around them. They operate in the shadows of governments they sponsor and help organize mindless people caught up in the circumstances of life by taking advantage to fill the vacuum by supporting hate groups that help them achieve their purpose. This includes leaders of cults and religions. The lesser spirits will control the population by seducing man through mind control, using people with lack of knowledge of their possession, destroying mankind without mercy by using forbitten technology that infringe on God's timeline.

Genesis 6:1-4 "And it came to pass, when men began to multiply on the face of the earth, and daughters were born unto them, [2] That the sons of God saw the daughters of men that they were fair; and they took them wives *of all which they chose. [3] And the Lord said, my spirit shall not always strive with man, for that he also is flesh: yet his days shall be an hundred and twenty years. [4] There were giants in the earth in those days and also after that, when the sons of God came in unto the daughters of men, and they bare children to them, the same became <u>mighty men which were of old, men of renown</u>.*" I constantly repeat these scriptures to keep you on tract as my source of biblical inspiration.

I hope you now have a better understanding of why we see the present-day church world in the state it's in and where it all began. These seeds of renowned breeds are genetically altered transformations that came through Ham's linage after the flood. In our time, among Christians, this fruit will show a mixture of law with grace. What we see now is the mixture of the religious spirits binding the ignorant believers back under the law to promote their own agendas in the name of God. Remember, Christ came to free us from the law. Through Jesuit sponsored seminary schools, these men of renown can be seen in the pulpits across the nation in denominations and cults. The part of this church that caters to the worldly pleasures as in…. *1 Tim. 5:6 "But she that liveth in pleasure is dead while she liveth." Rev. 3:17 "Because thou sayest, I am rich, and increased with goods, and have need of nothing; and knowest not that thou art wretched, and miserable, and poor, and blind, and naked."* This church does not know what spirit they are of…. *Proverbs 16:25 "There is a way that seemeth right unto a man, but the end thereof are the ways of death." <u>Hosea 4:6</u> "My people are destroyed for lack of knowledge: because thou hast rejected knowledge, I will also reject thee, that thou shalt be no priest to me: seeing thou hast forgotten the law of thy God, I will also forget thy children."* They will not heed to the prophet's call because they do not believe the spirit of the prophets of old are at work today in men. God is the same yesterday today and forever.

Now Let's Compare God's Chosen People in their Exodus and wilderness.

Numbers 16:1-2 "Now Korah, the son of Izhar, the son of Kohath, the son of Levi, and Dathan and Abiram, the sons of Eliab, and On, the son of Peleth, sons of Reuben, took men: [2] And they rose up before Moses, with certain of the children of Israel, two hundred and fifty princes of the assembly, <u>famous in the</u> <u>congregation, men of renown</u>."

Here we see a congregation of a mixed multitude, coming against the servant of God, Moses, a Son of God by birthright. This is one of the signs of these seed that became apostate because of their being mixed with Egyptian blood (the world) but of Hebrew descent. These seeds of enmity came up in them and contended with Moses. Remember, God was against them in the beginning to the point that they caused the flood, now these seed are reappearing among God's chosen people as tares in the band of Coran.

Now go back to the scripture Ecclesiastes 1:9. This is the work of the adversary in the seeds of a mixed multitude. **_Numbers 16:33_ _"They, and all that appertained to them, went down alive into the pit, and the earth closed upon them: and they perished from among the congregation."_** We see God's anger kindled to the point of destruction of that wicked seed. They were alive in flesh but dead as tares and God destroyed them all after having them assemble in one place to be caught in God's break in wrong place at the right time orchestrated by God and sent to the pit when he opened the earth's gateway to the abyss and sent them there. This DNA is in their children who survived their wilderness. This will be done for the last time at the battle of Armageddon.

Jude 1:11 _"Woe unto them! for they have gone in the_ _way of Cain_, _(cursed seed) and ran greedily (or riotously ASV) after the error of Balaam for_ _reward_, _and_ _charity_, _(in this life) when they feast with you, feeding themselves without fear: clouds they are without water, carried about of winds; trees whose fruit withereth, without fruit, twice dead, plucked up by the roots; 2 Corinthians 6:17 (KJV)_ [17] **Wherefore come out from among them, and be ye separate, saith the Lord, and touch not the unclean thing; and I will receive you,"** Under grace, we are given a chance to claim our birth right, however, it is evident that some of us will make the wrong choice as they did before Moses. History will repeat itself in our time when they ignore God's messengers and prophets and will be led to a place for destruction in our time during the tribulation and destroyed.

Psalm 55:13-15 _"But it was thou, a man mine equal, my guide, and mine acquaintance. [14] We took sweet counsel together and walked unto the house of God in company. [15] Let death seize upon them and let them go down quick into hell: for wickedness is in their dwellings, and among them."_

David's prophecy of the future of this seed that will be there with Christ in Judas who walked with Christ, took sweet counsel, he was exposed to the fullness in the presents of God and yet betrayed him. Judas blasphemed the holy one of God. These seeds, in apostate Christians, will do the same thing to you. God will give them a chance to reject Him through no name servants who will be like David before Goliath, the John the Baptist of today. That's why he said … *Matthew 10:36 (NASB77)* [36] *and A MAN'S ENEMIES WILL BE THE MEMBERS OF HIS HOUSEHOLD.*

These giants of **renowned in academic theology statue** of whom we regard as authorities of the knowledge of God. In our fall away, Satan has his own elect; people given over to him to serve in the grand scheme of earth's timeline under man's rule as vessels of dishonor. These no name messengers, elected by God, are sent to judge them so they can be turned over to receive the judgment of a reprobate because they were liars among the people of God. They will have their opportunity to repent before they are given a strong delusion. Like Eve, the lessons when you read is not to be taken for granted, for they are written for our learning. Keep your eyes on God and listen to His voice and act on his words and you will stay pure in spirit, soul and body. *1 Thessalonians 4:7 (KJV)* [7] *For God hath not called us unto uncleanness, but unto holiness. Isaiah 50:7 "For the Lord God will help me; therefore, shall I not be confounded: therefore, have I set my face like a flint, and I know that I shall not be ashamed."*

Peter took a step of faith in the water with his eyes on Jesus. When he took his eyes off Jesus for a moment and would have perished but Jesus showed him mercy and saved him. This is the last generation that will see the end of all evil put down by God Himself. Men in our government are now gathering against the servants of God. The Sons of God as in the spirit of Moses and the Elijah, God will assemble these kingdoms in a place to be caught in God's break once again and be destroyed.

Daniel 7:25"And he shall speak great words against the most High, and shall wear out the saints of the most High, and think to change times and laws: and they shall be given into his hand until a time and times and the dividing of time. This is the time Satan has been given to finish his course on the way to the lake of fire. Anytime Satan gets a hand in God's work, it goes beyond decent and order. Now you see why God hates these seeds. When Moses cursed these **renowned** men for usurping authority over God's heritage, they were mixed seeds and therefore had to be cut off.

When one takes a vow to stand on God's word without compromise, the world and compromised Christians will hate you and come against you as these did to Moses. *John 15:18-20 (ASV)* [18] *If the world hateth you, ye know that it hath hated me before it hated you.* [19] *If ye were of the world, the world would love its own: but because ye are not of the world, but I chose you out of the world, therefore the world hateth you.* [20] *Remember the word that I said unto you; A servant is not greater than his lord. If they persecuted me, they will also persecute you; if they kept my word, they will keep yours also. Luke 6:22-26 (ASV) "*[22] *Blessed are ye, when men shall hate you, and when they shall separate you from their company, and reproach you, and cast out your name as evil, for the Son of man's sake. Matthew 5:12 "Rejoice and be exceeding glad: for great is your reward in heaven:* (These are seeds of the enmity in false sisters and brothers that are now against you.) [23] *Rejoice <u>in that day</u>, and leap for joy: for behold, your reward is great in heaven; for in the same manner did their fathers unto the prophets* [24] *But woe unto you that are rich! for ye have received your consolation.* [25] *Woe unto you, ye that are full now! for ye shall hunger. Woe unto you, ye that laugh now! for ye shall mourn and weep.* [26] *Woe unto you, when all men shall speak well of you! for in the same manner did their fathers to the false prophets."*

The Lord also told me that your pass life has nothing to do with Him calling you; this was ordained in His sovereign will before the world was formed. That's why you were at the appointed time, removed from where you were and put on the shelf, He open your eyes, gave you ears to hear what the Holy Spirit is now going to prepare you for what he has predestined to do in your vessel; remold you to perfection, and prepare you to become meat for the master's use in your rest. The time has come for God to get the glory that only He deserves. As He told me, remember, you were but dust. *<u>Hebrews 4:9</u> "There remaineth therefore a rest to the people of God."*

<u>Who Is the "Man-Child" and when will he be manifested?</u>

The **first** man child was Adam. The **second** man-child was manifested when Mary gave birth to Jesus. At that time, He was the manifested son of God from heaven that would take away the sins of the first man-child Adam, created a natural man but spiritual in his existence. Isaiah (53) prophesied what he would look like, and Isaiah (61) tells what he came to do. *Rev. 12:5 And she brought forth a man child, who was to rule all nations with a rod of iron: and her child was caught up unto God, and to his throne.*

This was and is the manifested son of God to the Jews whom they rejected, where-by all, through His sacrifice, can claim our birth rite by Him reversing the curse of the first fallen man child, Adam. This second man child; Jesus, restored the first works in Adam, ascended back to the throne of the father as the only begotten son of God in the Earth. **Rev. 12:13 "And when the dragon saw that he was cast unto the earth, he persecuted the woman which brought forth <u>the man child.</u>** His second coming will be manifested in His elects, walking in the fullness that the church never achieved, just as the Jews never achieved the recognition of the world as the promise to Abraham as head of all nations. The tribulation is where all will be corrected and achieved. The church will be glorified in the sight of the entire world as the only church born of God where the entire world will see Him as **"One lord, one faith and one baptism"** This is the last **man child** manifested in His elects; then caught out as His body in glory when all is fulfilled of the prophets and the mystery of Godliness is seen in man, made perfect operating in the fullness of Christ. **Lastly,** Israel in her tribulation, God will revive the lost tribe of Judah hidden among his people as were God's elects in the church, this tribe of elects is where Israel will be glorified in the final battle near the end of the tribulation period.

Isaiah 66:7 <u>"Before she travailed, she brought forth; before her pain came, <u>she was delivered of a man child</u>. 8Who hath heard such a thing? who hath seen such things? Shall the earth be made to bring forth in one day? or shall a nation be born at once? for as soon as Zion travailed, <u>she brought forth her children</u>." Through the lion of the tribe of Judah; this will be the third travail of Zion that will establish the Kingdom of Christ on earth. **Psalm 78:68 <u>"But chose the tribe of Judah, the mount Zion which he loved."**

In my travels around this state and parts of the country, I found a few people who were having this same experience in their lives. They were disillusioned with the present assemblies and had started home fellowships. Many who are closed minded, blinded by traditions of men, are fellow confessing Christians contending with you today, by our lack of knowledge, treating you as a backslider because you left the assembly building.

God's elects are now being separated out unto himself, humbled to rest while God prepares to use these vessels to do what we have never done, keep His presence as often as we assemble so all would be healed, delivered and set free and leave being made whole, the glory of God's presents returned in the assembly believing in **"one God one faith and one baptism."** Being schooled in the mysteries kept to be revealed to this last generation is one of which only God can contain the degree of these revelations in me to keep me stable in a time like this; unless you meet someone of like mind, your conversation is only between you the son and God and whom he chooses to bless through you who in turn will become a blessing to you. AMEN (Updated for Release 12/2014)

INSIGHTS BEYOND
THE GRAVE

Background scripture:

Peter 3:19 (RSV) **"[19] in which he went and preached to the spirits in prison,"**

Recently, I was in the presents of some fellow saints and heard some expounding on the subject of **"Spirits in Prison",** though I once thought on this subject briefly, what I heard caught my attention to do and in-depth study. I ask the Holy Spirit to give me some scriptures to clarify what I had heard. This is what I researched in the word. There are some mysteries men cannot receive that are written in the scriptures. The Holy Ghost will reveal to those given ears to hear.

Long standing traditional teachings will cause many of you to be closed minded and reject anything new. These in part teachings are the result of the way you were indoctrinated. *Matthew "27:63 (RSV)* [63] *and said, "Sir, we remember how that impostor said, while he was still alive, after three days I will rise again."* It was during this period when his spirit left the cross, he preached to **"the spirits in prison"** in the underworld in Paradise. (1Pet.3:9) These were those who lived righteously but had to be preached the gospel of the kingdom to be introduced to the Son of God who was shrouded in the Old Testament. They were bound by Satan through their sins of omission in the flesh under the righteousness of law of sin and death.

Since no sin could inter heaven, Jesus became the sacrifice for their sins, releases them to be transported to the third heaven.

The law did not make them sinless. The spirit is from God but for the sins must be remitted before their soul can be translated to the third heaven. Paradise is where they were retained until the Christ became the sacrifice to take away those sins in the flesh and release their souls. When Jesus revealed himself in the underworld by preaching to their spirits, they were bound by Satan justifying the accusations of their sin nature because no sin can enter heaven. This was the state of the Old Testament Saints; they received him and were release from the spirit of the sin bondage unto death as Christ became the sacrifice for their sins committed under the old covenant.

He preached the gospel of the kingdom to them; they all received him and at that time he took the keys to Paradise, and the power of life and death from Satan, translated them out of Paradise along with the pennant thief to the third heaven. This was the works done in the underworld in the Earth. When he rose, he gave these keys to Peter on the day of Pentecost, all that now receive him have been given the power over death, hell and the grave.

This will be manifested through living by every word that proceeded from the mouth of God. ***Revelation 1:18 (RSV)_*** *"[18] and the living one; I died, and behold I am alive for evermore, and I have the keys of Death and Hades."* (When he rose) ***Matthew 27:52-53 (RSV)*** *"[52] the tombs also were opened, and many bodies of the saints who had fallen asleep were raised, [53] and coming out of the tombs after his resurrection they went into the holy city and appeared to many."* God reveal this to David in the psalms) ***Psalms 86:13 (RSV)*** *"[13] For great is thy steadfast love toward me; thou hast delivered my soul from the depths of Sheol (hell). Isaiah 14:15 (RSV) "[15] But you are brought down to Sheol, (hell) to the depths of the Pit".*

It is noteworthy to see that all these statements were made by Old Testament saints. The underworld work gave them a chance to receive the truth direct from Jesus representing his mercy for those whose hearts were right by obeying the law. God did not judge them without giving them a second chance to hear and see the sacrifice that freed them from their bodies of sin. Now all must come through Christ. Paradice was left open to receive the souls under grace that will be resurrected when Christ returns a second time to receive his church. I have heard men preach imaginary sermons that tell people, you go straight to heaven when you die. If that was the case, why would there be a resurrection?

Ezekiel 31:16-17 (RSV) *"16 I will make the nations quake at the sound of its fall, when I cast it down to Sheol (hell) with those who go down to the Pit; and all the trees of Eden, the choice and best of Lebanon, all that drink water, will be comforted in the <u>nether world</u>. 17 They also shall go down to Sheol with it, to those who are slain by the sword; yea, those who dwelt under its shadow among the nations shall perish."* These are they who die in battles to save others from harm in wars and acts that caused them to lose their lives while trying to save others. God remembered their sacrifice and gave them a chance to hear the everlasting gospel as the penitent thief and be given grace and mercy.

Ezekiel 32:21 (RSV) *"21 The mighty chiefs shall speak of them, with their helpers, out of the midst of Sheol (hell) `They have come down, they lie still`, the <u>uncircumcised, slain by the sword</u>."* This is a prophecy concerning those who died in wars fighting for the liberty of Israel and this nation. Under grace, the way they died, obeying their masters, their cries out to the lord in death, God will treat them as he did the pennant thief and give them a chance to hear the everlasting gospel in the underworld when Christ visits them in Paradise again in the two witnesses.

Remember paradise was left vacant after the first resurrection for what? *Acts 2:27-31 (RSV)* *"27 For thou wilt not abandon my soul to Hades, nor let thy Holy One see corruption. 28 Thou hast made known to me the ways of life; thou wilt make me full of gladness with thy presence.' 29 "Brethren, I may say to you confidently of the patriarch David that he both died and was buried, and his tomb is with us to this day. 30 Being therefore a prophet, and knowing that God had sworn with an oath to him that he would set one of his descendants upon his throne, 31 he foresaw and spoke of the resurrection of the Christ, that he was not abandoned to Hades, (hell) nor did his flesh see corruption."* In the book of Acts, Paul describes the hope of the Old Testament Saint by revelation of the Holy Spirit to be delivered from what we know today by the advent of the scriptures, what Jesus told the pennant thief about **"Paradise"** (Luke 23:43) Jesus is the only one that went back to heaven when he died because that's where he came from.

You came from the dirt, therefore to the dirt you return while your soul is parked in Paradise.

We are now in the New Testament; the scriptures will shed light on the dispensation of grace for those with ears to hear. In the judgment, no one will have and excuse before the Lord, what about those that have never heard the gospel of any kind in their life. Would they not have a legitimate excuse before the lord?) *Matthew 24:14 (KJV) And this gospel of the kingdom shall be preached in all the world for a witness unto all nations; and then shall the end come.* Note, the key word in this verse is **"all the world."** This gospel is for those outside the kingdom who have never known or heard whether there be a God or not. Just like Paul met people that had never heard whether there was a Holy Ghost in Acts. Those who have received Jesus are already in the kingdom and are now being used to carry that gospel that was hid from them that were lost. *2 Corinthians 4:3 (KJV)_ "3 But if our gospel be hid, it is hid to them that are lost:"* Now hold on to your hats saints, this will cause some of you to stumble at this statement. Translations will be the order of the day as the children of disobedience are handed over to the devil for the destruction of their flesh to enter heaven. They are the residue in Rev. 14:17-20, after the second resurrection in Rev. 14:15-16.

They will be the clusters to complete the quick work before the second sickle harvest in … (Rev. 14:18) … *1 Thessalonians 4:17 (KJV) "17 Then we which are alive and remain shall be caught up together with them in the clouds, to meet the Lord in the air: and so shall we ever be with the Lord. Rev 14:18 (KJV) And another angel came out from the altar, which had power over fire; and cried with a loud cry to him that had the sharp sickle, saying, thrust in thy sharp sickle, and gather the clusters of the vine of the earth; for her grapes are fully ripe.* (These are in the second and third resurrection during the tribulation. Remember the first is when Christ rose from the dead.)

Revelation 7:14 (KJV) "14 And I said unto him, Sir, thou knowest. And he said to me, these are they which came out of great tribulation, and have washed their robes, and made them white in the blood of the Lamb." Revelation 14:6 (KJV) "6 And I saw <u>another angel fly in the midst of heaven, having the everlasting gospel to preach unto them that dwell on the earth</u>, and to every nation, and kindred, and tongue, and people," The fact that they are ministering spirits, who are they ministering too? At this point, God will give those who were captives of the devil the opportunity to hear this everlasting gospel for three days in the underworld, preached by these two witnesses in (Rev.11:3). Angels are ministering spirits that operate in humans who shall again **"preach to the spirits in prison"** to these souls in captivity who gave their lives for the liberty of others. Just as the pennant thief received Christ, many others who died under conditions beyond their control; only those whose hearts were right under grace who cried out for mercy at death will be given the opportunity to receive Christ by hearing the everlasting gospel at that time, repent and be translated as the Old Testament saints were. (Ecclesiastes.1:9)

This gospel preached in the underworld for three days by the two witnesses; will precede the second translation of the tribulation Saints as Christ did in the first resurrection. (Rev. 14:15-16) *Revelation 14:18 (KJV)* *"¹⁸ And another angel came out from the altar, which had power over fire; and cried with a loud cry to him that had the sharp sickle, saying, Thrust in thy sharp sickle, and <u>gather the clusters</u> of the vine of the earth; for her grapes are fully ripe"* These are the children of disobedience (or unwise virgins prayed for by the saints) who are being resurrected out of great tribulation, translated in the second sickle which will be the third reaping of the residue during the **first thunder. 1 Corinthians 5:5 (KJV)** **⁵ To deliver such an one unto Satan for the destruction of the flesh, that the spirit may be saved <u>in the day of the Lord Jesus</u>.)**

Isaiah 61:1 (KJV) *"¹ The Spirit of the Lord GOD is upon me; because the LORD hath anointed me to preach good tidings unto the meek; he hath sent me to bind up the brokenhearted, to proclaim <u>liberty to the captives,</u> and <u>the opening of the prison to them that are bound</u>"* These are the spirits in prison, held in captivity in Paradise. As I said, hold on to your hats, there's more; I have read **Mary K. Baxter's** book how God gave her a tour of hell; one thing I notice, those Jesus spoke to had confessed him in their life and had a chance to repent but waited too long and died guilty of sins of omission, lost their souls by overstaying their day of grace.

They had all been warned on Earth in their life but refused to heed. They lived this privilege to dishonor. Not one account did I read where he spoke to an outright sinner, although they were begging for mercy when he passed them in their cells. Now the afterlife experiences are people who had been given mercy when they cried out to the Lord as the thief on the cross and those who had callings on their lives that Satan tried to take out before they run the course, God has predestined for them. Another thing I also noticed that those in hell as confessing Christians in their life were crying to him for a second chance but were refused. That's why he said, let a man examine himself by the word if you want to know if you have eternal life while we are still on this side of hell.

Revelation 20:13 (RSV) "[13] and the sea gave up the dead in it, Death and Hades gave up the dead in them, and all were judged by what they had done" Revelation 21:8 (KJV) "[8] But the fearful, and unbelieving, and the abominable, and murderers, and whoremongers, and sorcerers, and idolaters, and all liars, shall have their part in the lake which burneth with fire and brimstone: which is the second death." Where God is concern, He is all knowing, therefore, throughout the ages, God has used the devil in man to this end to carry out His master plan of redemption. Therefore, raising up some to honor and some to dishonor. Those that are raised up for honor will enter his kingdom while the others to dishonor will be used to perfect them and turned over to the devil to be destroyed. *2 Timothy 2:20-21 (KJV) "[20] But in a great house there are not only vessels of gold and of silver, but also of wood and of earth; and some to <u>honour</u>, and some <u>to dishonour</u>. [21] If a man therefore purge himself from these, he shall be a vessel unto honour, sanctified, and meet for the master's use, and prepared unto every good work."*

What does the bible say about suicide?

Exodus 20:13 "Thou shalt not kill." As you read the Old Testament, it is very apparent that killing was permitted as in the wars the Israelites fault. Who are we to question the sovereignty of God's predestination in preserving his chosen elect? These vessels of honor and dishonor are being raised together to do with whatever He chooses. We are given life as a privilege of his own will and if He chooses you to live for eternity with him, did you have anything to do with it? Your life is a gift from God; therefore, if you judge yourself unworthy of everlasting life when it is taken at your own hands, your fate is of your father the devil. This is another sin where there's no forgiveness.

Who are some of the people that took their lives in the bible?

Samson:

Judges 16:28-31 "And Samson called unto the LORD, and said, O Lord GOD, remember me, I pray thee, and strengthen me, I pray thee, only this once, O God, that I may be at once avenged of the Philistines for my two eyes. 29And Samson took hold of the two middle pillars upon which the house stood, and on which it was borne up, of the one with his right hand, and of the other with his left. 30And Samson said, Let me die with the Philistines. And he bowed himself with all his might; and the house fell upon the lords, and upon all the people that were therein. So the dead which he slew at his death were more than they which he slew in his life. 31Then his brethren and all the house of his father came down, and took him, and brought him up, and buried him between Zorah and Eshtaol in the burying place of Manoah his father. And he judged Israel twenty years."

Samson was a judge of Israel who was under the **Nasserite Vow,** never to cut his hair. He was not only disobedient to his parents by mixing with strange women, which was his weakness. His disobedience caused him to lose his sight which brought him under bondage to the Philistines through the enemy in his flesh. This is a type and shadow literally happening to Samson. Those who are spiritually blind will also be led into the enemies' camp as unwise virgins and destroyed. The Philistine found out his weakness through a woman. Samson gave place to the devil that used a woman to reveal his secret.

This is repeated over and over throughout the Bible because there's no new sin; it just repeats itself throughout ages. When Samson realized what he had done, as an elect, the only way back was to sacrifice his life to destroy the enemy of Israel. This act was God's mercy upon him as an elect. He was saved in death. God had to turn him over to Satan for the destruction of the flesh for his disobedience, but his soul was saved. Thank God for mercy. (1 Cor. 5:5)

Saul, Israel's first king

1 Samuel 31:4-5 "Then said Saul unto his armourbearer, draw thy sword, and thrust me through therewith; lest these uncircumcised come and thrust me through, and abuse me. But his armourbearer would not; for he was *sore afraid. Therefore, <u>Saul took a sword, and fell upon it.</u> 5And when his armourbearer saw that Saul was dead, he fell likewise upon his sword, and died with him."*

This is an example of what the people chose over what God chooses to be a ruler over His people. Saul catered to the people and disobeyed God, therefore, causing his judgment to be swift and sure. He was the first of #45 kings of his people as an anointed. This will be repeated in the gentiles in President #45, as the leaders of this nation under this covenant **"In God We Trust."** He will be a president put in that office that will cater to the will of the people and be put out of office by God.

This is what Satan used to take his soul and God turned him over to the devil to be destroyed in battle by his own hand. What we see in this death is a man who chose the will of the people over God, being sent to hell at his own hand. Saul had many times to repent but could not resist the will of the people and therefore lost his soul. Our government officials are now being judged because they have been duped by these false prophets that give them false messages as mediums of this day. The last President that will serve as the king of the free world as a gentile, will repeat that same history the will end the reign the cycle of gentile kings. Many preachers will make this choice in these last days to continue to serve the will of the people for their own gain as vessels of dishonor and commit spiritual suicide. This type of suicide will take you to hell. He was given the privilege to become a vessel of honor but by his own will became a vessel of dishonor and so will many of our Presidents in this nation.

Ahithophel

2 Samuel 17:23 "And when Ahithophel saw that his counsel was not followed, he saddled his ass, and arose, and gat him home to his house, to his city, and put his household in order, and hanged himself, and died, and was buried in the sepulchre of his father." In this context, Ahithophel spoke against God's chosen king. God caused Absalom to take another course, thus when Ahithophel fail, he hanged himself. His spirit will also be in many of these Christian patriot movements working against the government that will cause them to be destroyed.

Under the law, anyone who spoke against the king was put to death; therefore, the consequences of his action cause him to commit suicide.

I see many political activists talk show host doing the same thing as speaking evil against our own government as a nation divided. This is the enemy using our ignorance as confessing Christians to conquer us from within. Remember the scriptures said that many will be destroyed by lack of knowledge. All true Christians will pray for these wicked leaders and take a stand to defend the integrity of the truth in the God we say we serve. As Christians, our power is in corporate prayer as a single body of believers. It is the prophets calling to warn the government authorities of the consequences of their action against the will of God. If you are a born-again Christian, you will expose the wickedness of our leaders and do as we were commanded, pray for God to change their hearts. That's the power we gave up by taking matters into our own hands as religious patriots. This will be the fate of many that speak against those in kingdom authority as heads of governments. I see God raising up evil men and speaking through them to judge those who follow their pernicious ways without this vision. *Jude 1:10 (KJV) But these speak evil of those things which they know not: but what they know naturally, as brute beasts, in those things they corrupt themselves. Jude 1:8 (KJV) Likewise also these filthy dreamers defile the flesh, despise dominion, and speak evil of dignities. Ephesians 5:11 (KJV) And have no fellowship with the unfruitful works of darkness, but rather reprove them.*

Judas

Matthew 27:1-3 "When the morning was come, all the chief priests and elders of the people took counsel against Jesus to put him to death: 2And when they had bound him, they led him away, and delivered him to Pontius Pilate the governor. 3Then Judas, which had betrayeth him, when he saw that he was condemned, repented himself, and brought again the thirty pieces of silver to the chief priests and elders, <u>Matthew 27:5</u> And he cast down the pieces of silver in the temple, and departed, and went and hanged himself." Here we see again a man chosen to serve this purpose and to be given over to destruction as a vessel of dishonor. Being blind by the devil by the will of God to show us what it is to not know what spirit you are of and what he will allow you to do to serve his purpose.

The sovereignty of God is demonstrated as purpose in time orchestrated in His own will. *Isaiah 46:10 (KJV) [10] Declaring the end from the beginning, and from ancient times the things that are not yet done, saying, My counsel shall stand, and I will do all my pleasure*: Judas went to hell as a vessel of dishonor. He was never meant to go to heaven as in God's foreordained by his actions; God raised him up to fulfill his word spoken by his prophets. In these accounts of the lives of these men, each reasoned with-in themselves their action and the consequences. **Samson** failed God but was given mercy, sacrificed himself out of true repentance. **Saul's** motives were to escape the enemy's abuse as a king. **Judas** blasphemed the holy one of Israel and took his own life for betraying an innocent person and went to hell. This also shows how God can raise a vessel of dishonor to walk with you as a vessel of dishonor. This I have also experienced firsthand. As I have said in the beginning, all men cannot receive certain mysteries that are locked in the bible. I invite you to seek God about what you have just read or just table it if you cannot receive it because this was one of the mysteries, he shared with me as he did with Enoch.

Finally, most of this will not be relevant to those that know beyond a shadow of doubt that they have been begotten by the gospel, they shall be preserved through all these things. In summary, your mind can only be contained when God has taken you over; therefore, you can only comprehend his thoughts when he is in control of the temple. Just like Enoch could not reveal the knowledge of God to a wicked people that will come after the flood; this knowledge will cause man to destroy himself ahead of God's predestined scheduled events of the sovereign timeline. I am not saying I am like Enoch; this is what I have come to see. Very few men have been given the privileged to know God to this degree in His word.

Some of these writings will be very strange to the average believer as Peter once said about Paul and he walked with Jesus. *2 Peter 3:16 (KJV) "As also in all his epistles, <u>speaking in them of these things; in which are some things hard to be understood,</u> which they that are unlearned and unstable wrest, as they do also the other scriptures, unto their own destruction.,"* that is why it is given to those he has given ears to hear. (Updated for released Feb. 2015)

AMERICA'S LAST DAYS
OF FREEDOM

Opening introduction:

In this chronicle, I will provide a background that will lead up to the end of this subject. These writings are for those who have been given ears to hear it. Many years as a confessing Christian, being brought up in a religious environment, I did not receive the Holy Spirit until I ask God for it some twenty-five years later. All that time I was deeply religious using my own thoughts about God. The religious environment I was in taught me that you had to lay down all your sins first before you could receive the Holy Ghost. Now I make this statement because all up until that time, I received what I knew about God second handed. No one laid hands on me to receive the Holy Spirit; I came to see my sins because all those years, I live like most other Christians who live the way they think about God. When God drew me in by his spirit, I had many questions I needed to know the right answers too. You are now reading the answers to some of them. One morning in the year of 04, He spoke to my heart and said, **"quit thinking and my Holy Spirit will tell you what you need to know."**

This was what he showed me I needed to do in this verse... *Isaiah 55:7 (KJV) "7 Let the wicked forsake his way, and the unrighteous man his thoughts: and let him return unto the LORD, and he will have mercy upon him; and to our God, for he will abundantly pardon. 8 For my thoughts are not your thoughts, neither are your ways my ways, saith the LORD.*" Quit thinking, now how can I avoid not thinking? One must be persuaded to see that you were not created with a thought.

The reality of our meager beginnings and the advent of Adam's sin, we are born under a curse; therefore, we are all evil until we are born again, that's why I never had peace and rest in God. I also thought I was a good person *... Luke 18:19 (KJV)* [19] *And Jesus said unto him, why callest thou me good? none is good, save one, that is, God.* The Holy Spirit was sent to convict man of this reality. We are either guided by our five senses as a sinner, or as a chosen vessel by God's Holy Spirit; therefore, in our thinking, we are good in our own sight.

If we do not believe what God said about who is good, we set ourselves up to be deceived by blind guides as angels disguise in human beings. We forget the natural man has no good in him. God, through the scripture has brought me to a rest by revelation of himself and just what I am without him. I need not question God about anything anymore; I just believe **He is** and what he said about me; the Holy Spirit answers all my questions. I believe all the promises made to me and act on His word as the conditions to be met to receive what he died to give me.

I have not had great dreams or vision as some, when he approached me in the spirit, I said as Mary, your word is good enough for me and he put the faith in my heart to believe what he has said. This is what he has taught me as a believer; one who receives and acts on the word is considered his disciples. This is the discipleship of being led by the Holy Spirit. *John 1:12 (KJV)* "[12] *But as many as received him, to them gave he power to become the sons of God, even to them that believe on his name:*"

Now, that we have established a disciple as one who follows the teachings of Jesus Christ as a doer, not man' structured order as noted in this seminary trained traditions of men. Let's see where it all began. The world has a beginning and ending as the **Alpha** and the **Omega** and so does everything in it. To see where we are today is to see the end from the beginning of all that has been recorded in the bible about this time of the end. Since the fall of man, God's redemptive plan has been to reconcile to himself a remnant in each time, age, dispensation and generation. This is God's sovereignty, set in motion from the beginning before the foundation of the world; however, our reference is to this time as recorded in the bible. To understand the rise and fall of all things in history as recorded in the scriptures, you must believe God's version of creation.

The answer is before the world was, I AM. That statement is beyond our comprehension without a revelation. We do not know the reality of sin and its consequences until we hear the gospel. That's the nature of the natural man. Lets see sins origin from the bible perspective.

Genesis 3:1-6 (KJV) *"1 Now the serpent was more subtil than any beast of the field which the LORD God had made. And he said unto the woman, Yea, hath God said, Ye shall not eat of every tree of the garden? 2 And the woman said unto the serpent, We may eat of the fruit of the trees of the garden: 3 But of the fruit of the tree which is in the midst of the garden, God hath said, Ye shall not eat of it, neither shall ye touch it, lest ye die. 4 And the serpent said unto the woman, Ye shall not surely die: 5 For God doth know that in the day ye eat thereof, then your <u>eyes shall be opened, and ye shall be as gods, knowing good and evil.</u> 6 And when the woman saw that the tree was good for food, and that it was pleasant to the eyes, (lust of the eyes) and a tree to be desired to make one wise, she took of the fruit thereof, and did eat, (lust of the flesh for the prides of life.) and gave also unto her husband with her; and he did eat." (This is what made him a natural man.) Genesis 1:26 (KJV) "26 And God said, Let us make man in <u>our image,</u> <u>after our likeness:</u> and let them have dominion over the fish of the sea, and over the fowl of the air, and over the cattle, and over all the earth, and over every creeping thing that creepeth upon the earth. Genesis 2:18-20 (KJV) 18 And the LORD God said, It is not good that the man should be alone; I will make him an help meet for him. 19 <u>And out of the ground</u> the LORD God formed every beast of the field, and every fowl of the air; and brought them unto Adam to see what he would call them: and whatsoever Adam called every living creature that was the name thereof. 20 And Adam gave names to all cattle, and to the fowl of the air, and to every beast of the field; but for Adam there was not found an help meet for him."* He knew his creator as standing in his image, it was the mind of God speaking through Adam that named all the animals and having conversations daily with himself in the form of a natural man but spiritual in his origin and intellect. Therefore, he had no conception of natural things other than to do what he was told to do … to preserve his natural environment as in keeping the garden that was to preserve his natural state for eternity.

As the first Emmanuel representing God among his creation in the earth; he walked in dominion of all God created. Now what he was given that no other created being had; the free will of his intellect to choose. Since it was not good for him to be alone, God gave him a helpmate out of him, opposite of himself in the flesh as a woman but equal in the spirit as a companion of comfort (she represents the comforter) that made him a whole as one Join together by God. That same comforter is now the spirit of God inside of every born-again believer to make him one with God.

Now you know why he alone knows where your rib mate is. The consequences of his free will are the choices we make outside of the will of God as described in Gen. 3:1-6. They were of one spirit; whatever he did she would do, perfectly matched and one in agreement, whatever she did he would do. This is what being one in spirit is all about, as joined by God. Now if you forget this for a moment and use your free will to think outside of the will of God for you, that's stated in His word, this is the origin of our sins. We forget that we were a piece of dust formed in his image without a thought until he blew the breath of life in what he formed; therefore, Adam only had God's thoughts.

By now I hope you are beginning to get the picture of the two natures of the fallen man. Now he must choose life, which is to obey his creator and live forever or death as to listen to the thoughts of the devil which has already been condemned. ***Deuteronomy 30:19 (KJV)*** *"19 I call heaven and earth to record this day against you, that I have set before you life and death, blessing and cursing: therefore choose life, that both thou and thy seed may live:* Your obedience to God will save your children.

Proverbs 18:21 (KJV) *21 Death and life are in the power of the tongue: and they that love it shall eat the fruit thereof."* What will cause you to choose right is God's spirit? ***John 6:44 (KJV)*** *44 No man can come to me, except the Father which hath sent me draw him: and I will raise him up at the last day.*

All our life experiences are based on receiving or rejecting truth; trying to decide to do good or evil. Our choices are based on what spirit we are of; these are life's realities. God's elect's life is planned from the foundation of the world to live for eternity. It is He, that will use life's circumstances to teach you and persuade you to come into His presence through the word. What Adam did was use his free will to act on the word of a condemned fallen angel, disguised in Eve's fall, using her voice as a serpent which in time to come, your only hope of not being deceived is the unction anointing of the mind of God that knows his own voice.

What happen to Adam, by acting on Satan's words by partaken of the forbidden fruit offered through his counter-part Eve, he also received his curse and became a natural man separated from God in the spirit and if you listen to Satan, you will remain natural. *Genesis 3:7 (KJV) "⁷ And the eyes of them both were opened, and they knew that they were naked; and they sewed fig leaves together and made themselves aprons."* He became as the creation a natural view of heaven in earth but now defiled and alienated from God. This was evident when God called for him in … *Genesis 3:8-11 (KJV) "⁸ And they heard the voice of the LORD God walking in the garden in the cool of the day: and Adam and his wife hid themselves from the presence of the LORD God amongst the trees of the garden. ⁹ And the LORD God called unto Adam, and said unto him, Where art thou? ¹⁰ And he said, I heard thy voice in the garden, and I was afraid, because I was naked; and I hid myself. ¹¹ And he said, Who told thee that thou wast naked?*

In the spirit world, there is no concept of natural things; therefore, you are dead in the spirit to the flesh. This is where he saw himself for the first time in the flesh. He was reduced to walking by his five senses where he felt fear for the first time now as a natural man. He will become double minded, unable to understand until he is redeemed by Christ in the underworld when he preaches to their spirits in prison to be born again.

From that time on, the two natures will be at war in his thoughts. *Hast thou eaten of the tree, whereof I commanded thee that thou shouldest not eat?"* The only knowledge worth having is what God tells you and you act upon it by faith; anything other than His words will defile you. This has now become history written for our learning. The history of the world has been written from the end back to the beginning of time. (Isaiah 46:10) That's why Satan do not want you to study the word; he does not want you to become born from above to learn the secret of his defeat.

What God seek to share with man is the reality of Him by faith. *Hebrews 11:6 (KJV) "⁶ But without faith it is impossible to please him: for he that cometh to God must believe that he is, and that he is a rewarder of them that diligently seek him." All this is God's doing in our life for His purposes. Remember, John 6:44 (KJV) "⁴⁴ No man can come to me, except the Father which hath sent me draw him: and I will raise him up at the last day."* You cannot come to God except He draws you. (John 6:44) That's why there are so many confessing Christians who do not know what spirit they are of; they were convicted from those born from below in the assemblies of Satan. It is not our nature to desire to serve God after the fall. If you are now reading this material and feel a strong conviction to change; that's him drawing you in by his spirit. Our former father the devil is already condemned; he can only produce religious spirit that begat religious spirits and we will never know what spirit we are of until God open our eyes and ears to hear His voice again ... *Jeremiah 7:28 (NKJV) ²⁸ "So you shall say to them, 'This is a nation that does not obey the voice of the LORD their God nor receive correction. Truth has perished and has been cut off from their mouth. Matthew 7:13-15 (KJV) "¹³ Enter ye in at the strait gate: for wide is the gate, and broad is the way, that leadeth to destruction, and many there be which go in thereat: ¹⁴ Because strait is the gate, and narrow is the way, which leadeth unto life, and few there be that find it."*

The loss of the apostle's doctrine over the past two thousand plus years, have caused us all to miss the mark of perfection. Unless you give God back what he gave you, he cannot use you to His glory. *Romans 12:1 (KJV) "¹ I beseech you therefore, brethren, by the mercies of God, that ye present your bodies a living sacrifice, holy, acceptable unto God, which is your reasonable service."* Just as Christ sacrificed himself for you; you must sacrifice yourself for others. In you, he demonstrates this greater agape love that comes out of you as you die to self that shows his nature and character to the world as the new Adam.

John 15:13 (KJV) "¹³ Greater love hath no man than this, that a man lay down his life for his friends. Matthew 22:14 (KJV) ¹⁴ For many are called, but few are chosen. Matthew 7:21 (KJV) ²¹ Not everyone that saith unto me, Lord, Lord, shall enter into the kingdom of heaven; but he that doeth the will of my Father which is in heaven. Zechariah 4:6 (KJV) ...⁶ Not by might, nor by power, but by my spirit, saith the LORD of hosts. 1 Timothy 4:1 (KJV) ¹ Now the Spirit speaketh expressly, that in the latter times some shall depart from the faith, giving heed to seducing spirits, and doctrines of devils;"

Many pastors will see this reality when God opens their eyes as to how they have robbed the people in the name of God without being delivered from the devil as often as they assemble. It has been said by Present Obama, **"America is no longer a Christian nation."** Without your knowing, that statement sealed our fate, by the church being in the state it is in, many, carried away in these new doctrines that seem right for the times. In time, they will use a national crisis to close your doors.

This new doctrine will be dictated by what the president **(king of the free world)** believes to be right. This is the doctrine of the devils that have determined our fate as Sodom and Gomorrah. By approving sodomy, same sex marriage, and homosexuality. These agendas are of those who practice such lascivious behavior is condoned by president #44. Now we will be destroyed as Sodom and Gomorrah by the fires of nuclear disasters, meteors showers and an asteroid.

As a president elected by the people, he will be #44, as a President that will represent the change of moral laws against God's order. His changes will complete the end of the laws protecting our freedoms; fulfilling … *Daniel 7:25 (KJV)* [25] *and he shall speak great words against the most High, and shall wear out the saints of the most High, and think to change times and laws: and they shall be given into his hand until a time and times and the dividing of time"*. President #44 is not the antichrist; although his theology in practice **is** Anti-Christian, he will be instrumental in fueling the body that will come against the true saints.

Contrary to false teachings, the antichrist is not a single man; he is the beast principality of seduced Christians that will persecute the true church just as the antichrist body of the Sadducees and Pharisees, killed Jesus in the name of God not knowing what spirit they were of, so will the false church. Apostle John in his epistle tells us who is an antichrist … *1 John 2:18 (KJV)* [18] *Little children, it is the last time: and as ye have heard that antichrist shall come, even now are there <u>many antichrists</u>; whereby we know that it is the last time."*

We see here what constitutes an antichrist; anyone who come against the teachings of Christ. *1 John 4:3 (KJV)* [3] *And every spirit that confesseth not that Jesus Christ is come in the flesh is not of God: and this is that spirit <u>of antichrist, whereof ye have heard that it should come; and even now already</u>*

is it in the world." Now what is John saying? … Anyone born of the spirit of Christ will not continue to practice sin in his mortal body. *2 Timothy 2:19 (KJV) "19 Nevertheless the foundation of God standeth sure, having this seal, The Lord knoweth them that are his. And, Let every one that nameth the name of Christ depart from iniquity. John 15:18 (KJV) 18 If the world hate you, ye know that it hated me before it hated you.*"

Although President #44 shows all the signs of being an evil man, He is where he is by the will of God to serve his purpose in this nation's history. President #44 fulfills Dr. King's prophecy dream that one day a man would be judged by the content of his character, not the color of his skin. Obama is that person as an instrument of false hope that will bring about a change that will confound him in the end.

He also represents the prayers of the slaves upon whose backs this nation was cultivated. In whose farsighted prayers, prayed that one day the equality would be recognized in a man of color would be raised up to national status as he now fulfills; having the ability to speak great words at the right time in history that blind the people to look beyond his color and be persuaded by the content of his character is what Dr King prophesied before he was killed by this nation, he was raised up to warn. The church community of color got just what they asked for as a seduced sectarian, bigoted, segregated confessing Christian community. This to them is their Messiah of change. Being separated and seduced made them ripe as a religious community. Though he means well in his own way, the powers that control the White House are in control of the agenda, all of which serves God's purpose. In the future reality, he will see his idea of change result in bondage to the system. Only a few Presidents have known of the reality of this hidden power group that is behind the government. Those that did not follow their agenda were killed.

Many traditional churches will be judged for their continued segregation in their assemblies. This present-day church under the 501c-3 is no longer the conscious of the state. President #44 inherited the legacy of a nation being judged by God. The powers that be, knew this and therefore kept him in office that fulfills this prophecy of our end. However, in their madness, they will try to defy biblical history. *Jude 1:10 (KJV) 10 But these speak evil of those things which they know not: but what they know naturally, as brute beasts, in those things they corrupt themselves.*" No true Christian has hatred for our head authorities; we are to pray for them because we are not ignorant of who is in charge, God.

The Holy Spirit is colorless. Therefore, those born from above will be colorblind. The lack of God's standard of holiness is where we see the rise of so many false teachings. Men call themselves Christians and yet speak evil of our sitting dignitaries in their rhetoric and not the gospel in pulpits their credentials represent. The Republican's supposed to be the roots of conservative right thinking that made this nation our Republic, has become a party of division of which is demonstrated by their actions, working along party loyalties, not in the best interest of preserving our liberties, are destroying our government from within. They broke a law that said never speak evil of a king over a nation God has anointed to rule his people, in so doing, put a curse on this nation that's manifested in division. *2 Peter 2:10 (KJV)* [10] *But chiefly them that walk after the flesh in the lust of uncleanness and despise government. Presumptuous are they, self-willed, they are not afraid to speak evil of dignities. John 3:8 (KJV)* [8] *The wind bloweth where it listeth, and thou hearest the sound thereof, but canst not tell whence it cometh, and whither it goeth: so is every one that is born of the Spirit."* The evidence are the results of where it has blown; therefore, when assemblies receive an outpouring of that mighty rushing wind <u>again</u>, real Christian's will be colorblind.

If you have been studying these chronicles, it should by now be easier to comprehend. America as a nation is doomed by the same sin that judged Israel's disobedience to God's law; thinking themselves more highly than they should, exchanged the true God for idols. **"Hear old Israel, the lord our God is one"**. God put the words in our **DECLARATION of INDEPENDENCE that CONSTITUTES** the liberties that all will have the right to serve the true and only living God free of oppression from the government. That is in our **BILL of RIGHTS** sealed with a covenant **"IN GOD WE TRUST,"** the one God. Because of this covenant, every president will have to answer to God for his term to uphold these liberties granted to a free society.

This covenant fulfills the promise made to Abraham that this blessing will come upon the Gentiles after his chosen people rejected their Messiah.

On July 4th, 1776, in the assembly of the Continental congress, witnessed by those who signed their names on that declaration, that prophecy was fulfilled. The founding fathers declared to the world our independence from her mother, Great Britain that... **"We, the people of the United States, in order to form a more perfect union, establish justice, insure domestic Tranquility, provide for the common defense, promote the general welfare, and secure the Blessings of Liberty to ourselves and our posterity, do ordain and establish this constitution of the UNITED STATES of AMERICA."**

Historically, I want you to see the inspiration of God in men that had a religious knowledge of deity in one God. True patriots fear God: these men task under God's divine hand, directing the affairs of these men, spoke with such inspiration that we inscribed those words on our monuments commemorating their acts that established this nation. Now every President that does not **"uphold these principles truths to be self-evident that all men are created equal and is endowed by our creator certain inalienable rights to life liberty and the pursuit of happiness"** to serve the lord our God as one, shall be an instrument of Satan's desire to dismantle our nation's freedoms to bring us under bondage to our enemies.

God used President Lincoln to remind the nation of its religious root in his speech at Gettysburg. In my observation of this nation's history, this is where we began to fall into the hands of evil men. This was revealed to me about Lincoln's personal struggles. He was greatly resisted in his own household during his presidency, yet the will of God prevailed. History shows us that someone will lose their life to save lives as was Lincoln's life in the end when he issued the proclamation against the wishes of these powers in the southern dixie-crats slavery policy. If you are a student of Biblical history, it has always cost lives to bring change that benefits mankind.

Beware of the people in high places as presidents. This nation's strength was established on a strong male footprint; in the final days as a sign, women will begin to dominate the government in high places. This will be the Jezebel spirit emerging that brought down Ahab by seduction. This speech of Daniel Webster is the patriotic spirit manifested in Barabbas that is very much alive today. **"I shall exert faculty I possess in aiding to prevent the constitution from being nullified, destroyed, or impaired; and, even though I should see it fall, I will still, with a voice feeble, perhaps, but earnest as ever issued from human lips, and with fidelity** and zeal which nothing shall extinguish, call on the people to come to its rescue." (Daniel Webster) These are the people who cry "we must take back America and make her great again." Its roots originated in a patriotic religious spirit, spearheaded in the return of the Barabbas spirit, penetrated the church to increase its numbers by compromising that put them under state control such as the 501C-3, a government charter that will judge them unacceptable when this nation goes into judgment.

Read the chronicle on "**Barabbas, The Last stand of the Patriot's**." The sign that we have changed the times and laws (Dan.7:25) came from President Obama's declaration "**America is no longer a Christian nation**" to the elects, this was our sign to prepare to die. This declaration to the homosexual community will cause Christians to have to take a stand against changing the laws of nature to legally cohabitate with the same sex in a matrimony state. This platform has created a stronghold to promote their agenda that has led this nation into moral decadence that carries the curse of Sodom on it. Satan has been given a time and authority to persecute all the saints that come against this decree. This will bring back "**The Great Separation**" in the "**Battle for Souls**" of church and state that will lead up to the final tribulation that will glorify the church in victory. September 11, 2008, ended the seven years of grace of the last generation of the Gentiles which began at the end of the 1967 war with Israel and Syria that recaptured the Abraham land grant that included the City of David: Jerusalem. Now all is set for the return of Christ to the throne in the city of David.

The year 2008, closed the time of the gentile church age. That year begin the transition period to the tribulation, the new beginning (8) The watchmen will bring the vision as John the Baptist did; warn the people to prepare for the coming return of Christ. We are to prepare in the spirit for the fires of tribulation. Revelation 3:18 declared that this last church body represented by the description in the preceding verses 14-17 is the state of that church. Verse 18 is where the separation will begin when overnight our lives will change in America when the economy crashes. It will take a miracle to reverse the predicament this country finds itself in financially.

The hidden powers behind this government made sure of that when they implemented the planned downfall. *Revelation 18:17 (KJV)* "*17 For in one hour so great riches is come to nought. And every shipmaster, and all the*

company in ships, and sailors, and as many as trade by sea, stood afar off,"
This will be the start of the great tribulation that will birth the MAN-
CHILD true church (Rev.12:13) the bride of Christ. Those of you who
continue to believe the false teaching of RAPTURE before tribulation,
will be caught in God's break. When you hear this warning from his
messenger. *Hebrews 3:15 "(KJV)* [15] *While it is said, today if ye will hear his
voice, harden not your hearts, as in the provocation."* You will be given a
chance to repent when you hear the word from the prophets and messengers
of our time just as you are now hearing from one.

The chronicle, **"The Timeline of Events."** It is evident that we are entering
Matthew 24; this is the footman stage preceding the Four Horseman
in Revelation six. The only escape is in God, the conditions that God
will allow Satan to carry this out is described in the chronicle **"What
Will Happen during the Tribulation Siege"**. Soon the internet will go
offline for the public when the monetary system changes and the NEW
WORLD ORDER Bush senior declared in his inaugural address will
begin to emerge. There are two nations' the bible is written too, Israel
and the Gentile.

The nation established to receive the Abraham covenant that will be
instrumental in the restoration of Israel as a nation; America, containing
all the nations of the world that Paul was sent to evangelize. Once this
has been completed, this will end with the last generation in that nation,
forty years after the 1967 war. This is where we are now in our time; just
look at the signs all around, you will see tribulation is at the door. It is no
mistake that we are fighting in Iraq, (a return to the Old Babylon to be
judged) as history, once again, is repeated in the bible.

What happen to us on (9/11/01) is a direct result of our covert oppressive
and aggressive policies carried out by our CIA as self-appointed policemen
of the world that has toppled smaller nations and left them to exist in abject
poverty. Some of these nations are inhabited by descendants of Ishmael.
America has broken the covenant he caused our forefathers to make; we
were to trust in one God. As a result, God has given us a strong delusion
to blind us as he did Israel in their rebellion. What we see are the people
in government making decisions that are not in the best interest of our
present liberties.

These are the sleeper cells planted in this country during the cold war era to gain citizenship, attend our institutions of higher learning to get in positions of government to change the laws for this time and to prepare this nation to be handed over to the New World Order. This is the curse for turning to other gods that are the cymbals in our capital buildings and on our statures that parallel the history of Rome; that is, to go down at the hand of greed, corruption, over taxation and immorality. God has allowed us to sale ourselves to the enemy and now they are coming to collect.

Now we will see how Abraham's sin with Hagar comes back with a vengeance on us as a friend of Israel. They are children of the slave women and now slaves of Satan doomed for destruction. They will be given a spirit to cause them to sacrifice themselves just as true Christian are called to do by Christ. The Koran, their bible, will give them a false hope that caused them to self-destruct as a reward to get to heaven. Satan will use the seed given over to him to cause chaos among the nations in the last days.

This false teaching, under a strong delusion, God will use them to exact vengeance that will be the means of their self-destruction. They will be used to run interference as to bring acts of terror on enemy nations. This will make America, known to them as the great Satan, a primary target. These are the seeds God discarded to be destroyed at the end. All the word must be fulfilled, God has given these seeds to Satan to use them to carry out God's will, fulfilling all things according to the words of the prophets.

America has appointed itself as the Policemen of the World; therefore, they will be the primary victim of the world's wrath. God gave us a strong delusion to deliver us into the hands of our enemies as he did Israel when they turned to idols. America has lost the vision of the founding fathers and will now be weaken at the hand of smaller nations while the greater enemy, Russia and China just sit back and wait for us to collapse from within, without mercy, walk in and take no prisoners. China purchased our nation's real estate as a resort of our own greed is coming to collect what's theirs. We sold the title deed to America to China and other nations. They financed our greed for these luxury toys to continue our lifestyle. 9/11/01, the last seven years, the Trojan horse sneaked in our compromised boarders to wake up the sleeper cells that have for the past sixty years gained high places in our government.

This shadow government is now carrying out their agenda. Bush Jr, the seed of Bush senior, used the Supreme Court to usurp authority over the people's vote to put him in office. All are part of evil seeds to carry out this countries destruction by turning the power over to the major co-operations outside our boarders with contracts that will give them the power to corrupt every elected official in this country as a paid servant to change laws to their own profit economically.

Such is the state of our representatives in the congress and senate, paid to change the laws to their favor. We as a capitalist society have become so corrupt to the point God had Obama to use the word change as his motto. Only those that have been given eyes to see will discern these times. Bush Jr.'s election was to complete the agenda set in motion by his father; that is to go to Iraq to speed our economic downfall in this last seven years to be condemned when we entered Iraq as to reunite the Old and New Babylon to receive the former Babylon's fate, "911" will be our sign that the judgement has begun. When the towels fall. (Ezekiel 26:9.)

God will now confound the government to play into the hands of her enemies as we will see a great divide among the parties. The Supreme Court, our last beacon of the hope for justice to uphold the law; you will see the decisions that indicate the blinders have reached them to become a politically dominated court to change laws for the times. (Daniel 7:25). "911" was masterminded by this hidden **Deep State,** using covert agencies on an international scale as they have done through-out the history of this nation, used Muslim extremist to be the fall people and war as their means to topple nations and take them over by financing both sides to achieve their objective of world domination.

Without the revelations of the Holy Spirit to discern these signs of the times, there is no way we would see what's coming. On January 21, 2010, The Supreme Court Handed over our freedoms to the Corporations by overturning McCain-Feingold's campaign law that will in these last elections, make our vote null and void to where it will make elections easy to manipulate doubt among the people and will lead to the corruption of our election process in the future. These foreign corporations will now control the politicians.

Russia tried for eight years to defeat Afghanistan, and it collapsed their economy. The international community became victim of Russia's scheme, given to them by God for his purposes, to open the door to democracy as a front, allowed them to regroup their military to fulfill the prophecy of the destruction coming from the armies of the **North** against Israel; (Ezekiel 38:15-16) Russia and China. (The Communist sisters) All these events are designed to culminate into fulfilling prophecy relevant to our times. Now with all our technology, it has become an apparent quagmire with no dignified way out, like Vietnam, we are fighting the wrong enemy and now our leaders are beginning to see the handwriting on the wall as King Nebuchadnezzar's son in Babylon of his day; saw the parallels.

America's last stand in history

This is Noah's seven days before the rain. This time we will see the fire. The hatred, three thousand plus years in the making of the descendants of Ishmael and the children of Abraham's concubines, can only be solved by destruction, not appeasement; such is the case in **Afghanistan**. This terrain has been left the same for four thousand years as unchartered territory. Our leaders are like Saul; they want to take some spoils of an enemy that is bent on destroying you. With God's leading, what did Israel learn when they went against God; they lost the battle.

These people are under the same mark as God put on Cain. Anyone that tries to destroy them will become their victims. God caused us to set foot on their soils to enrage them to ware down our military as they did Russia's. This is the politics of our leaders, blinded by God. We are following a path in history that will bring about a revived Roman Empire that will reveal the Pope as their Cesar, as a capitalist nation, in the end will fall from within by its own greed, immorality and corruption as history repeats itself. The Government has now been legally given over to the N.W.O. by the Supreme Court; freedom as Americans is now over, the cooperations funded by the New World Order that owns The World Bank and our federal reserve banking system, will now run these countries.

These signs of 2010 the four horsemen of the book of revelation are now being prepared to be loosed; when the economy collapses tribulation will become full circle, no one will escape but the children of God and those chosen to repopulate the millennium. My life is on hold while I am at rest, waiting for the event that will complete the transformation as we are preparing to come out of the wilderness in the fullness of Christ. This book, completed as of this final entry, contains the full chronicled topics of our end time scenarios as written. Our fate as victims of blind guides will have us pleading for God's mercy. If you have received these messages, please join with me in prayer for our fellow brothers and sisters by laying down our lives for their sake in the love of Christ. The John the Baptist ministry is little known to this church world.

Just as he was a forerunner of Christ, history will be repeated as we come to re-introduce Christ with the message, warning of his wrath. The skeptic's rhetoric will continue right on up to the day of destruction as did in the days of Noah. They call Noah a fool by saying it is going to rain and got caught in God's break after one hundred-twenty years of warning. My message of the coming siege of America is a repeat of what Noah experienced.

Concerning the messages within this book, the year given for me to start publishing these chronicles was eleven. The numbers 11/11 the prior three years have been witnessed by many; however, I never related it to writing books. The first copy was completed for Print on January 11, 2011. This is the eleventh year, the other eleven is in God's timing as to when the fires of tribulation will commence. I am also in waiting for twenty-five years in Arizona at the time of this message to see what that brings as to that number.

"Holy Spirit, give us a word for this time to all that will hear in Jesus' name." Amen *Deuteronomy 11:26 (KJV)* [26] *Behold, I set before you this day a blessing and a curse; Jeremiah 21:8 (KJV)* [8] *And unto this people thou shalt say, thus saith the LORD; Behold, I set before you the way of life, and the way of death. Proverbs 18:21 (KJV)* [21] *Death and life are in the power of the tongue: and they that love it shall eat the fruit thereof. Deuteronomy 30:19 (KJV)* [19] *I call heaven and earth to record this day against you, that I have set before you life and death, blessing and cursing: therefore choose life, that both thou and thy seed may live: Joshua 24:15 (KJV)* [15] *And if it seem evil unto you to serve the LORD, choose you this day whom ye will serve; whether the gods which your fathers served that were on the other side of the flood, or the gods of the Amorites, in whose land ye dwell: but as for me and my house, we will serve the lord. Revelation 3:20 (KJV)* [20] *Behold, I stand at the door, and knock: if any man hear my voice, and open the door, I will come in to him, and will sup with him, and he with me. Revelation 22:17 (KJV)* [17] *And the Spirit and the bride say, Come. And let him that heareth say, Come. And let him that is athirst come. And whosoever will, let him take the water of life freely.* (Updated for release in 2014)

THE MYSTERY OF GODLINESS AND THE MYSTERY OF INIQUITY

The study of this subject under the anointing of the Holy Spirit proves to be one of the most enlightening revelations I have ever had. The study of these two subjects, I pray, will enhance your understanding of these two mysteries that have eluded the church world throughout the centuries. These are the things kept being revealed to the end-time generation that the church fails to receive that caused the great apostasy. When Jesus was speaking to the Jews (his own) He often spoke in parables and prophesied to his people because of their hard hearts. When they rejected Him, He spoke this prophecy? **John 5:43** *"I am come in my Father's name, and ye receive me not: <u>if another shall come in his own name, him ye will receive.</u>*

You may ask yourself, who is the other to come? My beloved brothers and sisters, this is where this whole mystery begins as you read this revelation, you will no doubt see what I came to see by the Holy Spirit, the source of all our shortcomings and sins as confessing Christians. Now my dear brothers and sisters, this is what the Spirit has to say to the church about where Satan gets his power over you.

Hosea 4:6 (KJV) *⁶ My people are destroyed for lack of knowledge: because thou hast rejected knowledge, I will also reject thee, that thou shalt be no priest to me: seeing thou hast forgotten the law of thy God, I will also forget*

212

thy children. Matthew 7:13-14 (KJV) [13] *Enter ye in at the strait gate: for wide is the gate, and broad is the way, that leadeth to destruction, and many there be which go in thereat:* [14] *Because strait is the gate, and narrow is the way, which leadeth unto life, and few there be that find it. 1 Peter 5:8 (KJV)* [8] *Be sober, be vigilant; because your adversary the devil, as a roaring lion, walketh about, seeking whom he may devour:*

What the church has fail to see is this reality of our sin nature. All mankind as of Adam's sin is born children of the devil and only God can deliver us from him. We must be delivered from seducing spirits that have controlled our intellect. Our blindness will never be known until God opens our eyes. This gospel consisting of the doctrine of Jesus Christ, when preached in the purity and power of true holiness will reveal Jesus to those that have ears to hear, open their eyes to see the reality of the new creature.

We must receive the Holy Spirit to give us the power to do right and live a sinless life. *Acts 1:8 (KJV)* [8] *But ye shall receive power, after that the Holy Ghost is come upon you: and ye shall be witnesses unto me both in Jerusalem, and in all Judaea, and in Samaria, and unto the uttermost part of the earth. Acts 3:19 (KJV)* [19] *Repent ye therefore, and be converted, that your sins may be blotted out, when the times of refreshing shall come from the presence of the Lord; Matthew 18:3 (KJV)* [3] *And said, Verily I say unto you, except ye be converted, and become as little children, ye shall not enter into the kingdom of heaven. This is the state of our hearts before we hear the real gospel. Acts 28:27 (KJV)* [27] *For the heart of this people is waxed gross, and their ears are dull of hearing and their eyes have they closed; lest they should see with their eyes, and hear with their ears, and understand with their heart, and should be converted, and I should heal them. Jeremiah 17:9 (KJV)* [9] *The heart is deceitful above all things, and desperately wicked: who can know it?*

The spirit that convicts you will determine what spirit you are of and the only way you will know who is of God is by his fruit. Those who are converted will be able to discern the right fruit. When Jesus told Peter **"when you come to be converted you can strengthen your brother,"** When you are walking in the perfect will of God, you will not be ignorant about what spirit is operating in your presence. This is the work of the Holy Spirit when you surrender your will … *Romans 11:25 (KJV)* [25] *For I would not, brethren, that ye should be ignorant of this mystery, lest ye should be wise* *in your own conceits; that blindness in part is happened to Israel, <u>until the fulness of the Gentiles be come in.</u>*

This is where we are now in that time. *1 Corinthians 12:1 (KJV)* [1] *Now concerning spiritual gifts, brethren, I would not have you ignorant. 2 Corinthians 2:11 (KJV)* [11] *Lest Satan should get an advantage of us: for we are not ignorant of his devices. 1 Corinthians 14:38 (KJV)* [38] *But if any man be ignorant, let him be ignorant. 2 Thessalonians 2:7 (KJV)* [7] *For the mystery of iniquity doth already work: only he who now letteth will let, until he be taken out of the way.*

Acts 1:2 (KJV) [2] *Until the day in which he was taken up, after that he through the Holy Ghost had given commandments unto the apostles whom he had chosen: Hebrews 10:15 -17* [15] *Whereof the Holy Ghost also is a witness to us: for after that he had said before,* [16] *This is the covenant that I will make with them after those days, saith the Lord, I will put my laws into their hearts, and in their minds will I write them;* [17] *And their sins and iniquities will I remember no more.* This is what it is to be born again.

John 6:44 (KJV) [44] *No man can come to me, except the Father which hath sent me draw him: and I will raise him up at the last day.* This statement will shock many confessing Christians; no one can enter the sovereign will of God except He bid you to come by His spirit. Why would he tell us that **"few there be that find it"**? Only God can bring you into his presence because he is doing the choosing not man and his theology. When the Holy Ghost showed me this revelation, I did not have to ask any more questions about heaven while being on Earth.

The only one going back to heaven is Christ in you. That's why he said … *Matthew 10:22 (KJV)* [22] *And ye shall be hated of all men for my name's sake: but he that endureth to the end shall be saved.* When you surrender, they are doing it to him all over again to him in your body and if you will be a willing and obedient servant until the end, you get to go back to heaven with him … *Hebrews 12:1 (KJV)* [1] *Wherefore seeing we also are compassed about with so great a cloud of witnesses, let us lay aside every weight, and the sin which doth so easily beset us, and let us run with patience the race that is set before us. Ecclesiastes 9:11 (NASB77)* [11] *I again saw under the sun that the race is not to the swift, and the battle is not to the warriors, and neither is bread to the wise, nor wealth to the discerning, nor favor to men of ability; for time and chance overtake them all. Matthew 22:14 (KJV) [14] For many are called, but few are chosen. Romans 12:1-2 (KJV) [1] I beseech you therefore, brethren, by the mercies of God, that ye present your bodies a living sacrifice, holy, acceptable unto God, which is your reasonable service. [2] And be not conformed to this world: but be ye transformed by the renewing of your mind, that ye may prove what is that good, and acceptable, and perfect, will of God. 1 Corinthians 2:16 (KJV) [16] For who hath known the mind of the Lord, that he may instruct him? But we have the mind of Christ. 2 Corinthians 5:17 (NASB77) [17] Therefore, if any man is in Christ, he is a new creature; the old things passed away; behold, new things have come. Romans 8:9 (KJV) [9] But ye are not in the flesh, but in the Spirit, if so be that the Spirit of God dwell in you. Now if any man have not the Spirit of Christ, he is none of his.*

What I found to be the key that will open the door to revelation knowledge is total surrender of your will, then we can become that child that depends on his father for his very existence. *Isaiah 55:7-8 (KJV) "[7] Let the wicked forsake his way, and the unrighteous man his thoughts: and let him return unto the LORD, and he will have mercy upon him; and to our God, for he will abundantly pardon. [8] For my thoughts are not your thoughts, neither are your ways my ways, saith the LORD."* Why do we still sin willfully as a confessing Christian?

We identify our Christianity after flesh and blood instead of Christ. Most of us do not believe that we can live free from sin or perfect and that's a great error in the teachings down on the level of modern theology. This doctrine leads to unbelief that denies Christ came in the flesh to perfect you. As John puts it; this is antichrist teachings.

1 John 4:3 (KJV) "[3] And every spirit that confesseth not that Jesus Christ is come in the flesh is not of God: and this is that spirit of antichrist, whereof ye have heard that it should come; and even now already is it in the world." Another great mystery about the antichrist; hirelings, trained in seminary institutions are Satan's agents of false teachings. He is the origin of all the wickedness manifested in time past to this present day. They are manifested in the warfare of our minds in the choices we make, whether good or evil. Each choice has its own fruit as an identifier as to who is in control of the vessel.

The prophets of the Old Testament spoke on this wise.

Isaiah 5:24 (NASB77) Isaiah 5:24 (KJV) ²⁴ *Therefore as the fire devoureth the stubble, and the flame consumeth the chaff, so their root shall be as rottenness, and their blossom shall go up as dust: because they have cast away the law of the LORD of hosts, and despised the word of the Holy One of Israel.* Those who are in Christ are in his church of which he is the foundation stone that is laid first, and then built upon. *Isaiah 30:27-28 "Behold, the name of the LORD cometh from far, burning with his anger, and the burden thereof is heavy: his lips are full of indignation, and his tongue as a devouring fire: 28And his breath, as an overflowing stream, shall reach to the midst of the neck, to sift the nations with the sieve of vanity and there shall be a bridle in the jaws of the people, causing them to err. (2 Thessalonians 2:11 (KJV) "11And for this cause God shall send them strong delusion, that they should believe a lie.* "This will come full circle in this last generation that shall see these things in their entirety in their midst. *Isaiah 14:12 "How art thou fallen from heaven, O Lucifer, son of the morning! how art thou cut down to the ground, which didst weaken the nations!"*

Hear we see where Satan will show his iniquity in all nations and people. They will be manifested on this wise … *Ephesians 6:12 (KJV)* ¹² *For we wrestle not against flesh and blood, but against principalities, against powers, against the rulers of the darkness of this world, against spiritual wickedness in high places. Daniel saw him as… Daniel 7:8 (KJV)* ⁸ *I considered the horns, and, behold, there came up among them another little horn, before whom there were three of the first horns plucked up by the roots: and, behold, in this horn were eyes like the eyes of man, and a mouth speaking great things.* These are men in great positions of power that will begin to … *Daniel 7:25 (KJV)* ²⁵ *And he shall speak great words against the most High, and <u>shall wear out the saints</u> of the most High, and think <u>to change times and laws:</u> and they shall be given into his hand until a time and times and the dividing of time.* This prophecy in our time represents the state of the church that will go through tribulation to be revived by being an apostate state of dry bones. (Ezekiel. 37)

This will be a time when *Matthew 24:12 (KJV)* ¹² *And because iniquity shall abound, the love of many shall wax cold. Daniel 8:23 (KJV)* ²³ *And in the latter time of their kingdom, when the transgressors are come to the full, a <u>king of fierce countenance</u>, and understanding dark sentences, shall stand* *up. Daniel 9:26 (KJV" 26 And after threescore and two weeks shall Messiah be cut off, but not for himself: and the people of the prince that shall come shall destroy the city and the sanctuary; and the end thereof shall be with a flood, and unto the end of the war desolations are determined. Daniel 11:36 (KJV) 36 And the king shall do according to his will; and he shall exalt himself, and magnify himself above every god, and shall speak marvelous things against the God of gods, and shall prosper till the indignation be accomplished: for that that is determined shall be done."* These are earthly principalities empowered by the son of perdition, Satan to begin the final assault for supremacy over the Earth. This is the seven years of tribulation that this spiritual warfare in heaven, manifested in the Earth among wicked men.

This is the activity of Satan as revealed in the New Testament:

2 Thes. 2:3-8 "Let no man deceive you by any means: for that day shall not come, except there come a falling away first, and that man of sin be revealed, the son of perdition; 4Who opposeth and exalteth himself above all that is called God, or that is worshipped; so that he as God sitteth in the temple of God, shewing himself that he is God. The antichrist, setting in the temple is not talking about a building but in his own body as the false Christ.

He will be duplicating what Christ did as the son of God; this time, he is the son of the devil who will be seen as a god to the people who have been deceived into thinking he is the solution to all the world's problems. There will not be another temple built in Jerusalem in our lifetime. The mystery of Godliness is Christ became the last sacrifice that ushered in the new covenant; therefore, all reference to the pass covenant of animal sacrifice had to be destroyed. This prophecy came to pass in seventy A.D. when the Romans destroyed Solomon's temple of sacrifice.

The revelation of the New Testament gospel is now you must become the sacrifice to be received in heaven; you are the new spirit filled tabernacle where God dwells in you as the holy of holies twenty-four seven to perform his will in the earth as he will in heaven. *5Remember ye not, that, when I was yet with you, I told you these things? 6And now ye know what withholdeth that he might be revealed in his time.7For the mystery of iniquity doth already work: only he who now letteth will let, until he be taken out of the way. 8And then shall that Wicked be revealed, whom the Lord shall consume with the spirit of his mouth and shall destroy with the brightness of his coming." 2 Thessalonians 2:3-8 (NLT)* [3] *Don't be fooled by what they say. For that day will not come until there is a great rebellion against God and the man of lawlessness is revealed—the one who brings destruction.* [4] *He will exalt himself and defy everything that people call god and every object of worship. He will even sit in the temple of God, claiming that he himself is God.* [5] *Don't you remember that I told you about all this when I was with you?* [6] *And you know what is holding him back, <u>for he can be revealed only when his time comes</u>.* [7] *For this lawlessness is already at work secretly, <u>and it will remain secret until the one who is holding it back steps out of the way.</u>* [8] *Then the man of lawlessness will be revealed, but the Lord Jesus will kill him with the breath of his mouth and destroy him by the splendor of his coming. Christ will himself expose him as the false prophet or antichrist at his coming.*

These mysteries are now being revealed to those that have ears to hear.*1 John 2:18 Little children, it is the last time: and as ye have heard that antichrist shall come, even now are there many antichrists; whereby we know that it is the last time. Rev. 13:1-8 "And I stood upon the sand of the sea, and saw a beast rise up out of the sea, having seven heads and ten horns, and upon his horns ten crowns, and upon his heads the name of blasphemy. 2And the beast which I saw was like unto a leopard, (China) and his feet were as the feet of a bear, (Russia) and his mouth as the mouth of a lion (America): and the dragon gave him his power and his seat, and great authority. 3And I saw <u>one of his heads</u> as it were wounded to death …* During World War II, Great Britain was wounded as a nation but recovered... **and his deadly wound was healed: and all the world wondered after the beas**t. This is the first stage of the beast system; the United Nation will bring them all together as the head of the first stage of the beast man in the same scenario that will rise and shows himself later when this antichrist man is struck down when Satan is cast out of heaven and is resurrected in him.

They will bring all nations together to bring stability to the world's economy for a while by establishing an international headquarters as the first stage of world dominance; The United Nations. *4And they worshipped the dragon which gave able to make war with him? 5And there was given unto him a mouth speaking great things and blasphemies; and power was given unto him to continue forty and two months. 6And he opened his mouth in blasphemy against God, to blaspheme his name, and his tabernacle, and them* *that dwell in heaven. 7And it was given unto him to make war with the saints, and to overcome them: and power was given him over all kindreds, and tongues, and nations. 8And all that dwell upon the earth shall worship him, whose names are not written in the book of life of the Lamb slain <u>from the foundation of the world.</u>"*

They will begin to set the stage for the kingdoms that will be the ten toes. **(Daniel 2:42)** After they have successfully caused all nations to come under this New World Order; the beast system known to the world as The United Nations. God will cause them to provoke World War III thinking they will succeed in reducing the world's population for the New World Order to live in a world they have created by deception to perpetuate their own agenda; a utopia, masterminded by these renown megalomaniacs manifesting alien DNA.

Now here's where this revelation shows the great contrast between Satan and Christ.

1. Christ came from above.

John 6:38 "For I came down from heaven, not to do mine own will, but the will of him that   sent me."

The Antichrist came from below. *Rev. 11:7 "And when they shall have finished their testimony, the beast that   ascendeth <u>out of the bottomless pit</u> shall make war against them, and shall overcome them, and kill them."*

2. Christ came in his father. <u>*John 5:43*</u> *"I am come in my Father's name, and ye receive me not: if another shall come in his own name, him ye will receive.*

The Antichrist came in his own name.

<u>*John 5:43*</u> *I am come in my Father's name, and ye receive me not: if another shall come <u>in his own name</u>, him ye will receive."*

3. Christ humbled himself.

<u>*Philip. 2:8*</u> *"And being found in fashion as a man, he humble himself, and became obedient unto death, even the death of the cross."*

The Antichrist Exalts himself. <u>*2 Thes. 2:4*</u> *"Who opposeth and exalteth himself above all that is called God, or that is worshipped; so that he as God sitteth in the temple of God, shewing himself that he is God."*

4. Christ despised.

Isaiah 53:3 "He is despised and rejected of men; a man of sorrows and acquainted with grief: and we hid as it were our faces from him; he was despised, and we esteemed him not."

The Antichrist admired.

Rev. 13:3-4 "And I saw one of his heads as it were wounded to death; and his deadly wound was healed: <u>and all the world wondered after the beast."</u>

5. Christ exalted.

Philip. 2:9 "Wherefore God also hath highly exalted him, and given him a name which is above every name:"

The Antichrist cast down to hell.

Isaiah 14:14-15 "I will ascend above the heights of the clouds; I will be like the most High. <u>15 Yet thou shalt be brought down to hell, to the sides of the pit."</u>

6. Christ came to do the Father's will.

John 6:38 "For I came down from heaven, not to do mine own will, but the will of him that sent me."

The Antichrist to do his own will.

Daniel 11:36 "And the king shall do according to his will; and he shall exalt himself, and magnify himself above every god, and shall speak marvellous things against the God of gods and shall prosper till the indignation be accomplished: for that that is determined shall be done."

7. Christ came to save.

Luke 19:10 "For the Son of man is come to seek and to save that which was lost."

The Antichrist comes to destroy.

Daniel 8:24 "And his power shall be mighty, but not by his own power:

and he shall <u>destroy wonderfully</u>, and shall prosper, and practise, and shall destroy the mighty and the holy people."

8. Christ the good shepherd.

John 10:14 "I am the good shepherd, and know my sheep, and am known of mine."

The Antichrist is the idol.

Leviticus 19:4 (NLT) Do not put your trust in idols or make gods of metal for yourselves. I, the LORD, am your God.

9. Christ represents truth.

John 14:6_"Jesus saith unto him, I am the way, the truth, and the life: no man cometh unto the father, but by me"

The Antichrist the liar.

Jn 8:44 (KJV) Ye are of your father the devil, and the lusts of your father ye will do. He was a murderer from the beginning, and abode not in the truth, because there is no truth in him. When he speaketh a lie, he speaketh of his own: for he is a liar, and the father of it.

10. Christ the Holy One.

Mark 1:24 "Saying, Let us alone; what have we to do with thee, thou Jesus of

Nazareth? art thou come to destroy us? I know thee who thou art, the <u>Holy One of God."</u>

The Antichrist, The Man of Sin.

_2 Thes. 2:3 "Let no man deceive you by any means: for that day shall not come, except there come a falling away first, and that <u>man of sin be</u> revealed, the son of perdition;

11. Christ, The Son of God.

Luke 1:35_"And the angel answered and said unto her, The Holy   G h o s t shall come upon thee, and the power of the Highest shall overshadow thee:

therefore also that holy thing which shall be born of thee shall be called the Son of God."

The Antichrist, The Son of Perdition

2 Thes. 2:3 "Let no man deceive you by any means: for that day shall not come, except there come a falling away first, and that man of sin be revealed, the son of perdition;"

12. Finally, Christ the Mystery of Godliness. *1 Tim. 3:16 "And without controversy great is the mystery of godliness: God was manifest in the flesh, justified in the Spirit, received up into glory."*

The Antichrist, The mystery of Iniquity

2 Thes. 2:7 "For the mystery of iniquity doth already work: only he who now letteth will let, until he be taken out of the way." Michael, the Archangel, has been given the power to restrain Satan from destroying the world ahead of time. He is now preparing to release him to complete the destruction of wicked man, rearrange the geography of the Earth back to the first millennium and to rest the Earth in the last or seventh millennium in perfect righteousness.

This one profound statement that Paul makes, reveals the state of the church that will be seduced by their own willing ignorance. *2 Thes. 2:3 "Let no man deceive you by any means: for that day shall not come, except there come a falling away first, and that man of sin be revealed, the son of perdition;" These false teachings will take its toll in the form of ... I Timothy 4:1 (KJV) [1] Now the Spirit speaketh expressly, that in the latter times some shall depart from the faith, giving heed to seducing spirits, and doctrines of devils; 2 Timothy 3:5 (KJV) [5] Having a form of godliness, but denying the power thereof: from such turn away.*

This is what the Holy Spirit has to say to man

Psalm 119:104 (KJV) [104] Through thy precepts (God's word) I get understanding: therefore, I hate every false way. Proverbs 4:7 (KJV) [7] Wisdom is the principal thing; therefore, get wisdom: and with all thy getting get understanding. This is the leading of the Holy Spirit, not man.

Proverbs 4:5 (KJV) [5] *Get wisdom, get understanding: forget it not; neither decline from the words of my mouth. Matthew 4:4 (KJV)* [4]*Man shall not live by bread alone, but by every word that proceedeth out of the mouth of God. Psalm 1:1-2 (KJV)* [1] *Blessed is the man that walketh not in the counsel of the ungodly, nor standeth in the way of sinners, nor sitteth in the seat of the scornful.* [2] *But his delight is in the law of the LORD; and in his law doth he meditate day and night. 2 Timothy 2:7 (KJV)* [7] *Consider what I say; and the Lord give thee understanding in all things. Proverbs 6:16-19 (KJV)* [16] *These six things doth the LORD hate: yea, seven are an abomination unto him:* [17] *A proud look, a lying tongue, and hands that shed innocent blood,* [18] *An heart that deviseth wicked imaginations, feet that be swift in running to mischief,* [19] *A false witness that speaketh lies, and he that soweth discord among brethren. 2 Timothy 2:20 (KJV)* [20] *But in a great house there are not only vessels of gold and of silver, but also of wood and of earth; and some to honour, and some to dishonour.*

This is a truth I learn from God when he revealed to me his ways. The only way you will be able to know you are a vessel of honor or of dishonor is revealed in these passages of scripture. This is the fruit the vessel of honor produces.

Galatians 5:22-23 (KJV) "[22] *But the fruit of the Spirit is <u>love, joy, peace, longsuffering, gentleness, goodness, faith,</u>* [23] *<u>Meekness, temperance</u>: against such there is no law."* This is the fruit the vessel of dishonor produces. *Galatians 5:19-21 (KJV)* "[19] *Now the works of the flesh are manifest, which are these; <u>Adultery, fornication, uncleanness, lasciviousness,</u>* [20] *<u>Idolatry, witchcraft, hatred, variance, emulations, wrath, strife, seditions, heresies,</u>* [21] *<u>Envyings, murders, drunkenness, revellings,</u> and such like: of the which I tell you before, as I have also told you in time past, that they which do such things shall not inherit the kingdom of God."*

God is speaking to all who confess to be of him not to be guilty of these sins of omission. These are the hidden spirits, manifested in them that killed Jesus in the name of God because they were blinded by their own thoughts to think that they were doing the right thing. They were religious men who were given the truth but got seduce by Satan that cause them to act out of God's will do things in their own way; therefore, could not see God among them. Thinking themselves wise became fools as tools of the devil, used as vessels of dishonor to carry out the will of God.

When one confesses salvation unless, it is the work of God's sovereign will, all you have become is a religious person. Notice I did not say Christian because those that persecute their own brothers and sisters in the name of God are not Christians but vessels of dishonor or antichrist. At this time under grace and truth, God is choosing out his vessel of honor to be used for his glory. This is election.

All who will be used in this capacity are as John the Baptist, at rest separated to him. **Hebrews 4:*1 (KJV)* ¹ *Let us therefore fear, lest, a promise being left us of entering into his rest, any of you should seem to come short of it.* If all we have done in our ignorance have caused this division among us, no wonder he has said ... *Matthew 24:22 (KJV)* ²² *And except those days should be shortened, there should no flesh be saved: but for the elect's sake those days shall be shortened. John 15:16 (KJV)* ¹⁶ *Ye have not chosen me, but I have chosen you, and ordained you, that ye should go and bring forth fruit, and that your fruit should remain: that whatsoever ye shall ask of the Father in my name, he may give it you. John 15:19 (KJV)* ¹⁹ *If ye were of the world, the world would love his own: but because ye are not of the world, but I have chosen you out of the world, therefore the world hateth you.*

Not obeying the word of your times will cause you to error by giving place to seducing spirits that have led to this great falling away. No matter what God is telling me; I am also tempered in the spirit not to desire anything outside of the perfect will of God for my life ... let me be clear, the things I'm tempted with are not from God, it's my love for him that keeps me from yielding to it. You must be honest about your vulnerabilities that only your love for God can deliver you from. All he has shared with me has been for me and to me; yes, I am telling you all these things to let you see what we must be delivered from, ourselves. We are in the world with all these temptations, God's love in you can keep you restrained by giving you the power that comes with the Holy Spirit to keep you from the evils of this world while you are in it. This is a work in progress for us all to strive for in our obedience to abide under that covering where no weapon formed against you will prevail.

Like Paul, I strive daily to keep myself under the blood and it has not been easy as coming from sin to salvation. The anointing that breaks all the yokes of bondage, looses you from oppression and finally set you free from captivity, is what he did when he walked with the father. If I come preaching or teaching without this anointing that Christ in me, all I am doing is beating the air with hard speeches as Paul said. This is what I believe; as having removed my fears, doubt and unbelief to see him perform his word that has given me a testimony of deliverance in all I have trusted in his word by acting on it. However, the reason I do not see this on that level, there is too much doubt in the people I am speaking to in this great fall away from the faith. *Ephesians 2:2 (KJV) ² Wherein in time past ye walked according to the course of this world, according to the prince of the power of the air, the spirit that now worketh in the children of disobedience: 1 Corinthians 9:27 (KJV) ²⁷ But I keep under my body and bring it into subjection: lest that by any means, when I have preached to others, I myself should be a castaway. Hebrews 2:4 (KJV) ⁴ God also bearing them witness, both with signs and wonders, and with divers miracles, and gifts of the Holy Ghost, according to his own will?*

I am at rest waiting on God's anointing; if **Hebrews 2:4** is not being confirmed in your ministry, you went ahead of God; therefore, Jesus is not with you. This is known as the permissive will of God which operates according to your faith not being in the perfect will of God. Now you should be able to see why this revelation in the last generation will be rejected before the start of the tribulation. It fulfills this scripture *... Revelation 12:9 (KJV) ⁹ And the great dragon was cast out, that old serpent, called the Devil, and Satan, which deceiveth the whole world: he was cast out into the earth, and his angels were cast out with him.* This includes the church of our times of the end. It is hard for men in leadership to admit their wrongs concerning the truth unless we are truly convicted. We have had two thousand years to the point that if God had not sent revivals periodically to remind us of his presents, we would not be here today.

Just like the Israelites did not recognize God speaking in Jesus as their Messiah standing there in the flesh, that's how far they were blinded through misinterpreting the law. We as confessing Christians, error in strange here say doctrines until we believe we are right because so many others who are like minded are doing the same things. This is how we fall away without even knowing it. This is the great delusion that many will choose to continue in and become vessels of dishonor by their own choice.

This I know for certain, if God had not chosen me and bid me to come by his spirit, there is no way I would have come to this level of understanding of the perfect will of God on my own. I now live as a surrendered vessel as to … *Matthew 6:25 (KJV)* [25] *Therefore I say unto you, Take no thought for your life, what ye shall eat, or what ye shall drink; nor yet for your body, what ye shall put on. Is not the life more than meat, and the body than raiment? Job 14:1 (KJV)* [1] *Man that is born of a woman is of few days, and full of trouble. 2 Timothy 3:12 (KJV)* [12] *Yea, and all that will live godly in Christ Jesus shall suffer persecution. James 4:14 (KJV)* [14] *Whereas ye know not what shall be on the morrow. For what is your life? It is even a vapour that appeareth for a little time, and then vanisheth away. Philippians 4:11 (KJV)* [11] *Not that I speak in respect of want: for I have learned, in whatsoever state I am, therewith to be content.* With all the things the devil use to keep us thinking in the natural, I can see for me without God's choosing, there is no way I can get to heaven. *Psalm 27:14 (KJV)* [14] *Wait on the LORD: be of good courage, and he shall strengthen thine heart: wait, I say, on the LORD. Luke 18:8 (KJV)* [8] *I tell you that he will avenge them speedily. Nevertheless, when the Son of man cometh, shall he find faith on the earth?"* In all my studying of the scripture, I have come to see that a few have been chosen from each time, each age, each generation and each dispensation to make up the numberless multitude and only God has known the end of these mysteries that have yet to be reveal to man.

Revelation 7:9 (KJV) [9] *After this I beheld, and, lo, a great multitude, which no man could number, of all nations, and kindreds, and people, and tongues, stood before the throne, and before the Lamb, clothed with white robes, and palms in their hands;* I stand in awe at what has been revealed to me and yet there are not many with ears to hear it. Whether we want to admit it or not; this is a fact … *Romans 3:11 (KJV)* [11] *There is none that understandeth, there is none that seeketh after God. Isaiah 53:1 (KJV)* [1] *Who hath believed our report? and to whom is the arm of the LORD revealed? John 12:38 (KJV)* [38] *That the saying of Esaias the prophet might be fulfilled, which he spake, Lord, who hath believed our report? and to whom hath the arm of the Lord been revealed.*

This is what the Holy Spirit told me about man outside of the will of God. The only thing God requires of you is what he made from the dust and put in your body. It takes the spirit of God to humble us to where we will give place to each other as an equal in the spirit. *Isaiah 64:6 (KJV)* [6] *But we are all as an unclean thing, and all our righteousnesses are as filthy rags;*

and we all do fade as a leaf; and our iniquities, like the wind, have taken us away. Ecclesiastes 1:9 (KJV) ⁹ *The thing that hath been, it is that which shall be; and that which is done is that which shall be done: and there is no new thing under the sun. Ecclesiastes 4:4 (KJV)* ⁴ *Again, I considered all travail, and every right work, that for this a man is envied of his neighbour. This is also vanity and vexation of spirit. Ecclesiastes 4:6 (KJV)* ⁶ *Better is an handful with quietness, than both the hands full with travail and vexation of spirit. Psalm 107:30 (KJV)* ³⁰ *Then are they glad because they be quiet; so he bringeth them unto their desired haven. 1 Thessalonians 4:11 (KJV)* ¹¹ *And that ye study to be quiet, and to do your own business, and to work with your own hands, as we commanded you; Luke 6:42 (KJV)* ⁴² *Either how canst thou say to thy brother, Brother, let me pull out the mote that is in thine eye, when thou thyself beholdest not the beam that is in thine own eye? Thou hypocrite, cast out first the beam out of thine own eye, and then shalt thou see clearly to pull out the mote that is in thy brother's eye.*

This is how the Holy Spirit talks to me through the scriptures about myself. Therefore, he had to bring me to rest. Look at all these things he is showing me about myself that must first be dealt with in ME! ... that I did not know until he opened my eyes. *Psalm 69:9 (KJV)* ⁹ *For the zeal of thine house hath eaten me up; and the reproaches of them that reproached thee are fallen upon me.* In retrospect, I see my whole life before me as a preacher in time past, zeal without knowledge neither knowing what spirit I was of until Christ opened my eyes which is the sum of this revelation and testimony as to where I have come today by God's grace and mercy. I, in my ignorance rebelled all the way here. These expressions are God's work in me to his own will because he had chosen me for this purpose; I am just as confounded as you as to why he has given me this privilege. No wonder Paul said when he had this encounter, **"what will you have me do."** I too have seen my whole life before my face just as he has described it in the word.

This is our state at birth, The Natural or Carnal man

1 Corinthians 3:1-3 (KJV) ¹ *And I, brethren, could not speak unto you as unto spiritual, but as unto carnal, even as unto babes in Christ.* ² *I have fed you with milk, and not with meat: for hitherto ye were not able to bear it, neither yet now are ye able.* ³ *For ye are yet carnal: for whereas there is among you envying, and strife, and divisions, are ye not carnal, and walk as men? 1 Corinthians 2:14 (KJV) ¹⁴ But the natural man receiveth not the things of the Spirit of God: for they are foolishness unto him: neither can he know them, because they are spiritually discerned. 1 Corinthians 3:1 (KJV) "¹ And I, brethren, could not speak unto you as unto spiritual, but as unto carnal, even as unto babes in Christ."*

The Holy Spirit addresses the soul part of us as a sinner. He speaks to the heart of our very existence, the heart of your emotions which are governed by our five senses. The limits of our intellect are through these five gateways to the heart of man. What we **see**, what we **smell**, what we **hear**, what we **taste**, and what we **touch**. These natural gateways all are the soul of our existence, operating through our brain power responding to seducing spirits using the natural circumstances that open us to imaginations, conscience, memory, reasoning and affections. This is who you are as a child of the devil. Until we are converted, this is known as the carnal man ruled by the influences of circumstances governed by his thought processes through the five gates of the senses.

The New Spirit Man

2 Corinthians 5:17 (KJV) ¹⁷ Therefore if any man be in Christ, he is a new creature: old things are passed away; behold, all things are become new. This is the restored Adam, revived by the quickening power of the spoken word through holy men walking in the spirit of Christ as led by the spirit of God choosing whom he will in the earth to come to him by his spirit for this reason ... *John 6:44 (KJV) ⁴⁴ No man can come to me, except the Father which hath sent me draw him: and I will raise him up at the last day.*

You see, God is choosing who is going to heaven. Therefore, these are born from above because only the Holy Spirit connects you to heaven where the perfect and sovereign will of God can be performed in the Earth through yield vessels led by the Holy Spirit. This is the spiritual man that has been converted that will produce the fruit as in ... *Galatians 5:22-23 (KJV) ²² But the fruit of the Spirit is love, joy, peace, longsuffering, gentleness, goodness, faith, ²³ Meekness, temperance: against such there is no law.* As these prevail in you, God through you will produce fruit that remain.

This is only seen in those chosen by God that has gone through conversion by being proved in the wilderness separated to God to become meat for the master's use. Now you see why **"few there be that find it."** No one that is chosen by God will escape a wilderness experience. This is where the natural man dies, and the spirit man is revived. Only God can bring you through this experience as he did in Jesus. God came in the flesh as Jesus, Emanuel, meaning God among us in human form as the second Adam. He is holy and will not compromise one jot or tittle of his word because he is perfect. This time he will past the test of temptation to overcome the natural man that will quicken all whom God will choose to be restored as new creations. These are the elects chosen to be used of God to preserve his presence in the Earth; without his presence, the wickedness that is in man will have caused the whole earth to be destroyed a head of schedule. Case in point, Noah and the Ark, the first tribulation period and we are approaching the second, and lastly the whole earth to be renovated after the millennium.

Finally: in my final summation of what the Holy Spirit has made known to me in these chronicle essays? *Ecclesiastes 1:9 (KJV)* [9] *The thing that hath been, it is that which shall be; and that which is done is that which shall be done: and there is no new thing under the sun.*

THE JEWS

The Jews rejected **God the father** by departing from the law given to Moses. Second: **they rejected him as the Son of God**, the Messiah. Third: **they rejected him as the Holy Spirit** in the stoning of Stephen. That final act put them in darkness by the veil when they sent him to the cross, sealing their fate at the hand of a gentile who washed his hands of innocent blood. Now I know many of you never have heard this statement before; Pilate, washing his hands, cleared the gentiles of this sin and opens the door to all God's creation that ushered in the time of grace. God foreknew that this final rejection of Deacon Stephen who represented the fullness of the Holy Ghost as the First martyr would seal their fate until he returns. **Acts 15:16 (NASB77)** [16] **AFTER THESE THINGS I will return, AND I WILL REBUILD THE TABERNACLE OF DAVID WHICH HAS FALLEN, AND I WILL REBUILD ITS RUINS, AND I WILL RESTORE IT,**

Here we see that Jesus said that he would rebuild the temple during the millennium. From the cross to now, no sacrifice by any Jew will be received because the pure lamb has been slain in Christ. In seventy A.D. the natural temple was destroyed, now our bodies must become the sacrifice through Christ. In the last days, this attempt to rebuild the temple will become an act of war in the middle east because of the temple mount.

THE GENTILES

I sit here with only one reply, have mercy on me. We in our time of the gentiles have done the same thing. We have rejected Christ and gone about to establish our own righteousness; have put ourselves back in the natural temples he condemned and divided ourselves with doctrines of our own choosing. Baptism is no longer a sign of conversion but a symbol to be interpreted in the many doctrines that have come from false teachings. The Holy Ghost has been replaced with a man speaking for him in a natural temple. Instead of one body, there are now three; the body that serves under the law, the body that serves Jesus only and the body that serves a ghost that's not holy. Now you know why if he did not have an elect, there would be no flesh to save. I thank God for having mercy on all he has chosen to serve him, beyond this, no flesh will be saved. (Updated for release 11/2014)

THE BEAST AND THE
FALSE PROPHET

We are living in the last days of bible prophecy. God is the same yesterday today and forever. God is revealing the hidden revelations kept to be revealed to this last generation. In this book of chronicles, I have written over a seven-year period, where I sat at the feet of the Holy Spirit to receive these revelation truths. This knowledge, kept to revealed at the end of the last generation, I know may prove controversial to some self-professed bible scholars of this age that have attempted to interpret what was not meant to be revealed until the time was right.

I can only say to those who get to read these chronicles and essays, judge them by and through the spirit of the prophets of old. I myself have been taken back with what he has revealed to me during that seven-year period from 2004 through 2011. Politically, we are coming to a point where world leaders will have to conclude that to survive what will be the inevitable at that time of natural as well as man-made disasters, for the sake of mankind's own preservation, he would have to create a new world order and a planned population reduction.

They will have to enact a peace treaty for the good of the survival of mankind in the form of a New World Order government. The inhumane acts of war that threatened the extinction of humankind will be evident in the signs noted in the gospel of Matthew twenty-four. Jesus foretold the signs at the end of that last generation. God is now choosing out his elect remnant during this transition period to earth's second tribulation where the fullness of Christ in his elect will once again, arrest the attention of the world in the Elijah showdown with the antichrist religions. What we see in the changing attitudes of the people are spirits of Satan being manifested as evil man get worst and worst.

All false teachings and false prophets shall be shown up as children of the devil. *John 8:44 (KJV) Ye are of your father the devil, and the lusts of your father ye will do. He was a murderer from the beginning, and abode not in the truth, because there is no truth in him. When he speaketh a lie, he speaketh of his own: for he is a liar, and the father of it.* We have forgotten what we were from the beginning, just dust. One day in God's plans, he decided to select a place to turn this void into a living thing of beauty on the level of heaven. Only it will be a natural version of its existence. He called this place Eden; then, out of that dust, he created an image of himself, put him in the garden to dress it and keep it. Just as God has his son as his companion in heaven, all the animals were created with companion mates ... so, he took out of him a mate to become his counterparts as his comforter.

They, being spiritual in origin, had no concept of the natural environment they were placed in. When Adam sinned, his mind was invaded with another thought; from that time on he was defiled and transformed into a natural brute beast like all the other animals. He is no longer the expressed image of his father God, because of this curse; he now will be the expressed image of his new father the devil. Before man was created, he was just a piece of dust, no thoughts, no mind, just the image of his creator, God.

He was not alive until God breathe himself into Adam. He, at that time became as God in the Earth to lord over his creation as master of the cosmos and universal things in a dominion capacity as a natural version of himself, acting in the knowledge from his creator, God. Adam demonstrated what one would be like to be born from above. When God breathe on him, he received the Holy Spirit. Adam was the first to receive the Holy Spirit in the earth. The power Adam had was so great the devil chose not to approach him but his counterpart ... Eve, his weaker side.

Now some of you are saying, where is he going with this? It's because I am speaking to a generation that has no concept of truth as noted in the present apostasy of our religious state, the Holy Spirit must give us a lesson in our historical origin to bring us into another preparation for a latter rain. He's making this so plain on the level that a fool or a wayfaring man need not understand. The fact that we were not created having a thought, now you see where the two natures are manifested in sin are at enmity with each other as archrivals, demonstrated in Cain and Able: the first two seeds after the fall. Cain became the devils seed, Abel God's. There was no reason for procreation before the fall; this was a result of his flesh activated in a natural body looking upon his counterpart with a lust he never knew was in him until that moment he desired to copulate with her.

Now you know why he created them male and female; he knew the end from the beginning. Now, you either have the mind of God or the mind of the devil. The mind of God is spiritual, the mind of the devil is natural; there is no in-between. This void in human existence will be filled with our lying father, the devil. That's where we will see the sum of these two bodies against each other as in Cain and Abel. This warfare between these seeds from the same house will cause the destruction of the Earth in the end if God would allow it.

Throughout times, ages and dispensations to come, mankind will have to be born again to understand spiritual things. *1 Peter 1:23 (KJV)* [23] *Being born again, not of corruptible seed, but of incorruptible, by the word of God, which liveth and abideth forever.* The incorruptible will be the ones God chooses to carry out his sovereign will in the Earth, such as Abel replaced by Seth. *Matthew 7:14-16 (KJV)* [14] *Because strait is the gate, and narrow is the way, which leadeth unto life, and few there be that find it.* [15] *Beware of false prophets, which come to you in sheep's clothing, but inwardly they are ravening wolves.* [16] *Ye shall know them by their fruits. Do men gather grapes of thorns, or figs of thistles?*

We are born as puppets in the hands of the devil until God cuts the cords by selecting his own, if not selected, you will remain Satan's puppet until you die, never having lived. Outside of God, all your life will be measured in the accomplishments of the natural world. We spend our energies chasing after the elusive meager elements of this world that will pass away and take you with them. The one book man refuses to study will be the book that judges him. The history of the world has been written in the bible. It is a great mystery that only God through the Holy Spirit can help you understand. That's why we must be born again to have the ability to understand spiritual things. Now let's examine the thought process of man to determine the source of the branch that produces his fruit. This will be the only distinction between the two bodies.

The revelation of the perfect will of God is revealed by the Holy Spirit as **"The Mystery of Iniquity and the Mystery of Godliness."** These scriptures show the contrast of our daily walk in truth *2 Thessalonians 2:7 (KJV)* [7] *For the mystery of iniquity doth already work: only he who now letteth will let, until he be taken out of the way. 1 Timothy 3:16 (KJV)* [16] *And without controversy great is the mystery of godliness: God was manifest in the flesh, justified in the Spirit, seen of angels, preached unto the Gentiles, believed on in the world, received up into glory. Luke 24:45 (KJV)* [45] *Then opened he their understanding, that they might understand the scriptures,* When God told me to quit thinking, the reason I didn't understand what he meant is ... I was not fully surrendered to his thoughts that would transform me to his ways.

Psalm 119:104 (KJV) [104] *Through thy precepts I get understanding: therefore I hate every false way. Jeremiah 3:15 (KJV* [15] *And I will give you pastors according to mine heart, which shall feed you with knowledge and understanding. Psalm 1:1-6 (KJV)* [1] *Blessed is the man that walketh not in the counsel of the ungodly, nor standeth in the way of sinners, nor sitteth in the seat of the scornful.* [2] *But his delight is in thelaw of the LORD; and in his law doth he meditate day and night.* [3] *And he shall be like a tree planted by the rivers of water, that bringeth forth his fruit in his season; his leaf also shall not wither; and whatsoever he doeth shall prosper.* [4] *The ungodly are not so: but are like the chaff which the wind driveth away.* [5] *Therefore the ungodly shall not stand in the judgment, nor sinners in the congregation of the righteous.* [6] *For the LORD knoweth the way of the righteous: but the way of the ungodly shall perish. 1 John 2:20 (KJV)* [20] *But ye have an unction from the Holy One, and ye know all things.*

All Godly pastors will be known by their fruit of the spirit that will remain because the Holy Spirit will be their instructor to guide them to perfection. Those that God send will represent God in the flesh and this environment will be known by the evidence of signs, wonders and miracles as people are healed, delivered and set free. *Proverbs 4:1 (KJV)* [1] *Hear, ye children, the instruction of a father, and attend to know understanding. Proverbs 9:6 (KJV) ⁶ Forsake the foolish, and live; and go in the way of understanding. Proverbs 13:15 (KJV) ¹⁵ Good understanding giveth favour: but the way of transgressors is hard.*

Proverbs 15:14 (KJV) ¹⁴ The heart of him that hath understanding seeketh knowledge: but the mouth of fools feedeth on foolishness. Proverbs 18:2 (KJV) ² A fool hath no delight in understanding, but that his heart may discover itself. Proverbs 20:5 (KJV) ⁵ Counsel in the heart of man is like deep water; but a man of understanding will draw it out. Jeremiah 17:9 (KJV) ⁹ The heart is deceitful above all things, and desperately wicked: who can know it? Jeremiah 4:22 (KJV) ²² For my people is foolish, they have not known me; they are sottish children, and they have none understanding: they are wise to do evil, but to do good they have no knowledge.

This is what ungodly leaders will cause you to do by not waiting on God to fulfill their calling, the enemy of your soul will use blind guides through those born from below by seducing spirits to steer you onto the broad way that will cause all who follow them to fall short of God's glory. *Daniel 11:35 (KJV) ³⁵ And some of them of understanding shall fall, to try them, and to purge, and to make them white, <u>even to the time of the end:</u> <u>because it is yet for a time appointed</u>.*

We cannot help God, but many will error for lack of knowledge and try to make you what he himself is not. We know them by their bible name as hypocrites. The man without God is a wild beast loosed in a field of blind sheep; all that encounter him, suffer brutality and death. This beast that man will become has to be restrained by God or else Satan will use him to destroy the world ahead of schedule. Just like the mind of God gives us the ability of God, so will, the mind of the devil gives his children the ability to do supernatural evil. You should by now be able to see where this is leading to in our time, a great confrontation.

I used to ask God a lot of questions until one day he said to me, *"quit thinking and I will tell you what you need to know"*. *Isaiah 55:7-8 (KJV) ⁷ Let the wicked forsake his way,* what he was telling me, I was too wicked and had he answered me at times, it would have destroyed me. *and the unrighteous man his thoughts:* You would have to come into a transformation where he must prepare you to receive his thoughts. *and let him return unto the LORD, and he will have mercy upon him; and to our God, for he will abundantly pardon.*

This will become a new way of life by him exposing your heart and cause you to repent of the hidden evils within him so he can take over the temple. [8] **For my thoughts are not your thoughts, neither are your ways my ways, saith the LORD.** At that time he will purge you by requiring you to … *Romans 12:1-2 (KJV)* [1] *I beseech you therefore, brethren, by the mercies of God, that ye present your bodies a living sacrifice, holy, acceptable unto God, which is your reasonable service.* [2] *And be not conformed to this world: but be ye transformed by the renewing of your mind, that ye may prove what is that good, and acceptable, and perfect, will of God.*

Now you are going to become the new Adam that will do battle with the devil to take the kingdom back by force. *Matthew 11:12 (KJV)* [12] *And from the days of John the Baptist until now the kingdom of heaven suffereth violence, and the violent take it by force.* Our warfare will be between the **Beast** and the **False Prophet**. The spiritual warfare will take place in our minds first and be manifested through spiritually dead souls of the devil's children. The children of the devil's kingdom will be the multitude of souls he will command in his army against Christ; get it, **antichrist**.

These will be in the form of … *Ephesians 6:12-13 (KJV)* [12] *For we wrestle not against flesh and blood, but against principalities, against powers, against the rulers of the darkness of this world, against spiritual wickedness in high places.* [13] *Wherefore take unto you the whole armour of God that ye may be able to withstand in the evil day, and having done all, to stand.* The power of God works by agape love which comes from the father. This is what Christ did to give you this power … *John 15:13 (KJV)* [13] *Greater love hath no man than this that a man lay down his life for his friends.*

The devils power is manifested in … *Galatians 5:19-21 (KJV)* [19] *Now the works of the flesh are manifest, which are these; Adultery, fornication, uncleanness, lasciviousness,* [20] *Idolatry, witchcraft, hatred, variance, emulations, wrath, strife, seditions, heresies,* [21] *Envyings, murders, drunkenness, revellings, and such like: of the which I tell you before, as I have also told you in time past, that they which do such things shall not inherit the kingdom of God.* (Seventeen evil spirits) These are the fruits of the children of the devil that are contrary to the fruits of the Holy Spirit

... This is what will judge 98 percent of confessing Christians to be guilty of sins of omission that will cause hell to be enlarged.) *Galatians 5:22-23 (KJV)* [22] *But the fruit of the Spirit is <u>love</u>, <u>joy</u>, <u>peace</u>, <u>longsuffering</u>, <u>gentleness</u>, <u>goodness</u>, <u>faith</u>,* [23] *<u>Meekness</u>, <u>temperance</u>: against such there is no law.*

After the resurrection, the **"Holy Spirit, God inside you"** ... will cause you to live above the law. It is only in your receiving mode of the word and acting in faith on that word as you are led by the Holy Spirit. Your salvation gives you this power of God as you walk by faith. The sanctification part of your walk comes as you lay aside your sins and weights as God reveals in your heart until one day people will begin to see more of God's fruit than yours.

The curse of Adam's sin, the beast in you as a child of the devil, is reversed at the time of your repentance; from that time on, the mercy of God will prevail by your walking in obedience. God does not need any man's help when it comes to deliverance; what we see are those confessing to be of him having need to die through fasting and prayer and feasting on the word for revelations from the Holy Spirit, given as needed during your training.

Demonic powers are defeated by perfect love. When you are led to fast by the spirit of God, your flesh must be contained and the image of Christ must be seen; the demons grouped in legions, can only be broken when they see the image of Christ in your forehead. It is not that you were perfect; this is a work of God for his purposes. Through lack of knowledge, Satan has got the advantage over confessing Christians that has caused all of us to fall short of his glory. Satan will divide the minds of man into many strange doctrines to keep him conquered. The Ishmaelite, descendants of Hagar, the bond woman's seed of Abraham will reap havoc and terror to reclaim his birth right in the last days in great numbers. Through-out each time, age, and dispensation. *Luke 19:10 (KJV)* [10] *For the Son of man is come to seek and to save that which was lost.*

GOD IS DOING THE SEEKING AND SAVING, NOT MAN. God never told you to save anyone but yourself first before he can use you to save others. (Acts 2:38) The beast system of false teaching, through constant warfare, will over time, ware out the saints that had the apostle's doctrine. During this time, will empower principalities to make laws that stop the power of God. *Daniel 7:25 (KJV)* [25] *And he shall speak great words against the most High, <u>and shall wear out the saints of the most High</u>, <u>and think to change times and laws:</u> and they shall be given into his hand until a time antimes and the dividing of time.* All the prophets' messages have pointed to this end-time confrontation. This will be manifested in seven years of chaos that will change the Earth's geography back to the first millennium. In my previous chronicles, God revealed this revelation that Daniel and John were told not to write.

The context on this subject is to get you to see why we need God to reclaim our birth right to live for eternity with him. The bible was written by holy men... *2 Peter 1:21 (KJV)* [21] *For the prophecy came not in old time by the will of man: but holy men of God spake as they were moved by the Holy Ghost.* God set in motion after choosing him a people, a plan of redemption after the flood, wrote the Torah through Moses; now we can be judged by what his standards are to receive eternal life. In the Old Testament, the Beast Man was contained in righteousness. Man failed the test of the law and was brought under the captivity of the Beast-Man. He used the natural circumstances of life to generate fear, doubt and unbelief. The theology of the False Prophet will seduce him to think that he is serving God but, without knowing ... *2 Timothy 3:5 (KJV)* [5] *Having a form of godliness but denying the power thereof: from such turn away.* The thin line of deception is of such that only God can discern it. All God's elects will have this unction. *Proverbs 14:12 (KJV)* [12] *There is a way which seemeth right unto a man, but the end thereof are the ways of death. 1 John 2:20 (KJV)* [20] *But ye have an unction from the Holy One, and ye know all things.*

Many will error on the side of disobedience after hearing God's true prophets and messengers and become unfruitful as the unwise virgins and be given over to suffer at the hands of an ungodly world and be sacrificed to the Beast System. The seven years of tribulation will be the war in the spirit world for supremacy between Michael and Satan. The natural part will be manifested in the Earth among saints and the sinners. Satan's children are as convinced as he is that they will prevail.

That's the nature of the beast man without God, that's what man will become. The end of this battle has already been predicted. *Revelation 19:20 (KJV)* [20] *And the beast was taken, and with himthe false prophet that wrought miracles before him, with which he deceived them that had received the mark of the beast, and them that worshipped his image. These both were cast alive into a lake of fire burning with brimstone.* (Updated for Released 11/2014)

THERE IS NO MONEY IN
TELLING THE TRUTH

Background scripture:

1 Corinthians 8:5 (KJV) "*5 For though there be that are called gods, whether in heaven or in earth, (as there be gods many, and lords many", Malachi 3:10-12 (KJV) Mal 3:10 (KJV)* Bring ye all the tithes into the storehouse, that there may be meat in mine house, and prove me now herewith, saith the **LORD** *of hosts, if I will not open you the windows of heaven, and pour you out a blessing, that there shall not be room enough to receive it. 11 And I will rebuke the devourer for your sakes, and he shall not destroy the fruits of your ground; neither shall your vine cast her fruit before the time in the field, saith the LORD of hosts. 12 And all nations shall call you blessed: for ye shall be a delightsome land, saith the LORD of hosts.*" When we are influence by man's theology, Satan will set us up as gods or Popes in the pulpits. *Matthew 16:24 (KJV)* *24 Then said Jesus unto his disciples, If any man will come after me, let him deny himself, and take up his cross, and follow me.*

Now that I observe things through the eyes of God, the above scriptures used by most theologians trained under the influence of seminary teaching, have with-out a revelation bound and robbed their assemblies by mixing law with grace. This article is designed to provoke the celebrity TV community. I ask the Holy Spirit to give me Scriptures and commentary on what I saw.

The influence of Hollywood is quite apparent among the TV celebrity ministries. I am sure that most of them mean well in their endeavors to preach the gospel. *John 8:32 (KJV)* *32 And ye shall know the truth and the truth shall make you free.* Until I was delivered from myself, self-examination and submission to the word of God brought me into the reality of the real gospel. It was not until I surrendered my will, my thoughts and my ways that I began to understand God's ways. The Holy Spirit is God's mind to communicate through yield vessels; however, many of us fail to enter the strait gate that leads to the rest from your labor so he can begin his that lead you to everlasting life. (Matt. 7:13-14)

If you have been reading my chronicles, you will see that I write from the standpoint of a personal testimony of my transformation in progress by acting on what the word says. It has been by revelations that I have come to know truth, not dreams or visions. Now I see what it is to have the mind of Christ. When you surrender, you are prevented from judging others when you come to the knowledge that none of us can throw stones at each other. This reality one must see to be used by the Holy Spirit ... *Matthew 7:3-5 (KJV)* *3 And why beholdest thou the mote that is in thy brother's eye, but considerest not the beam that is in thine own eye? 4 Or how wilt thou say to thy brother, Let me pull out the mote out of thine eye; and, behold, a beam is in thine own eye? 5 Thou hypocrite, first cast out the beam out of thine own eye; and then shalt thou see clearly to cast out the mote out of thy brother's eye. Matthew 22:14 (KJV) For many are called, but few are chosen. 1 Corinthians 1:26 (KJV) 26 For ye see your calling, brethren, how that not many wise men after the flesh, not many mighty, not many noble, are called:*

When we become delivered from ourselves, then and only then will demon spirits see the image of Christ in our foreheads and instantly move when the word is spoken in faith, if this does not happen, examine yourself as to who is speaking, God or flesh. Unbelief will not move the devil. This waiting process will include fasting and much prayer to break the flesh as Jesus did in his wilderness. I was one of those who entered the ministry without waiting on my calling. I, like many others was sincere but my decision was based on the opinion of man.

Divided by denominational doctrines, theological seminary teachings have reduced the pastor to a motivational speaker out for hire to acquire worldly gain. This present day preaching in my observation through the Holy Spirit borders on a literary knowledge of the word using real-life circumstances, based in logical theology to relate their version of truth. It sounds good, preaches well, but has no depth that reaches the heart to bring forth fruit of repentance that remain. I have observed this thin line of deception by not waiting on your calling to be sanctified, set apart, and sent to the wilderness to die to self so God can send you as himself represented in your body. These are the few there be that find him and make their calling and election sure.

The way Christ taught in the four Gospels in comparison to what we see demonstrated in modern-day theology, leaves much to be desired of truth for this reason … *Matthew 16:24 (KJV) "24 Then said Jesus unto his disciples, If any man will come after me, let him deny himself, and take up his cross, and follow me. Hosea 4:6 (KJV) 6 My people are destroyed for lack of knowledge: because thou hast rejected knowledge, I will also reject thee, that thou shalt be no priest to me: seeing thou hast forgotten the law of thy God, I will also forget thy children. 1 Peter 4:1 (KJV) 1 Forasmuch then as Christ hath suffered for us in the flesh, arm yourselves likewise with the same mind: for he that hath suffered in the flesh hath ceased from sin;"*

Does this sound like you will be loved as a celebrity preacher if you were to come the way of Christ's teachings, *2 John 1:7 (KJV) 7 For many deceivers are entered into the world, who confess not that Jesus Christ is come in the flesh. This is a deceiver and an antichrist.* Except for those elected, we are a far cry from the truth. The reason being, as having my eyes open by the spirit, we have been indoctrinated in denominational sectarian traditions over generations of teachings that we believe are right, some have become self-appointed authorities.

Our **"first impression of the gospel is not always right."** Read my chronicle under that title. This in part is due to many others that are practicing operating in the same traditions. Over the years, I have seen moves of God, but the Holy Spirit revealed to me that they were only in part because we have never reached the fullness of Christ; therefore, that piece we sought him for was manifested in error and the fruit did not remain to the good of God's glory in these movements. As organized assemblies, have we profited from these movements? No, we are still divided by identifying ourselves by what movement you believe in. We really do not know what spirit we are of. This sets us up for another judgment; *Proverbs 16:25*

(KJV) ²⁵ *There is a way that seemeth right unto a man, but the end thereof are the ways of death.*

Now God has set in these end times, a time to send out his prophets and messengers once again to warn his divided body to set their house in order. *1 Peter 4:17 (KJV)* ¹⁷ *For the time is come that judgment must begin at the house of God: and if it first begin at us, what shall the end be of them that obey not the gospel of God? Amos 3:7 (KJV)* ⁷ *Surely the Lord GOD will do nothing, but he revealeth his secret unto his servants the prophets. Ephesians 3:5 (KJV)* ⁵ *Which in other ages was not made known unto the sons of men, as it is now revealed unto his holy apostles and prophets by the Spirit;*

He is talking about apostles and prophets, and messengers, raised up the same way as in the Old Testament. We have forgotten the scriptures that tell us that there is ... *Ephesians 4:5 (KJV)* ⁵ *One Lord, one faith, one baptism, Malachi 3:6-7 (KJV)* ⁶ *For I am the LORD, I change not; therefore, ye sons of Jacob are not consumed.* ⁷ *Even from the days of your fathers ye are gone away from mine ordinances and have not kept them. Return unto me, and I will return unto you, saith the LORD of hosts. But ye said, wherein shall we return?"*

I am a witness, if you are deceived you will never know it until God opens your eyes. Another reality, old long-standing traditions have assemblies still steeped in hidden prejudices, bigotry, denominational sectarianism, and cult like separations that cut you off from spiritual realities. If we are truly discerning the times, most of us are operating in, many are under a strong delusion to think that this kind of division is going to be caught up into heaven. I was influenced by these faith movements in my early years only to find that it was not the course God had chosen for me. I had to endure stiff rebukes and chastening before eventually it would cost me all I had to walk with God. Now I always live in the reality that it will cost me all again to keep him.

The path God has chosen for me leaves me no room for self; therefore, *"to whom much is given, much will be required."* The standard God set for me is total surrender. *John 15:16 (KJV)* ¹⁶ *Ye have not chosen me, but I have chosen you, and ordained you, that ye should go and bring forth fruit, and that your fruit should remain: that whatsoever ye shall ask of the Father in my name, he may give it you.* When I started noticing a pattern in those sent to me to mentor spiritually, whatever was said to them through me to do, when they acted on that word in agreement, they would call me back rejoicing in the answer.

It has cost me many associations to walk this straight path God put before me and I have not found it grievous to walk with him, though it has not been that easy. I got to know him in my suffering. He has always been with me. *1 Peter 4:1 (KJV)* [1] *Forasmuch then as Christ hath suffered for us in the flesh, arm yourselves likewise with the same mind: for he that hath suffered in the flesh hath ceased from sin;* It is not as though I have arrived but having my footsteps ordered by him, I am learning to die daily. I have learned this truth also; Satan never wants you to know the reality of your new creation authority. This reality of knowing that ... *1 John 4:4 (KJV)* [4] *Ye are of God, little children, and have overcome them: because greater is he that is in you, than he that is in the world. Isaiah 54:17 (KJV)* [17] *No weapon that is formed against thee shall prosper; and every tongue that shall rise against thee in judgment thou shalt condemn. This is the heritage of the servants of the LORD, and their righteousness is of me, saith the LORD.* It is not about things on Earth but things heavenly.

That's why Jesus told his disciples' not to carry anything on their journey because what you have is more precious than silver and gold. (Mark 6:8) From that time on, it is God walking in you speaking His words; now who can defy the words of God in a vessel that walks by faith. It is not about building your kingdom but his. There is not another kingdom that will stand against His. The house you build is inhabited by a wolf in sheep clothing. The house God builds is inhabited by his spirit. When the real test come, only those sheep shepherded by God will remain because they know his voice. God separated me from those who did not walk this straight path. I had to suffer being made to look like I was wrong to obey God. We are living in the last days where all this is about to become a reality as God turns up the heat to purify his temples, he has chosen to dwell in him. (Rev. 3:18)

Christ never went around telling everyone who he is; reason being, the father can speak for himself. The title will follow the office. If you must tell people who you are, it is evident that you went out ahead of him. This example Jesus gave when he asked, *"who do men say I am"?* (Mark 8:29) All who God send, will carry a sign of his presence by standing for and acting on this doctrine without compromise will see miracles no man can perform; is not this the sign the apostles carried and as many that received him performed the same miracles when he sent them out. Now these things that shows his acts are written for our learning to the example as the apostles to see the same things when we come together. God has not change. We have been influenced by those who lead us to seek him by using the principles of faith that works without salvation because all have been given to power to gain all this world has to offer by just practicing the principles of faith. *Mark 16:17 (KJV)* [17] *And these signs shall follow them that believe; In my name shall they cast out devils; they shall speak with new tongues.*

When you read the verses in Malachi 3:8-13, here is where I see the people are being robbed by lack of knowledge; you may read this account in the chronicle **"Tithes and offerings"** This is where it becomes a curse when you do not bring the whole council of the word of God to the assemblies that caused them in the early church to sell their possessions and give it all to the poor. That's what I had to do also.

What this revelation of the gospel caused them to do? … Read the above-mentioned chronicle about the revelation of the new creature in Christ that made them see what they had, was more precious than money or possessions. That's why you do not see tithes mentioned in the new covenant because being set free from the world means you are in possession of it as the new Adam restored. Now with God in you, all you need is what it takes to get through the day because he in you has no needs that are not already supplied.

You live in the reality of this is not your home and these meagerly elements have no relevance to your new home in eternity. Being free of all entanglements of Satan's strings that bound you to this Earth, then you will know what being free really means. Everything you get will be a blessing, having no needs that are not supplied; you will seek the welfare of others. This is what it is to be converted in the New Testament teachings.

All who are called to this ministry are separated unto God and are at rest as the John the Baptist being prepared for the fullness to come of the wilderness in the fullness and take the kingdom back from the devil by force. (Matt. 11:12) The days of hard speeches and testimonies with no sign are over. Those elected will carry the same sign as the first apostles because they are hand-picked by God for his full occupation to glorify himself in the tribulation. We have been beating the air in self, many of us mean well, as I did but, we were just debating with each other trying to prove who has more of God. Now let us examine ourselves, repent and wait on God. (Updated for Release 11/2014)

SEEDS OF GENERATIONS PAST

In this chronicle, the Holy Spirit will reveal the hidden evils of generations past. Many of us do not understand that past generations of sin in the bloodline are carried down through your off springs as corrupt DNA, until that sin is renounced in that blood line; therefore, reversing the curse on his seeds. *2 Peter 2:14 (KJV)* [14] *Having eyes full of adultery, and that cannot cease from sin; beguiling unstable souls: an heart they have exercised with covetous practices; cursed children:* This is what you must be delivered from.

Every word in the bible is speaking to confessing Christians, not to the world. If we who confess to being of him do not produce his fruit, where is the hope for the world? One of the mysteries of Adam's curse, Satan took possession of his body to procreate seeds of destruction. This is evident in Cain, as the scripture say...*1 John 3:12 (KJV)* [12] *Not as Cain, who was of that wicked one, and slew his brother. And wherefore slew he him? Because his own works were evil, and his brother's righteous.* The cursed bloodline seeds of generations past can only be reversed through repentance; for this cause... *Romans 5:12 (KJV)* [12] *Wherefore, as by one man sin entered into the world, and death by sin; and so death passed upon all men, for that all have sinned*: Religious leaders born from below will cause you to be in this state ... *2 Timothy 3:7 (KJV)* [7] *Ever learning, and never able to come to the knowledge of the truth.* This is what Jesus told his own religious leaders when they did not recognize him as their Messiah. *Luke 9:55 (KJV)* [55] *But he turned, and rebuked them, and said, Ye know not what manner of spirit ye are of.*

This is evident when our fruit as confessing Christians are contrary to the fruit of the spirit. Many of us are not delivered from these past generational sins in the family. The gospel that revealed these sins has been lost; therefore, we are a defiled body of confessing Christians. These are the types of sins manifested through lack of knowledge… **unforgiveness** which prevents God from hearing your prayers. This will cause anxieties and stress which will cloud the mind of pure thought.

Diseases and **sickness** get their roots from these sins, and you cannot be healed until this root is cursed through forgiveness. Satan's kingdom is ruled in his children through fear. So as a man thinks so is he. Born in sin, Satan's DNA brought sickness and disease. That's what fear generates that's manifested in his sibling as we were all born. (John 8:44) This is what Paul warned the Corinthians about … *1 Corinthians 11:30 (KJV/NLT)* [30] *That is why many of you are weak and sick and some have even died.* The real gospel calls us to come to the only one that can deliver as in … *Matthew 11:28 (KJV/NLT)* [28] *Then Jesus said, "Come to me, all of you who are weary and carry heavy burdens, and I will give you rest. Hebrews 4:9 (KJV)* [9] *There remaineth therefore a rest to the people of God.* The above description in un-forgiveness causes tensions that keep us from rest naturally and spiritually. This causes one worry, leading to heart trouble which is seeded by hidden anger. **Fears** of the unknown are the most devastating to our physical body; it produces tensions that unleash toxins in the body that leads to cancer. As Job once said …. *Job 3:25 (KJV)* [25] *For the thing which I greatly feared is come upon me, and that which I was afraid of is come unto me.* This is what will cause you to overcome everything God will allow the devil to bring upon you and be an overcomer, Faith without fear, doubt and unbelief. That's the kind of faith he seeks to find if you continue to act on every word of his. You see, Jesus represented perfection as the word of God. That's why when he said **"Be thou made whole"** to everyone he healed. Now if you can believe like that so will you and die like John of old age.

God knew Job had a hidden fear and used Satan to bring it out. God also testified of Job's perfection, therefore this fear had to be removed to complete his perfect love in God. (1 John 4:18) Fear activates generational curses where sickness is concern of those in the bloodline that had these diseases. It gives one a view of past family histories in this area. That's why I do not think on the past sins I have been forgiven for. Medical science trace your family history of these dreaded diseases that cause you to fear. *Numbers 32:22 (KJV)* ²³ *But if ye will not do so, behold, ye have sinned against the LORD: and be sure your sin will find you out.* I have discovered that our worst sin is unbelief. All this is addressing Christians for their sin of unbelief which is replaced by fear. Our fears are from unbelief, what it does is cause you to live short of what God has given you; that is perfect deliverance from all the oppressions of the devil. Despite all this, God is ... *Romans 8:28 (KJV)* ²⁸ *And we know that all things work together for good to them that love God, to them who are the called according to his purpose.*

When God has made known to us his perfect will, by us identifying ourselves as children of God ... our unbelief will give the devil the right to destroy us by ... *Hosea 4:6 (KJV)* ⁶ *My people are destroyed for <u>lack of knowledge</u>: because thou hast rejected knowledge, I will also reject thee, that thou shalt be no priest to me: seeing thou hast forgotten the law of thy God, I will also forget thy children.* Now this statement will be rejected by many of you, anything less than perfection gives no glory to God. It has been my experience to see that we do not understand what perfection is? Perfection is ... *Luke 4:4 (KJV)* ⁴ *And Jesus answered him, saying, It is written, That man shall not live by bread alone, but by every word of God.* The only thing pure in the sight of God is his spoken word; therefore ... *Isaiah 1:19 (KJV)* ¹⁹ *If ye be willing and obedient, ye shall eat the good of the land:*

God can only give you what is good in his sight, that's why Jesus always said ... *Mark 6:56 (KJV)* ⁵⁶ *And whithersoever he entered, into villages, or cities, or country, they laid the sick in the streets, and besought him that they might touch if it were but the border of his garment: and as <u>many as touched him were made whole</u>.* He was the quickening spirit restoring all that believed in him back to a new Adam.

The **spirit of resentment** caused maladies that block production of vital fluids in the joints that cause rheumatoid arthritis and asthma. Asthma can be triggered by anxiety or fear that causes fluid to accumulate in the walls of the bronchial passages which restrict air flow and leads to shortness of breath. It can be associated to things around you planted in your mind and if you believe that nature cause it, then nature will trigger it. This is saying what I fear one day may return on me. Being converted is not looking at the circumstances that you already control by the word spoken in faith that delivered you from the world; you now are in control of these circumstances.

The Holy Spirit only speaks life to you. ***Proverbs 18:21 (KJV)*** [21] ***Death and life are in the power of the tongue: and they that love it shall eat the fruit thereof.*** The opposite of blessing is cursing and as children of the devil, you see why we are always cursing each other when God is the only one with that power; therefore, if you take his place, Satan will cause you to curse yourself as a judge with the same words. If you love God, you will be blessing instead of cursing.

Once I was in a religious environment and thought that works are what gained favor with God, I later learn … ***1 Samuel 15:22 (KJV/NLT)*** [22] ***Samuel said, Hath the LORD as great delight in burnt offerings and sacrifices, as in obeying the voice of the LORD? Behold, to obey is better than sacrifice, and to hearken than the fat of rams. 1 Samuel 15:22 (NLT)*** [22] ***But Samuel replied, "What is more pleasing to the LORD: your burnt offerings and sacrifices or your obedience to his voice? Obedience is far better than sacrifice. Listening to him is much better than offering the fat of rams.***

This is a direct result of mixing law with grace. Law will give you a works mentality; Grace will give you a deliverance mentality by obeying the word. That's how God proves to you he is real. Grace is what came after the law to usher in the new covenant that gave us the Holy Spirit which by obedience is above the law because God is doing the works. Read the **Red** letters in the four gospels as to what his works are. Coming from sin to salvation, God is … ***Romans 8:28 (KJV)*** [28] ***And we know that all things work together for good to them that love God, to them who are the called according to his purpose.*** According to our confession, we are now ***"to live by every word that proceeds out of the mouth of God."*** This is the whole perfect man, Jesus inside of you walking perfect as you obey walking in dominion of all things as the new Adam. Let me remind you that the Holy Spirit is revealing the secret of where all diseases come from in family bloodline past generations and the conditions that gives Satan the right to inflict them and where is the cure.

When you have **out of control fear** as in the sudden attacks that we face in life, the adrenal glands cause body functions to stress into energy overload. It is like turning up the burner on a stove when the meal is cooked; something gets burned. You can burn up a whole day's energy if you remain in that state for one half hour. God knew this would cause us to have premature heart attacks, so he put a function in the brain that causes us to faint, thus preserving our life. By lack of knowledge, we jeopardize our health, shorten our lives, cause sickness and diseases and while trying to figure all these things out, not being in a spiritual environment that demonstrates this kind of faith, many will have to go to the world's system of doctors and hospital for a cure. This is where Satan gets to steal your organs that will ultimately cause your early demise.

They now have the technology to detect the problem but only God has the cure. God will have mercy on you, and you may lose an organ or two, but you are not delivered. Satan is having a field day parading you before God Day and night, in fear justifying stealing your organs, and causing prolonged suffering through unbelief. The only power over all these things is the word of God spoken in faith. Therefore, no sickness or disease can remain in you once God has allowed it to show you his power over the devil by standing on his word. It's your own personal Elijah showdown to prove to the devil the God you serve is your deliverer which cannot void his word spoken in faith.

This is how he uses the devil to perfect his ways in us. You see, the devil now becomes the instrument to perfect you because he drives you to believe and trust God though his word which he has said ... *Isaiah 55:11 (KJV)* [11] *So shall my word be that goeth forth out of my mouth: it shall not return unto me void, but it shall accomplish that which I please, and it shall prosper in the thing whereto I sent it. Isa 53:5 (KJV) But he was wounded for our transgressions, he was bruised for our iniquities: the chastisement of our peace was upon him; and with his <u>stripes we are healed.</u>* When you come to the knowledge of the truth, that's when you become a convert in the lord. We are coming from sin to salvation and Jesus has won our victory over our enemy. He uses the devil to teach us the errors of our ways by allowing him to do these things that will later bring him glory. When God has achieved his purpose, you will be delivered if you have unwavering faith in his word. Your test is in his timing not yours. While we are in this fleshy temple, Satan can hinder you, but he can no longer harm you as to prevent what God has chosen your vessel to do. Your unbelief becomes your enemy. God in that believer has proved he is the greater one in him by faith by acting on the word. You must be willing to die to prove his word. If you die waiting on his word, you will get the reward of eternal life because that is what his word is, eternal life.

In summary, if life and death are in the power of every believer's tongue, then the key to walking this God given privilege is to live by every word that precede of the mouth of God. Beloved, I have suffered many things throughout my life. In my profession, I was exposed to many deadly diseases and never was infected.

My Testimony

"I have had a crippling injury and completely recovered, I was chastened with severe form of a skin disease that lasted for two and a half months, diagnosed with glaucoma and told that I was going blind, paralyze from a fall, completely recovered with-in eleven days, rejected by the brethren for my stand on the doctrine, lost a family, all my material possessions and had them restored doubled in this life. (Mark 10:29-30) All this is what God did to confirm His word as real to me; that's why I am in a place at this time where there's nothing that can take the place of his word in me. My only desire is to let Him come out of this wilderness in the fullness of this latter rain."

Love one another, despite what they do to you, think pure thoughts, follow peace with all men and live holy as being a doer of the word by example of good works. Support those that have been a spiritual blessing to you. That's giving into the true gospel that saves and deliver souls. That's why I over time as in my spiritual growth have had to sell-out, forsake, deny myself to support this stand to walk like the apostles did, over the years, all have left me but a few. I have outlived two wives. I am now at the age eighty at the time I'm updating this chronicle, a little worn but not tired, ready to finish my course when that day comes for him to be glorified in me when I leave this wilderness for the last time. It is my desire to experience the fullness of God and see him put the devil under my feet as a fitting memorial that shows him how much I love him for giving me this privilege to have a relationship that shows that he has not changed. He and he alone has given me this opportunity to share this testimony for the last time and go home to live with him for eternity. I want to return his gratitude by letting others see him as the deliverer in me. AMEN (Updated for release in 2/2024)

THE WHOLE TRUTH
SO HELP ME GOD

My testimony

Background Scriptures:

John 16:13 (KJV) "*¹³ Howbeit when he, the Spirit of truth, is come, he will guide you into all truth: for he shall not speak of himself; but whatsoever he shall hear, that shall he speak: and he will shew you things to come. John 20:31 (KJV) ³¹ But these are written, that ye might believe that Jesus is the Christ, the Son of God; and that believing ye might have life through his name. Romans 2:16 (KJV)* <u>16 In the day when</u> *God shall judge the secrets of men by Jesus Christ according to my gospel. Romans 8:11 (KJV) ¹¹ But if the Spirit of him that raised up Jesus from the dead dwell in you, he that raised up Christ from the dead shall also quicken your mortal bodies by his Spirit that dwelleth in you. Romans 15:5 (KJV) ⁵ Now the God of patience and consolation grant you to be likeminded one toward another according to Christ Jesus: Revelation 1:9 (KJV) ⁹ I John, who also am your brother, and companion in tribulation, and in the kingdom and patience of Jesus Christ, was in the isle that is called Patmos, for the word of God, and for the testimony of Jesus Christ. Revelation 1:2 (KJV) ² Who bare record of the word of God, and of the testimony of Jesus Christ, and of all things that he saw. Romans 16:24 (KJV) ²⁴ The grace of our Lord Jesus Christ be with you all. Amen.*"

While at rest, the Holy Spirit has been opening my mind to revelations of the hidden mysteries in the word. What he revealed was so radical to what I was taught in time past, all I could say is have mercy on me as a confessing Christian living in sin. As he revealed my heart, I saw these sins of omission, unbelief and lack of faith; I really did not know what I thought I knew. The depth of this revelation brought tears of repentance to my eyes. This book is an updated version, containing all my completed chronicles in the third layer. My first release unedited titled ... **"God the Same Yesterday Today and Forever"** is a testament to this fact of how I was brought to rest to receive the truth about this more excellent way. As time progressed, I begin to see that this was going to be a layered revelation in stages.

Just as John was banished on the island of Patmos, so was I separated from all outside influences in my life to become a scribe to write these revelations as dictated to me without any dreams of visions, the message to this last generation. I did not know when I was writing these truths that it would eventually become a book until one morning I compiled these chronicles together, I began to see it was a book with a word to this last generation that will be a warning of the coming second stage tribulation of earth's transition to a new time continuum.

This book for me was difficult to write and to read because of the revelations and content. I had no formal training in writing. I am a self-taught computer user. I could get no one to do any editing. To my surprise, it all unfolded through Scriptural links as the Holy Spirit was rightly dividing the word of truth to see how God shows mercy by sending his prophets and messengers to warn us as in ... *Amos 3:7 (KJV)* [7] *Surely the Lord GOD will do nothing, but he revealeth his secret unto his servants the prophets. &Ephesians 3:5 (KJV)* [5] *Which in other ages was not made known unto the sons of men, as it is now revealed unto his holy apostles and prophets by the Spirit;* ... to warn as many that receive them, less we all would perish by not having the vision of the times. God is calling out his chosen elect to reveal the history that will be repeated among the gentiles just as it was done to Israel in time past. Only this time, it will be two-fold in our judgement during the tribulation period.

The conditions that will lead up to a repeat of the time of Noah as to our state at the time of our visitation. Satan has divided the church into many factions, by seducing men to become renowned in academic status, to go after earthly fame thereby deceiving the whole world and the souls of many confessing Christians. When I was writing these chronicles, I knew the nature of some of these revelations would be very controversial to the traditional Christian. I was prepared to take the rejection that comes with being a messenger at an early age in my life. God designed my life to endure a lot of rejection, I spent many hours alone in my closet weeping because he put the ability to take all kinds of abuse like a lamb. He gifted me with abilities that put me into situations and positions that required a higher education in my profession. I never took my abilities serious because for me it was just natural but to those around me in the medical field, I was treated with much respect because I knew how to stay in my place not being formally educated with this ability that was a great benefit to a pathologist diagnostic ability to have a technician like me at his disposal.

Over the course of thirty-five years as a professional, occupying positions bypassing the qualifications, I endured the opposition from peers that felt they were more deserving. I am so grateful to God who gave me the integrity to stand as a good soldier to open doors for other people of color in the south, when I relocated back to my home state in North Carolina, working in an all-white environment as the first man of color in authority in one of the newly integrated southern hospitals in 1972. I had a unique experience growing up, I got along well with white boys my age like Buckwheat in "The Little Rascals." The only incident I recall as a young boy that was racially motivated … I was on my way home from a movie theater when a group of white boys stopped me and gave me a Pepsi Cola bath. I was so dumb to what they were doing, I was trying to drink it as they shook the bottle to spray me with. I heard one say "This Nigger is crazy" … They got back in the car and left. I have never been able to hold anything in my heart against anyone, regardless of what they did against me. It's easy for me to forget and let go. That was my grandmother's character she passed on to me. I won the respect of my peers of an opposite race. I recall when I left that position to take another, how I was so moved by the tears of those I taught and trained despite the circumstances, acknowledged how my life had an impact on them that they would never forget. That's when I saw what my grandmother taught me that I put into action, *"people are taught to be prejudice, they are not born that way."* I saw firsthand what love and compassion can do to change the hearts of people taught wrong beliefs. I became to them as a man of color, the exception. One of the pathologists told me to my face, we needed someone with credentials like yours for this lab to be accredited, it was not my decision to hire someone like you. (By the way, he was of German descent.) These are some of the things I had to hear from those raised in a prejudice environment. You are a credit to your race, if I were going to have a negro for a friend, it would be one like you, you are smart to be a colored fellow.

Little did I know that God was about to reward me in this new position, I was given a budget with the freedom to modernize the Histology Lab I supervised. I can identify with Sidney Portier in the Movie **"In the Heat of the Night"** Mr. Tibbs" In my new position, they called me **"Mr. Riddley."** That title of respect followed me to the end of my career. When I resettled in Arizona in 1988 where I met and later married my second wife. In the year 2004 until today, I was being tutored by the Holy Spirit in this more excellent way over these years of study. Being no longer affiliated with an assembly, God would send the circumstance to test me in the fruits of His spirit. These tests were painful and hard because I did not fully understand the nature of dying to the flesh, none the less, this was the course God chose for my life.

I am blessed in that I have a sister and mother who believed in what God was doing in me and now a wife and daughter that was going to be used to perfect me. Their standing with me during the years of rejection proved to be much encouragement to me in the latter years to this present day. After having experienced what I went through to be at this place in my life. We have a three-cord relationship that has never been broken among these tests. My sister has suffered sickness in the flesh for most of her married life. I suffered rejections, I have never known my mother to be sick throughout her life and is now in her nighties.

I am more of an orator in the word than a writer, that's why now I can see why God chooses the lease among men to confound the so called wise. I have a form of dyslexia that makes me a slow person when it comes to reading and learning. In school, I was considered a candidate for special education classes. We did not have that kind of evaluation when I attended school; therefore, I was one of the class dummies. I am truly in awe when I look at how this all came about; although I paid a high price in my ignorance, only God could have redeemed me from such disastrous circumstances that took its toll on my life. In retrospect, looking back at how I was rescued from many situations and circumstances … God was intervening in my life using these experiences for the good to bring me to an understanding, while preserving me for the purpose I was born.

That's why in writing these books, it's in the form of a testimony as to how I was brought into his presence out of the volume of his books. These revelations of what is about to take place in the world that will be the end of all things as we know it; what else is there for me or you who receive these revelations but to prepare for your redemption. Understanding election is the most wonderful revelation I have ever received, to walk in divine care, not to have a worry. That's why we are told not to be entangled with the cares of this life for the short span we are here.

Being moved in the spirit as to your actions is quite different from being moved by your feelings and emotions, which is our flesh nature. This is where you will notice where compassion will dictate what will be done in the spirit world as being led by the spirit. While we are being used, we are waiting for the day of our redemption and departure from this world. We are dying to this world that shall soon pass away and at the same time experiencing what it is to be contained and used by the Holy Spirit. This is the joy of being delivered from the cares of this life to know that what will happen to us in this body is happening to Jesus all over again, this time in you. His words are alive to me; my ability to love unconditionally in any circumstance is a testament of his love in me.

I have found that his work in me when I surrendered, will speak for itself through those around you who needed to see and ensample to what this life is all about. These are some of the things God brought to my mind that I was not always aware of what he was doing at those times in these circumstances of my life.

At age twenty-one, I was called to go to war in Vietnam, a Jewish doctor told me this war is not for you and signed my papers that sent me back home. Over these years, this is how I saw God was protecting me. In my profession, I was exposed to a highly contagious deadly disease that did not infect me; exposed to Tuberculosis many times while performing autopsies but tested negative.

Took a flu shot and nearly died from it but refused to be hospitalized, cured from Shingles completely in six days. Diagnosed with Glaucoma and told I was going blind at age fifty-five. Suffered a massive Hematoma in the back of my head because of a fall that paralyzed me from the neck down and told I would not walk normal again, recovered completely in eleven days, A victim of a head-on auto crash that left my wife with broken bones, I was removed without a scratch or an injury. He has proved to be the greater one in me when I was unaware of many of these situations could have taken me out.

After experiencing what God did to protect me, as I reflect in the awe of having been brought to this place, when I had no knowledge of what he was doing until my eyes were open to this to see these revelations that cost me everything to be at this place in him, to God be the glory. When he separated me from those I ministered with, I knew why but could not explain to the point of their understanding because God open my eyes to see their faults that if I continued these attachments, would influence what he was about to finish in me.

When I had my visitation with Satan in a motel room after being left behind by the evangelistic group, I came to Arizona in early 1988. That experience would have taken the life right out of me if God had not allowed it. Satan's presents is too horrible to describe; ... the evil in him will take the life right out of you. God gave me that experience so I would know he is the only one that can save me from him. I have walked into everything he told me I would. My God gifted profession gave me a talent that physicians could see and recognize these talents being used to their benefit as a gifted medical and autopsy Assistant. All they had to do was tell me the medical history and what they were seeking to find, I could dissect that area of the body to pinpoint the revelations from a medical standpoint. I knew where to find every organ in the body and its function.

God retired me in 2005 from **Burrow Neurological Institute** in Phoenix Arizona; after, where I begin writing these chronicles. After the death of my second wife in October 2020, it was during those years we became a work in progress as God used her to keep me focused. I know that not long, my course will soon be finished ... like Paul, I am preparing my vessel to be offered up in glory as a soldier in this army that shall glorify him for the last time in my mortal body in victory. Only the Holy Spirit can declare the whole truth through those God has chosen to deliver his testimony. That's' why I refer this to having my Enoch moments. I thank God who sent my wife in my life as a companion to preserve me in this wilderness for the pass thirty-two years. In preparing me, she saw what God was doing in me an held me to a higher standard that kept me on the straight and narrow. In her own words before she passed, she said, I got to have my own Abraham. I am now one month from the age of seventy-eight, in excellent health at the time of this update. To God be the glory. (Updated for release in 9/2021)

WHY DO BAD THINGS HAPPEN TO GOOD PEOPLE?

What is the devil here to do?

John 10:10 (KJV) [10] *The thief cometh not, but for to steal, and to kill, and to destroy: I am come that they might have life, and that they might have it more abundantly.*

Why must we suffer?

1 Peter 4:12 (KJV) [12] *Beloved, think it not strange concerning the fiery trial which is to try you, as though some strange thing happened unto you:* In my observations, when it comes to suffering, it is not the nature of the natural man to willingly suffer. This is where I see the church have left the foundation laid by Christ. Love of him will enable you to suffer as he did because he is the only one that can save you by walking in his footsteps. You already have the victory. Being on devil territory, your trial is in believing that he does not have the rights to what is yours. Therefore ... *Matthew 11:12 (KJV)* [12] *And from the days of John the Baptist until now the kingdom of heaven suffereth violence, and the violent take it by force.* The strength of your love and faith is the test. *1 Thessalonians 3:4 (KJV)* [4] *For verily, when we were with you, we told you before that we should suffer tribulation; even as it came to pass, and ye know.* You suffer because you represent good in the presents of evil. The seeds of enmity cause those in sin to persecute you when you show up the devil in them that are not ready to change.

They are not comfortable in your presence. *2 Timothy 3:12 (KJV)* [12] *Yea, and all that will live godly in Christ Jesus shall suffer persecution.* That is why you are singled out by those who hate what you represent.

Revelation 2:10 (KJV) [10] *Fear none of those things which thou shalt suffer: behold, the devil shall cast some of you into prison, that ye may be tried; and ye shall have tribulation ten days: <u>be thou faithful unto death</u>, and I will give thee a crown of life.* This type of suffering will become the ultimate test of endurance unto death. It may come in these forms, sickness, infirmities, circumstances beyond your control or whatever God will allow to keep you looking to him unto death. He knows us better than we know ourselves and will not suffer you more than you can bare, even unto death. *Acts 14:22 (KJV)* [22] *Confirming the souls of the disciples, and exhorting them to continue in the faith, and that we must through much tribulation enter into the kingdom of God.*

What does suffering produce?

Galatians 5:22-23 (KJV) [22] **But the fruit of the Spirit is love, joy, peace, longsuffering, gentleness, goodness, faith,** [23] **Meekness, temperance: against such there is no law.** If you want to be like Christ, you must surrender your will so he can produce his fruits in you. You will only show what you have given place to.

What one must be ready to do?

Isaiah 55:7-8 (NKJV) [7] *Let the wicked forsake his way, And the unrighteous man his thoughts; Let him return to the LORD, And He will have mercy on him; And to our God, For He will abundantly pardon.* [8] *"For My thoughts are not your thoughts, nor are your ways My ways," says the LORD. 1 Corinthians 15:31 (KJV)* [31] *I protest by your rejoicing which I have in Christ Jesus our Lord, I die daily.* I must admit this, sadly, in all the time I spent going to the assemblies, no one delt with these sins of omission as they apply to Christians. That's where I came into the revelation of what it is to be born from below. That thin line of deception is hidden in unrepented sins of omission. Let us all examine ourselves because these sins below are still found in confessing Christians.

Galatians 5:19-21 (KJV) [19] *Now the works of the flesh are manifest, which are these; <u>Adultery, fornication, uncleanness, lasciviousness</u>,* [20] *Idolatry,* *witchcraft, hatred, variance, emulations, wrath, strife, seditions, heresies,* [21] *Envyings, murders, drunkenness, revellings, and such like: of the which I tell you before, as I have also told you in time past, that they which do such things shall not inherit the kingdom of God.* Now you know why he said … *Luke 6:46 (NKJV)* [46] *"But why do you call Me 'Lord, Lord,' and do not do the things which I say? Matthew 7:21 (NKJV)* [21] *"Not everyone who says to Me, 'Lord, Lord,' shall enter the kingdom of heaven, but he who does the will of My Father in heaven. Matthew 7:22 (NKJV)* [22] *Many will say to Me in that day, 'Lord, Lord, have we not prophesied in Your name, cast out demons in Your name, and done many wonders in Your name?' Matthew 7:23 (NKJV)* [23] *And then I will declare to them, 'I never knew you; depart from Me, you who practice lawlessness!'* These are the sins that will keep you from having eternal life if not confessed and forsaken before you die. Amen

(Completed for print 10/2014)

WHICH GODS DO YOU SERVE?

Background Scriptures:

The Holy Spirit speaks out of the volumes of the word

Luke 18:8 (KJV) ⁸ *I tell you that he will avenge them speedily. Nevertheless, when the Son of man cometh, shall he find faith on the earth? Jeremiah 33:3 (KJV/NLT)* ³ *Call unto me, and I will answer thee, and shew thee great and mighty things, which thou knowest not.* **Jeremiah 33:3 (NLT)** ³ **Ask me and I will tell you remarkable secrets you do not know about things to come.** *1 Thessalonians 4:11 (KJV)* ¹¹ *And that ye study to be quiet, and to do your own business, and to work with your own hands, as we commanded you;* **1 Thessalonians 4:11 (NLT)** ¹¹ **Make it your goal to live a quiet life, minding your own business and working with your hands, just as we instructed you before.** *Psalm 46:10 (KJV)* ¹⁰ *Be still and know that I am God: I will be exalted among the heathen, I will be exalted in the earth. Jeremiah 24:7 (KJV)* ⁷ *And I will give them an heart to know me, that I am the Lord: and they shall be my people, and I will be their God: for they shall return unto me with their whole heart. Hebrews 8:10 (KJV)* ¹⁰ *For this is the covenant that I will make with the house of Israel after those days, saith the Lord; I will put my laws into their mind and write them in their hearts: and I will be to them a God, and they shall be to me a people. James 4:7 (KJV)* ⁷ *Submit yourselves therefore to God.*

Resist the devil, and he will flee from you. Romans 8:27 (KJV) [27] *And he that searcheth the hearts knoweth what is the mind of the Spirit, because he maketh intercession for the saints according to the will of God.* **Romans 8:27 (NLT)** [27] **And the Father who knows all hearts knows what the Spirit is saying, for the Spirit pleads for us believers in harmony with God's own will.** *Romans 15:6 (KJV)* [6] *That ye may with one mind and one mouth glorify God, even the Father of our Lord Jesus Christ. 1 Thessalonians 5:23 (KJV)* [23] *And the very God of peace sanctify you wholly; and I pray God your whole spirit and soul and body be preserved blameless unto the coming of our Lord Jesus Christ.*

The Holy Spirit speaks through the above scriptures to lay the background and foundation as to how to approach God to receive answers to the questions that will give you perfect peace. When it comes to Christianity, there is a discernable lack of knowledge regarding the perfect will of God. You have heard me explain in other chronicles how I came to know the secrets to understanding the perfect will of God. You must learn that it is not about you but all about God. As I have said before, the key is the surrender of self and your will.

There are so many things God wants to tell us about heavenly things that are far beyond the things of this world; that is why he requires our complete attention to be on him and in him. *Isaiah 50:7 (KJV)* [7] *For the Lord GOD will help me; therefore, shall I not be confounded: therefore, have I set my face like a flint, and I know that I shall not be ashamed.* God wants us to know all about him so he can show others around you who he is when you are not ashamed of him. *Colossians 4:6 (KJV)* [6] *Let your speech be always with grace, seasoned with salt, that ye may know how ye ought to answer every man.* It is in our surrendered state that the Holy Spirit will have an answer for those who inquire of Him not you; if your body belongs to him then he is speaking for himself. Now that He has laid the background to answer some of the most common questions, let's perform a self-examination to see in whom or what you believe in.

Question: #1

Why do bad things always happen to good people?

Answer:

1 Peter 4:12 (KJV) [12] *Beloved, think it not strange concerning the fiery trial which is to try you, as though some strange thing happened unto you:* All the bible teaches about trouble that will come upon those who obey the word is not to say that you are wrong. Remember, this is the reason for study so you will have and understanding, it is Christ who is during the suffering all over; this time in your body when you surrender your will. *2 Timothy 3:12 (KJV)* [12] *Yea, and all that will live godly in Christ Jesus shall suffer persecution. Psalm 94:13 (KJV)* [13] *That thou mayest give him rest from the days of adversity, until the pit be digged for the wicked.* It is his ability through your love for him that will enable you to suffer, not being a shame.

Question: #2

Why do we still get sick and die as Christians?

Answer:

2 Thessalonians 3:2 (KJV) [2] *And that we may be delivered from unreasonable and wicked men: for all men have not faith. Matthew 9:29 (KJV)* [29] *Then touched he their eyes, saying, according to your faith be it unto you. Mark 11:22 (KJV)* [22] *And Jesus answering saith unto them, Have faith in God.* We are called to live and walk by faith in the spoken word of God in the finished works of Christ. We all are capable of walking in the fullness of what Christ delivered us from, sickness and diseases with the devil under your feet. *1 Peter 2:24 (KJV)* [24] *Who his own self bare our sins in his own body on the tree, that we, being dead to sins, should live unto righteousness: by whose stripes ye were healed.*

A good explanation of the works of the devil is explained in Deut. 28:15 through the end of the chapter. The first through the fifteenth verse of this chapter is the promise to those that obey. Now let's see what Paul said in ... *1 Corinthians 11:24-30 (KJV/NLT)* [24] *And when he had given thanks, he brake it, and said, Take, eat: this is my body, which is broken for you: this do in remembrance of me.* ²⁵ *After the same manner also he took the cup, when he had supped, saying, this cup is the new testament in my blood: this do ye, as oft as ye drink it, in remembrance of me.* ²⁶ *For as often as ye eat this bread, and drink this cup, ye do shew the Lord's death till he come.* ²⁷ <u>*Wherefore whosoever shall eat this bread, and drink this cup of the Lord, unworthily, shall be guilty of the body and blood of the Lord.*</u> ²⁸ *But let a man examine himself, and so let him eat of that bread, and drink of that cup.* ²⁹ *For he that eateth and drinketh unworthily, eateth and drinketh damnation to himself, not discerning the Lord's body.* <u>30 *For this cause many are weak and sickly among you, and many sleep.*</u>

1 Corinthians 11:24-30 (NLT) ²⁴ *and gave thanks to God for it. Then he broke it in pieces and said, "This is my body, which is given for you. Do this to remember me."* ²⁵ *In the same way, he took the cup of wine after supper, saying, "This cup is the new covenant between God and his people—an agreement confirmed with my blood. Do these to remember me as often as you drink it?"* ²⁶ *For every time you eat this bread and drink this cup, you are announcing the Lord's death until he comes again.* ²⁷ *So anyone who eats this bread or drinks this cup of the Lord unworthily is guilty of sinning against the body and blood of the Lord.* ²⁸ *That is why you should examine yourself before eating the bread and drinking the cup.* ²⁹ *For if you eat the bread or drink the cup without honoring the body of Christ, you are eating and drinking God's judgment upon yourself.* ³⁰ *That is why many of you are weak and sick and some have even died.*

This is not a ritual but an act you perform before God knowing what you are doing. If you are not ready to give your whole spirit soul and body to the lord, do not partake of this because of the curse that will come on you for lying before God and willfully continuing in sins of omission, unbelief and disobedience, will give Satan the right to destroy your flesh through sickness, disease or bondage to those things you refuse to let go in your past. If you are not ready to forsake all he said in his word that you must, you will not live the privilege of being totally delivered from the devil. Other things will become your priorities and eventually your gods. Just do not deny him when you are faced with a trial; that will keep you out of heaven.

Question; #3

Can we live perfect?

Answer: Matthew 5:48 (KJV) [48] *Be ye therefore perfect, even as your Father which is in heaven is perfect.* What makes one perfect is … *"living by every word that proceeded out of the mouth of God"* (Matthew 4:4) When we say we cannot live perfect, we are denying that Jesus came in the flesh. When we come to the reality of what being born again mean, that is converted, we will not willfully be sinning. Under grace and truth, God's mercy is upon us as his chosen and the enemy is used to bring us into perfection by what He allow him to do to show us the error of our ways. You will know why repentance is daily when you see the evils that are in your body that still cause you to sin. *1 John 2:1 (KJV)* [1] *My little children, these things write I unto you, that ye sin not. And if any man sin, we have an advocate with the Father, Jesus Christ the righteous:*

When you are being drawn in by his spirit, He sees you perfect in Christ finished works. If you obey as he leads, you are perfect in his sight. *2 Timothy 2:15 (KJV)* [15] *Study to shew thyself approved unto God, a workman that needeth not to be ashamed, rightly dividing the word of truth;* therefore, if we do not this, we will be … *Hosea 4:6 (KJV)* [6] *My people are destroyed for lack of knowledge: because thou hast rejected knowledge, I will also reject thee, that thou shalt be no priest to me: seeing thou hast forgotten the law of thy God, I will also forget thy children.* You see, when we confess to be of God and do not obey his word; the devil has a right to do to you what Christ delivered you from, the ability not to sin. The devil can cause your children to go astray by being disobedient to God, your children will be disobedient to you. *1 John 2:1 (KJV)* [1] *My little children, these things write I unto you, that ye sin not. And if any man sin, we have an advocate with the Father, Jesus Christ the righteous:*

Question: #4

How do you know you have been born again? I did not feel anything.

Answer:

In time past I associated my born-again experience with a feeling; the trouble with that is, the fruit will show what spirit you are of. You can feel anything you imagine and believe it to be true. Jesus said, **"by the fruit you shall know them,"** or in other words who is born from above ... *1 Peter 1:23 (KJV)* [23] *Being born again, not of corruptible seed, but of incorruptible, by the word of God, which liveth and abideth forever.* The first fruit on the straight and narrow is love. *Romans 8:9 (KJV)* [9] *But ye are not in the flesh, but in the Spirit, if so be that the Spirit of God dwell in you. Now if any man have not the Spirit of Christ, he is none of his.* If you still love the world ... *1 John 2:15 (KJV)* [15] *Love not the world, neither the things that are in the world. If any man love the world, the love of the Father is not in him.*

Question: #5

When we have done all the good we know, why do our children turn and do bad things?

Answer:

Proverbs 22:6 (KJV) [6] *Train up a child in the way he should go: and when he is old, he will not depart from it.* The key words in the above verse are **"the way he should go,"** As confessing Christian parents, we are to lead by example. The bible teaches us to obey the word of God so that we may become examples of good works. We are to lay the foundation for them to build upon that brings stability and meaning to their lives walking by faith, letting them see the source of all help is God. The word taught them by example is what will not come back void. If you are hypercritical in your lifestyle as a confessing Christian, you are casting a snare to be passed upon your children. God has a unique work for each of our children you have dedicated to him; therefore, what God will allow to bring that child to him will be on the bases of what you have allowed God to teach him through you during the years that were to shape his or her character.

Question: #6

Are we all children of God?

Answer: Since Adam sinned, there are now two sets of children. *John 6:44 (KJV)* [44] *No man can come to me, except the Father which hath sent me draw him: and I will raise him up at the last day. 1 John 3:10 (KJV) "[10] In this the children of God are manifest, and the children of the devil: whosoever doeth not righteousness is not of God, neither he that loveth not his brother. 1 John 3:9 (KJV) [9] Whosoever is born of God doth not commit sin; for his seed remaineth in him: and he cannot sin, because he is born of God. John 8:44 (KJV) [44] Ye are of your father the devil, and the lusts of your father ye will do. He was a murderer from the beginning, and abode not in the truth, because there is no truth in him. When he speaketh a lie, he speaketh of his own: for he is a liar, and the father of it. Matthew 19:17 (KJV) [17] And he said unto him, why callest thou me good? There is none good but one, that is, God: but if thou wilt enter into life, keep the commandments." Matthew 7:21 (KJV) 21 Not everyone that saith unto me, Lord, Lord, shall enter into the kingdom of heaven; but he that doeth the will of my Father which is in heaven. Matthew 7:22 (KJV) [22] Many will say to me in that day, Lord, Lord, have we not prophesied in thy name? and in thy name have cast out devils? and in thy name done many wonderful works? Matthew 7:23 (KJV) [23] And then will I profess unto them, I never knew you: depart from me, ye that work iniquity. God's chosen John6:44, Satan's, John 8:44* Now let's examine the scriptures above to see what God has said about this question.

Many believe that all good people will go to heaven, as you see, your goodness will not get you to heaven if you are not born again and being led of the Holy Spirit. *Isaiah 64:6 (KJV) "[6] But we are all as an unclean thing, and all our righteousnesses are as filthy rags; and we all do fade as a leaf; and our iniquities, like the wind, have taken us away. Psalm 51:5 (KJV) [5] Behold, I was shapen in iniquity; and in sin did my mother conceive me.*

This is what God said about us in His sight. If our parents were born in sin, so are we all sinners in need of salvation as Adam and Eve's off springs. Hell will be full of **nuns, virgins,** and **good people** who die not in the perfect will of God because of false teachings. They were seduced by the devil with lying spirits. Read the chronicle ... **"How Satan deceived the** whole world." *1 Corinthians 13:3 (KJV)* *"3 And though I bestow all my goods to feed the poor, and though I give my body to be burned, and have not charity, (love) it profiteth me nothing. Romans 3:23 (KJV)* 23 *For all have sinned and come short of the glory of God; Isaiah 64:6 (KJV)* 6 *But we are all as an unclean thing, and all our righteousness are as filthy rags; and we all do fade as a leaf; and our iniquities, like the wind, have taken us away. Matthew 16:26 (KJV)* 26 *For what is a man profited, if he shall gain the whole world, and lose his own soul? Or what shall a man give in exchange for his soul?"*

I once thought that being good as a Christian will get you to heaven until the Holy Spirit corrected me in the word about what God said is what I will be judged by. As you see, we have nothing to justify our approach to God but the blood of his son Jesus. Even as Christians, our sins of omission by willing lack of knowledge will cause us to miss heaven. *Galatians 5:19-21 (KJV)* 19 *Now the works of the flesh are manifest, which are these; Adultery, fornication, uncleanness, lasciviousness,* 20 *Idolatry, witchcraft, hatred, variance, emulations, wrath, strife, seditions, heresies,* 21 *Envyings, murders, drunkenness, revellings, and such like: of the which I tell you before, as I have also told you in time past, that they which do such things shall not inherit the kingdom of God.*

He is talking to Christians, who depended on their pastor to tell them the truth without studying behind what is being said. That will be your fault, not the pastors. The real Holy Spirit will not guide you wrong and there is a false one in them that are born from below under these false doctrines as you see by the fruits above. That's the one that have you not knowing what spirit you are of.

Question #7

Do you identify yourself with a religious organization?

Answer:

John 15:26 (KJV) 26 *But when the Comforter is come, whom I will send unto you from the Father, even the Spirit of truth, which proceedeth from the Father, he shall testify of me: John 16:13 (KJV)* 13 *Howbeit when he, the Spirit of truth, is come, he will guide you into all truth: for he shall not speak of himself; but whatsoever he shall hear, that shall he speak: and he will shew you things to come. God told Peter "when you come to be converted strengthen your brother." Colossians 2:16 (KJV)* [16] *Let no man therefore judge you in meat, or in drink, or in respect of an <u>holyday</u>, or of the <u>new moon</u>, or of the <u>sabbath days</u>:*

What he means, God will speak for himself in you and will not identify himself with an organization. *1 Peter 3:15 (KJV)* [15] *But sanctify the Lord God in your hearts: and be ready always to give an answer to every man that asketh you a reason of the hope that is in you with meekness and fear: 2 Corinthians 5:12 (KJV)* [12] *For we commend not ourselves again unto you, but give you occasion to glory on our behalf, that ye may have somewhat to answer them which glory in appearance, and not in heart. 2 Corinthians 5:12 (NLT)* [12] *Are we commending ourselves to you again? No, we are giving you a reason to be proud of us, so you can answer those who brag about having a <u>spectacular ministry</u> rather than having a sincere heart.* No glory to flesh. A sign of false teaching is self-glory as to say, look what I or we have done.

Question #8

Do you practice the pagan holidays such as … Easter, Day of the Dead, Saint Nicolas Day (Christmas), St Patrick's Day, Valentine's Day, and etcetera?

Answer:

Do a search on the goddess Estar. After we come to the knowledge of the truth and still willingly associate Christ resurrection with painted eggs and a bunny rabbit is beyond me. However, I did at one time before I came into truth some twenty years ago. *Exodus 20:3 (KJV)* [3] *Thou shalt have no other gods before me. When you take this stand, you will see who loves God.*

Christmas

Jeremiah 10:2-5 (KJV) [2] *Thus saith the Lord, Learn not the way of the heathen, and be not dismayed at the signs of heaven; for the heathen are dismayed at them.* [3] *For the customs of the people are vain: for one cutteth a tree out of the forest, the work of the hands of the workman, with the axe.* [4] *They deck it with silver and with gold; they fasten it with nails and with hammers that it move not.* [5] *They are upright as the palm tree, but speak not: they must needs be borne, because they cannot go. Be not afraid of them; for they cannot do evil, neither also is it in them to do good.*

Santa is Satan spelled backwards, the god of materialism. In other words, you are seeking the things he offers you in this world on his terms that will bring you under bondage. This seducing spirit will cause you to sacrifice in vain to give to people that do not need it for the sake of tradition and favor. Satan will rob you in the process by putting yourself into the bondage of debt to win the favor of people that do not care that much for you but will take advantage of your generosity. Even in giving, we have not been able to discern to whom is worthy of the need.

St Patrick's Day & day of the dead

Exodus 23:24 (KJV) [24] *Thou shalt not bow down to their gods, nor serve them, nor do after their works: but thou shalt utterly overthrow them, and quite break down their images. Colossians 2:18 (KJV)* [18] *Let no man beguile you of your reward in a voluntary humility and worshipping of angels, intruding into those things which he hath not seen, vainly puffed up by his fleshly mind, John 15:19 (KJV)* [19] *If ye were of the world, the world would love his own: but because ye are not of the world, but I have chosen you out of the world, therefore the world hateth you. Luke 9:60 (KJV)* [60] *Jesus said unto him, Let the dead bury their dead: but go thou and preach the kingdom of God.* These are they who bow down to dead saints and worship their dead loved ones and try to keep their spirits alive by not letting go, open the door for Satan to create illusions in your imaginations that will cause you to see what you want to see. This is a form of witchcraft, seeking the dead. If you cannot find this endorsed in the bible by God, then you are into idol worship.

Question #9

Do you seek to gain all this world' goods for yourself?

Matthew 6:33 (KJV) [33] *But seek ye first the kingdom of God, and his righteousness; and all these things shall be added unto you. 1John 2:15 (KJV)* [15] *Love not the world, neither the things that are in the world. If any man love the world, the love of the Father is not in him. Luke 9:23 (KJV)* [23] *And he said to them all, If any man will come after me, let him deny himself, and take up his cross daily, and follow me. Colossians 3:1 (KJV)* [1] *If ye then be risen with Christ, seek those things which are above, where Christ sitteth on the right hand of God. Matthew 6:20 (KJV)* [20] *But lay up for yourselves treasures in heaven, where neither moth nor rust doth corrupt, and where thieves do not break through nor steal: Mark 10:25 (KJV)* [25] *It is easier for a camel to go through the eye of a needle, than for a rich man to enter into the kingdom of God. 1 John 3:17 (KJV)* [17] *But whoso hath this world's good, and seeth his brother have need, and shutteth up his bowels of compassion from him, how dwelleth the love of God in him? Mark 8:36 (KJV)* [36] *For what shall it profit a man, if he shall gain the whole world, and lose his own soul?*

When we learn the revelation of the new creature, we will not need to carry anything with us but Jesus. His presence is more precious than silver and gold. When he shows up, people get healed, delivered and set free. Now can your material possessions buy that. This is the gift that causes men to give of their possessions to others when Jesus shows up in you. **Matthew 16:26 (KJV) For what is a man profited, if he shall gain the whole world, and lose his own soul? or what shall a man give in exchange for his soul?**

Question #10

Is God first in your thought life?

Isaiah 55:7-8 (NKJV) [7] *Let the wicked forsake his way, And the unrighteous man his thoughts; Let him return to the LORD, And He will have mercy on him; And to our God, For He will abundantly pardon.* [8] *"For My thoughts are not your thoughts, Nor are your ways My ways," says the LORD. Proverbs 3:6 (KJV)* [6] *In all thy ways acknowledge him, and he shall direct thy paths. Isaiah 26:3 (KJV)* [3] *Thou wilt keep him in perfect peace, whose mind is stayed on thee: because he trusteth in thee. The one thing that will separate true believers from those that are lukewarm, they no longer trust in themselves but God. 2 Corinthians 10:5 (KJV) 5 Casting down imaginations, and every high thing that exalteth itself against the knowledge of God and bringing into captivity every thought to the obedience of Christ; James 4:15 (KJV) 15 For that ye ought to say, If the Lord will, we shall live, and do this, or that.* When we fully fall in love with the Lord, we will seek his wisdom in all areas of our life.

Question #11

Do you believe all confessing Christian go to Heaven?

Matthew 7:21 (KJV) 21 Not everyone that saith unto me, Lord, Lord, shall enter into the kingdom of heaven; but he that doeth the will of my Father which is in heaven. Luke 13:24 (KJV) 24 Strive to enter in at the strait gate: for many, I say unto you, will seek to enter in, and shall not be able. To say that all Christians go to heaven is against what the word said is required of all who name His name must do. There are seventeen sins of omission that Christians commit that will keep them out of heaven. In … *Galatians 5:17-21 (KJV) 17 For the flesh lusteth against the Spirit, and the Spirit against the flesh: and these are contrary the one to the other: <u>so that ye cannot do the things that ye would.</u> 18 But if ye be led of the Spirit, ye are not under the law. 19 Now the works of the flesh are manifest, which are these; <u>Adultery</u>, <u>fornication</u>, <u>uncleanness</u>, <u>lasciviousness</u>, 20 <u>Idolatry</u>, <u>witchcraft</u>, <u>hatred</u>, <u>variance</u>, <u>emulations</u>, <u>wrath</u>, <u>strife</u>, <u>seditions</u>, <u>heresies</u>, 21 <u>Envyings</u>, <u>murders</u>, <u>drunkenness</u>, <u>revellings</u>, and such like: of the which I tell you before, as I have also told you in time past, <u>that they which do such things shall not inherit the kingdom of God</u>.* These sins if un-confessed will take you to hell. The word of God is addressed to Confessing Christians as a guide to what God requires to be received in heaven not what you think or feel. *Romans 3:4 (KJV) 4 God forbid: yea, let God be true, but every man a liar; Revelation 21:8 (KJV) 8 But the fearful, and unbelieving, and the abominable, and murderers, and whoremongers, and sorcerers, and idolaters, and all liars, shall have their part in the lake which burneth with fire and brimstone: which is the second death."*

Question # 12

Do you believe every word of God is truth?

Hebrews 11:6 (KJV) [6] *But without faith it is impossible to please him: for he that cometh to God must believe that he is, and that he is a rewarder of them that diligently seek him.* Most people believe there is a God but cannot serve him on his terms given in the word. Every word in the bible is truth. The circumstances under which God used man despite his faults is what people tend to question the bible's validity by not being born from above.

He allowed the weakness of those he used to be seen in them to show his greatness at man's weakest point to see what he can do in and through us. *2 Corinthians 12:9 (NKJV)* [9] **And He said to me,** *"My grace is sufficient for you, for My strength is made perfect in weakness." Therefore, most gladly I will rather boast in my infirmities, that the power of Christ may rest upon me. 2 Timothy 3:16 (KJV)* [16] *All scripture is given by inspiration of God, and is profitable for doctrine, for reproof, for correction, for instruction in righteousness: 2 Timothy 2:15 (KJV)* [15] *Study to shew thyself approved unto God, a workman that needeth not to be ashamed, rightly dividing the word of truth. John 16:13 (KJV)* [13] *Howbeit when he, the Spirit of truth, is come, he will guide you into all truth: for he shall not speak of himself; but whatsoever he shall hear, that shall he speak: and he will shew you things to come.*

The truth can only be demonstrated in yield vessels being made to honor. That is why no one can come to God until He draws you in by his spirit. The Holy Spirit will teach you and guide you into all truth in the spoken word. This is what makes ordinary men become extraordinary human beings. God's greatness is shown in the least of men by his own standards. AMEN (Updated for Released 5/2017)

WHAT WILL HAPPEN DURING THE TRIBULATION SIEGE?

Contrary to the lies perpetrated in the pulpits across the nation, the Church is going to be purified in the first half of the tribulation. If you are new to these Chronicles, please read them before you form an opinion. We are living in the time of the end of this last generation Jesus spoke about in *Luke 21:32, Matthew 24:34 (KJV)* "*32 Verily I say unto you, this generation shall not pass away, till all be fulfilled.*" That generation started at the end of the 1967 war with Syria when Israel took back their capital, Jerusalem. The Gentile nation that inherited Abraham's blessing **(America)** will begin to be judged at the end of the forty years after 2008. The warning would come to the Church on Sept. 11, 2001, that would signal the last seven years that would end the time of the gentiles to rule in 2008. The seventieth week of Daniel 9:24 will be the beginning of the end of man's rule on earth. This transition will be known as the tribulation period.

In the year of 2008, God's hand will be seen by His elects as a sign that he has now taken over the affairs of man and begin to move in his sovereign will. What happen after 08 will marked the fulfillment of… *Matthew 24:8 (KJV)* "*8 All these are the beginning of sorrows.*" The time of the gentiles is now coming to an end. We are now entering the season of the tribulation. The head domino **America** is about to fall and so will all her enemies after God has allowed them to destroy her. In my sessions with the Holy Spirit, God gave me a revelation that showed His other side. They rejected the true prophet's vision; therefore, Satan has kept this from the present-day church by false teachings and the doctrine to live godly is to gain.

The principals that do not require salvation to get results, just what Satan told Jesus in the wilderness in … *Matthew 4:9 (KJV)* *"⁹ And saith unto him, all these things will I give thee, if thou wilt fall down and worship me."* All Satan had to do is, press the church into divisions that will remove the apostle's doctrine that laid the foundation to holiness, something the devil cannot get around. This deception in the form of a false sense of reality and security is where we find ourselves as a divided body about to be brought into judgment when this becomes apparent of our state of apostasy. *Revelation 3:17-18 (KJV)* *"¹⁷ Because thou sayest, I am rich, and increased with goods, and have need of nothing; and knowest not that thou art wretched, and miserable, and poor, and blind, and naked: ¹⁸ I counsel thee to buy of me gold tried in the fire, that thou mayest be rich; and white raiment, that thou mayest be clothed, and that the shame of thy nakedness do not appear; and anoint thine eyes with eye salve, that thou mayest see."* My beloved brothers and sisters, these verses without a shadow of doubt confirmed the last day Church will be purified in the first half by the fires of tribulation. What the world will see along with a willingly blind Church, what the devil failed to tell them when they were seduced, the price of delusion. What it is to name the name of the lord and not depart from iniquity. This is the other side of God that the Church has failed to see. All the prophecies unfolding currently are events under God's control, using the devil to carry them out.

 If we are listening and watching as elects, we have no alternative but to die to self. Our country has the curse of Sodomy on it, legalized under President #44's watch as king of the free world. Though God revealed this to me years ago while studying the book of Revelation, when I got to this chapter, if I were not prepared, I would have gotten sick at what was revealed to me. *Revelation 10:4 (KJV)* *"⁴ And when the seven thunders had uttered their voices, I was about to write: and I heard a voice from heaven saying unto me, seal up those things which the seven thunders uttered, and write them not."*

What I was told was only reserved to be revealed just before the tribulation begins. Whether you believe it or not, we as a body divided into parts of the truth, building our separate kingdoms in what God has allowed in His permissive will. We will see many natural disasters in this nation and around the world as signs of His coming. Many of you will stumble at this statement, the beginning stages of the tribulation are upon us. This was the only revelation I was given about the **Seven Thunders** at that time. The children of disobedience that were prayed for as unwise virgins, will experience the **first thunder** for rejecting God's messengers.

During the years of 2009+, the coming chaos in this nation will lead to marshal law being declared in major cities. This judgment will begin under President #44's watch when he legalized Homosexuality. The parables of the wise virgins are those who saw this act of abomination legalized in a Christian nation, refused to take a stan as a unified church body against that declaration, brought the judgement. The foolish virgins, mixed with the tares, became the children of disobedient, luke-warmers, will spiritually be outside of the gate of refuge. Those that the intercessors prayed for by name, will be delivered into the hands of Satan for the destruction of their flesh that their souls might be saved. Paul gave us this revelation in ... *1 Corinthians 5:5 (KJV) "⁵ To deliver such an one unto Satan for the destruction of the flesh, that the spirit may be saved in the day of the Lord Jesus. Jeremiah 5:12 (KJV) ¹² They have belied the LORD, and said, it is not he; neither shall evil come upon us; neither shall we see sword nor famine:"* Those that did not believe we are going through tribulation will boast in their ignorance. Beloved, this is that time that we will see as elects much sorrow for these fellow saints who find themselves in that 98 percent predicament. I, like Jeremiah, find myself at times, lamenting over what I see coming that many are not prepared to endure.

These are the prayers of the saints being answered for our loved ones. Because we laid downed our lives when we were called, just as Jesus did, our sacrifice for them will cause them to be saved. In the meantime, this is what they will suffer for their disobedience along with the world; amid **famine, death, widespread diseases, bloodshed, war and natural disasters as in Revelation six** to where mass graves will have to be used to bury the dead. God will give us a view of this scene in the coming pandemic where death will take over a hundred thousand lives in a short period of time. We will see men as brute beast result to a two-fold brutality that will exceed the evils we saw manifested in Hitler when the famine comes to your doors ... *Isaiah 36:12 (KJV) "¹² But Rabshakeh said, Hath my master sent me to thy master and to thee to speak these words? hath he not sent me to the men that sit upon the wall, that they may eat their own dung, and drink their own piss* *with you?" Jeremiah 5:12 (KJV/NLT)* [12] *They have lied about the Lord and said, 'He won't bother us! No disasters will come upon us. There will be no war or famine. Jeremiah 19:9 (KJV)* ["9] *And I will cause them to eat the flesh of their sons and the flesh of their daughters, and they shall eat everyone the flesh of his friend* in the siege *and straitness, wherewith their enemies, and they that seek their* lives, shall straiten them. *Ezekiel 5:10 (KJV)* ["10] *Therefore the fathers shall eat the sons in the midst of thee, and the sons shall eat their fathers; and* I will execute judgments in thee, *and the whole remnant of thee will I scatter into all the winds."* This is an insight of what will be happening during the seven thunders in the book of revelation. This is what John saw that the lord would not let be written at that time. It will be sealed until the last generation of gentiles. Now you are that generation that will get to see the other side of **sinners in the hands of an angry God.** They are being delivered up for the destruction of their flesh to get to heaven for their disobedience and some will become food in times of famine. *Micah 3:3 (KJV)* [3] *Who also* eat the flesh of my people, *and flay their skin from off them; and they break their bones, and chop them in pieces, as for the pot, and as flesh within the caldron.* (A pot used for cooking human remains.)

These scriptures are taken from New Living Translation [second edition] for clarity. Compare to King James.

<u>This is History being repeated upon the Gentiles</u>

Matthew 24:19 (KJV/NLT) "[19] **How terrible it will be for pregnant women and for nursing mothers in those days. Deuteronomy 28:57 (KJV/NLT)** [57] **She will hide from them the afterbirth and the new baby she has borne, so that she herself can secretly eat them. She will have nothing else to eat during the siege and terrible distress that your enemy will inflict on all your towns."** History repeats itself in cycles of time, as with the Jews in their siege for their disobedience so will we. <u>Deuteronomy 28:53-56 (NLT)</u> [53] **"The siege and terrible distress of the enemy's attack will be so severe that you will eat the flesh of your own sons and daughters, whom the Lord your God has given you.** [54] **The most tenderhearted man among you will have no compassion for his own brother, his beloved wife, and his surviving children.** [55] **He will refuse to share with them the flesh he is devouring—the flesh of one of his own children—because he has nothing else to eat during the siege and terrible distress that your enemy will inflict on all your towns.** [56] **The**

most tender and delicate woman among you—so delicate she would not so much as touch the ground with her foot—will be selfish toward the husband she loves and toward her own son or daughter."

Matthew 24:19 (KJV) [19] *And woe unto them that are with child, and to them that give suck in those days!* (What will she result to survive ... *Deuteronomy 28:57 (KJV)* [57] *And toward her young one that cometh out from between her feet, and toward her children which she shall bear: for she shall eat them for want of all things secretly in the siege and straitness, wherewith thine enemy shall distress thee in thy gates."* This is the result of a reprobate brut mind with the will to survive, the ultimate spirit of delusion. *"The Walking Dead,"* human beings reduced to brute beast cannibalism. *2 Peter 2:12 (KJV)* ["12] *But these, as natural brute beasts, made to be taken and destroyed, speak evil of the things that they understand not; and shall utterly perish in their own corruption;"* These scriptures reflect horrible times and conditions during the tribulation siege.

This is what cannot be revealed in our current state of APOSTACY. Now to be revealed to the children of disobedience, what they will have to face this as the unwise virgins after the doors of refuge are closed to heaven. The second sickle angel reaping in **Rev.14:17-20** is the portal open to heaven where they will be received. Great tribulation will be in the last half. Since the church will be glorified during the first period and removed by the first sickle angels in **Rev. 14:15-16**, when the two witnesses complete their work in the underworld in Jerusalem. God does not need to reveal what will be happening to those undergoing His wrath in the final **six thunders**, though the mystery is shrouded in the scriptures, just as John did not need to write it down, neither did I at the time I receive this message. It will be much worse than these things I put in print.

The remaining horror is what the wicked will be suffering when the church is gone. This is to be noted about the curse that will return on this country for aborting babies to the tune of seventy million at the time of this updating. The hidden description of the **Seven Thunders** is revealed in my prior two books before this final works went to print containing all my chronicles, covering my Enoch moment revelations as well as prophetic events from Genesis to Revelation, given me over a seven-year period. This is the blood sacrifice we offered up to Satan for our creature comforts, the murder of our unborn children. Our sins as a nation have come up before God. This is our punishment. God will allow the Chinese army to exact this judgment on us. Their army of millions of young men is a direct result of a policy to sacrifice many baby girls to build a large army of men to join with their communist sister, Russia. They made a pact to wait until we are militarily weakened through these vein wars we are fighting and natural disaster that will deplete the national treasury and cause the collapse of our economy.

This is a part of the revelation of what will be happening during the beginning stages of the thunder judgments. This is where time will be cut short to save the church. The Chinese will enter from the west coast during the seizure, they will take no prisoners. Your young wives and daughters will be sacrificed to them as their reward. These young men have never had a woman. The punishment for our disobedient as confessing Christians, will be their spoils to their reward where-in they will be rape by a savage demonically possessed army without mercy and killed. The extent of their savagery is of such as to what they will do to our young daughters and wives, I am forbidden to give the details. This was done to Israel's women in their siege, their babies were ripped from their bodies for food. Many will die in the slaughter as martyrs. Women with child will be killed and the unborn babies ripped from their stomachs to be eaten by the invading soldiers. We as a nation will reap what we have sown at the hand of our enemies two-fold as the double for double judgement. ***Revelation 18:6 (NKJV)*** *⁶ Render to her just as she rendered to you, and <u>repay her double according</u> to her works; in the cup which she has mixed, <u>mix double for her</u>.* This is the curse of Sodom and Gomorrah. This is sad, but this is what happen to Israel in their siege and God would have to repent to his own people and Sodom and Gomorrah, if we were allowed to escape. This is one on the most grievous messages I have ever had to sit, hear and write down to tell the people of this generation. In case you are wondering about trying to prepare provisions to endure these conditions, you will become the victims of trying to defy God's promise to provide for his own as he did the children in the wilderness for not having the faith to trust him to take care of you. If you are entertaining fear now because of this time of uncertainty, you need to pray for deliverance because most of the churched people I see in this state are in that 98 percent of apostasy. AMEN (Updated 6/2018)

MARRIAGE DIVORCE AND REMARRIAGE AS CHRISTIANS

Background scripture:

Matthew 19:6 (KJV) *⁶ Wherefore they are no more twain, but one flesh. What therefore God hath joined together, let not man put asunder.* **Matthew 19:6 (NLT)** **⁶ Since they are no longer two but one, let no one split apart what God has joined together."** *Matthew 19:8-10 (KJV)* *⁸ He saith unto them, Moses because of the hardness of your hearts suffered you to put away your wives: but from the beginning it was not so. ⁹ And I say unto you, whosoever shall put away his wife, except it be for fornication, and shall marry another, committeth adultery: and whoso marrieth her which is put away doth commit adultery. ¹⁰ His disciples say unto him, If the case of the man be so with his wife, it is not good to marry.* **Matthew 19:8-10 (NLT)** **⁸ Jesus replied, "Moses permitted divorce only as a concession to your hard hearts, but it was not what God had originally intended. ⁹ And I tell you this, whoever divorces his wife and marries someone else commits adultery—unless his wife has been unfaithful." ¹⁰ Jesus' disciples then said to him, "If this is the case, it is better not to marry!"** *John 4:18 (KJV)* *¹⁸ For thou hast had five husbands; and he whom thou now hast is not thy husband:*

In my conviction, I have been forgiven and delivered from my sins of the past, having been freed from condemnation and man's doctrine, I am transparent about my life. I am in my second marriage which means I no longer qualify to hold an office under the five ministerial graces while my former spouse is alive as outlined in the following scriptures. He has not changed his word; you are in error and therefore will become a stumbling block. Those that are in that state as pastors and church leaders, does not have the favor of God on them. *1 Timothy 3:2-6 (KJV)* [2] *A bishop then must be blameless, the husband of one wife, vigilant, sober, of good behaviour, given to hospitality, apt to teach;* [3] *Not given to wine, no striker, not greedy of filthy lucre; but patient, not a brawler, not covetous;* [4] *One that ruleth well his own house, having his children in subjection with all gravity;* [5] *(For if a man know not how to rule his own house, how shall he take care of the church of God?)* [6] *Not a novice, lest being lifted up with pride he fall into the condemnation of the devil.*

The qualifications are the same for all officers in the body of Christ, which includes Deacon's verse, **8-12.** I started preaching while married to my first wife. When I got saved, she was not ready to follow the same path. Ten years into this marriage, having a religious background as a child growing up, after having two sons living in a large city, I returned to my hometown and went back to that same religious background I was brought up in. I had no knowledge of true convictions only what the denomination view of it was.

I served well under my pastor on up through the ranks in the assembly, taught Sunday school with a passion for the truth but did not know at the time the error of my ways. After four years serving under elders, I felt what I thought was the call to preach; after all those in the circle I traveled felt it was my time. In the year of September 1977, I preached my first sermon; at the end of which you could hear a pin drop.

This was in a Pentecostal Holiness church use to a lot of hollowing, jumping and shouting when someone preached, God used me despite my ignorance. I am a natural orator in this area and spoke with boldness that offended many that were in attendance. What was said did not go over well with the other ministers in attendance.

From what I can recall, for forty-five minutes, I covered a lot of unpopular subjects in the message from the word standpoint which cut to the root of that denomination's belief. One of which was women pastors and how we have been denying the faith taught in the bible, not a hearsay sermon. I did not expect to experience what came after that night from those I had known and fellowshipped with for years on the ministry circuit. They would have nothing to do with me after that night. Each appointment I had after that night; I was never invited back.

I did not know I went ahead of God and therefore, operated in His permissive will by not waiting on Him. I had a zeal for truth, if the bible said it, I said it, though my conviction showed some influence of man's doctrine, ultimately it led to a tragedy that led to my divorce. Now I have been converted and have nothing to fear or hide any more, I speak as a man freed from my past as being under the blood. I was convicted by God Himself in my second marriage.

All I have related to you who read this as a direct result of that born from above experience, being drawn in by His spirit as the work that God needs no man's help. What I found out through the teachings of the Holy Spirit; I was carnal thinking I was spiritual. I know this may come as a shocker to most of you as it was to me; this is what it is to be deceived and not know it. What God revealed to me that He has not changed one word he has spoken to His creation He set in motion and ordained before the foundation of the world knowing the end from the beginning? *Isaiah 46:10 (KJV)* [10] *Declaring the end from the beginning, and from ancient times the things that are not yet done, saying, my counsel shall stand, and I will do all my pleasure:*

I can but only speak that which I was given to know about myself in answer to this question once I came to this knowledge of this more perfect way of God. I received the Holy Spirit after I was convicted of my state seven years into my second marriage in the basement of my present home. I did not understand what I thought God's word meant and operated as a carnal Christian in His permissive will, when the time was right, He convicted me of my sins of omission for lack of knowledge. He did not have to use anyone else to do this, just His Holy Spirit.

These sins of omission along with many others was a second marriage. He showed me through time how He had not changed His word and gave me an understanding of grace and mercy. This was the same conviction as the woman at the well. It takes God through the Holy Spirit to convict you of sin not man. The reason why I was told to quit thinking, that is where I was justifying my sins of omission. I had to be made to see that by God not man. Most of us are guilty of many of the same sins of omission that has us blinded by our own thoughts because of others in the same predicaments we use to justify our actions who happen to be confessing Christians like you.

When God approach me in the spirit, he referred to me his **friend**, son, **end time messenger** and **servant**, not as a vessel to be used in one of the five ministerial graces. I later found out through revelation that I no longer qualified to wear one of these special titles because of this reproach of a second marriage. If we let the Holy Spirit do what God sent him to do, we would know our places in the kingdom as God has put us, not man.

Second marriages:

Matthew 19:8-10 (KJV) [8] He saith unto them, Moses because of the hardness of your hearts suffered you to put away your wives: but from the beginning it was not so. [9] And I say unto you, whosoever shall put away his wife, except it be for fornication, and shall marry another, committeth adultery: and whoso marrieth her which is put away doth commit adultery. [10] His disciples say unto him, If the case of the man be so with his wife, it is not good to marry. Matthew 19:8-10 (NLT) [8] Jesus replied, "Moses permitted divorce only as a concession to your hard hearts, but it was not what God had originally intended. [9] And I tell you this, whoever divorces his wife and marries someone else commits adultery—unless his wife has been unfaithful." [10] Jesus' disciples then said to him, "If this is the case, it is better not to marry!"

Let's see what the Holy Spirit teach about what God meant when the words were spoken to Christ. We are born in sin shaped in iniquity; therefore, we are victims of lack of knowledge of the perfect will of God as confessing Christians. God did not join many of us together. We were influence by having our senses exercised through the five gates of sin by what we see, taste, smell, touch and feel and the lust that causes Satan to seduce us to use our judgment instead of waiting on God by not knowing what spirit we are of.

We were operating in the realm of the natural man by using our own thoughts. A lasting satisfaction and peace throughout your life for eternity is only found living in God's perfect agape love. You must first fall in love with God as seeking His kingdom to be able to fall in love with your rib mate to have the joys in this life that will add no sorrow.

Therefore, God must do the adding and choosing. *Isaiah 55:8 (KJV)* [8] *For my thoughts are not your thoughts, neither are your ways my ways, saith the Lord. Isaiah 55:12 (KJV)* [12] *For ye shall go out with joy and be led forth with peace: the mountains and the hills shall break forth before you into singing, and all the trees of the field shall clap their hands.*

Adam oversaw all God created, as a new creature, all creation will now bow to you as respect to their creator God now in you; now this is your heritage as a new creature. We have never reached the fullness of God in Christ. Adam's dominion was over all God's creation. *Matthew 17:20 (KJV)* [20] *And Jesus said unto them, Because of your unbelief: for verily I say unto you, If ye have faith as a grain of mustard seed, ye shall say unto this mountain, Remove hence to yonder place; and it shall remove; and nothing shall be impossible unto you.*

This is what you have inherited as a priest of God; if Satan can keep you from ever coming to the knowledge of that truth, you will never come into that place of real peace and rest. God will not send you a wife or a husband to oppress you if you are a converted Christian. Remember, it is your rib mate he will add to you to make you whole, and God only knows who that person is. You cannot fulfill a need that only God can supply. He already knows who's in need of a helpmate from the day you were born. I have seen people who were hurt by their choices of a mate and when they were freed, chose to live as eunuchs the rest of their lives by letting their flesh die because of the pain and heartbreak of that experience.

Others that lose their mates in death as loving couples choose to remain unmarried having fulfilled that part of their life. Just as I in the death of my wife. All do not have this capability, only to those it has been given. A second marriage never corrects the problem you encountered in the first when that departed husband or wife still lives. I was not convicted of the sin I committed as a Christian is adultery in a second marriage. The woman at the well had five husbands when she was convicted that she was living in sin. So, will all who have not come under subjection to truth defile them self in multiple marriages. Under grace and truth, the mercy of God is upon you until you are convicted as the woman at the well, you will have to repent as she did and **stop with that one you have** as to go and sin no more.

If you marry again, after having come to the knowledge of the truth, this is willfully sinning. Therefore, will be cast into outer darkness as an adulterous person cut off from God. Especially if you are holding the office as a pastor. Let me be clear, I speak this by permission; adultery will not keep you out of heaven if you never commit it again once you have been convicted.

You will not qualify to hold an office of leadership as stated in the five ministerial graces in (Eph. 4:11-12). You will be used as a servant because your state will make you a reproach in the sight of those that will inquire according to the scriptures of your qualification that are not in line with God's word which has not changed. Your work will not prosper with fruit that remains if you choose to operate in one of these ordained offices, having two wives, you will become a reproach. Remember what Christ told the Pharisees when they asked about what Moses allowed them to do as stated in (**Matt. 19:8-10**). When we submit to the mind of God, His choices will keep you in perfect peace.

John 14:27 (KJV) [27] *Peace I leave with you, my peace I give unto you: not as the world giveth, give I unto you. Let not your heart be troubled, neither let it be afraid. Amos 3:3 (KJV)* [3] *Can two walk together, except they be agreed?* When we are born from above, God Knows what you need and has said He will supply it. Therefore, if you need a wife or a woman a husband, God knows where your rib mate is and has already prepared them for you. Your footsteps will be ordered by Him not you if you are truly convicted by the spirit of Christ.

Second marriages bring with them not only the sin of adultery while the divorced mate still lives. Your body is already defiled in another's bedroom if you are not a virgin, that will be a wound in the heart when you must face the person that has slept with him or her before you. It carries a spirit of jealousy and envy or even bitterness to those whose heart have been wounded by a departing mate. Crossed seeds do not mix well as stepfathers and stepmothers. This is the price you must pay for your mistake by not letting God choose. It will bring with it, temptations that will trouble your spirit if you do not learn to die. Only when one chooses to remarry after a mate has died and the joining to another is likewise a widower or a virgin is this acceptable in the sight of God. Just let him do the choosing. It is the duty of pastors with one wife to have holy women and men in the assembly to teach the younger men and women the value of chastity as young Christians.

It is of a great pleasure for the woman to present her virginity to the man God will send to her in need of a mate. Avoid fornication at all costs. This is what God seek to give to every believer and what He will add, brings you no sorrow. ***Hebrews 13:4 (KJV)*** [4] ***Marriage is honourable in all, and the bed undefiled: but whoremongers and adulterers God will judge.*** (Updated 2/2021)

A MESSAGE TO THE MARRIED AND UNMARRIED

"This is an updated answer by request in times like these"

God used two wives to complete my calling, this is what I learned as a husband. **"Marriage Divorce and Remarriage."** This is an addition to that chronicle to the young at heart when considering marriage.

Hebrews 13:4 "(NKJV) ⁴ Marriage is honorable among all, and the bed undefiled; but fornicators and adulterers God will judge. 1 Corinthians 7:34 (NKJV) ³⁴ There is a difference between a wife and a virgin. The unmarried woman cares about the things of the Lord, that she may be holy both in body and in spirit. But she who is married cares about the things of the world--how she may please her husband. Proverbs 22:6 (NKJV) ⁶ Train up a child in the way he should go, and when he is old he will not depart from it. Hebrews 13:17 (NKJV) ¹⁷ Obey those who rule over you, and be submissive, for they watch out for your souls, as those who must give account. Let them do so with joy and not with grief, for that would be unprofitable for you."

I was inspired to re-write this updated chronicle on the bassist of sound scripturally based revelation knowledge that covers the whole council of the truth. The truth about the state of marriage today is a result of once again, the fall away from a Godly walk that's reflective of lack of knowledge in the application of truth. Let's be honest with ourselves and to each other.

I have found this place of Eden in our marriage that's in this living in the experience. The reality is, we have not lived what we have confessed that can caused the word not to come back void in our lives and children. We have brought them up to be good but not holy committed to the truth that will guide them when they leave. The mixture of carnality with truth, many of us living a carnal application of acting in our feelings as to use our judgment in decision making that lead to fleshy choices rather than spiritual. Statistics don't lie when it comes to the reality of divisions in the home that have led the church down the road to compete with the world when it comes to divorces.

I speak reflective of this last generation's realities of having a false sense of security and reality. I suffered this tragedy and God gave me a second chance to get it right. Many of us as confessing Christian parents have not prepared them to face the realities of these times with all these temptations facing us daily. Many have become the spoils of seducing spirits we see by their choices that reflect what they have not been taught by example. When God call me out and separated me from the assembly environment in 2004, it was to get my attention that led me to focus on his words alone as being re-taught by and through the Holy Spirit. In my alone time meditation studies, He began to reveal the full council of the word to me that I had never known to this degree. God was revealing His perfect will to me to make my calling and election sure.

These revelations are not new but are what we have strayed from in the application of our teachings. Old long-standing traditions have become a taboo in the ministry of the full council of the word. We don't deal with the details that end up defeating many of us. We have come to the point to go outside of the church to get intimate advice from the world in search of answers in our marriages. One thing I learned from having this experience, He reveals what need to be taught in that time to combat sinful seducing spirits that we are faced with in the reality of our daily temptations. I came to see my own shortcoming as I look at my life in retrospect, now being taught by revelation. So as now settled in this wisdom, I can share it with you that have ears to hear it. The lack of strong doctrinal leadership reflective of what the apostles taught that was administered through five ministerial gifts to the church to make us perfect is what we failed to see demonstrated among us as coming up through the ranks: the perfect knowledge by example. (Eph.4:11-12)

Through these gifts, God will reveal what we need to hear at the appropriate time. Without the vision of your times, these divisions have led to many divorces among us. I became a victim of all these things I am writing about as now being re-taught by the Holy Spirit. The parenting gaps, reflected from a spiritual standpoint, is the hypocrisy our children were exposed too, that has given them a false sense of spiritual realities. What I was taught from my childhood was what my parents were taught; when I came face to face with the world, I found I was not mentally equipped to deal with the temptations I faced, and neither were many of you. The evidence is to see the path some of us took. We are not capable of deciding who we want to live with for the rest of our life; from a spiritual standpoint, most of our thoughts are carnal, that's because our flesh has played a part in our decision making. If you want to avoid making life changing bad mistakes … **Matthew 6:33 "(NKJV) [33] But seek first the kingdom of God and His righteousness, and all these things shall be added to you."**

 If you are unmarried as a confessing Christian, fall in love with God first; then, who He has for you is already planned and will walk into your life as directed by God … **Matthew 19:6 "(NKJV) [6] So then, they are no longer two but one flesh. Therefore, what God has joined together, let not man separate."** Now what I'm about to tell you may seem too extreme, which reflects how far we are removed from truth. Regardless of what you may think, we, in my observations, living in a compromised standard of holiness, God has not changed his word; we will be judged by what God gave you to know and act on that will add no sorrow … **Proverbs 10:22 "(NKJV) [22] The blessing of the LORD makes one rich, And He adds no sorrow with it."** If you want this life changing experience, you must … **Romans 12:1-2 "(NKJV) [1] I beseech you therefore, brethren, by the mercies of God, that you present your bodies a living sacrifice, (First) holy, acceptable to God, which is your reasonable service. [2] And do not be conformed to this world, but be transformed by the renewing of your mind, that you may prove what is that good and acceptable and perfect will of God."** You must let God give you that born-again experience from above to become a virtuous woman or that man of honor, as God's priest in the earth. When both of you are born from above, you will become one in Christ and will follow the word's instructions as to your place here in the flesh.

What is a virtuous woman like? **Proverbs 31:10-14 "(NKJV)** [10] **Who can find a virtuous wife? For her worth is far above rubies.** [11] **The heart of her husband safely trusts her; So, he will have no lack of gain.** [12] **She does him good and not evil All the days of her life.** [13] **She seeks wool and flax, and willingly works with her hands.** [14] **She is like the merchant ships, she brings her food from afar."** Now that's a proverb 31 woman. This is what she will be to the man God send to her to live till death do they part. God put pleasures that comes alive in your most intimate moment that will keep you both satisfied with a strong love bond that only God can keep alive in you both that honor Him in all the glory. The Sunday school teachers are to teach the congregation as males teaching male and women teaching women when it comes to these intimate gender subjects.

Warning, this is graphically expressed as to couples that God put together

These common everyday interactions are to help you in your daily application of the word. The reality of you both coming from sin to salvation is to let His love guide you both as you walk in forgiveness that helps you overcome each other's faults. Your bodies are alive in sin, therefore, there are chemicals such as Testosterone in the male that operate through the eye gate as well as Hormonal activity in the women reproductive system that she will not understand without proper holy advise from another Godly woman. This is that sinful nature that gave Adam a desire to come together with Eve for procreation when they sinned. Your body at that time became sensitive to tempting stimulations that will come through these five natural carnal gates to your flesh; what you **see,** what you **feel,** what you **taste**, what you **touch**, and what you **hear**. That's that flesh part of you that will lead to continuing in sin. That's Satan's power over you as born in sin until you give the body back to Christ. Spiritually, you respond on a 90/10 body function system from a flesh standpoint.

You see, this is the mystery that will make you one in Christ. True love from Christ contains that 90 percent of your flesh and the other 10% by touch activates all the pleasure put there by God when he joined you two together, what you will feel at that time goes farther that the physical act of having sex, it's what will give you that feeling of climatic euphoria each time you come together that will cause you to be content with each other until death do you part. You see, in the lord, sex is a spiritual thing that only God can contain when you both give yourself to him.

Now the husband … **Ephesians 5:25 "(NKJV)** [25] **Husbands, love your wives, just as Christ also loved the church and gave Himself for her, Colossians 3:19 (NKJV)** [9] **Husbands, love your wives and do not be bitter toward them. 1 Peter 3:7 (NKJV)** [7] Husbands, likewise, dwell with them with understanding, giving honor to the wife, as to the weaker vessel, and as being heirs together of the grace of life, that your prayers may not be hindered." God's love is enough to keep you both satisfied sexually and emotionally. That's why you must be join by him. Being in the flesh and coming from a sinful pass, all will not be able to contain themselves in this area, if you are having a problem in this area, God is greater than your flesh until such a time he sees fit to send you a helpmate … **1 Corinthians 7:9 "(NKJV)** [9] **but if they cannot exercise self-control, let them marry. For it is better to marry than to burn with passion."** The pleasure of sexual relations is to be enjoyed in marriage for procreation only … **Hebrews 13:4 (KJV)** [4] **Marriage** *is* **honourable in all, and the bed undefiled: but whoremongers and adulterers God will judge.** Now this is an area of intimacy, some have asked about their sex life before they were married. Being born in sin, some may be born with an overactive passion that causes you to burn in your flesh with unholy desires. Therefore, if you find it difficult to contain, then it's better you marry. God has made provisions for you both that requires you both to keep your intimacy holy without defiling you both by keeping adultery and fornication out of your marriage. Therefore, keep your intimacy in your bedroom for the rest of your life together. Having the right spirit in you both in marriage, you will know what is right and acceptable in the sight of God. **1 Corinthians 7:14 "(NKJV)** [14] **For the unbelieving husband is sanctified by the wife, and the unbelieving wife is sanctified by the husband; otherwise, your children would be unclean, but now they are holy."** (Except for fasting) … **1 Corinthians 7:5 (NKJV)** [5] **Do not deprive one another except with consent for a time, that you may give yourselves to fasting and prayer; and come together again so that Satan does not tempt you because of your lack of self-control."** Here again, an active sex life in marriage must be controlled by having a healthy love fir each other that will help you contain yourself during that time. Remember, we are to love God first to keep from being tempted beyond that you are able to bare.

No husband or wife as a Christian, should let the world compete for the affection you have for each other; women, don't do as Eve and leave your covering by becoming entrapped to give place to a weakness when you belong to the lord first and then your Husband. This is how ... **2 Timothy 3:6 "(KJV) ⁶ For of this sort are they which creep into houses, and lead captive silly women laden with sins, led away with divers lusts,"** The test of your love as the bread provider and priest is to honor your wife in the presence of the opposite gender. Everyone is not dead to the flesh that you may confide in; only God can direct you to that kind of person at the time you need to be comforted. Don't share your intimate secrets between you and your spouse to others; this may lead to a test of their conviction not being in your best interest. Whatever it takes to be at peace, do it. Don't be critical of each other as couples, it shows a lack of love. There's a time for reproof and correction but only in love, led by God. He will teach you both how to follow peace when you study his word together. Never approach God in prayer with a critical spirit, always approach him with a meek and submissive spirit when making your request to Him; that's for all who serve him. These are some things you will have to contend with that's between you and God. I will not forget my wife telling me when I was not treating her right, I'm going to tell God on you. She never had that problem out of me again.

The flesh has a mind of its own as overcoming the desires that were in you as a sinner. **1 Corinthians 10:13 "(NKJV) ¹³ No temptation has overtaken you except such as is common to man; but God is faithful, who will not allow you to be tempted beyond what you are able, but with the temptation will also make the way of escape, that you may be able to bear it."** When I read the story of Hosea in the bible as to why God led him to marry a prostitute who continued her activity during their marriage, this is what led me to believe that God prepares his servants for what he has given them to do. To make a point, his wife was a representation of the state of Israel as a whoring nation in search of another god. All things were done literally in the Old Testament. That was the literal type and shadow of things to come in the spirit. Under grace and truth according to ... **Matthew 5:28 "(NKJV) ²⁸ But I say to you that whoever looks at**

a woman to lust for her has already committed adultery with her in his heart."

When you are joined in the spirit, you will not withhold the pleasures due to you both as being one. That is one of the real joys of being married in the lord. Remember, **Hebrews 13:4 "(NKJV)** **4 Marriage is honorable among all, and the bed undefiled; but fornicators and adulterers God will judge."** Even when you come to Christ after having married, God can still make you one in spirit if you are willing to do things his way. This I put to test in my second time around that got her saved and sanctified, as in ... **1 Corinthians 7:14"(NKJV)** **14 For the unbelieving husband is sanctified by the wife, and the unbelieving wife is sanctified by the husband; otherwise, your children would be unclean, but now they are holy."** Here's what I have been made to see? When Adam and Eve sinned, their flesh came alive for the first time to see that they were different. That difference is what attracted them to come together for procreation by mixing both seeds that will produce the miracle of creating another human in their image. This is a seed bloodline that will become a link to your origin. Only in marriage is this acceptable in the lord. That's why fornication and adultery carry a curse when two sets of siblings are from the same woman as a divorced spouse still lives. Under grace, if this happened before you come to the knowledge of the truth, you can be forgiven. Your desires can now be released from the bondage as being forgiven of condemnation when you come to the knowledge of this truth in a legal state of matrimony. Remember men, the woman came out of your side, not his back.

Study to maintain your place as equals to become one in operation as being made whole in the lord ... **1 Peter 3:1 "(NKJV)** **1 Wives, likewise, be submissive to your own husbands,** **that even if some do not obey the word, they, without a word, may be won by the conduct of their wives,"** When the two of you are one in spirit, it's the most powerful force on earth. Don't look outside of your marriage to find solutions to what God has already instructed you to do. He does not need outside help that he has already outlined in his instructional word for you both; He is in you to give you the strength to endure all the temptations that you will encounter in your life in him; just do it in the order he has set in his word ... **1 Corinthians 11:3 "(NKJV)** **3 But I want you to know that the head** of every man is Christ, the head of woman is man, and the head of Christ is God." This order is where God receives your prayers as a married couple as being confessing Christians. Don't tell him what he already knows about your spouse, you are to come in his love to ask him to help your spouse overcome a fault you are having difficulty with submitting to.

The single and un-married

Now as un-married believing Christians, these are the teachings … **1 Corinthians 7:34 "(NKJV) ³⁴ There is a difference between a wife and a virgin. The unmarried woman cares about the things of the Lord, that she may be holy both in body and in spirit. But she who is married cares about the things of the world--how she may please her husband."** When one chooses to take a wife or a husband, the man must by these teachings, strive to be the Adam as priest of his house, having dominion ruling in love with respect toward his helpmate. To prove this, I put God's word to the test; I wanted my wife to refer to me as her Abraham. It took twenty-five years to hear this come out of her mouth. His word did not come back void.

The wife is to be his Eve as seeking to please not only her husband but learning from Eve's mistake in the garden not to leave her husband's side to shame or disgrace him in public. Men, you must remember to live as a faith servant as Abraham to represent the lord so your wife's admiration will be as Sarah's towards Abraham. Though I was not as perfect as Abraham's faith, but God honored my steadfastness to prove his word. That's what I wanted. This is what you must be ready to do if you are contemplating marriage. I was not taught this in my assembly experience, but God has had mercy on me to re-teach me himself for your benefit. The Holy Spirit showed me about the weaker part of the woman that Satan use to disgrace the male image of God in the man when you are not one. The reality is, you both are different and coming from sin will become a work in progress.

This is where parenting has a lot to do with a child's training as to the right direction God would have them go in their life. They are to be trained by example … **Proverbs 22:6 "(NKJV) ⁶ Train up a child in the way he should go, and when he is old, he will not depart from it."** I believe that the woman as mothers have a special link to her children to produce the kind of child that will not forget what they have been taught. **James 5:20**

"(NKJV) ²⁰ let him know that he who turns a sinner from the error of his way will save a soul from death and cover a multitude of sins." In marriage, agree when it comes to disciplining your children. If you are double minded in this area, so will your children be in their disobedience to you. That's your God given duty as a mother, let God teach you how to raise a child to give back to Him that will bring him glory and make your husband admire your training of his seeds. Read the Proverbs to get a perspective of how to raise wise children. Remember Samuel.

<u>If you are not ready to do this as a confessing Christian God's way, it's best not to marry.</u> Therefore, for this cause, many young men and women in prison are the curse into bondage as the devil's servants by not having good examples in their up-bringing. Always let God's word rule your heart as guided by the Holy Spirit, not your emotions. In counseling, I have discerned, there are some people God did not let them bring children into this world because their emotional state would corrupt their off springs to rule over them and fill the prisons. Be careful not to let your children become the ruler over you as a parent. You will become a victim of this state ... **Isaiah 3:12 (KJV)** ¹² *As for* **my people, children** *are* **their oppressors, and women rule over them. O my people, they which lead thee cause** *thee* **to err, and destroy the way of thy paths.** Don't let outside worldly opinions influence your action to work against truth. Avoid being intimidated by those you once held in high regard. **2 Peter 3:18 "(NKJV) ¹⁸ but grow in the grace and knowledge of our Lord and Savior Jesus Christ. To Him be the glory both now and forever."** We have but a short time on this earth as Christians to get it right so let's not waste time on matters of non-spiritual concerns.

That's why I'm so passionate about getting it right as to point you to what God taught me out of His word as the truth that sets you free. When you come out of the world, these are the things you are to sanctify yourself from as in ... **Galatians 5:19-21 "(NKJV) ¹⁹ Now the works of the flesh are evident, which are: <u>adultery, fornication, uncleanness, lewdness,</u> ²⁰ <u>idolatry, sorcery, hatred, contentions, jealousies, outbursts of wrath, selfish ambitions, dissensions, heresies,</u> ²¹ <u>envy, murders, drunkenness, revelries,</u> and the like; of which I tell you beforehand, just as I also told you in time past, that <u>those who practice such things will not inherit the kingdom of God.</u>"** Some of us are still guilty of some of these sins of omission as I was when I had my encounter, so don't think you are all that good because you have not physically done some of these things. **Isaiah 64:6 "(KJV)** [6] **But we are all as an unclean thing, and all our righteousness are as filthy rags; and we all do fade as a leaf; and our iniquities, like the wind, have taken us away. 2 Corinthians 10:5 (KJV)** [5] **Casting down imaginations, and every high thing that exalteth itself against the knowledge of God, and bringing into captivity every thought to the obedience of Christ;"**

Don't take these things for granted that many in that 98 percent are going to be lost for that reason. The devil carries around a black book to write these things down that you don't repent from doing and use them to justify taking your soul in the judgment. Many of us caught up in some of these error teachings, like to think our loved ones are in heaven. Beloved I don't mean to offend you or cause you to doubt your salvation, just be sure you know God is going to be your judge out of what he said in his word, your fruit of him will leave your testimony, not what we feel or think. After over twenty years of living in the error of sins of omission, I now know that God cannot compromise his word. These things were written for our learning and each of us are responsible for saving your own soul. Let me be clear! I was on my way to hell as a sincere confessing Christian, if God had not chosen me to be called as one of his elects, I believe I would still be blind to these realities today. That's that 98 percent of confessing Christians, I have been telling you I had difficulty believing that will be replaced in these end time when I heard it spoken in a prophecy in 1988.

Get a good concordance dictionary and look up each one that you may be able to judge yourself by knowledge of understanding the perfect will of God in the truth. **Hosea 4:6 "(KJV)** [6] **My people are destroyed for lack of knowledge: because thou hast rejected knowledge, I will also reject thee, that thou shalt be no priest to me: seeing thou hast forgotten the law of thy God, I will also forget thy children."**

These fruits in Gal. 5:22-23, came with the Holy Spirit in those born from above; however, what I have experienced in being rejected for revealing these truths is from those steeped in traditional teachings. They are not the doer of the word. You don't want to be ... **Daniel 5:27 "(NKJV)** [27] **You have been weighed in the balances and found wanting;** or ... **2 Timothy 3:7 (KJV)** [7] **Ever learning, and never able to come to the knowledge of the** truth." so judge yourself on the bassist of the knowledge of the truth that tells you where you are going before you leave here. **1 Corinthians 11:31 "(NKJV)** [31] **For if we would judge ourselves, we would not be judged."**

The church assembly is supposed to be a house of prayer; in this great fall away, this is what it has become …**Matthew 21:13 "(NKJV)** [13] **And He said to them, "It is written, 'My house shall be called a house of prayer,' but you have made it a 'den of thieves.' "**These new teachings in the state of apostasy, many leaders have not let the whole council of the word be taught in their kingdom building assemblies. This is the snare that comes with being seminary trained. They have compromised the truth under the 501c-3 mark and now must guard what they say in their assemblies as now being politically correct by robbing them of their unjustified tithes to keep their assemblies full to pay the bills. You are already blessed in him because he, in you, has no needs and that's our faith in him … our needs are already provided for in him. Beloved, learn to be content through self-denial as dying to self so people can see him in you as a Godly husband or a Godly wife. Our priorities have been misplaced by the cares of this life. Don't forget, being single in the lord is a blessing; indeed, so don't be in a hurry to be entangled if you are not ready to submit to being a husband or a wife, to follow his word as an example of a believer. Being single, you are free indeed, only answerable to the lord and those over you as your masters in the flesh on the earth. AMEN (Updated for re-release 8/2021)

AMERICA'S DECLINE INTO SODOM & GOMORRAH

The decline of moral decadence in America has evolved into another Sodom and Gomorrah. This is what I have come to see through the inspiration of the Holy Spirit leading up to what is about to happen in this nation's judgment. We refuse to heed to the history God has shown us in his word as confessing Christians, how he deals with this sin that is manifested in cursed seeds as a direct result of Adam's sin. Satan can plant perverted seeds in opposite gender off springs by now having living host. When Satan was dethroned in heaven, he became a perverted disembodied spirit that knows no bounds of evil when manifested. Having access to living temples of God's creation in the earth. This happened when he entered Eve in the garden.

This manifestation is how Satan will mock God's male image by putting male dominate seeds in a female's body and likewise a female dominate seed in a male's body. This will cause those born under this curse to become closet homosexuals and transgenders. It is generationally passed through a curse bloodline seed. When this was discovered in the Old Testament, the instructions God gave to his people? *Leviticus 20:13 (KJV)* [13] *If a man also lie with mankind, as he lieth with a woman, both of them have committed an abomination: they shall surely be put to death; their blood shall be upon them. (Paralleled in NLT) Leviticus 20:13 (NLT)* [13] *"The penalty for homosexual acts is death to both parties. They have committed a detestable act and are guilty of a capital offense. Leviticus 20:23 (KJV)* ²³ *And ye shall not walk in the manners of the nation, which I cast out before you: (Sodom and Gomorrah) for they committed all these things, and therefore I abhorred them. Genesis 19:4-8 (KJV)* ⁴ *But before they lay down, the men of the city, even the men of Sodom, compassed the house round, both old and young, all the people from every quarter:* ⁵ *And they called unto Lot, and said unto him, Where are the men which came in to thee this night? bring them out unto us, that we may know them.* ⁶ *And Lot went out at the door unto them, and shut the door after him,* ⁷ *And said, I pray you, brethren, do not so wickedly.* ⁸ *Behold now, I have two daughters which have not known man; let me, I pray you,* <u>*bring them out unto you, and do ye to them as is good in your eyes:*</u> *only unto these men do nothing; for therefore came they under the shadow of my roof.*

What I want you to see in these eight verses, living among this kind of evil will make you passive to the point of becoming like lot, willing to offer up his two daughters as a sacrifice to a wicked mob because he had forgotten all about God's divine protection for his household was with him as visiting angels. Lot represents a confessing Christian that say they know God but lack convictions by compromising to please flesh.

Which brings this to a point of reference; here in the western world, we have sacrificed our children for the pleasures of this world from a spiritual standpoint by ignoring as Christians, God's moral laws against nature. Our seduction did not come overnight to this place in time where it is acceptable in our society. Man, in his flesh, is no match for the devil. He is a spirit being created to live for eternity in the lake of fire for him and those angels that followed him. To get us to where we are, all he had to do is just ware us out to this point of compromise if we never come to the knowledge of the truth, we will be judged unworthy by our sins of omission.

This apostate church world, now promoting this kind of behavior, see their congregations infected with members possessed with these spirits. *Romans 1:27-28 (KJV)* ²⁷ *And likewise also the men, leaving the natural use of the woman, burned in their lust one toward another; men with men working that which is unseemly, and receiving in themselves that recompense of their error which was meet.* ²⁸ *And even as they did not like to retain God in their knowledge, God gave them over to a reprobate mind, to do those things which are not convenient.* We were blinded by Jesuit trained seminary teachers of bible principals.

301

In the Antediluvian age of Adam, man was being judge by his conscious to the point that ... *Acts 17:30 (KJV)* [30] *And the times of this ignorance God winked at; but now commandeth all men everywhere to repent:* This was before the law until his angels cohabited with the daughters of mankind ... *Genesis 6:5 (KJV)* [5] *And GOD saw that the wickedness of man was great in the earth, and that every imagination of the thoughts of his heart was only evil continually.* Keep this in mind because it will become apparent that we have reached this point in time also to repeat history. The lewd behavior behind closed doors in a nation cursed with this spirit that God hates to the point of extinction. This state of perversion caused the flood and the destruction of Sodom and Gomorrah by fire because of these acts in open sex orgies of all kinds of perversions such as ... *Leviticus 18:23 (KJV)* [23] *Neither shalt thou lie with any beast to defile thyself therewith: neither shall any woman stand before a beast to lie down thereto: it is confusion.* (Paralleled with NLT) **Leviticus 18:23 (NLT)** [23] **"A man must never defile himself by having sexual intercourse with an animal, and a woman must never present herself to a male animal in order to have intercourse with it; this is a terrible perversion.**

Warning! The following content contains sexually explicit material

Just see how openly sexuality is paraded in the flesh in this generation. If we are honest with ourselves as a former sinner, you know that the only power that keeps you from sinning as in your past is your love for God. This type of perversion will manifest itself in creatures of advantage. Perversion knows no bounds; it will lead to lying with lower creatures.

What you see is another animal in a human body having sex with an animal of another species. Yes, people are doing these things behind closed doors. It's known as bestiality. This is what God calls confusion in the mind by not being able to distinguish his species is that of non-human and becomes like that lower species in their immoral co-habitation desires.

This is what he calls lewd and lascivious behavior. I know this may shock you; all they need is a body, they don't care about the gender or species it is, it's a spirit in the wrong species in human form or in animal form, just like homosexuality is a spirit in the wrong body. This is how Satan mock God's creation when Adam Sinned. These are the disembodied seducing spirits, when you give place to them in your curiosity, can enter you and cause you to perform these cohabitation acts. These pleasures effect your brain chemistry that cause you to become addicted to sex. They are only known when they manifest.

The degree of activity may not be known in the outset and may lie dormant and manifest at a later age in its host. In the past, persons with these tendencies that see no outlet in a moral society will lived a double life as a closet sexual deviates and closet homosexuals that may practice this behavior in secret. Well, now we are seeing them come out as having gained positions in high places to change laws according to the times. (Daniel. 7:25) our president #44, set his approval by endorsing this behavior as **king of this free world,** open that door to the legalization as a nation under a covenant with God.

When this happens, we will have sealed our fate by fire as did Sodom and Gomorrah. God would have to repent to them in the judgment if we were to escape after having done even worse to the point that we will receive double judgment as confessing Christians and as a nation. We have a written history of what God did to those who came to this state of moral decadence in the past. This has been written in biblical history for our learning as a warning that as a nation, if we are guilty of these sins, we will suffer the same fate as Sodom and Gomorrah.

These are seeds of generation past, hidden in the bloodline waiting for the right time to come out as they are accepted as equals in society. You cannot legislate morality; ask the Catholic Church. This same spirit is manifested in pedophilia as taking advantage of innocent children in sexual contact. This accounts for the increase in incestuous behavior toward your own children. Beware of those who indulge in strong drinks, drugs and alcohol, it will be the downfall of this society. Under President #44, we have now openly endorsed this behavior. They now have a platform to change the laws of nature forbidden by God. Any city that caters to these spirits will be destroyed without remedy and never rise again. As Americans, this now becomes a given in that, this judgment cannot be reversed, or else God would have to change his word and that's not going to happen. This day is now upon us as the signs of the times, pointing to an eminent collapse in this nation. This decree is what caused natural disasters to intensify in these strongholds of Satan as God's anger is kindled.

The day President #44 declared **"we are no longer a Christian nation"** and endorsed a pro homosexual policy; we were doomed. Now get ready for this on the eminent horizon... *Joel 2:2 (KJV)* [2] *A day of darkness* (When this happen, in that day, all churches under the 501-C3 charter will be closed by the government if they don't embrace this new society.*) and of gloominess, a day of clouds and of thick darkness, as the morning spread upon the mountains: a great people and a strong; there hath not been ever the like, neither shall be any more after it, even to the years of many generations.* Now we are at that generation where history is about to repeat itself again.

Like the Jews, a vail of darkness is now over America and her hypocrisy is exposed. Her enemies have found her out ... **Joel 2:2 (NLT)** [2] **It is a day of darkness and gloom, a day of thick clouds and deep blackness. Suddenly, like dawn spreading across the mountains, a mighty army appears! How great and powerful they are! The likes of them have not been seen before and never will be seen again.** God will cause our enemies to steal our technology that was meant for our good and defense, be taken through capitalist greed in this country and be sold to enemies in the government to pass these top secret projects to enemy nations of which some of them have roots that will use it to destroy us; and, in the end, then themselves. I can see this nation's elections coming to an end with this curse upon us beyond president # 45. The #46 will be the return of #44's spirit as elected by the people, will have an ultra-liberal agenda so God can deliver us into the hands of our enemies as the judgment endorse under President #44. Both #44 and #45's spirit will hold this nation's government hostage. These are false prophecies that say they will return.

The chronicle titled **"Revelation Revealed", "During the Tribulation Siege" "Nowhere to Run- Nowhere to Hide"** explains the course of events we are about to face. All this indicate, we are about to be judged with the same fate as Sodom and Gomorrah after the wars that will cause our destruction from within. The meteorites and asteroids will reduce this nation to ash as fire and brimstone rain down on us. We will be extinct as a nation on Earth to be found no more at all. *Revelation 18:21 (KJV) And a mighty angel took up a stone like a great millstone, and cast it into the sea, saying, thus with violence shall that great city Babylon* (Modern America) *be thrown down, and shall be found no more at all*. (Updated & released 3/2023)

THE RETURN OF THE BARABBAS PATRIOT

Question; Are you a modern-day Christian Barabbas?

Background scriptures:

Mark 15:7 (KJV) [7] *And there was one named Barabbas, which lay bound with them that had made insurrection with him, who had committed murder in the insurrection. Matthew 27:21-22 (KJV)* [21] *The governor answered and said unto them, whether of the twain will ye that I release unto you? They said, Barabbas.* [22] *Pilate saith unto them, what shall I do then with Jesus which is called Christ? They all say unto him, let him be crucified. Mark 15:15 (KJV)* [15] *And so Pilate, willing to content the people, released Barabbas unto them, and delivered Jesus, when he had scourged him, to be crucified.*

"Holy Spirit reveal the mystery surrounding Barabbas and why he was released".
AMEN

The history of the sacrificial customs of the Jews will be a type and shadow in the revelation of grace and truth. In the ceremonial aspect of the atonement for sins, a pure lamb without blemish had to be selected to atone for the annual sins of the people as a nation at the feast of the Passover. At the same time a scapegoat was selected also to represent in his release of their sins to wonder in the desert that their sins had been removed. Therefore, it is called the scapegoat. Satan, down through the ages use man too in high places to plot their own destruction in the form of insurrections from within as attempting to take over God's government. Spiritually, let's look at these two subjects in biblical history: one **Jesus** the other **Barabbas**.

They are both Jews accused of crimes against the two nations; Jesus falsely accused of blaspheming Jewish laws among his people for saying he was the son of God and Barabbas, for and insurrection that resulted in the death of a Roman soldier. One is innocent, the other guilty. Now they are paraded before Pilate to be judged. Jesus now represents the sacrificial lamb readied for the slaughter and Barabbas represents the scapegoat, full of sin. Spiritually, what this scene means, Barabbas represents Christians who takes matters into their own hands when they think God is not doing what they think he should do to change what they believe is righteous. Their zeal for God to contrive with evil intent to make a wrong right in their own outside of the will of God, will get you destroyed as a confessing evangelical Christian. Although he means well ... *Romans 10:2 (KJV)* [2] *For I bear them record that they have a zeal of God, but not according to knowledge.*

Zeal as a confessing Christian in disobedience to the authorities that results in attempting to overthrow the government God has established ... will cause you to parish at the hand of the devil for violating this scripture... *Amos 9:10 (KJV)* [10] *All the sinners of my people shall die by the sword, which say, the evil shall not overtake nor prevent us. This will be the saying of those who say "we must take back America" Matthew 26:52 (KJV)* [52] *Then said Jesus unto him, put up again thy sword into his place: for all they that take the sword shall perish with the sword.* I have heard some of these well-known prophets telling people to buy guns to protect themselves. That's what will happen when you get too involved with the world, you will forget God's divine promise to protect you.

The Barabbas spirit that tried to overthrow the Roman government in defense of Jewish law got him a death sentence. But we had another nation within a nation of which Pilate was trying to keep the peace in his position with both that presented him with a dilemma that God had orchestrated to transform the old to become a type and shadow of things to come that will be spiritually represented. The spiritual significance of Barabbas' release will allow his spirit to return in Christians in the latter times as patriot

Christians, attempting to do the same thing and repeat history. This whole scene is a type and shadow of an end time scenario we are now about to see repeated in these patriot movements across the nation. They will be victims of history repeating itself. This time, all will be destroyed at the hand of the government they rose and attempted to overthrow.

This is what Barabbas did not know, all who think you are going to change what the prophets have spoken in time past that is now coming to pass, you are fools indeed. This is the knowledge Daniel spoke that has increased to the point that if Christ tarried any longer, man would re-create himself. **(Dan.12:4)** The technology surveillance in use has all these movements activities monitored as did the Romans in the day of Barabbas. The moment you rise, these laws that have been enacted will give them the power to take you out and leave no prisoners. This is that Barabbas spirit returning to be judged, and this time destroyed. Do not underestimate the power in the hands of this unscrupulous government. God has given them a time to do all they planned. They are the foreigners planted in this country that are here to take it over, when we break this covenant with God, in the end, they will ultimately destroy all that is in this nation, including themselves.

Check out their DNA, it has reached this status of megalomania. This is what the present church in delusion failed to see without a vision from a biblical perspective by rejecting the true prophets' warnings. The founding fathers under the influence of the of the Holy Spirit directing their activities, not that they were all that religious, many owned slaves and practiced Freemasonry that design the layout of Washington as a sign of their power over future government operations as they wrote the constitutional by-law and bill of rights that will guarantee the liberties of all that set foot on this soil, the freedom to serve the one true God will have that right.

Our right to bear arms as intended by these men assembled in that CONTINENTAL CONGRESS was not intended to be used to overthrow a government set up by God to fulfill the Abraham covenant in this nation with the seal, IN GOD WE TRUST. All who will attempt this from within will be destroyed. That's why the south lost the civil war; they were fighting against the covenant for not freeing the people that became their slaves when that covenant made us all free men under God. It is the changing of the laws of God that made us the nation we have become. The reason, we are the last nation reserved for the final destruction at the hands of our enemies, we are the economic stability of the world as a capitalist nation.

The Jesuits and their institutions of higher learning through their seminaries system, brought the Christian church to this end as their means justified the end as to the seduction that removed the apostle's doctrine and divided the assemblies to bring in hirelings. They changed the assembly into a corporate body of a structured order that would operate like a worldly corporation with a non-profit status so they can be monitored in their division, teaching these new doctrines. They will have to file a 501c-3 that will give the government the right to close their doors if they do not comply with the dictates of that charter. Now! we will become the **great whore** by being seduced by the Roman Catholic Church. We are at the point in history where we have no power to defend ourselves as we will learn from fighting these long undeclared wars as self-appointed policemen of the world, will end in ultimate defeat. God would have to apologize to Israel if we can commit the same crimes as going after other gods if we were to escape. These are the darkest days in the history of America and yet none seem to recognize the consequences are irreversible when you choose to ignore the history that brought us into existence. We have been exposed to those who aligned themselves with us as allies as being hypocritical. Now they are going to withdraw their support, and in that day, when we need it most, they will dissert us to join the invading armies of the North, Russia and China as in Ezekiel. 38. (Updated 5/2016)

TO MEDIA MINISTRIES

"There is no Fame in Telling the Truth"

Background picture:

1 Corinthians 8:5 (KJV) "5 For though there be that are called gods, whether in heaven or in earth, (as there be gods many, and lords many", When we are influence by man's theology, Satan will set us up as gods or popes in the pulpits. *Matthew 16:24 (KJV) ²⁴ Then said Jesus unto his disciples, If any man will come after me, let him deny himself, and take up his cross, and follow me. Mark 7:9 (KJV) And he said unto them, Full well ye reject the commandment of God, that ye may keep your own tradition.*

This article is designed to provoke the celebrity Christian TV community. I ask the Holy Spirit to give me Scriptures and commentary on what I saw. The influence of Hollywood is quite apparent among the TV celebrity ministries. I am sure that most of them mean well in their endeavors to preach the gospel as I was. *John 8:32 (KJV) ³² And ye shall know the truth, and the truth shall make you free.* Until I was delivered from myself to the point that self-examination and submission to the word of God brought me into the reality of the real gospel. It was not until I surrendered my will, my thoughts and my ways that I began to understand God's ways. In all that I am revealing to you who get to read this, it was to me first being set apart from all else is where I got to see myself.

The Holy Spirit is God's mind to communicate through yield vessels; however, many of us fail to enter the strait gate that leads to peace, rest and everlasting life. **(Matthew 7:13-14)** If you have been reading my chronicles, you will see that I write from the standpoint of a personal testimony of my transformation in progress by acting on what the words say. All this is to prepare me for his final battle for souls. It has been by revelations that I have come to know the truth. When you surrender, you are prevented from judging others when you come to the knowledge that none of us can throw stones at each other.

We all came from sin. We do not have a revelation that the doers of the word life, will be the judge to the sinner. Your actions must follow God's words, that' why Jesus said believe me for my works sake. Most preachers will answer that question as to say, look what I have built in the name of God without realizing he is preaching another gospel that cause their them not remain under the stress of a hard trial. The whole council of the truth must be declared among you to be perfected.

When the word said **"judge not that you be not judged"** we are already judged by the word, as a sinner and as a saint. Being born in sin, we are going to hell with our father the devil if we do not repent; remember the women caught in the very act of adultery, Jesus, being perfect did not judge her while in the flesh because he was going to be the sin sacrifice for her. Therefore, we cannot judge anyone else. Now ask yourself this question, did you come from heaven, are you better than Jesus? We have already been judged by what the word of God as a sinner or a saint, the difference as saints, God's love brought us into the kingdom so that same love in us enables Jesus to be lifted to draw others by loving not judging. This reality one must-see to be used by the Holy Spirit.

When you judge, the Holy Spirit is grieve …. **Matthew 7:3-5 (KJV) [3] And why beholdest thou the mote that is in thy brother's eye, but considerest not the beam that is in thine own eye? [4] Or how wilt thou say to thy brother, let me pull out the mote out of thine eye; and, behold, a beam is in thine own eye? [5] Thou hypocrite, first cast out the beam out of thine own eye; and then shalt thou see clearly to cast out the mote out of thy brother's eye.** This is when you become converted. **Matthew 22:14 (KJV) [14] For many are called, but few are chosen. 1 Corinthians 1:26 (KJV) [26] For ye see your calling, brethren, how that not many wise men after the flesh, not many mighty, not many noble, are called:**

When we become delivered from ourselves, then and only then will demon spirits see the image of Christ in our foreheads and instantly move at the word spoken in faith through the inspiration of the Holy Spirit. When this does not happen, examine yourself as to who is speaking, God or flesh. God is the one addressing the devil in you through the power of the spoken word. When the demons saw Jesus, they recognized him; likewise, they will recognize him again in you. This waiting process will include fasting and much prayer to break the flesh as Jesus did in his wilderness to come out in the fullness of God. I was one of those who entered the ministry without waiting on my calling. I, like many others was sincere but my decision was based on the opinion of man. Divided by denominational doctrines and theological seminary teachings, we have reduced the pastor to a motivational speaker using biblical principles and precepts to acquire a renowned status in the world for material gain as we see how this doctrine is applied as hirelings in the pulpits.

This present day preaching in my observation through the Holy Spirit, borders on a literary knowledge of the word using real-life circumstances to relate their version of truth. It sounds good, preaches well, but has no depth that reaches the heart to bring forth fruit of repentance that remain. Holiness is foreign in this doctrine with an element of a seeker friendly compromise delivery. Those who receive some form of deliverance through men with gifts, later find themselves back in the same state they were. In my observations, I have observed this thin line of deception by not waiting on your calling to be sanctified, set apart, and sent to the wilderness to die to self so God can send you as himself represented in your body. These are the few there be that find him and make their calling and election sure. Those that hear them will make their calling and election sure also.

The way Christ taught in the four Gospels in comparison to what we see demonstrated in modern-day theology, leaves much to be desired of truth for this reason ... *Matthew 16:24 (KJV) "24 Then said Jesus unto his disciples, If any man will come after me, let him deny himself, and take up his cross, and follow me. Hosea 4:6 (KJV) 6 My people are destroyed for lack of knowledge: because thou hast rejected knowledge, I will also reject thee, that thou shalt be no priest to me: seeing thou hast forgotten the law of thy God, I will also forget thy children. 1 Peter 4:1 (KJV) 1 Forasmuch then as Christ hath suffered for us in the flesh, arm yourselves likewise with the same mind: for he that hath suffered in the flesh hath ceased from sin;"*

Does this sound like you will be loved as a celebrity preacher if you were to come the way of Christ teachings, *2 John 1:7 (KJV)* [7] *For many deceivers are entered into the world, who confess not that Jesus Christ is come in the flesh. This is a deceiver and an antichrist.* Except for those elected, we are a far cry from the truth. The reason being, as having my eyes open by the spirit of truth, we have been indoctrinated in denominational traditions over generations of teachings to the point that we believe we are right, and some have become self-appointed authorities. I have listened to men that have been teaching bible prophecy for forty years or more do not have this revelation of the new thing that' going to confound many in this generation. *Isaiah 43:19 (KJV)* [19] *Behold, I will do a new thing; now it shall spring forth; shall ye not know it? I will even make a way in the wilderness, and rivers in the desert.*

Our first impression of the gospel is not always right. This in part is due to many others that are practicing the same traditions. Over time, I have seen moves of God, what the Holy Spirit revealed to me that they were only in part because we have never reached the fullness of Christ. Therefore, that piece we sought him for was manifested in error and the fruit did not remain to the good of God's glory in these movements.

As organized assemblies, have we profited from these movements? No, we are still divided by identifying ourselves by what movement or denomination you believe in and some even say? We are non-denominational; now what does that mean. It is evident that many have yet to come to the knowledge of the truth THAT HE, the Holy Spirit speaks for himself. In my experience as contending for the return of the apostle's doctrine, if we really went this way, the world would really be nowhere near the assembly except to get saved. We really do not know what spirit we are of. This sets us up for another judgment … *Proverbs 16:25 (KJV)* [25] *There is a way that seemeth right unto a man, but the end thereof are the ways of death.*

Now that God has set in these end times a time to send out his prophets and messengers once again to warn his divided body to set their house in order. *1 Peter 4:17 (KJV)* [17] *For the time is come that judgment must begin at the house of God: and if it first begin at us, what shall the end be of them that obey not the gospel of God? Amos 3:7 (KJV)* [7] *Surely the Lord GOD will do nothing, but he revealeth his secret unto his servants the prophets. Ephesians 3:5 (KJV)* [5] *Which in other ages was not made known unto the sons of men, as it is now revealed unto his holy apostles and prophets by the Spirit.* He is talking about apostles and prophets and   raised up as he did in the Old Testament in our time. They will be the ones to open the visions the prophets spoke in time past to be revealed in this time. They will have the Vision to what the prophets of old spoke concerning the end times and those who refuse to hear it, will perish.

We have forgotten the scriptures that tell us that there is ... *Ephesians 4:5 (KJV)* ⁵ *One Lord, one faith, one baptism,* I am a witness, if you are deceived, you will never know it until God opens your eyes. Another reality, old long-standing traditions, carried through generations of teachings, have assemblies still steeped in hidden pride, prejudices, bigotry, denominational sectarianism, which have cut off many of these spiritual realities. If we are truly discerning the times, most of us are operating in a strong delusion to think that this kind of division is going to be caught up into heaven.

That's why there must be another Pentecost, the church He established, must be one when he returns. I was influenced by these faith movements in my early years only to find that it was not the course God had chosen for me. I had to endure stiff rebukes and chastening before eventually it would cost me all I had to walk with God and that I am yet to arrive to that degree. I always live in the reality that it will cost me all again to keep him. The path God has chosen for me leaves me no room for self, therefore, I'm convicted by what I know to be right. The standard God set for me is total surrender.

John 15:16 (KJV) ¹⁶ *Ye have not chosen me, but I have chosen you, and ordained you, that ye should go and bring forth fruit, and that your fruit should remain: that whatsoever ye shall ask of the Father in my name, he may give it you.*   I have seen noted ministers come in from the field to retire in the comfort of establishing universities catering to their worldly fame status they have acquired just to hear men speak well of them, now are becoming commentators of rhetoric and false doctrine.

When I started noticing a pattern in those, he sent to me to mentor spiritually, whatever was said to them through me to do, when they acted on that word in agreement, they would call me back rejoicing in the answer. It has cost me many associations to walk this straight path God put before me and I have not found it grievous to walk with him. I stumbled many times but kept walking. No, I have not reached that place of perfection, that will be when he fully takes possession of the vessel. In my efforts to obey, I got to know what he went through for me to be here with him at this time. *1 Peter 4:1 (KJV)* [1] *Forasmuch then as Christ hath suffered for us in the flesh, arm yourselves likewise with the same mind: for he that hath suffered in the flesh hath ceased from sin.*

It is not as though I have arrived but striving to let my footsteps be ordered by him, I am learning to die daily. I have learned this truth also; Satan never wants you to know the reality of your new creation power. This reality of knowing that … *1 John 4:4 (KJV)* [4] *Ye are of God, little children, and have overcome them: because greater is he that is in you, than he that is in the world. Isaiah 54:17 (KJV)* [17] *No weapon that is formed against thee shall prosper; and every tongue that shall rise against thee in judgment thou shalt condemn. This is the heritage of the servants of the LORD, and their righteousness is of me, saith the LORD.* It is not about things on Earth but things heavenly. That is why Jesus told his disciples not to carry anything on their journey because what you have is more precious than silver and gold. Those I bless through you will provide your needs. **(Mark 6:8)** From that time on, it is God walking in you speaking His words. Now who can defy the words of God in a chosen vessel. It is not about building your kingdom but his. The house you build is inhabited by a wolf in sheep clothing.

The house God builds is inhabited by the spirit of truth. When the real test come, only those sheep in the house of God will remain. When God open my eyes to this, he separated me from those who did not walk this straight path. I had to suffer being rejected to the point of being given a false word by a brother who meant well but was being used by the devil. We are living in the last days where all this is about to become a reality as God turns up the heat to purify his temples, chosen to dwell in him. (Rev. 3:18) Christ did not go around telling people who he was because in him the father is able to speak for himself, therefore, the title followed the office he served in.

If you must tell people who you are, it is evident that you went out ahead of him and is evident why your fruit has not remained. This is the example Jesus gave when he asked, **"who do men say I am"**. All who God send will carry a sign of his presence by performing miracles as coming out of the volume of his books. Is not this sign the apostles carried with them and all who believed and received Christ will have the same power when he sent them out? The reason we do not see this on that level, there's little faith for these kinds of miracles. *Mark 16:17 (KJV)* [17] *And these signs shall follow them that believe; In my name shall they cast out devils; they shall speak with new tongues;* Now all who receive Christ have the same power. All who are called to this ministry are separated unto God and are at rest as the John the Baptists being prepared for the fullness to come out in the day of provocation from the wilderness in the fullness and take the kingdom back from the devil by force and some will lose their heads to the glory of God. **(Matt. 11:12)** The days of hard speeches and testimonies with no sign are over. Those elected will carry the same sign as the first apostles because they are hand-picked by God for his full occupation to glorify himself in the tribulation as in the latter rain. We have been beating the air in self, many of us mean well, as I did but, we were just debating with each other trying to prove who knows more about God. Now let us examine ourselves, repent and wait on God. (Updated for Release 11/2019)

WHAT WILL BE THE CONDITIONS BEFORE THE RAPTURE?

Background Scripture:

1 Thessalonians 4:16-18 (KJV) [16] **For the Lord himself shall descend from heaven with a shout, with the voice of the archangel, and with the trump of God: and the dead in Christ shall rise first:** [17] **Then we which are alive and remain shall be caught up together with them in the clouds, to meet the Lord in the air: and so shall we ever be with the Lord.** [18] **Wherefore comfort one another with these words.**

The largest misconception by far in doctrinal teaching in this present-day church world as Christians, that is, we are going to escape the tribulation and be raptured before it all begin. Those of you with eyes to see and ears to hear will have a clear understanding of why this single doctrine will cause hell to enlarge itself to receive multitudes of deceived confessing Christians. They will be taken over by fears of the times. This mystery, revealed in the previous chronicle, prove to be so controversial to even down right rejected by the many to the point that I have asked the Holy Spirit to be more specific and to the point as to this mystery that has 98 percent of the church world in disbelief.

Fact One; We are not all serving the same God. There is only .... *Ephesians*

4:5 (KJV) [5] *One Lord, one faith, one baptism, Fact two;* We are not believing that there is only one doctrine. *1 Timothy 1:6-7 (KJV)* [6] *From which some having swerved have turned aside unto vain jangling;* [7] *Desiring to be teachers of the law; understanding neither what they say, nor whereof they affirm. 2 John 1:10 (KJV)* [10] *If there come any unto you, and bring not this doctrine, receive him not into your house, neither bid him God speed:* What is this doctrine that many seem to have missed? This I asked the Holy Spirit also when he got my attention. The four gospels declared through Christ, set the foundation for all that come after him. This will be explained in those used to bring this revelation in the epistles' that followed to complete the New Testament. What should all who minister be declaring? *1 Corinthians 2:2 (KJV)* [2] *For I determined not to know anything among you, save Jesus Christ, and him crucified.* Once I asked a minister, why do you say you know him, yet keep all these pagan holidays that are not scriptural. He had no reply.

This is the doctrine that will convict and save souls with fruit that remain. The whole council declared in righteousness and true holiness will produce this fruit. Your leader must follow Christ example when one comes to be converted in the knowledge of truth by the surrendering of your will to Christ so he can be birth in you by receiving his Holy Spirit. He then is activated to teach and guide you by revelation in the application of truth so you will not be ignorant in the application of the word. This includes all things relevant to the time you are living in. This will be evident in the church operating in the fullness by having the whole council of God declared among them in the spirit of (Eph. 5:11-12). Christ must be crucified in you for the Holy Spirit to have the liberty to teach and manifest him-self in the body to this degree with Christ as the head, not man.

As I have said in these chronicles in the pass and now say again; it is God's way or no way will for truth be revealed. Now let all who minister examine ourselves to see where we fall short. It is the mind of Christ that is the head of his body. Outside of his doctrine, you are none of his. *Romans 8:9 (KJV)* [9] *But ye are not in the flesh, but in the Spirit, if so be that the Spirit of God dwell in you. Now if any man have not the Spirit of Christ, he is none of his.* Our thoughts and ways will usurp over the thoughts of God and there in is the error of our ways. Therefore, we must forsake our thoughts for this reason. At this point in time, there is about to be a great separation of the wheat and the tares during the tribulation that will be a shock to the church world.

Many of our hearts are not in the right place where the love of God has the effect it had when Jesus showed up. As a messenger of God with the end time vision for those who have ears to hear, this is what I am experiencing … **Matthew 13:15-24 (KJV/NLT** [15] **For this people's heart is waxed gross, and their ears are dull of hearing, and their eyes they have closed; lest at any time they should see with their eyes, and hear with their ears, and should understand with their heart, and should be converted, and I should heal them. Matthew 13:15 (NLT)** [15] **For the hearts of these people are hardened, and their ears cannot hear, and they have closed their eyes— so their eyes cannot see, and their ears cannot hear, and their hearts cannot understand, and they cannot turn to me and let me heal them.'** *(KJV)* [16] *But blessed are your eyes, for they see: and your ears, for they hear.* [17] *For verily I say unto you, that many prophets and righteous men have desired to see those things which ye see and have not seen them; and to hear those things which ye hear, and have not heard them.* **Matthew 13:17 (NLT)** [17] **I assure you, many prophets and godly people have longed to see and hear what you have seen and heard, but they could not.** (These are the revelations being revealed to this end time generation.) [18] **Hear ye therefore the parable of the sower.**

Matthew 13:18 (NLT) [18] **"Now here is the explanation of the story I told about the farmer sowing grain:** *(KJV)* [19] *(When any one heareth the word of the kingdom, and understandeth it not, then cometh the wicked one, and catcheth away that which was sown in his heart. This is he which received seed by the way side.* **Matthew 13:19 (NLT)** [19] **The seed that fell on the hard path represents those who hear the Good News about the Kingdom and don't understand it. Then the evil one comes and snatches the seed away from their hearts.** *(KJV)* [20] *But he that received the seed into stony places, the same is he that heareth the word, and anon with joy receiveth it.* **Matthew 13:20 (NLT)** [20] **The rocky soil represents those who hear the message and receive it with joy.** *(KJV)* [21] *Yet hath he does not root in himself, but endureth for a while: for when tribulation or persecution ariseth because of the word, by and by he is offended.* (They did not receive the word in their hearts.) [22] *He also that received seed among the thorns is he that heareth the word; and the care of this world, and the deceitfulness of* *riches, choke the word, and he becometh unfruitful.* These are deceived into thinking that godliness is gain as seen in some of these faith movement teachings. If the word of faith is our boast, what about the rich men that has gained this entire world's goods?

Matthew 5:45 (KJV) [45] *That ye may be the children of your Father which is in heaven: for he maketh his sun to rise on the evil and on the good, and sendeth rain on the just and on the unjust.* [23] *But he that received seed into the good ground is he that heareth the word, and understandeth it; which also beareth fruit, and bringeth forth, some an hundredfold, some sixty, some thirty.* (This is the fruit that is sawn in the elects that will remain.) [24] *Another parable put he forth unto them, saying, The kingdom of heaven is likened unto a man which sowed good seed in his field:* [25] *But while men slept, his enemy came and sowed tares among the wheat, and went his way.* [26] *But when the blade was sprung up, and brought forth fruit, then appeared the tares also.* [27] *So the servants of the householder came and said unto him, Sir, didst not thou sow good seed in thy field? from whence then hath it tears?* [28] *He said unto them, An enemy hath done this. The servants said unto him, wilt thou then that we go and gather them up?* [29] *But he said, Nay; lest while ye gather up the tares, ye root up also the wheat with them.* [30] *Let both grow together until the harvest: and in the time of harvest I will say to the reapers, Gather ye together first the tares, and bind them in bundles to burn them: but gather the wheat into my barn.*

This is where the present-day church as seen in the spirit world in apostasy. Many are not prepared for the shock when they confront the truth of God. As Daniel spoke in *Daniel 7:25 (KJV)* [25] ___*And he shall speak great words against the most High and shall wear out the saints of the most High.*___ Throughout time, the Gentiles age from the advent of the resurrection of Jesus Christ, the persecution of the church down through time has brought it to its present state of divisions.

This could only happen by the original doctrine being compromised to where we see the church and the world sitting in the same assembly. Spiritually, what this represents in doctrinal teachings are the many divisions because of carnal influence usurping the teachings of the Holy Spirit. This is largely in part due to theological seminarian influence in interpretations of scripture. The Holy Spirit in every elected believer chosen by God will speak the truth that brings the persecution Jesus encountered to adhere to the teachings he received from the father. God would have to repent if we were to escape because of teaching another compromised doctrine. *2 John 1:10 (KJV)* [10] *If there come any unto you, and bring not this doctrine, receive him not into your house, neither bid him God speed:*

In our flesh, we do not choose to suffer; that's why God does the choosing because the power to do the will of God comes through his Holy Spirit. *Zechariah 4:6 (NKJV)* [6] **So he answered and said to me: «This is the word of the *LORD* to Zerubbabel: 'Not by might nor by power, but by My Spirit,' Says the *LORD* of hosts. John 6:54 (KJV)** [54] *Whoso eateth my flesh, and drinketh my blood, hath eternal life; and I will raise him up at the last day.* Just as the Holy Spirit raised him from the dead in you, he will give you the power to be raised up from the dead in him at the resurrection. The Holy Spirit interprets this as the suffering of Christ.

Matthew 10:22 (KJV) [22] *And ye shall be hated of all men for my name's sake: but he that endureth to the end shall be saved.* This is evident when the flesh caters to the will of the people to escape rejection through compromise. This opens the door to your heart to commit the sins of omission. (Gal.5:19-21) In the sight of God (your judge) this will take you to hell. *1 Corinthians 4:14 (KJV)* [14] *I write not these things to shame you, but as my beloved sons I warn you. 1 Corinthians 6:5 (KJV)* [5] *I speak to your shame. Is it so, that there is not a wise man among you? no, not one that shall be able to judge between his brethren?* Those whose lives are beyond reproach will become a witness against you.

1 Corinthians 15:34 (KJV) [34] *Awake to righteousness, and sin not; <u>for some have not the knowledge of God;</u> I speak this to your shame. Hebrews 12:2 (KJV)* [2] *Looking unto Jesus the author and finisher of our faith; who for the joy that was set before him endured the cross, despising the shame, and is set down at the right hand of the throne of God. Revelation 3:18 (KJV)* [18] *I counsel thee to buy of me gold tried in the fire, that thou mayest be rich; and white raiment, that thou mayest be clothed, and that the shame of thy nakedness do not appear; and anoint thine eyes with eyesalve, that thou mayest see.*

In most of these writings given to me by and through the Holy Spirit, I see him repeatedly, reminding us. That's to get our attention before he requires your soul. Many are not prepared spiritually to endure. Except for his elects, this so-called church (wheat) and the worldly Christian (tares) are as the same, growing together and their lack of knowledge represents the blindness of no consciousness of their sinful state before God, the final judge. Unless this warning from his messengers brings them to repentance, there would be no church to save. Thank God for election. Our carnal nature gives way to deception; for this cause, we must ... *Isaiah 55:7-8 (KJV)* *⁷ Let the wicked forsake his way, and the unrighteous man his thoughts: and let him return unto the Lord, and he will have mercy upon him; and to our God, for he will abundantly pardon. ⁸ For my thoughts are not your thoughts, neither are your ways my ways, saith the Lord.*

This is the bases of the division in the interpretations that have led to many doctrines that represent the mind of man speaking without the anointing of the Holy Spirit which is the mind of God speaking the unadulterated truth. He does not lie to you; the devil in man is the liar when you know not what spirit you are of. This thin line of deception that church leaders think that when everyone speaks well of you, that is good. *Luke 6:26 (KJV)* *²⁶ Woe unto you, when all men shall speak well of you! for so did their fathers to the false prophets.* The Woe on the so call spiritual leaders, are the lies they have indorsed that have caused this present-day church assembly to be deceived living with a false since of reality and security.

I like to give you a good understanding as the Holy Spirit gave me before I could call myself a Christian, just what I was saying before God that I will be held accountable. Leading up to the subject in question; are we going through a part of the tribulation. *Jeremiah 5:12 (KJV)* *¹² They have belied the Lord, and said, it is not he; neither shall evil come upon us; neither shall we see sword nor famine: Matthew 24:3-6 (KJV) ³ And as he sat upon the mount of Olives, the disciples came unto him privately, saying, Tell us, when shall these things be? and what shall be the sign of thy coming, and of the end of the world? ⁴ And Jesus answered and said unto them, Take heed that no man deceive you. ⁵ For many shall come in my name, saying, I am Christ; and shall deceive many. ⁶ And ye shall hear of wars and rumours of wars: see that ye be not troubled: for all these things must come to pass, but the end is not yet.*

Christ was prophesying of the time from his departure until he returns of generations of men getting worse and worse. *2 Timothy 3:13 (KJV)* *¹³ But evil men and seducers shall wax worse and worse, deceiving, and being deceived.* The time at this point in the present day spiritually is.... *Joel 2:2 (KJV)* *² A day of darkness and of gloominess, a day of clouds and of thick darkness, as the morning spread upon the mountains: a great people and a strong; there hath not been ever the , neither shall be any more after it, even to the years of many generations.* What the church has failed to see on a large scale, their state poses no threat to the world neither is their light to the extent that Christ can be seen. This is the curse upon the church under the state with the mark **501C-3** state-controlled religion. What was once a great manifestation is no more on the scale of the early apostle's assembly. It appears the world and the churches are one in the same. The signs and wonders that demonstrate Christ as the deliverer is not present in this body of confessing Christians at this time of the end.

What we see are the gifts working in division as individual works but not as a unit of one body with Christ at the helm. The doctrine, over time has been changed to represent the traditions of the Pharisees and scribes when Jesus first encountered them. What did he say ... *Mark 7:8 (KJV)* [8] *For laying aside the commandment of God, ye hold the tradition of men, as the washing of pots and cups: and many other such like things ye do.* [9] *And he said unto them, Full well ye reject the commandment of God, that ye may keep your own tradition. 2 Corinthians 3:6 (KJV)* [6] *Who also hath made us able ministers of the New Testament; not of the letter, but of the spirit: for the letter killeth, but the spirit giveth life.*

This is where we are in these end times. How does he describe this church? *Revelation 3:16-17 (KJV)* [16] *So then because thou art lukewarm, and neither cold nor hot, I will spue thee out of my mouth.* [17] *Because thou sayest, I am rich, and increased with goods, and have need of nothing; and knowest not that thou art wretched, and miserable, and poor, and blind, and naked:* What is the word to them at the end of time before they enter the tribulation? *Revelation 3:18 (KJV)* [18] *I counsel thee to buy of me gold tried in the fire, that thou mayest be rich; and white raiment, that thou mayest be clothed, and that the shame of thy nakedness do not appear; and anoint thine eyes with eye salve, that thou mayest see.*

You would have to be blind not to see that this describes this electronic church that does not know it's connected to the beast system to promote these doctrines that the government now controls. This is evident by having a **501C-3** to operate under government charters. This process did not happen overnight; over time through being seduced to this present end ... *Daniel 7:25 (KJV)* [25] *And he shall speak great words against the most*

High, and shall <u>wear out the saints of the most High</u>, and think to change times and laws: and they shall be given into his hand until a time and times and the dividing of time. Now to bring the confessing church body back to the apostles' doctrine. All our worldly gains will have to be removed so God can show himself as God, beside him there is no other. **Rev. 3:18** are the fires in the beginning to set the stage of tribulation to show the real God of the universe. Only those in truth will rise to the occasion to begin to do the exploits we have never seen performed in the elect of God.

Daniel 11:32 (KJV) [32] *And such as do wickedly against the covenant shall he corrupt by flatteries: but the people that do know their God shall be strong and do exploits.* Many deceived Christians who still lack the faith to act on the word will be in great fear when all is gone overnight. The only God that will come to the aid of his chosen people will be the God of Abraham, Isaac and Jacob. Showing to the whole world that there is only .... *Ephesians 4:5 (KJV)* [5] *One Lord, one faith, one baptism, Romans 14:11-13 (KJV)* [11] *For it is written, As I live, saith the Lord, every knee shall bow to me, and every tongue shall confess to God. -*[12] *So then every one of us shall give account of himself to God.* [13] *<u>Let us not therefore judge one another anymore</u>: but judge this rather, that no man put a stumbling block or an occasion to fall in his brother's way.*

This time for those that are call is a time of self-examination and preparation as wise virgins that heeded to the call, making them ready for his glory. If we continue to judge one another, it is evident you miss that call. There are many well-meaning pastors with one wife who are not far from the kingdom but because of this error in their teachings, I pray will repent on their day of visitation from the prophets and profit eternal life for the good they have done with earnest hearts before God. It is not the desire of God to see them given over to a delusion to join the antichrist body and be our persecutors during the church time in tribulation.

When they are not raptured as they told their congregations, many they lied too will seek to kill them for leading them down this broad road. The fact that God has chosen to show this vision to me does not make me something special, it's to me first now in return, I pray in love that other eyes will be open to hear what **"Thus say the lord"** this time while many ... *Joel 3:14 (KJV)* [14] *Multitudes, multitudes in the valley of decision: for the day of the Lord is near in the valley of decision.* This is the time that

... Isaiah 5:14 (KJV) [14] *Therefore hell hath enlarged herself and opened her mouth without measure: and their glory, and their multitude, and their pomp, and he that rejoiceth, shall descend into it.*

The great mystery being revealed by the Holy Spirit to this end time generation was kept back by Daniel and John because of the apostasy that would seduce the church down through the ages ... *Matthew 24:22 (KJV)* [22] *And except those days should be shortened, there should no flesh be saved: but for the elect's sake those days shall be shortened.* The fear that will come upon many in false teachings will cause them to be trapped into the beast system their churches were under and receive the mark through this electronic media system that will rise in the New World Order and become part of the New World Religion as the antichrist. Are you saying my church has the mark of the beast? All who are alive will see what will cause every tongue to confess that he is God when your denominations or movement god is consumed in the Elijah show down as a false god and a liar. When the **seals** of Revelation are broken, the **trumpets** begin to sound, the **thunders** begin to roar in the elements begin to melt when the **vials** are poured out without mixture, everything described in the chronicle **"The Book of Revelation Revealed," "During the tribulation siege,"** and **"Through the Prophets Eyes"** are the fires that will separate the wheat from the tares to birth the true church out of great tribulation.

The last trumpets will remove the church, and the **first thunder** will be the residue of the children of disobedience gathering. (Revelation 14:18) Many will perish in his wrath. The conditions at the time of the translation are described in this chronicle " **"During the Tribulation Siege"** and **"America's Last days of Freedom"**. *1 Corinthians 15:52 (KJV)* [52] *In a moment, in the twinkling of an eye, at the last trump: for the trumpet shall sound, and the dead shall be raised incorruptible, and we shall be changed.*

This is the time that must be shortened for the saints in tribulation when God has completed their purification. No one will know the moment or hour, but I was given a sign. The time that nobody knows will be on the Jewish calendar before the new moon; that is the time that nobody will know until he appears as in the sky. *1 Thessalonians 4:16 (KJV)* [16] *For the Lord himself shall descend from heaven with a shout, with the voice of the archangel, and with the trump of God: and the dead in Christ shall rise first: Revelation 14:15-16 (KJV)* [15] *And another angel came out of the temple, crying with a loud voice to him that sat on the cloud, Thrust in thy sickle, and reap: for the time is come for thee to reap; for the harvest of the earth is ripe.* ¹⁶ *And he that sat on the cloud thrust in his sickle on the earth; and the earth was reaped. Revelation 12:1-2 (KJV)* ¹ *And there appeared a great wonder in heaven; a woman clothed with the sun, and the moon under her feet, and upon her head a crown <u>of twelve stars:</u>* (The remnant of the tribes of Israel*) ² And she being with <u>child cried</u>, (The Church) travailing in birth, and pained to be delivered. 1Thes.4:17 (KJV)* <u>17 Then we which are alive and remain shall be caught up together with them in the clouds, to meet the Lord in the air: and so shall we ever be with the Lord.</u>

Revelation 14:17-18 (KJV) ¹⁷ *And another angel came out of the temple which is in heaven, he also having a sharp sickle.* ¹⁸ *And another angel came out from the altar, which had power over fire; and cried with a loud cry to him that had the sharp sickle, saying, thrust in thy sharp sickle, and <u>gather the clusters of the vine of the earth; for her grapes are fully ripe</u>.* This was the great mystery Daniel and John could not reveal. The first resurrection of the New Testament translation saints takes place after the last trumpet. After this, the wrath of God will be poured out without mixture. *Colossians 3:6 (KJV)* ⁶ *For which things' sake the wrath of God cometh on the <u>children of disobedience:</u> Romans 9:22 (KJV)* ²² *What if God, willing to shew his wrath, and to make his power known, endured with much longsuffering the vessels of wrath fitted to destruction:* This is reserved for the children of disobedience; they will suffer the **first thunder** for their disobedience as unwise virgins and be reaped as the **residue or cluster** out of the wine press in the second sickle of **Rev. 14:17-18(KJV)**. After this there will be no flesh saved but those souls reserved to repopulate the millennium. What Daniel and John were told not to write is revealed as the conditions at the time the church is being purified.

I pray this revelation will give those with eyes to see and ears to hear a clearer understanding of the tribulation that will bring back the body of believers to … **Ephesians 4:5 (KJV)** ⁵ **One Lord, one faith, one baptism. Revelation 3:18 (KJV)** ¹⁸ **I counsel thee to buy of me gold tried in the fire, that thou mayest be rich; and white raiment, that thou mayest be clothed, and that the shame of thy nakedness do not appear; and anoint thine eyes with eye salve, that thou mayest see.** (Updated for release in 10/2023)

THE POWER OF THE
NEWS MEDIA

"The news for the people too
busy to hear the truth"

This message came to me while watching the news as reported in these channels on the four major networks: ABC, FOX, MSNBC and CNN. As a watchman, this is the shallow controlled news to the public. I watch this news on television as well as interesting movies. What I see in these movies that are coming out of Hollywood, are my visions of the future. Since I am not a dreamer, God is sending a pictorial view of our future in the form of entertainment. In the spirit, I discern the method of the rhetoric, void of truth in all these media programs. These four news networks in my observation spiritually, are feeding their rhetoric from three extremes that feeds negative energy which has resulted in the political state of this nation.

Little do people know the covenant on this nation is the same as Israel and we are to uphold these biblical truths that all men are created equal and within this nation as free servants of the one true God. This right is accorded to every citizen regardless of race, creed or color or nation of origin. What has emerged in these later days is a direct result of the bios rhetoric coming from these four major networks, designed to wake up hidden spirits if hate, using this media platform provided by these networks controlled by the NWO. This nation's president in the sight of God, represent the office of **the king of the free gentile world**, chosen by God to protect Israel; therefore, to speak against your leader as a Christian fuel the negative energy that gives the devil power to increase his activity in the spirit world. As children of the devil, the world cannot help but speak negative but to have confessing Christians sharing the same rhetoric under the Abraham covenant is like speaking death to a once great society.

Now, let's look at what these three networks have to do with this? FOX represents the extreme conservative right while MSNBC the opposite extreme liberal left and CNN is in the middle as an independent. What do we see in this type of media representation? They have the worldwide network of the internet (**beast system**) that's contributing to the controlling of the American public. These Medias are controlled by the people behind the New World Order. All the communication technology invented in this nation is being used to bring us all into a system that has reduced us as a people who now only must know how to use their fingers to get instant gratification from these gadgets of new technology inventions. Therefore, not having to think for themselves, all are wondering after this beastly idol, the internet aided by your smart i-phones. **Rev. 13:3-4**.

These four media outlets are now being used to shape our minds and opinions by using so called authorities from four points of view to convince us that we must choose a side and support us, we will do all the work for you. This generation of tech-no-nerds raised without love are being used to invent technologies that will produce these lying signs and holographic wonders that the world has not been allowed to see. This now brings us to the two political parties, the Democrats and the Republicans; however, the last generation will be victims of the political system as voters.

The state of the political parties will give rise to an independent movement that will appeal to this millennial generation. FOX is the medium for the Republican agenda while MSNBC, the medium for the Democrats and CNN feeds from both as striving to be in the middle as an independent. All three gives you choices along your political beliefs and the rhetoric from these three points of view are used to influence your opinions because you now do not have to think anymore, technology has dumbed you down to where the pace at which you are going mentally and physically leaves no room for you to make your own decisions.

You now depend on the experts to tell you what to think. The same goes for medical advice. Unfortunately, Christians have been seduced to serve the idols of this last generation to the point that they have without knowing God has left them, will choose to follow the beast system. They have given themselves over willingly by submitting to come under subjection to government controlled organized assemblies by taking the mark **501-c3.** These splintered divisions caused the church to be conquered by this government' mark. By there being many different forms of religions, the government had to regulate them by ordering them all to take a 501-C3 government charter to operate. This was set up originally for the world to support their causes under government approved tax free not for profit sponsorship. Now, let's get down to the president's position as the representative of the free world. Many Christians, without knowing are bowing down to the beast; why? The Holy Ghost is not ignorant and therefore those who are born from above will have the unction of the mind of Christ with the power to resist these temptations.

When I was ministering, I was not led to go down that road for that reason. There is nothing in this world that is not controlled by God; he has set all things in motion from the foundation of the world the end from the beginning. (Isa. 46:10) The mind of Christ in you then takes the posture of prayer as the weapons of our warfare. The energy we release in speaking the words of God are far more powerful than the words of the children of the devil. All the presidents who have held this office will have to give an account to God in the judgment for how he conducted himself as a king in this position in the free world, America. As Christians, we are to send up prayers to God for those whose agendas are against our liberties and freedoms granted in our constitution and the laws of God that will change the hearts of these wicked men in this office to execute executive orders against our freedoms. That is the power of prayer.

If the church had remained the conscious of the state, our country would fear a real Christian majority with the ear of God to hear their prayers as did the nation of Israel. Had we remained faithful to this covenant, we would still be a free nation. Instead, we followed our counterpart's path, Israel to go after the glittering idols the devil dangled before us and sold our birth right to exist to our enemy China, Japan and many other nations, will produce the idols we will begin to serve as the meagerly idols of this world. As Israel found out, God is no longer with us. The devil used the nations in his kingdom to offer us their resources in exchange for a few of our secrets to gain a foothold of power. This is how we have been deceived as a nation and handed over to our enemies posing as favoring our democracy only to use this technology to come and defeat, inspired by the powers that's ushering in this New World Order.

When they have achieved their objectives; that is, to collapse us from within and take control of the spoils and divides them among themselves. God has given them this plan, knowing the end from the beginning that brings us to where we are today, on the brink of economic collapse. This is what is fueling the speed of negative energy from these media networks, used to speak evil to divide this nation from within. The present division we see is dismantling our government from with-in through these three Medias controlled by these powers to bring us to the point where every thought and intent is to perpetuate evil continually. The two political parties as evident in this division in our present government's inability to act in the best interest of our liberties.

The people that depend on your local and national news as in the three networks described above, will be the victims of controlled manipulative communications. All this negative energy has overshadowed the prayers of a defeated church world. If you have read the previous chronicles, you should be well informed of this result of our present state as a nation, unprepared to endure. This is the result of a nation that have said **"In God We Trust"** as a covenant that has reserved us as a nation to receive the Abraham blessing for one purpose, to be responsible for the restoration of Israel as a nation.

All the prophecies must be fulfilled in the scriptures, now we have fulfilled our purpose as Gentiles coming to the end of our existence. This is God's final revelation in the closing of the books. Man's time to be is no more and the previous chronicles reveal what we are now about to face in the world as we come to an end of the sixth millennium. Those elected in this last generation are sealed to spend eternity with their creator; those that do not hear them not shall be used to purify them in the fires of tribulation and be destroyed. The power of the media is manifested in how we are adversely affected by riding waves of negative spiritual energy that play into our fears of what we are willingly ignorantly of and choose to ignore. AMEN (Updated Release 3/2023)

WHAT IS IT ABOUT GOD'S LOVE WE DON'T GET?

Background Scriptures:

1 John 3:1 (KJV) ¹ *Behold, what manner of love the Father hath bestowed upon us, that we should be called the sons of God: therefore, the world knoweth us not, because it knew him not. Luke 14:26 (KJV)* ²⁶ *If any man come to me, and hate not his father, and mother, and wife, and children, and brethren, and sisters, yea, and his own life also, he cannot be my disciple. Luke 18:18-22 (KJV)* ¹⁸ *And a certain ruler asked him, saying, Good Master, what shall I do to inherit eternal life?* ¹⁹ *And Jesus said unto him, why callest thou me good? none is good, save one, that is, God.* ²⁰ *Thou knowest the commandments, Do not commit adultery, Do not kill, Do not steal, Do not bear false witness, Honour thy father and thy mother.* ²¹ *And he said, <u>All these have I kept from my youth up</u>.* ²² *Now when Jesus heard these things, he said unto him, Yet lackest thou one thing: <u>sell all that thou hast</u>, and distribute unto the poor, and thou shalt have treasure in heaven: and come, follow me. Luke 16:13 (KJV)* ¹³ *No servant can serve two masters: for either he will hate the one, and love the other; or else he will hold to the one, and despise the other. Ye cannot serve God and mammon. 1 John 2:15 (KJV)* ¹⁵ *Love not the world, neither the things that are in the world. <u>If any man love the world, the love of the Father is not in him.</u>*

I, like many confessing Christians in my early encounter with the word, quoted scripture from a literal understanding with no knowledge of the contextual meaning. Voided of faith, I saw how we are destroyed by the devil for lack of knowledge. God sent his Holy Spirit to teach us all things but what we have received through blind guides in their best intentions, caused us to operate in the wrong spirit as ... *"ever learning but never able to come to the knowledge of the truth". (1 Timothy 3:7)*

The revelation we missed is, the work is the lord's using our bodies. All these scriptures above are pointing to Christ in you to perform what we are not capable of doing without him. *John 12:32(KJV)* [32] *And I, if I be lifted up from the earth, will draw all men unto me.* It has come to my understanding that if Jesus is to live; you must die; the two of us cannot occupy the same house without recognizing who is in control. Now I know why he said, **"few there be that find it."** *(Matthew 7:14) Amos 3:3 (KJV)* [3] *Can two walk together, except they be agreed?* You see, the way to Christ is to surrender and let Him make you an ensample in his word. Now, who do you know that is walking in Christ as he walked on earth? Christ demonstrated the Agape love and when you surrender your will, others will see this kind of love in you.

This is what became known to me, now I strive to let Him be. You have heard me say how I was brought into this rest; I did not come on my own. I found out I was elected before the foundation of the world, when the time he had preordained for this to happen, His spirit drew me in and took over my life. This experience leaves you with a testimony of what was done and how it was done. This is where we learn to testify of him. I cannot express in words what it is like to be able to love unconditionally; this is an experience of his power to be able to endure hurts, insults, rejections and hold no remorse in your heart. You only see the good as to what that person can be and being a surrendered vessel, God lift himself in this way that gets the attention of those he has open to receive salvation.

This gives meaning to my life that is beyond words; he now is the doer of the word as I surrender my ways. This is what I have experienced. It is manifested more in deeds that follow His words; only when the two are combined are the bassists of a miracle. I have found also that this love is not demonstrated in words alone but in actions and deeds. You will be placed in circumstances to test your obedience and faith so God can get the glory when others testify of him working through you. This I learn why self must die for this kind of love to be seen. I noticed that my ability to discern is becoming keener in the circumstances of life. If Christ is not the center focus of your life, you will not be perfect in this kind of love.

You cannot speak everything you hear the spirit tell you about others. Some things he shows and tells you are to make you aware of the circumstances. You will not be given this favor until you surrender your will. What makes most of us become a judge is when we are seduced to think of ourselves more highly than we should because of what we have been given to know. It will become a test to see if you will remain as that little child. We are to ... *1 Thessalonians 4:11 (KJV)* [11] *And that ye study to be quiet, and to do your own business, and to work with your own hands, as we commanded you; I know why Paul told Timothy to .... 2 Timothy 2:15 (KJV)* [15] *Study to shew thyself approved unto God, a workman that needeth not to be ashamed, rightly dividing the word of truth.* He will reward you when you diligently seek him in obedience through his word.

When he introduces himself, you will never be the same person you were before you met him. Those of you with religious spirits that justify your sins by saying, we cannot be as perfect as Christ have not been converted. If you can find in the word that Christ endorsed these sins that defiled his body by continuing in sins as described in *Galatians 5:17-21 (KJV)* [17] *For the flesh lusteth against the Spirit, and the Spirit against the flesh: and these are contrary the one to the other: so that ye cannot do the things that ye would.* [18] *But if ye be led of the Spirit, ye are not under the law.* [19] *Now the works of the flesh are manifest, which are these; Adultery, fornication, uncleanness, lasciviousness,* [20] *Idolatry, witchcraft, hatred, variance, emulations, wrath, strife, seditions, heresies,* [21] *Envying, murders, drunkenness, revellings, and such like: of the which I tell you before, as I have also told you in time past, that they which do such things shall not inherit the kingdom of heaven Jude 1:8 (KJV)* [8] *Likewise also these filthy dreamers defile the flesh, despise dominion, and speak evil of dignities.*

You see, when he said be still, he is trying to get our attention. In an assembly where the doctrine is down on man's level of logical seminary theology, there is no deep convictions, the assemblies occupied with all these spirits, becomes an unholy environment, therefore, the Holy Spirit cannot operate. *Ecclesiastes 12:14 (KJV) For God shall bring every work into judgment, with every secret thing, whether it be good, or whether it be evil.*

Why do you think Satan is always keeping us busy, so we will miss God by keeping us entangled with the cares of this life? Even in your service to your local assembly, it is the few that become too entangled to have an active spiritual life. They will carry the weight of those that want to be associated with an assembly by name only. This is where I saw many in these assemblies burdened with administrative task that have no spiritual benefit to the people; otherwise, you are zeal fully working in your own strength to please the organization without even knowing this is their problem holding them back from spiritual growth. Without knowing what you are doing is not in line with the apostle's doctrine as taught by Christ.

Deliverance will be replaced with programs that need people to run them and these men will label them as their ministries and call it working for God. *2 Timothy 2:4 (KJV)* [4] *No man that warreth entangleth himself with the affairs of this life; that he may please him who hath chosen him to be a soldier.* There are many soldiers call to battle, but only one general has the battle plans for victory, that's why we all must work as one. Even the false teachers know how to keep you under their bonds as their servant is to have you all under control. Remember, *Amos 3:3 (KJV)* [3] *Can two walk together, except they be agreed?*

When one is drafted by the Holy Spirit, (elected) the first thing you recognize is who is in authority; next, your indoctrination begins, only those who endure the test of perfect obedience are sent out on the battlefields. They become the true patriots of the gospel of truth whose victory is guaranteed if you follow the general's orders, your enemy will be defeated. That soldier goes to battle knowing that he may become a casualty; the motivation for which he serves unto death was the inspiration he received in his indoctrination, he is made to see that the rewards are far greater than his sacrifice. *John 15:13 (KJV)* [13] *Greater love hath no man than this that a man lay down his life for his friends.*

When I see our leaders of this nation sacrificing the lives of innocent soldiers for their own political agendas, I know these young men are just following orders. My heart goes out to them in prayer for their sacrifice for our nation's pride in vain glory. These are the wars we will never win. God will hear the cries of these innocent soldiers as they are led to the slaughter at the hands of corrupt politicians in government. When I was call to military service in the **Vietnam war,** A Jewish doctor told me, this war is not for you; gave me a letter to give to the CO at the induction center. I was sent home and reclassified as 1-Y.

All who fall in love with Christ will love fellow brothers and sisters who have been begotten of the same love in the spirit. This is his family of obedient children. *1 John 2:20 (KJV)* [20] *But ye have an <u>unction</u> from the Holy One, and ye know all things. John 13:35 (KJV)* [35] *By this shall all men know that ye are my disciples, if ye have love one to another.* This love is purified as our minds are renewed day by day. The closer you get to Him, your fears will leave, your faith will get stronger, and confidence increased. When things start to happen to you like they did to Christ, you know you must be on the right road. That is because you are more conscious of sin than those around you as your deeds become more righteous. You see, it is his love that caused you to obey.

You, in singleness of heart, is seeking to save yourself from the wickedness around you by not giving place to the seducing spirits that lead you to sin. When we come to be converted, we will have the mind of Christ. I see an increase in the activity in the spirit world. Many who are not stable are being seduced without their knowing; while those of us who are aware of this activity in the spirit world are getting closer to the Lord; others, clinging to worldly traditions of idol worship as God turns up the heat in the activities of this world. This is what you are about to see happen in every confessing Christian? When God takes away all our creature comforts, we will see the hidden spirits you were not delivered from, show themselves. *Matthew 12:33 (KJV)* [33] *Either make the tree good, and his fruit good; or else make the tree corrupt, and his fruit corrupt: for the tree is known by his fruit. Ephesians 5:11-12 (KJV)* [11] *And have no fellowship with the unfruitful works of darkness, but rather reprove them. James 1:8 (KJV)* [8] *A double minded man is unstable in all his ways.* Only when you are provoked in a crisis will this spirit show who possesses the vessel.

Each time I have an occasion to enter a church building; it is like going back in time. Having eyes to see and ears to hear invokes the spirit of intersession that others may see what you see. The perfect love manifested in compassion for souls that will be lost if no one plead for them. Apostle John, the beloved disciple, gave us his account of what it was like to walk in this love. After the resurrection, testified in his epistles of what it was like to be in his presence. The power of this love in him gave him the ability to endure all that the devil put on him and die an old man of natural causes on the island of Patmos. That same power is in you.

He truly experienced what it was like to have no weapon formed against him to prevail. All that I have found in the bible especially the New Testament points us to this kind of love that lets Jesus be seen in us. Only God can judge because he has the power to cast you into hell, not man. If you are not moved with compassion by what you see, you are not yet perfect in love. *Isaiah 54:17 (KJV)* [17] *No weapon that is formed against thee shall prosper; and every tongue that shall rise against thee in judgment thou shalt condemn. This is the heritage of the servants of the Lord, and their righteousness is of me, saith the Lord. 1 John 4:4 (KJV)* [4] *Ye are of God, little children, and have overcome them: because greater is he that is in you, than he that is in the world.* My dear brothers and sisters, this is the power of love. AMEN (Released 3/11)

WHICH GODS ARE YOUR IDOLS?

Background Scripture:

Proverbs 16:25 (KJV) "*25 There is a way that seemeth right unto a man, but the end thereof are the ways of death. Proverbs 18:21 (KJV) 21 Death and life are in the power of the tongue: and they that love it shall eat the fruit thereof. Luke 6:46 (KJV) 46 And why call ye me, Lord, Lord, and do not the things which I say? John 14:15 (KJV) 15 If ye love me, keep my commandments.*

Matthew 12:34 (KJV) 34 O generation of vipers, how can ye, being evil, speak good things? for out of the abundance of the heart the mouth speaketh. Proverbs 6:2 (KJV) 2 Thou art snared with the words of thy mouth, thou art taken with the words of thy mouth. John 8:44-45 (KJV) 44 Ye are of your father the devil, and the lusts of your father ye will do. He was a murderer from the beginning, and abode not in the truth, because there is no truth in him. When he speaketh a lie, he speaketh of his own: for he is a liar, and the father of it. 45 And because I tell you the truth, ye believe me not.

Many of us do not have a righteous understanding of what is an idol. As I sit in meditation, the Holy Spirit revealed this to me. *"My people only know me in part and therefore serve me in part. Their testimonies identify themselves with the denomination they were convicted in or the movement they believe in. They do not recognize that these teachings are under the law, will cause you to become a modern-day Pharisee. This form of separatism is why there*

are divisions among you. As I told you in time past and now tell you again" ...
2 Peter 2:1 (KJV) "¹ But there were false prophets also among the people, even as there shall be false teachers among you, who privily shall bring in damnable heresies, even denying the Lord that bought them, and bring upon themselves swift destruction. 1 John 4:1 (KJV) ¹ Beloved, believe not every spirit, but try the spirits whether they are of God: because many false prophets are gone out into the world."

THE REAL GOSPEL WILL JUDGE YOU AND EXPOSE THEM AS LIERS. They thought Jesus had a devil, don't be surprised when you begin to walk like this, some will also depart from you and say the same of you; for some, it will be true. When you decide to eat His flesh and drink of His blood, false brothering will walk away from you too.

Only those elected will carry the true gospel that represent and demonstrate the presents of the Holy Spirit. These are the few among the people that will be persecuted as doers of the word because ...*1 John 2:27 (KJV)" ²⁷ But the anointing which ye have received of him abideth in you, and ye need not that any man teach you: but as the same anointing teacheth you of all things, and is truth, and is no lie, and even as it hath taught you, ye shall abide in him. Matthew 7:21-22-23 (KJV) ²¹ Not everyone that saith unto me, Lord, Lord, shall enter into the kingdom of heaven; but he that doeth the will of my Father which is in heaven. ²² Many will say to me in that day, Lord, Lord, have we not prophesied in thy name? and in thy name have cast out devils? and in thy name done many wonderful works? ²³ And then will I profess unto them, I never knew you: depart from me, ye that work iniquity." James 2:10 (KJV) ¹⁰ For whosoever shall keep the whole law, and yet offend in one point, he is guilty of all.*

Now, are you ready to be a Christian? Before God separated me from the present-day assemblies, I, like many of you believed in part and thought I had it all together as a Christian. Many of you will reject these truths as strange doctrine because you have been indoctrinated in denominations or movements you identify yourself with. Without knowing, this has become your idol; now you see how easy it is to be deceived to worship your denomination's belief as an idol that can only point you to a man. That's what has us *"ever learning and never able to come to the knowledge of the truth"*. When someone ask, what are you, most will say, **I'm non-denominational, Baptist, Catholic, Methodist, Jehovah's Witness,**

Mormon, Episcopalian, Muslin, etcetera. What all this means, you don't have a clear understanding of who you are because false teaching has brought us down to believe in your denominations or movements' doctrines. This is the theology of man that identify how divided we have become under man's doctrines ... *Mark 7:9 (KJV)* *"⁹ And he said unto them, Full well ye reject the commandment of God, that ye may keep your own tradition."* In the chronicle titled ... **"Living in the reality of the new birth,"** these seven characteristics of those who are born again as to being subject to the Holy Spirit's teachings. They don't go around telling everyone who they are. When you are truly born again, the Holy Spirit speaks for himself. *John 15:26 (KJV)* ²⁶ *But when the Comforter is come, whom I will send unto you from the Father, even the Spirit of truth, which proceedeth from the Father, he shall testify of me: John 16:13 (KJV)* ¹³ *Howbeit when he, the Spirit of truth, is come, he will guide you into all truth: for he shall not speak of himself; but whatsoever he shall hear, that shall he speak: and he will shew you things to come.* The Holy Spirit manifests himself in those who have surrendered their will to the father in true repentance.

These are the called-out ones used to bring those the father has called to repentance and teach those in error this more excellent way in the perfect will of God. Do not be shocked at this statement; you don't have to be a pastor, prophet, evangelist, teacher or an apostle to do this; just a servant as a yield vessel under grace is all that is required to be used of God. This I speak from my own experience as a servant, I have been used in a few of these graces just by being available.

As I have said, it is not in the title but in just being obedient in the Spirit and you will be used. If I claim one of the offices in myself, with two living wives at that time, I would be a reproach to the truth. It's only when God reveals himself to you, He becomes real. False dreams and visions do not reveal this kind of truth because they are from the devil. This is through a relationship by constant fellowship and praying in a submissive spirit that does not question him. I understand how easy it is to be deceived and not know it; I was myself until God open my eyes. As I have said in time past, you will never know you are deceived until God give you ears to hear the truth that reaches the heart that brings conviction of your shortcomings.

That's when the Holy Spirit is drawing you to come into to the kingdom as one of his children. *John 6:44 (KJV)* ⁴⁴ *No man can come to me, except the Father which hath sent me draw him: and I will raise him up at the last day. Revelation 3:20 (KJV)* [20] *Behold, I stand at the door, and knock: if any man hear my voice, and open the door, I will come into him, and will sup with him, and he with me.* You see, God is not associated with anything on earth because He is heavenly, those who are born from above are ... *Colossians 3:1-2 (KJV)* [1] *If ye then be risen with Christ, seek those things which are above, where Christ sitteth on the right hand of God.* [2] *Set your affection on things above, not on things on the earth. John 4:24 (KJV)* [24] *God is a Spirit: and they that worship him must worship him in spirit and in truth. Romans 8:9 (KJV)* [9] *But ye are not in the flesh, but in the Spirit, if so be that the Spirit of God dwell in you. Now if any man have not the Spirit of Christ, he is none of his.*

This is the mind of God. The only assembly God dwells in is of one mind when they come together as on the day of Pentecost under the anointing of the Holy Spirit, this is the oneness that brings his presence. Now, you are the temples that brings the presents of the Holy Spirit when you assemble as in the days of the early apostles. *2 Corinthians 6:16 (KJV)* "[16] *And what agreement hath <u>the temple of God with idols</u>? for ye are the temple of the living God; as God hath said, I will dwell in them, and walk in them; and I will be their God, and they shall be my people. Ephesians 5:11 (KJV)* [11] *And have no fellowship with the unfruitful works of darkness, but rather reprove them. 2 Corinthians 6:17 (KJV)* [17] *Wherefore come out from among them, and be ye separate, saith the Lord, and touch not the unclean thing; and I will receive you.*" If a pastor is not an ensample of the works of Christ, that is, seeing people healed, delivered from demons, opening the eyes of the blind and freeing all that are oppressed of the devil, **(Isaiah. 61:1-5 KJV)** Many will say as I did in ignorance, that is not my calling; well, why would he say *"these signs will follow them that believe"* I did not see it followed by an office. That is why he said, it is according to your faith. This He spoke to his apostles before the ascension to be imparted into as many as receive him. Wherever He finds faith, He can use any one of faith to speak the word. Remember, when Ananias laid hand on Paul to receive his sight, we all are his priest. *Matthew 9:29 (KJV)* [29] **Then touched he their eyes, saying,** *according to your faith be it unto you.*

My dear brothers and sisters, I was shocked too when God revealed this to me after opening my eyes to truth. This is what it is to be born of the spirit. We are told to … *2 Timothy 2:15 (KJV)* [15] *Study to shew thyself approved unto God, a workman that needeth not to be ashamed, rightly dividing the word of truth.* We are to be Bereans in the word to keep from being deceived. *Acts 17:11 (KJV)* [11] *These were more noble than those in Thessalonica, in that they received the word with all readiness of mind, and searched the scriptures daily, whether those things were so.*

I rely on the Holy Spirit to rightly divide the word to me in the spirit because he is the master teacher. As you see in these writings, the supporting scriptures are to establish who is speaking. These sayings given to me in the spirit are too hard for some to receive because this represents where we are supposed to be after two thousand years of the presents of the Holy Spirit. I find myself weeping in sorrow as many have departed from me as being separated from brethren as John the Baptist to receive this revelation. Some I had to separate myself because they could not receive this type of meat, sadly, many have been confessing Christians longer than I.

Another thing I notice, we as brethren … do not take to subjecting ourselves to one another in the spirit as equals. Many times, when I shared what God was saying to me, many were offended because of the depth of what was being said provoked them to envy as being a leader in the assembly, show their hidden pride. I have taken to interceding for them that their eyes and ears will be open to truth in this more perfect way of God as mine is.

We have been taught that we cannot live perfect, it is for this reason that many having rejected some of these teachings, remain influenced in traditional teaching by willing ignorance, will reject the truth of God to keep their denominational belief or hold to their own opinion in error. The scriptures say we are to live and be as though we are in *"no continual city but ever seeking one to come," (Heb. 13:14 KJV) not "ever learning but never able to come to the knowledge of the truth".* Now the next time someone enquire of your faith, let the Holy Spirit testify of Himself. (Updated for release 5/2019)

INSIGHTS FROM YOUR
END TIME MESSENGER

"What to watch for in time to come"

Many confessing Christians are unaware of the realities of the spiritual forces at work to defeat you in every aspect of your life. As one of God's servants raised up to mentor those assign to me, it is evident by the situational circumstances, many have missed this final vision; therefore, will not endure. There is a discernable increase in the activity of the spirits of oppression in the lives of some confessing Christians. *1 Peter 4:12 "(KJV)* **12** Beloved, think it not strange concerning the fiery trial which is to try you, as though some strange thing happened unto you: *1 Peter 4:4 (KJV)* **4** Wherein they think it strange that ye run not with them to the same excess of riot, speaking evil of you": **1 Peter 4:4 (NLT)** **4 Of course, your former friends are very surprised when you no longer join them in the wicked things they do, and they say evil things about you."**

What I see happening is in the realm where Satan has been given the authority to increase his activity against the believers who act on God's word, we who are dying daily are fully aware of the increased activity of Satan. The Holy Spirit will keep you aware of this by discernment. His efforts to hinder our continued progress in this warfare in the spirit world are in the things we refuse to give up.

2 Timothy 3:12 (KJV)" **12** *Yea, and all that will live godly in Christ Jesus shall suffer persecution."* We are being crucified while in this wilderness as was Jesus by being separated out unto himself. We are to continue in faith in his spoken word, knowing that we are in control of our destiny awaiting our day of redemption. We are preparing to suffer with Christ therefore … *Acts 14:22 "(KJV)* [22] *Confirming the souls of the disciples, and exhorting them to continue in the faith, and that we must through much tribulation enter into the kingdom of God."* It is unfortunate that the church world has been presented the side of God through false teaching as in the doctrine of rapture and prosperity. This hidden church will be re-united into one body in the latter rain, believing in one God as at Pentecost, exercising the faith that made it all possible. The reason why things are changing around you is that we are all being tested for your loyalties to choose who you will serve by separating the doers from the hearers only.

In these times, the activity in the spirit world has been stepped up another level, anything that can be used against you, will, which includes members of your own household will manifest spirits of Cain, causing the death of their bloodline to save themselves. Some of us have had it somewhat relatively easy in our created comfort zones; it has given us a false since of reality and security. The sudden changes in our circumstances are seen in the lives of people around you. America and the world are in a time of international reckoning. We are about to be tested to see who your god is when he reveals your heart by your action in the coming tribulation. This is the reason for tribulation to show the world, who is the one true God and this time, take them home in the rapture.

We are going to be given a choice to separate our self from those used to persecute you in the name of God through the spirit as an antichrist child of the devil. The reason we are told to separate yourself from them is to gain strength to resist the devil using them.

You who are employed in the workplace are going to have to trust God by doing good for those used to oppress you. Everything we will encounter as confessing Christians is covered in the word. Therefore, if we are not studying and dying to self, we are not engrafting the strength of the word that is necessary for our spiritual growth. You will not be able to resist these temptations in the form of sudden trials if your flesh is still alive. Remember, Peter's denial was in thinking he had the ability to do what only God can, resist the devil without the power of God. If you are not born from above, you will do the same thing.

You must live in the reality of being a new creature which means Christ living, moving and having his being in your vessel. These things are now coming upon us through these spirits around you. This is going to be our last trial that will separate the believers from the unbelievers for his glory. If you are having it good and are well loved, check yourself out, you may be compromising to get along. Remember, obedience to the word of God will attract persecution form those you offend by you being a doer of the word. *Luke 6:26 (KJV) "26 Woe unto you, when all men shall speak well of you! for so did their fathers to the false prophets."* If you are really converted, your mind will be on heavenly things. This is what makes it easy to suffer because you live in the reality of the power of God in you by the new birth and is now able to stand in his strength, his power and his might. Knowing all things are yours but all you need is what it takes to get through each day.

This is a time to be still. Many in traditional assemblies will not receive this vision of the times because we have been taught that we must win souls in our own strength as working for God instead of working with him. That is the error in theology as taught by man's traditions when in fact, it only contributes to separate kingdom building in the name of God. Why is there so much division at this end time? God knows who he has purposed to save through you, that is why we are told to "be still and know that I am God." *Isaiah 55:8 (KJV) "8 For my thoughts are not your thoughts, neither are your ways my ways, saith the LORD."* Beloved, don't be offended when I make this statement? We all need to repent to put ourselves in the perfect will of God. All this is a result of what God has allowed in his permissive will because he will not impose upon your will unless you are chosen as one of his elects. I was shocked too when he showed me how I was out of his will when the time came for my eyes to be open by election only. How do I know this? He opened my eyes when I thought I was right to see how wrong I was in his permissive will. That is how I knew it was God speaking to me.

I had to be given a hard rebuked to get my attention. Do not remain in that 98 percent that refuse to believe that we still have prophets and messengers as in the Old Testament in this time. It is unfortunate that we are deceived to this degree as I was because of long standing traditions that have through many generations seared our minds in a state of willing ignorance; delusional to think that the very word we say we believe, out of context in its application shall be a witness against us if we do not repent.

The John the Baptist ministry will return in his messengers as it did to introduce Christ. This time, he will warn us of his return to set the body back to our first love and prepare for the fires during the tribulation with this word of warning. ***Revelation 3:18 (KJV) "18 I counsel thee to buy of me gold tried in the fire, that thou mayest be rich; and white raiment, that thou mayest be clothed, and that the shame of thy nakedness do not appear; and anoint thine eyes with eye salve, that thou mayest see."***

It will be the last warning. The guardian angel or angels assign to as many as be saved are subject to your free will, they have their instructions from God. We must agree with God's will as being born from above to become one with the spirits in the third heaven. We who live in that reality and faith, have complete authority over the spirits in the second heaven. If we are walking in the spirit as led of God in all things, his spirit is one with the word and these guardian angels will not let Satan's host of wicked spirits touch you for this reason ... **1 John 4:4 (KJV)" ⁴Ye are of God, little children, and have overcome them: because greater is *he that is in you, than he that is in the world. Therefore, Psalm 91:10 (KJV) ¹⁰There shall no evil befall thee, neither shall any plague come nigh thy dwelling. Isaiah 54:17 (KJV) ¹⁷No weapon that is formed against thee shall prosper; and every tongue that shall rise against thee in judgment thou shalt condemn. This is the heritage of the servants of the LORD, and their righteousness is of me, saith the LORD."***

You see, when you come to the knowledge that you are a chosen vessel, you will humble and obey and the above scriptures are the promises and the angel or angels on assignment are given the authority by you speaking what God tells you to speak, protect you from the evils of this world while you are in this world.

That's the prayer Jesus prayed to make us one in the earth with him and the father in heaven. The wicked spirits in the second heaven can no longer hinder our prayers prayed in the will of our father. These keys Satan no longer has, now you can bypass the second heaven and go directly into the throne room in the third heaven that Paul saw and heard and find grace to help you in time of need. Daniel's prayers were hindered for twenty-one days trying to get through the second heaven. This is where the angels that rebelled with Satan dwells.

They are waiting to be judged and are now wondering wicked spirits waiting to be assigned a body every time there is a birth in the earth, Satan assigns a body to them until it is claimed by God for his use. Satan has the right to use the body now because of Adam's sin until God claims it for his use because he gave it life.

Jesus delivered us from the power of all these innumerable wicked spirits to enter you by receiving him and told us to never look back as remembering what happen to Lot's wife. *Luke 9:62 And Jesus said unto him, no man, having put his hand to the plough, and looking back, is fit for the kingdom of God.* When they are cast out, this is what happens? ... *Luke 11:24-6 (KJV)* [24] *When the unclean spirit is gone out of a man, he walketh through dry places, seeking rest; and finding none, he saith, I will return unto my house whence I came out.* [25] *And when he cometh, he findeth it swept and garnished.* [26] *Then goeth he, and taketh to him seven other spirits more wicked than himself; and they enter in, and dwell there: and the last state of that man is worse than the first.* Spiritually, this is what happens when we confess salvation; our temple was cleaned by faith when you receive Christ.

Satan was put out, all the doors to your temple were closed and your temple was sealed and made ready for Jesus to fully occupy the entire house. He will operate from inside out because all the doors to your temple were closed and sealed from within. Only you can open those doors. What goes into the heart from the spoken word of God will be what comes out of the mouth. The five gates to the natural world are where Satan will try to return to the vessel he was put out of. That's what you will see, taste, smell and touch and feel. Now, he will have to get your permission to come back in. It is your free will to choose when he presents all the enticements of the world you once loved. When you received the report of the finished works Christ did for you, your body became the temple at that moment by faith in the spoken word which brought about a heartfelt conviction.

When Satan returns and knocks, if you do not recognize him disguised as Jesus, **which is now <u>inside</u> and not outside,** in that deception, open that door to your soul, you will at that time, becoming a religious person with a dual personality when you break the seal to open the door to your soul again. Satan enters, you will not know what spirit you are of until you hear the real gospel again that reveals who is with-in by the fruit. That is why you must continue to walk in the spirit by faith without doubt that gives place to the Holy Spirit to do the discerning and take authority over Satan. The reason we fall short of the fullness of this authority, **2 Corinthians 4:3 (KJV) "3 But if our gospel be hid, it is hid to them that are lost":** To understand this verse is to have the knowledge of the spirit world and the faith to believe the greater one in you is now in control of your spirit, soul and body. If you entertain any doubts, these become the cracks in the seals he enters that spoils the fruit by not continuing in the truth.

This is how ... **Hosea 4:6 (KJV)" 6 My people are destroyed for lack of knowledge: because thou hast rejected knowledge, I will also reject thee, that thou shalt be no priest to me: seeing thou hast forgotten the law of thy God, I will also forget thy children."** The people with religious spirits will reject the truth because they are still in love with the world. They are not aware that the old man is still in charge of their thoughts.

They will not know who their real father is. That is what it is to be blind. Blind men without direction will stumble and fall. **1 John 5:16 (KJV)" 16 If any man see his brother sin a sin which is not unto death, he shall ask, and he shall give him life for them that sin not unto death. <u>There is a sin unto death: I do not say that he shall pray for it.</u>"** Those that walk-in truth is to help those who are confessing just like you to see the true light by example to keep them from dying in the sins that come with religious spirits. The sin that Judas committed after having sat in the presence of God and turned him over to the devil can only be committed by those that come to the knowledge of the truth. This kind of blasphemy will not be forgiven. **1 John 5:17 (KJV) "17 All unrighteousness is sin: <u>and there is a sin not unto death</u>."**

These are the sins not unto death that you can be forgiven for if you repent before you die; these are the sins that many will ... **Daniel 5:27 (KJV) 27; Thou art weighed in the balances, and art found wanting.** They represent lack of knowledge and willful sinning that will send you to hell if any of these seven-teen sins are found in you when God requires your soul .... **Galatians 5:19-21 (KJV) "19 Now the works of the flesh are manifest, which are these; <u>Adultery, fornication, uncleanness, lasciviousness</u>, 20 <u>Idolatry, witchcraft, hatred, variance, emulations, wrath, strife, seditions, heresies</u>, 21 <u>Envying, murders, drunkenness, revellings</u>, and such like: of the which I** *tell you before, as I have also told you in time past, that <u>they which do such things shall not inherit the kingdom of God..</u>"*

Galatians 5:19-21 (NLT) [19] **When you follow the desires of your sinful nature, your lives will produce these evil results: <u>sexual immorality, impure thoughts, eagerness for lustful pleasure,</u>** [20] **idolatry, <u>participation in demonic activities, hostility, quarreling, jealousy, outbursts of anger, selfish ambition, divisions, the feeling that everyone is wrong except those in your own little group,</u>** [21] **<u>envy, drunkenness, wild parties,</u> and other kinds of sin. Let me tell you again, as I have before, that anyone living that sort of life will not inherit the Kingdom of God."**

These are the sins committed by lukewarm confessing Christians with shallow convictions or a false view of Christianity, if un-confessed, cause you to be luke-warm and be spit out of God's mouth in the judgment. This represents to God that you have not made up your mind as to who you are going to serve, he makes the choice for you by handing you to the devil for being in that state when he requires your soul. If not confessed before you die, as sated at the end of this verse, you will go to hell. If you are not living in the reality of your new birth, you will not have the strength to resist these spirits of temptation we war with in our minds daily. Considering how many Christians say they are born again, when tested, only then will the spirit you are of be seen and speak for it-self.

Remember, the Pharisees and Sadducees did not know this reality until Jesus told them (John 8:44) and they still killed him not knowing that they were of, the devil that made them do it. They were acting under his influence to fulfill the scriptures. God had already given them over to the devil. God knew their hearts were hardened against truth. Lukewarm Christians in the same spirit will deliver those born again flesh dead blood brought Christians in the days ahead when the test comes again in the downfall of this nation very soon. What I have been made to see, it will take all of me surrendered to see the fullness of him. All that are led into this wilderness will see that in part done away with. *1 Corinthians 13:9-10 (KJV) "9 For we know in part, and we prophesy in part.* [10] *But when that which is perfect is come, then that which is in part shall be done away.* Christ will be in his elects and they that receive them will be added to the kingdom to replace those in that 98 percent that's going to repeat history by not knowing his voice when he calls. They are going to do what the Jews did, reject him in you. Many of their children will be brought in to replace them to fill the house at the marriage supper of the lamb. The world will see the real Jesus in glory returned as head of his body of believers. All will bow down, worship and confess that he is God when our idol gods are shown up as such in the tribulation. (Completed for release 6/2018)

THE PRIORITY SINNERS PRAYER SHOULD BE?

"Lord, deliver me from myself"

Coming from a traditional assembly teaching in my early years, as I look back at where I came from as to where I am now, all I can say in comparison is? I was a victim of traditional assembly teachings. Now, this is the shocker. I thought I was Saved because of repeating these verses ... *Romans 10:9-10 (KJV) "⁹ That if thou shalt confess with thy mouth the Lord Jesus, and shalt believe in thine heart that God hath raised him from the dead, thou shalt be saved. ¹⁰ For with the heart man believeth unto righteousness; and with the mouth confession is made unto salvation.* This is the truth. *Hebrews 4:2 (KJV) ² for unto us was the gospel preached, as well as unto them: but the word preached did not profit them, not being mixed with faith in them that heard it;"* furthermore, to show you how dumb I was, each time I joined a new church, I would get baptized. I heard what was quoted to me as truth, but where I went wrong, it was not with a Godly understanding of the context or with a demonstration of faith and power in an environment to produce the right fruit. That is what some seminary theologist have over time, brought to the assemblies.

When I was convicted by the Holy Spirit some twenty years later, yes! It was that long before God himself convicted me in a second marriage. You see, because I was a chosen vessel, I was used despite of my ignorance while married to my first wife because God's hand was upon me working all things out to his good, giving me experiences that will help others while I was operating in his permissive will. What I was exposed to in my initial conviction was a shallow view of the gospel, taught down on the level of the re-organized assembly, operating under theological teachings down on the level of man's influence; the structured order of service that put the Holy Ghost in the background and man in the foreground. This is what it is to be seduced into strange doctrines and not even know it. This was my first encounter with the so-called gospel. Without knowing, I was ... *2 Timothy 3:7 (KJV)* [7] *Ever learning, and never able to come to the knowledge of the truth.* This is what will happen when you think you have a better way of winning souls than the Holy Spirit. Each of us is responsible for the salvation of our souls by keeping the word in the forefront of our new life we have committed to Christ as to continue in him. This is the conviction that comes through the Holy Ghost anointing in the preaching of the gospel that comes with a demonstration of faith in them that heard it.

This is where you see the sovereign will of God, selecting souls for his kingdom. We cannot live a life as a new creature until we yield to the leading of the Holy Spirit. Anything less than the apostle's doctrine of Jesus Christ will not produce fruit that remain. *John 12:32 (KJV)* "*32 And I, if I be lifted up from the earth, will draw all men unto me.*" It is for this reason that ... *John 6:44 (KJV)* "*44 No man can come to me, except the Father which hath sent me draw him: and I will raise him up at the last day.*" Down on the level of traditional teachings, where there is no anointing, Jesus cannot show himself as the deliverer. Therefore, you are deceived into a vein representation by man presenting the gospel the way he sees it instead of having the vision from the anointing of the Holy Spirit. God will not override your free will because he gave us that free will to choose who you will serve.

Now you see why we fall short just by being persuaded by the wrong teacher. I was a victim of all that and God let me go for twenty years and used me despite this until he was ready to have the Holy Spirit to bring me into his presence for the purpose I was born. Now that should shake you up if you are a confessing Christian living in sin without convictions of it. *Matthew 22:14 (KJV)* "*14 For many are called, but few are chosen. 1 Corinthians 1:26 (KJV)* [26] *For ye see your calling, brethren, how that not many wise men after the flesh, not many mighty, not many noble, are called: 1 Corinthians 1:26 (NLT)* [26] *Remember, dear brothers and sisters, that few of you were wise in the world's eyes, or powerful, or wealthy when God called you. John 15:16 (KJV* [16] *Ye have not chosen me, but I have chosen you, and ordained you, that ye should go and bring forth fruit, and that your fruit should remain: that whatsoever ye shall ask of the Father in my name, he may give it you."*

Now you should see as I did when my eyes were open why my fruit was corrupt as demonstrated in my shortcomings. All of us know we should do good but without the real gospel as demonstrated in faith, purity and power of holiness, we cannot overcome the temptations that are in this world that keeps us under the influence of sin. *Hosea 4:6 (KJV)* [6] *My people are destroyed for lack of knowledge: because thou hast rejected knowledge, I will also reject thee, that thou shalt be no priest to me: seeing thou hast forgotten the law of thy God, I will also forget thy children.* Except you receive the real Holy Ghost, you will not have the power to resist the devil. Notice, I said, **real** Holy Ghost; you see, there is a **false one** that will cause you to appear religious around others but show corrupt fruit … *1 John 2:20 (KJV)* [20] *But ye have an unction from the Holy One, and ye know all things. John 13:18 (KJV)* "[18] *I speak not of you all: I know whom I have chosen: but that the scripture may be fulfilled, He that eateth bread with me hath lifted up his heel against me."* The doers of the word will always suffer at the hands of those who are offended by being shown up as false brothering.

Only those chosen will do the will of the father because they are chosen. If any good is done through you, it is the work of God using you as a vessel of honor or of dishonor. It is up to you to know who is in possession of your vessel. The real Holy Ghost will keep sin from remaining in the assembly, by lifting God's standard of holiness that brings real conviction to produce the fruit of the Holy Spirit that will remain. That's why Jesus said … *John 3:14 (KJV)* [14] *And as Moses lifted up the serpent in the wilderness, even so must the Son of man be lifted up: John 12:32 (KJV)* [32] *And I, if I be lifted up from the earth, will draw all men unto me.*

Why do some of us have such a hard time staying saved after we have confessed salvation? Some pastors have preached the doctrine; **"that once save always save"** is a false doctrine that originated in the split that divided and separated the Baptist assemblies. This is the result of living in a compromised environment practicing the principles of truth without the Holy Spirit. Now I am not judging the Baptist, but labels get their names by reason of divisions in doctrinal theology by these denominational names they identify themselves with.

This is the gap as was in the days when john was baptizing teaching of one that was going to come with the anointing, Jesus. *Acts 19:1-5 (KJV) "1 And it came to pass, that, while Apollos was at Corinth, Paul having passed through the upper coasts came to Ephesus: and finding certain disciples, 2 He said unto them, Have ye received the Holy Ghost since ye believed? And they said unto him, <u>we have not so much as heard whether there be any Holy Ghost.</u> 3 And he said unto them, unto what then were ye baptized? And they said, Unto John's baptism. 4 Then said Paul, John verily baptized with the baptism of repentance, saying unto the people, that they should believe on him which should come after him, that is, on Christ Jesus. 5 When they heard this, they were baptized in the name of the Lord Jesus.*

Now to show you how ignorant some pastors are, my pastor told me not to claim the Holy Ghost because I was not ready for him at the time; so, I never did because I thought it was claiming too much, so I kept trying to earn him. It would be twenty years later before God convicted me himself that all I had to do is receive him. That is when I was delivered from the law. Your salvation is one day at a time, that's why Jesus said … *Matthew 6:34 (KJV) "34 Take therefore no thought for the morrow: for the morrow shall take thought for the things of itself. Sufficient unto the day is the evil thereof."* Spirits are subject to spirits, do not be willingly ignorant to think that you can be with the world and not be influenced. I am telling you from the experiences God allowed me to go through that open my eyes and mind when he brought me into the revelation of his truth. I saw myself in a state of helplessness on my way to hell if it had not been for his mercy by choosing me for salvation.

The Apostles all died at the hands of well-meaning ignorant Pharisees and Sadducees except John to uphold these truths as evidence of the risen Christ that those who received him would walk the same way. *2 Timothy 3:12 (KJV) "12 Yea, and all that will live godly in Christ Jesus shall suffer persecution"* No child of the devil chooses to suffer; your father the devil hate the image you stand in. He seeks to dehumanize you in the most horrible ways God allows him to bring you to conviction. Living as deceived children of the devil, if you are not chosen, in God's sight, you have never lived. This may come as a shock to you, we all were children of the devil at birth. God in his predestination, chooses those to be saved through times and ages to preserve what he has already set in motion to happen. When your time comes for the invitation, that is your day to choose your destiny for eternity.

All will be given that choice at some point in your life. Our warfare in the spirit is with those Satan deceived with religious spirits as born from below under false teaching in the name of God; they! will be your persecutors. Since Adam sinned, Satan has the right to procreate his own seeds as manifested in Cain. When Eve sinned, he took possession of her soul and now he had a means to bring his seeds into the world. All he had to do is get Eve to seduce Adam to partake of her sin by taking a bite of the forbidden fruit and partake of her disobedience. Satan spoke to Adam using Eve's voice. Satan now has the means to deliver his seeds into her womb to procreate his own children while living as cursed seeds of the devil.

The sin DNA entered both. His plan was now complete. He had her to seduce Adam and when he yielded, he possessed his soul also; therefore, we all are born in a fallen state until God chooses you as one of his seeds in his foreknowledge as one of his elects. Regardless of what you have been taught by man, I am thoroughly convinced that if you think you have eternal life, you will never know it until God opens your eyes to **His** truth that will be the judge of who goes to heaven.

The will of the lord has to be done on earth as in heaven; therefore, God must choose you to come into his kingdom as his disciples for his will to be done on Earth. *John 6:44 (NASB77)* [44] *"No one can come to Me, unless the Father who sent Me draws him; and I will raise him up on the last day. Matthew 7:21 (KJV) "21 Not everyone that saith unto me, Lord, Lord, shall enter into the kingdom of heaven; but he that doeth the will of my Father which is in heaven." Matthew 7:21 (NLT)* [21] *"Not all people who sound religious are really godly. They may refer to me as 'Lord,' but they still won't enter the Kingdom of Heaven. The decisive issue is whether they obey my Father in heaven."* It is the father that chooses you to do his will not you, your will is of your father the devil. That is why you must be delivered from your old nature.

That's what he told the Pharisees and Sadducees ... *John 8:44 (KJV)"* [44] *Ye are of your father the devil, and the lusts of your father ye will do. He was a murderer from the beginning, and abode not in the truth, because there is no truth in him. When he speaketh a lie, he speaketh of his own: for he is a liar, and the father of it."* So, if we as confessing   are living a lie, we are just a religious child of the devil deceived into thinking we are all right. *Proverbs 16:25 (NASB77)* [25] There is a way which seems right to a man, *but its end is the way of death.*

You will never know it until God opens your ears to the true gospel that brings the conviction of your sins of omission. I convicted my second wife by example by doing what I did not do in my first marriage. **First,** I became the priest of my own house before I could be used to help others. I made many mistakes during that time but never gave up my faith in the word; God had mercy on me and worked all things out to my good for his purposes. These things the Holy Spirit taught me for seven years, separated me from all that I find that is not pleasing to him in his perfect will for me and that's by Knowledge of the leading of the Holy Spirit. Outside of his word, I know nothing that would profit me eternal life. I am fully persuaded to be still and wait for this final and last anointing as coming out of this wilderness in the fullness.

We in these times have never seen the fullness of the works He said He would do because we have only known in part; the division in doctrines have kept this body from becoming one. God once again is about to show the world who He is in his chosen elects. His head is now on this new body of believers prepared to do the exploits to his glory. When I wanted to know why so many of us fail to come to perfect obedience, this was my answer .... *2 Timothy 2:4 (KJV) "4 No man that warreth entangleth himself with the affairs of this life; that he may please him who hath chosen him to be a soldier. Romans 8:7 (KJV)* [7] *Because the carnal mind is enmity against God: for it is not subject to the law of God, neither indeed can be. Luke 9:23 (KJV)* [23] *And he said to them all, If any man will come after me, let him deny himself, and <u>take up his cross daily</u>, and follow me. 2 Thessalonians 3:2 (KJV)* [2] *And that we may be delivered from unreasonable and wicked men: for all men have not faith."* You are only saved one day at a time. No wonder Peter said, **"who then can be saved"** when he heard what Jesus said about what it would take to enter the kingdom of heaven.

Remember, he denied him because he did not have the power to resist the devil when the test came, and so will you if you are not born from above of the Holy Spirit of God. Those that draw back when it comes to the witness of the spirit, if you were convicted by the Holy Ghost, he will speak for himself. After Pentecost, he never denied him again. Those that are called by God may experience fear at times because we are still in the flesh body; if you disobey you will be chastised as sons. The secret to Christ being seen in you is by dying daily to your self will; then you will know the reality of being born again as living in a conscious state of obedience by the leading of the Holy Spirit. Sadly, you will see many around you who mean well but you know they are not ready for what we are about to see happen very soon. They are constantly talking about tomorrow that has not yet come and what I want to buy, sale, get and gain.

Matthew 6:34 (KJV) "34 Take therefore no thought for the morrow: for the morrow shall take thought for the things of itself. Sufficient unto the day is the evil thereof. If ye were of the world, the world would love his own: but because ye are not of the world, but I have chosen you out of the world, therefore the world hateth you.

The sign of a new creature is?

*2 Corinthians 6:17 (KJV) ¹⁷ Wherefore come out from among them, and be ye separate, saith the Lord, and touch not the unclean thing; and I will receive you, 1 Thessalonians 4:7 (KJV) ⁷ For God hath not called us unto uncleanness, but unto holiness. 1 Peter 1:15 (KJV) ¹⁵ But as he which hath called you is holy, so be ye holy in all manner of conversation; 1 John 3:13 (KJV) ¹³ Marvel not, my brethren, if the world hate you. (*This you will also experience through those confessing to be saved but are not convicted of their sins of omission.) *John 15:18 (KJV) ¹⁸ If the world hate you, ye know that it hated me before it hated you.* In reading the account of the first sermon spoken through the inspiration of the Holy Spirit in Peter, at the very end of that message ... *Acts 2:40 (KJV) "⁴⁰ And with many other words did he testify and exhort, saying, Save yourselves from this untoward generation."* Now you see, it is all about saving yourself first as to become a convert of the Holy Spirit and this is what God ask of you in return .... *Romans 12:1-2 (KJV) "¹ "* I beseech you therefore, brethren, by the mercies of God, that ye present your bodies a living sacrifice, holy, acceptable unto God, which is your reasonable service." *² And be not conformed to this world: but be ye transformed by the renewing of your mind, that ye may prove what is that good, and acceptable, and perfect, will of God." Romans 12:1-2 (NLT) ¹ And* *so, dear brothers and sisters, I plead with you to give your bodies to God. Let them be a living and holy sacrifice—the kind he will accept. When you think of what he has done for you, is this too much to ask?² Don't copy the behavior and customs of this world, but let God transform you into a new person by changing the way you think. Then you will know what God wants you to do, and you will know how good and pleasing and perfect his will really is." (When you come to realize that) ... 1 Corinthians 6:19 (KJV)¹⁹ What? know ye not that your body is the temple of the Holy Ghost which is in you, which ye have of God, and ye are not your own? 1 John 4:4 (NKJV)⁴ You are of God, little children, and have overcome them, because He who is in you is greater than he who is in the world.*

This is the difference in a converted believer given ears to hear that is called by election as were the apostles. The fruit that came from them was of God and in their blood was the New Testament completed. Now ask yourself, **are you ready to be a Christian as a disciple of Christ? "Let a man examine himself"** You can know whether you are a vessel of **honor** or **dishonor** just by the studying and engrafting the word of God not only as a hearer, but this revelation comes by being a doer of the word. I have come to see that I am a work in progress by the hand of the lord and my only guarantee of eternal life is obedience unto my death in the flesh so I can live in the reality of the resurrected Christ in me. I do not have the power in myself to do that; that is why I had to give him my temple, his strength in me only can resist the devil's temptation we face daily.

The persecution that come upon you, will test your love for him, casting all my cares upon him so the faith he seeks to find will be in you when he returns. The great mystery that is going to be a shocker to the church world very soon is that 98 percent of confessing Christians, following the teachings of man's theology based on bible principles that work without being saved. It is your responsibility to search the scriptures to see if your spiritual leaders are following in the footsteps of Christ, many will be found weighted in the balance of too many sins of omission to go to heaven.

You see, the world lives in fear of the unknown; this is what will cause them to receive the mark of their father the devil. Why do you think he said come out from among them; they are already dead. The dead live with the dead; play with the dead and will bury their dead. This is what God said of Satan's kingdom ... **Luke 9:60 (KJV) "⁶⁰Jesus said unto him, Let the**

dead bury their dead: but go thou and preach the kingdom of God." that will cause men to live forever. Who you love cannot be hidden from those who know God's ways? *Ephesians 5:11 (KJV)* [11] *And have no fellowship with the unfruitful works of darkness, but rather reprove them.* I was in that 98 percent with a shallow view of the gospel at best, until God open my eyes to his truth. Without a heartfelt conviction unto obedience, it will not be enough to get to heaven in times of great fear and perplexity. Only God has the power over the devil when he (God) is in you, keep you from evil by your willing obedience to his word. Satan will use circumstances that generate great fear like this present pandemic to capture many souls.

If we believe he is, and don't do what he called us to do? *John 8:24 (KJV)* [24] *I said therefore unto you, that ye shall die in your sins: for if ye believe not that I am he, ye shall die in your sins. Hebrews 11:6 (KJV) "6 But without faith it is impossible to please him: for he that cometh to God must believe that he is, and that he is a rewarder of them that diligently seek him."* This is a hard saying because we as individual believers must answer to these saying that will judge us while we are here. God has made this an individual choice to give up your will in exchange for his. *Jeremiah 17:9 (KJV) "9* The heart is deceitful above all things, and desperately wicked: <u>who can know it</u>?* "If you are not dead, what's hidden in your heart will be seen. This is the mercy of God to get you to repent and save yourself. *1 Thessalonians 5:22-23 (KJV) "22 Abstain from all appearance of evil. [23] And the very God of peace sanctify you wholly; and I pray God your whole spirit and soul and body are preserved blameless unto the coming of our Lord Jesus Christ."*

We are kept by obeying. This is what our church leaders have resulted too to attract the youth; allow dirty sensual dancing in the assemblies. Without your knowing, you are calling evil good and good evil. *Isaiah 5:20 (KJV) "20 Woe unto them that call evil good, and good evil; that put darkness for light, and light for darkness; that put bitter for sweet, and sweet for bitter!"* We, as confessing Christian, wonder why our children are going astray; there is not much the church has to offer in trying to compete with the world. This is what religion's do. I have never forgotten when God revealed to me that 98% of the church is not prepared to enter heaven. I know that statement will not go over well with this present-day church doctrine. As one minister said to me ... we all can't be that wrong.

Remember the parable of the marriage of the last supper and those that left Egypt, none of them went into the promise land, only their children. In these last days, I experience many that say they know him but don't recognize his voice when he is speaking, they will reject him in the call and some of their children will take their place. *Luke 14:16-24 (NASB77)* [16] *But He said to him, "A certain man was giving a big dinner, and he invited many;* [17] *and at the dinner hour he sent his slave to say to those who had been invited, 'Come; for everything is ready now.'* [18] *"But they all alike began to make excuses. The first one said to him, 'I have bought a piece of land and I need to go out and look at it; please consider me excused.'* [19] *"And another one said, 'I have bought five yoke of oxen, and I am going to try them out; please consider me excused.'* [20] *"And another one said, 'I have married a wife, and for that reason I cannot come.'* [21] *"And the slave came back and reported this to his master. Then the head of the household became angry and said to his slave, 'Go out at once into the streets and lanes of the city and bring in here the poor and crippled and blind and lame.'* [22] *"And the slave said, 'Master, what you commanded has been done, and still there is room.'* [23] «And the master said to the slave, ‹Go out into the highways and along the hedges, and compel them to come in, **that my house may be filled**. [24] 'For I tell you, none of those men who were invited shall taste of my dinner."*

That 2 percent is the remnant elect that will be taken out of this confessing church and the rest will be those the church rejected that will take their place in this dispensation of the last generation by the elects in the world that God has been preserved to be reaped out of great tribulation. If it were not for them, no flesh would be saved. Yes, the very scum of this world that this present-day church in the **Laodicean** spirit of our times, in their pride, steeped in tradition, and living in a false sense of reality and security, are about to see their little kingdoms crumble. God is going to let them see their state as ... *Revelation 3:16-17 (KJV) 16 So then because thou art lukewarm, and neither cold nor hot, I will spue thee out of my mouth.* [17] *Because thou sayest, I am rich, and increased with goods, and have need of nothing; and knowest not that thou art wretched, and miserable, and poor, and blind, and naked: Revelation 3:16-17 (NLT)* [16] *But since you are like lukewarm water, neither hot nor cold, I will spit you out of my mouth!* [17] *You say, 'I am rich. I have everything I want. I don't need a thing!' And you don't realize that you are wretched and miserable and poor and blind and naked. Isaiah 5:14 (KJV) Therefore, hell hath enlarged herself, and opened her mouth without measure: and their glory, and their multitude, and their pomp, and* *he that rejoiceth, shall descend into it.* No matter what denomination, cult teachings or religious movement you identify yourself with, it will be tested whether it be of God in the Elijah show down.

We have changed the order of the assemblies as men by becoming victims of Jezebel spirits as stated also in *... Revelation 2:18-25 (KJV ")* [18] *And unto the angel of the church in* <u>*Thyatira*</u> *write; These things saith the Son of God, who hath his eyes like unto a flame of fire, and his feet are like fine brass;" (This is the way John saw Jesus in his vision in heaven.)* [19] *I know thy works, and charity, and service, and faith, and thy patience, and thy works; and the last to be more than the first."* (This is also pointing to this last generation where we will see all these religions converging together into what will later become a one world religion during the tribulation: a false church body. This we know by revelation as the body of the antichrist.) [20] *Notwithstanding I have a few things against thee, because thou* <u>*sufferest that woman Jezebel,*</u> *which calleth herself a prophetess,"* Women in charge as leaders in the assemblies. There is no scripture to show God has changed his mind and replaced Adam with Eve when she was of Adam in the beginning. Woman may prophesy but according to scripture cannot usurp authority over the male image of God. *1 Corinthians 11:12 (KJV)* [12] *For as the woman is of the man, even so is the man also by the woman; but all things of God.* There is nothing mention about Eve when it comes to the sin nature, that's because she is of the man and therefore only became the means by which the man lost his authority over the Earth. Just think, when all these women pastors are told that they have been operating in God's permissive will, have not submitted to the authority that God has set as head of his house, the man. That's one of the reasons he must return in the latter rain to set his house in order that gives him the glory and take us home.

The male image as priest of His house, then and only then will you see the true jezebel that Elijah met show herself and turn and persecute the church as an antichrist spirit. This spirit will facilitate the initiation of the war for gender supremacy in religions that will give rise to the true church in the tribulation. The usurping of the weaker vessel over the male image will be the downfall of many marriages. As I have mentioned, this spirit in a previous chronicle, the female is this spirit's gender of choice because of her physical attributes.

1 Tim.2:12) to teach and to seduce my servants to commit fornication, and to eat things sacrificed unto idols. (This is what God has against the priest of the house that changed the order to give women the right to usurp authority over the man.) [21] *And I gave her space to repent of her fornication;* (To put her in Adam's stead as head is what fornication mean in this context. Eve was of Adam not Adam of Eve in the beginning. This represents he has another woman and by his own will, allowed her to seduce him to commit fornication that changed the order of the church.

Women are to teach women. The two are equal in the spirit but in the flesh state she now is to be subject to the male image of God because of her sin in the garden and God has not changed that order in the earth.) *(1 Corinthians 11:8 (KJV) "8 For the man is not of the woman; but the woman of the man. 1 Timothy 2:12 (KJV) 12 But I suffer not a woman to teach, nor to usurp authority over the man, but to be in silence".) … and she repented not.* [22] *Behold, I will cast her into a bed, and them that commit adultery with her into great tribulation …* (This is the time God has purposed to set his house in order), **except they repent of their deeds.** (This is in reference to changing the order of his house.) [23] *And I will kill her children with death;* (This is the curse that will be upon all that remain after they have been expose as false teachers, will be lost.) *and all the churches shall know that I am he which searcheth the reins and hearts: and I will give unto every one of you according to your works.* [24] *But unto you I say, and unto the rest in Thyatira, as many as have not this doctrine, and which have not known the depths of Satan, as they speak; I will put upon you none other burden. 25 But that which ye have already hold fast till I come."* This has reference to those who did not give place to this spirit.

God knows the hearts of all he has given ears to hear that did not know they were wrong and repent and separate themselves, as those on the day of Pentecost that consented to kill Jesus. He will have mercy on them for being under the influence of their false leaders if they repent. He knows who is sincere in heart and these are the ones that will be given ears to hear. Only God know these things because he is doing the choosing. The reason why we all judge at times depends on the way or by whom the gospel was presented at the time you heard what we thought was the truth. If Christ was not lifted in love, you will not produce the right fruit. A genetically altered gospel **(man's word engrafted with God's word)** will produce fruit that change the appearance of what the real fruit should look like. These are the assemblies that we see producing this corrupt fruit that comes out of these sinner's prayers that have many not knowing what spirit they are of, made them a religious child of the devil. I hope you have a better understanding that salvation is more than just saying a sinner's prayer. If not for his mercy and his sovereign will, I would be on my way to hell today. Remember, you will be judged by what God has said it will take to get to heaven, not the pastors, preachers or evangelist that excite you into a frenzy of emotion, rob you and invite you to take a front row seat in hell. (Updated for release 2/2021)

THE BROAD ROAD

Background scripture:

Matthew 7:13-16 (KJV) [13] *Enter ye in at the strait gate: for wide is the gate, and broad is the way, that leadeth to destruction, and many there be which go in there at:* [14] *Because strait is the gate, and narrow is the way, which leadeth unto life, and few there be that find it. Matthew 7:15-16 (KJV)* [15] *Beware of false prophets, which come to you in sheep's clothing, but inwardly they are ravening wolves.* [16] *Ye shall know them by their fruits. Do men gather grapes of thorns, or figs of thistles?* **Matthew 7:13-14 (NLT)** [13] **"You can enter God's Kingdom only through the narrow gate. The highway to hell is broad, and its gate is wide for the many who choose the easy way.** [14] **But the gateway to life is small, and the road is narrow, and only a few ever find it." Matthew 7:15-16 (NLT2)** [15] **"Beware of false prophets who come disguised as harmless sheep but are really vicious wolves.** [16] **You can identify them by their fruit, that is, by the way they act. Can you pick grapes from thornbushes, or figs from thistles?**

I have found that studying under the teachings of the Holy Spirit, the word is so layered with revelation, there is just no end to what God will share with those whose mind he has open to truth. Each time I do a study on a topic of his leading; he will take the same scriptures he has given in the past and open a deeper truth to the same scripture; many that read these chronicles will see that I am not that educated as you see in my writing style.

This you see by my grammatical expressions, thanks to my word processor,

I have somewhat improved a little. I, like the writers of the King James Version, express these revelations in everyday common colloquial terms. I am not a polished writer as you may see by the some of my phrases; I just write it the way he tells me because he knows who he has prepared to hear it. God is serious, if we take him for granted thinking that he did not mean what he said the way he said it, you will be the victim of your own thoughts and judge yourself unfit to enter his kingdom.

If your body is his, and the mind is his, his thoughts drive you to study of his word; that is how your soul is fed the knowledge to set you on target to enter his kingdom. That's why he has told us ... *Isaiah 50:7 (KJV) "7 For the Lord GOD will help me; therefore, shall I not be confounded: therefore, have I set my face like a flint, and I know that I shall not be ashamed.* His method on the road to glory is designed to humble you because his glory is far greater than any man can perform. He has such great love that this is how he shows it ... *Isaiah 54:7-8 (KJV) 7 For a small moment have I forsaken thee; but with great mercies will I gather thee. 8 In a little wrath I hid my face from thee for a moment, but with everlasting kindness will I have mercy on thee, saith the LORD thy Redeemer.* (If we would just obey,) *Isaiah 54:17 (KJV) 17 No weapon that is formed against thee shall prosper; and every tongue that shall rise against thee in judgment thou shalt condemn. This is the heritage of the servants of the LORD, and their righteousness is of me, saith the LORD.* This is the promise that nothing on this Earth can harm you is living in the reality that he is the greater one in you. *Hebrews 13:5 (KJV) 5 Let your conversation be without covetousness; and be content with such things as ye have: for he hath said, I will never leave thee, nor forsake thee."* Godly love leads to contentment because this brings peace by understanding. The world's contentment is only for a moment because their spirit is open to lust for adventure. Just as we can lose our love for one another over time in our marriages without the love of God, we treat Him the same way by leaving our first love.

This is what causes us all to fall short of our full potential in him. It prevents you from being delivered from yourself. Therefore, I strive to obey when he lets me see just how un-grateful, we are, in the way we return his love and kindness. Remember what happen in the wilderness when they kept forgetting what God had done for them ... they were turned over to the devil and left in there to die. That is what its like to overstay your day of grace. In my own sorrow, I am convicted to tears at my ways and actions when his love reminds me by forgetting what he has done to get me here. When you really love someone, it hurts you to hurt them unintentionally. You see, the **broad road** has so many tempting things in our daily life, only your love for God will keep you loyal to him just as it would to your wife or husband.

Many of us have sinned in this area of our life yet God did not forsake us but forgave us and cleaned up our mess as only he can. I have said in time past; we don't choose to serve him, he chooses us and persuades us to serve him out of love and gratitude for his kind acts to our benefit that no one else could perform but him for you. When he reveals our hearts and lets us see how the cares of this life are taking his place, this is where we fail him in perfect obedience. That is why I am glad to be on the receiving end of his mercy, love and forgiveness when he corrects me in an error or a sin of omission that cause me to repent. Many of us have not come to that place of humble humility to be this transparent about ourselves. It is better to repent now and change than to be weighed in the balance in the judgment and found wanting.

That is why those that are taught under the law will judge you because it carries the spirit of the Pharisees in their error that showed no compassion in their daily administration of the law. If you were that perfect all would know who you are because the works would show that Christ has returned, the entire world will know when that day arrives in our temple. Remember the woman about to be stone. **John 8:7 (NLT) [7] They kept demanding an answer, so he stood up again and said, "All right, stone her. But let those who have never sinned throw the first stones!"** Jesus did not send anyone to hell while he was here because he was laying the foundation to let us see this reality. He became the sacrifice for sins for the new covenant that will give all who receive him through repenting as John the Baptist forewarned.

All who would lay another foundation after Christ will be judged by the word of God. The elects are dealt with as sons because they are chosen from the foundation of the world. Those that receive Christ by the kind acts He performs through them, make their calling and election sure as they obey. Now this brings us to this question? **Why is there so few that find it?** We cannot receive him until his spirit breaks the grip of Satan's influence over our minds that reach our heart and draws us into his kingdom by his spirit for this reason … *John 3:5 (KJV) "5 Jesus answered, Verily, verily, I say unto thee, except a man be born of water and of the Spirit, he cannot enter into the kingdom of God. John 6:44 (KJV)* [44] *No man can come to me, except the Father which hath sent me draw him: and I will raise him up at the last day."*

Some are predestined by election at an appointed time, he draws them in by his spirit. They will be used to bring others in the kingdom by the leading of the Holy Spirit. That is how he selects us for eternal life. That shocked me too. We all must do the same thing; obey to receive the same reward as in the parable of the vineyard. When I look back at how he designed all of my experiences to bring me into the greater understanding of his ways, which include the loss of all things that is now my past; few will ever understand the meaning of this statement … *Matthew 19:29 (KJV) And every one that hath forsaken houses, or brethren, or sisters, or father, or mother, or wife, or children, or lands, for my name's sake, shall receive an hundredfold, and shall inherit everlasting life.*

To let you see what I had to go through as one of my experiences; God had me in a predicament that I could not go to my own biological grandmother's funeral, it was her love and care that I was under spiritually that showed me how to walk this way as a young child. My mother and sister continued to show this love to me when I was being rejected by my peers. Yes, I cried when this happened to me because I was ridiculed by other family members by being the first of her grandchildren and did not attend her funeral. God had to give me this experience literally so I could be made to see the depth of what I was being prepared to do as a minister of his word during the tribulation. In the coming days and years, people that hear this word must be willing to walk away from all in this world to save their lives, including their families. This is that day that … *Psalm 95:8 "(KJV)* [8] *Harden not your heart, as in the provocation, and as in the day of temptation in the wilderness:"* What did God do; all that did not repent were left there to die. All that are a part of this call are preparing to receive their glorified bodies in finishing our course to be taken home to heaven in the rapture.

You will have to forsake all that is dear to you on this Earth during that time to go to heaven because these are the choices you will be given. It is to this degree that I am persuaded to let nothing prevent me from letting him finish what he has spent all these years perfecting in me and I have not arrived at that place of perfection to his glory. God is no respecter of persons and will do the same for you what he is doing in me, so do not think I am an exception. Now I know why he said quit thinking. Yes, I am still waiting to arrive at that place of perfect love that can only be accomplished in his fullness. When Satan seduced us to enter by way of the **broad road,** it is as a mirage because nothing is lasting, things are coming and going so fast until there is no stopping to smell the roses.

There always seems to be so much to see and do. That same spirit is in the present-day assemblies that keep you so busy doing works for God that pleases your leaders instead of God. That's why so many are ... *2 Timothy 3:7 (KJV)* [7] *Ever learning, and never able to come to the knowledge of the truth...* Whoever you open your spirit other than God will control you to the point of bondage. When you enter the straight path, your mind set is to follow your leader as you see him following Christ. You must be still and focus your face on Jesus and remember Peter's experience on the water when he took his eyes off Jesus, he began to sink. The sum of our short comings are the short cuts and turns we take trying to get around these trials that are designed by God to perfect us. These are the wrecks in our lives. Obedience to God only can calm these waves in our lives. When we let Satan get his hand on the helm that God gave us to guide us in to calm seas; we will always end up on a reef.

I have also come to see that our greatest enemy is fear of the unknown. This represents the lack of faith to love and trust God to do what he said. It is perfecting our love that will cast out all your fears and turn it to faith. All the promises are a guarantee that you in him will arrive at your destination by acting in faith on his words that cannot fail.

Hebrews 11:6 (KJV) "6 But without faith it is impossible to please him: for he that cometh to God must believe that he is, and that he is a rewarder of them that diligently seek him." When Jesus walked on water, he had no need to consider the circumstances he allowed Satan to create because he was in control of them all. In my youth, I use to hear the old saints say, you must have a **"no so"** salvation. Over the years I have come to see that is true, you cannot serve God out of ignorance to his word. Satan is a formidable opponent, you are just a piece of dust, only God can deal with him when he sees His image in your forehead as his defeat. If the shield of faith in his spoken word is not in your forehead, Satan will not move. That is your shield of armor.

All the things in this world such as the lust of the eyes, the lust of the flesh and the prides of this world will be used to replace the time you need to learn how to defeat him. He will keep you doing everything but receiving the word that tells you how he was defeated by Christ so when he calls your bluff, you do not have enough knowledge to keep him from destroying you through fear. *1 John 4:18 (NKJV)* ¹⁸ **There is no fear in love; but perfect love casts out fear, because fear involves torment. But he who fears has not been made perfect in love.** *Hosea 4:6 (KJV) "6 My people are destroyed for lack of knowledge: because thou hast rejected knowledge, I will also reject thee, that thou shalt be no priest to me: seeing thou hast forgotten the law of thy God, I will also forget thy children."* You want to know why our children are rebelling against us as confessing Christians, examine yourself through the word and you will see that your children reflect your obedience or disobedience to God by the way they respect you and others around them.

This was the case in my past if you are honest and delivered to the point of transparency your own past sins. We forget we were supposed to be the guiding light that they too would come to know the lord. We in our zeal are so busy trying to set everybody else's house in order and forgot about our own. The devil will take your misguided zeal and devotion and cause you to run ahead of God. For some, have caused you to bury your children before they bury you. It caused me to lose everything dear to me, but God turned it around and made it a blessing. If you are called by God, the first order of priorities by God is self-deliverance. This is evident as a leader when your own house is not in order; what did God say about that? ... *1 Timothy 3:5 (KJV)* ⁵ *"For if a man know not how to rule his own house, how shall he take care of the church of God?"*

If we forget the lord your children will forget you and this is the sin that comes back on the priest as head of his house for not leading and the mother for not chastening and teaching the fruit of her body so they will not bring you to shame. The wife's priority is not to preach to others but to bring honor to her husband by training his seeds up in the way they should go that they too, will know the God you serve by example will be a present help to them when they go astray and guide them back to that foundation that was laid by God in you. I wish I was taught like this in my early exposure to Christianity.

Now I must give you some comfort in this area; we are in a very wicked time and Satan will take advantage of every mistake you make. Some of our children will have to go astray as in the parable of the prodigal son because of the influences the world may have on them. These are realities you will have to face when that time come, what you have taught them of God by example will not return void if your heart was in the right place during the training. You will have to release that child into the hands of the lord to bring him or her back. Remember, the only thing that should be as a priority in your prayers are whatever it takes to bring that child back to God, no matter what they must go through to get them there. In my prayers, I ask God to do whatever it takes to keep that child from going to hell. *Isaiah 3:12 (KJV)* [12] "*As for my people, children are their oppressors, and women rule over them. O my people, they which lead thee cause thee to err, and destroy the way of thy paths."*

The assemblies that compromise truth to get large numbers, represents those that take the **broad road** and cause you to miss God. These same busy scheduled lifestyles which include working for God instead of working with him, comes from teachings of the law mixed with grace; this will cause you to do good works and not be led by the spirit of God in all things. This is the spirit of the church of **Thyatira.** They also mixed law with grace, lost their way that led to a change of the order of the home and the house of God as women started emerging as leaders. In my past, these teaching brought me much persecution to be banished from my own hometown which is a stronghold of women pastors. This is where I see the error when he got my attention.

We, as Christians, are not mare human being but spirit beings in a flesh body as the new Adam, empowered by the Holy Ghost to do extraordinary things. We were totally delivered when Christ said, **"it is finished."** The mind of God only responds to his words not ours. When we pray, we are to put him in remembrance of his word and through faith, patience and long suffering, he will bring it to pass instantly or in his own time and the word mixed in faith will not come back void.

There are two of us; the old flesh man contending with the new spirit man. They both are in the same body. The old flesh man does not want to give up the world and the new spirit man's mind is in heavenly places and only responds to the word of God. That is why he said ... *1 Corinthians 2:16 (KJV)* [16] *For who hath known the mind of the Lord, that he may instruct him? But we have the mind of Christ. Romans 8:9 (KJV)* [9] *But ye are not in the flesh, but in the Spirit, if so be that the Spirit of God dwell in you. Now if any man have not the Spirit of Christ, he is none of his.* Now before you conquer the old man, there are some realities you are going to have to deal with to break these spiritual strongholds you see that may still have your mind under their influence. Just because you said you are saved don't think that you will never have any more problems with the old man again.

I am glad Paul was transparent enough to let us see this reality when he had to deal with his own will over the father's will. This is how he expressed it ... **Romans 7:15-25 (NLT)** [15] **I don't really understand myself, for I want to do what is right, but I don't do it. Instead, I do what I hate.** [16] **But if I know that what I am doing is wrong, this shows that I agree that the law is good.** [17] **So I am not the one doing wrong; it is sin living in me that does it.** [18] **And I know that nothing good lives in me, that is, in my sinful nature. I want to do what is right, but I can't.** [19] **I want to do what is good, but I don't. I don't want to do what is wrong, but I do it anyway.** [20] **But if I do what I don't want to do, I am not really the one doing wrong; it is sin living in me that does it.** [21] **I have discovered this principle of life—that when I want to do what is right, I inevitably do what is wrong.** [22] **I love God's law with all my heart.** [23] **But there is another power within me that is at war with my mind. This power makes me a slave to the sin that is still within me.** [24] **Oh, what a miserable person I am! Who will free me from this life that is dominated by sin and death?** [25] **Thank God! The answer is in Jesus Christ our Lord. So, you see how it is: In my mind I really want to obey God's law, but because of my sinful nature I am a slave to sin.**

We must learn to die of these daily temptations here on earth to be truly converted. When we surrender our will, this will be your fight for the rest of your life as a confessing Christian. That old sin nature will fight against your mind, thoughts, and ways to keep us from being renewed day by day into the new Adam. This is an inside job that brings Christ to the forefront of our lives where the world can see him in you. *2 Corinthians 5:17 (KJV)* [17] *"Therefore if any man be in Christ, he is a new creature: old things are passed away; behold, all things are become new."* The reality of the Holy Spirit is manifested in humble Christians who let go their pride to please God. Although it is available to all, only a few will live the privilege. Only those that obey will drink of that living water of life by feeding on that living bread and drinking that water daily, as in eating his flesh and drinking his blood as being used in hope for their day of redemption to be absent from the body and present with the lord for eternity. They have pass from death to life, as having their love perfected in Christ.

Now, are you going to turn away, because these sayings are too hard for you also? Remember the rich man. There are many that are teaching and preaching in part in their own strength coupled with a little faith. In my observations through the Holy Ghost, many are separated, seduced on the **broad road** to teach the principles of truth that leads to the material wealth of this world and personal gain that comes with using these principles without having to change your sinful ways. This is what contributed to the sins of omission. **Gal. 5:19-21** Satan will lead you to building your own kingdoms and not pointing them to the Kingdom of God in holiness.

If you are not totally surrendered to the will of God, this is his permissive will. This error has led to these present divisions by the names we identify ourselves with on our kingdom assemblies. We now teach in part but not the whole council of the word. Therefore, we can now choose to serve God according to the part that fits our comfort zone. This is the doctrine of the **Laodicean** spirit which holds the doctrine of the **Nicolaitan's** that put man up as gods. *1 Corinthians 8:5 (KJV)* [5] *"For though there be that are called gods, whether in heaven or in earth, as there be gods many, and lords many"* If your leader is pushing the organizations causes more than bringing you to the knowledge of the truth, you are being miss-led and therefore, will not produce the right fruit under pressure of life's trials.

This has reference to too many leaders operating outside the body that seek to glorify themselves; **this!** is what God hates. They will be given over to a delusion if they do not repent and become an antichrist in the days ahead by being blind as to not know what spirit **they** are of and will now repeat what the Pharisees and Sadducees did to Jesus, come against you as an antichrist and deliver you up to death. They are judged and condemned by the same word they refused to receive. Many of them have a piece of truth that appeals to man's intellect as to the way he sees God and have created a comfort zone that has led to this false sense of reality and security. You will never become holy by living in one part of truth. You can have faith in a lot of things and not be holy.

James 2:10 (KJV) [10] *"For whosoever shall keep the whole law, and yet offend in one point, he is guilty of all. 1 Thessalonians 5:23 (KJV)* [23] *And the very God of peace sanctify you wholly; and I pray God your whole spirit and soul and body be preserved blameless unto the coming of our Lord Jesus Christ. 1 Thessalonians 4:7 (KJV)* [7] *For God hath not called us unto uncleanness, but unto holiness. Hebrews 12:14 (KJV)* [14] *Follow peace with all men, and holiness, without which no man shall see the Lord:"* People have asked me, are you a prophet? My reply, I am just a messenger, warning of the return of Christ, this time in his wrath. All I know is that in the year 2004, God begin to speak to me in my quiet prayer time meditations. When I began to see that he was dictating a vision of this time in the form of a warning. I begin to write them down over a seven-year period.

These truths not only shook my foundation to the point of repentance. I saw the side of God that the devil hid from them that are lost. *2 Corinthians 4:3 (KJV)* [3] *"But if our gospel be hid, it is hid to them that are lost:"* That's when I saw these sides; wrath, anger and judgment but in his administration, mercy. I saw compassion and all that comprise the fruits of his spirit towards mankind as his created image.

I was like a deer in front of bright headlights, I could see for the first time what had been hid behind those blinding lights; Satan was driving an eighteen-wheeler and I was in a compact car on the wrong side of the road, on my way to a head on collision if I did not turn back into the right lane. Now in my tearful prayer times, I lament over what I see. I am like peter, in all I have done in rebellion, I am not worthy to be used for this privilege.

I thank God for leading me into his secrete closet where the Holy Spirit taught me all these heavenly things and reveal mysteries, I never heard no man teach but are locked in his word. This is what I have written about in these books without an editor that is helping me get delivered from myself. I now rely on his teachings to correct the errors of my ways. He gave me an ear to hear his voice through many sources. He uses people as vessels of honor and dishonor for his purposes. If you are not able to see and hear in the spirit, you will reject the people he uses to speak this kind of truth through because of a discernable error of your ways that judge them that may be used in your own household. People with life's wisdom, knowledge and a certain degree of understanding can speak truthful sayings and not even be of it; you must be wise enough to hear God speaking to you through them and yet not partake of their evil deeds. This is the vessel of dishonor being used by God to help you become a vessel of honor.

When he gave me the revelation to vessels of **honor** and **dishonor**, the only thing I wanted to know was, which one was I? Walking with God by receiving his words in obedience is the key that unlocks the door to the deeper life and produces the faith that enables you to move those mountains by the word of faith. Do not be shocked at this statement; if you think you are doing something for God, you are already deceived. What he is doing through you is to your benefit when you come to see who is doing the work, you were to rest from your labor in the law.

Hebrews 4:9 (KJV) [9] *There remaineth therefore a rest to the people of God.* (He is the present help in you for this reason) … *Zechariah 4:6 (KJV) "6 Then he answered and spake unto me, saying, This is the word of the LORD unto Zerubbabel, saying, <u>Not by might, nor by power, but by my spirit, saith the LORD of hosts.</u>"* That's why he said) … *Romans 8:14 (KJV)* [14] *"For as many as are led by the Spirit of God, they are the sons of God."* I have come to realize all I need is what it will take to get through each day; whether it be money, strength, food, clothing, or transportation, all those things are his needs in your fleshly body and since it all belongs to him, that's why he said … *Matthew 6:25 (KJV)* [25] *" Therefore I say unto you, Take no thought for your life, what ye shall eat, or what ye shall drink; nor yet for your body, what ye shall put on. Is not the life more than meat, and the body than raiment? Matthew 6:34 (KJV)* [34] *Take therefore no thought for the morrow: for the morrow shall take thought for the things of itself. Sufficient unto the day is the evil thereof. Philippians 4:11 (NKJV)* [11] **Not that I speak in regard to need, for I have learned in whatever state I am, to be content:** *Philippians 4:19 (KJV)* [19] *But my God shall supply all your need according to his riches in glory by Christ Jesus. 2 Corinthians 5:7 (KJV)* [7] *(For we walk by faith, not by sight:"*

Keeping his commandments is what puts you in his perfect will. Therefore, whatever you may ask in his will, he will give it you. You, walking in his will, will not ask a miss because the spirit knows what to ask according to what's in his good pleasure to give you; it is God's mind speaking back to himself the things needed while in your flesh. When I was separated from the brothering, one reason, some had their own agendas by thinking themselves more highly than they should. This separation was caused by God to deal with each of us individually as to what he had called us to do approaching the tribulation. All those who repent when he visits them will be used. Some continued in the error of their ways by refusing to humble themselves.

You cannot have too many leaders in the same house sowing discord. Just as I to saw the error of my ways and repented, so will all he has chosen. I am greatly comforted by the Holy Spirit in my present state never to trust in my flesh again. To God be the glory. (Updated for release 2/2020)

THE TWO PERCENTERS

Background scriptures:

Isaiah 58:3 (KJV) [3] *"Wherefore have we fasted, say they, and thou seest not? Wherefore have we afflicted our soul, and thou takest no knowledge? Behold, in the day of your fast ye find pleasure, and exact all your labours. Isaiah 58:3 (NLT)* [3] *`We have fasted before you!' they say. `Why aren't you impressed? We have done much penance, and you don't even notice it!' "I will tell you why! It's because you are living for yourselves even while you are fasting. You keep right on oppressing your workers.* I have known those who have went on long fast and God didn't meet them. God does not except this kind of sacrifice unless it is absolute; therefore, the devil will give you a false vision and you will not even know it until God opens your eyes to truth. This is where many false visions have led many into false doctrines and teachings, seeking ordination to offices, not being qualified or beyond reproach to receive that anointing.

Hebrews 10:38 (KJV) [38] *Now the just shall live by faith: but if any man draw back, my soul shall have no pleasure in him. Ezekiel 33:11 (KJV)* [11] *Say unto them, As I live, saith the Lord GOD, I have no pleasure in the death of the wicked; but that the wicked turn from his way and live: turn ye, turn ye from your evil ways; for why will ye die, O house of Israel?"* False dreams and visions are where we will see the great deceptions of the church world being led in that 98 percent that will cause hell to enlarge itself. The inspiration behind this chronicle came from watching the protest of that 99 percent controlled by that 1 percent. Their march on Wall Street shows the state of the mindset as an oppressed middle class of the haves and the have knots from a worldly point of view.

Another interesting parallel, both parties of government that have caused this divide are playing into the hands of our enemies. The Democrats for the have knots and the Republicans for the haves. The spirit behind these two parties is one in the same because both are controlled by the **deep state** shadow government. Their agenda to control the world's population is by dividing this country from within. They use our laws to bring this nation under their control legally by manipulating circumstances that will cause the people to surrender our God given liberties. All who are reading the signs that are evident in these election cycles, this country has reached the end of our self-preservation economically. We are now at a point beyond recovery. With a deficit of thirty-two trillion dollars, we cannot pay the interest, let alone the debt. The current sitting president #44 has renounced the covenant made by our founding earthly fathers of this nation, **"In God We Trust"** by saying; **"America is no longer a Christian nation."** He is a true liberal Democrat whose seed is of a bad faction of the tribes of Ismael, being Americanized, set his approval on the sins of immorality that is against the biblical teachings of the foundation of this nation.

According to biblical history, this sign represents we have reached the end of time as a gentile nation set up by God to be responsible for the restoration of the national status of Israel. The #45 will be the president to fulfill this prophecy. *Isaiah 5:14 (KJV) "14 Therefore hell hath enlarged herself and opened her mouth without measure: and their glory, and their multitude, and their pomp, and he that rejoiceth, shall descend into it."* The above scripture is indicative of the remnant of this end time generation that shall see what Matthew's gospel stated, as in ... *Matthew 24:34 (KJV) "34 Verily I say unto you, this generation shall not pass, till all these things be fulfilled."*

The year "2013" was the end of the extension after the seven years of grace of 911. Every born-again believer walking in the right spirit, will see an increased persecution from skeptics who reject your stand on the current social scene endorsing the sodomy lifestyle legalized under President #44. Therefore, we are separated from those who refused to heed to the call. The elects shall suffer to bring back the glory of the risen Christ in tribulation that 98 percent of the church world refuses to believe that they are not going through the first three- and one-half years of tribulation.

This is where the church Christ died for will be purified and removed. All these doctrines that have led to this willing ignorance to ignore these signs will be the means the devil will justify their destruction as blind guides. Beloved, as a messenger of God with this revelation of the end of times, I have no pleasure in what I see and know; in fact, my only encouragement is in the comfort of the Holy Spirit and a few believers that share these same revelations. You be the judge of who or what I am by the words of this testimony. The spirit of prophecy will prove itself. I did not choose this course, who wants to be rejected 98 percent of the time when many in the church-world do not want to hear this truth. This work is of God. I truly know how those who carried messages like this long before me felt by being rejected as the barer of bad and good news. The good news is ... all who receive this message will be as the wise virgins and save themselves; those who refuse will face great fear as their blind guides that led them to believe the lies of the false doctrines they promoted.

When you can see the hearts of those deceived by false prophets being seared in their fate by rejecting this message, you will weep too. *2 Thessalonians 2:11 (KJV)* [11] *"And for this cause God shall send them strong delusion, that they should believe a lie:"* The kind of faith Christ will be looking to find is in those who have it in their hearts and not in their heads. This kind of faith is available to all but only a few will find it. **(Matthew 7:14)** I must be transparent; God has kept me silent and separated to himself for seven years in the writing of these revelations. My desire is for those in my immediate surroundings to recognize when the lord is speaking, therefore, I must follow peace in all things until the time he has appointed me to come out of this wilderness in him. Many are not in a place that they can look beyond the flesh and hear Jesus' speaking.

I let God show his love through me that you may be comforted also. I have had my bitter chastening from the lord which included a **forty-day fast** in this area during those seven years to bring me to this conscious state of his being in me. Only God can change hearts as I have experience but only if you humble yourself in total obedience can some strong holds be broken by fasting and prayer. I really believe there is nothing too hard for God if you are willing to pay the price to put his word to the test.

Hebrews 10:38 (KJV) ³⁸ *"Now the just shall live by faith: but if any man draw back, my soul shall have no pleasure in him. Hebrews 11:6 (KJV)* ⁶ *But without faith it is impossible to please him: for he that cometh to God must believe that he is, and that he is a rewarder of them that diligently seek him. John 6:37 (KJV)* ³⁷ *All that the Father giveth me shall come to me; and him that cometh to me I will in no wise cast out. 2 Thessalonians 3:2 (KJV)* ² *And that we may be delivered from unreasonable and wicked men: <u>for all men have not faith.</u>"*

This last part underlined is indicative of to whom it is given. You cannot make people have faith in God. A measure of faith is given to everyone whether saved or unsaved. As for believers, the reason we have such a hard time believing and developing our faith in God, we are acting for the Holy Spirit by speaking without convictions which includes our thoughts usurping authority over his. The Holy Spirit has a language that talks only to God, the more he gets to talk to God about you, as praying in the spirit, the stronger you will become in faith. He builds you up to believe in God's word and persuade you to let him speak it to pass. Now you know why we are told to be still and quiet before the lord and spend time in your closet praying in your prayer language for that reason.

When you are obedient in faith toward God, people will see God in you and be blessed by his presence in you. If you believe God is, the only way you can let him be seen is by faith in his spoken word; if not, your prayers will not be answered. How can he demonstrate the power of his word if you do not believe, how can he perform it? *Jeremiah 1:12 (KJV) Then said the LORD unto me, thou hast well seen for I will hasten my word to perform it.* We are about to see in whom or what we have believed be tested. This time, you will be making a choice to live for eternity in heaven or hell. Unfortunately, 98 percent of this confessing Christian world is not prepared to past that test. The 2 percent used to reap from this current church harvest that will gather those in the highways and byways to replace that 98 percent selected to take their place in the parable of the marriage supper of the lamb. Like Israel, we are doomed to repeat history also.

These are the souls that will replace them when the church world rejects his messengers who told them to prepare for the coming of the bridegroom.

This is the multitude that will be taken from this last generation. This is what the John the Baptist ministry will do at the appointed time when the church world rejects this warning in the first call. *1 Peter 4:17 (KJV)* [17] *"For the time is come that judgment must begin at the house of God: and if it first begins at us, what shall the end be of them that obey not the gospel of God? Luke 14:24)* [24] *For I say unto you, that none of those men which were bidden shall taste of my supper. (1 Peter 4:18-19 (NASB77)* [18] *AND IF IT IS WITH DIFFICULTY THAT THE RIGHTEOUS IS SAVED, WHAT WILL BECOME OF THE GODLESS MAN AND THE SINNER?* [19] *Therefore, let those also who suffer according to the will of God entrust their souls to a faithful Creator in doing what is right.*

God at that time will reject the lukewarm confessing Christians by spitting them out of his mouth. America sent missionaries all over the world from seminaries and religious denominations to spread their doctrines in these nations and now, we are in need to be evangelized. We have become a valley of dry bones with only a few as chosen remnants. Many of them will be saved during our persecution, as we become like the third world nations we see destroyed by war. Those chosen to carry this gospel are seeing signs wonders and miracles in these third world nations because of their persecution. We have become a non-fertile missionary field, steeped in pride as national patriots. This is a hard statement; many churches are caught up in this false since of reality and security, captivated and seduced in the spirit of **Laodicea,** practicing the doctrine of the **Nicolaitans,** lording over God's heritage that caused 98 percent as members of man's kingdoms on Earth. Every time I hear a pastor call those in his assemblies his members, the Holy Spirit is grieved. I was once told by a pastor; these are my babies; you need to get your own.

When they see how they have been deceived after rejecting the true prophets, fear will cause many to take the mark spiritually by having faith in the wrong gods. Your 501c-3 is the literal natural mark. I mention briefly in another chronicle of how many of these teachers have resulted to teaching biblical principles that work without salvation. Even the world use these principles to get wealthy in their teaching seminars. This is the **broad road** that leads you around suffering and rejection. The wilderness temptation shows by knowledge of truth, Satan did not have anything to offer Jesus because he was the one there with the father when he created him.

Satan thought by him being in the flesh he could trick him to yield to temptation like Adam. What he did not realize, he was speaking to the second Adam that created the first Adam, representing God among his people that created Satan also. That's why this scripture states ... *Deuteronomy 8:18 (KJV) "18 But thou shalt remember the LORD thy God: for it is he that giveth thee power to get wealth,* (not Satan) *that he may establish his covenant which he sware unto thy fathers, as it is this day."* *Isaiah 46:9-11 (KJV)* ⁹ *Remember the former things of old: for I am God, and there is none else; I am God, and there is none like me,* ¹⁰ *Declaring the end from the beginning, and from ancient times the things that are not yet done, saying, My counsel shall stand, and I will do all my pleasure:* ¹¹ *Calling a ravenous bird from the east, the man that executeth my counsel from a far country: yea, I have spoken it, I will also bring it to pass; I have purposed it, I will also do it.*

Satan has been given a temporary title deed to the earth that God owns, and we are paying the mortgage. All he has to offer you is what you can see, feel, taste, touch and hear while on the Earth on his way to his last stop, seeking as many souls as possible he can to take with him to the lake of fire. All he has will be appealing to his children as natural carnal human beings. The natural man's five gates to his soul are our warfare in the mind daily against good and evil. I am nobody's judge; the word of God has that covered.

When we study as a student of the Holy Spirit and not the seminarians as man see him, we would know by observation who is right and who is wrong just by revelation knowledge of the truth. One thing I have observed by seminary trained pastors; they do not stress the holiness message. *Hebrews 12:14 (KJV)* ¹⁴ *Follow peace with all men, and holiness, without which no man shall see the Lord: 1 Thessalonians 4:7 (KJV)* ⁷ *For God hath not called us unto uncleanness, but unto holiness.* Therefore, they have become good speakers and purveyors of knowledge. I must admit, I have learned a great deal of historical knowledge from them. What I have found through the teachings of the Holy Spirit's anointing, God desires to reveal himself through his word. Remember, we are destroyed by lack of this knowledge and in our ignorance; we will become a judge of others if we are not tempered in our knowledge of truth.

If you do not fall in love with God, Satan will cause you to be puffed up in the very thing God hates, blinded by your own pride. The temptation to think of yourself more highly than you ought, will contend with you when we learn something others do not know. That is why we must first be converted before God can use you to convert others to himself not you. This spirit that seduced those who went into their wilderness with a shallow conviction, sent there by man, took the bait Satan offered to build these mega kingdom assemblies, while those on the other extreme came out judging everyone as though they were the only ones right. I distinctly remember that about Elijah after killing all of Jezebel' prophets, thought he was the only one right.

What he did not realize, as a prophet, speaking what God tells you to say will not make you popular among the people confessing to be of God in name only. We who carry messages like this will be tempted at times in our rejections. *Luke 6:26 (KJV)* [26] *"Woe unto you, when all men shall speak well of you! for so did their fathers to the false prophets."*

Though in many situations, it will appear that you are the only one speaking with this vision at times, God has others who are being fed as you speak that are holding their peace for God's reasons. We will love people who will tell us what we want to hear. As you see, the word does the judging; just make sure you are being led to say what you are saying. Through the mind of the spirit, I see some good being done in many well-meaning ministers, however, because of the discernable error in doctrines and interpretations, I choose to have no part with those who teach only principles that does not require salvation to work for you by just using the name of the lord. Satan uses his false prophets to rob you in the name of God, to think that to be godly is to gain.

Why do we as confessing Christians go to these false preachers and get in lines as ignorant Christians to buy the Holy Spirit when we have been given him freely from God; lack of knowledge of faith to believe the word of truth. *Luke 11:13 (KJV)* [13] *If ye then, being evil, know how to give good gifts unto your children: how much more shall your heavenly Father give the Holy Spirit to them that ask him? Hebrews 12:1 (KJV)* [1] *"Wherefore seeing we also are compassed about with so great a cloud of witnesses, let us lay aside every weight, and the sin which doth so easily beset us, and let us run with patience the race that is set before us, James 1:4 (KJV)* [4] But let patience have her perfect work, that ye may be perfect and entire, wanting nothing."* It takes patience to acquire the blessings of God that adds no sorrow. Patient is the fruit many confessing Christians lack because they too, are caught up in the cares of this life. We in America, the nation that received the gentile blessing of Abraham for one purpose; to be instrumental in the restoration of Israel as a nation, that sign was fulfilled in 1967 when they regained their capital. (Matt. 24:34)

As you see, at the end of nearly sixteen hundred years only eight souls were selected to repopulate the Earth that has led up to this time of our end. A remnant will be saved to repopulate the Earth for the last time at the end of the tribulation period. Many of their children will be saved to replace their deceived hypocritical parents that raised them in these false teachings. I know this is hard to believe, but the evidence precedes us in history of how God dealt with a world whose inhabitants have now reach the state of ... *Genesis 6:5-7 (KJV)* [5] *"And GOD saw that the wickedness of man was great in the earth, and that every imagination of the thoughts of his heart was only evil continually.* [6] *And it repented the LORD that he had made man on the earth, and it grieved him at his heart.* [7] *And the LORD said, I will destroy man whom I have created from the face of the earth; both man, and beast, and the creeping thing, and the fowls of the air; for it repenteth me that I have made them."* This to me is my Enoch moment, let me give you some insight into the numberless multitude as spoken in ... *Revelation 7:9 (KJV)* "[9] *After this I beheld, and, lo, a great multitude, which no man could number, of all nations, and kindreds, and people, and tongues, stood before the throne, and before the Lamb, clothed with white robes, and palms in their hands;"* *John 10:16 (NASB77)* [16] *"And I have other sheep, which are not of this fold; I must bring them also, and they shall hear My voice; and they shall become one flock with one shepherd.*

These are people taken from each time, age and dispensation which include those that will be taken in the first and last millennium and a times unknown to man. God speaks to the end of time which includes all the prophecies being fulfilled. *(Isaiah 46:10)* Remember, there was no birth control when God told man to repopulate the earth; man lived up to nine hundred and sixty-nine years planting these seeds to repopulate the earth which had few mountains but many streams of water before the flood. There are hidden things that cannot be told to us in this last dispensation because of our state of apostasy that will only be known by those when we get to heaven about that numberless multitude.

Although the world existed before the creation as spoken in Genesis when God said, **"replenish the Earth." (Gen.1:28)** There is no evidence from biblical history of this world was inhabited by other beings. Where the bible is silent is where Satan gave birth to science, speculation and probabilities. If man could live to get to 969 years old, just think of how big some of these animals had to be breathing 100% oxygen made them become what we know as mammals. What they call prehistoric are mammals that God allowed to become extinct because they were too large to be taken on the ark and would not have survived after?

God led only the species that would be able to survive after the flood because they would only live no more than 120 years at best for some species as the ocean dwelling creatures.

When archaeologist begin to dig through the layers of petrified mud, it became evident that some of these animals died in a live fresh state because of intact with-in layers of petrified mud that had become as hardened rock in certain parts of the world that they were discovered. Some were found with undigested food in their well-preserved state. The flood transported them all over the world. Humans made in the Image of God can by diet in certain regions of the world, have been documented to live to get 175 after many generations of polluting the earth, it has been reduced 120 or less. The flood changed the geography of the world and the heavenly bodies. During the tribulation, the Earth's geography will be changed back to the first millennium at the end by a miracle of God, those chosen to repopulate the millennium will see this great wonder.

The deep valleys and canyons we see today are a result of flood waters that came up out of the ground and from the sky that changed the atmospheric pressure and cause the loss of pure oxygen after the flood that led to a shortened life span. Men have been jailed by the **deep state** for revealing this knowledge to confound scientific theories about this mystery. They have the ancient record of this truth in the Vatican.

God's fallen angels knew this and when they emerged in fallen man, caused them to withhold certain knowledge that would give birth to science that will serve the purpose of their agendas as God had given them for the ages to come. That is why you are now being told the truth before the time of the end. Various parts of the Earth were populated with large beast that was not pre-Adam. The Earth will be repopulated in the last millennium of the natural man after the tribulation with no devil to tempt him, this time because of the presence of the Kingdom of Christ.

This will be the second stage of the reformation of Earth at the end of the tribulation. John saw the new heaven and Earth that will come at the end of the last millennium that will represent the number eight (the new beginning). Only one third of the land mass was left after the flood. The natural disasters described in the book of Revelation is in the form of symbolic mysteries are the calamities changing the world's geography back to the first millennium. We will come to know it in our time as **"Climate Change."** The third World War will precede these subsequent natural disasters such as ... the stars falling, fragmented asteroid meteorites obliterating the western hemisphere, ultraviolet rays, (purifying the earth by killing off all remaining biological and defiled life forms). These are mysteries that have been kept hidden from this present world.

I pray that by this revelation, you will see that God has magnified his word above his name and not one word will be compromised to let you in heaven if you do not repent when you are warned. You see why no one chooses to be the barer of this kind of news. After my tragic divorce, I found myself transplanted in Phoenix Arizona, away from all my past. It took a second marriage to preserve me to this point in my life to become an end time messenger to this last generation. I still am left at times with this reality that only the presence of the lord to comfort me. There is not much I have to look forward to but to finish my course and go home.

As a child, living with an undiagnosed form of dyslexia, could not read well, wrote things wrong on my papers when I knew I was right in my mind, made me look like a dummy in school. I can now understand rejection and ridicule. I endured it at an early age in my life being criticized and buffeted for my faults. God has let me see, like those who have gone before me with this message, how he and he alone has kept me all these years to preserve me for the purpose I was born. The wickedness of this time is so great, when my course is finished, I will be offered up alone as Stephen, Paul and John the Baptist when my time comes to an end. I know in my testimonies at times in these chronicles may seem I have not had it so easy most of my life and that is true in my private life. While following peace with my fellow man, I have had to endure much rejection, suffer long periods of oppression from well-meaning confessing Christians.

I have always seen myself as the least among men. That is what kept me humble in my God given profession and cause me to excel among my peers because God made me a taker of abuse with no remorse. My grandmother taught me that. I know now that what I had to experience in my latter years was to perfect my character. I can relate to those he sends to me to mentor. To him be the glory. (Updated for release 1/2021)

WHAT DOES THE WORD SAY ABOUT OUR DEPARTED LOVED ONES?

Background scriptures:

Matthew 22:30 (KJV) [30] *For in the resurrection they neither marry, nor are given in marriage, <u>but are as the angels of God in heaven</u>. Luke 20:35 (KJV)* [35] *But they which shall be <u>accounted worthy to obtain that world,</u> and the resurrection from the dead, neither marry, nor are given in marriage: Matthew 22:30 (NLT)* [30] *For when the dead rise, they will neither marry nor be given in marriage. In this respect they will be like the angels in heaven. Galatians 3:28 (KJV)* [28] *There is neither Jew nor Greek, there is neither bond nor free, there is neither male nor female: for ye are all one in Christ Jesus. John 8:32 (KJV)* [32] *And ye shall know the truth, and the truth shall make you free.*

Recently, I was asked by a dear sister about whether we will meet our departed loved ones such as husbands and wives in heaven and be united again as on earth? Only God know the secrets in men hearts at death that will judge your destiny. We look on the outer appearance and are influenced by our life here on earth because of carnal false teachings that incorporate imagination into the unknown. Many of us have not been convicted to see the spiritual truth about the two natures of man that boarders on THE UNCONFESSED SINS OF OMISSION. (Gal.5:19-21)

My reply was what Jesus told the Pharisees and the scribes when they ask the question about the resurrection as to who would have the wife of the widow that married seven brothers in search of an heir. This was Jesus's reply… *Mark 12:23 (KJV)* [23] *In the resurrection therefore, when they shall rise, whose wife shall she be of them? for the seven had her to wife. Matthew 22:29-33 (KJV)* [29] *Jesus answered and said unto them, <u>Ye do err, not knowing the scriptures,</u> nor the power of God.* [32] *I am the God of Abraham, and the God of Isaac, and the God of Jacob? God is not the God of the dead, but of the living.* [33] *And when the multitude heard this, they were astonished at his doctrine. Galatians 3:28 (KJV)* [28] *There is neither Jew nor Greek, there is neither bond nor free, there is neither male nor female: for ye are all one in Christ Jesus.*

What was he saying? If you are not walking in the spirit as though you are in heaven, that is an indication that you are not ready to leave this earth. That's why Paul said we are passing from this cursed earthly body by dying daily to become as ministering angels in the spirit to be glorified in a new body to spend eternity with God. The standard we are striving to achieve is perfect transformation in body, mind and spirit. We as new creatures are the restored Adams to set over universal and Earthly things in this vast cosmos God has created for those he loves. Now look up at the sky, that is the numberless multitude needed to rule these unseen worlds. You will only know the full mystery when you receive the new glorified body. That knowledge cannot be contained in your flesh state. When you set your mind to speak the truth, I have found that you will draw some of the same replies as did those in Christ time on earth, now represented again in you. Now do not get the impression that I have arrived, this is what we all must be striving for.

The Holy Spirit is revealing the truth about our state and his mercy on us as he speaks through me. In our flesh, through false teaching, we have been told lies and imaginary tales from the pulpits that God is going to let you continue in heaven as you were on the earth. If he said that we are as angels in heaven, they are sexless, that's why Mary Magdalene did not recognize Christ until he spoke. That's because all things will become new with no reference to the flesh. There will be no remembrance of your past life here on earth. That is the whole point of your dying to your natural state. All that was relevant to this life as you are forgiven of past sins, is thrown in the lake of remembrance no more. *John 20:15-16" (KJV)* *15 Jesus saith unto her, Woman, why weepest thou? whom seekest thou? She, supposing him to be the gardener, saith unto him, Sir, if thou have borne him hence, tell me where thou hast laid him, and I will take him away. 16 Jesus saith unto her, Mary. She turned herself, and saith unto him, Rabboni; which is to say, Master."* His glorified state was a new look. She knew his voice and so will everyone born from above, when the call is made in the resurrection of your spirit not your body in the grave.

There's neither male nor female as spirit being ... we are there for his pleasure in his service to worship and serve God in spirit only ... it was his truth that got us there. You will have the mind of God. His mind is heavenly; therefore, if you keep it stayed on him, you are in perfect peace as Paul said, waiting to be absent from your body and be present with the lord. This change represents the death of the old you that was in the flesh when we pass from this life into a sexless existence. Why would he use the apostles to preach the gospel of death to the flesh to become a new creature to walk as Adam did before the fall from that state of being a spirit being in flesh form. This time you will become a spirit being with a new glorified body in heaven. There will be no memory of you past life. All that was thrown in God's Lake, never to be returned because it represents your pass life in sin, and no sin will enter heaven.

God set the standard back to the fullness when he said. *2 Corinthians 5:17 (KJV) 17 Therefore if any man be in Christ, he is a new creature: old things are passed away; behold, all things are become new.* When Christ explain the concept of spiritual things to Nicodemus, that is why it was so difficult for him to understand because he was carnal. *1 Peter 4:6 (KJV) 6 For this cause was the gospel preached also to them that are dead, that they might be judged according to men in the flesh, but live according to God in the spirit. Galatians 5:16 (KJV) 16 This I say then, walk in the Spirit, and ye shall not fulfill the lust of the flesh.*

You must die to the flesh for Christ to be resurrected in the fullness; that is his standard of perfection as stated in Eph. 4:11-12 and Matthew 5:48. They were astonished at his doctrine because his standard **is** perfection. Now let me comfort you through the Holy Spirit. God knew Man was going to fail him, that's why he created them male and female in the natural world, He gave them sex organs that will serve his purpose to repopulate the earth after the fall. His flesh came alive with the lust that came with the spirit of his new father the devil when he yields to Eve and ate the forbidden fruit. Some of us are foolish enough to question God about his sovereign will that was set in motion before we were created while you are a mass of dirt, waiting to be formed in his image. Like clay instructing the potter. *Romans 9:21 (NKJV)* [21] *Does not the potter have power over the clay, from the same lump to make one vessel for honor and another for dishonor?*

This is the activity of our new father, using you to mock God in our ignorance. That is why he created them male and female in the beginning and after they sinned, you might as well go ahead and repopulate the Earth so I can select me sons from among them in their fallen state to show my glory in the Earth through a pre-determined timeline I have given man to subdue the Earth back into his possession. This is where we see for the first time His mercy and compassion for mankind to bring him back into his presents just by obeying every word he said. Look what happen to Adam when he listened to the devil speaking with Eve's voice and got judged instantly to receive the fate of separation and death. When we choose to ignore what God said, we become willingly ignorant. We are already judge by his spoken word because the opposite of being blessed is being cursed; that's the state we all were born.

Now we are under the new covenant, we all can from sin; therefore, we cannot judge each other sense none of us came from heaven. This is the blessed life that will lead you into eternity. This is what is required to remain in right standing here on Earth in the flesh … *John 3:3 (KJV)* [3] *Jesus answered and said unto him, Verily, verily, I say unto thee, except a man be born again, he cannot see the kingdom of God. John 3:6-7 (KJV)* [6] *That which is born of the flesh is flesh; and that which is born of the Spirit is spirit.* [7] *Marvel not that I said unto thee, Ye must be born again. … 1 John 2:1 (KJV)* [1] *My little children, these things write I unto you, that ye sin not. And if any man sin, we have an advocate with the Father, Jesus Christ the righteous: 1 John 1:9 (KJV)* [9] *If we confess our sins, he is faithful and just to forgive us our sins, and to cleanse us from all unrighteousness.*

This is the true meaning of mercy and grace administered by God, who judge man's heart by his word. Why do we have such a hard time believing truth to the point of conviction to act on it as a sign to Him we believe he is who he said he is? Now my dear brothers and sisters, let's read in more detailed explanations what Paul said about his own struggles while in his flesh. We must see the need for this power that comes only from God's mercy on us when we obey his words. Therefore, I repent daily like Job did daily sacrifices. In my state, there is no good in me. This is what keeps you in right standing daily. Remember, the sins of omission. (Gal. 5:19-21**) Matthew 6:34 (NKJV)** [34] **Therefore, do not worry about tomorrow, for tomorrow will worry about its own things. Sufficient for the day is its own trouble.**

All that will strive to live Godly will come face to face with these realities ... (Compare to KJV) **Romans 7:14-25 (NLT) "**[14] **So the trouble is not with the law, for it is spiritual and good. <u>The trouble is with me</u>, for I am all too human, a slave to sin.** (This is your struggle with that old you.) [15] **I don't really understand myself, for I want to do what is right, but I don't do it. Instead, I do what I hate.** [16] **But if I know that what I am doing is wrong, this shows that I agree that the law is good.** (Our convictions bring us to a reality where God can show himself as a present and only help.) [17] **So I am not the one doing wrong; it is sin living in me that does it.** [18] **And<u> I know that nothing good lives in me,</u>** (This is the old you at war in your mind; once these strong holes were occupied by the devil, now they are contending in your thoughts to regain control of your mind.) **that is, in my sinful nature. I want to do what is right, but I can't.** [19] **I want to do what is good, but I don't. I don't want to do what is wrong, but I do it anyway.** (After we are saved, this is where you will see the need to be delivered from your old self.)[20] **But if I do what I don't want to do, I am not really the one doing wrong; it is sin living in me that does it.** (This is where the power of God shows himself as the greater power in you not yielding to sin, but you must give place to him to help you overcome that temptation.) [21] **I have discovered this principle of life—that when I want to do what is right, I inevitably do what is wrong.** (This is a stage of weakness.) [22] **I love God's law with all my heart.** [23] **But there is another power within me that is at war with my mind. This power makes me a slave to the sin that is still within me.** (When Adam sinned, instantly the spirit of lust came into him and transformed his state of mind into strange desires for Eve he never had before because he was dead in the flesh to sin.) [24] **Oh, what a miserable person I am!** (This is going to be your test of your will to resist these temptations on a daily bassist.) **Who will free me from this life that is dominated by sin and death?** (Now here's your answer.) [25] **Thank God! The answer is in Jesus Christ our Lord. So, you see how it is: In my mind I really want to obey God's law, but because of my sinful nature I am a slave to sin."**

Many of us do not have this degree of understanding to overcome these temptation because we do not have strong ensamples to help you by Godly prayer, overcome the burdens and get you delivered from your old self. Therefore, we must live by every word of God to be perfect in his sight. Under the new covenant, we are made the righteousness of God in Christ through obedience. I have noticed that most theologians put Paul on a higher level of grace as to speak of him as though we are not capable of living like that. Paul was another man in God's appointed time chosen to do what he did in the same spirit of the Holy Ghost we have been given as the chosen in our day. What I see in his life is his testimony of how the power of God caused him to do and experience extraordinary things that only God can do in an elected yield vessel, you are no different and that same spirit is now in you to do even greater exploits. All that is required is to do what he gave you the power to do. This was his message then and is the same message now concerning God's power that gives us the ability to do extraordinary things.

Compare to KJV `

Romans 8:1-9 (NLT) "1 So now there is no condemnation for those who belong to Christ Jesus. [2] And because you belong to him, the power of the life-giving Spirit has freed you from the power of sin that leads to death. [3] The Law of Moses was unable to save us because of the weakness of our sinful nature. So, God did what the law could not do. He sent his own Son in a body like the body's we sinners have. And in that body God declared an end to sin's control over us by giving his Son as a sacrifice for our sins. [4] He did this so that the just requirement of the law would be fully satisfied for us, who no longer follow our sinful nature but instead follow the Spirit. [5] Those who are dominated by the sinful nature think about sinful things, but those who are controlled by the Holy Spirit think about things that please the Spirit. [6] So letting your sinful nature control your mind leads to death. But letting the Spirit control your mind leads to life and peace. [7] For the sinful nature is always hostile to God. It never did obey God's laws, and it never will. [8] That's why those who are still under the control of their sinful nature

can never please God. ⁹ But you are not controlled by your sinful nature. You are controlled by the Spirit if you have the Spirit of God living in you. And remember that those who do not have the Spirit of Christ living in them do not belong to him at all."

What I have been made to see by the Holy Spirit' teachings in the New Testament, to get us back to the dominion of Adam, we must die again to be fully restored to the power of God in our flesh to keep us from sinning. God has made provision for all things we encounter in the fleshly state of life while on earth. This includes marriage and having children to carry out his sovereign will set in motion on Earth.

There is nothing to compare with heaven other than to come to your death in the flesh in the Earth. This is the perfect new man and without Christ in you, the world will never see him in the fullness to bring forth fruit that remain as it did in all the chosen apostles. In their blood sacrifices, upheld his standard and Paul's testimony is the comforting source of this power. Though we cannot fully comprehend while in the flesh what heaven will be like, Those God has given a short tour and send them back, is to give us hope to live in the reality that there is a heaven. What God shows us in the life of Paul is the power that made him an extraordinary human being is also in you to do the same. This was his testimony of what he experienced from that power of God delivering him despite his infirmities expressed in Romans 7 & 8 concerning the fleshly nature of man. That's why I don't entertain unbelief.

The reason why I laid the foundation in this manner is to show you the difference in the two dimensions of time continuum between life on earth and what' to expect in the worlds to come that we cannot fully comprehend in the flesh. If we believe the reality of there is a God who is eternal, he has set conditions on what he requires to live with him for eternity.

He sent his Holy Spirit to give us the power to be as He. That's why we who are at peace with God are …. *2 Corinthians 10:5 (KJV) ⁵ Casting down imaginations, and every high thing that exalteth itself against the knowledge of God and bringing into captivity every thought to the obedience of Christ; 1 Corinthians 2:2 (KJV) ² For I determined not to know anything among you, save Jesus Christ, and him crucified.*

What he has said about what heaven is like leaves nothing to be added to his word without bringing condemnation to yourself. It was revealed to me that there will be no knowledge of what we did while in the flesh on earth because what's in God's mind will be in your mind and if he throws your sins in the lake of remembrance no more, there will be no knowledge of them in you in heaven. **Now do you still want to go to heaven on these terms.** God is a spirit, and you will be as he for eternity as his servants. The new creature in Christ will have no memory of the flesh in heaven because there will be no evil thoughts in him. That's why you are called a **"new creatures, old things are passed away".** You will not recognize your loved one as in this world because the spirit world is sexless and, in that state, there is no memory of flesh as we become angelic beings when our spirit and soul is redeemed, our bodies are returned to the dust of the Earth it is not going to raise in that fleshly corrupted state. As now spirit being, your natural body has served its purpose and what was done in it in the flesh is buried with it and returns to dust. That's why there will be no bodily resurrection in the natural part that is returned to the dust. This is all spiritual.

I still have some skepticism when I hear of these stories of communication with long lost loved ones in heaven. I still do not have a sound scripturally based revelation in this area. The only place I found is where Saul used the devil to contact Samuel and that sealed his fate as a child of the devil. I know this may come as a shock to some of you who would rather believe a lie   because of soul bond ties you refused to let go, it is the enemy of your soul that is keeping them alive for the sake of your feeling. However, these are the lies feeding off your imaginations, you choose to believe. *2 Corinthians 10:5 (KJV)* [5] *Casting down imaginations, and every high thing that exalteth itself against the knowledge of God and bringing into captivity every thought to the obedience of Christ.* The reality of this truth will become apparent when you breathe your last breath. Hell will be full of good people here on earth that did not claim their birthright to live in eternity with their creator. Many of them were told that being good will get you to heaven.

To be born again is to have your mind set in heavenly places in the one that redeemed you as one of his own to be with him for eternity. His spirit made you back into the image of God to get to heaven because he is the only one that can look on his face and live. *1 John 3:2 (KJV)* [2] *Beloved, now are we the sons of God, and it doth not yet appear what we shall be: but we know that, when he shall appear, we shall be like him; for we shall see him as he is. Matthew 4:4 (KJV)* [4] *But he answered and said, it is written, Man shall not live by bread alone, but by every word that proceedeth out of the mouth of God. Luke 18:8 (KJV)* [8] *I tell you that he will avenge them speedily. Nevertheless, when the Son of man cometh, shall he find faith on the earth? Matthew 7:21 (KJV)* [21] *Not everyone that saith unto me, Lord, Lord, shall enter into the kingdom of heaven; but he that doeth the will of my Father which is in heaven. Luke 6:46 (NKJV)* [46] *"But why do you call Me 'Lord, Lord,' and do not do the things which I say? 1 John 4:1 (KJV)* [1] Beloved, believe not every spirit, but try the spirits whether they are of God: because many false prophets are *gone out into the world. Luke 21:34 (KJV)* [34] *And take heed to yourselves, lest at any time your hearts be overcharged with surfeiting, and drunkenness, and cares of this life, and so that day come upon you unawares.*

In time past, I was more devoted to an organized religious denomination than I was to the word of God while being instructed in the traditions of that denomination's belief. I was captivated by the spirit of religion that comes from below and is of the devil. My pastor meant well but I later found him indoctrinated in what that denomination believed as man interpreted. This I found out when I preached my first sermon in his pulpit as a loyal servant of his for four years. I was brought in question about the interpretation of what God said over what man said and had my first encounter as Peter; to decide to obey man or God.

A lot has happened to me since that day. We are now in the last days, the persecution the early saints paid for in their blood to keep the standards of this doctrine will now be our sacrifice in blood in these last days to bring the glory back to this church. Christ in you will once again put the devil under His church feet and take those found in him home for eternity. *Matthew 11:12 (KJV)* [12] *And from the days of John the Baptist until now the kingdom of heaven suffereth violence, and the violent take it by force. Mark 13:9 (KJV)* [9] *But take heed to yourselves: for they shall deliver you up to councils; and in the synagogues ye shall be beaten: and ye shall be brought before rulers and kings for my sake, for a testimony against them.*

Those of us who have received this vision for our times are looking forward to our day of redemption. The fact that God has magnified his word above his name is what we all will be judged by as confessing Christians. Regardless of what your pastor said, God will hold you responsible for what he has said in his word in the judgment, so do your repenting now as I did when he showed me my sins of omission. Follow and support those that sacrifice themselves to bring you messages like this to warn you. Take self-examination to make your calling and election sure as they follow Christ. God has assigned them to be the true watchman of your souls. They are the ones you should give support as they are suffering for your sake to uphold the integrity of this word so the fruit will remain in all that receive them who walk in the same spirit as were in the original apostles. We are the few. (Updated for release 3/2020)

GOD'S FINAL WARNING

"The signs of the times"

The largest misconception by far in doctrinal teaching in the present-day church world is the saints are going to escape the tribulation; that is, be translated before it all began. All who are living in the last generation will repeat what the saints suffered in the former rain to return the church back to the original apostle's doctrine before the true church can be raptured. Unless you die before the time of Jacob's trouble commences in this end time, you must be purified in the fires of tribulation. *Revelation 3:18 (KJV)* [18] *I counsel thee to buy of me gold tried in the fire, that thou mayest be rich; and white raiment, that thou mayest be clothed, and that the shame of thy nakedness do not appear; and anoint thine eyes with eyesalve, that thou mayest see.* The church must return to a new Pentecost as one body as in the beginning. That is why there must be a latter rain. On my first missionary journey around the state of Arizona, I met a pastor that said to me, I don't believe God would allow his children to suffer any of the tribulation. Those of you with eyes to see and ears to hear will have a clear understanding of why this single doctrine will cause …. *Isaiah 5:14 (KJV)* [14] *Therefore hell hath enlarged herself and opened her mouth without measure: and their glory, and their multitude, and their pomp, and he that rejoiceth, shall descend into it.*… Multitudes of deceived confessing Christians who serve God on the bassist of their feeling and emotions and doctrinal hearsay, that's not according to revelation knowledge will be caught in God's break shaking without the power. *Hosea 4:6 (NASB77)* [6] *My people are destroyed for lack of knowledge. Because you have rejected knowledge, I also will reject you from being my priest. Since you have forgotten the law of your God, I also will forget your children.* Our Children in this last generation are paying the price for our hypocrisy. Many of them will take their parents' place.

Fact One; We are not all serving the same God. There is only .... *"Ephesians 4:5 (KJV) ⁵ One Lord, one faith, one baptism,"* ... containing the only doctrine that made man whole into one body, not separate in part as we have become has divided the kingdom of God in the earth.

Fact two; We do not believe that there is only one doctrine. *1 Timothy 1:6-7 (KJV) ⁶ From which some having swerved have turned aside unto vain jangling; ⁷ Desiring to be teachers of the law; understanding neither what they say, nor whereof they affirm.* **1 Timothy 1:6-7 (NLT) ⁶ But some people have missed this whole point. They have turned away from these things and spend their time in meaningless discussions. ⁷ They want to be known as teachers of the Law of Moses, but they don't know what they are talking about, even though they speak so confidently.** *2 John 1:10 (KJV) ¹⁰ If there come any unto you, and bring not this doctrine, receive him not into your house, neither bid him God speed:* This new doctrine, introduced through seminary train men to become self-kingdom builders as hireling speakers and not deliverers. This is the evidence of the great fall away. This is that thin line of deception that over generations of doctrinal changes by straying away from the Pentecostal experience of one body in the former rain to many; is now divided by denominational name calling.

The four gospels declared through Christ, set the foundation for all that come after him. This will be explained and demonstrated in those used to bring this revelation in the epistles that followed to complete the New Testament in their blood. All who are called to minister this doctrine after they have been converted, will have this mind set towards the fellow brothers ... *1 Corinthians 2:2 (KJV)² For I determined not to know anything among you, save Jesus Christ, and him crucified;* After you have been crucified in him, this doctrine will produce that fruit which will remain in the whole council of the five ministerial graces, complete us to become a spirit filled unified body with Christ as its head. In my travels, where I find a person that believes for a miracle, received one. If you base your leadership on knowledge more than convictions that border on self-denial and Godly faith, you will not see these signs, wonders or miracles. *Hebrews 4:2 (KJV) ² For unto us was the gospel preached, as well as unto them: but the word preached did not profit them, not being mixed with faith in them that heard it.* Now pastors are no more that glorified self-help speakers that can tell you everything about what's in the bible but do not believe we can do what the original apostles did. Many have said we do not have that in our time, God did that to give us the bible, but no one can live that perfect. *Matthew 5:48 (NKJV)* [48] *Therefore you shall be perfect, just as your Father in heaven is perfect.* That's why you don't see deliverance in many assemblies because of unbelief and not knowing who you represent. *John 8:43 (NKJV)* [43] *Why do you not understand My speech? Because you are not able to listen to My word. Mark 7:9 (NKJV)* [9] *He said to them, "All too well you reject the commandment of God, that you may keep your tradition.*

This same Holy Ghost sent back on the day of Pentecost must be in your converted leader for this to become a reality. This will be judged by the fruit of your leader as their measure of faith in God. Those who have been converted (Christ in you) as he told peter will become the rock which this foundation will be built upon as the apostles demonstrated and that body will produce the same signs of all that believe as in the early church. The Holy Spirit is activated to teach and guide you by revelation knowledge in the application of truth, so you will not be ignorant in rightly dividing the word once you are born in the truth of the apostle's doctrine. This includes all things relevant to your time on earth. This will be evident in the church operating in the fullness by having the whole council of God declared among them in the spirit of **(Eph. 4:11-12)**, the perfect knowledge. When Christ is being crucified in you, the Holy Spirit will have the liberty to teach and manifest him-self in your body to this degree.

The fullness of Christ will be manifested when self is crucified completely. It is the mind of Christ that is the head of his body. *1 Corinthians 2:16 (KJV)* [16] *For who hath known the mind of the Lord, that he may instruct him? But we have the mind of Christ.* Outside of his doctrine, you are none of his. (Romans.8:9) I wish I had an example like this in my early encounter, I would not have wrecked my life to find Him to become a better servant of God. I am so grateful to have been chosen by God to be and instrument to be used in this more excellent way for these latter days. I look forward to the day to be absent from this body and present with the lord for eternity. *Romans 8:9 (KJV)* [9] *But ye are not in the flesh, but in the Spirit, if so be that the Spirit of God dwell in you. Now if any man have not the Spirit of Christ, he is none of his.* Logical theology as taught in seminaries will usurp over the Holy Spirit of God and there in is the error of many pastors and teachers. Therefore, we must forsake our thoughts for this reason ... *Isaiah 55:8 (KJV)* [8] *<u>For my thoughts are not your thoughts, neither are your ways my ways</u>, saith the Lord.* But the reality we see that's evident among the church world ... *Isaiah 53:6 (NKJV)* [6] *All we like sheep have gone astray; We have turned, everyone, to his own way; And the LORD has laid on Him the iniquity of us all. Therefore ... 2 Timothy 3:7 (NKJV)* [7] *always learning and never able to come to the knowledge of the truth.*

This is the bassist of the division in the interpretations that have led to many doctrines that represent the mind of man speaking without the anointing of the Holy Spirit who is the mind of God that speaks the unadulterated truth. He does not lie to you; the devil in man is the liar when you know not what spirit you are of. I taught this in a full gospel assembly and got expelled for upholding this doctrine because I was told that you will never grow a church teaching this hard. The Woe on the spiritual leaders who have endorsed the lies that caused many of these present-day church assemblies to be deceived will become the blood of the souls on their hands for teaching lies.

They were sent into the seminary wilderness by Satan to receive what they thought was Christ but was not being led by Christ, and took the devils bate ... *Matthew 4:9 (NKJV)* [9] *And he said to Him, "All these things I will give You if You will fall down and worship me."* That's how we got hirelings to build mega assemblies under the 501c-3 as non-profit corporations. When I was convicted of my state and brought to rest, it was for God to prepare me during that time for his sovereign calling on my life. I was set aside for seven years. If God did not have a purpose for me being born, I would still be as those who find themselves as I did when this last word of warning came to me.

Jeremiah 5:12 (KJV) [12] *They have belied the Lord, and said, it is not he; neither shall evil come upon us; neither shall we see sword nor famine: Jeremiah 5:12 (NLT)* [12] *"They have lied about the LORD and said, 'He won't bother us! No disasters will come upon us. There will be no war or . Matthew 24:3-6 (KJV)* [3] *And as he sat upon the Mount of Olives, the disciples came unto him privately, saying, tell us, when shall these things be?*

and what shall be the sign of thy coming, and of the end of the world? [4] *And Jesus answered and said unto them, take heed that no man deceive you.* [5] *For many shall come in my name, saying, I am Christ; and shall deceive many.* [6] *And ye shall hear of wars and rumours of wars: see that ye be not troubled: for all these things must come to pass, but the end is not yet.*

Christ was prophesying of the time from his departure, what would happen to them as well as all who follow him until he returns. During that time, as generations of men will get worse and worse; however, the very last generation will receive a specific word and a revelation that had to be withheld because the church will be splintered into many new doctrines. This revelation had to be hidden that was kept back to be revealed at that time. Throughout times, ages and dispensations, God's elect will preserve his presence and timeline of man on Earth. *2 Timothy 3:13 (KJV)* [13] *But evil men and seducers shall wax worse and worse, deceiving, and being deceived.* We are at the end of that time he was prophesying of the generation that would not pass till all is fulfilled.

This is where we are today that this prophecy is coming to pass. *Joel 2:2 (KJV)* [2] *A Day of darkness and of gloominess, a day of clouds and of thick darkness, as the morning spread upon the mountains: a great people and a strong; there hath not been ever the like, neither shall be any more after it, <u>even to the years of many generations.</u>* What we all failed to see at this time of the end on a large scale, our state as a church pose no threat to the world neither is there a light to the extent that Christ can be seen or feared. This is the curse upon the church, under the state as a **501-c3** organization. This without their knowing is their mark that put them under the beast system. They are state controlled, and division is how they were conquered. In other words, the state has control over what God can say or do when we come together.

In the days ahead when the laws are changed, you will see what this really means. This was not the intent of the founding fathers in the beginning; we were to become the conscious of the state, had we upheld that standard of righteousness, justice, and equality, overseen by a body of believers worshipping in true holiness, that would have been our distinction as a Christian nation to keep us from acts of Tierney on our soil as was the covenant made with Israel.

We were to hold our elected representatives responsible for protecting our liberties by praying over every representative we sent to Washington. To a certain extent, we have by this anointing, held this position among nations that they feared us because of the power and blessings that came with this covenant. What was once a great Christian nation that a few held to the doctrine that brought eras of revivals is no more on the scale of the early apostles; unfortunately, many no longer believe in the same God the apostles preached … just as the Jews, we have rejected that doctrine in favor of man's traditions.

We now operate in teaching in-part truths and self-help principles with gifts that have led to this present spiritual dilemma. That is the reason why we do not see these signs in the church that caught the attention of the world as it did in their time. When I traveled in those ministerial circles, before I came to this revelation, hearing many say … we do not have prophets like that anymore; this statement today represents no vision for your times which explains our present state of spiritual blindness. Many well-known prophets that carry the title have been compromised by the world by making zealous predictions that did not come true. It appears the world and the churches are one in the same. The signs wonders and miracles that demonstrate Christ as the deliverer is not present in this body of confessing Christians; those with gifts, operate as separate kingdoms.

The reproaches we have come to see in those that say they are of God … have lost their power by compromising the truth. The doctrine, over time has been changed to represent the traditions of the Pharisees, Sadducees and scribes when Jesus first encountered them. Their Traditions separated them from the laws of Moses and divided their body into two separate sects of beliefs; the Pharisees believed in the resurrection while the Sadducees believe there is none. They were in that darkness for four hundred years to where they could not recognize their own Messiah when he arrived. Today, under grace and truth, this is an ongoing argument in the assemblies.

That same spirit has injected man's thoughts that have us divided by false interpretation of scripture such as some are divided by rapture before tribulation and others who say that to be Godly is to gain; now who is right? What did Jesus say? … *Mark 7:8 (KJV)* [8]*For laying aside the commandment of God, ye hold the tradition of men, as the washing of pots and cups: and many other such like things ye do.* [9]*And he said unto them,*

Full well ye reject the commandment of God, that ye may keep your own tradition. 2 Corinthians 3:6 (KJV) [6] *Who also hath made us able ministers of the New Testament; not of the letter, but of the spirit: for the letter killeth, but the spirit giveth life.* The seminaries can qualify you on the bassist of the letter but until you are converted as Peter (Christ rebirth in you), you are just hireling speakers in the pulpit marketing yourself on the bases of your knowledge, degrees, and accolades to become renowned authorities among your peers in your own strength as demonstrated in the electronic media where they all get to perform and compete for your pocketbook. Many of them with gifts of the spirit, use them primarily to get personal fame and gain.

I wonder why God did not allow me to be blessed with the money to market these books, only to publish them. I later learned, as a scribe to be entrusted with these revelations, it would come to me in three layers over time. Therefore, I never wanted to draw any attention to myself when I saw this was ongoing. The Holy Spirit is not a liar; Jesus brought the truth to life when He came out of the volumes of the books and rose from the dead. **You see, the Sadducees were wrong**. This is where we are in these end times. With all these new doctrines, such as rapture and prosperity and other cult religions that have come out of these divisions, our confused state is the reason why we must go through the fires of tribulation, Rev.3:18) as the three Hebrew boys in their test to see who are the true sons of God.

Revelation 3:16-17 (KJV) [16] *So then because thou art lukewarm, and neither cold nor hot, I will spue thee out of my mouth.* [17] *Because thou sayest, I am rich, and increased with goods, and have need of nothing; and knowest not that thou art wretched, and miserable, and poor, and blind, and naked:* This type of blindness with no prophetic vision will cause us to ignore these signs of the prophets raised up in this time as were under the law to interpret what they said of old that applies to our time. Therefore, history repeats itself when the church, naming his name rejects them by not knowing His voice. *Matthew 16:3 (KJV)* [3] *And in the morning, it will be foul weather today: for the sky is red and lowring. O ye hypocrites, ye can discern the face of the sky; but can ye not discern the signs of the times?* What is this word the prophets will bring before we enter the tribulation? *1 Peter 4:17 (KJV) For the time is come that judgment must begin at the house of God: and if it first begins at us, what shall the end be of them that obey not the gospel of God? Revelation 3:18 (KJV)* [18] *I counsel thee to <u>buy of me gold tried in the fire,</u> that thou mayest be rich; and white raiment, that thou mayest be clothed, and that the shame of thy nakedness do not appear; and anoint thine eyes with eye salve, that thou mayest see.*

You would have to be blind not to see that this describes this electronic church media that does not know it is connected to the beast system to promote these doctrines that the government now controls. They, as 501c-3 corporations, will commercialize by compromising what they stand for to raise money to fund programs that do not deliver the people. This is evident by having a 501C-3 to operate under a government charter. The internet, meant for good, will be how Satan will use it in our time to enter our minds by way of being **"the prince of the power of the air;"** through doctrines introduced to create mass confusion, use this media platform that will contribute to these divisions. It has become the technology of confusion. It carries too much information for your mind to process.

When it comes to truth, most will tell you what they saw over the internet or what their pastor said. The Wikipedia is its fuel and most of us Christians are riding on it. After seven years with the lord being tutored by the Holy Spirit, when I had the liberty to examine the prophecies given to me, that's when I saw for the first time what this technology has produced. It is a doorway to your mind and is presently destroying the standard of holiness and robbing you of your attention span and patience among the few Christians left. No wonder God said … *Matthew 24:24 (KJV)* [24] *For there shall arise false Christs, and false prophets, and shall shew great signs and wonders; insomuch that, if it were possible, they shall deceive the very elect* … That's why the days will have to be shortened in our time to save the saints. (Matthew 24:22) Wickedness does not get better but worst.

What Jesus demonstrated when he walked the earth advertised itself, brought attention to the one true God and cause the authorities to fear him by demonstrating that he is the higher power by the authority and miracles he performed. Now if we are His temples and He is not being seen to this degree, something is wrong in the way we are being taught. This deception did not happen overnight. Satan's **Deep State** seduced this present church where now the principalities are boldly speaking words against the most high as President Obama in declaring **"we are no longer a Christian nation."** Although that may be true by observation, God is warning his elects that a seed of Ishmael has reached the White House. You will see this by his action in the days to come before his time is up.

Daniel 7:25 (KJV) [25] *And he shall speak great words against the most High and shall <u>wear out the saints of the most High</u>, and think to change times and laws: and they shall be given into his hand until a time and times and the dividing of time.* DURING THE SECOND HALF OF THE TRIBULATION IS WHERE THE CHURCH WILL BE PURIFIED AND TAKEN OUT WITH THE JEWS, WHEN THE TWO WITNESSES RISE IN THE RESSURRECTION OF THOSE UNDER GRACE. (Rev.14:15-16, Rev. 11:11) Now to bring the confessing church body back to the apostle's doctrine, all our worldly gains must be removed when this false sense of security is exposed in our economic collapse. God will show himself as the God who showed up with the Hebrew boys when they were thrown into our fiery furnace, they that know him will see him do these exploits. **Rev. 3:18** will be our fiery furnace during the tribulation where God will show himself by bringing the former rain restoration that will lead his elects into the latter rain by performing great exploits.

Only those in truth will rise to the occasion to begin to do the exploits we have never seen performed in the elect. Just like the three Hebrew boys knew the real God and He showed himself by saving them from the fiery furnace, the same will happen for those in the great confrontation of good and evil: God in the fullness of his elects and Satan in the fullness as the man of sin.

Daniel 11:32 (KJV) [32] *And such as do wickedly against the covenant shall he corrupt by flatteries:* (All the false pastors and teachers will begin to be exposed as a true of false Shepard.) *but the people that do know their God shall be strong and do exploits.* The only God that will come to the aid of his chosen people will be the God of Abraham, Isaac and Jacob. This is the Elijah show down where the whole world will get to see. *Ephesians 4:5 (KJV)* [5] *One Lord, one faith, one baptism, Romans 14:11-13 (KJV)* [11] *For it is written, As I live, saith the Lord, every knee shall bow to me, and every tongue shall confess to God.* -[12] *So then every one of us shall give account of himself to God.* [13] <u>*Let us not therefore judge one another anymore:*</u> *but judge this rather, that no man put a stumbling block or an occasion to fall in his brother's way. 1 Corinthians 2:2 (KJV)* [2] *For I determined not to know anything among you, save Jesus Christ, and him crucified.*

Those who are called, this is a time of self-examination in preparation as wise virgins that heeded the call by making their calling and election sure, getting ready for his glory. They are in their secret closets in prayer, setting their house in order as wise virgins that their house might be saved. If we continue to judge one another in the flesh, it is evident you miss the call. You may say, I am judging … only if you are seeing this in your fleshy mind as man speaking. Everyone in this call has returned to their inner tabernacle of prayer to set their house to be restored to their first love.

This statement will not be well received in the traditional assembly environment; as chosen temples of God, we are waiting in our latter-day upper room for the former and latter rain again to put flesh on these dry bones being revived. **(Ezekiel 37)** There are many well-meaning pastors and teachers whose lives are like Nicodemus, not far from the kingdom. The error in our teaching as were in mine is the same zeal that was not according to the perfect fruit God can except. This is where we are found operating in our own separate kingdoms. This doctrine will attract large following without a standard of holiness. I pray they will repent as I did on their day of visitation when the prophets warn you. You be the judge of what you are reading and compare it with what the apostle's taught and preached that got them killed. Remember that woe on those all will speak well of. God is sending his messenger as he did in the days of the apostles, and they are being rejected as were Christ in his days on earth.

Do not suffer your congregation to be given over to a delusion because of your pride of being exposed and be led to do what the Sanhedrin did to Jesus again as gentiles, join the Antichrist bodies and be our persecutors, kill the prophets in our time during the tribulation in the name of God. When the shock of not being translated as they were told by their pastors, after God cause the stock market to rise so high to when it takes the final dive, it will take all the rich and financially connected down with it. This nation will be under martial law and all will lose including his people, rich and poor alike and only those that know the real God will rise in the fullness of God to do the exploits. You at that time will be deciding to live for eternity with Christ or give in to fear and be marked for eternal separation.

The wealth of the wicked will be returned to the just during this quick work. This window will be between three or six months. The rich will see where the true riches are and make what resources they have available before the economy completely collapses. I pray in love that others will be opened to hear what **"Thus say the lord"** through the spirit of the prophets when ... Joel **3:14 (KJV)** [14] **Multitudes, multitudes in the valley of decision: for the day of the Lord is near in the valley of decision.** This is that time when ... *Isaiah 5:14 (KJV)* [14] *Therefore hell hath enlarged herself and opened her mouth without measure: and their glory, and their multitude, and their pomp, and he that rejoiceth, shall descend into it.* Please do not harden your heart, your destiny is above.

I see the Holy Spirit constantly using this verse as a warning not to harden your heart on your day of visitation. The great mystery that was kept back by Daniel and John to be revealed by his Holy prophets and messengers to this end time generation of the apostate church world is ... *Matthew 24:22 (KJV)* *"[22] And except those days should be shortened, there should no flesh be saved: but for the elect's sake those days shall be shortened."* The fear that will come upon those that have been lied too, will cause many, trapped into the beast system their churches were under to receive the mark of that system to go into a state of delusion to join this new world religion. You may ask, what is this fire of tribulation? All who are alive will see what will cause every tongue to confess when your denomination or cult god is consumed in the Elijah show down as a false god and a liar. When the **seals** of Revelation are broken, the **trumpets** began to sound, the **thunders** begin to roar, and the **vials** described in the chronicle, **"The Book of Revelation Revealed"** are the fires that will separates the wheat from the tares to birth the true church out of great tribulation. The last trumpet is where the first resurrection of the New Testament saints will occur, **(Revelation 14:15-16)** and the **first thunders** will be the horror the children of disobedience will suffer as the residue in the second sickle of **(Rev. 14:17-18).** The first thunder will sound after the last trumpet. This is the time that must be shortened for the saints in tribulation when God has completed their purification.

This is a side note:

Under grace and truth, these are two feasts that cover all the law for all believers under grace. In the spirit, Christ living in us is a constant **feast in your tabernacles** waiting under grace and truth to be taken out at the **feast of the last trumpet**. Christ in you is the fulfillment of the law.

All the rest applies to the Old Testament law administered in carnality. There-in is the error in the application of truth by mixing law with grace. We, under grace worship God in the spirit of truth. The law in the Old Covenant was administered in carnality. The tabernacle is now within man. These divisions came out of mixing law with grace.

Revelation 12:1-2 (KJV) [1] *And there appeared a great wonder in heaven; a woman clothed with the sun, and the moon under her feet, and upon her head a crown of <u>twelve stars:</u>* [2] *And she being <u>with child cried</u>, travailing in birth, and pained to be delivered.* (The twelve stars are the remnant <u>taken from the twelve tribe of Israel</u>; is the mystery of the 144,000. The child in travail is the church; both are waiting to be delivered at the last trumpet. That's when the two witnesses will rise as at that time as noted in… *Revelation 14:15-16 (NASB77)* [15] *And another angel came out of the temple, crying out with a loud voice to Him who sat on the cloud, "Put in your sickle and reap, because the hour to reap has come, because the harvest of the earth is ripe."* [16] *And He who sat on the cloud swung His sickle over the earth; and the earth was reaped. 1 Thessalonians 4:16 (KJV)* [16] *For the Lord himself shall descend from heaven with a shout, with the voice of the archangel, and with the <u>trump of God</u>:* (This is our feast of the trumpets that will take us out at the sounding of the last trumpet.) *Ezekiel 37:12 "(KJV)* [12] *Therefore prophesy and say unto them, thus saith the Lord GOD; Behold, O my people, I will open your graves, and cause you to come up out of your graves, and <u>bring you into the land of Israel.</u>"* … *and the dead in Christ shall rise first: 1 Corinthians 15:52 (NASB77)* [52] *in a moment, in the twinkling of an eye, <u>at the last trumpet; for the trumpet will sound, and the dead will be raised imperishable, and we shall be changed. and the earth was reaped.</u>* The underlined passage above tells us the translation will take place in Israel as stated in Revelation 11:11.

This is the church and Israel being translated in the second resurrection with the two witnesses as the first fruits of the New Testament Saints. Christ resurrection was the first fruits of the Father. *1Thes. 4:17 (KJV)* [17] *Then we which are alive and remain shall be caught up together with them in the clouds, to meet the Lord in the air: and so, shall we ever be with the Lord. Revelation 14:17-18 (KJV)* [17] *And another angel came out of the temple, which is in heaven, he also having a sharp sickle.* [18] *And another angel came out from the altar, which had power over fire; and cried with a loud cry to* *him that had the sharp sickle, saying, thrust in sharp sickle, and <u>gather the</u> <u>clusters of the vine of the earth; for her grapes are fully ripe</u>. 1 Corinthians 5:5 (KJV)* [5] *To deliver such an one unto Satan for the destruction of the flesh, that the spirit may be saved in the day of the Lord Jesus.* These are the children of disobedience being reaped out of the winepress as their bodies are turned over to the devil for the destruction of their flesh through the prayers of the righteous. *Ephesians 5:6 (KJV)* [6] *Let no man deceive you with vain words: for because of these things cometh the wrath of God upon the children of disobedience.*

Revelation 11:13 (KJV) [13] *And the same hour was there a great earthquake, and the tenth part of the city fell, and in the earthquake, were slain of men seven thousand: and the remnant were affrighted and gave glory to the God of heaven*. (This is the remnant saved to repopulate the millennium.) **Isaiah 26:20 (NKJV)** [20] *Come, my people, enter your chambers*, **and shut your doors behind you; Hide yourself, as it were, for a little moment, Until the indignation is past.** *Matthew 24:29 (KJV)* [29] *Immediately after the tribulation of those days shall the sun be darkened, and the moon shall not give her light, and the stars shall fall from heaven, and the powers of the heavens shall be shaken:* THE ENTIRE WORLD WILL SEE THE RESSURRECTION OF THE DEAD IN CHRIST AT THAT TIME. They will not be driving cars or on planes as the movies depicted. Only the military will have vehicles.

Remember, there was an earthquake when Jesus rose to translate the first fruits. These are some the great mysteries Daniel and John could not reveal as the scriptural timeline of the events that led up to the translation. The first translation of the New Testament saints takes place after the last trumpet. After this, the wrath of God will be poured out without mixture. *Colossians 3:6 (KJV)* [6] *For which things' sake the wrath of God cometh on the children of disobedience:* These are the worldly children of the devil that was used by him to bring the judgements upon the world; now will suffer God's wrath. **Romans 9:22 (KJV)** [22] **What if God, willing to shew his wrath, and to make his power known, endured with much longsuffering the vessels of wrath fitted to destruction:** This is reserved for the children of disobedience; they will suffer the **first thunder** for their disobedience as un-wise virgins and be reaped as the **<u>residue or cluster</u>** out of the wine press in the second sickle of **Rev. 14:17-18.**

They are saved because of the righteous saints that gave their lives as a sacrifice to God who heard their prayers and granted them mercy. They had to suffer the destruction of their flesh as being handed over to the world for the destruction of their flesh that their souls might be saved. What's happening to them as suffering the first thunder is described in Micah 3:3. After this there will be no flesh saved but those souls reserved to repopulate the millennium. I pray these revelations will give those with eyes to see and ears to hear a clearer understanding of the tribulation period that will bring back the body of believers to ... *Ephesians 4:5 (KJV)* [5] *One Lord, one faith, one baptism.* (That is why there must be a tribulation period.) *Revelation 3:18 (KJV)* [18] *I counsel thee to buy of me gold tried in the fire, that thou mayest be rich; and white raiment, that thou mayest be clothed, and that the shame of thy nakedness do not appear; and anoint thine eyes with eyesalve, that thou mayest see.*

Please seek the Lord while he has this door open for you to save yourself from the destruction and carnage that's surely coming upon America and the world very soon. I know now why you must be called by God to speak words like this that few confessing Christians will have ears to hear. May God have mercy on all that call upon his name. (Updated for release 1/2017)

GET READY TO GO HOME

"Salvation, the third layer revelations"

Background Scripture:

Ephesians 2:2 (NKJV) [2] *in which you once walked according to the course of this world, according to the <u>prince of the power of the air</u>, the spirit who now works in the sons of disobedience, John 4:23-24 (NKJV)* [23] *But the hour is coming, and now is, when the true worshipers will worship the Father in spirit and truth; for the Father is seeking such to worship Him.* [24] *God is Spirit, and those who worship Him must worship in spirit and truth." 1 John 4:4 (KJV)* [4] *Ye are of God, little children, and have overcome them: because greater is he that is in you, than he that is in the world. Isaiah 54:17 (KJV)* [17] *No weapon that is formed against thee shall prosper; and every tongue that shall rise against thee in judgment thou shalt condemn. This is the heritage of the servants of the LORD, and their righteousness is of me, saith the LORD.*

Many confessing Christians have not come to the reality of our state as a confessing body of believers in Jesus Christ. Truly God is our judge, but our state is a far cry from the apostle's doctrine as presented on the day of Pentecost. Our divisions as a body of believers have reached the state of not being able to recognize where the true body is. As Jesus stated on one occasion to the Pharisees, it appears that we know not who we truly represent by being guided by the same traditions that cause the Pharisees to be rejected by Christ. *Mark 7:9 (NKJV)* [9] *He said to them, "All too well you reject the commandment of God, that you may keep your tradition.*

In my studies under the guidance of the Holy Spirit, I discovered the three layers that lead to spiritual maturity that brings you into the reality of walking in the spirit as a new creation. This third layer is to be converted to where Christ can be seen in his fullness. That's where we have never come under this new covenant. This is the evidence of the times that reflect the great fall-away from the former rain that came on the day of Pentecost in one body.

Now let's break down the revelation in the background scriptures. Once I was told of a person that read some of my chronicles, according to what God said in his word, not many of us are where we should be in these end times. I recalled what Peter said when Jesus told him what we must do to get to heaven. *Mark 10:26 (NKJV)* [26] *And they were greatly astonished, saying among themselves, "Who then can be saved?"* Read that whole chapter. This has been the most humbling experience to see yourself as God sees you through the volumes of what his word said about who is going to heaven. When this revelation came to me, I was grieved at what I had been made to see. *Matthew 7:22 (KJV)* [22] *Many will say to me in that day, Lord, Lord, have we not prophesied in thy name? and in thy name have cast out devils? and in thy name done many wonderful works? Luke 13:27-28 (KJV)* [27] *But he shall say, I tell you, I know you not whence ye are; depart from me, all ye workers of iniquity.* [28] *There shall be weeping and gnashing of teeth, when ye shall see Abraham, and Isaac, and Jacob, and all the prophets, in the kingdom of God, and you yourselves thrust out.*

What I have observed, that has contributed to our present state of apostate blindness, is the seminary system that re-organized the way the body operates. It makes the Holy Spirit look like he is not smart enough to conduct the assembly service, so Satan sent our leaders to one of his seminary institutions to trained pastors, teachers and leaders to put some structure and order into the manner of conducting the services; now that's tradition. We no longer worship God in the spirit but in a pre-determined order that put the Holy Spirit out of operation. We now entertain the knowledge of the truth without a demonstration to see God perform the healings and deliverance that set you free. They put the emphasis on getting save without coming to the knowledge of knowing what truth is in practice. It sounds good, preaches well, you learn a lot of knowledge of the bible, but attracts followers without deep convictions.

The new qualifications to become a leader or a pastor will now employ the marketing of these leaders with their academic accolades that come out of these seminaries as hirelings, qualified authorities to teach and preach the gospel. This is what led to ... *2 Timothy 3:7 (NKJV)* [7] *always learning and never able to come to the knowledge of the truth.* This will require government involvement to regulate these newly formed religious corporations under what we have come to know as 501c-3 non-profit corporate status that will allow you to collect money in the name of their religions. They, being trained in biblical principle teachings, will use the bible to justify robbing their contributors under a tide system in the Old Testament for the Jews, will establish their kingdom that will operate like worldly programs. Deliverance is no longer seen in this compromised religious gathering. What they fail to see is, that 501c-3 identifies them as a Christian organization, operating under a worldly charter to be monitored by the government.

They, without realizing, have put themselves under the state that can close you down at any time in a national crisis. This is what we see being implemented during this pandemic as a test of government controls, you willingly gave them in exchange to run a legal religious corporation. You will fall under the same regulation as all the other worldly corporations. That's your natural mark by forgetting where the body of Christ is in the spirit. One thing this pandemic has shown us, we really do not know what spirit we are of by not seeing how far we have fallen from the truth. 98 percent of the church world is being controlled by fear because it shows you are in love with the world as one of Satan's religious bodies, deceived over time by being influence by one of these new doctrines. You will have a choice to choose what fits your comfort zone lifestyle without making any changes to the way you live. *Proverbs 16:25 (NKJV)* [25] *There is a way that seems right to a man, But its end is the way of death.*

I know my observations are not that well received in a time of this great fall-away. Many church leaders have become hardened to a word like this that infringe upon their pride to admit what is an obvious truth that applies to those that find themselves in this state as a confessing Christian body. God is speaking to the leaders that have cause many that followed them to be in this predicament. This pandemic shows us what it is, not to have the faith that keep us from being overtaken with fear that is here to collect the souls of those without faith in the God they serve to keep them from fear.

Now this is where you are, by not entering the third layer, Satan now rides the airways capturing those in fear and taking them out as the **"prince of the power of the air,"** using the media that has shortened your attention span to keep you from coming to the knowledge of the truth. This is that time Jesus was talking about when he said ... **Luke 18:8 (NKJV) [8] I tell you that He will avenge them speedily. Nevertheless, when the Son of Man comes, will He really find faith on the earth?" Luke 12:40 (NKJV) [40] Therefore you also be ready, for the Son of Man is coming at an hour you do not expect."**

God closed the door to all the assemblies to get our attention so he can bring us back to ... **John 4:23-24 (NKJV) [23] But the hour is coming, and now is, when the true worshipers will worship the Father in spirit and truth; for the Father is seeking such to worship Him. [24] God *is* Spirit, and those who worship Him must worship in spirit and truth."** This is where he wants to show you where he is and has been since you confess to be saved; in you, not one of Satan's religious temples. If we had ... **2 Timothy 2:15 (NKJV) [15] Be diligent to present yourself approved to God, a worker who does not need to be ashamed, rightly dividing the word of truth."** The Holy Spirit would have made that become a reality to keep you from being deceived by following men who mean well but are marked as hireling pastors and teachers. They will not receive you without these credentials to speak in their assemblies, in their minds, you have no creditable authority. That's what the Pharisees told Jesus. They do not believe in prophets being sent by God as he did in the Old Testament. Therefore, they will not have the vision of the truth to be told to them of their times. They can no longer recognize the voice of God when he come to warn them. *Proverbs 29:18 (KJV) [18] Where there is no vision, the people perish: but he that keepeth the law, happy is he. Proverbs 16:25 (KJV) [25] There is a way that seemeth right unto a man, but the end thereof are the ways of death.*

When God begin to deal with me about the book of Revelation, I knew at that time I was going to embark upon a controversial journey and experience what all true messengers of old experienced, rejection by modern day theologians in the same spirit of the Pharisees. They could not recognize their own Messiah after memorizing in the Torah, what he would look like and what he will do. Likewise, these modern-day theologians in the authority of their accolades, will not recognize his voice when he speaks while saying they know him. They are the Barabbas type patriot Christians, trying to **take back America to make her great again**, are unaware we have legalized Sodomy as a Christian nation. That's the curse that cannot be reversed. Therefore, unless their eyes are open to repent of their ungodly deeds, they are on the way to hell by taking up arms. **Matthew 26:52 (NKJV)** [52] **But Jesus said to him, "Put your sword in its place, for all who take the sword will perish by the sword.**

The wake-up revelation that the world is not ready for, in the end, will see what all they have done is created the means for their own self destruction. That's the **end game** that will bring about the new time continuum. The battle of all battles, this time mankind is fighting the army of God with his angels in the battle of armor getting.

My beloved brothers and sisters, men like me become known after they are dead. I am sure the apostles did not know that people would be quoting them as instruments used to pen down God's instructions to live with him in eternity. All of which suffered at the hand of well-meaning evil men that thought they were acting in the will of God, kill them in the name of God. This is the antichrist spirit in most confessing Christians who lack knowledge of who they are. That's because you were brought up in a religious organization without ever knowing what spirit they were of. **Hosea 4:6 (NKJV)** [6] <u>**My people are destroyed for lack of knowledge. Because you have rejected knowledge**</u>**, I also will reject you from being priest for Me; Because you have forgotten the law of your God, I also will forget your children.**

This is the last time we will have to examine ourselves as to what we believe is truth compared to the way we live. That's why Jesus said, **"by the fruit, you shall know them."** I will remain the least known to this present-day church because my message is for those that have been given ears to hear and God knows who they are. They will come to God in this last revival in the battle for souls. God will have compassion on this last generation of children as victims of their parent's Christian hypocrisy. Except for the elects, we are all guilty in the sight of God.

To the point if he did not raise up an elect, there would be nothing to come back for. It is through them, God has preserved this world from premature destruction at the hands of evil men who thought as their father once did in heaven, they could defy the God that created them and overtake his kingdom. It is amazing how Satan can make some of us believe there's no God while he believes and tremble. **James 2:19 (NKJV)** **[19] You believe that there is one God. You do well. Even the demons believe--and tremble!** When Satan met Jesus in the wilderness, he offered him everything that was possible to obtain in this world to make you look like a god, and if you except his offer as I stated in my previous chronicles, you will be … **2 Timothy 3:7 (NKJV) [7] always learning and never able to come to the knowledge of the truth.** That's where we get speakers as hirelings, dispensing knowledge but brings no deliverance. Satan is the author of religions that bring you a counterfeit gospel that will rob, steal and in the end cause you to lose your soul. You are responsible for your own salvation. We all are as equals in God's kingdom. The bible is our instructions as to how to obtain salvation and to keep it as being instructed by the Holy Spirit to … *2 Timothy 2:15 (KJV) [15] Study to shew thyself approved unto God, a workman that needeth not to be ashamed, rightly dividing the word of truth.* This is how you will … *Acts 2:40 (KJV) [40] And with many other words did he testify and exhort, saying, <u>Save yourselves from this untoward generation.</u>*

The key to entering this third layer revelation of salvation is to … *Isaiah 55:7-8 (KJV) [7] Let the wicked forsake his way, and the unrighteous man his thoughts: and let him return unto the LORD, and he will have mercy upon him; and to our God, for he will abundantly pardon. [8] For my thoughts are not your thoughts, neither are your ways my ways, saith the LORD.* For some of us, our sins of the past will be hard to overcome because the nature of some of them, you will have to die from this world and all its seducing desires to obtain that level of deliverance. Most of us will live out our lives as confessing Christians suffering the things of the world that God will use to keep you saved because of hidden things suppressed with-in you that if you were given these liberties, cause you to lose your soul.

That's why some will suffer until death because that's what it takes to keep you serving God until you die. God knows everything about you so when you trusted him to keep you saved, he saw what's in your heart that would work against you as coming from a sinful life and began at that time to … *Romans 8:28 (KJV) [28] And we know that all things work together for good to them that love God, to them who are the called according to his purpose.* The few that would walk this privilege Jesus died to give us all, they loved him as John did and suffered none of these things in the flesh without being delivered. Their faith never questioned God's ability to deliver them out of the trials they faced in this life because they lived in the reality that … *1 John 4:4 (KJV)* ⁴ *Ye are of God, little children, and have overcome them: because greater is he that is in you, than he that is in the world. Isaiah 54:17 (KJV)* ¹⁷ *No weapon that is formed against thee shall prosper; and every tongue that shall rise against thee in judgment thou shalt condemn. This is the heritage of the servants of the LORD, and their righteousness is of me, saith the LORD.* Now you have the time to answer the question by self-examination during this pandemic because we all are being judged for the last time to decide who you are going to serve. What man has devised in this warfare, only God can save you from. Just remember, this type of fear we are experiencing is a war in the spirit world for souls to reduce the population of the world these megalomaniacs, using forbidden technologies that has brought us to this end as in the days of Noah. If God tarried any longer, we who survive would be ruled by mindless robots. That's why we are in the transition stage of the next cross-over into a new time continuum. AMEN (Completed 7/2021)

THROUGH THE PROPHET'S EYES

The Revelation of the signs in Matthew 24 & Luke :21

This description will be witnessed in the book of Revelation.

Introduction:

I stand in awe of this privilege to be used as a scribe and messenger of this end time generation. God is releasing these hidden mystery revelations, kept being revealed to this last generation prior to the tribulation.

It is a warning as to what is to come that no one will be able to escape. Whatever you have prepared as for your own provisions, for many, may become the means of your own destruction. Desperate hordes of people such as your NEIGHBORS, CRIMINALS and THE ENVADING ARMIES will turn men into brute beast with an instinct to survive. There will be nowhere to run or hide. America's judgment will be double to that of Israel's in history because of the sodomy curse. In the end, the only thing left standing is Israel's capital city Jerusalem and a few cities near her for the return of Christ to reign during the millennium.

Everything will be rebuilt during the millennium. This chronicle is the final prophetic summery of the scriptural scenarios leading up to the book of Revelation to the point that America will no longer exist as a nation on this Earth. This chronicle was written in two parts; the first was printed in my first two books. This part three, I kept back for this final publication. What I saw because of these revelations was so hard to hear in God's anger, the stench of our sins has reached his nostrils. Since the release of the first book, part one in 2011, as a messenger watchman raised up for these end times through the Holy Spirit's leading, I have selected the layered versions of these chronicles and combined them into this final release. What I have been privileged to hear has been a shock to me too as you will read. Now I know why he said, this is for those who have ears to hear.

The advent of "911" was a wakeup call to America and the Church world; we were given **seven days** in America to repent as Noah's seven days before the judgment. The churches were not in a place to endure so the prophets in the spirit of Elijah prayed for a delay to give God's people a stay in judgment. The prayers of the elected prophets extended it to **seven years to get his people in position to make war in the spirit.** When we did not repent, our nation entered a strong delusion because of our pride ... *Proverbs 16:18 (KJV) "Pride goeth before destruction, and an haughty spirit before a fall,"* We were led into undeclared wars by false intelligence reports at the hands of a shadow organization that is plotting the destruction of this nations under a false vision that will lead into a new time continuum when all is revealed.

We, the citizens are being provoked by the same seducing spirit of pride; without knowing, are giving up our rights and liberties in the name of freedom through a new law known as the **"Patriot Act."** At the end of these seven years, God will begin to judge the whole world and there will be no more delay. This has been updated and shortened from the original chronicle in my last two books is the third layer of Revelation to this generation.

Background scripture:

2 Chronicles.7:14 "If my people, which are called by my name, shall humble themselves, and pray, and seek my face, and turn from their wicked ways; then will I hear from heaven, and will forgive their sin, and will heal their land." When this word came to Israel, their state was to the point of no return; it became their judgment. When God use the word **if** in this context in our time in history, judgment is about to follow as history will now repeat itself.

Signs of America's decline

America has overstepped her bounds as self-appointed policemen of the world by committing acts of aggression without divine direction. Departing from God's grace has serious consequences that will result in ultimate defeat. **Vietnam** was the first of the signs of a false vision by our actions to begin the process of crashing our economy. **Desert Storm** was to ensure our continual flow of oil to protect our vested interest in the Middle East that our technology produced.

The War on Terrorism, provoked by the "911" event, led us to follow Russia's path in Afghanistan that will cause our economy to collapse in the future. Our troops being deployed on two Middle Eastern soils will play into fulfilling bible prophecy. God led Israel into captivity when they departed from his laws that kept their enemies in fear of their God. Our Nation's military was the most feared in the world because of our position as the world's leader in military technology. These young Americans will become the vein sacrifices that will lead to our internal economic collapse as did Russia. Our economic collapse and ultimate siege will be the ends of our own doings. These Middle Eastern nations that descended from Ishmael will contribute to our downfall and ultimate defeat as the enemy from with-in. **Jer. 51:55 NLT** [55]**For the LORD is destroying Babylon. (America) He will silence her. Waves of enemies' pound against her; the noise of battle rings through the city.** Revelation 18 is a description of that gentile nation, **(the modern-day "Mystery Babylon")** that will bring about its own end and ultimate destruction by departing from God that established it with a covenant. **"In God, We Trust" America, the Modern Babylon** of this day.

What Jeremiah describes in the passage above will result in the innocent lives of our young soldiers being lost as the destruction of our troops in that area by action motivated by blind pride and war hungry political leaders in Washington; in their greed, will rob the treasury and cause us all to suffer at the hands of our enemies. The technology we invented was transferred to our enemies by spies in the camp. We will soon see these losses due to fighting two undeclared long wars begin to compromise America's ability to defend herself. This technology will become the new warfare that will be waged first in the cyber world. President Obama will try to use diplomatic means, play into the hand of our enemies as a war weary nation on the verge of collapse.

This will play into our enemy's plans and cause much unrest as the Middle Eastern Tribal nation's fight for power and control among themselves. President Obama is a seed of their roots is in a unique position to take advantage of executive orders to benefit the wave growth of the Hispanic and Muslim population by his actions on their behalf. This is the quagmire he inherited that will make it exceedingly difficult to appeal to the nation's masses on both sides in his last term. will keep him in office for a second term. When civil unrest erupts in our cities, because of many injustices that will lead to a return of racial tensions along with a collapsing economy, the nation will be in a quagmire with no dignified way out. The end of presidential cycle, # 45 will galvanize the republic with a spirit that will end the cycle of kings of the free world and prepare the nation for judgement.

Point two, History of the times

What we see is a nation in blindness and the elected saints of this end time are the chosen ones to restore the glory of the church in midst of her tribulation as one body. Sept.11, 2001 marked the beginning of her sorrows; the church will now, learn the mystery of the gospel that was kept and hid from the church-world through willing ignorance to them that are lost; now revealed to this generation. This was our warning. *Ezekiel 26:9 "And he shall set engines (Airplanes) of war against thy walls, and with his axes he shall break down thy towers." (World Trade Center)* <u>Isaiah 30:25</u> *(KJV) And there shall be upon every high mountain, and upon every high hill, rivers and streams of waters in the day of the great slaughter, <u>when the towers fall</u>."* This is describing the World Trade Towers on the river of Manhattan.

This was the fulfilling of this prophecy which will be a sign to that nation that she is about to come under judgment for her sins. *Amos 3:7 "Surely the Lord God will do nothing, but he revealeth his secret unto his servants the prophets."* President **Reagan** *warned us in his term, I will never forget using this phrase,* **VOODOO Economics**. This has reference to spending money we do not have. If our currency is the economic stability of the world, countries will cater to us to gain access to our technology and unscrupulous generosity. Our pride has made us an easy target to be provoked by war ready politicians under the influence of the **deep state** to fight undeclared wars on credit that will be the means of our future internal economic collapse. **"If we ever forget that we are a nation under God; we are a nation gone under." (President Reagan)**

President Clinton, the first of the baby boomers, used by the hidden power structure in Washington whose agenda is to crash this nation's economy to bring us into to the European common market by default. **President Kennedy** did not buy into this de-escalation of the cold war and thus had to be taken out by this hidden covert power structure in our government funding deep cover operations as depicted in the chronicle; **"The Deep State,"** undercover mercenaries to cause international crisis by using right wing misguided pawns as scapegoats.

I must make this comment, this so-called curse that is on the Kennedy family came through their father, Joseph P. Kennedy who refused to corporate with them and therefore, if any member of his family tried creating their legacy by carrying out the father's plan to dominant this country's government, their fate will make national news as did other presidents who died in office by some mysterious means.

President **Clinton** was groomed to push through executive orders by-passing congress to render our military, in a weaken state to be under the control of the United Nations multinational forces in times of national crisis such as martial law. The timing was right during his presidency to win the hearts of the less fortunate that will be the means of his popularity that will appeal to the working class when he leaves office among the minorities.

His presidency as the first of the baby boomers will disgrace the oval office by releasing the sodomy spirit through his immoral behavior that made national news. His wife will rise as the return of Jezebel in high places in her contention for power. They will deliberately compromise our borders to create a national crisis. It will become a political dilemma that neither side will be able to do anything before it becomes a national crisis. It will cause a significant increase in the Hispanic population to reach critical mass and will become an opening for our Middle Eastern enemies to come in and set up terror cells that will link them to their mother countries.

This will allow the Islamic terrorist (our enemy from within), to set up internal chaos. Communist influence will use this unbalanced social dilemma to their advantage to spark civil unrest among the races that will lead to a national crisis. This is Russian influence through families planted in this nation during the cold war as immigrant families spies to move when the time is right. We will see the revelation of these executive orders that sidelined our national guard and bring UN troops and multinational forces to our front doors and in our neighborhoods. Military strategists learned that when a nation is to be taken down, it is advantageous to use troops of another country to accomplish control.

Joel 2:9 (KJV) "9 They shall run to and fro in <u>the city</u>; they shall run upon <u>the wall</u>; they shall <u>climb up upon the houses</u>; they shall enter in at the <u>windows like a thief</u>." This is what they will do when martial law is declared. Our disobedience as a nation will give rise to these evil powers at the hand of God using enemy forces to inflict the sorrows spoken of in **Matthew 24:8** Remember, Satan got his power from the **Laodicea** lukewarm church, which he divided by removing the prayer meeting out of the corporate assemblies through seducing spirits and doctrine of devils. 98 percent of the present church has no idea of what is about to happen in this country because of false teaching.

Now, this is what I have observed spiritually of our time? Every religious organization believes they have the right doctrine; therefore, they are always judging one another. This in part is due to the Jesuit influence of the Catholic Church that built and financed these seminaries and institutions of higher learning to penetrate Christianity. Through these institutions, Satan has transformed the Christian church body into a form that will facilitate this grand delusion that we see today as pastors become Popes in the pulpits. **"Their end justifies the means".** This is noted by the degrees that qualifies the pastor as a hireling in the pulpit. This principle is applied in the corporate world as you see them hand down their family legacies to their children. This false teaching will repeat biblical history when the rapture is delayed because of this error in doctrinal teaching. **Man cannot reveal what has not been given him to know.**

PROJECTION FOR THE YEARS AFTER 2008+

1. The cost to fight the terrorist will compromise our military preparedness and further bring about economic

and Political instability. We will see the return of the Barabbas patriot spirit.

2. China will rise to become a major player in cheap labor. Major US corporations will take advantage of this opportunity to outsource to cut labor cost by reducing operating cost to stay in the black at a cost of revealing our manufacturing technology secrets to our enemy.

3. Illegal immigrants will become a major work force, undermining jobs that will decrease union labor, collapse the middle class and contribute to the return of racial tensions.

4. Banks will create a crisis that will cause them to rob the Federal bank to keep the country afloat.

5. Medical care will skyrocket as the economy weakens and becomes almost nonexistent to many. Hospitals begin to merge; many will not be able to provide medical care for lack of dwindling operating funds; thus, viral epidemic outbreaks will reduce the world's population drastically. **Rev.6:8**

6. Over 100,000 lives will be lost in this country before the church wakes up to the call to repentance that will bring about the outpouring of the Holy Spirit as God revive his church. (**Joel 2:28**) *Rev. 22:10_"And he saith unto me, Seal not the sayings of the prophecy of this book: for the time is at hand"*.

This reflects the mystery kept being revealed to this last generation. The timeline of projections is a collection from other prophecies. These are the few that agreed with my spirit to put them in print. Many I did not write because they gave specific dates and that to me is a red flag of a prophet's zeal. Only God knows the specific day he has appoint to judge all things. *Luke 17:20 (KJV)* [20] *And when he was demanded of the Pharisees, when the kingdom of God should come, he answered them and said, The kingdom of God cometh not with observation:*

In the meantime, this is the course of events that will be unfolding this biblical mystery to the church preparing to enter its tribulation. Man has penetrated the forbidden zone of creation, which is ... decoding the human DNA infringing on re-creation. This was brought in by these German scientists we took after the war. This beast in our time of grace is spiritual in that it exercises mind control. The 501C-3 is the mark that put the church under government control because there were too many of us saying we are the right ones and to keep them from taking advantage of those who would become victims of these organized religions, this is the mark they gave you as a house divided as 501C-3 state-chartered religions. Now the church poses no threat to the government. You just gave up your legal and spiritual rights to call out the government. The church world will embrace political correctness. In time of national crisis, they now can close your assemblies.

When John said through the Holy Spirit ... *1 John 4:4 (KJV) Ye are of God, little children, and have overcome them: because greater is he that is in you, than he that is in the world*: ... we all say we are serving the same god, but the fruit show we know not what spirit we are of or have become. The spirit of God is not deceived. I speak this way because I was once under the influence of this spirit. Many will suffer as children of disobedience. He did not say that you were not His children, being part of this system; they did not come out from among them when the call was made. This is what you will suffer ... *Ephesians 5:6 (KJV) Let no man deceive you with vain words: for because of these things cometh the wrath of God upon the children of disobedience.* Read the parable of the foolish virgins. **(Matthew 25:4-13, & Colossians.3:6)** regarding the church and the world.

When the stock market loses a thousand points in one week, the new world controllers are resetting the financial structure to comply with their global agenda. This is to ensure that those who are rich and well connected with their wealth will be brought down also. They will begin manipulating the stock market to appear to make record making gains, but it will be just a prop plot to take over the nation when God have them to pull the plug over-night. *Revelation 18:8 (KJV)* [8] *Therefore shall her plagues come in one day, death, and mourning, and famine; and she shall be utterly burned with fire: for strong is the Lord God who judgeth her.* When all their wealth is gone, many will attempt suicide, but God will not let them get away without paying for their sins against their fellow men.

All 501-C3 churches will be ordered closed, by reasons the "**New World Order**" charter of world government taking control. This will be the first evidence of an emerging ten regent world international government law imposed by United Nation to rule over all world governments. Rome (The city situated on seven hills.) **(Rev. 13:1)** will become the center focus of the "**New World Religion;**" a revived Roman Empire where-in the pope is now the Caesar. Satan empowered them to bring order out of chaos. The man that demonstrates this wisdom will produce signs and wonders by the spirit of illusions that will convince all to follow him to be the savior of the world. I am not saying the Antichrist will be a Pope, but the Roman Catholic Church will be the religious catalyst used to bring about this change because of their position in the religious world at that time. Muslims believe their messiah will be the one to bring peace and control to the world with them as the master race in charge.

Now this is a false prophecy, but the man that rise out of the chaos with this wisdom can only be manifested during a defeated church that will allow Satan to show himself as a god man who at that time will produce these great lying signs and wonders. The elect of God walking in the fullness will gravely wound him before Satan comes and revive him. This is where we get the term **Antichrist**; He will represent the new world religion that the Roman Catholic Church brought together in times of world crisis. He will become their leader of this religious body. God is allowing all this to happen to fulfill all prophecy relating to this time in history, so they can be destroyed all at once as a body united against Christ, **Antichrist**.

Matthew 24:3-4 (ASV) "3 And as he sat on the mount of Olives, the disciples came unto him privately, saying, tell us, when shall these things be? and what shall be the sign of thy coming, and of the end of the world? 4 And Jesus answered and said unto them, take heed that no man lead you astray." The Church, under the control of the state, their prophets will be trying to predict by observations of the times and will be making false predictions giving dates that will discredit them when what they predicted do not happen as they said it would. This will make the church a perfect candidate for this deception.

You will see the religious patriots rise as Barabbas to come against the state … brought down when they take up arms again. *Amos 9:10 (KJV)* "*All the sinners of my people shall die by the sword*, (This is addressing patriot Christians who take up arms to defend themselves.) *which say, the evil shall not overtake nor prevent us.*" They will be under the delusion that, they can take back America or make it great again. They are the Barabbas patriots of today.

What will become apparent leading up to the time of full-blown tribulation, during this time many natural as well as man-made disasters will be occurring in many parts of the world. In a united new religious front, God will send a spirit that will cause all religions to come together that have rejected his prophets for the common good of the survival of mankind. We see this happening already among religious organizations as they began to embrace the Pope. Rodney King left this phrase I have heard used in a lot of situations. **"Can't we all just get along?"** This will be spearheaded by the last Pope in office at that time. This pre-antichrist movement will appeal to those preaching the doctrine of **rapture** and **prosperity**. Without realizing they are at the end of America's prosperity reign, having this kind of faith to gain the world's goods instead of delivering souls into the kingdom; instead, robbed them in the name of God to justify building their kingdom for their personal gain will be the woe on them in the judgment. These spirits will be tolerant of each other's religious practices and will begin to come together.

Their charities will be extended abroad instead of taking care of those in the homeland first. *1 John 3:17 (KJV)* [17] *But whoso hath this world's good, and seeth his brother have need, and shutteth up his bowels of compassion from him, how dwelleth the love of God in him?* Our priority is to take of our own first before we can deliver the heathen nations. We have failed to show this love among ourselves; therefore, we have not been an example to the rest of the world where Christianity is concern; this is evident by being the world's leading crime producing nation. The day we cease to honor the covenant our forefathers made in the declaration of this Nation's independence by putting **"In God We Trust"** on our legal tender, showing His sovereignty over us, **"we will cease to be a nation under God's protection,"** President Reagan's warning.

Now to show that these hidden powers that are currently present in Washington today, ruling behind the scenes through generations, have been waiting for the opportunity to accomplish their agenda. One of the last acts of the use of our currency that will be a sign of the end our election cycles by popular vote, is the legalized purchase of our government officials we sent to Washington to represent the people. This will be evident by the Supreme Court's actions in interpreting the law from a political standpoint that will change campaign laws. On the back of a dollar bill, you will see **"In God We Trust"** and two cymbals: **"NUVUS ORDO SECLORUM"** (New World Order) the other, **"EPLURIBUS UNUM"** (Out of Many One). This is no accident but by design represents members of a secret organization known as the illuminated ones or **Illuminati's** that in our time will be known as Bilderbergers. The Deep State's think tank to bring about the new world order.

There are two presidents I have heard use these terms. George H. Bush introduced us to the New World Order in his inaugural address. President William Jefferson Clinton used the term **"EPLURIBUS UNUM"** on occasions. These cymbals date back to the Knights Temblor's which are now known as the Knights of Malta of which came the Scull & Bones Sorority, Satan worshipers and have one purpose, to take control of the governments and religious organizations.

This seed roots can be traced back to the Roman Empire that plundered nations as Knight's Templars (Keepers of the treasures) disguised in a false religious form now known as Jesuit'. They orchestrated the rise of the Roman Catholic Church to ensure the survival of all the plunders of the Roman Empire would be kept out of the hands of pilferers and placed in the care of the military company known now as the Jesuit order.

Under a satanic vision, they evolved into a separate religious self-governing state that will pose no threat to existing nations and governments. This advantage will give them the opportunity to use their wealth to finance their nation within a nation. We are warring with a formidable opponent; Satan's deep cover with tentacles rooted all over the world with an agenda to rule a one world religions and governments as the **Beast** that gave power to the **false prophet**.

They will pit nations against each other to the point of war to achieve their objectives to bring them under control by financing both sides; therefore, taking control of them both in the end. America as self-appointed policemen of the world will be caught up in the web of Ishmael's descendant's; our covert CIA will finance a secret terror army that will be used to terrorize nations in these end times to claim an illegitimate birth right. This will make the Middle East a hot bed for launching their terror on nations that are not friendly to their cause.

Matthew 24:7-8 (ASV) "⁷ For nation shall rise against nation, and kingdom against kingdom; and there shall be famines and earthquakes in divers places. ⁸ But all these things are the beginning of travail." (Or sorrows) If we kept this covenant, we would become that nation all nations will covet after, other religious faction will target us for our Christian declaration.

Joshua showed us how God fights for his people in war as a nation. Now, in view of our past, we have reached the generation that shall witness the downfall of America as this comes in the form of natural as well as man-made disasters on our soil for departing from God. **"⁹Then shall they deliver you up unto tribulation and shall kill you: and ye shall be hated of all the nations for my name's sake.** (Our enemies in the end will turn against us as we begin to show weakness by divisions in our government agencies. All whose names are written in the lamb's book of life will stand on Bible truth as elects that will be used to lift a standard of holiness against this spirit.) **¹⁰ And then shall many stumble, and shall deliver up one another, and shall hate one another.**

This hatred will be directed against Christians who take a stand against this legalized immorality in high places. Israel and America are as one under grace in that, if we cease to stand with them as a nation, God will turn our enemies against us to be destroyed. These signs are emerging under the Obama Presidency that is contributing to these natural disasters. We made a covenant with God for divine protection. **"Hear oh Israel the**

Lord our God is one" and to **America, "In God we trust"** [11] **And many false prophets shall arise and shall lead many astray."** Our current sitting president has declared **"we are no longer a Christian nation."** Our so-called Christian assemblies are infected with the Barabbas patriot spirit to think that they can take back America are about to see history repeated as in these last days.

The seduction of the church brought denominational division; (man's ways) will be the error that will cause many to be destroyed as victims of false teachings. Just as the Sanhedrin killed Stephen who represented the fullness of the Holy Spirit, severed their tides with God as a nation at that time; the destruction of their natural temple will come seventy years later. *Daniel 7:25 (KJV) And he shall speak great words against the most High and shall wear out the saints of the most High, and think to change times and laws: and they shall be given into his hand until a time and times and the dividing of time.* This will happen during the first four years of transition to the tribulation will be at the end of the seventh year in 2008 under the last president to be elected by the people; Obama. Whoever follows will be put in office by the Electoral College or used to bring judgement on this nation by the people's vote. The year of thirteen will be a false surge in the economy to further deceive this nation with a false sense of security.

This will mark the end of the extended judgment of the last generation of gentiles after the 911 sign ended the seven years of grace. You will see this spirit exposed all the way up to the Supreme Court. **"**[12] ***And because iniquity shall be multiplied, the love of the many shall wax cold.*** People with-out a Godly mentality will result to evil continually. This is apostasy. [13] **But he that endureth to the end, the same shall be saved.** Those that take heed to the prophet's warning will not be ignorant and save themselves; many will give up their lives in glory standing against authorities. [14] ***And this gospel of the kingdom shall be preached in the whole world for a testimony unto all the nations; and then shall the end come."*** God will send the spirit of John the Baptist that will began to preach the unadulterated word to warn the people to flee from the wrath of God as he prepares to make way for the return of Christ by lifting His standard against the false bride (the Antichrist body) His bride (the true church) in glory.

Four years after 911 grace period, this is the footman stage. God will be preparing his elects. At the end of this period will be a false surge of the economy. The stock market will start to go up and down during the Obama presidency. When we draw back in defense of Israel; thereafter, there will be one disaster after another all over the country. When the economy crashes, the enemy of our soul will set the stage for his assault against the church, when the first seal is broken in Revelation six. This will be the time of the horsemen. Out rides the **white horse,** representing the spirit of Christ bringing the restoration of the former rain. Therefore, we need to be in the spirit; there are **two** spirits appearing now.

The spirit of Christ precedes the false spirit that will be seen in the Antichrist body of seduced Christians. God must empower his elects first to come out of the wilderness or else they will be deceived also. The **second spirit** will be the false manifestation of Christ that would deceive the very elect if God had not sealed them with this unction anointing before Satan arrived. **Daniel 12:3 (NASB77) "And those who have insight will shine brightly like the brightness of the expanse of heaven, and those who lead the many to righteousness, like the stars forever and ever.** You must remember this is taking place in the spirit realm in the war with Satan before he is cast out into the Earth preparing for the great confrontation of the Elijah showdown during the tribulation. *Revelation 19:11 (KJV) And I saw heaven opened and behold a <u>white horse;</u> and he that sat upon him was called Faithful and True, and in righteousness he doth judge and make war.*

This is what God is preparing his elects to do. Through His elects, He will take back the kingdom by force and prepare for the latter rain outpouring in the fullness of himself. This confrontation with the corporate body of the Antichrist is what will be known as the Elijah show down. This latter rain shall restore the church and put the devil under her feet for the last time. When this is finished, they will be taken out.

All the wealth of the wicked will be returned to the just for this quick work. The kingdom of heaven at that time will suffer violence and God will be in His elects, taking the kingdom back by force. *Matthew 11:12 (KJV) And from the days of John the Baptist until now the kingdom of heaven suffereth violence, and the violent take it by force. "15 When therefore ye see the abomination of desolation, which was spoken of through Daniel the prophet, standing in the holy place (<u>let him that readeth understand</u>),"*

This underlined section has two meaning; **first,** is a type and shadow that literally happen to Israel during their siege that Jeremiah prophesied, and Daniel verified that would come in their time **... Daniel 9:2 (NASB77) in the first year of his reign I, <u>Daniel</u>, observed in the books the number of the years which was revealed as the word of the LORD to <u>Jeremiah</u> the prophet for the completion of the <u>desolations of Jerusalem, namely, seventy years.</u> Luke 21:6 (NASB77) "As for these things which you are looking at, the days will come in which there will not be left one stone upon another which will not be torn down." Mathew 24:16 (NASB77) then let those who are in Judea flee to the mountains;** This context has reference to those he was speaking too in the synagogue about what will happen to them in the fall of Jerusalem.

The **second time** will be Spiritual, the church in the new covenant is your body being invaded by seducing spirits as Christians that present another god in a form that will represent an abomination as being occupied with another god; Satan. **2 Tim. 3:5 (NASB77) holding to a form of godliness, although they have denied its power; and avoid such men as these.**

In this period **A.D.,** Satan will wear out the saints. **(Daniel 7:25)** All those born of the spirit of Christ will flee these assemblies that Satan has taken over with a false doctrine when God opens their eyes. This is what he means when he said come out from among them and I will receive you or protect you. The new covenant in our time is the abomination and desolation that will bring down confessing Christians as temples of God who refuse to flee from these church buildings in the last days that name the name of God but deny His presents by their action. They will become the Antichrist bodies by not knowing what spirit they are of. Jesus addresses both the church and Israel, parallel together in tribulation in the last seven years of man's rule on Earth.

The gentile's judgment will be in the first half and Israel's in the second when the Thunder judgment comes after the last trumpet. The church, having been purified, along with Israel's remnant will be caught out by the sickle angels in **Rev. 14:15-18** and **Rev. 11:11.** There will be safe havens for both bodies of the remnant that will be saved to repopulate the earth during the millennium. *Isaiah 26:20 (KJV)* [20] *Come, my people, enter thou into thy chambers, and shut thy doors about thee: hide thyself as it were for a little moment, until the indignation be over-past.*

Many will reject the call by being carnal Christians and will be caught in God's break. The prophets have the vision and those who choose to ignore them will perish. Those preserved needs will be divinely met due to their acts of obedience; they are being purified. Others will be delivered up before the Antichrist system for the testimony of Jesus Christ will be martyred.

This is a mystery of the souls reserved to repopulate the millennium; they have never been indoctrinated by man. Their witness will be when they see how God preserved them through all the horrors of the tribulation and see Christ coming back to reign as the only God that gave them the privilege to see all those great wonders by him during the tribulation. This will make them loyal to the one true God that showed up with great power to deliver them during that time.

The next scene is the world at mid tribulation when the siege of the nation's takes place. *Matthew 24:19-21 "(KJV)* [19] *But woe unto them that are with child and to them that give suck in those days!"* (This is what pregnant women without God must do to survive when their babies are born?) *Deuteronomy 28:57 (KJV) And toward her young one that cometh out from between her feet, and toward her children which she shall bear: for she shall eat them for want of all things secretly in the siege and straitness, wherewith thine enemy shall distress thee in thy gate*s. (Siege of this nation) [20] *And pray ye that your flight be not in the winter, neither on a Sabbath:* One of the signs that will precede the natural disasters will be a large under sea earthquake that will cause a slight shift in the axes of the Earth, the latitudes will take a slight shift; this is what will contribute to climate changes and diverse whether patterns along with those manipulated by man.

This is the second stage of restoring the original latitude that caused what happen when the earth was flooded. There will be places where the temperatures will reach as low as -46 degrees and many who live in these arrears will die because of no power or heat. The **Sabbath** will be the day of the lord's wrath on the nations in judgment because he will rise out of his Sabbath rest. [21] *for then shall be great tribulation, such as hath not been from the beginning of the world until now, no, nor ever shall be."* This describes (**Rev. 12:1-8**) the church and Israel being purified (**Rev.3:18**) through the fires of tribulation waiting to be delivered. (**Rev.14:15-18**) The mystery of the book of Revelation was reserves to be revealed to end time elected chosen vessels of God, to interpret what the prophet spoke in time past; many have only managed to wrest the scriptures in this area by using logical observation theology.

God has reserved a word to be given in each time, age and dispensation. What you have been reading was not meant to be known until now. *Daniel 12:9 (KJV) And he said, go thy way, Daniel: for the words are closed up and sealed till the time of the end.* Now this next passage is a witness to John from Daniel's prophecy as the last of the apostles that walked with Christ given the privilege to write the last book to the New Testament of the coming apocalypse.

What he was told not to write in the following verse was reserved for the prophets and messengers raised up at the end of the gentile age to reveal what he told Daniel and John not to write. The interpretation will be given to these end time prophets and messengers in the scriptures what has been hidden from those who were seeking for what was not to be revealed until that time of the end.

Revelation 10:4 (KJV) And when the seven thunders had uttered their voices, I was about to write: and I heard a voice from heaven saying unto me, seal up those things which the seven thunders uttered, and write them not. What Daniel was told to seal up and John told not to write is so horrible; I had difficulty writing it myself concerning the **seven thunders**. I was only allowed to write down the revelation to the **first thunder** at that time. That's because the children of disobedience will suffer the **first thunder**.

In my spirit, this was so horrible, no wonder John was told not to write it down. Now to explain why he was told not to write it down was for this reason. God foreknew the church would go into apostasy and therefore, reject the words of God down through the generations to where they will not receive these prophets and messengers as I have experience; you be the judge of what you are reading by the message relayed. This is where I found on my first missionary tour in the state of Arizona that 98 percent of the churches rejected this vision. This is what John and Daniel were told not to write, that can only be revealed at the right time by the spirit to those that have ears to hear, what's ahead for the hard-hearted and children of disobedience. To think that God would allow such a thing and to understand why; you would have to see the conditions in the world at this time as described by Jesus on Mount Olivet to his disciples in Matthew twenty-four. In his opening statement, he tells the apostles that it is only given to you to know what's ahead of your ministry, what would happen to you and at the end of that last generation, this mystery will be revealed.

When the siege takes place, people in that nation will be interned into concentration camps set up by FEMA; yes, your own government. They have been preparing these camps since 2008. You will not be brought there to be fed but to die as rejects of the new society whose agenda is to reduce the world's population to several hundred million because of this advance technology will control humanity if they succeed. This is what the people must result too as a means of their survival? **Jeremiah 19:9 (ASV) ⁹ And I will cause them to eat the flesh of their sons and the flesh of their daughters; and they shall eat everyone the flesh of his friend, in the siege and in the distress, wherewith their enemies, and they that seek their life, shall distress them. Ezekiel 5:10 (ASV) ¹⁰ Therefore the fathers shall eat the sons in the midst of thee, and the sons shall eat their fathers; and I will execute judgments on thee; and the whole remnant of thee will I scatter unto all the winds. Micah 3:3 (ASV) ³ who also eat the flesh of my people, and flay their skin from off them, and break their bones, and chop them in pieces, as for the pot, and as flesh within the caldron.** (This is a large pot that will be used to cook human remains. My God! … have mercy.)

Side Bar page insert

When God started giving me these detailed revelations about our times, it was a hard word to receive. This is history repeating itself, as you see; this is what happened to Israel when they were given over to their enemies in their siege.

Deuteronomy 28:53-57 (NLT) ⁵³ The siege will be so severe that you will eat the flesh of your own sons and daughters, whom the LORD your God has given you. ⁵⁴ The most tenderhearted man among you will have no compassion for his own brother, his beloved wife, and his surviving children. ⁵⁵ He will refuse to give them a share of the flesh he is devouring—the flesh of one of his own children—because he has nothing else to eat during the siege that your enemy will inflict on all your towns. ⁵⁶ The most tender and delicate woman among you—so delicate she would not so much as touch her feet to the ground—will

be cruel to the husband she loves and to her own son or daughter. [57] **She will hide from them the afterbirth and the new baby she has borne, so that she herself can secretly eat them. (Matt.24:19) … She will have nothing else to eat during the siege and terrible distress that your enemy will inflict on all your towns.**

(Compare with KJV) This part I have reserved just to explain the implications spoken in **Micah 3:3.** Let's examine this verse in detail. **Micah 3:3 (ASV)** "[3] **who also <u>eat the flesh of my people,</u>** these are the lukewarm children of disobedience who were prayed for … being led to the slaughter who would not leave these worldly assemblies when they were told; at the time, in their death or martyrdom will be received in heaven but their bodies will become food at that time. Someone gave their life in prayer to save them, and God remembered. These saints suffered as Samson for their disobedience, are brought up before the lord as described in **Rev. 8:1-3;** these are the prayers of the righteous who gave their lives through self-denial as sons of God that they might be saved are being received from their intercessors to be spared ...**and flay their skin from off them,** they are as sheep led to the slaughter literally is what's happening to them. **and break their bones, and chop them in pieces, as for the pot, …** The world with no presents of God in their mentality, men will become as brute beast cannibals with no conscious, **"The walking Dead"** this is what they will do to survive.

2 Peter 2:12 (KJV) But these, as <u>natural brute beasts, made to be   and destroyed,</u> speak evil of the things that they understand not; and shall utterly perish in their own corruption; brute beast cannibalism. Remember, **(Rev. 6:4-8)** is present in the land; no food, worldwide chaos as famine takes its toll on mankind …. **and as flesh within the <u>caldron.</u>"** They will have large pots that will be used to cook the remains of their own kind. In this verse, God identifies them as **"<u>eating the flesh of my people.</u>"** Women with child will have their bellies ripped open at delivery; fresh babies from the womb will be a delicacy as food. Hungry soldiers will rip the babies from pregnant mothers for their food; no wonder God did not want to reveal this to an apostate church before the time. **(Matthew 24:19, Deut. 28:57)**

After this revelation, I just had to take a break and digest what was being communicated to me. I can agree, this saying is too hard and to think that God is going to allow this to happen to His people is unthinkable, but we have it said right out of the scriptures. I can't kick against the truth. Now I must admit, I have never related these scriptures to **(Rev. 10:4)**. I understand now why this revelation was never made known about our future as man's doctrines would replace the doctrine of Jesus Christ. We have been hood-winked to only see the good side of God; for this cause, many will be caught in God's break, unprepared by false teaching. That's why the church will not receive the full report of the doctrine of Jesus Christ now because they have been told they will be translated before it all begins. We have been hood winked by our own leaders. I know this is very hard to hear or imagine that God is going to let such as these evils be seen in man to this degree.

The signs are already leading to this very soon to becoming a reality. In the time I have taken to study the word under this anointing, I noticed that history is always repeating itself; the mystery layers of knowledge in the right context is few and far between, especially where the church and Israel are concern. This is the work of the Holy Ghost in these latter days as many as received him, manifested in the true **"Sons of God."** I know there will be many people that will reject these revelations when they read this section of the chronicle. Even some departed from me because this was too hard. They had reservations about this part, but I will let it stand the test of a true or a false prophecy regarding our times.

Now you may continue in Matthew

[22] And except those days should be shortened, there should no flesh be saved: but for the elect's sake those days shall be shortened. [23] Then if any man shall say unto you, Lo, here is Christ, or there; believe it not. [24] For there shall arise false Christs, and false prophets, and shall shew great signs and wonders; insomuch that, if it were possible, they shall deceive the very elect. When God seals all his elects that will be used for his glory, this will be the unction mark on their fore-heads in the spirit that John spoke about. *1 John 2:20 (KJV)* [20] But ye have an unction from the Holy One, and ye know all things.

At the same time, all vessels of dishonor will be sealed for judgment. The demons saw this mark on Paul but not on the **"son of sceva"** in (Acts 19:14); these demons in people will kill you for provoking them in your ignorance. The elects will discern the lying signs and wonders of Satan's false prophets and will triumph over them through the spirits of Moses and Elijah. Some theologians have disputed about these two prophets that one is Enoch instead of Moses.

Moses death is one of the mysteries that is also revealed. We get a view of this when Satan disputed with Michael about his body. If Satan had to ask where his body was, this means he did not see it in a grave; now where was it? **Jude 1:9 (NASB77) But Michael the archangel, when he disputed with the devil and argued about the body of Moses, did not dare pronounce against him a railing judgment, but said, " The Lord rebuke you."** God translated him too. The spirit of Moses dealt with Pharaoh and brought down his army. Therefore, his spirit will return in those selected to bring down the beast in the government system. This is the mystery of why they were translated not to see death in their flesh. Their spirit had to remain alive to return to earth in those selected to operate in their spirit as the two witnesses.

Enoch was taken because he walked in perfect harmony with God for three hundred years until one day, he had a Star-Tract translation where his atoms disintegrated as a human being never to return to Earth. His dispensation of his time ended at the flood. Moses and Elijah time is still in this dispensation of time; therefore, their spirits can be translated back into a body of flesh because they never died on Earth.

Enoch's life was in the Antediluvian of Adam; therefore, after the flood, all was closed that pertained to the evils of that age. Therefore, you do not see his books as part of the new world's scriptures and anyone who teach from the remnant of this knowledge, as doctrine will corrupt the law and the New Testament doctrine by adding to what was never intended to be known to that degree in this dispensation of time. That is why the book of Enoch is not part of the bible. The mystery of that time was passed on to Moses to write the Genesis of the books of the law that will govern His chosen people in the Old Testament bible time that will apply throughout all time after the flood in a new dispensation of man's time on Earth.

This is another great mystery of the tribulation, the spirit of the two witnesses will be manifested on this wise during the tribulation, in a cooperate body; under grace, this is their spirit returning in a chosen body by God to perform a pre-destine work; not as we are told in the parable in

Rev 11:3; this is a type and shadow of these two prophets that will appear literally in Israel in their time of tribulation. These two prophets' spirit will be moving in those chosen in the body of the church in the latter rain. These are the revelational mysteries of this time to help us understand what will be happening in the spirit on a greater level.

Their work during the tribulation will be manifested in the gentile church on this wise. Those operating in the spirit of Moses will judge the people in government and high places in the principalities and those operating in the spirit of Elijah will be exposing the false prophets. This will be a battle in the spirit by the elects that will defeat the **Beast** and the **False Prophet**. After they judge the gentile nations, they will appear literally in Israel as a sign given them by the Old Testament prophets. *Revelation 11:3 (KJV)* [3] *And I will give power unto my two witnesses, and they shall prophesy a thousand two hundred and threescore days, clothed in sackcloth.* They will judge the gentile nation in the spirit to glorify the body of Christ, then will appear in the form of two men in Israel in their judgment. Their appearance in sackcloth will be as Jews in Jerusalem is their sign.

This is their last work on Earth; when their work is completed, God will allow them to be killed. After three days in the underworld to **"preach to the spirits in prison,"** whose hearts were rights under God's grace in accordance with the manner of their sacrifice at death but bound by sins in the flesh, just as Christ did when he freed the souls in captivity in Paradise as the blood sacrifice for their sins and took them back with him to the third heaven.

The paradise mystery

This mystery of what was done in Paradise was the subject of one of my previous chronicles printed in books one and two about the spirit world. Paradise was left vacant to receive the blessed merciful that will obtain mercy. These are people who died under circumstances like the pennate thief, only they gave their lives in sacrifice for the greater good of others. These are some soldiers who found God on the battlefield and ask for mercy before their death and those like that pinnate thief who saw the reality of Christ for the first time and ask for mercy. They must hear the gospel while in Paradise as preached by the two witnesses and receive the blood of Christ for their sins. They are the **"spirits in prison,"** bound by sins of omission that will obtain mercy through Christ as preached by the two witnesses.

At this point and time, you should see this mystery unfolding in the chronological order as the Holy Ghost is revealing these mysteries. This next verse confirms that the church is going through tribulation. *Matthew 24:29 (KJV) "Immediately after the tribulation of those days shall the sun be darkened, and the moon shall not give her light, and the stars shall fall from heaven, and the powers of the heavens shall be shaken:"* There will be clouds from nuclear explosions during the wars, after this, meteorite showers will hit this nation and have the same effect as brimstone because of the sodomy curse on this nation.

The ozone layer will open to let the ultraviolet rays purify the earth in the end. God is rearranging the Earth's geography and purifying it for the millennium. In the book of Revelation, this is the second stage of Earth being set back to where the atmospheric pressure will be restored to 100 percent oxygen which will sustain life again for one thousand years. **Matt. 24:31 (NASB77)** *"And He will send forth His angels with A GREAT TRUMPET, and THEY WILL GATHER TOGETHER His elect from the four winds, from one end of the sky to the other.* (This verse described is linked to the book of Revelation as to when the rapture takes place. *(Rev. 14:15-18) Isiah 46:10 (KJV) Declaring the end from the beginning, and from ancient times the things that are not yet done, saying, my counsel shall stand, and I will do all my pleasure:*

The above scripture tells us that God has set time back to the first millennium to rest the Earth for one thousand years. This is the second resurrection after Christ where the rapture takes place as the first translated saints of the New Testament. As I said earlier, only God has that date on his calendar. This is the state of the church at that time. *Galatians 4:19 (KJV) "My little children, of whom I travail in birth again until Christ be formed in you."* Tribulation is where this travail of the church to purification to become like Christ. This is where … *Joel 3:14 "Multitudes, multitudes in the valley of decision: for the day of the Lord is near in the valley of decision."* God will give the people of the Earth another chance to repent before the church is taken out. **Matthew 24:33 (NASB77) even so you too, when you see all these things, recognize that He is near, right at the door.** The punishment of those that refused to hear the warning because they did not know that they were hearing from God and not man; will prove to be to their own destruction. The next series of verses represent the extreme conditions just before the church's harvest. **Isaiah 13:16 (NLT)** [16] **Their little children will be dashed to death before their eyes. Their homes will be sacked, and their wives will be raped by attacking hordes.**

This happened in Israel's siege. This to me is another horror of the tribulation; when the economy collapses in this country, prisoners will be loosed and reap havoc during the siege. Carnage and murders will be as neighbor turn against neighbor. You don't want to be out of God's will with young wives and daughters at that time. This is where many with guns will kill off great numbers of the population among themselves as part of the chaos to survive. That's why they wouldn't let our Congress pass any new gun laws. They wanted the population to buy as many guns as possible you needed to kill your neighbors.

They knew this type of chaos would be to their favor to help reduce the population in many cities and towns; after this carnage, the soldiers will move in. Just like you see them do in the movies. This is something we all are familiar with by watching disaster movies; what happens to the women as these demonic possessed men rape them because of advantage of being in a state of a lawless environment. **Lamentation. 5:11 Our enemies rape the women and young girls in Jerusalem and throughout the towns of Judah."** You will see this repeated during the Middle Eastern wars for tribal control; they will rape the women in captivity in the towns they take over. When the siege take place, to the surprise of most people, the government already know where to go where Christians are concern. You gave all your information about you over the internet when you marked your organization under the 501C-3 government charter. This will be a surprise to these patriot movements; this time the Barabbas patriot spirit will not escape; they will have no mercy on them and kill them all to achieve their objectives.

Hosea 13:16 (NLT) "The people of Samaria must bear the consequences of their guilt because they rebelled against their God. (They mixed with people who served other gods, this judgment is on America.) **They will be killed by an invading army, their little ones dashed to death against the ground, their pregnant women ripped open by swords."** This is a hard saying, soldiers will rip open the womb of pregnant women to take their babies for food; they are demon possessed marked by the lives of aborted baby girls, this is what they will do to survive as revealed earlier in the book of **Deut. 28:55-57.**

Members of your family who you thought loved you will give you up to the authorities to save their own lives. Your Judas could be sleeping in your own bed ... many will become food to the zombie like masses of people that lost their minds, desperate to survive, as they become brut beast cannibals. They are marked in their foreheads by the beast and are literally the "**walking dead.**"

Famine will be in the land as Micah 3:3 tells you, these zombie like beast men will hunt you down for food. God is using Hollywood to show you your destiny in **"The Walking Dead,"** series, as man will become as part of the falling away as their love wax cold when the great persecution begins ... *Matt. 24:12, Mark 13:11 "But when they shall lead you, and deliver you up, take no thought beforehand what ye shall speak, neither do ye premeditate: but whatsoever shall be given you in that hour, that speak ye: for it is not ye that speak, but the Holy Ghost. Matt. 24:22 "And except those days should be shortened, there should no flesh be saved: but for the elect's sake those days shall be shortened."* Does this look like you have been raptured. There are two versions of this chronicle; the first was released in my first two books. This version I held this back for the final printing and to be given as a warning to pastors. Many of them are not far from the kingdom as he told Nicodemus.

There are some covert activities going on behind the scenes in our government that I could not reveal now because they arc not to be known to a people already judged; what they have done in these secrete covert operations, by using this forbidden technology that caused the flood. It will become the means of our self-imposed bondage and destruction in the hands of our enemies. Our extinction will come in the cross over of a new time continuum. *Revelation 18:6 (KJV) Reward her even as she rewarded you, and <u>double unto her double</u> according to her works: in the cup which she hath filled fill to her double. Revelation 18:21 (KJV) And a mighty angel took up a stone like a great millstone, and cast it into the sea, saying, thus with violence <u>shall that great city Babylon be thrown down, and shall be found no more at all.</u>*

The end of the tribulation from a geographic standpoint, America will no longer exist. This is what was revealed to me about her in the millennium. The curse of Sodom and Gomorrah was upon America; it will be a forbidden zone during the millennium like in the original movie **"Planet of the Apes."** This is what America will be like after the rapture.

How long will this be?

Daniel 8:14 (KJV) *"*[14] *And he said unto me, unto two thousand and three hundred days; then shall the sanctuary be cleansed."* This is the time of the judgment of the church and nations. You must choose what family you want to be in. *Matt. 10:35-36 For I am come to set a man at variance against his father, and the daughter against her mother, and the daughter in law against her mother-in-law. [36] And a man's foes shall be they of his own household." Luke 21:22 "For these be the days of vengeance, that all things which are written may be fulfilled". Luke 21:24 "And they shall fall by the edge of the sword and shall be led away captive into all nations: and Jerusalem shall be trodden down of the Gentiles, until the times of the Gentiles be fulfilled."*

Just as Israel lost their place as a nation, through the rejection of their messiah, they were scattered into all nations before the advent of **May 15, 1948,** which marked the end of their exile as a people chosen by God. This sign will mark the beginning stages of the closing of the Gentile age which will end (40) years after the 1967 war that re-captured the Abraham land grant and Jerusalem, the capital city. Any attempts to make them give back any of this land will cause God's anger will suffer us to be confounded as a national government and will suffer widespread natural disasters. This will come to the forefront where all will see by their inaction along party loyalties. America's covenant was to ensure the restoration of Israel as a nation. That was completed after the 1967 war where they regain their capital city, Jerusalem. This set the stage that will end with twenty years of a false since of prosperity and security and the last twenty years will bring the sorrows as this nation will be confounded and politically divided against itself to be given over to her enemies for destruction.

This will set the stage for Christ to return to sit on the throne of David. The last seven years after 9/11/2001 will be the warning sign that will become more intense at the end of the seven years. As in the days of Noah so shall it be in these last days. This delusion coupled with our pride; none will heed to the warning signs in this nation. After the door was closed to the Ark, God waited seven days before the judgment came. Sept. 11, 2001, until that same month in 08, our seven days will be in years in our time after the World Trade Towers fall. *(Ezekiel 26:9) 2 Thes.2:11 "And for this cause God shall send them strong delusion, that they should believe a lie" 2 Thes. 2:3 "Let no man deceive you by any means: for that day shall not come, except there comes a falling away first, and that man of sin be revealed, the son of perdition;" 2 Thes.3:2 "And that we may be delivered from unreasonable and wicked men: for all men have not faith.* Generations of false teachings will cause many to reject this side of God.

This part of that verse underlined refers to rejecting the word that will save them; they will not have the faith to act on the words of warning to be saved. *[3] But the Lord is faithful, who shall establish you, and keep you from evil."* This is to the saints in tribulation. Many of us are still deceived without even knowing it. I see the final judgment was extended for the past four years but now the signs are rapidly descending upon us to the point that a fool or a wayfaring man can see something is wrong. All who endured the persecution to be purified will be in the rapture when the first sickle angel appears with Christ to reap a ripe harvest in **Rev. 14:15-16**

This is a note to all pastors

In my first missionary journey in 04, God retired me from my job. I was sent by God on January 4th to March 11 for (40) days, in the year of 05. I, and two other brothers, visited 153 churches throughout the state of Arizona where I have lived for the past thirty years; only four assemblies received this message at that time. That was my wake-up call to the state of the church for me. In retrospect, throughout most of my adult life since the day I preached my first sermon in Sept. of 1977; my life has never been the same. Without ever knowing the full scope of what would happen to me, the way God as a little boy, I recall … was giving me a unique life experience that will mature me into a soldier of his teaching and training for these last years of this gospel that has been hid from them that are lost; it is the sum of our own willing ignorance.

These unknown nobodies like me, are raised up being criticized for our uncompromising stand by our peers. In my early years, having a form of un-diagnose dyslexia that showed in my inability to read beyond a third-grade level. I see it as a blessing because it enabled me to take rejection and criticism at a young age without becoming bitter by being made to look like one of the class dummies.

I am now holding fellow brethren in prayer daily in hopes to reverse the decision of the activity of the enemy I see working against them in their lives. Only God could have kept me in waiting to this present day by giving me a piece of his mind has kept me at peace through all my experiences to bring me to this present place of rest. What you are privileged to read in these chronicles are things during those years from 2004 until this present day that have brought me much grief and sorrow and many separations. The only thing left for me is what he has prepared me all these years to die from, so he can finish the course he has predestined for this body of his use. I strive daily to be obedient by his power, so I can endure to the end. I have seen the end of all things and what he is now telling you. This world as we know it shall soon be no more.

My beloved brothers and sisters with ears to hear and eyes to see, I appeal to you all in tears to take heed to what has been revealed to you as well as to me as a final warning. The floodgates of a fiery hell are being opened and heated by God's anger over what the enemy of our soul has brought his created world too. If you are alarmed by the daily bad news scene, I am afraid it's only going to get worst. This is His present state of mind for mankind that has been repeated in this last generation? *Genesis 6:5-7 (KJV)* "And GOD saw that the wickedness of man was great in the earth, and that every imagination of the thoughts of his heart was only evil continually *6 And it repented the LORD that he had made man on the earth, and it grieved him at his heart. 7 And the LORD said, I will destroy man whom I have created from the face of the earth; both man, and beast, and the creeping thing, and the fowls of the air; for it repenteth me that I have made them. Isaiah 5:14 (KJV) Therefore hell hath enlarged herself and opened her mouth without measure: and their glory, and their multitude, and their pomp, and he that rejoiceth, shall descend into it."* May God have mercy on all that call upon his name. Thus, is the end of this revelation. AMEN

REVELATION, THE FINAL LAYER REVEALED

Revelation Chart Timeline

Event		Timeline
1:1-20	Christ Testimony	End of the age
2: -3:2	The seven churches	Ditto
4:1-8:5	Opening of the seals	Tribulation begins
8:6 -11:19	The seven trumpets	Mid tribulation
17:1-20:15	The trumpet events	Judgment of nations
12:1-14:14	The last trumpet	The first thunder
14:15 -18	The resurrection	Church removed
15:1- 16:1	The seven vials	Thunder judgement
21:1-21	Restoration of earth	White throne judge
22:1-22	New Jerusalem	Brought down
This will be the beginning stages of the new Earth		

The horrific details are revealed in the previous witness of the prophetic timeline presentation chronicles from a Matthew 24: & Luke 21: as revealed to His messengers. Other details are witnessed in this chronicle view of the book of Revelation. The supporting chronicles are listed below.

"The conditions leading up to the translation," "Nowhere to Run, Nowhere to Hide," "What will happen during

the tribulation siege." These are the chronicles of the prophetic timeline as foretold by Old Testament prophets; now made simple by interpretation of what we really need to know, be revealed now through his holy prophets and messengers raised up as in old times to make known the revelation of these mysteries to this last generation.

Background Scripture:

Daniel 12:9 (KJV) [9] *And he said, go thy way, Daniel: for the words are closed up and <u>sealed till the time of the end</u>.* **Daniel 12:9 (NLT)** "[9] **But he said, "Go now, Daniel, for what I have said is kept secret and sealed until the time of the end." Rev 10:4 (KJV) And when the seven thunders had uttered their voices, I was about to write: and I heard a voice from heaven saying unto me, seal up those things which the seven thunders uttered, and write them not. Revelation 10:4 (NLT)** [4] **When the seven thunders spoke, I was about to write. But I heard a voice from heaven saying, "Keep secret what the seven thunders said, and do not write it down."** *Ephesians 3:5 (KJV)* [5] *Which in other ages was not made known unto the sons of men, as it is now revealed unto his holy apostles and prophets by the Spirit.*

The following scriptures are taken from the King James Paralleled in the English version for clarity, with the New Living Translation (Second edition), English Standard Version (ESV) and the NASB1977 version as helps translations to interpretation; used in compliance with the guidelines by permission. I have found these versions to be most consistent with the spirit of interpretation in today's English language from **KJV & ASV** bibles. These versions are distinguished by case slanting.

Now the mystery third layer can be revealed ... **Revelation 1:1-7 (NLT)** "[1] **This is a revelation from Jesus Christ, which God gave him to show his servants the events that must soon take place. He sent an angel to present this revelation to his servant John,** [2] **who faithfully reported everything he saw. This is his report of the word of God and the testimony of Jesus Christ.** [3] **God blesses the one who reads the words of this prophecy to the church, and he blesses all who listen to its message and obey what it says, for the time is near.** [4] **This letter is from John to the seven churches in the province of Asia. Grace and peace to you from the one who is, who** always was, and who is still to come; from the sevenfold Spirit before his throne; ⁵ and from Jesus Christ. He is the faithful witness to these things, the first to rise from the dead, and the ruler of all the kings of the world. All glory to him who loves us and has freed us from our sins by shedding his blood for us. ⁶ He has made us a Kingdom of priests for God his Father. All glory and power to him forever and ever! Amen. ⁷ Look! He comes with the clouds of heaven. And everyone will see him— even those who pierced him. And all the nations of the world will mourn for him. Yes! Amen!" [v. 8-10]

God establishes **HIMSELF AS THE ALMIGHTY,** the Beginning of all things and the End of all things. [verse 9] John, a fellow companion of Christ in suffering, banished on the island of Patmos to receive this testimony of Jesus Christ. John describes the coming kingdom that is prepared for all who remain faithful to their calling to the end. *Acts 14:22 (KJV) "Confirming the souls of the disciples, and exhorting them to continue in the faith, and that we must through much tribulation enter into the kingdom of God. James 1:2-4 My brethren, count it all joy when ye fall into divers temptations; 3Knowing this, that the trying of your faith worketh patience. 4But let patience have her perfect work, that ye may be perfect and entire, wanting nothing. Romans 8:17 And if children, then heirs; heirs of God, and joint heirs with Christ; if so be that we suffer with him, that we may be also glorified together. 2 Tim. 2:12 If we suffer, we shall also reign with him: if we deny him, he also will deny us."*

John is in the spirit on the Island of Patmos to write the book of Revelation

John is not the revelator, as most pastors imply, he did not reveal these mysteries; although he was given an understanding of some parts, but most of this book is a summary of what all the major and minor prophet spoke in time past, words that will hold mysteries of past, present and future mysteries to be revealed to this end time generation.

There is not much in the book of Revelation that reveals its mystery as you will see by supporting scriptures that will lead into the background context to open the mystery of this book as the Holy Spirit tells us just enough to prepare those, given ears to hear, the mystery in this manner. **Isaiah 28:10-13 (NASB77)** ¹⁰ **"For He says, ' Order on order, order on** order, Line on line, line on line, A little here, a little there.'" [11] Indeed, He will speak to this people Through stammering lips and a foreign tongue, [12] He who said to them, "Here is rest, give rest to the weary," And "Here is repose," but they would not listen. [13] So the word of the LORD to them will be, " Order on order, order on order, Line on line, line on line, A little here, a little there," That they may go and stumble backward, be broken, snared, and taken captive.

This last verse above underlined, explains the state the church will be in at the time this mystery is revealed. We will see why there is much confusion in its interpretations. Now you can be the judge of what is being revealed as to what is truth by the master teacher, the Holy Spirit. John is merely a witness, giving his testimony as being one of the original apostles, chosen to complete the end of the New Testament.

Both Daniel and John wrote these books in their latter years as prophets to bear witness to the words of God that will be revealed to a future generation at God's appointed time. As prophets, they are the two witnesses God showed a portion of what he told them not to write down. Jesus foretold in Matthew twenty-four. Prophets and messengers will be raised up in the last days as John the Baptist of that day to reveal these mysteries at the end of the time of many generations as told by Daniel. I am not saying I am he; you be the judge. The fact that he can speak for himself, here, I am just the scribe.

The Beginning:

Revelation 1:10-11 (NLT) [10] **It was the Lord's Day, and I was worshiping in the Spirit. Suddenly, I heard behind me a loud voice like a trumpet blast.** [11] **It said, "Write in a book everything you see, and send it to the seven churches in the cities of Ephesus, Smyrna, Pergamum, Thyatira, Sardis, Philadelphia, and Laodicea."**

This is the word of God manifested in the seven spirits of God to the seven churches, a final word of commendation, exaltation, rebuke, impending judgment and warnings coming up to the end of time man was given to subdue the Earth: the sixth millennium.

The letter to the spirit of the seventh church **Laodicea** is the final state of the people in those assemblies this mystery will be revealed. We are the temples that will represent this apostasy that have all these spirits in their assemblies mixed and growing together as the wheat and tares, possessed with all seven of these spirits. He will begin the separation in Revelation six in the breaking of the seals.

Chapter two

[v.1] The church of <u>Ephesus</u> the love loss church.
[v.8] <u>Smyrna,</u> the persecuted church.
[v.12] <u>Pergamos</u>, the compromising church.
[v.18] <u>Thyatira,</u> the corrupt church
[Ch. 3: v.1] <u>Sardis</u>, the dead church.
[v7] <u>Philadelphia</u>, the faithful church.
[v.14] <u>Laodicea</u>, the lukewarm church.

During the time of grace, these spirits describe the seven-fold nature of the different spirits that will identify the state of individual confessing Christians in the body of these assemblies that may be found growing together in the same church from a spiritual point of view in the church age. Your temple represents a spirit in the believers that is in the assembly when they come together under grace. **Matthew 7:16 (NASB77)** [16] **"<u>You will know them by their fruits.</u> Grapes are not gathered from thorn bushes, nor figs from thistles, are they?** *Matthew 7:20 (KJV)* [20] *Wherefore by their fruits ye shall know them.*

Now as you examine the characteristics of these assemblies, you now are to examine yourself by what's being said about these spirits in the churches because these are spirits in the bodies of believers. Every word God speaks about these seven spirits represents the way you have received him, that fruit will show.

The point of reference in our time is the spirit of the last church body, **Laodicea.** Let's examine the characteristics of this church for reference; its primary teachings are faith based positive concepts taken from the bible as self-help empowerment. The church spirit of the last days of our time will have evolved into a new doctrine that will explain why there must be a tribulation period. When John was writing this part of the vision, it was to the assemblies primarily apostle Paul established in these areas of the Middle east and Asia Minor to remind them of their state in the sight of God.

The mystery of this last church will characterize what all these spirits combined into one body will teach in part until that which is perfect returns. This doctrine we will come to know in our time as the doctrine of **rapture** & **prosperity**.

In verse (16 & 17) this church is self-indulged and spiritually deluded. It will be splintered into the doctrine of the **Nicolaitan's** that cause all who are indoctrinated to worship man. Pastors in their pre-eminence will perform as popes in the pulpits, robbing the people in the name of God, giving self-help speeches as hirelings to motivate their members to think that to be godly is to gain. This will be their appearance.

a.   **Wealthy**
b.   **Have need of nothing**
c.   **Has a good outer appearance**

These represent an outward appearance of Godliness, but unaware of what spirit they are of; seduced into the principles of faith which is the word in part that works without salvation. This will give rise to positive self-empowerment; teaching principles of truth that will cause men to get wealthy in the name of God by not knowing what spirit possesses him. **Deuteronomy 8:18 (NASB77) "But you shall remember the LORD your God, for it is He who is giving you power to make wealth, that He may confirm His covenant which He swore to your fathers, as it is this day."** This refers to the Jews that God gave a royal priest status as a nation would be wealthy. The temptations that came with that status made them think of themselves more highly than they should.

Ecclesiastes 1:9 (NLT) [9] History merely repeats itself. It has all been done before. Nothing under the sun is truly new.

God gave this principal to his people to make them independent of any other nation as a natural people. That's why Jews are wealthy and are the target of enemy nations because they can create an economic block of financial power when they come together using this principle. In the last days, this doctrine will cause the gentiles to lose sight of God as their source of wealth and seek their wealth in their own power and lose their souls; all in the name of God. They name the name of God but have no standard of holiness with a false sense of humility … what you see is an assembly deceived into thinking it is in the perfect will of God.

1 Timothy 6:5 (NASB77) and constant friction between men of depraved mind and deprived of the truths, who suppose that godliness is a means of gain." As the Holy Spirit departs, they will deny the power of God by their promotion of worldly programs as a substitute for deliverance in their assemblies. They will operate as religious corporations under a government charter 501-c3 as a seduced body now under government control. With this kingdom building mentality as being Seminary trained, they will transfer their self-help religious corporations to their children. This deception that circumvents the lack of deliverance, representing they know not of what spirit they are of or have become as did the Pharisees and Sadducees when Jesus rebuked them. **Luke 9:55 (NASB77) "But He turned and rebuked them, [and said, "You do not know what kind of spirit you are of;"** *Mark 7:9 (KJV) And he said unto them, Full well ye reject the commandment of God, that ye may keep your own tradition.* Under the new covenant, you are the new spiritual temple after Christ's resurrection. The natural temple was destroyed in 70 A. D. Christ in you will not compromise his doctrine to build a mega assembly. It is built on the foundation Christ left on one soul at a time and this is the fruit that will remain, just as he handpicked his apostles.

This will be your new family. These assemblies, under state control will pose no threat to the principalities that be; they lack revelation knowledge of truth … having been brought under subjection of government control as (501C-3 organizations as legalized charities.

The land grant God gave Israel had only one requirement under the laws of Moses, to give a tenth of all their substance to the Levite priestly tribe that will administer the law for your needs and the needs of the poor. Pastors have used this in conjunction with Malachi 3:10 to justify robbing the innocent under grace and truth to build their legacy kingdoms. This is not the doctrine of the New Testament as Christ taught and demonstrated. When he said not to be entangled with the bondages of this world, this is true freedom. All his promises have guaranteed we will have more than enough during this short life span. This was not a tax. Here again, we see that God gave them all things freely with a promise that they will never be in bondage to any nation nor any sickness in their midst if they keep this royal priesthood status of the law as his chosen people. **(Deut. 28:1-15)**

When they fail victim to seducing spirits and desired to be like the heathens, this is where they would be brought under the world's system of taxation when Rome took over their land, this was their 501C-3 bondage of paying tax to a heathen government that took the land God gave then freely. This bondage will be what they willingly requested as desiring an earthly king; they must sacrifice their sons in war and their daughters as servants and concubines to the king. He warned them that they would have to give up their rights to a king when they wanted to be like the other nations on earth to have a natural ruler over them. The churches supposed to be free of government control as Christians, operating in the apostle's doctrine that cause all that received Christ to help their neighbor in need by sharing their blessing that demonstrated a love greater than silver and gold with the poor. Instead, we have managed to create a welfare state in the church by the people not getting delivered.

The intent of the founding fathers is that the church would become the conscious of the state to keep our government officials inspired to keep this covenant with God as a Christian nation that would guarantee our continual freedoms and liberties as in **"In God We Trust."** The gospel under this covenant will proclaim … Mt **10:8 (KJV) Heal the sick, cleanse the lepers, raise the dead, cast out devils: freely ye have received, freely give.** This is what God gave to his church that Christ paid for in his blood that distinguishes us as a people who united as gentiles under this doctrine that will know their God. Now! Can you see where we all have fallen from?

This is what God sees that has happen to His diluted church?

a. **They are naked**
b. **Blind & spiritually poor**
c. **Lukewarm & indifferent**

In this state, **1 Timothy 6:5 (KJV) Perverse disputings of men of corrupt minds, and destitute of the truth, supposing that gain is godliness: from such withdraw thyself. 2 Timothy 3:7 (KJV) [7] Ever learning, and never able to come to the knowledge of the truth.** Exercising the faith for of outward show; they now will receive in part and will only know in part until their eyes are open when the prophets and messengers bring this vision of the final warning of our fallen state. The book of Revelation describes the sum of what we are as his creations, a people, a nation and a church have evolved into moral decadence as we become so wicked to change God's truth into a lie that will cause the end of this final age to save the world from destruction by man. We have been ... *Proverbs 6:2 (KJV) "Thou art snared with the words of thy mouth, thou art taken with the words of thy mouth. (We are serving in this state ... Proverbs 14:12(KJV) There is a way which seemeth right unto a man, but the end thereof are the ways of death. 2 Timothy 3:7 (KJV)* [7] Ever learning, and never able to come to the knowledge of the truth." God's mercy is extended in this warning which shows His love for this end-time church.

We must now repent after we have been warned by the prophets in... **(Amos 3:7 (NLT)** [7] **Indeed, the Sovereign Lord never does anything until he reveals his plans to his servants the prophets. Ephesians 3:5 (NLT)** [5] **God did not reveal it to previous generations, but now by his Spirit he has revealed it to his holy apostles and prophets.** *Joel 2:1-4 (KJV) Blow ye the trumpet in Zion, and sound an alarm in my holy mountain: let all the inhabitants of the land tremble: for the day of the LORD cometh, for it is nigh at hand; 2A day of darkness and of gloominess, a day of clouds and of thick darkness, as the morning spread upon the mountains: a great people and a strong; there hath not been ever the like, neither shall be any more after it, even to the years of many generations*".

The above underlined verse describes the present state of the church at the time of this warning, the end of the sixth millennium as ... *Matthew 24:34 (KJV)* [34] *Verily I say unto you, this generation shall not pass, till all these things be fulfilled.* The church, in its lukewarm state, being shocked with a hard word, will reject these messengers warning them to repent or face impending tribulation and doom, as Israel did in their time. Jesus tells them .... *Rev. 3:18(KJV) "I counsel thee to buy of me gold tried in the fire, that thou mayest be rich; and white raiment, that thou mayest be clothed, and that the shame of thy nakedness do not appear; and anoint thine eyes with eye salve, that thou mayest see."*

Chapter 4

In my early years as a baby Christian, I was taught when the angel told

John this in ... *Rev. 4:1(KJV) "After this I looked, and, behold, a door was opened in heaven: and the first voice which I heard was as it were of a trumpet talking with me; which said, <u>come up hither,</u> and I will show thee things which must be hereafter;* ... that meant, the church was being translated or raptured; many theologians use this interpretation today as the key verse to justify the rapture doctrine.

As I examine the context of this verse under the leading of the Holy Spirit, there is a great error of deception in this doctrine being taught in the Laodicea church time. This is in direct contrast to the verse in **Rev. 3:18, Matthew 24:29 and Acts 14:22.** Here we see in (4:1) John describes that he is in a state of spiritual captivity, in other words, caught up in the Holy Spirit to write the book of Revelation. The mystery of the twenty-four elders; they are witnesses to the word of God spoken in the earth; twelve for the Jews and twelve for the gentiles. *<u>Jeremiah 23:18(KJV)</u> "For who hath stood in the counsel of the LORD, and hath perceived and heard his word? who hath marked his word, and heard it?" They are the judges of the true and false prophets as stated in... Jeremiah 23:21(KJV) I have not sent these prophets, yet they ran: I have not spoken to them, yet they prophesied. Their righteousness is judging the spoken word in the earth. 1 Cor. 6:2(KJV) "Do ye not know that the saints shall judge the world? and if the world shall be judged by you, are ye unworthy to judge the smallest matters?"*

[Rev.4:5-11] These verses represent the awesomeness of God and His heavenly host and divine authority over all things in heaven and earth as the judge. All the glory and worship by the heavenly host including the four and twenty elders, are praising the lamb that was slain before the foundation of the world as the only one worthy to open the seals.

Chapter 5:

There's no one In heaven worthy to open the seven seals that Daniel was told to seal and now witnessed to John would be revealed through the end time prophets and messengers before the tribulation. *Daniel 12:4(KJV) "But thou, O Daniel, shut up the words, and <u>seal the book</u>, even to <u>the time of the end</u>: many shall run to and fro, and knowledge shall be increased; Ezekiel 2:9-10 (KJV) And when I looked, behold, an hand was sent unto me; and, lo, a roll of a book was therein; 10And he spread it before me; and <u>it was</u>*

written within and without: and there was written therein lamentations, and mourning, and woe."

Now what was written in these scrolls that had to be sealed is now about to be revealed to the end time prophets and messengers. This is John's witness…**Revelation 10:4 (NLT)** [4] **When the seven thunders spoke, I was about to write. But I heard a voice from heaven saying, "Keep secret what the seven thunders said, and do not write it down."** [verse 5-6] Jesus, in His triumphant victory, has prevailed as the lion of the tribe of Judah, succeeded in crushing the devil under His feet. God separates out His chosen elects to send them into the wilderness before the judgment to prepare them to receive the fullness of Him as the John the Baptist of this day before the tribulation. Read what they were sent in the wilderness to do in the chronicle **"Preparation for Glory"** (The wilderness experience).

Historical Background

Genesis 12:1-5(KJV) "Now the LORD had said unto Abram, Get thee out of thy country, and from thy kindred, and from thy father's house, unto a land that I will shew thee: 2And I will make of thee a great nation, and I will bless thee, and make thy name great; and thou shalt be a blessing:3And I will bless them that bless thee, and curse him that curseth thee: and in thee shall all families of the earth be blessed.4So Abram departed, as the LORD had spoken unto him; and Lot went with him: and Abram was seventy and five years old when he departed out of Haran. 5And Abram took Sarai his wife, and Lot his brother's son, and rejecting you more thatall their substance that they had gathered, and the souls that they had gotten in Haran; and they went forth to go into the land of Canaan; and into the land of Canaan they came. Genesis 3:15 (KJV) and I will put enmity between thee and the woman, and between thy seed and her seed; it shall bruise thy head, and thou shalt bruise his heel;"

Adam's sin brought the second manifestation of the seed of enmity as in Cain. Again, Satan will use a woman to seduce her husband to produce another line of seeds of enmity in Abraham's linage to produce descendants that would represent what happened in the enmity that came between Cain and Abel. When Abraham laid with Hagar, which produced Ishmael; Abraham did not fully wait on God to fulfill the promise through Sarah, her unbelief, became party to this sin just as Adam's became party to Eve's sin will be repeated throughout times, ages and dispensations.

Now, we see the historical account of God's divine predestination to reverse the decision of the enemy through these acts of disobedience in their efforts to help God. This, through time would bring about the destruction of God's people as well as the church of Christ.

[**Rev. 5:7**] As Jesus accepts the scroll from the father; He has now been given the authority to judge the world by opening the seals. *Daniel 12:9(KJV) "And he said, go thy way, Daniel: for the words are closed up and sealed till the time of the end."* What has been kept hidden from man is now to be revealed in the breaking of the seals.

[**Rev.5:8**] The great mysteries revealed in the seven seals are what Daniel could not reveal when he saw them; Christ himself preparing to try the **Church** operating in the **Laodicea spirit,** as these seals are open, (**Rev.3:18**) is where every tongue shall confess Him in the end as the only God. *Philippians 2:11(KJV) "And that every tongue should confess that Jesus Christ is Lord, to the glory of God the Father."*

[**Rev.5:9-14**] The lamb that was slain before the foundation of the world is now being worshiped by the heavenly host before the opening of the seals.

The first seal

Rev. 6:1-8; this is the ... *Matthew 24:8(KJV) "All these are the beginning of sorrows."* What we see here in the beginning of the opening of the seals, are the fulfillment of ... **Matt. 24: verses 1-34.** To avoid repetition, this account is in the previous chronicle, "**Through the Eyes of the Prophets**"

The **white horse** is Christ coming in the spirit with the former rain to his elects to restore what we lost in His body; our first love in the former rain. These are the elects, chosen to spearhead the latter rain. At the same time a false spirit of the Antichrist that has deceived the whole world by false teachings will come full circle. This false teaching of rapture will put them in a state thinking they will not be here during the tribulation; therefore, many will become lukewarm. When this reality comes full circle, great fear will overtake them by rejecting the vision of the prophets because they were told they would be gone.

The spirit of Christ will enter his chosen vessels in the fullness to prepare for the great tribulation. At that time … ***Matthew 11:12 (KJV)*** [12] ***And from the days of John the Baptist until now the kingdom of heaven suffereth violence, and the violent take it by force.*** The confrontation of the fullness of the devil against the fullness of Christ will be at war in our temples. This is revival in Ezekiel thirty-seven as in the dry bones … His chosen elects of the church and Israel will prepare to conquer its enemies once and for all in doing battle with the Antichrist as the **Man Child.** This Antichrist body will consist of many that were deceived in that 98 percent that rejected his prophets and messengers. This is that end time generation which Jesus spoke about to his disciples in Matthew twenty-four.

The second seal

Revelation 6:3-4 (NLT) "[3] When the Lamb broke the second seal, I heard the second living being say, "Come!" [4] Then another horse appeared a <u>Red</u> one. Its rider was given a mighty sword and the authority to take peace from the earth. And there was war and slaughter everywhere." (Matthew 24: -7(KJV) "For nation shall rise against nation, and kingdom against kingdom: and there shall be famines, and pestilences, and earthquakes, in divers places.") The horror of these events will be revealed in the coming chapters as a witness to other chronicles. These are the beginning stages leading up to World War III among the nations.

The Third Seal

Rev. 6:5-6(KJV) "And when he had opened the <u>third seal</u>, I heard the third beast say, Come and see. And I beheld, and lo <u>a black horse</u>; and he that sat on him had a pair of balances in his hand. [6] And I heard a voice during the four beasts say, A measure of wheat for a penny, and three measures of barley for a penny; and see thou hurt not the oil and the wine." This will be a time of extreme famine in the Earth. Many will die of hunger before they resort to cannibalism. Only those with the mark can get food and will pay an extremely high price for just the bare necessities of life. The **oil** and the **wine;** the oil is the anointed elects, the wine is those being purified in the press to perfection back to the Pentecostal accord, washed in the <u>blood</u> of the lamb. **Rev. 3:18**

The fourth seal

Rev. 6:7-8(KJV) "And when he had opened the fourth seal, I heard the voice of the fourth beast say, Come and see. 8And I looked and behold a pale horse: and his name that sat on him was Death, and Hell followed with him. And power was given unto them over the fourth part of the earth, to kill with sword, and with hunger and with death, and with the beasts of the earth."

This continuation of events taking place as described in **Matthew 24.** A great many of the lukewarm Christians, living in their created comfort zone lifestyles, will be claim for hell; lukewarm represents a pale spirit that is neither for nor against anything. Their state in God's sight is dead while they are living ... otherwise, they just have not made up their minds who to serve; that's why they will be spit out of his mouth. This will mark them for death while they are still living. Great fear will overtake many of them and they will lose their minds when they see that they have been deceived and given over to receive the mark will become as zombies; the **"Walking Dead"** while they are living. Now you know why there are movies about the walking dead, God is showing you your future.

This is that wait and see attitude. Many will be turned over to the devil as part of that 98 percent that have rejected the prophets. This will be the consequences of the last three seals that will cause this scripture to be fulfilled. *"Isaiah 5:14 (KJV)* [14] *Therefore hell hath enlarged herself and opened her mouth without measure: and their glory, and their multitude, and their pomp, and he that rejoiceth, shall descend into it."* The hand of God in judgment is the same way He judged His people in time pass; **"The great Separation"** of the wheat from the tares and bringing forth His body out of great persecution. This is **the Body of Christ in tribulation,** coming forth as pure gold, as His bride through the fires of tribulation. **(Rev.3:18)**

The fifth seal

Rev 6:9-10 (KJV) And when he had opened the fifth seal, I saw under the altar the souls of them that were slain for the word of God, and for the testimony which they held: [10] *And they cried with a loud voice, saying, how long, O Lord, holy and true, dost thou not judge and avenge our blood on them that dwell on the earth?* The souls of those martyred for the testimony of Jesus Christ pleading for their fellow brothers who are undergoing great tribulation and persecution to be redeemed out of the earth while He exact vengeance. America and the world are being judged as described in ... *Rev. 19:2(KJV) "For true and righteous are his judgments: for he hath judged the great whore, which did corrupt the earth with her fornication, and hath avenged the blood of his servants at her hand."* This is God's punishment for our sins as a nation and as a people that named his name and did not depart from iniquity. These gentile nations were warned as was Israel, as a nation and a people before judgment came. America,(The Modern Babylon) will become an immoral habitation of Sodomy spirits seducing the world.

Rev. 6:11 "And white robes were given unto every one of them; and it was said unto them, that they should rest yet for a little season, until their fellow servants also and their brethren, that should be killed as they were, should be fulfilled." As the saints are being martyred to be received in heaven, they are given their rewards and garments of praise as over comers in the blood of the lamb while God is exacting His judgment in the earth as stated in ... *Exodus 32:35(KJV) "And the LORD plagued the people, because they made the calf, which Aaron made.* Aaron represents **pastors** who erected idols (**large assemblies**) that turn the body of Christ back to the natural idol temples; therefore, deceiving them of the revelation of where the true temple is; **their bodies in the spirit**. They would bound them by mixing law with grace by lack of revelation knowledge. This will lead to divisions and captivity and into bondage to the government they were to oversee to protect the liberties of our religious freedoms.

The evidence of not knowing what spirit they are of, when members of these assemblies accuse you of not being a member of the church body as in their natural assembly buildings. They will use this verse out of context by saying ... *Hebrews 10:25 (KJV) "Not forsaking the assembling of ourselves together, as the manner of some is; but exhorting one another: and so much the more, as ye see the day approaching"* ... While those in truth will ... *1 Corinthians 2:2 (KJV) [2] For I determined not to know anything among you, save Jesus Christ, and him crucified. 2 Corinthians 6:17 (KJV) [17] Wherefore come out from among them, and be ye separate, saith the Lord, and touch not the unclean thing; and I will receive you, Ephesians 5:11 "And have no fellowship with the unfruitful works of darkness, but rather reprove them."* *Amos 3:3 (KJV) [3] Can two walk together, except they be agreed?*

This form of division will lead to judging those who are not connected to these idol assemblies. God's people know each other when they meet. They are few and far between. That's an observation I experience by fellow confessing Christian not being able to recognize his voice. My beloved brothers and sisters, there are not many that will endure the truth of God that comes with persecution from your fellow brethren in these traditional assemblies. This is America's judgment for turning to idolatry. We did what the Jesuit's taught us in their seminaries, build buildings as idols of deception and produced Popes in the pulpits.

The sixth seal

Rev. 6:12-13(KJV) "And I beheld when he had opened <u>*the sixth seal,*</u> *and, lo, there was a great earthquake; and the sun became black as sackcloth of hair, and the moon became as blood; 13 And the stars of heaven fell unto the earth, even as a fig tree casteth her untimely figs, when she is shaken of a mighty wind."* The chronological order of the book of Revelation is one of the mysteries that have eluded many that have studied this book through the ages without this vision that was not revealed. The opening chart should shed son light as to the course of events. Even Clarence Larkin who drew diagrams of timelines in his book was not given this revelation according to his charts. His book titled **"Dispensational truths & Rightly Dividing the Word of Truth."**

These events take a twist and what is happening now is described in … *Rev. 11:13(KJV) "And the same hour was there a great earthquake, and the tenth part of the city fell, and in the earthquake, were slain of men seven thousand: and the remnant were affrighted and gave glory to the God of heaven."* These that are frightened are those that will be preserved for the millennium that will see all these great wonders; they have never been indoctrinated by man. *Luke 21:11 (KJV) And great earthquakes shall be in divers places, and famines, and pestilences; and fearful sights and great signs shall there be from heaven.* This will be an ongoing occurrence during the breaking of the seals. God will seal all that shall be gathered for eternity to be purified in the great tribulation back **to "One lord, one faith and one baptism."** (Eph.4:5) This is also the time that Satan is about to be cast out of heaven because his work will be finished there as the accuser when all the saints are sealed for translation.

Daniel 9:26 (KJV) And after threescore and two weeks shall Messiah be cut off, but not for himself: and the people of the prince that shall come shall destroy the city and the sanctuary; and the end thereof shall be with a flood, and unto the end of the war desolations are determined. This is coming up to the end of the first half years of tribulation. Matthew twenty-four and Luke twenty-one describe the literal events of natural disasters in diverse places all over the world that will be the headlines of the day. The **Beast** System: at that time, you will not have any possessions or housing unless you have the mark of the beast. All property will belong to the state, though you may have your home paid off, it sets on the state property; that's their claim to your property when there's no money to pay your taxes. All your money will be lost in the crash. They will change the money system so that those who withdraw their money, it will become just worthless paper in the new system.

Rev. 6:14-17(KJV) "And the heaven departed as a scroll when it is rolled together; and every mountain and island were moved out of their places. 15 And the kings of the earth, and the great men, and the rich men, and the chief captains, and the mighty men, and every bondman, and every free man, hid themselves in the dens and in the rocks of the mountains; 16 And said to the mountains and rocks, <u>Fall on us, and hide us from the face of him that sitteth on the throne, and from the wrath of the Lamb:</u> 17 For the great day of his wrath is come; and who shall be able to Stan."

These events are so devastating to the point of producing cataclysmic natural disasters in all nations and within America; some using forbidden technology to manipulate elements in nature. This is the Sodomy curse in the great day of the lord as described in ... *Romans 1:18-32 (KJV) For the wrath of God is revealed from heaven against all ungodliness and unrighteousness of men, who hold the truth in unrighteousness; 19 Because that which may be known of God is manifest in them; for God hath shewed it unto them. 20 For the invisible things of him from the creation of the world are clearly seen, being understood by the things that are made, even his eternal power and Godhead; so that they are without excuse: 21 Because that, when they knew God, they glorified him not as God neither were thankful; but became vain in their imaginations, and their foolish heart was darkened. 22 Professing themselves to be wise, they became fools, 23 And changed the glory of the un-corruptible God into an image made like to corruptible man, and to birds, and four-footed beasts, and creeping things. 24 Wherefore God also gave them up to uncleanness through the lusts of their own hearts, to dishonour their own bodies between themselves: 25 Who changed the truth of God into a lie and worshipped and served the creature more than the Creator, who is blessed forever. Amen. 26 For this cause God gave them up unto vile affections: for even their women did change the natural use into that which is against nature: 27 And likewise also the men, leaving the natural use of the woman, burned in their lust one toward another; men with men working that which is unseemly, and receiving in themselves that recompense of their error which was meet.* I never imagined I would live to see the president of the United States, stand in the Oval Office representing the **King of the free world,** identify himself as a Christian, and out of the same mouth declared that **"we are no longer a Christian nation".** It is the evidence of a foreign seed has entered the highest office of this nation as an instrument used to bring this nation into bondage by changing God's laws under his watch.

He has insulted our Christianity claims as a nation by endorsing homosexuality as a legal lifestyle. This decree by a president elected by the people, justified a curse that sealed our fate as Sodom and Gomorrah. God would have to repent to them if we were to escape this judgment. *Romans 1:28-32* "And even as they did not like to retain God in their knowledge, God gave them over to a reprobate mind, to do those things which are not convenient; *29* Being filled with all unrighteousness, fornication, wickedness, covetousness, maliciousness; full of envy, murder, debate, deceit, malignity; whisperers, *30* Backbiters, haters of God, despiteful, proud, boasters, inventors of evil things, disobedient to parents, *31* Without understanding, covenant breakers, without natural affection, implacable, unmerciful: *32-who knowing the judgment of God, that they which commit such things are worthy of death, not only do the same, but have pleasure in them that do them." Romans 2:5 (KJV) But after thy hardness and impenitent heart treasurest up unto thyself wrath against the day of wrath and revelation of the righteous judgment of God."* This is what is happening among the ungodly. The children of disobedience will suffer with them in the second half before they are gathered in the second sickle as the clusters. **(Rev.14:18-20)**

Chapter 7

Verses 1-8 what's happening here, God is preparing His elect for spiritual war with the principalities in heaven in the battle for souls; God's elects are sealed to endure the tribulations are walking in the fullness of the latter rain as the **Man Child**. Since Satan tricked David to number His people, this was the law that God gave them in ... *Numbers 1:49(KJV) "Only thou shalt not number the tribe of Levi, neither take the sum of them among the children of Israel:"* This law was violated by David in ... **1 Chronicles 27:23-24. Isaiah 10:22 (KJV) "For though thy people Israel be as the sand of the sea, yet a <u>remnant of them shall return</u>: the consumption decreed shall overflow with righteousness. Isaiah 11:11 And it shall come to pass in that day, that the Lord shall set his hand again the second time to recover the <u>remnant of his people, which shall be left</u>, from Assyria, and from Egypt, and from Pathros, and from Cush, and from Elam, and from Shinar, and from Hamath, and from the islands of the sea."**

David, as king, made a decree that cannot be changed; violated God's command. In **Rev.7:5-8** is the remnant of Israel's elect sealed in that 144,000 representing the twelve tribes gathered from all nations. God foreknew this and had John to write that mystery to be revealed for this time. *Rev. 14:4(KJV) "These are they which were not defiled with women; for they are virgins. These are they which follow the Lamb whithersoever he goeth. These were redeemed from among men, being the first <u>fruits unto God and to the Lamb.</u> Galatians 6:16 And as many as walk according to this rule, peace be on them, and mercy, and upon the Israel of God."* To prevent Jerusalem from being destroyed, "The lion of the tribe of Judah," Christ himself will cause a miracle to take place in this remnant tribe as he did with them in the 1967 war that destroyed the Syrian armies. Once again, through the tribe of Judah in the valley of amour getting, the armies of the North will fill that valley with blood to the horse's bridle. (Ezekiel chapters 38-39)

Revelation 7:9 (KJV) [9] After this I beheld, and, lo, a great multitude, <u>which no man could number</u>, of all nations, and kindreds, and people, and tongues, stood before the throne, and before the Lamb, clothed with white robes, and palms in their hands; This numberless multitudes consist of a mystery that is behind the interpretation of this scripture ... *John 10:16 (KJV) And other sheep I have, which are not of this fold: them also I must bring, and they shall hear my voice; and there shall be one fold, and one shepherd.* The forbidden knowledge of this number takes into an account of time hidden from man of which all life from time of things unspeakable to the end of the last millennium; sealed to spend eternity with God and His son. Chronologically, the order of this book, some chapters will pre-describe the events in the later chapters. John is seeing visions in no continual order, **it contains prophecies, Past, present and future.** We are now in the last generation where all who are alive shall see what Jesus was telling his disciples on the Mount of Olives as spoken in time passed by the true prophets to be fulfilled in this present future.

Revelation 7:10-17 (NLT) [10] **And they were shouting with a mighty shout, "Salvation comes from our God who sits on the throne and from the Lamb!"** [11] **And all the angels were standing around the throne and around the elders and the four living beings. And they fell before the throne with their faces to the ground and worshiped God.** [12] **They sang, "Amen! Blessing and glory and wisdom and thanksgiving and honor and power and strength belong to our God forever and ever! Amen."** [13] **Then one of the twenty-four elders asked me, "Who are these who are clothed in white? Where did they come from?"** [14] **And I said to him, "Sir, you are the one who knows." Then he said to me, "These are the ones who died in the great tribulation.** (The elder is giving him a view of the future saints going through tribulation.)**They have washed their robes in the blood of the Lamb and made them white.** [15] **"That is why they stand in front of God's throne and serve him day and night in his Temple. And he who sits on the throne will give them shelter.** [16] <u>**They will never again be hungry or thirsty; they will never be scorched by the heat of the sun.**</u>

This part underlined shows that many Christians will not live the full privilege unto their death of being free from <u>sickness</u>, <u>hunger</u>, <u>diseases</u>, <u>disaster</u> and <u>elements</u> from the skies; but held to their confession of salvation in faith unto death. God will still get the glory out of them in their death. The ozone layer will be open during the last half of the tribulation to purify the earth. This is where the children of disobedience will suffer the first thunder with ultraviolet rays that will burn them also. [17] **For the Lamb on the throne will be their Shepherd. He will lead them to springs of life-giving water. And God will wipe every tear from their eyes."**

These are the martyred saints during the great tribulation. At this point, these saints who have undergone the great tribulation, overcoming by the blood of the lamb, through the war in heaven between Michael and the devil trying to prevent the reaping of the harvest. Michael has triumph over the devil in the body of Christ to prepare the way for the saints to be translated into heaven to receive her rewards.

The chapters below are describing what is happening in heaven in the war with the principalities as Michael and the heavenly angels in **Ephesians 6:12** is taking place in the spirit and manifested in the earth in the evil activity of men at war with themselves and the saints.

Chapter 8:

The seventh seal

God Receives the Prayers if the Righteous

<u>Rev. 8:1</u> **"And when he had opened the <u>seventh seal</u>, there was silence in heaven about the space of half an hour."** The intercessory prayers of the saints are being received for the preservation of the children of disobedience. All those whose names are now coming before the lord are being sealed with power not to deny his name. They will be led as sheep to the slaughter. What will happen to them is described in more detail in the chronicle **"What will happen during the Tribulation siege."**

[Rev. 8: 2-6] describes the activity around the throne for a space of a half hour. He is now receiving the prayers of the righteous for them that are sealed to endure the first thunder.

The first trumpet

Revelation 8:7 (KJV) The <u>first</u> angel sounded, and there followed hail and fire mingled with blood, and they were cast upon the earth: and the third part of trees was burnt up, and all green grass was burnt up. This verse describes the aftermath of a horrific event such as a nuclear disaster. Russia and China will have ravaged the United States and nuclear bombs were exploded from within during the siege to prevent them from taking this cursed land.

Matthew 24:15-19 "When ye therefore shall see the abomination of desolation, spoken of by Daniel the prophet, stand in the holy place, <u>whoso readeth, let him understand</u>: 16Then let them which be in Judaea flee into the mountains:

17Let him which is on the housetop not come down to take anything out of his house: 18Neither let him which is in the field return back to take his clothes.

There are two revelations in verse (15 & 17). The **first** is natural as what happen in seventy A.D. to the natural temple as to what the Jews had to do to escape in the siege and the **second** is the spiritual temple we have become as confessing Christians. We, as his temples have now become an abomination for not forsaking our worldly garments, if we do not repent when he shows us the error of our ways, our garments are full of worldly spots if we don't flee from these assemblies of idolatry, we will be unacceptable at the marriage supper and therefore, left behind.

19And woe unto them that are with child, and to them that give suck in those days!" Deut. 28:57 (NLT) [57] *She will hide from them the afterbirth and the new baby she has borne, so that she herself can secretly eat them. She will have nothing else to eat during the siege and terrible distress that your enemy will inflict on all your towns.* Pregnant women will be abandoned in the siege; their children will be taken away from them for food. Our young wives and daughters will become the spoils of the released criminals, and the invading armies of China and Russia. It is during this period that the saints are being purified for the translated in the first resurrection of the New Testament saints to escape the coming wrath that will be noted in the coming chapters.

The second trumpet

(Rev. 8:8-9) The indescribable things that are to be experienced that caused the powers of heaven to be shaken as natural disasters such as earthquakes exploding larva reducing mountains to ash; this is the re-organization of the Earth's geography, getting ready for the millennium. What man thought he had created with this forbidden technology will be the end of his own doom. *Matthew 24:21-22(KJV) For then shall be great tribulation, such as was not since the beginning of the world to this time, no, nor ever shall be. 22And except those days should be shortened, there should no flesh be saved: but for the elect's sake those days shall be shortened. Rev. 13:10(KJV) He that leadeth into captivity shall go into captivity: he that killeth with the sword must be killed with the sword. Here is the patience and the faith of the saints.*

Many patriot Christians that resort to defending themselves will be killed without mercy during the siege. Their false view of Christianity will cause them to become zealots to defend the church. The scapegoat patriot spirit in Barabbas will return in them and lead them into captivity. They will judge themselves to be delivered into bondage and killed. *Amos 9:10 (KJV)* [10] *All the sinners of my people shall die by the sword, which say, the evil shall not overtake nor prevent us.* This is their punishment for rebelling against the doctrine in their attempts to take back America.

The third trumpet

Revelation 8:10-11 (KJV) [10] *And the third angel sounded, and there fell a great star from heaven, burning as it were a lamp, and it fell upon the third part of the rivers, and upon the fountains of waters;* [11] *And the name of the star is called* <u>Wormwood</u>: *and the third part of the waters became wormwood; and many men died of the waters, because they were made bitter.* This is a result of an asteroid hitting the Earth, dead sea life. America's destruction will be first natural disaster, wars will speed up economic collapse, foreign invasion, meteorite showers and finally a fragment of an asteroid will ultimately change this nations geography before the end that will leave this nation uninhabitable. Some of this will happen before the saints are removed.

The fourth trumpet

Revelation 8:12-13 (KJV) [12] *And the fourth angel sounded, and the third part of the sun was smitten, and the third part of the moon, and the third part of the stars; so, as the third part of them was darkened, and the day shone not for a third part of it, (Those that are prophesying, this will be the three days of darkness. It' a false prophecy that came through the Catholic Church.) and the night likewise.* [13] *And I beheld, and heard an angel flying through the midst of heaven, saying with a loud voice, Woe, woe, woe, to the inhabiters of the earth by reason of the other voices of the trumpet of the three angels, which are yet to sound!*

Darkness will once again be in the Earth as when Moses and Aaron were before Pharaoh in Egypt but in certain parts under that judgment. This is the work of the two witnesses in the last half of the tribulation. These are the natural elements described in … **Matthew 24:29-30 (KJV)** [29] **Immediately after the tribulation of those days shall the sun be darkened, and the moon shall not give her light, and the stars shall fall from heaven, and**

the powers of the heavens shall be shaken: [30] **And then shall appear the sign of the Son of man in heaven: and then shall all the tribes of the earth mourn, and they shall see the Son of man coming in the clouds of heaven with power and great glory.** This leads up to rapture.

This darkness is the result of an asteroid meteor shower that will take out the western hemisphere, which includes America. Scientists have already detected it but it will be too late when they learn it is on a collision course with earth. One will come close by as a warning before the final fragment of that larger one impacts the western hemisphere. This is what's being described in the verses above. We will be raptured just before this when the two witnesses finish their work in the final judgment of the Jews in the second half that will be cut short. It would have the same impact as in the movie **"Deep impact.** The **first** of the three woes will precede the sounding of the fifth trumpet.

The fifth trumpet

Revelation 9:1-6 (KJV) [1] *And the fifth angel* <u>*sounded,*</u> *and I saw a star fall from heaven unto the earth: and to him was given the key of the bottomless pit.* [2] *And he opened the bottomless pit; and there arose a smoke out of the pit, as the smoke of a great furnace; and the sun and the air were darkened by reason of the smoke of the pit.* The demon spirits from the bottomless pit are being loosed after all saints are sealed, Satan is cast out of heaven and begin his assault through the wicked-on Earth. One of the signs that will be apparent at that time is an increase in mass suicide murder demons released to commit mayhem in the Earth. This is when tribulation becomes full circle in the Earth. [4] **And it was commanded them that they should not hurt the grass of the earth, neither any green thing, neither any tree; but only those men which have not the seal of God in their foreheads.**

These are the places of habitation for the people sealed to survive the tribulation. They are the chosen to repopulate the millennium. **(Zechariah 13:8-9 "(KJV)** [8] **And it shall come to pass, that in all the land, saith the LORD, two parts therein shall be cut off and die; but the third shall be left therein.** [9] <u>**And I will bring the third part through the fire,**</u> **and will refine them as silver is refined, and will try them as gold is tried: they shall call on my name, and I will hear them: I will say, it is my people: and they shall say, The LORD is my God. (Isaiah 26:20 (KJV)** [20] **Come,** my people, enter thou into thy chambers, and shut thy doors about thee: hide thyself as it were for a little moment, until the indignation be over-past)." (cont.) [5] And to them it was given that they should not kill them, but that they should be tormented five months: and their torment was as the torment of a scorpion, when he striketh a man. [6] And in those days shall men seek death and shall not find it; and shall desire to die, and death shall flee from them.

This is the environment that will create a zombie like state of mind as deceived Christians who would not repent are given over to the devil for their sins of omission, they will be inhabited by legions of demons. This is when this scripture will be fulfilled ... *Matthew 12:45 "(KJV)* [45] *Then goeth he, and taketh with himself seven other spirits more wicked than himself, and they enter in and dwell there: and the last state of that man is worse than the first. Even so shall it be also unto this wicked generation"*.

At this point, I would like to explain something about the children of disobedience. Those that have the protection of the prayers of the righteous will be saved by their intercessors whose sacrifice of their lives for those loved by them. Many pastors, whose assemblies refused to take heed to the prophet's warning, will cause many in their congregation to be lost through false teachings. When I came into this knowledge as seeing things through the mind of Christ. There are very few humble educated pastors and teachers that can discern the voice of God. This to me has become a sad experience when rejected by them for speaking the truth, seeing that they know not what spirit they are of.

Men who were seduced to become hirelings as in marketing themselves on the bassist of their academic accolades are the most responsible for this movement into this doctrine that led to the Laodicea spirit. I call this the begging spirit they received from the devil that led them to go ahead of God when the devil offered them the riches in the name of God, using Mal.3:10 to justify robbing the people that brought this woe on them to build their family owned 501-C3 earthly kingdoms. These spirits will open the door for the devil to walk in their assemblies and commit murder. Without knowing, your compromised state has given him this authority to open the door for these seven spirits of Revelation two to enter your assembly as you compromise the doctrine to invite unbelievers in to help build your kingdom. God will restrain these suicide spirits so none of the wicked shall escape their punishment on Earth in large numbers.

As men's hearts wax worst and worst, members of your own household who have rejected God in the call to repent are marked in the spirit will turn you over to authorities that are seeking all Christians to be put to death. Legions of the worst demon spirits will be loosed on Earth during that time from the bottomless pit when the church is removed. They will torment all that remain without mercy. This will happen to the children of disobedience during the first thunder. All that rejected God were given a strong delusion as people, nations and deceived Christians that will be possessed with these demon spirits. These are the seven spirits that are worst that the ones you had. The invading army of China, controlled by a principality demon, will be merciless and kill all American men on site and **rape your young wives and daughters** as their reward for all the aborted babies women consented to be killed. They will be ravaged like the babies were when they were aborted.

The two witnesses in the Earth were the ones that kept them restrained for the church and Israel during their tribulation. After the three and one-half days in the Earth to preach to the spirits in prison, they will rise like Christ did on the third day. The spirit of these two witnesses will be as the **manifested sons of God** among the people of the world as Jesus walking in the fullness of the Godhead bodily. The spirit of Moses will expose the people in high places in governments and the spirit of Elijah will expose all false prophets in the exploits they will do that will expose the lying signs. Many will be martyred, and some will not see death when we all are translated in the final rapture.

Revelation 9:7-12 (RSV) [7] *In appearance the locusts were like horses arrayed for battle; on their heads were what looked like crowns of gold; their faces were like human faces,* [8] *their hair like women's hair, and their teeth like lions' teeth;* [9] *they had scales like iron breastplates, and the noise of their wings was like the noise of many <u>chariots with horses rushing into battle</u>.* [10] *They have <u>tails like scorpions, and stings</u>, and their power of hurting men for five months lies in their tails.* [11] *They have as king over them the angel of the bottomless pit; his name in Hebrew is Abad'don, and in Greek he is called Apollyon.* [12] *The first woe has passed; behold, two woes are still to come.*

These are nations at war. The scorpions here are Apache attack helicopters, tanks and jets plains described in ... *(Joel 2:3-7 (KJV) A fire devoureth before them; and behind them a flame burneth: the <u>land is as the garden of Eden</u>* (This is war on American soil, China and Russia are coming the take their garden of Eden. This invasion will last six months and 70% of Americans will have been destroyed.) *Before them, and behind them a desolate wilderness; yea, and nothing shall escape them. (*This is the invading army) *4The appearance of them is as the appearance of horses; and as horsemen, so shall they run. 5 Like the noise of chariots on the tops of mountains shall they leap,* (scorpions and chariots don't leap over mountains, but helicopters do.) *like the noise of a flame of fire that devoured the stubble, as a strong people set in battle array. 6 Before their face the people shall be much pained: all faces shall gather blackness. 7 They shall run like mighty men; they <u>shall climb the wall like men of war</u>.*

John was not being given the revelation to what he is seeing; therefore, the only thing he could compare to what he was seeing was what he had seen in his time; therefore, a scorpion in his time would be a helicopter today, flying over a mountain shooting rockets out of its tail; chariots would be tanks. These host of demon spirits, loosed to possess this army that will number the two hundred million to eventually invade Israel.) *and they shall march everyone on his ways, and they shall not break their ranks:* John, here the Prophet, is describing an end time attack vessel, the only thing he had to compare it with was scorpions and chariot vessels running to war.

The sixth trumpet

This vision describes what will be happening near the end of the tribulation during World War III: Read the chronicle titled: **"The Epic View of WWIII".**

Revelation 9:13-21 (NLT) [13] *Then the sixth angel blew his trumpet, and I heard a voice speaking from the four horns of the gold altar that stands in the presence of God.* [14] *And the voice said to the sixth angel who held the trumpet, "Release the four angels who are bound at the great Euphrates River."* [15] *Then the four angels who had been prepared for this <u>hour and day and month and year</u> were turned loose to kill one-third the people on earth.*

This is World War III taking place. All nations in this area are banding together to become this final war army. [16] *I heard the size of their army,*

470

which was 200 million mounted troops. [17] And in my vision, I saw the horses and the riders sitting on them. The riders wore armor that was fiery red and dark blue and yellow. (Look for these colors to be worn by the invading armies. They are coming to shed blood on a mass level.) The horses had heads like lions, and fire and smoke and burning sulfur billowed from their mouths. (Military armored attack tanks.) [18] One-third the people on earth were killed by these three plagues by the fire and smoke and burning sulfur that came from the mouths of the horses. [19] Their power was in their mouths and in their tails. (Apache helicopters and tanks) For their tails had heads like snakes, with the power to injure people. [20] But the people who did not die in these plagues still refused to repent of their evil deeds and turn to God. They continued to worship demons and idols made of gold, silver, bronze, stone, and wood— idols that can neither see nor hear nor walk! [21] And they did not repent of their murders or their witchcraft or their sexual immorality or their thefts. They still think they are going to rebound out of this chaos.

Chapter Ten

Revelation 10:1-11 (NLT) [1] Then I saw another mighty angel coming down from heaven, surrounded by a cloud, with a rainbow over his head. His face shone like the sun, and his feet were like pillars of fire. [2] And in his hand, was a small scroll that had been opened. He stood with his right foot on the sea and his left foot on the land. [3] And he gave a great shout like the roar of a lion. And when he shouted, the seven thunders answered. This is the mystery that will be withheld from mankind. Now we will see what Daniel & John was told not to write that was sealed in the seven thunders. [4] *"When the seven thunders spoke, I was about to write. But I heard a voice from heaven saying, "Keep secret what the seven thunders said, and do not write it down."* This revelation was so horrible when I revealed it the first time in the chronicle **"Through the Eyes of the Prophets"**, the controversial nature of this revelation caused some to depart from me because these sayings were too hard. They couldn't believe God would let something like that happen to people. I did not want to write it again. These are the things Daniel and John were told not to write at the time they saw the vision.

(Compare with KJV)

Jeremiah 19:9 (NLT) 9 I will see to it that your enemies lay siege to the city until all the food is gone. Then those trapped inside will eat

their own sons and daughters and friends. They will be driven to utter despair. *Matthew 24:19 (KJV)" 19 And woe unto them that are with child, and to them that give suck in those days!* Deuteronomy 28:57 (NLT) ⁵⁷ She will hide from them the afterbirth and the new baby she has borne, so that she herself can secretly eat them. She will have nothing else to eat during the siege and terrible distress that your enemy will inflict on all your towns. Ezekiel 5:10 (NLT) ¹⁰ Parents will eat their own children, and children will eat their parents. I will punish you and scatter to the winds the <u>few who survive.</u> This is Israel's punishment for her sins against God, now have come upon us as the nation this covenant was given too, as gentiles, we too have departed from God and now is about to experience the same judgment.

Deuteronomy 28:53-56 (NLT) ⁵³ "The siege and terrible distress of the enemy's attack will be so severe that you will eat the flesh of your own sons and daughters, whom the Lord your God has given you. ⁵⁴ The most tenderhearted man among you will have no compassion for his own brother, his beloved wife, and his surviving children. Deuteronomy 28:55-58 (NLT) ⁵⁵ He will refuse to share with them the flesh he is devouring—the flesh of one of his own children—because he has nothing else to eat during the siege and terrible distress that your enemy will inflict on all your towns. ⁵⁶ The most tender and delicate woman among you—so delicate she would not so much as touch the ground with her foot—will be selfish toward the husband she loves and toward her own son or daughter. ⁵⁷ She will hide from them the afterbirth and the new baby she has borne, so that she herself can secretly eat them. She will have nothing else to eat during the siege and terrible distress that your enemy will inflict on all your towns. ⁵⁸ "If you refuse to obey all the words of instruction that are written in this book, and if you do not fear the glorious and awesome name of the Lord your God," Micah 3:3 (KJV) ³ *Who also eat the flesh of my people, and flay their skin from off them; and they break their bones, and chop them in pieces, as for the pot, and as flesh within the caldron.* <u>Micah 3:3 (NLT)</u> Yes, <u>you eat my people's flesh,</u> strip off their skin, and break their bones. You chop them up like meat for the cooking pot.

Christians being punished for their disobedience will become food for the worldly. This revelation was not to be given until the end of the last

472

generation that would experience the tribulation. Now you know why John was told not to write it down. If you are a lukewarm Christian and not being held up in prayer by someone who loves you more than you love God, this is your fate.

Rev.10:5-11(KJV) [5] *Then the angel I saw standing on the sea and on the land raised his right hand toward heaven.* [6] *He swore an oath in the name of the one who lives forever and ever, who created the heavens and everything in them, the earth and everything in it, and the sea and everything in it. He said, "There will be no more delay. This statement represents the fullness of time of man has come.* [7] **When** (at this time) *the seventh angel blows his trumpet, God's mysterious plan will be fulfilled.* (This mystery of when the rapture will take place will be revealed in coming chapters.) *It will happen just as he announced it to his servants the prophets."* [8] *Then the voice from heaven spoke to me again: "Go and take the open scroll from the hand of the angel who is standing on the sea and on the land."* [9] *So I went to the angel and told him to give me the small scroll. "Yes, take it and eat it," he said. "It will be sweet as honey in your mouth, but it will turn sour in your stomach!"* [10] *So I took the small scroll from the hand of the angel, and I ate it! It was sweet in my mouth, but when I swallowed it, it turned sour in my stomach.* The scroll of the seven thunders was given to John to digest in the spirit to be revealed through another at the end of the last generation. [11] *Then I was told, "You must prophesy again about many peoples, nations, languages, and kings."* This represents the spirit of prophecy will continue until the time of the end.

Chapter Eleven

Revelation 11:1-17 (NLT) [1] **Then I was given a measuring stick, and I was told, "Go and measure the Temple of God and the altar and count the number of worshipers.** [2] **But do not measure the outer courtyard, for it has been turned over to the nations.** (The times of the Gentiles will be the dispensation of Christ until he returns for his bride in the outer court to rapture her at the right time in tribulation.) **They will trample the holy city for 42 months.** [3] **And I will give power to my two witnesses, and they will be clothed in burlap and will prophesy during those 1,260 days."** [4] **These two prophets are the two olive trees and the two lamp stands that stand before the Lord of all the earth.** [5] **If anyone tries to harm them, fire flashes from their mouths and consumes their enemies. This is**

how anyone who tries to harm them must die. [6] They have power to shut the sky so that no rain will fall for as long as they prophesy. And they have the power to turn the rivers and oceans into blood, and to strike the earth with every kind of plague as often as they wish. [7] When they complete their testimony, the beast that comes up out of the bottomless pit will declare war against them, and he will conquer them and kill them. (What these two witnesses will be doing will be manifested in the spirit during the first half of the tribulation in the elected saints that will reap havoc on the people in the world as Moses did, calling down plaques on earth and shaking the heavens before they show up in Jerusalem on the streets literally to fulfill the prophecies they were told to look for.) [8] And their bodies will lie in the main street of Jerusalem, the city that is figuratively called "Sodom" and "Egypt, the city where their Lord was crucified. Sodom, represents America the Gentiles and Egypt, represents His people turning back to the world. Hold on to your hats, there are many saints who were in churches that were held captive under false doctrine. God knew their hearts and gave them mercy through the prayers of the righteous. Paradise was left vacant to receive the "blessed merciful that will obtain mercy".

These are they who die in wars fighting for the liberty of others in just causes, laid down their lives for the greater good, called out to God in their final hour. *James 4:14 (KJV)* [14] *Whereas ye know not what shall be on the morrow. For what is your life? It is even a vapour, that appeareth for a little time, and then vanisheth away.* They are as the pennant thief who are convicted before death and cry out to the lord for mercy. They will receive mercy as to hear the real gospel and receive Christ to take away their sins in the flesh and be forgiven before they can be translated just as the penitent thief. This is the work repeated in the two witnesses when they preach to the "Spirits in Prison" as Christ did during the three days in the underworld.

Many of the soldiers in the wars fault in this country and Israel gave their lives under these circumstances by obeying the government under a false sign, sent these innocent young men to their death. Their blood cries out to God against this nation for this injustice. The two witnesses in the spirit of Christ will do that work in the underworld during this period. They are in the underworld to "preach to these spirits in prison" as did

Christ to the saints of old, but now to the merciful in Paradise that will obtain mercy and then resurrected when they are raised. **Rev. 14:15-16.**

We see the same pattern here as when Christ was in the underworld to **preach to the spirits in prison;** (Ecclesiastes 1:9) all that died under the old covenant had to be introduced to Christ and receive him in paradise as the sacrifice for their sins of omission before they could be translated into the third heaven. Satan held them by having sins of omission. They were righteous by the law, but their sins remained in their flesh at death until Jesus became the sacrifice for their sins.

Now, the two witnesses will do the same to those innocent souls who were sincere in heart and victims as described above who were sacrificed innocently in wars and victims of injustices but cried out to God before their death for mercy. This is mercy for those during the times of a famine of the word in the earth during the great fall-away. The blood of many innocent souls is on churches of this nation. Only God knows who they all are. If you find this hard to receive, just table it. This was one of my Enoch moments. Believe me; I know what it is like to be rejected for breaking with the traditions of seminary trained men. This revelation has cut to the heart of many believers I shared it with. I am currently standing the gap for them as children of disobedience. **(Eccl. 1:9) 9** <u>**And for three and a half days**</u>**, all peoples, tribes, languages, and nations will stare at their bodies. No one will be allowed to bury them.** [10] **All the people who belong to this world will gloat over them and give presents to each other to celebrate the death of the two prophets who had tormented them.** [11] **But after three and a half days, God breathed life into them, and they stood up! Terror struck all who were staring at them.**

I know this passage will be quite controversial, considering all the books that have been written about Revelation and the two witnesses. They represent the glorified elects that were represented in the returned in the spirit of Moses and Elijah that will be martyred for the glory of God that cut short the time of their tribulation to save the souls in Christ. This is the **translation** or **rapture** that the entire world will see <u>just before the tribulation comes to an end</u>. This is time cut short to save the saints.

God is preparing to remove his people at his appointed time. *(Ezekiel 37:13 (KJV) "13 And ye shall know that I am the LORD, when I have opened your graves, O my people, and brought you up out of your graves,")* Rev. continued **(NLT) then a loud voice from heaven called to the two prophets, "<u>Come up here!</u>" And they rose to heaven in a cloud as their enemies watched.** (This is the call that will affect the resurrection of the saints, **at the end not before.** You will not be driving cars or riding on plains as movies depict. Only the military will have vehicles at the time.) [13] **At the same time there was a terrible earthquake that destroyed a tenth of the city. Seven thousand people died in that earthquake, and everyone else was terrified and gave glory to the God of heaven.**

When Jesus died on the cross, there was an eclipse and a great earthquake; this same natural phenomenon will happen at the resurrection of the saints that will arrest the attention of the world. [14] **The second terror is past, but look, the third terror is coming quickly."**

The seventh trumpet

<u>**This is the point in time that is reserved for the final purification before translation; the hour that no man knows.**</u>

At this point, I would like to insert the mystery of the blood moons; they are the sign that does not date events. That's why those that go by these observations will always use their imagination and predict false prophecies that does not come true. I have found those that are mixing law with grace are reading Jewish signs that are natural. Under the new covenant all things are spiritual in discerning the times. *Rev. 11:15-17(KJV)* [15] *Then the seventh angel blew his trumpet, and there were loud voices shouting in heaven: "The world has now become the Kingdom of our Lord and of his Christ, and he will reign forever and ever."* [16] *The twenty-four elders sitting on their thrones before God fell with their faces to the ground and worshiped him.* [17] *And they said, "We give thanks to you, Lord God, the Almighty, the one who is and who always was, for now you have assumed your great power and have begun to reign.* This is the period that the two witnesses will rise and be translated at God's appointed time as described in the coming chapter of Rev. 14:15-16; this is describing what's leading up to that event is Rev.11:11.

Rev. 11:18-19(JKV) 18And the nations were angry, and thy wrath is come, and the time of the dead, that they should be judged, and that thou shouldest give reward unto thy servants the prophets, and to the saints, and them that fear thy name, small and great; and shouldest destroy them which destroy the earth. 19 And the temple of God was opened in heaven, and there was seen in his temple the ark of his testament: and there were lightning's, and voices, and thundering, and an earthquake, and great hail."

The destruction of the Modern Mystery Babylon, (**America**) will come by never seen natural disasters on Earth before first. This is the footman stage of Revelation; the horseman state will come when the crash of the economy come in a stock dive that will not rebound. These chronicles are from completed notes of revelations that have been expanded to reflect the final third layer of truth the Lord has been sharing with me since 2002 to this present day. God has revealed to me that he is steal translating his word to those with ears to hear, although we are few, I am not the only one.

Most King James only bible readers in traditional denominational teachings are not open to being completely delivered by limiting their knowledge of truth. That's why we must be born from above by keeping our minds on heavenly knowledge to be open to his ways as to what he uses to speak through. Most of our experiences in traditional assemblies are not open to this level of truth that lets the Holy Spirit do the teaching that completely delivers you and sets you free to see God in all things as the master of the circumstances of this life. There is no way I could withstand what has been revealed to me if he had not contained me in the process of my teaching and training. The contexts of the previous chapters are describing the events before the translation takes place, leading up to the rapture. John did not see these things in the order of their occurrences. This is now, the work of the Holy Spirit to put this puzzle together.

Revelation 12:1-8 (NLT) **1 Then I witnessed in heaven an event of great significance. I saw a woman clothed with the sun, with the moon beneath her feet, and a crown of twelve stars on her head. 2 She was pregnant, and she cried out because of her labor pains and the agony of giving birth. 3 Then I witnessed in heaven another significant event. I saw a large red dragon with seven heads and ten horns, with seven crowns on his heads.** (The Jesuits army of false teachers sit in their headquarters on the top of seven hills in Rome had to conquer all three major religions and bring them together as one. Rome is situated on seven hills. **4 His tail swept away one-third of the stars in the sky, and he threw them to the**

earth. He stood in front of the woman as she was about to give birth, ready to devour her baby as soon as it was born.

When Satan rebelled, he took a third of the angel in rebellion with him and they are now preparing to come against the saints in the Earth in the fullness of their demonic power when he is cast out. The woe now, there are not enough bodies to hold these demon spirits, many with the mark will contain legions of spirits, that's why they will be the **"walking dead"** ... [5] **She gave birth to a son who was to rule all nations with an iron rod. And her child was snatched away from the dragon and was caught up to God and to his throne.** This is the type and shadow of the church in pain and travail awaiting translation in the in the spirit in the second half of the tribulation; it is the spiritual version of Joseph and Mary's flight from Herod' decree by escaping to Egypt to save the **child Jesus**. God will have safe havens to protect them until that time. Satan is trying to prevent this but is powerless to do so because God's sovereignty is at work here. [6] **And the woman fled into the wilderness, where God had prepared a place to care for her for 1,260 days.** The papacy reign that was called the dark ages was will be the number of days the church will do battle with Satan aided by the spirit of the two witnesses and gravely wound him. [7] **Then there was war in heaven. Michael and his angels fought against the dragon and his angels.** [8] **And the dragon lost the battle, and he and his angels were forced out of heaven.** This war in the spirit world will be manifested in the natural in peoples of all nations as the course of events described in the previous chapters; Satan being cast out of heaven into the Earth. The parallels are the events of the **seals** the **trumpets** and the **first thunder**. The **seals** are the beginning of sorrows, while the **trumpets** and the **thunders** are the result of God's wrath being carried out by Satan and the **vials** will bring the destruction of mankind. Remember, God oversees all things using Satan to carry out what the prophets have foretold in time past.

Rev. 12:9 "The huge serpent was thrown down. That ancient snake, named Devil and Satan, <u>the deceiver of the whole world</u>, was thrown down to earth. Its angels were thrown down with it." The bottomless pit contained the demons or disembodied spirits that was ruled by these fallen angelic principalities now in the earth being loosed to torment the wicked on the earth. <u>**Luke 8:31**</u> **"The demons begged Jesus not to order**

them to go into the bottomless pit." Some of these were too wicked to be allowed to roam on the Earth.

These came out the pit in legions to possess a person's body. All who receive the mark will be possessed by these legions of demons and cursed for eternity; that's when they will be returned to the pit with their father, the devil, by way of the lake of fire. When those marked see no hope of being saved, they will curse God in their torment. That's why those Jesus met in the man at Gadara, did not want to be sent back to hell but could wander as disembodied spirits when they ask Jesus to go into the swine. These are the suicide demons that will return and commit mass suicides in these last days.

Some are seeking their homes from whence they were cast out, waiting for an opportunity to return. That's why Jesus gave us this picture in ... *Matthew 12:43-44 (KJV) When the unclean spirit is gone out of a man, he walketh through dry places, seeking rest, and findeth none. 44 Then he saith, I will return into my house from whence I came out; and when he is come, he findeth it empty, swept, and garnished."*

All who reject God under these false teachings will be possessed by these spirits and be condemned to spend eternity in hell with them for giving place to these seducing spirits that led them down the broad road to destruction and eternal separation. They will curse God for condemning them when they are possessed with these demons.

Matthew 12:45 (KJV) <u>Then goeth he, and taketh with himself seven other spirits more wicked than himself, and they enter in and dwell there: and the last state of that man is worse than the first</u>. Even so shall it be also unto this wicked generation. This is where many will lose their minds and be as Zombies and others will curse God in their torment. They will also cause men to result to cannibalism to survive.

Revelation 12:10-13 (NLT) "[10] Then I heard a loud voice shouting across the heavens, "It has come at last— salvation and power and the Kingdom of our God, and the authority of his Christ. For the accuser of our brothers and sisters has been thrown down to earth— the one who accuses them before our God day and night."

These chapters leading up to the 14ᵗʰ are describing what's going on

between these times. God used plagues in Pharaoh's time. Now, God will allow Satan to use them in a greater more destructive way with double the punishment. We will **suffer double judgment** in the final closing days of tribulation. This is the end of man's rule of the earth, the sixth millennium. God will allow Satan to release these more powerful demonic spirits to destroy those given over to him as he sees fit, then God will bring him down. [11] **And they have defeated him by the blood of the Lamb and by their testimony. And they did not love their lives so much that they were afraid to die. 12 Be glad for this reason, heavens and those who live in them. How horrible it is for the earth and the sea because the Devil has come down to them with fierce anger, knowing that he has little time left.**[13] **When the dragon realized that he had been thrown down to the earth, he pursued the woman who had given birth to** the male child. The fullness of Christ going against the devil in the final days of the tribulation to glorify his bride by putting all these principalities under her feet as his bride whose victory will be glorified as coming forth without spot or wrinkle to be presented to Christ. This is His gift from the Father that justified His death burial and resurrection.

Revelation 12:14-17 (NLT) [14] **But she was given two wings like those of a great eagle, so she could fly to the place prepared for her in the wilderness. There she would be cared for and protected from the dragon for a time, times, and half a time.** [15] **Then the dragon tried to drown the woman with a flood of water that flowed from his mouth.** [16] **But the earth helped her by opening its mouth and swallowing the river that gushed out from the mouth of the dragon.** [17] **And the dragon was angry at the woman and declared war against the rest of her children—all who keep God's commandments and maintain their testimony for Jesus.**

All the above events are taking place during the confrontation with good and evil for the last time that will put Satan and his host of demons under the church's feet. This will be that deadly wound that the pre-antichrist man of sin will suffer at the hand of the church in tribulation and when Satan is cast down and enter him … he will rise in him and all will wonder at this marvel and be further deceived. If God's mind is not in you, you will be deceived; that's what it means to have this unction at that time.

Chapter 13:1-2, this scene takes place in the transition of world powers completing the first half of tribulation. **Rev. 13:1-2 "And I stood upon**

the sand of the sea, and saw a beast rise up out of the sea, having <u>seven heads</u> and <u>ten horns.</u>;" representing the seat of the New World Government and Religion. Rome is situated on seven hills. The peace pact designed to bring order out of chaos will be a mutual calm of nations for the good of preserving mankind. This will set the stage for a reorganization that will unite all nations and religions for the good of all; **"NOVUS ORDO SECLORUM"** (N.W.O.) There will be seven banking institutions, representing the ten divisions as the toes of Daniel interpretation of that stature, (The Beast System) will control the world's financial transactions; once this is in place, it will become a cashless society. All this will happen amazingly fast as God is shortening the time.

Rome will be their new headquarters after the destruction of America and be split into ten regional governments under one world ruler. This will be the new revived Roman Empire.) **2And the beast which I saw was like unto a <u>leopard</u>, and his feet were as the feet of a <u>bear</u>, and his mouth as the mouth of a <u>lion</u>: and the dragon gave him his power, and his seat, and great authority."** In our time these cymbals represent Russia (the **bear**), China (the **Leopard**) and America (the **lion**).

The chaos that will come about to usher in the New World Order is where the world will see this corporate body of leaders rise with the solution to all the world's problems. This is the spirit of the Antichrist released in the fullness of his power in the earth. Contrary to what we have been told, the man of sin is a principality ruling a body of people. Satan is the man of sin manifested in this principality.

Remember, the reason we did not know these things is because we have been blinded by keeping our carnal Christian traditions, when the Jesuits introduced logical theology where men had to go to seminary to be qualified as pastors using what they taught us to become, popes in the pulpits. I have no boast, if God had not chosen to use me in this way; I would be as deceived as those who reject these words. This is the time God has given these principalities the power as having their minds illuminated, **(Illuminati's)** possessed with a strand of fallen angel DNA that will show these megalomania personalities that will allow Satan to use them to gain control of the world.

This is the course of events that's happening during the breaking of the

seals and the sounding of the **trumpets.** The **thunders** will happen when the **bear** and the **leopard** take over the **lion.** Great Britain and America are mother and daughter, **(Ezekiel 16:44)** when they are bought down economically; this beast system represented the rise of the eighth kingdom which is of the seventh will precede the wrath of God.

Rev. 13:3-4 (KJV) "And I saw one of his heads as it were wounded to death; and his deadly wound was healed: and all the world wondered after the beast. ⁴And they worshipped the dragon which gave power unto the beast: and they worshipped the beast, saying, who is like unto the beast? who is able to make war with him?" Great Britain was crippled during World War II and revived through the beast system, saved by the daughter's help, out of which came the establishment of the United Nations in America to bring all nations under one head with an agenda to eventually rule the world. This is the first stage of the rise.

Rev. 13:5-6(KJV) "And there was given unto him a mouth speaking great things and blasphemies; and power was given unto him to continue forty and two-months. (We at this point are entering the second half of the tribulation). *⁶And he opened his mouth in blasphemy against God, to blaspheme his name, and his tabernacle, and them that dwell in heaven."* (Satan will exercise worldwide supremacy fulfilling Daniel's prophecy in) *... Daniel 7:25 "And he shall speak great words against the most High and shall wear out the saints of the most High, and think to change times and laws: and they shall be given into his hand until a time and times and the dividing of time."* **(3½ years)** The last president elected by the people will speak these words against the God and seal our fate as a nation.

Those whose name are written in the lamb's book of life are sealed; those not chosen, have already been marked with Satan's number of men. Even among confessing lukewarm Christians, GOD KNOWS WHO HE HAS CHOSEN FOR HIS GLORY. The sealing takes place, in the spirit, and at the same time the Antichrist body is being sealed in their foreheads in the spirit with Satan's number which is the natural fallen state **666** is man's number. Now to explain this number further, in the natural order, the **first six** is the days of creation, the **second six** is the day of man, the **third six** is the time he will be given in the natural to subdue the Earth; six thousand years. He, in his fallen state is considered the beast man; the children of the devil, identified with this number as the natural order in his fallen state, **666. (2 Peter 2:12, John 8:44)** God's people will know each other. This mystery gives us insight into the religious organization that will introduce the man of sin.

On the Popes Crown are these Roman inscriptions.

"VICARIUS – FELII - DEI"

The numerology interpretation is as follows ...

V=5, I=1, C=100, A=0, R=0, I=1, O=0, U=5, S=0 Total = 112

F=0, I=1, L=50, L=1, L=1 total =53

D=500, E=0, I=1 Total =501

The grand total is 666

This represents the religious organization that will bring the antichrist to the national forefront of acceptance. The Antichrist body, the false church, will be united against the true church as were in the days of Christ in the Sanhedrin. The body of the Sadducees and Pharisees united against Him. These were the Antichrist John said were already in the world. They represented the Antichrist body of his time on earth. That's why John said in **1 John 2:18** that he was already here manifested in these two bodies in his day. Keep and eye on Trumps' son-in-law, Jerad Christner. He owns a high finance building in New York with the numbers **"666."** He negotiated the peace that recognized in our time Jerusalem as their capital and influenced Trump, operating in the spirit of King Cyrus of old to tell them to begin preparations to rebuild the Jerusalem temple.

Revelation 13:7-9 (NLT) [7] **And the beast was allowed to wage war against God's holy people and to conquer them. And he was given authority to rule over every tribe and people and language and nation.** [8] **And all the people who belong to this world worshiped the beast. They are the ones whose names were not written in the Book of Life before the world was made—the Book that belongs to the Lamb who was slaughtered.** [9] **Anyone with ears to hear should listen and understand.**

When God the Holy Ghost speaks, those whose hearts and minds have been prepared will be drawn by the Holy Spirit will have ears to hear. The fact that no one can come to the Lord except the spirit of God draws him **(John 6:44)** is the mystery of how God has chosen His number throughout times, ages, dispensations and in each generation which will comprise the heavenly host of saints is the mystery of this number that no man can number. That is why we are warned, the day we hear the voice of God tugging at our heart to make your calling and election sure. That word will be a witness against us, and some might not be given a second chance.

Rev. 13:10(KJV) "He that leadeth into captivity shall go into captivity: he that killeth with the sword must be killed with the sword. Here is the patience and the faith of the saints." Pastors of the flock, as blind guides who would not continue in the apostle's doctrine, will cause many souls to be lost if they do not repent when God visited them through His prophets, they will be given over into captivity to the devil as their father to suffer his fate in the lake of fire. *(2 Thes. 2:11 And for this cause God shall send them strong delusion, that they should believe a lie:" Romans 2:5 "But after thy hardness and impenitent heart treasurest up unto thyself wrath against the day of wrath and revelation of the righteous judgment of God;")*

Those who have been rejected by God as pastors will be evident by their Antichrist nature marked to be a child of the devil. They will become your persecutors as the Pharisees and Sadducees did to Jesus, so they will do to you. *Rev.13:11-15(KJV) "And I beheld another beast coming up out of the earth; and he had two horns like a lamb, and he spake as a dragon. 12 And he exerciseth all the power of the first beast before him, and causeth the earth and them which dwell therein to worship the first beast, whose deadly wound was healed .* Satan will now exercise great powers in the earth having released the spirit of the false prophet to come full circle in a new world religion which will captivate and persuade all to follow this new image of worship he has created.

This image will be likened to that in … **Daniel 3:15 (NLT) [15] I will give you one more chance to bow down and worship the statue I have made when you hear the sound of the musical instruments. But if you refuse, you will be thrown immediately into the blazing furnace. And then what god will be able to rescue you from my power?"** This beast image will be introduced in a new forbidden technology. Read the chronicle **"The mystery of the mark of the beast"** All who will not take the mark will be killed. *(KJV) 13 And he doeth great wonders, so that he maketh fire come* *down from heaven on the earth in the sight of men, [14] And deceiveth them that dwell on the earth by the means of those miracles which he had power to do in the sight of the beast; saying to them that dwell on the earth, that they should make an image to the beast, which had the wound by a sword, and did live. [15] And he had power to give life unto the image of the beast,"* This new technology will have the ability to speak and control human minds. The internet is the beast that has been used to set the stage for the greatest illusions that will be the hall mark of this technology. When Steve Jobs introduce his smart i-phone, he gave the power to the beast ... *that the image of the beast should both speak,* (she is an advance AI form of **Seri** on your smart phone.) *and cause that as many as would not worship the image of the beast should be killed.* New technologies, not introduced to the world, will set the world up for these illusions on a grand scale. The internet smart phone, **(the talking beast)** will be the means to implement the test for the mark of the beast.

The reason, you will have already been marked in the spirit with-out knowing it for rejecting God. **That is! The spirit of delusion**. This technology will be used to dumb down the world's population by control of the media. When all are captivated by this technology, Steve Jobs knowledge from his strand of Nephilim DNA will introduce a forbidden technology so advance, it will exercise mind control through an app that will be tested through a revamp version of the Pokémon game. This app carries a code that is unique as your fingerprint, the wavelength to your brain. When opened, will bypass your conscious and connect to your brain's subconscious control center. When a person is being hypnotized, this is the area of the brain that's controlled by outside commands. Those who have been seduced through the introduction of video games will be the most immediate to respond, when they open this app.

What you saw them do by congregating in public places and designated meeting areas converging in groups, is proof of how effective this tool will be to mind control. This is how you will receive the mark without your knowing through a post hypnotic app on your i-phone. This is that grand delusion that will facilitate the greatest illusions of them all; Satan coming through the airways as the **"prince of the power of the air."** Through this media as a spirit being will now control the world through fear. What we fail to see under grace and truth, all things are spiritually discerned. The more you are distracted by this world, the less likely you are to receive revelation of what's going on around you in the circumstances of your life.

Revelational observations

False teachings over generations will have you thinking you are right, when there is no rapture as you were told, fear will cause you to take the mark as a deceived religious child of the devil. New technologies that have not been introduced to the world will enable them to produce great lying signs and holographic wonders in the heavenlies that will cause all to marvel at this beastly technology. Waves of seducing spirits will always precede to set the world up for such delusions. Strange sighting of UFO like events, great illusions will appear in the sky. Those chem-trails are not just smoke from the jet engines. One reason evil men are waxing worse; the skies are heavily charged with micro nanite energy waves that is affecting our ability to control our action by these negatively charged waves implanted with positive micro–Nano technology can affect our brain functions as in a 5G wavelength. They are what can link your brain's **matrix** to respond to these suggestions. That's why a 4G & 5G network is needed. This is the forbidden technology that's contributing to the end of another time continuum as in the days of Noah.

This is the forbidden knowledge zone that caused the flood. The internet has been the first wave to link your mind to be controlled by these implanted waves, link to your brain functions that have caused us all to wonder after this beast created by this technology to dumb down the world to bring us under control. This deep cover black opt agency used mad scientist with no regard for human life to de-code the human gene DNA that will give man the ability to recreate himself and gifted techno genius Geeks to create and operate technologies like those in the Netflix series **"Persons of Interest"** is a perfect picture of this shadow organization with this technology that is contributing to this end of man's state on Earth. The new i-phone ten has facial recognition technology that requires your facial picture to activate it; the profile is then sent to a national database for future use by the government. Their activities as black opts agencies are hidden even from current sitting presidents.

The general population, under AI control is where the internet technology was introduced to control your mind by destroying the fruit of patience and taking over your thoughts. In other words, your mind has been hacked. This instant gratification will contribute to violet confrontations when provoked. This is the effect it will have on some people's brain chemistry; as you see, all are now wondering after this beast; the internet. Satan, as the **"prince of the power of the air,"** arrived in the spirit through this technology which is now the beast in a spiritual form in these last days. It was invented in the mother country but the technology to advance it came from America, the **modern-day mystery Babylon** that solved the world's communication problem that led to mind control.

I know this information is shocking as in the manner it was revealed to me; that's why I could not release this version until now. The evidence is how we have become so dependent on these techno toys for our stability. This technology in the hands of our enemies will be used to destroy us. Just as we have techno geeks to wright these algorisms that operate this technology; you also have these geeks to hack them. This is the new cyber warfare that can take down a nation just by tapping a few keys on a computer. The Russians have mastered the use of this cyber technology they stole from us through spies planted in our government. The next president, put in office by another election default, is where it will become a reality by the action of the people around him.

Social media:

Without your knowing, all those posting of your personal information on social media of your life will be the means of your own self-imposed bondage. These are signs, you are already seduced by this beast that is now evidenced by your action to post such details about yourself. This is the effect it had upon you that took over your mind that caused you to post such details as things we see over this beast that you have given place in your mind. This tool for me has been the way God showed me how the enemy has used this mass seduction of 98 percent among confessing Christians through this electronic church media. What was meant for good, during religious divisions, will be the means that will contribute to this mass confusion.

Revelation Continued ...

Revelation 13:16-18 (NLT) [16] **He required everyone—small and great, rich and poor, free and slave—to be given a mark on the right hand or on the forehead.** [17] **And no one could buy or sell anything without that mark,**

which was either the name of the beast or the number representing his name. [18] Wisdom is needed here. Let the one with understanding solve the meaning of the number of the beast, for it is the number of a man. **His number is 666.** This mystery was revealed earlier of the three sixes.

Chapter 14:1-2 (KJV) "And I looked, and, lo, a Lamb stood on the mount Sion, and with him an hundred forty and four thousand, having <u>his Father's name written in their foreheads</u>. 2And I heard a voice from heaven, as the voice of many waters, and as the voice of a great thunder: and I heard the voice of harpers harping with their harps:"

Satan does everything like God because he knows nothing new. Just as God sealed all the saints in their foreheads, which is seen in heaven, evident on the 144,000 and the numberless multitude, all that were condemned are sealed at the same time in Satan's body with the number that represents the natural order of life that he reduced man to **666,** representing his natural condemned state, is the number of the man of sin.

This is a spiritual mark on your forehead for all the demons to identify who they have the authority to possess you as the devil's children. Those saints in Christ will have a special sign in the spirit on their foreheads that represents their defeat as the image of Christ. They have the true testimony of Christ and will be with the twelve tribes of Israel chosen by God before the foundation of the world to bare the true testimony of Jesus Christ.

Rev. 14:3-5(KJV) "And they sung as it were a new song before the throne, and before the four beasts, and the elders: and no man could learn that song but the <u>hundred and forty and four thousand, which were redeemed from the earth.</u> 4These are they which were <u>not defiled with women; for they are virgins.</u> These are they which follow the Lamb whithersoever he goeth. These were <u>redeemed from among men</u>, being the <u>first fruits</u> unto God and to the Lamb." 5 "And in their mouth was found no guile: for they are without fault before the throne of God." Rev. 5:9 "And they sung a new song, saying, Thou art worthy to take the book, and to open the seals thereof: for thou wast slain, and hast <u>redeemed us to God by thy blood out of every kindred, and tongue, and people, and nation;"</u> Ephes. 5:27(KJV) "That he might present it to himself a glorious church, not having spot, or wrinkle, or any such thing; but that it should be holy and without blemish." This is the heritage of the saints rewarded.

Rev. 14:6-7 "And I saw another angel fly in the midst of heaven, having the everlasting gospel to preach unto them that dwell on the earth, and to every nation, and kindred, and tongue, and people, 7Saying with a loud voice, Fear God, and give glory to him; for the hour of his judgment is come: and worship him that made heaven, and earth, and the sea, and the fountains of waters. (<u>Matthew 24:14</u> "And this gospel of the kingdom shall be preached in all the world for a witness unto all nations; and then shall the end come."

All previous revelations lead up to the translation of the saints. Here's wisdom, the two witnesses' power in the true church body will hold back the judgment until this gospel has been declared to every soul on the face of the Earth and in the Earth as held captive in the underworld that some of you might find difficult to believe; as I said, these were my Enoch moments. Then, man's time is complete in the Earth for the first translation of the New Testament saints.

Rev. 14:8-13 (KJV) "And there followed another angel, saying, Babylon is fallen, is fallen, that great city, because she made all nations drink of the wine of the wrath of her fornication. 9 And the third angel followed them, saying with a loud voice, If any man worship the beast and his image, and receive his mark in his forehead, or in his hand, 10The same shall drink of the wine of the wrath of God, which is poured out without mixture into the cup of his indignation; and he shall be tormented with <u>fire and brimstone</u> in the presence of the holy angels, and in the presence of the Lamb: (All the people left in America will be incinerated when the meteorite showers hit this country as the Sodomy curse is fulfilled.) 11And the smoke of their torment ascendeth up for ever and ever: and they have no rest day nor night, who worship the beast and his image, and whosoever receiveth the mark of his name.12Here is the patience of the saints: here are they that keep the commandments of God, and the faith of Jesus. [13] And I heard a voice from heaven saying unto me, Write, blessed are the dead which die in the Lord from henceforth: Yea, saith the Spirit that they may rest from their labours; and their works do follow them.

Some pastors and leaders were anointed to carry a word in their ministry on Earth and their works will still bless men after they are gone in the flesh. America the modern Babylon has been given over to her enemies for destruction and God is now preparing to remove the church in tribulation which was aided by the spirit of the two witnesses. Israel's visitation in the second half of the tribulation will be a literal sign to them when they show up demonstrating great power over the Antichrist until they are martyred. The spirit of Moses will bring down the beast governments, the spirit of Elijah will expose the false prophets in the earth.

What has transpired in this nation as well as others but primarily, America has undergone the brunt of God's judgment. When the two witnesses have **"preach to the spirits in prison"** in the underworld, the entire world will see this resurrection at the end of the sixth day of man's time on Earth. (Revelation 11:11) *Matthew 24:29 (KJV)* [29] *Immediately after the tribulation of those days shall the sun be darkened, and the moon shall not give her light, and the stars shall fall from heaven, and the powers of the heavens shall be shaken: Revelation 12:1-2 (KJV)* [1] *And there appeared a great wonder in heaven; a woman clothed with the sun, and the moon under her feet, and upon her head a crown of* <u>*twelve stars:*</u> [2] <u>*And she being with child cried, travailing in birth*</u>*, and pained to be delivered.*

The twelve stars are the remnant twelve tribes of Israel; the woman, travailing in birth is the church. They both are waiting to be translated out of great tribulation at the sounding of the **seventh trumpet**. This is where time will be cut short as they are purified in the fires of tribulation. **(Rev. 3:18)** This is the moment God only knows but has given us a sign as for his coming. The sign of the new moon on the Jewish calendar; no one knows until they see it appear … so shall it be at his coming.

Rev. 14:14-15 "Then and I looked, and behold a white cloud, and upon the cloud one sat like unto the Son of man, having on his head a golden crown, and in his hand a sharp sickle. 15And another angel came out of the temple, crying with a loud voice to him that sat on the cloud, <u>*Thrust in thy sickle, and reap: for the time is come for thee to reap; for the harvest of the earth is ripe.*</u>*" 1 Thessalonians 4:16-17 (KJV)* [16] *"For the Lord himself shall descend from heaven with a shout, with the voice of the archangel, 1 Corinthians 15:52 (KJV) "In a moment, in the twinkling of an eye,* <u>*at the last trump:*</u> *for the trumpet shall sound, and the dead shall be raised incorruptible, and we shall be changed." … Ezekiel 37:12 "(KJV)* [12] Therefore prophesy and say unto them, *thus saith the Lord GOD; Behold, O my people, I will open your graves, and cause you to come up* <u>*out of your graves,*</u> *and* <u>*bring you into the land of Israel.*</u>*"* (Israel is the center of the world, the translation of all the saints will take place as the two witnesses rise on the third day as they are received up into the third heaven to begin the judgment of the saints to receive their rewards.) [17] ***Then we which <u>are alive and remain shall be caught up together with them in the clouds</u>, to meet the Lord in the air: and so shall we ever be with the Lord." Luke 17:20 (KJV) And when he was demanded of the Pharisees, when the kingdom of God should come, he answered them and said, the kingdom of God <u>cometh not with observation</u>:*** These are signs in Matthew twenty-four of the times in the end, tells all the elected saints to prepare as wise virgins awaiting their redemption to be **translated** as the glorified saints, the bride triumphant over the devil.

The entire world will witness this great event take place in the sky that will happen at God's appointed time in the second half of the tribulation. God will now hear the intercessory prayers being received for the children of disobedience, the unwise virgins. (**Rev.8:1-4**.) As punishment, they will now be handed over to the beast system these false churches were in when they refused to separate from that are now being handed over to the devil for destruction of the flesh that their souls might be saved. They did not prepare when they were warned and will suffer this fate of the unwise virgins. Paul gave us an insight into this in ... **1 Corinthians 5:5 (NASB77) [5] I have decided to deliver such a one to Satan for the destruction of his flesh, that his spirit may be saved <u>in the day of the Lord Jesus</u>.**

As you see, this is the day of the lord. When this is completed, God sends the second angel to receive the residue of the harvest. These are they that were prayed for above by the saints as described in... ***Rev. 8:1-4 "And when he had opened the seventh seal, there was silence in heaven about the space of half an hour. 2 And I saw the seven angels which stood before God; and to them were given seven trumpets. 3 And another angel came and stood at the altar, having a golden censer; and there was given unto him much incense, that he should offer it with the prayers of all saints upon the golden altar which was before the throne. 4 And the smoke of the incense, which came with the prayers of the saints, ascended up before God out of the angel's hand." 1 Peter 3:12 (KJV) "[12] For the eyes of the Lord are over the righteous, and his ears are open unto their prayers: but the face of the Lord is against them that do evil."***

These saints are now being reaped out of the wine press in great tribulation. This is that cluster. What is happening to them is described in the chronicle **"What will happen during the Tribulation siege"** of those who did not escape in the first sickle. (**Rev.14:15-16 (KJV)** This was only meant to be revealed at the end of the last generation.

Rev. 14:17--20 "And another angel came out from the altar, which had power over fire; and cried with a loud cry to him that had the sharp sickle, saying, thrust in thy sharp sickle, and <u>gather the clusters</u> of the vine of the earth; for her grapes are fully ripe. These are the children of disobedience being received as they were led as sheep to the slaughter, gathered at death in the second sickle in the above verse who suffered the horrors of the **first thunder.** They had to suffer through great tribulation for their disobedience. *19And the angel thrust in his sickle into the earth, and gathered the vine of the earth, and cast it into the great winepress of the wrath of God. 20And the winepress was trodden without the city, and blood came out of the winepress, even unto the horse bridles, by the space of a thousand and six hundred furlongs."* My beloved brothers and sisters, the foolish virgins suffered the **first thunder** for not taking heed to the messengers of God in the first call. I too, have this burden on me for those I love to plead for their souls. **Joel 2:2-3 (NASB77) As the dawn is spread over the mountains, so there is a great and mighty people; There has never been anything like it, nor will there be again after it to the years of many generations.** (This is that time for this prophecy to be fulfilled as stated in the Matthew twenty-four account.) **3 A fire consumes before them, and behind them a flame burns. The land is like the Garden of Eden before them, but a desolate wilderness behind them, and nothing at all escapes them."**

This is the second layer of the above scriptures. At this point, there should be no misunderstanding of this parable of the **wise and foolish virgins.** When the door was shut, what they would suffer could only be experienced not written. These foolish virgins were His children also but did not take heed to warning. Their lives were spared by those who prayed and gave their lives in prayer for them. God foreknew how far the church would fall into false teaching and held this revelation back to be revealed now.

Rev. 15:1-2(KJV) "And I saw another sign in heaven, great and marvellous, seven angels having the seven last plagues; <u>for in them is filled up the wrath of God</u>. 2And I saw as it were a sea of glass mingled with fire: and them that had gotten the victory over the beast, and over his image, and over his mark, and over the number of his name, stand on the sea of glass, having the harps of God." <u>Rev. 7:14</u> "And I said unto him, Sir, thou knowest. And *he said to me, these are they which came out of great tribulation, and have washed their robes, and made them white in the blood of the Lamb."* These are they who suffered the destruction of their flesh, the remnant of God's heritage redeemed out of the winepress as children of disobedience. They are before the throne with the redeemed worshiping God.

Revelation 15:3-8 (NLT) ^3 **And they were singing the song of Moses, the servant of God, and the song of the Lamb: "Great and marvelous are your works, O Lord God, the Almighty. Just and true are your ways, O King of the nations.** ^4 **Who will not fear you, Lord, and glorify your name? For you alone are holy. All nations will come and worship before you, for your righteous deeds have been revealed."** ^5 **Then I looked and saw that the Temple in heaven, God's Tabernacle, was thrown wide open.** ^6 **The seven angels who were holding the seven plagues came out of the Temple. They were clothed in spotless white linen with gold sashes across their chests.** ^7 **Then one of the four living beings handed each of the seven angels a gold bowl** (or vial) **filled with the wrath of God, who lives forever and ever.** ^8 **The Temple was filled with smoke from God's glory and power. No one could enter the Temple until the seven angels had completed pouring out the seven plagues.**

The church is gone. The wrath is now being prepared without mixture. What is about to happen in the Earth is so horrible, it was forbidden to be written until now where-in this is that generation that would experience the wrath of God; if revealed in time past, all would lose hope of being save. This is the other side of God that is revealed by an intimate relationship of his choice as Enoch had with God who told him how He would execute His wrath in the last days. **Jude 1:14-15, Heb.11:5** gives his account; to think that I have been chosen to hear such things as you are now reading is still beyond my comprehension.

Chapter 16:

What is about to happen in the earth, represents God withdrawing His hand and Satan carrying out His wrath that would result in the destruction of the whole Earth if God did not intervene. False teachings caused this mystery to be withheld from the church until this present day. Satan, manifested in the spirit of this advanced technology as the **"prince of the**

power of the air," Michael and his angels have kept him restrained so man in his fallen state can run his course in the Earth.

2 Thessalonians 2:7 (NASB77) For the mystery of lawlessness is already at work; only he who now restrains will do so until he is taken out of the way. The angels that have these demons restrained are loosening these evil demonic spirits to inflict these things in the **final six Thunders** which need not be revealed for it was reserved for the wicked to experience not the saints. These are the turn of events occurring for those who have received the mark of the beast. This mystery is described in **Ezekiel chapter seven** and the book of **Lamentations** is a brief description of the last six thunders the wicked will suffer. Although the reality will be much worst. One of the signs I see before this goes to print is found in *Jeremiah 50:32 (KJV)* [32] *And the proudest shall stumble and fall, and none shall raise him up: and I will kindle a fire in his cities, and it shall devour all round about him.* It is evident that these fires around our cities are signs that we are getting ready to burn. The more God's anger is provoked, the greater the disasters.

Revelation 16:1-2 (NLT) [1] **Then I heard a mighty voice from the Temple say to the seven angels, "Go your ways and pour out on the earth the seven bowls** (or vials) **containing God's wrath."**

The First Vial

[2] **So the first angel left the Temple and poured out his bowl on the earth, and horrible, malignant sores broke out on everyone who had the mark of the beast and who worshiped his statue.**

During World War III, America, destroyed by the invasion of Russia and China. Finally, a nuclear explosion, sickness and diseases are widespread because of the fallout. Grievous sores are being suffered by the wicked; finally, here come the meteors showers that shall cause us to exist no more at all. God caused someone from within to push the M.A.D self-destruct button that will prevent our invading enemies from using this land which now has the curse of Sodom and Gomorrah on it. This is the spirit of Moses witness as before the Egyptians; this time America, in these last days shall receive doubled judgment as in the wrath of God and will exist no more at all.

The Second Vial

Revelation 16:3-4 (NLT) ³ **Then the second angel poured out his bowl on the sea, and it became like the blood of a corpse. And everything in the sea died.** War, Nuclear fallout, and natural disasters have left the nations in perils of great suffering.

The Third Vial

(KJV)⁴ Then the third angel poured out his bowl on the rivers and springs, and they became blood. ⁵And I heard the angel of the waters say, thou art righteous, O Lord, which art, and wast, and shalt be, because thou hast judged thus … ⁶For they have <u>shed the blood of saints and prophets</u>, and thou hast given them blood to drink; for they are worthy. God avenges the saints for their suffering at the hands of evil men for Christ's sake by giving them the same plaque of blood to drink as in Egypt.

Revelation 16:7-21 (NLT) ⁷ **And I heard a voice from the altar, saying, "Yes, O Lord God, the Almighty, your judgments are true and just.**

The Fourth Vial

⁸ **Then the fourth angel poured out his bowl on the sun, causing it to scorch everyone with its fire.** This is the effects of solar flares from the sun hitting the Earth destroying the Ozone layer. ⁹ **Everyone was burned by this blast of heat, and they cursed the name of God, who had control over all these plagues. They did not repent of their sins and turn to God and give him glory.**

This may come as a shock to some of you, these people do not know they are in the tribulation because God sent them a false sign; they think they are going to overcome all this and go on to recover just like in the movie **"2012."** They have literally built arks in places they hope will cause them to survive. They are marked with the spirit of delusion to be sent to their self-destruction. You may notice in these writings; I have watched many movies; God used them to give me a visual account as he was giving the world a vision of its future from Hollywood. I didn't get this through dreams or literal visions, it was all by dictation and I am just the scribe.

I used to wonder why I never had dreams and visions as many others to confirm these revelations, what he did through me was so unique, that is why His way is past finding out. He used the media to give me a pictorial view from these movies that represented how his ways are not predictable until your eyes are open to His ways. The internet is the **"Matrix"** of mind control; the beast that speaks through your smart phone is **Seri** through your phone and **Alexa** in your home. The smart chips are used to tract your every move and conversation through a government agency. Only they have this technology to keep you from knowing what they are doing. Foreign plants in high offices have turned our secrets over to their mother countries. The enemy between nations have turned us against ourselves from within.

The Fifth Vial

(NLT) [10] **Then the fifth angel poured out his bowl on the throne of the beast, and his kingdom was plunged into darkness. His subjects ground their teeth in anguish,** (This is the cloud left by an asteroid hitting the earth.) [11] **and they cursed the God of heaven for their pains and sores. But they did not repent of their evil deeds and turn to God.** Being marked, there is no escape. They will curse God out of hate.

The Sixth Vial

(NLT) [12] **Then the sixth angel poured out his bowl on the great Euphrates River, and it dried up so that the kings from the east could march their armies toward the west without hindrance.** [13] **And I saw three evil spirits that looked like frogs leap from the mouths of the dragon, the beast, and the false prophet.** [14] **They are demonic spirits who work miracles and go out to all the rulers of the world to gather them for battle against the Lord on that great judgment day of God the Almighty.** (God is sending these spirits that will cause all the evil nations to band together for battle in the valley to prepare for Armageddon.) [15] **"Look, I will come as unexpectedly as a thief! Blessed are all who are watching for me, who keep their clothing ready, so they will not have to walk around naked and ashamed."** That' what the church did, they literally walked necked before God without shame. Those that will see all this are prepared to survive the tribulation to repopulate the millennium. **Revelation 16:16 (NLT)** [16] **And the demonic spirits gathered all the rulers and their armies to a place with the Hebrew name Armageddon.**

The Seventh Vial

(NLT) [17] Then the seventh angel poured out his bowl into the air. And a mighty shout came from the throne in the Temple, saying, "It is finished!" [18] Then the thunder crashed and rolled, and lightning flashed. And a great earthquake struck—the worst since people were placed on the earth. (God is rearranging the Geography of the Earth, flattening the high ground for the millennium reign.) [19] The great city of Babylon (America) split into three sections, and the cities of many nations fell into heaps of rubble. This is what God did to the wicked band of Koran in the wilderness, now again in this last segment of the tribulation; America will become a place of no habitation by humankind as a cursed land. It will be no more.

Revelation 18:21 (KJV) "And a mighty angel took up a stone like a great millstone, and cast it into the sea, saying, thus with violence shall that great city Babylon be thrown down, and shall be found no more at all." … So, God remembered all of Babylon's sins, and he made her drink the cup that was filled with the wine of his fierce wrath. (America will be no more) [20] *And every island disappeared, and all the mountains were leveled.* [21] *There was a terrible hailstorm, and hailstones weighing seventy-five pounds fell from the sky onto the people below. They cursed God because of the terrible plague of the hailstorm.* In the beginning, the water came up out of the earth as a fountain; as these mountains crumble by the pounding of these great balls of ice, this will be the ground water that once again will water the earth.

During the millennial reign, the remnant will be able to come to Jerusalem on dry leveled earth. All the natural disasters will put the earth back in the state where man can live for one thousand years. During this time, the Earth will be populated with man and animals, living in harmony together as in Eden with no devil to tempt them... **Isaiah 46:10 (NLT) Only I can tell you the future before it even happens. Everything I plan will come to pass, for I do whatever I wish.** The remnant will be like Adam put back in the garden without the devil to temp them. This new sheepfold will consist of people of all nations, kindred and tongues, living in harmony together all over the world and Jesus as their Sheppard. (Praise the Lord!) **20And every island fled away, and the mountains were not found. 21And there fell upon men a great hail out of heaven, every** stone about the weight of a talent: and men blasphemed God because of the plague of the hail; for the plague thereof was exceeding great.

When these vials are finished, the geography of the earth will have changed. This is another of the great mysteries revealed to me. When Adam sinned, it changed the whole universe and cosmos because Satan was unleashed back into the heavenly bodies; this changed the order of all things in the cosmos which will lead to the birth of science, false prediction, astrological projections, and mystery UFO sightings that will be the means of false signs that will give them lying spirits to deceive these vessels raised up for dishonor; especially in the last days.

Ezekiel 14:9 (NLT) "And if a prophet is deceived into giving a message, it is because <u>I, the LORD, have deceived that prophet.</u> I will lift my fist against such prophets and cut them off from the community of Israel. There are many prophecies about the last days that were foretold by men that were not chosen. During this time of Jacob's trouble, all false prophets will be exposed that God did not choose. What these reserved to repopulate the millennium will see is a realignment of the universe back to where it was before Adam sinned and Satan bound. They will marvel at how such a small demon angel could have done this to the Earth.

The 2012 false prophecies are cut off at that point and the true prophecies, vessels of honor, will reveal the end of the revelations that was not to be told to wicked men. The same delusion we had about **Y2K** will repeat again in **2012**. This time it will set the world up for this coming great illusion that will bring destruction, angels in the form of E T's. This is the second stage of the worlds realigned in preparation for the completion of the new heaven and earth that will come after the millennium.

The next two chapters, 17 & 18 does not represent a chronological order of events. It is describing events that are in the middle of the tribulation as previously described in earlier chapters.

Rev. 17:1-3(KJV) "And there came one of the seven angels which had the seven vials, and talked with me, saying unto me, Come hither; I will shew unto thee the judgment of the great whore that sitteth upon many waters 2With whom the kings of the earth have committed fornication, and the inhabitants of the earth have been made drunk with the wine of her fornication".3 "So he carried me away in the spirit into the wilderness: and

I saw a woman sit upon a scarlet coloured beast, full of names of blasphemy, having seven heads and ten horns." The failure of Christianity to keep the doctrine of Jesus Christ where-in is the spirit of prophecy declaring the whole council of God as the focus in the assemblies. They assembled to their own shame.

Rev. 17:4-5 "And the woman was arrayed in purple and scarlet colour, and decked with gold and precious stones and pearls, having a golden cup in her hand full of abominations and filthiness of her fornication: 5And upon her forehead was a name written, MYSTERY, BABYLON THE GREAT, THE MOTHER OF HARLOTS AND ABOMINATIONS OF THE EARTH."

This mystery is revealed when America developed the technology that gave the world the ability to communicate all over the world in real time and be understood. America, the spiritual Babylon produced the technology that became our beast system, traveling through the airways, the internet. America, the mystery Babylon, was given over to the Beast System for her sins of fornication and sodomy which allowed all the religions she embraced by lowering the standards to worship in idols erected by man. God set her free to worship the gods they chose, revoking the covenant of the founders of this nation, **"In God We Trust"** to America and to Israel, **"Hear o' Israel, the lord our God is one;"** ... under grace, a Jew and a Gentile are serving the one God.

America having served her purpose as the nation blessed to restore Israel back to national status and become their protectors, will become a dead heap to the rest of the world by turning back to the heathen gods. Remember, under grace and truth, everything takes on a spiritual meaning. Man is to worship the God of Abraham, Isaac and Jacob in Spirit and in truth.

Rev. 17:6-7 "And I saw the woman drunken with the blood of the saints, and with the blood of the martyrs of Jesus: and when I saw her, I wondered with great admiration. 7And the angel said unto me, where fore didst thou marvel? I will tell thee the mystery of the woman, and of the <u>beast that carrieth her</u>, which hath the seven heads and ten horns." This beast principality will control the world's economy, caused the fall of America and Great Britain, the last two kingdoms. Out of which gave birth to the eighth kingdom. This will give place to the establishment of a ten-regional world government.

(The ten toes in Nebuchadnezzar's dream) The papacy was a separate wealthy religious nation situated on seven hills, therefore, will be the place of the administration of wealth in the world after America is destroyed.

Rev. 17:8 "The beast that thou sawest was and is not; and shall ascend <u>out of the bottomless pit,</u> and go into perdition: and they that dwell on the earth shall wonder, whose names were not written in the book of life from the foundation of the world, when they behold <u>the beast that was, is not, and yet is</u>." This set the stage for Satan as the great illusionist. He, Satan produced great lying signs and wonders that if it were possible; they would have deceived the very elect. These signs will be in the form of great illusions that all will wonder after. The key part of this verse is **"the beast that was, is not, yet is;"** that's the great **illusionist,** Satan that will captivate the world's attention and cause all to wonder after this eighth wonder of this world.

Rev. 17:9-11 "And here is the mind which hath wisdom. The seven heads are seven mountains, on which the woman sitteth. In this context, Rome is depicted as the mother of all harlots' sense her wealth was used to seed false doctrines. Her headquarters situated on seven hills, evolved as the **New World Religion;** a new version of the revived Roman Empire who's **"means justified the end"** that united all religions into one. [10] *And there are seven kings: five are fallen, and one is, and the other is not yet come; and when he cometh, he must continue a short space.* [11] *And <u>the beast that was, and is not,</u> even he is the eighth, and is of the seven, and goeth into perdition.*

This is Daniel's interpretation of the past kingdoms, now we are getting ready for the last kingdoms represented in the ten toes of the dream. **(The New World Order) and is of the seven ...** (the final kingdom incorporating all others with-in, are the sons of perdition bringing all into captivity) ... *and goeth into perdition.* Satan, having ruled the past empires as the **Son of Perdition,** God will now allow him to succeed finally in deceiving the whole world. **(Jerimiah 51:25; Daniel 2:44-45)** God will crush all ten toes of these kingdoms in the end.

Rev. 17:12(KJV) 12And the ten horns which thou sawest are <u>ten kings, which have received no kingdom yet;</u> but receive power as kings one hour with the beast." These kingdoms that shall come will be ruled by the beast principalities, The **Sons of Perdition (Satan)** but separate. The little horn that was wounded **(Rev.13:3)** to death by the church will give rise to this eighth wonder of the world. When Satan is cast out of heaven and incarnate himself into this Pre-Antichrist forerunner when he is struck down and rise in the fullness as the man of sin, Satan himself, a **New World Religion** of Satan worshipers. He will have the solution to all the worlds' problems as a master illusionist on his way to the lake of fire. They have succeeded in overtaking the last two kingdoms, Great Britain and The United States. The European common union will become the new **beast system,** consisting of seven banking systems. It will be divided into ten regions of world government. (The ten toes or the beast with ten horns)

Rev. 17:13-15(KJV) "These have one mind and shall give their power and strength unto the beast. 14These shall make war with the Lamb, (Christ in *his body) and the Lamb shall overcome them: for he is Lord of lords, and King of kings: and they that are with him are called, and chosen, and faithful. 15 And he saith unto me, the waters which thou sawest, where the whore sitteth, are peoples, and multitudes, and nations, and tongues;"* (America). This is a war for spiritual supremacy which is known as the mystery of **Godliness** and the mystery of **Iniquity** which is at work in all the past events leading up to this final battle which has resulted in the destruction of America. **(2 Thessalonians. 2:7-8)**

Revelation. 17:16-17(KJV) "And the ten horns which thou sawest upon the beast, these shall hate the whore, [America] and shall make her desolate and naked, and shall eat her flesh, and burn her with fire. [Nuclear war and natural disasters] *17For God hath put in their hearts to fulfill his will, and to agree, and give their kingdom unto the beast, until the words of God shall be fulfilled."* America and Great Britain were brought into the common market by economic default. Like mother like daughter. **(Ezk.16:44)**

Rev. 17:18(KJV) "And the woman which thou sawest is that great city, which reigneth over the kings of the earth." This was the UN in America, the Babylon which birth the New World Order.

Revelation 18:1-3 (NLT) ¹*After all this I saw another angel come down from heaven with great authority, and the earth grew bright with his splendor.* ² *He gave a mighty shout: "Babylon is fallen—that great city is fallen! She has become a home for demons.* (This describes the downfall of America once the envy of all nations now has become a harlot among them.) *She is a hideout for every foul spirit, a hideout for every foul vulture and every foul* *and dreadful animal. ³ For all the nations have fallen because of the wine of her passionate immorality. The kings of the world have committed adultery with her. Because of her desires for extravagant luxury, the merchants of the world have grown rich." Rev. 17:4(KJV) "And the woman was arrayed in purple and scarlet color, and decked with gold and precious stones and pearls, having a golden cup in her hand full of abominations and filthiness of her fornication:"*

America's decadence, Like Israel, both in the end, fell victim to idol gods and false religion through greed, corrupt wealth, immorality, and over taxation, as did the history of the Roman Empire as a point about a capitalist society. Both will be punished by their enemies; however, Israel warned by their prophets, will repent. God is returning to his people to set up his kingdom for Christ to reign. Their great delusion will be reversed; only the elects will know this through the sovereignty of God's predestination in them. If not, they would be deceived also. **(Matt.24:24)**

Revelation 18:4-7 (NLT) ⁴ Then I heard another voice calling from heaven, "Come away from her, my people. Do not take part in her sins, or you will be punished with her.⁵ For her sins are piled as high as heaven, and God remembers her evil deeds. ⁶ Do to her as she has done to others. <u>Double her penalty for all her evil deeds.</u> She brewed a cup of terror for others, so brew <u>twice as much for her</u>."

America's CIA operating international covert organizations as an arm of the New World Order. with black opts divisions unknown to current sitting presidents; committed crimes that cause the suffering of many smaller nations who signed on as her allies. ⁷ **She glorified herself and lived in luxury, so match it now with torment and sorrow. She boasted in her heart, 'I am queen on my throne. I am no helpless widow, and I have no reason to mourn. Isaiah 51:19(KJV "These two things are come unto thee; who shall be sorry for thee? desolation, and destruction, and the famine, and the sword: by whom shall I comfort thee?"** This is America's sins coming up before God. The descendants of Ishmael will exact vengeance in the form of terrorism throughout the world. This will be a fight among themselves for tribal supremacy; because of their great numbers in many nations, their anger will be against all who come against them. The Koran they study will be their motivation spearheaded by the teachings of their false prophet Mohamed ... whos' vision is, all who are not like them are to be destroyed. The sin of disobedience that caused Abraham to lie with Hagar is coming back in great numbers with a vengeance to claim an illegitimate birth rite they do not have.

Romans 1:21(KJV) Because that, when they knew God, they glorified him not as God, neither were thankful; but became vain in their imaginations, and their foolish heart was darkened."This context represents the state of all these religions under a delusion by false visions; the apostate church possessed with the **Laodicea** spirit will be targeted by these tribal Muslim for our harlot religious behavior for legalizing sodomy as a Christian practice.

Revelation 18:8-20 (NLT) Therefore, these plagues will overtake her in <u>a single day</u>, death and mourning and famine. She will be completely consumed by fire, for the Lord God who judges her is mighty."

The second wave of the destruction on America will come through an economic collapse. This is interesting also I discovered; God collapsed Russia's economy so they could regroup to take us down when our judgment will come in the same scenario as theirs. These are signs of history that will repeat itself. Russia was in Afghanistan for eight years; it caused the collapse of their economy in 1992. Now we are in the same region, fighting the same people going into the eight years at the time of this writing and now our economy is about to collapse. Russia and China (Communist sisters) made a pact because of seeing how America's gullibility became apparent on the international scene by justifying a war under false information fed to them by the people behind the N.W.O. to speed up our collapse. This would fulfill bible prophecy concerning the modern-day Babylon when we put boots on the ground. It will become apparent to our enemies that we were making decisions not in the best interest of our continued liberties. God open Russia's eyes, having made this mistake, saw we were going down the same path, made a secret pact with her communist sister China and are waiting for our economic collapse. (Khrushchev said during his time as Russia's Premier; **"we will never have to go to war with the United States, history shows that they will collapse at the hand of their own greed."**

These wars will compromise our military's ability to defend the nation from with-in; in a weaken state, unable to defend ourselves with the aid of China will invade us from the West coast and Russia from Alaska and the

East coast begin to reap havoc on the remaining cities that will doom us as a nation. This will be the curse that China will inflict on us for killing the unborn, their male army was built on the blood of sacrificed baby girls. These young men have never had a woman, as a reward, our young wives and daughters will be their spoils as a reward to them for aborting seventy million babies as an apostate Christian nation.

They will rape and killed them. Those that read this, there will be no place to escape this judgment but the protection of Christ. The chronicle **"Nowhere to Run, Nowhere to Hide"** will give the biblical account. The children of disobedience will suffer this fate as did Israel's women during their invasion. *⁹And the kings of the world who committed adultery with her and enjoyed her great luxury will mourn for her as they see the smoke rising from her charred remains.¹⁰ They will stand at a distance, terrified by her great torment. They will cry out, "How terrible, how terrible for you, O Babylon, you great city! In a single moment, God's judgment came on you."¹¹ The merchants of the world will weep and mourn for her, for there is no one left to buy their goods. ¹² She bought great quantities of gold, silver, jewels, and pearls; fine linen, purple, silk, and scarlet cloth; things made of fragrant thyine wood, ivory goods, and objects made of expensive wood; and bronze, iron, and marble. ¹³ She also bought cinnamon, spice, incense, myrrh, frankincense, wine, olive oil, fine flour, wheat, cattle, sheep, horses, chariots, and bodies—that is, human slaves. 12 The merchandise of gold, and silver, and precious stones, and of pearls, and fine linen, and purple, and silk, and scarlet, and all thyine wood, and all manner vessels of ivory, and all manner vessels of most precious wood, and of brass, and iron, and marble, 13 And cinnamon, and odours, and ointments, and frankincense, and wine, and oil, and fine flour, and wheat, and beasts, and sheep, and horses, and chariots, and slaves, and souls of men."* (Many souls were lost because of her fornication with other false religions.) *14 And the fruits that thy soul lusted after are departed from thee, and all things which were dainty and goodly are departed from thee, and thou shalt find them no more at all. 15 The merchants of these things, which were made rich by her, shall stand afar off for the fear of her torment, weeping and wailing. 16 And saying, Alas, alas, that great city, that was clothed in fine linen, and purple, and scarlet, and decked with gold, and precious stones, and pearls! 17 For in one hour so great riches is come to nought.* This is the day to watch for as the elects to rise out of obscurity and take the kingdom back by force. The collapse of the economy will get the attention of the people when all is lost, many will seek to hear our words. This is when the dry bones will be revived; not before. They will not listen to you while they are wealthy and fat.

We will be the modern-day John the Baptist to make way for the coming of Christ to reign forever. *And every shipmaster, and all the company in ships, and sailors, and as many as trade by sea, stood afar off 18And cried when they saw the smoke of her burning, saying, what city is like unto this great city! 19And they cast dust on their heads, and cried, weeping and wailing, saying, Alas, alas, that great city, wherein were made rich all that had ships in the sea by reason of her costliness! for in one hour is she made desolate." 20 Rejoice over her, thou heaven, and ye holy apostles and prophets; for God hath avenged you on her.* This is the vengeance on America for the prophets that were killed as mentioned in ... *Rev. 16:6 "For they have shed the blood of saints and prophets, and thou hast given them blood to drink; for they are worthy."*

This is the time that these nuclear explosions in America will be set off from within. Like Israel, we also, killed our prophets as gentiles by rejecting their message putting them out of their assemblies and turning them over to the authorities in the end to be killed. We will be made an example when all is finished; we will cease to exist.

Rev. 18: 21-22 "And a mighty angel took up a stone like a great millstone, and cast it into the sea, saying, thus with violence shall that great city Babylon be thrown down, and shall be found no more at all. 22And the voice of harpers, and musicians, and of pipers, and trumpeters, shall be heard no more at all in thee; and no craftsman, of whatsoever craft he be, shall be found any more in thee; and the sound of a millstone shall be heard no more at all in thee;" This millstone being thrown down represents the sudden judgment in a moment of time without remedy; America is no more. All the nations mourn her destruction. A remnant that is preserved out of her will be protected in havens in another country.

Rev. 18:23-24 "And the light of a candle shall shine no more at all in thee; and the voice of the bridegroom and of the bride shall be heard no more at all in thee: for thy merchants were the great men of the earth; for by thy sorceries were all nations deceived. 24And in her was found the blood of prophets, and of saints, and of all that were slain upon the earth." The fact that

America is no more, all the saints gathered in the Harvest are preparing for the marriage supper of the lamb. In the end, the coming asteroids and meteorites will completely change the geography of the world and crush this land to where none will inhabit this land ever again; ultraviolet rays will purify the Earth' atmosphere.

Rev. 19:1-5 "And after these things I heard a great voice of much people in heaven, saying, Alleluia; Salvation, and glory, and honour, and power, unto the Lord our God: 2For true and righteous are his judgments: for he hath judged the great whore, which did corrupt the earth with her fornication, and hath avenged the blood of his servants at her hand. 3And again they said, Alleluia. And her smoke rose up for ever and ever. 4And the four and twenty elders and the four beasts fell down and worshipped God that sat on the throne, saying, Amen; Alleluia. 5And a voice came out of the throne, saying, praise our God, all ye his servants, and ye that fear him, both small and great."

The final chapters of this book lead up to the return of Christ; these multitudes comprise the hallelujah chorus and are praising Yahweh, the lord of all for avenging the blood of the saints and judging the great whore the American version of the papacy that defiled many nations with her false doctrines of religions and democracy that became a foul bird in her mockery is now no more. **(Isaiah 34:8-10)** This nation will be a cymbal of a cursed land, no one will go near it in the millennium. It will be the forbidden zone as in the first movie **"Planet of the Apes."**

Rev. 19:6-10 "And I heard as it were the voice of a great multitude, and as the voice of many waters, and as the voice of mighty thunderings, saying, Alleluia: for the Lord God omnipotent reigneth. 7Let us be glad and rejoice and give honour to him: for the marriage of the Lamb is come, and his wife hath made herself ready. 8And to her was granted that she should be arrayed in fine linen, clean and white: for the fine linen is the righteousness of saints. 9And he saith unto me, Write, blessed are they which are called unto the marriage supper of the Lamb. And he saith unto me, these are the true sayings of God. 10And I fell at his feet to worship him. And he said unto me, see thou do it not: I am thy fellow servant, and of thy brethren that have the testimony of Jesus: worship God: for <u>the testimony of Jesus is the spirit of prophecy.</u>"

The bride is being made ready to be presented to Christ; the marriage supper of the lamb begins. The purified church tried through the fires of tribulation, being presented without spot or wrinkle arrayed in the garments prepared for his bride.

Revelation 19:11-15 (NLT) [11] **Then I saw heaven opened, and a white horse was standing there. Its rider was named Faithful and True, for he judges fairly and wages a righteous war.** [12] **His eyes were like flames of fire, and on his head were many crowns. A name was written on him that no one understood except himself.** [13] **He wore a robe dipped in blood, and his title was the Word of God.** [14] **The armies of heaven, dressed in the finest of pure white linen, followed him on white horses.** [15] **From his mouth came a sharp sword to strike down the nations. He will rule them with an iron rod.**

During the millennium, there will be zero tolerance for any acts of disobedience; any nation that does not make the annual vigil to Jerusalem for the feast of tabernacles will be cut off and allowed to die. **He will release the fierce wrath of God, the Almighty, like juice flowing from a winepress. Revelation 19:16-21 (NLT)** [16] **On his robe at his thigh was written this title: King of all kings and Lord of all lords.** [17] **Then I saw an angel standing in the sun, shouting to the vultures flying high in the sky: "Come!**

Gather together for the great banquet God has prepared. [18] *Come and eat the flesh of kings, generals, and strong warriors; of horses and their riders; and of all humanity, both free and slave, small and great."* {These are the spoils of battle; the flesh of men, great and small fed to vultures in the end.} [19] *Then I saw the beast and the kings of the world and their armies gathered together to fight against the one sitting on the horse and his army.* {This is the final battle that will destroy them all; only a remnants will be left for the re-population of the Earth in the millennium in the end.} [20] *And the beast was captured, and with him the false prophet who did mighty miracles on behalf of the beast—miracles that deceived all who had accepted the mark of the beast and who worshiped his statue. Both the beast and his false prophet were thrown alive into the fiery lake of burning sulfur.*

This verse confirmed, the **Antichrist is a principality not a man,** although Satan was its head. We see these two principalities will be thrown in the lake of fire which deceived the whole world. This was the Antichrist principality that ruled the New World Religion (**False Prophet**) and (**The Beast**) the New World Order, the eighth kingdom. [21] *Their entire army was killed by the sharp sword that came from the mouth of the one riding the white horse. And the vultures all gorged themselves on the dead bodies.* Revelation 20:1-3 (NLT) [1] Then I saw an angel coming down from heaven with the key to the bottomless pit and a heavy chain in his hand. [2] He seized the dragon—that old serpent, who is the devil, Satan—and bound him in chains for a thousand years. [3] The angel threw him into the bottomless pit, which he then shut and locked so Satan could not deceive the nations anymore until the thousand years were finished. Afterward he must be released for a little while.

Rev. 20:1-3 (KJV) *"And I saw an angel come down from heaven, having the key of the bottomless pit and a great chain in his hand.* This is where all evil spirits will be bound. *2And he laid hold on the dragon, that old serpent, which is the Devil, and Satan, and bound him a thousand years,* Satan and all his spirits are now bound through the millennium. *3And cast him into the bottomless pit, and shut him up, and set a seal upon him, that he should deceive the nations no more, till the thousand years should be fulfilled: and after that he must be loosed a little season."*

Rev. 20:4-6 (KJV) *"And I saw thrones, and they sat upon them, and judgment was given unto them: and I saw the souls of them that were beheaded for the witness of Jesus, and for the word of God, and which had not worshipped the beast, neither his image, neither had received his mark upon their foreheads, or in their hands; and they lived and reigned with Christ a thousand years.* These are the saints who, during the tribulation, held to the testimony of Jesus Christ until death.} *5But the rest of the dead lived not again until the thousand years were finished.* Here we see another mystery revealed; only the tribulation saints who bare his testimony will be entrusted to reign with him during those thousand years with the 144,000 who were chosen to follow the lamb wherever he goes. This is the first resurrection. *6Blessed and holy is he that hath part in the first resurrection: on such the second death hath no power, but they shall be priests of God and of Christ and shall reign with him a thousand years."*

Rev. 20:7-10 *"And when the thousand years are expired, Satan shall be loosed out of his prison, 8And shall go out to deceive the nations which are in the four quarters of the earth, Gog and Magog, to gather them together to battle: the number of whom is as the sand of the sea. 9And they went up on the breadth of the earth, and compassed the camp of the saints about, and the beloved city:"*

These are the descendants of the Meshach and tubal Cain; the armies of the north, these are the kindred tribes given over to the devil, ruled by the Gog & Magog principality that were never meant to go to heaven as cursed seeds. A remnant will be saved for the millennium. Now every word must be fulfilled. No one is going to heaven without being tried for their loyalty; therefore, all that were born during the millennium must be tried and therefore Satan is loose for this purpose. Among that remnants were seeds to fulfill this prophecy... **Romans 14:11 (KJV) For it is written, As I live, saith the Lord, every knee shall bow to me, and every tongue shall confess to God.**

These were cursed seeds, never to go to heaven but were there only to fulfill that prophecy without their father to temp them to do evil. God does not share his glory with the devil; therefore, Satan had to be bound during the reign of Jesus Christ. Christ will fulfill what Israel never achieved because of their disobedience. This is a return of the perfect law age without the temptation of evil, Christ himself sitting on the throne of David in Jerusalem. He is the perfect version of Solomon. *10And the devil that deceived them was cast into the lake of fire and brimstone, where the <u>beast and the false prophet are</u>, and shall be tormented day and night for ever and ever."*

The Great White Throne Judgment

<u>*Rev. 20:11-15(KJV)*</u> *"And I saw a great white throne, and him that sat on it, from whose face the earth and the heaven fled away; and there was found no place for them. 12And I saw the dead, small and great, stand before God; and the books were opened: and another book was opened, which is the book of life: and the dead were judged out of those things which were written in the books, according to their works. 13And the sea gave up the dead which were in it; and death and hell delivered up the dead which were in them: and they were judged every man according to their works. 14And death and hell were cast into the lake of fire. This is the second death. <u>15And whosoever was not found written in the book of life was cast into the lake of fire.</u>"*

In this entire book as the Holy Spirit revealed to me ... **I see by revelation**

the mystery of what was written in those scrolls of the seven thunders could not be known to an apostate church. It was given to all men to know these mysteries, but only a few chosen elects with ears to hear whose names are written in the lamb's book of life will discern the revelation to these truths that they might teach others.

My beloved brothers and sisters, all these souls before the Great White Throne Judgment are those rejected by God, marked by the beast, are receiving their rewards for being used by their father the devil to carry out his evils through the principalities to this end, now receiving the same reward of their father the devil; by being cast in the lake of fire with him to be tormented forever.

(**Chapter 21:1-8)** Describes the remaking of the new heaven and the new Earth. (Verses 9-21) The new Jerusalem coming down to the new Earth. **(Verses 22-26)** describes the glory.

(Chapter22:1-5) John sees the river of life flowing from the throne of God. **(Verses 6-11)** describes the nearness of the end of the time of man.

Rev. 22:6-11(KJV) "And he said unto me, these sayings are faithful and true: and the Lord God of the holy prophets sent his angel to shew unto his servants the things which must shortly be done. 7Behold, I come quickly: blessed is he that keepeth the sayings of the prophecy of this book. 8And I John saw these things and heard them. And when I had heard and seen, I fell down to worship before the feet of the angel which shewed me these things. 9Then saith he unto me, See thou do it not: for I am thy fellow servant, and of thy brethren the prophets, and of them which keep the sayings of this book: worship Go 10And he saith unto me, Seal not the sayings of the prophecy of this book: for the time is at hand 11He that is unjust, let him be unjust still: and he which is filthy, let him be filthy still: and he that is righteous, let him be righteous still: and he that is holy, let him be holy still."

The Final Testimony of Jesus Christ to the Churches.

Rev. 22:12-17(KJV) "And, behold, I come quickly; and my reward is with me, to give every man according as his work shall be. 13I am Alpha and Omega, the beginning and the end, the first and the last. 14Blessed are they that do his commandments that they may have right to the tree of life and may enter in through the gates into the city. 15For without are dogs, and sorcerers, and whoremongers, and murderers, and idolaters, and whosoever loveth and maketh a lie. 16I Jesus have sent mine angel to testify unto you these things in the churches. I am the root and the offspring of David, and the bright and morning star. 17And the Spirit and the bride say, Come. And let him that heareth say, Come. And let him that is athirst come. And whosoever will, let him take the water of life freely."

This is God's final warning to this last Generation

Rev. 22:18-19 "For <u>I testify unto every man that heareth the words of the prophecy of this book, If any man shall add unto these things, God shall add unto him the plagues that are written in this book:</u> 19And if any man shall take away from the words of the book of this prophecy, God shall take away his part out of the book of life, and out of the holy city, and from the things which are written in this book".

The quickness of His coming.

Rev. 22:20-21(KJV) He which testifieth these things saith, surely, I come quickly. Amen. Even so, <u>come, Lord Jesus.</u> 21The grace of our Lord Jesus Christ be with you all. Amen.

As you have read this final expanded third layer of this chronicled of Prophecy that was reserved to be released at this time, There are things I was told what was so horrible, I could not put in print that many you who lack this knowledge would lose hope of being save. Many may be astonished if not dismayed at the revelations that cut into our deep-rooted beliefs. The most amazing revelation to me is to have been chosen and given ears to hear such things that were kept being revealed at the end time. This is the last generation of Gentiles before the tribulation. I understand that many will not be able to receive the shock of this information, however, table it and let the spirit of prophecy be tested. (**There is an audio CD version that can be had by request.**)

I have no fear of what men may do to me while Christ is in this body; however, he suffers himself to be taken out is my day of redemption, to him be the glory. I, **Steven B. Riddley** do testify that the words and comments are to be judged by the spirit of prophecy. (Updated inserts May 2024)

Foot note update (7/18/2024)

It is quite apparent. Our nation has been captivated by a blind sense of reality. The church has failed to educate us in the truth. We now have become victims of seducing spirits as being brought under captivity of men appointed by God to allow the devil to deceive not only this nation, but the whole world. Men possessed with megalomania personalities, are rising in this time of biblical history to fulfill what the prophets have spoken about this time. These men are being used in this short window of nations in a state of delusion, will captivate the minds of ignorant confessing Christians to revolt against their government without being aware of the state we are in the sight of the God we say we serve. Satan justified their use by a dead church that have ceased praying to restrain these men selected to carry out this dubious plan in this nation.

President **Obama #44,** put a curse on this nation that cannot be reversed. He, as **king of the free world,** legalized the sins of Sodom and **Biden** finished putting the seal of destruction on us by legalizing the sins of Gomorrah. What we are seeing in these natural disasters is God's anger displayed on a worldwide scale with America receiving the brunt of these disasters. The diverse manner of their occurrences is the unpredictable nature of them all over this nation. Now the whole country is captivated and controlled by a spirit that possesses **Donald Trump** to bring us to judgement to think that they can defy God and reverse this curse.

His place as president #45 is to show the America, its state of delusion by promoting a certified liar as displayed in a spirit of a pre-antichrist that will try to defy God's judgement to take back America for the devil to rule. God would have to apologize to Sodom and Gomorrah who did not legalize this behavior that got them judged for destruction. That's not going to happen because we legalized it while confessing to be a Christian nation. What we saw in that attempt to take him out is a parallel warning of how the antichrist will be struck down and rise to dominate the whole world. He is a form of a pre-antichrist spirit to bring the chaos that will cause the ultimate downfall of this nation to be handed over to her enemies as Israel as history is now being repeated among the gentiles. His defiance will cause all to are taken in by this spirit to fulfill his own prophecy of this nation being led into a bloodbath that will come out of this election.

We, as a nation, raised up to protect Israel have served that purpose. Now all eyes are on us as God get ready to exact this judgement. As found in Rev. 18:6, the two city judgement that will show you what I described above as the mysteries of America, whose name is described as The Mystery Modern Babylon in the spirit of the book of Revelation being revealed as the last nation to represent the third mystery Babylon John spoke about to be judge to bring the world into this second phase of the new time continuum as was in the days of Noah to complete the last millennium. Now, may God give you eyes to see and ears to hear what the spirit of God is saying to his church. AMEN

NOWHERE TO RUN,
NOWHERE TO HIDE

Opening scripture:

Isaiah 55:7-8 (KJV) "7 Let the wicked forsake his way, and the unrighteous man his thoughts: and let him return unto the LORD, and he will have mercy upon him; and to our God, for he will abundantly pardon. 8 For my thoughts are not your thoughts, neither are your ways my ways, saith the Lord." 2 Timothy 3:13 (KJV) 13 But evil men and seducers shall wax worse and worse, deceiving, and being deceived. *Matthew 11:28 (KJV)* 28 *Come unto me, all ye that labour and are heavy laden, and I will give you rest.* 2 **Thessalonians 2:3 (KJV)** 3 **Let no man deceive you by any means: for** *that day shall not come,* **except there come a falling away first, and that man of sin be revealed, the son of perdition;**

It is quite clear to me now what evil men will do under the influence of his father, the devil. If you think you are something, you will never humble yourself to God or man. In our thinking, we are good in our own sight. If we do not believe what God said about who is good, we set ourselves up to be deceived by those who present themselves as angels in disguise. We forget the natural man, in God's sight has no good in him. It is the nature of our father, (the devil) that ... *2 Timothy 3:13 (ASV) "But evil men and impostors shall wax worse and worse, deceiving and being deceived"* as his children. God, through the scripture has brought me to a rest by revelation of himself and just what I am without him. It is not possible for a child of the devil to do good all the time when their nature is evil.

Such is the case of choosing our leaders in government. We act surprise when we elect them and then see them sale out to special interest groups that change the purpose you sent them there to serve. I have not been given great dreams or vision as some; this direct experience with the Holy Spirit has made me skeptical to the point to do as Jesus did, wait for the fruit. Hollywood and the media are being used to show us our future in movies as a true visual depiction of the horrors that's coming, and we only see it as entertainment. When He approached me in the spirit and ask what I desired of him. I ask for his mind and said, your word is good enough for me; Only God could have put the faith in my heart to ask as well as believe what he has said. Truth is a shocker to a person who find he has lived a lie most of his life. The Holy Spirit taught me a believer receives the word and acts on it without question, there-in is he called a disciple. This discipleship is being led by the Holy Spirit daily. ***John 1:12 (KJV)*** *"¹² But as many as received him, to them gave them power to become the sons of God, even to them that believe on his name:"*

Now, we must follow the teachings of Jesus Christ not man; let us see where it all began. To see where we are today is to see the end from the beginning of all that has been recorded in biblical history about this time of the end as it's revealed. To understand the rise and fall of all things in history as recorded in the scriptures, you must believe God's version of creation. We do not know the reality of sin and its consequences until we become a victim; that's' when we are ready to hear truth. That is the nature of the natural man as a sinner.

Deuteronomy 30:19 (KJV) *"¹⁹ I call heaven and earth to record this day against you, that I have set before you life and death, blessing and cursing: therefore, choose life, <u>that both thou and thy seed may live:</u>* Disobedience will curse your bloodline seeds. ***Hosea 4:6 (KJV)*** *⁶ My people are destroyed for lack of knowledge: because thou hast rejected knowledge, I will also reject thee, that thou shalt be no priest to me: seeing thou hast forgotten the law of thy God, <u>I will also forget thy children.</u> **Proverbs 18:21 (KJV)*** *²¹ Death and life are in the power of the tongue: and they that love it shall eat the fruit thereof."* (What will cause you to choose right is God's spirit?) ***John 6:44***

515

(KJV) [44] <u>*No man can come to me, except the Father which hath sent me draw*</u> <u>*him:*</u> *and I will raise him up at the last day.*

God had to use parables of the natural to get us to understand spiritual things. In the spirit world, there is no concept of natural things, it then becomes as a type and shadow as in the Old Testament; therefore, you are led to die in the spirit to the flesh. Now that is not to say we will no longer have fleshy desires; remember, we came from sin to salvation. All we must do is confess our sins once we are convicted of them in our daily walk. *1 Corinthians 15:31 (KJV)* [31] *I protest by your rejoicing which I have in Christ Jesus our Lord, I die daily. Hebrews 11:6 (KJV)* "[6] *But without faith it is impossible to please him: for he that cometh to God* <u>*must believe that*</u> <u>*he is,*</u> *and that he is a rewarder of them that diligently seek him.*" All this is God's doing in our life for His purposes and to your good and His glory; you reap the benefits by being obedient to the end. Remember (**John 6:44**); the only saints that will endure to the end will be given the power to be raised up in the last days; that's why you must be born from above. He is the quickening power within you that is there to convict you when you sin.

When He goes back to heaven where he came from, by your being one with him, you will rise with him also. This is the promise if we continue in him; our former father the devil is already condemned. He does not want you ever to know the truth about his defeat; therefore, he will use the circumstances of life in this world to keep you blind and from ever coming to the knowledge of truth. He will have you … *2 Timothy 3:7 (KJV)* [7] **Ever learning, and never able to come to the knowledge of the truth.**

Matthew 7:13-15 (KJV) "[13] *Enter ye in at the strait gate: for wide is the gate, and broad is the way, that leadeth to destruction, and many there be which go in thereat:* [14] *Because strait is the gate, and narrow is the way, which leadeth unto life, and* <u>*few there be that find it.*</u>" I can see why he has kept me away from outside influences all this time to perfect me as his messenger without any help from man. Your leader must be an example of what you can become; that's why it's easy to teach the principles of the word without salvation than being a doer of the word. God gave man these principles that will give him the power to get wealth. The principals work without salvation in the name of the lord. The gospel we see a great majority operating in the pulpit, is like seeing self-help motivational speakers, using Malichi 3:10 in the name of God to get wealthy and build their legacy family kingdoms.

Now if we are to be like Jesus … then he is our example. This evidence shows when the word mixed with faith is a demonstration by those that receive him is rewarded by a manifestation. *Romans 12:1 (KJV) "¹ I beseech you therefore, brethren, by the mercies of God, that ye present your bodies a living sacrifice, holy, acceptable unto God, which is your reasonable service."* Just as Christ sacrificed himself for you; you must sacrifice yourself for others. In you, he demonstrates this greater love that comes out of you as you die to self that shows his nature and character in the world as the new Adam, walking in authority and dominion over the circumstances of life.

John 15:13 (KJV) "¹³ Greater love hath no man than this, that a man lay down his life for his friends. Matthew 22:14 (KJV) ¹⁴ For many are called, but few are chosen. Matthew 7:21 (KJV) ²¹ Not everyone that saith unto me, Lord, Lord, shall enter into the kingdom of heaven; but he that doeth the will of my Father which is in heaven. Zechariah 4:6 (KJV) …⁶ Not by might, nor by power, but by my spirit, saith the LORD of hosts. 1 Timothy 4:1 (KJV) ¹ Now the Spirit speaketh expressly, that in the latter times some shall depart from the faith, giving heed to seducing spirits, and doctrines of devils;"

It has been said by President Obama, **"America is no longer a Christian nation." Serving** as **king of the free world,** without knowing, he has broken the covenant of God in Christ in that statement. He will now dictate the agendas of the powers that put him in office as to what he believes to be right in their sight. This is the doctrine of the devils that have determined our fate as Sodom and Gomorrah by approving same sex marriage and homosexuality as a legal lifestyle. These are the agendas of those who practice such lascivious behavior and pedophilia, now condoned by a sitting president. This is the same decadence that brought down The Roman Empire. Based on the signs, if we see another president elected, it will be by the Electoral College. If we survive another election, it will be rigged by the powers controlling our government, by the hand of God for the purpose to speed up our destruction.

The change brought on by our current sitting president, circumvented the laws of God protecting our freedoms, fulfilling. *Daniel 7:25 (KJV) ²⁵ And he shall <u>speak great words against the most High</u>,* (This is when he renounce our Christian status.) **and** *shall <u>wear out the saints of the most</u> <u>High,</u>* (The church is under the control of the state; 501C-3*) and think to <u>change times and laws:</u>* (He will liberate the homosexual spirit of Sodomy that a previous president defiled in that office by the legalization of same sex marriages.) *and they shall be given into his hand until a time and times and the dividing of time".* This is the length of time Satan must accomplish his purpose; to set in motion the take-down of our society. President Obama's theology is Anti-Christian in practice and will cause the true church great persecution by allowing this law to pass during his time to serve as **"King of the free world."**

President Clinton brought this sodomy spirit into the Oval Office as a baby-boomer and now the next generation has unleashed it. Contrary to false teachings, the Antichrist is a body of seduced Christians led by man; although Satan is the god of it all, they will persecute the true church just as the Antichrist body of the Sadducees and Pharisees persecuted and finally killed Jesus in the name of God not knowing what spirit they were of and so will the false church with the same spirit repeat history as gentiles. Apostle John in his epistle tells us who is an antichrist ... *1 John 2:18 (KJV)* "[18] *Little children, it is the last time: and as ye have heard that antichrist shall come, even now are there <u>many antichrists</u>; whereby we know that it is the last time.*" We see here what constitutes an Antichrist; anyone who come against the teachings of Christ. **1 John 4:3 (KJV)** "[3] *And every spirit that confesseth not that Jesus Christ is come in the flesh is not of God: and this is that spirit <u>of antichrist, whereof ye have heard that</u> <u>it should come; and even now already is it in the world</u>.*"

Now what is John saying? ... *2 Timothy 2:19 (KJV)* "[19] *Nevertheless the foundation of God standeth sure, having this seal, The Lord knoweth them that are his. And, let everyone that nameth the name of Christ depart from iniquity. John 15:18 (KJV)* [18] *If the world hate you, ye know that it hated me before it hated you.*"

Although President Obama shows all the signs of evil convictions as were many of his predecessors, he was put there by the will of God to serve his purpose in history. Obama fulfills Dr. Martin Luther King's prophecy dream that one day a man would be judged by the content of his character, not the color of his skin. Obama is an instrument of false hope that will be used to bring about a change that will confound him in the end. His ability to speak great words at the right time in history is the same spirit that will cause many that are blind to follow the Antichrist; now he is not the Antichrist, although his actions are antichristian … it will show how far we have departed from the teaching the foundation of this nation's history in our schools; as Christians, we do not know the history behind our spiritual birth as a people and this generation is no longer taught the history of this nation's birth. The church community got just what they asked for as seduced Christians and just before our end comes, we will see all our evils exposed by whoever comes after him.

Many are still segregated among themselves, in sectarian false teachings that have caused many confessing Christians to think of themselves more highly than they should. This is the fruit of the Laodicea church. Obama to them was their Messiah of change. In the future reality, they will see his idea of change dictated by these powers will result in bondage to the system. In their assemblies. *Jude 1:10 (KJV)* [10] *But these speak evil of those things which they know not: but what they know naturally, as brute beasts, in those things they corrupt themselves."* No converted Christian has hatred for our head authorities; we are to pray for them because we are not ignorant of who is in charge; God.

The Holy Spirit has no identity to things natural such as class, race, creed or color. This character flaw is a result of not being delivered from past false teachings of racial or ethnic pride; for some, it has caused a superiority complex. The absence of God's love and a standard of holiness is where we see these false teachings that still harbor these prejudices that are being exposed in organized assemblies. Pastors and leaders are demonstrating these character flaws by speaking evil of our sitting dignitaries of authority from their bully pulpits every Sunday. The pastors raised up by God will teach the believer to pray for change in the hearts of men. We can discern by their action, the nature of agendas. *2 Peter 2:10 (KJV)* [10] *But chiefly them that walk after the flesh in the lust of uncleanness and despise government. Presumptuous are they, self-willed, they are not afraid to speak evil of dignities.* When one becomes converted, they will live in the love of the lord one day at a time. These are those born from above who see things in heavenly places and walk accordingly. *John 3:8 (KJV)* [8] *The wind bloweth where it listeth, and thou hearest the sound thereof, but canst not tell whence it cometh, and whither it goeth: so is every one that is born of the Spirit.*

What you will see in every born from above believer is the fruit of that spirit's source. When an assembly receives an outpouring of that mighty rushing wind <u>again</u>, you will be colorblind. These chronicles of our time should by now be easier to comprehend. No Jesus, no signs, wonders or miracles as were present in the early church. America as a nation is doomed by the same sin that judged Israel's disobedience of God's law; thinking themselves more highly than they should, exchanged the true God for idols. We in America, because of her status in the world, have appointed ourselves its policeman. **"Hear old Israel, the lord our God is one"** to **Israel and "In God We Trust."** to **America.** God put the words in our **DECLARATION of INDEPENDENCE** that **CONSTITUTES** the liberties that all will have the right to serve the one true and living God free of oppression from the government. That' in our **BILL of RIGHTS** sealed with a covenant **"IN GOD WE TRUST,"** the one God.

This covenant fulfills the promise made to Abraham that this blessing will come upon the Gentiles. Every citizen that had a part in its birth as a nation were to be given these same rights which included freed slaves. In the final days, this injustice of not granting to all it' citizens their equal rights, will return in an oppressed people in the form of civil unrest.

On July 4th, 1776 in the assembly of the **CONTINENTAL CONGRESS,** witnessed by those who signed their names on that **DECLARATION;** that prophecy was fulfilled. The founding fathers declared to the world our independence from the mother country, Great Britain that… **"We, the people of the United States, in order to form a more perfect union, establish justice, insure domestic tranquility, provide for the common defense, promote the general welfare, and secure the blessings of Liberty to ourselves and our posterity, do ordain and establish this constitution for the United States of America."** Historically, I want you to see the inspiration of God in men that had a religious knowledge of deity in one God but became hypocritical in its administration of equality. True patriots fear God.

They are the true Christian prayer worriers for this nation to keep these liberties. Satan has worn them out and killed many of them off. **(Daniel 7:25)** Now there are not enough prayer warriors left to keep Satan from having this time he has been given that will expose all the evils with-in mankind. The Holy Spirit has been snuffed out the church to make room for the new idols of religious symbols we have erected in the name of God as monuments of our own efforts to leave a legacy to yourself. The Jesuits seminaries have indoctrinated them to become popes in the pulpits promoting a form of religion that denies the power of God.

The founding fathers under God's divine hand directing their affairs, spoke with such inspiration that we inscribed those words on our monuments commemorating their acts that established this nation with liberties like no other nation on Earth; that is, to serve the one true God that established it.

Now every president that does not **"uphold these principles truths to be self-evident that all men are created equal and is endowed by our creator certain inalienable rights to life liberty and the pursuit of happiness"** to serve the lord our God as one, shall be an instrument of Satan to dismantle our nation's liberties and freedoms. God used President Lincoln to remind the nation of its religious root in his speech at Gettysburg. Those words came in one of the shortest speeches ever given by a sitting president. God gave him a vision that grieved him about this nation and that speech at Gettysburg reflected his state of mind at that time. In my observation of this nation's history, this is where we began to fall into the hands of unscrupulous evil men. President Lincoln represented a true Republican who at that time was greatly resisted in his own household during his presidency, yet the will of God prevailed.

The evidence of this deep cover shadow government is responsible for his death and others who does not follow their agenda. As I look back at the course of history up until this present day, I see women becoming more dominant in high places. Satan used women in this capacity to do his bidding; remember Eve. He knows natural men are still weakened by the female's physical attributes and use them to this end. Our abuse of them will come back with a vengeance. Now I don't' want anyone to get the impression that men are more important than women or that I have some disdain for women; I was put out of the assemblies and driven out of a city for revealing the true doctrine regarding this matter. God warn us when he pronounced this curse on Eve that put her subject to man in marriage as the image of God. Satan will now use this enmity between the sexes to war for supremacy and control in these last days.

Therefore, we must be born again to become subject to the will of God that will cause us to remain in our places as the doctrine of Christ administered through the Holy Spirit as equals in our rightful places among those whom God has joined together and profit from Eve' mistake. This has been written for our learning that we once again can be equals as new creatures in Christ. God gave us his precepts that govern our interactions with the male and female gender as part of the New Testament doctrine in Christ and it has not changed. We are still fighting for gender supremacy by not knowing what spirit we are of. No one wants to do it God's way. The failure of man's credibility has caused their women to rule over them. *Isaiah 3:12 (KJV)* [12] *As for my people, children are their oppressors, and women rule over them. O my people, they which lead thee cause thee to err, and destroy the way of thy paths.*

This speech of Daniel Webster is very much alive today. *"I shall exert faculty I possess in aiding to prevent the constitution from being nullified, destroyed, or impaired; and, even though I should see it fall, I will still, with a voice feeble, perhaps, but earnest as ever issued from human lips, and with fidelity and zeal which nothing shall extinguish, call on the people to come to its rescue."* (Daniel Webster) These are the people that cry **"We must take back America and make it great again."** Though it may seem inspiring, it is a form of misguided patriotism. They are not aware of the times; this expression of human emotion and a zeal will prove to be fatal to this movement in these last days as a nation under judgment. This will be the last stand of the <u>**"Barabbas Patriot spirit**</u>.

The sign that shows we have changed the times and laws **(Dan.7:25)** came from President Obama's declaration **"America is no longer a Christian nation;"** to the elects, this was our sign to prepare to die. Out of the mouth of **"the king of the free world,"** he has authorized Satan to begin persecuting all the saints that will come against these new laws that will bring about the separation of the wheat from the tares. The fact that the President has justified homosexuality as a legal status in his endorsement as **"king of the free world;"** will force all Christians to take a stand on your beliefs as a Christian on issues that have changed the truth of God into a lie. There are many **"Shades of Gray"** when it comes down to what we really do behind closed doors in our secret chambers when we entertain these spirits. This hidden lust for sexual fantasies that are now emerging that came with this spirit of Sodomy has been unleashed with a vengeance. The only power to resist these evils will be your love for God. As a watchman, I keep up with the wave of spirits unleashed from the spirit world. Our current sitting president constantly endorses this lifestyle nearly every time he gives a major speech. Only in a Sodomy environment with many shades of gray will release this form of bedroom pornography that many lukewarm Christians are seduced to buy and watch. The world's lust can never be satisfied as a natural brute beast man and many confessing Christians are not as dead to these desires as they should be.

In searching the internet, I must increase my prayers of conviction to avoid these temptations. I like being delivered to transparency about the matters that few will admit. In the days ahead, you will see why my prayers are for all that call upon his name will help many confessing Christians get delivered from these evils. September 11, 2008, ended the seven years of grace of this last generation of the Gentiles which began at the end of the 1967 war with Israel and Syria that recaptured much of the Abraham land grant that included the City of David: Jerusalem. Now, all is set for the return of Christ to the throne of David. What will speed up our collapse, when we try to force Israel to give up land recaptured? We, as a nation, will see more natural disasters and a great division in Government as a sign of God's anger. This shows, we are beginning to separate from those we were raised up to protect. If we refuse to protect Israel, God will no longer protect us.

The year 2008, closed the time of the gentile church age. We are entering a pre-trib phase where we will see the signs leading into tribulation. Whether we believe it or not, we are off springs of the Jews under grace as their protectors as they stand against the tyranny that threatens their existence as a nation. Two thousand and eight was the transition period to the tribulation that will begin to intensify in the years after. The watchmen must now do what John the Baptist did; warn the people to prepare for the coming return of Christ. We are to prepare in the spirit for the fires of tribulation. In this verses of Rev. 3:14-17 is the state of that church. Verse 18 is where the separation will begin when overnight our lives will change in America when the economy crashes as it did in 1929 and never return.

God' warning signs are once again being ignored. **Amos 3:7 (NASB77) Surely the Lord GOD does nothing Unless He reveals His secret counsel To His servants the prophets. Ephesians 3:5-6 (NASB77) which in** other generations was not made known to the sons of men, as it has now been revealed to His holy apostles and prophets in the Spirit; *Revelation 18:17 (KJV)* "¹⁷ *For in one hour so great riches is come to nought. And every shipmaster, and all the company in ships, and sailors, and as many as trade by sea, stood afar off,*" This will be the start of the great tribulation that will birth the **MANCHILD** true church **(Rev.12:13)** the bride of Christ, you who continue to believe the false teaching of **RAPTURE** before tribulation will be caught in God's break. You will be given a chance to repent when you hear the word from the prophets and messengers of our time as you are hearing now. The timeline of events have us in the footman stage preceding the Four Horseman in Revelation six. The only escape is in Christ. The conditions that God will allow Satan to carry this out are described in the chronicle, "**What Will Happen during the Tribulation Siege.**"

Soon the new internet will take the place of the world' monetary system when our current monetary system fails. The NEW WORLD ORDER that Bush senior declared in his inaugural address will evolve into ten regions as the new world government. There are two nations' the bible is written too, Israel and the Gentile. The nation established to receive the Abraham covenant blessings that will be instrumental in the restoration of Israel as a nation and be its protector; America, containing all the nations of the world that Paul was sent to, became the symbol of the gentile melting pot containing all the people of the world that inherited this blessing and the stability of the world.

Once this has been completed, this will end with the last generation in that nation, forty years after the 1967 war. *Matthew 24:34 (ASV)* ³⁴ *Verily I say unto you, this generation shall not pass away, till all these things be accomplished.* This is where we are now in our time; just look at the signs all around us; tribulation is at the door. September 11, 01 … is no mistake we are fighting in Iraq, **(a return to the old Babylon to be judged)** this is history repeated in the bible. What happens to us on "911" was a sign that we were going to be given a strong delusion to blind us as did Israel in their rebellion? What our pride as war hungry politicians in government, making decisions that are not in the best interest of our present liberties. Now we will see how Abraham's sin with Hagar comes back with a vengeance as to claim a false birth right. We, as a friend of Israel will be targeted by their great numbers all over the world.

They are children of the bond woman and now slaves of Satan, except for a remnant, they are doomed for destruction. A remnant of all tribes, kindred's and toques including Ishmael' seed will be saved for the re-population of the millennium. The descendants of Ishmael will be given a spirit of the doctrine taught in their Koran of self-sacrifice in harm's way as a reward for eternity. This false teaching, under a strong delusion, Satan will use them to exact vengeance that will be the means of their own self-destruction as a nation when they join the armies of the north.

They will be used to run interference as to bring acts of terror on enemy nations. This will make America, known to them as the great Satan and Israel our co-defenders in war, their primary targets. These are the seeds God discarded to be destroyed at the end. All the word must be fulfilled; God has given these seeds to Satan to use them to carry out his will to fulfill all things according to the words of the prophets. America has appointed herself as the Policemen of the World; therefore, we will be the primary victim of the world's wrath. America has lost the vision of the founding fathers and will now be weaken at the hand of smaller nations while the greater enemy, Russia and China, God has opened their eyes to see our path of destruction to the point that they will manipulate the current quagmire situation we find ourselves in fighting these wars designed to collapse our economy as did Russia'.

That is why God sent Russia there first to collapse their economy first to rebuild their army to fulfill Ezekiel thirty-eight and nine, so they will return to lead the armies of the north against Israel to fulfill this prophecy. All they must do now is just set back and wait for us to collapse, and do what Khrushchev said, divide the spoils among their communist sister, China.

China capitalized off our greed by manipulating our economy, providing a cheap labor force too good for our greedy manufacturers to resist; in return, we had to share our manufacturing secrets and technologies with them. In the future, they will intern use it to build up their own economies and turn against us. They will use our own money to purchase this nation's real estate through gains in great trade deficits. The excess money from our trade with China will be use it to finance our declining economy. Their stability is based on America remaining solvent as a nation.

We mortgage the title deed to America to China and enemy nations to finance our continued lifestyle that carries with it now, a false sense of security. Un-like Israel, we have become naive to our own vulnerabilities. In the beginning, God provided this nation with all the resources it needed for self-independence as he did with Israel. That distinction made all nations dependent on our technology as we become the means of their stability that will make America the envy of the world; that's why when we fall, so will the other nations with us because we like the head domino, when we fall, so will they. We are the means of their stability. (Rev. 18)

What wall street did with the help of greedy bankers, robbed the nation's treasury and created our economic instability to the point we had to give our technology secrets to our enemy nations to maintain a lifestyle no longer obtainable by today's economic standards. Soon, this will come back in the form of an uprising of the general population. The middle class will work harder and gain very little by new taxes designed to limit their prosperity. This was done legally by that 1 percent of the wealthiest people of the world that will aid them in creating the chaos in the future to crash our economy.

Bush Junior's vice president was a plant as the front man; his position by this shadow world government as being connected to the company that would gain the greatest profit from these wars that would ultimately rob the war chest that would collapse the economy. Do not put all the blame on Obama when this happens, if another president is elected, he will become their fall guy. Obama is the middle of the last three presidents that will complete the number of (45) kings of the gentile nation. He is the answer to the slaves' cries that is fulfilled in this present future. His speaking talents were worthy of them financing his return as President as a historical event that will probably not end on his watch. He justifies how far we as people of color with an identify problem in our history from slavery. We have not served the one God faithfully our masters introduced us too … had we obeyed that God, our deliverance would have come sooner; instead, Obama is the delayed prayers our ancestors got in the end when God raised him up as an answer to the prayers of the slaves who died in hope of being delivered. The key word we as watchers looked for was hope and change. His term in office will cause a return of the seeds of racial divisions.

We as people of color have not evolved as a people and served the God of our forefathers served as slave in the fields as one. We have fallen away too from the truth. **Up from slavery**, under conditions beyond our control, led to these division we have with-in our own race as a people of color. We are guilty of the same evils that have caused us to turn on each other also. The pride of having a man of color in the Oval Office shows we also have forgotten God also.

When this nation falls; so, will China, Russia and all other nations in the end. We, as a nation were set up by God to be the stability of the world's economies; therefore, when we seek to be its policemen, in the end our allies will become the victims of our true intentions and depart from us; that will contribute to our fall, so will all the others as stated in **(Revelation 18:18-21)** come under a one world government to survive. Sept. 11/2001, during those seven years, the Trojan horse sneaked into our compromised boarders to wake up the immigrant sleeper family cells sent in during the cold war as spy families that have for the past seventy years gained high positions in our government.

Their activity in high places will compromise our national security. This shadow government is now carrying out their agenda. They overthrew our vote to return Bush Jr, the seed of Bush senior, to stack the High court and return him to office to finish their agenda and change the laws they needed to legally take control of this country to usurped authority over the people's vote to him put him in office. All of them are part of a secret organization of a Satanic order of Skull and Bones origin; evil seeds to carry out this countries destruction by turning the power over to the major corporations outside our boarders with contracts that will buy out the Republic and its conservative party representatives to corrupt every elected official in this country as a paid servant to change laws to their own profit. It's unfortunate that we as free born citizens are seeing this boldly displayed with no regard for us as citizens.

You will see this in the days ahead in our two-party system of government. That is why God gave Obama a vision to use the words hope & change as his motto. Only those that have been given eyes to see will discern these times. Bush Jr.' election was to complete the agenda set in motion by his father as a member of the western division of this hidden shadow government that is orchestrating our economic downfall in these final years after 911; his vice president, planted in that position, influence his decisions to enter a second war by use of false intelligence. This son as president was not endowed with the wisdom to run this country as demonstrated when he had to speak off script and therefore was the perfect candidate during this period to aide in fulfilling their agenda. When he leaves office, you will not hear much from him for a while, he now realizes what he has done that cost the innocent lives of so many young men.

War has always been their means to speed up their agenda. Their headquarters being in this nation, through manipulation of past presidents have hood winked us into bondage. This is where you will see the Supreme Court, our last beacon of justice to uphold the law, hand down decisions that indicate the blinders have reached them to change laws along party loyalties and the times. **(Daniel 7:25)**

"911" was masterminded by their secret covert black opts division, used mercenaries on an international scale as they have done through-out this country's history, our CIA covert opts division in this nation has act as the world's policemen to cause wars as their means to topple nations and take then over by financing both sides to achieve their objective of world domination. Money is not their desire; they own the control rights to every country. God will let them carry out this grand delusion. All will be exposed during the tribulation.

Now, can you see God's hand in man's affairs? This plays into fulfilling biblical prophecy. Without these revelations by the Holy Spirit to read and discern these signs of the times, in conjunction with discerning actions of the people being used; there is no way we will see what is coming. I am only the scribe to write it down as was John and all the others moved on by the Holy Spirit. On January 21, 2010, The Supreme court handed over our freedoms to these corrupt corporations by overturning McCain-Feingold's campaign law that will in these last elections, make our vote null and void. These corporations with foreign roots will now control our politicians. When their plant gets in office by their support, he will have no choice but to yield to their demands.

Russia tried for eight years to defeat Afghanistan, and it collapsed their economy. The international community became victims of Russia's scheme, given to them by God for this purpose, to open the door to democracy as a front, allowed them to rob this nation through organized crime, this now corrupt regime would finance their recovery to regroup their military to fulfill the prophecy of the destruction coming from the armies of the **North** against Israel. (Ezekiel 38) This is the new Russia, headed by the old regimes, groomed a young leader, Putin to re-instate him when the time was right, to complete their objective.

Ezekiel 38:15-16 (NASB77) <u>**"And you will come from your place out of the remote parts of the north, you and many peoples with you,**</u> **all of them riding on horses, a great assembly and a mighty army; 16 and you will come up against My people Israel like a cloud to cover the land. It will come about in the last days that I shall bring you against My land, in order that the nations may know Me when I shall be sanctified through you before their eyes, O Gog;"** This is Israel's tribulation where God will glorify himself in their defeat.

Russia, China, and the nations of the seeds of Ishmael along with the residue of other nations will comprise this army. Now with all our technology, we are in an apparent quagmire with no dignified way out; like Vietnam, we are fighting the wrong enemy, now our leaders will begin to see the handwriting on the wall as in the days as the Babylon of old ... **Daniel 5:27 (NKJV)** [27] **TEKEL: You have been weighed in the balances and found wanting.** This is Noah's seven days before the rain. This time will be by fire. The hatred three thousand plus years in the making of the descendants of Ishmael can only be solved by destruction, not appeasement; such is the case in Afghanistan. This terrain has been left the same for four thousand years as un-chartered territory. In our case, we are there to test some of our new military technology, using satellite mapping from the sky.

Our leaders have become blind, they want to take some spoils of an enemy that is bent on destroying you. With-out the leading of the God we said we trust; the victory will be reversed. What did Israel learn when they went against God? They lost the battle. These people are under a curse never to become heirs of the kingdom by birth right. In that area of the Middle East, any nation that try to take them down will be brought down themselves. That is the curse on the descendants of Cain and Ismael; now

Russia and America will become victims by going against God' plan, set in motion from the beginning of man's time on earth. They, as nations, have become blind by their action against God. They are now possessed with Antichrist spirits as nations, their armies in their attempt to destroy Israel will cause them both to be destroyed. Russia, ruled as an antigod nation under Gog and Magog principalities in the spirit world.

They will never be a friend to America or Israel. Our allies will join them as that mighty army of the **north,** coming to destroy Israel when we fall along with the middle eastern territory nations because of the enmity of these two seeds. God caused us to set foot on their soils to enrage them to ware down our military as they did Russia's. This is the politics of our leaders, blinded by God. We are following a path in history as the Roman Empire; we will fall from within by our own greed, corruption, moral decadence and a corrupt taxation system as history repeats itself. This Government, by executive orders has now been legally given over to the N.W.O. by the Supreme Court; freedom in America through the **"Patriot Act"** is now over.

The cooperation's funded by the New World Order that owns The World Bank, took over the Federal Reserve Bank, now uses our own tax money to finance their agenda's that have us policing the world. The civil unrest in the world is because of people being oppressed to the point; they no longer have anything to lose, will be the spirit that will bring all nations to the brink of worldwide chaos. These conditions will play into the hand of the New World Order to justify their action on the world stage by reducing the world's population through withholding the regulations on gun laws so these patriots will kill off each other in the chaos in a systematic use of biological and cyber warfare to bring order out of chaos, under this term; **"EPLURIBUS UNUM"** for the good of mankind, **"out of many will become the one". That's when the world will be crying for peace that will bring the man of sin on the scene with the solution to all the world's problems.** The four horsemen of the book of revelation six have been loosed; when tribulation becomes full circle, no one will escape but those chosen to repopulate the millennium. What we see in this worldwide delusion, the devil is now increasing the activity of the footman in his last attempt to gather as many souls as possible for hell in this short time he has been given. *Isaiah 5:14 (KJV) Therefore, hell hath enlarged* *herself, and opened her mouth without measure: and their glory, and their multitude, and their pomp, and he that rejoiceth, shall descend into it.*

Victims of the times

If the circumstances of life are seemly overwhelming you now in the footman stage, what are you going to do when the horses arrive? They have us pitted against each other in this nation so we in out desperation, will turn on each other and kill each other in great numbers before the troops come in. That's why they will not let them pass any gun laws; they want the population to have as many guns as you can buy for this reason, to kill each other off as neighbor against neighbor in great numbers in the chaos when the food shortage comes, martial law is declared. This will become more apparent when Satan release the suicide demons held captive until now to commit mass murders. Those that was in the man Jesus met at Gadara are these type demons. They are Satan's killing agents; spirits that led those pigs to commit suicide when they went in them. Up until this end time they have been contained. Now Satan has justified their release to begin their assault on earth as we see the increase in mass suicides.

Just as it was in the days of Noah, so shall it be in these end times. People are oblivious to these times as the church lite are our, there is no vision of the spirit world because they are led by false prophet that seek their favor and tell them what they want to hear. In their defiance, they will ignore the warning signs as to go about as though things will always be the same. We too, will be eating, drinking, buying homes, marrying and giving in marriage right on up to the crash. On the morning of the great crash, many will be trapped in foreign lands with no way to get back ... others on high seas in luxury liners that will be attacked by enemy ships when the fall of this nation comes overnight. Hackers are in place to carry out cyber war by dismantling our infrastructure. As a capitalist society, we as a people of pride will fall by willing ignorance, living in a false since of reality and security, only to get caught in God's break with no way out. All hope will be gone.

The elects are chosen by God as were the apostles ... are preparing to come out of the wilderness in the fullness of Christ. When God showed me the error of my ways, I had no choice but to repent. I now spend my time while at rest in intercessory prayer for the souls in the balance whose fate as victims of blind guides, pleading for God's mercy upon them. The John the Baptist ministry was very short and not known to this church world; his movement of followers lasted for three years. The last six months, his message cut to the heart of his people and Rome before he was killed by a jezebel wife of by king Herod. The reason he was the greatest prophet, he got to see, introduce and baptize their Messiah. Although his ministry was noticeably short, it paralleled with Christ. He was rejected by a kingdom government as a forerunner of Christ. Dr Martin Luther King was our first sign of a prophet raised up to warn this nation who also killed him as did Israel killed their prophets. It has been my experience, having been rejected by the church world to prepare to go up against these kingdoms at the hands of a people doomed to self-destruction.

Holy Spirit give us a word for this time for all that will hear in Jesus's name. Amen

Deuteronomy 28:65 (KJV) And among *these nations* shalt <u>thou find no ease, neither shall the sole of thy foot have rest:</u> *but the LORD shall give thee there a <u>trembling heart,</u> (the spirit of fear that's coming will cause people to turn on each other and their hearts will fail.) and failing of eyes, and sorrow of mind: (many will lose their minds and be as zombies.) Deuteronomy 28:65 (NLT) There among those nations you will find no peace or place to rest. And the LORD will cause your heart to tremble, your eyesight to fail, and your soul to despair. Amos 9:10 (KJV) All the sinners of my people shall die by the sword, which say, the evil shall not overtake nor prevent us. (These are patriot Christians that armed themselves as the world did and made their own provisions to survive what they think will be temporary.) Matthew 26:52 (KJV) Then said Jesus unto him, put up again thy sword into his place: for all they that take the sword shall perish with the sword. Ezekiel 33:27 (KJV) Say thou thus unto them, thus saith the Lord GOD; As I live, surely they that are in the wastes shall fall by the sword, (invading armies) and him that is in the open field will I give to the beasts to be devoured, (Wild animals will hunt you down as food.) and they that be in the forts and in the caves shall die of the pestilence.* (These places you call safe havens in mountains, built for survival, will become your grave by these diseases.) *Ezekiel 33:27 (NLT) "Say to them, 'This is what the Sovereign LORD says: As surely as I live, those living in the ruins will die by the sword. And <u>I will send wild animals to eat those living in the open fields. Those hiding in the forts and caves will</u>*

die of disease. Deuteronomy 11:26 (KJV) [26] *Behold, I set before you this day a blessing and a curse; Jeremiah 21:8 (KJV)* [8] *And unto this people thou shalt say, thus saith the LORD; Behold, I set before you the <u>way of life</u>, and the <u>way of death.</u> Deuteronomy 30:19 (KJV)* [19] *I call heaven and earth to <u>record this day against you</u>, that I have set before you life and death, blessing and cursing: therefore choose life, that both thou and thy seed may live: Joshua 24:15 (KJV)* [15] *And if it seem evil unto you to serve the LORD, choose you this day whom ye will serve; whether the gods which your fathers served that were on <u>the other side of the flood</u>, or the gods of the Amorites, in whose land ye dwell: but as for me and my house,* This is to every believer that commit his way unto the lord. *we will serve the LORD.* **AMEN** (Updated and released 4/2018)

THE LAMB'S BOOK OF LIFE

Background scripture:

Revelation 3:5 (KJV) He that overcometh, the same shall be clothed in white raiment; and <u>I will not blot out his name out of the book of life</u>, but I will confess his name before my Father, and before his angels. Revelation 13:8 (KJV) And all that dwell upon the earth shall worship him, whose names are not written in the book of life of the Lamb slain from the foundation of the world. Revelation 20:12 (KJV) ¹² And I saw the dead, small and great, stand before God; and the <u>books</u> were opened: and <u>another book</u> was opened, which is the <u>book of life</u>: and the dead were judged out of those things which were written in the books, according to their works. Revelation 22:19 (KJV) <u>And if any man shall take away from the words of the book of this prophecy, God shall take away his part out of the book of life, and out of the holy city, and from the things which are written in this book.</u>

Many have found these revelations hard to receive. As victims of generations of false teachings; this revelation is in His timing ... *John 8:32 (KJV) And ye shall know the truth, and the truth shall make you free.* Now, let us examine the above scriptures in the right context of what will determine whose name will remain in the lamb's book of life and what will cause it to be blotted out? This is for those that have been taught the doctrine, **"Once Saved Always Saved"** *Revelation 13:8 (KJV) And all that dwell upon the earth shall worship him, (*Satan) *whose names <u>are not</u> written in the book of life of the Lamb slain from the foundation of the world.* Your name is written in the book of life the day you were born. ***Romans 10:13 (KJV) For whosoever shall call upon the name of the Lord shall be saved.*** Under grace and truth, that is when your name is written in the lamb's book of life. Is it possible to lose your salvation? **Revelation 3:5 (KJV) He that overcometh, the same shall be clothed in white raiment; and <u>I will not blot out his name</u> <u>out of the book of life</u>, but I will confess his name before my Father, and before his angels.** God by faith honors his part of the promise. Here-in is the revelation; only God through the Holy Spirit can speak for himself the witness of God in you after you have been born from above. If you are still following the ways of the world, you are born from below as a religious child of the devil, living in a way that seems right as a luke-warm confessing Christian.

John 14:17 (KJV) Even the Spirit of truth; whom the world cannot receive, because it seeth him not, neither knoweth him: but ye know him; for he dwelleth with you and shall be in you. John 16:13 (KJV) Howbeit when he, the Spirit of truth, is come, he will guide you into all truth: for he shall not speak of himself; but whatsoever he shall hear, that shall he speak: and he will shew you things to come. This is where many confessing Christians have been taught by well-meaning pastors the mindset that you have to work for God. Under traditional seminary training, you may be activating the wrong spirit; this may be why so many are trying to do good deeds and works to justify their salvation. Many have missed their calling by being sent by man as I was. If we must surrender to his will, then it is God that does the leading and this is where you see God at work and not man performing what only he can do; heal the sick, raise the dead and cast out demons. Even those with gifts of the spirit are often misused to gain wealth in this world.

Matthew 7:21 (KJV) Not everyone that saith unto me, Lord, Lord, shall into the kingdom of heaven; but he that doeth the will of my Father which is in heaven. Luke 6:46 (KJV) And why call ye me, Lord, Lord, and do not the things which I say? All who join a religious assembly by confessing Romans 10:9-10 will be saved because the word said it, but if that gospel was not received with a demonstration of faith as in the early church to them that heard it ... by lack of knowledge of how to apply the truth in faith without the whole council of God, you will not be walking in God's perfect will for you if He did not call you to do what you are doing. This is where many will be destroyed by lack of knowledge, operating in the wrong calling as being sent by man under the influence of Satan. This is the counter fit gospel that has come to look and sound like the real thing over many generations of teaching.

Since I have come to this knowledge, I have found many who confess salvation cannot receive the truth without being offended. WHY IS THAT? This is what He told the Sanhedrin? *Luke 13:35 (KJV) Behold, your house is left unto you desolate: and verily I say unto you, Ye shall not see me, until the time come when ye shall say, blessed is he that cometh in the name of the Lord.* When Jesus made that statement, he was before the people that name his name but rejected him because he did not keep their traditions by putting the money changers out of the temple and a veil of darkness fell between them and their seeds that will remain until he returns during the tribulation. Those that know Christ will walk in humble humility. We see now that our name can be blotted out of the **lamb's** book of life just by sins of omission. Galatians. 5:19-21. If one is born in sin, you must   your sins to receive salvation in Christ to be put on the strait road to heaven which is aided by having Jesus in control of your temple; up until that time, you are a child of the devil waiting for his judgment.

Revelation 20:15 (KJV) And whosoever <u>was not</u> found written in the book of life was cast into the lake of fire. All that call upon the name of the lord under a deep faith conviction that cuts to the core of your vary being, have the convictions to endure to the end. The doctrine of once saved always save is subject to this statement … *Matthew 24:13 (KJV) But he that shall endure unto the end, the same shall be saved. Matthew 7:21 (KJV)* [21] *Not everyone that saith unto me, Lord, Lord, shall enter into the kingdom of heaven; but he that doeth the will of my Father which is in heaven. Luke 6:46 (KJV)* [46] *And why call ye me, Lord, Lord, and do not the things which I say?* He is talking to confessing Christians.

Great multitudes of deceived confessing Christians, who were told once you confess your salvation, **you will not go to hell,** many were taught out of **the NIV version of the bible** that denies the real Chris. That's the work of the Jesuits teaching in the seminary schools to defile the Christian church. They are the ones that change the word and introduce a new doctrine, some are even cult like in their practices. One organization confesses to be His witnesses but remain in the world. They are victims of false Sheppard acting on the words of false angelic visitations, sent to take advantage of your sinful state circumstances to capture you into a false representation of Jesus. They will rob you of your money as tithing under the law and your birth-rite in the name of God through faith principal teachings. The great white throne judgment will be for the wicked dead and lukewarm confessing Christian that God spit out of his mouth with shallow convictions as victims of double-minded preachers who rejected the prophets. *Revelation 3:16 (KJV) So then because thou art lukewarm, and neither cold nor hot, <u>I will spue thee out of my mouth</u>.* He is talking to confessing Christians, at that time, their names were blotted out of the lamb's book of life. Just remember ... *Revelation 3:5 (KJV) He that overcometh, the same shall be clothed in white raiment; and <u>I will not blot out his name out of the book of life</u>, but I will confess his name before my Father, and before his angels. Revelation 22:19 (KJV) And if any man shall take away from the words of the book of this prophecy, <u>God shall take away his part out of the book</u> of life, and out of the holy city, and from the things which are written in this book.* This is the final layer of this finish work, updated to be revealed to this last generation of Gentiles and Jews that are not prepared to face what we have not been taught to believe on a large-scale, error in interpretations.

I can see now if he did not have an elect, none of us would be saved with some many different kingdoms works in the name of God. It is for this reason, why there must be a tribulation; we must return to the one true God that shall be the only one glorified in the end as God. This book of the hidden revelations of which I call them my Enoch moments because I was separated out and tutored by the Holy Spirit, not man. These expanded versions of all my sessions in this form as I call them chronicles, is at the request of my faithful friends who God moved on their hearts to contribute to these publications. I have not used an editor to keep in line with the other scribes of the bible, who wrote under direct inspiration of the Holy Spirit; this is the true prophet's message of current events and revelations of our times.

In summary:

Numbers 32:23 (KJV) [23] *But if ye will not do so, behold, ye have sinned against the LORD: and be sure your sin will find you out.*

Now on the National Front "In God, We Trust

Our nation is undergoing a national reckoning for sins of generations past. The evil done in past generations is being revealed for all to see. What we are unprepared to accept is, the reality of what these evils of the past as a confessing Christian nation, are now the curses upon us for our disobedience as did Israel's.

The enemy of our soul will now lead this generation into such carnage as our sins have found us out. That's why America is on fire ... *Jeremiah 50:32 "(KJV)* [32] *And the most proud shall stumble and fall, and none shall raise him up: and I will kindle a fire in his cities, and it shall devour all round about him."* Natural disasters are going to get greater and more devastating as God's anger grows against this wicked generation for the injustices to our own citizens as a sign that we will burn until we exist no more at all. **Revelation 18:9-24 (CEV)** [9] **Every king on earth who slept with her and shared in her luxury will mourn. They will weep, when they see the smoke from that fire.** [10] **Her sufferings will frighten them, and they will stand at a distance and say, "Pity that great and powerful city! Pity Babylon! In a single hour her judgment has come."** [11] **Every merchant on earth will mourn, because there is no one to buy their goods.** [12] *There won't be anyone to buy their gold, silver, jewels, pearls, fine linen, purple cloth, silk, scarlet cloth, sweet-smelling wood, fancy carvings of ivory and wood, as well as things made of bronze, iron, or marble.* [13] **No one will buy their cinnamon, spices, incense, myrrh, frankincense, wine, olive oil, fine flour, wheat, cattle, sheep, horses, chariots, slaves, and other humans.** [14] **Babylon, the things your heart desired have all escaped from you. Every luxury and all your glory will be lost forever. You will never get them back.** [15] *The merchants had become rich because of her. But when they saw her sufferings, they were terrified. They stood at a distance, crying and mourning.* [16] **Then they shouted, "Pity the great city of Babylon! She dressed in fine linen and wore purple and scarlet cloth. She had jewelry made of gold and precious stones and pearls.** [17] **Yet in a single hour her riches disappeared.** (This will happen when the economy crash) ... **Every ship captain and passenger and sailor stood at a distance, together with everyone who does business by traveling on the sea.** [18] **When they saw the smoke from her fire, they shouted, "This was the greatest city ever!"** [19] **They cried loudly, and in their sorrow they threw dust on their heads, as they said,**

"Pity the great city of Babylon! Everyone who sailed the seas became rich from her treasures. But in a single hour the city was destroyed. [20] The heavens should be happy with God's people and apostles and prophets. God has punished her for them." [21] A powerful angel then picked up a huge stone and threw it into the sea. The angel said, "This is how the great city of Babylon will be thrown down, never to rise again. [22] The music of harps and singers and of flutes and trumpets will no longer be heard. No workers will ever set up shop in that city, and the sound of grinding grain will be silenced forever. [23] Lamps will no longer shine anywhere in Babylon, and couples will never again say wedding vows there. Her merchants ruled the earth, and by her witchcraft she fooled all nations. [24] On the streets of Babylon is found the blood of God's people and of his prophets, and everyone else." This will be the downfall of a once great society. In the end, we turned on each other from within.

Through the inspiration of the Holy Spirit, what has been given me to understand of this time, all the sins of mankind are now being exposed. We as a people have no idea of what is behind these tragedies, now justified by Satan as we changed the laws against the male and female genders to become one in the same against the word of God. Thus, Satan has been given the full right to ravage this nation to fulfill all things spoken in the scriptures. We, titled as a Christian nation is linked by a covenant to the one true and only God, were told to trust in. As a nation, we inherited this covenant passed on from the Jews that rejected their Christ. We are that gentile nation, the recipients of the Abraham covenant. God birth this nation (America) with this covenant **"In God We Trust;"** the God of Abraham, Isaack and Jacob, and later, put it on our legal tender as a sign that would cause our currency to be coveted by all nations.

This will be the covenant cymbal of the blessings of wealth to all who will seek to be free to serve the one true God as Christians, born from above, free from governmental restraints to prosper by all the talented that come here to contribute to what would become a great society. It was God's intension for us to be the example and a light to all nations as a beacon of justice, mercy and compassion to its citizens. If we keep this covenant, God will prevent any nation from committing acts of aggression on our soil. We would become the stability of all nation's economy.

We have been protected by God's divine hand holding back what the devil that has already justified before God through the law of sin and death, our destruction. Man, through the enemy of his soul by not knowing what spirit possesses him, has reached the point of no return, has cursed this nation with eminent death and sudden destruction of himself at his own hand. Evil begets evil and good begets good; what we see in the world today is a direct result of Satan's reign of power over the world in the hearts of evil wicked souls he has possessed to the point that it now appears that he has deceived the whole world. (Revelation. 12:9) What we see happening that has many in awe at the magnitude of the evils we see man performing at this present time; speaking from the heart of my source of inspiration, the Holy Spirit ... those who have been studying these chronicles, this final entry through knowledge of the scriptures has been the source of my inspiration as coming out of the volume of the books. Everything happening in the world is a sign of the two forces in the spirit world at war with each manifested in the minds of the people used by the devil. The reason we see so much evil to where it appears to overtake the good that cause many to doubt God.

Many are denying what they have professed as Christians by being overwhelmed by these sudden changes in their environment and circumstances. These divisions in church doctrines have not prepared them to face truth. Many are perplexed in this present darkness. These signs are a direct result of sins committed against each other as confessing Christians by naming the name of the lord and willfully continue sinning has justified a curse upon our households. Satan has asked for the children of this last generation; justified by our hypocrisy as confessing Christians on such a large number. We are the reason for this rebellion of our children. Satan has asked for their lives. We sacrificed them to him when he offered us the prides of this life in exchange for the children of this last generation. This will be the sign of his influence over them; **they will mark themselves with tattoos and piercing, a sign to us of this claim.** It will be up to us to take them back when this revelation is revealed by this sign on them.

He has justified taking these spoils as we see them being abducted in such large numbers that it would alarm the public if they knew what has been done to some of our children. These seducing spirits are manifested in the rebellious nature in some of our children. Many are looking for some truth in something that is real. God will save many of them to replace the confessing Christians that are going to reject him. These children are suffering for our sins of omission and hypocrisy as Satan turn your young daughters over to our enemies as his spoils. He wants their lives not your things. That's the agreement you made when he said in … *Matthew 4:9 (KJV) "9 And saith unto him, all these things will I give thee, if thou wilt fall down and worship me."* His strong hole in Hollywood is where they go to sell their soul in exchange for worldly fame. The reason he wants your young daughters, carrying the title as a Christian nation, he wants a life for a life as justified by the abortions of the unborn. If you knew the real number of abortions performed in this country, you would see why he wants their lives. If you are guilty, just repent and forgive yourself; the door of forgiveness is still open at the time of this revelation.

I am now interceding daily as my sacrifice because of the shortness of time. I have two sons as well as an adopted extended family I am praying that God will have mercy and deliver them in their hour of trials. You see, I fail the first time around as a confessing Christian. After over twenty years in that state, I had a burning bush experience that cause the transformation of my life and mind when I fell on my face before the great **"I AM."** God had a sovereign calling on my life that cause me to have to experience many things through the word to be able to take the rejections that will identify me with his name. This is the price I am willing to pay for my past sins to keep those dear to me from going to hell. I am interceding and standing the gap for those he has put on my heart. If you were to examine yourself through the scriptures, you would see as I did that you have not done everything right as a confessing Christian. God is giving us all a chance to get right before his judgment falls on the world.

Time is no more, and we are in that last generation that will suffer the tribulation of the first church to bring back the reality of **"one lord, one faith and one baptism."** In the days ahead, as the wicked get worse and worse. All who have not confessed these sins of omission when our hearts are exposed will perish as the devil's children.

These are the sins that have justified what we are seeing on a national scale. As a church, failing to keep his standard of holiness, being given a choice to live for eternity in heaven or hell.

These are some of the charges God has against us as a church and a nation?

1. Reversing God's order of the law as male and female genders.

2. Renouncing our Christian heritage as a nation.

3. Renouncing our humane status in the inhumane treatment of fellow human beings.

4. Judging each other as a divided body.

5. Robbing the poor in the name of God.

Finally, Our presidents, along with the Supreme Court, changed the laws that guaranteed our liberties, like Israel in their past, we have return to the heathen gods of this world. We now will experience the carnage of a third world nation we said we would never become after our economy collapses. Our enemies will plunder the spoils of all we have gained since our birth as a nation and in the end; we will exist no more at all. The curse of Sodom and Gomorrah is upon us. We will burn to extinction when meteorites and asteroids take us out with fire and brimstone. The downfall of America is a result of ignoring the history of a past capitalist society, case in point, The Roman Empire. We will repeat history as they return in the form of a deep cover religious empire that will defile the whole world.

You have heard me say many times in these chronicles, history is repeating itself and to ignore its parallels, we will be the final victims as gentiles, lose our national status as a nation. Such is the case in America; we have followed early Rome's path in history right on up to the very same end as greed, corruption, unfair taxation and immorality will cause us to crumble from within. The evidence as well as the signs are presently before us; we just choose to ignore them. One observation I noticed with Israel and America, as nations link to deity, when they chose to ignore their link to the God of Abraham, Isaac and Jacob, He allowed their enemies to conquer them and led them into captivity as punishment for their sins.

This is the destiny that we will suffer during the tribulation for Israel and America. However, Israel will be saved from destruction by God because they are going to repent in the tribulation but only that remnant will be saved. The Holy Spirit has provided a scriptural and prophetic history of these events in these chronicles for those who have become students of his teaching held back from being revealed to this last generation. This, to me is the most grievous part about this knowledge; confessing Christians, choosing to be willingly ignorant as in the days of Noah, mock these messengers as part of that 98 percent that shall be caught in God's break. In great fear, many will ultimately be given over to the world they chose not to leave and be lost. When Jesus walked as the son of God on Earth, He did not quote chapter and verse when he spoke to the religious leaders of his time; instead, he reminded them of what he knew they had read daily in the Torah they had departed from; the heart of the law administered with justice, mercy and compassion. In his elects, he will remind these modern-day theologians of what they have become as a nation privileged to know and serve the one true God.

It is evident that we have chosen to be willingly ignorant; in so doing, we have ignored the curse that comes when you do not obey what he has commanded us to keep as conditions for this covering of divine protection. America will go down in the tribulation and God will once again come to the aid of his people and saved them through the tribe of Judah In the midst of their "911" that will catch them off guard as did America. It will lead to **World War Three** in the valley of Armor- getting. This time in Israel, in their second travail, will bring forth the hidden tribe of Judah. This is their third travail to perfection where Christ himself will sit on the throne and administer true righteousness and justice. His tribe will once again, lead the army that will defeat the Antichrist to save the Jerusalem capital left standing in the end. The first half will produce the true church that will put the devil under her feet. All the reconstruction will be done by those saved to repopulate the earth during the millennium for those living in that time, will live to get close to a thousand years old. The Earth will once again be beautiful without the presence of the devil.

About the rebuilding of the temple before the tribulation, according to the place it is scheduled to be built, we should hear more about its preparation given the signs of the times; however, given the signs, if it were to be rebuilt it should have been practically finished by now. As you have been told in these revelations of Jesus Christ, which include the mysteries kept back to be revealed to this last generation; they shall see all these things come to pass. The books are closed as to what the traditions of man have brought us too. This is the period of preparations for His return. (Zechariah 6:12-13) tells us that the new temple will come down with Christ to reign in the last millennium. God is saving his best for last. May God have mercy on all who call upon his name and be saved ... thus, ends the chapter of man's time to rule the earth. (Completed for final printing at the end of Obama's time in office.)

Let all things be judged by the spirit of prophecy.

These Chronicles of an unknown scribe called to pen down this revelation in simple form for all with ears to hear and eyes to see can understand. Authored by and through the inspiration of the Holy Spirit.

As Your End Time Messenger of God, I could not leave any of you who have read this message of the vision God gave me for this last generation without leaving you who may not know the lord without hope. The fact that you have this in hand is an act of God's mercy upon you to give you an opportunity to receive his mercy and save you from what is now soon, the inevitable. We all have enjoyed the blessing of living in this country, have had the privileges no other people on earth to live. What God has made known to us all is an opportunity to save ourselves. Sadly, many will reject this call and face the horrors expressed within these chronicles. If these revelations have convinced you of this as I was once a shallow believing Christian, lukewarm when I had my visitation from God to come into his perfect sovereign will, I had to repent.

1 John 1:9 (KJV) If we confess our sins, he is faithful and just to forgive us our sins, and to cleanse us from all unrighteousness. Romans 10:8 (KJV) But what saith it? The word is nigh thee, even in thy mouth, and in thy heart: that is, the word of faith, which we preach; Romans 10:9 (KJV) That if thou shalt confess with thy mouth the Lord Jesus, and shalt believe in thine heart that God hath raised him from the dead, thou shalt be saved. After having been told and entrusted with this vision, I strive daily to be ready when my time comes to enter eternity. This is my only hope of his promise to be saved from our hour of destruction. May God have mercy on all that call upon his name. AMEN

THE FOUNDATION FOR AMERICA, THE BEAUTIFUL

As a person of color, I am glad to have been born in America. This privilege has given me the right to put all the social ills behind me and worship in the true love of mankind as one.

We are a nation that has strayed away from the foundation of the Christian principles of its origin. The presents of all the evil at the time of our origination as a nation are about to see the reality of a melting pot boiling into an unseasoned stew with no taste for the pallets of the people it was to serve. The iron and the clay cannot be purified with this mixture until God adds the final ingredients.

We are being judged according to our constitution for not upholding these truths as a Christian nation to be self-evident that all men are created equal with the right to serve the God of Abraham, Isaac and Jacob that gave us this privilege to live under a divinely inspired constitution that's guaranteed to all its citizens, the freedom to serve **the one God we put our trust.** Now we are a nation in perils, whose liberties are in jeopardy of being taken away. As a nation of gentiles in Paul's gospel to be represented as a melting pot of all nations, kindred and tongues, have not administered equally, justice to its citizens its constitution guaranteed. Now we as that nation that has long endured the safety of our God are about to be judged for not upholding this constitution before Him.

As former president Abraham Lincoln's epiphany expressed at Gettysburg … after the emancipation, we now have had over a hundred years to correct the errors of the past. Now once again, this nation, in its current state of division, have by our own willful and prideful arrogance, will suffer the consequences of the enemy from within. All the good men with character in this government are dying off. Our national acts of willful injustices as a Christian nation, in the name of democracy, offended her allies, sacrifice in vain the lives of our young men in these wars in our attempt to police the world, jeopardized our liberties, suppressed our civil rights and our economic pursuit of happiness that seem no longer in our abilities to obtain in our presence state of corruption. We are headed to repeat history as the modern version of Roman capitalism to go down as the Babylon of old, never to be seen again under this curse of Sodom and Gomorrah.

Now that nation, when warned, killed its national prophet raised up by the God of its fathers. Having cut off their vision, now stands in division as a once great Republic; In her evils will oppress the true Christian who refuse to bow before a new beast system that seduced it. Surely our God will not judge us with-out giving us every opportunity to repent. *2 Chronicles 7:14 (KJV)* [14] *If my people, which are called by my name, shall humble themselves, and pray, and seek my face, and turn from their wicked ways; then will I hear from heaven, and will forgive their sin, and will heal their land.* This judgment now cannot be stayed because of the Sodomy curse upon us as the only nation in the history of time ages and dispensations, with a designated Christian origin, legalized sodomy as a nation. The is an insight into our future from one of his end time messengers. After having been rejected by this present-day church world; like those who carried messages like this to past generation to judge them that say they are Christians but are not by their action contrary to the fruit of the Holy Spirit. God is now sending his prophets and messenger to do the same thing in these last days. Those given ears to hear will become the wise virgins, will make themselves ready for the final call and prepare for their day of redemption.

I have outlived two wives to get to this place of peace and rest. I count it all joy of the things I suffered to be at this place in Christ spiritually to carry a message like Noah and find no ears to hear it because of the present state of the apostate church world. Like Jeremiah, I find myself lamenting at what I have been given to know that too many will suffer the judgement of false teaching that have them in a state to hear man over the voice of God, being given over to be judged by their unconfessed sins of omission when warned to repent. I now spend my time in intercessory prayer for the souls of my love ones and those who I may never meet that God will give them eyes to see and ears to hear that they might be saved as I prepare to come out of this wilderness to preach the everlasting gospel to those that shall take the place of those that have rejected this message in that 98 percent as a return of the days of Noah is upon us. AMEN (updated 2/2023)

FIRST IMPRESSIONS OF THE GOSPEL ARE NOT ALWAYS THE RIGHT ONES

"The mystery of self-deliverance"

It is my prayer and hope you who receive these chronicles are reading, studying and meditating on them. As I have mentioned in the previous chronicles, I was a confessing Christian for many years before I had what was a real corrective encounter with the truth. All that time, I was operating in the permissive will of God. I followed the influences of man's doctrine as in a denominational setting for eleven years. This was in May of 1972 when I joined the church I was brought up in under "The Disciples of Christ Denomination." I, as a child grew up under this teaching in name only as I would find out later. I was serious about pastors telling truth. When I attended convocational meetings, after the sessions were over, many of the pastors' smoked cigarettes as they huddled together joking and jesting about worldly things. I knew some of these men as a child. I grew up around a religious environment as a child. I now realize I am an answer to my grandmother's prayers. Little did I know for this to come to pass, I would embark upon a journey that would take thirty years to completely come to the knowledge of this truth of which resulted in me being separated from the assembly environment during the last seven years of that period.

I was a church hopper at the time as pastors would call you. I was looking for a man who practiced what he preached. This was my encounters with denominations and pastors. I went from my childhood denomination as Disciples of Christ to the Pentecostal Holiness Movement and finally the Full Gospel Assemblies. Although I visited some Baptist churches, some of their pastors even had girlfriends on the side. All this I experience in the years of my search for truth. You see, I was looking for it through man at the time. My lack of spiritual satisfaction led me to be baptized five times would end up in a domestic confusion that led to a near tragedy by having been labeled as a church hopper. In my zealous search, I neglected my family because of my tendency to be one tract minded in my pursuits. Now after the fact, I understand Paul's zeal before he had his encounter. During this time, I thought I was right because I could see other's faults and not my own. I saw what others did not notice without knowing I was judging them. I was a modern-day Pharisee.

God had always had his hand upon me, like Paul I was too zealous and blind to see him at the time. After being separated from my first wife, I traveled with an evangelist a crossed the country until I reached Phoenix Arizona. The evangelist group I traveled with disbanded, I was literally left behind. I did not need to watch a movie to know what that's like. Although I tried to reconcile with my ex-wife, I was divorce by having irreconcilable differences. When I found myself alone in a strange city, no one to call or communicate with because I had been ridiculed for separating from my family to prevent a major tragedy that would have resulted in the loss of my life through domestic circumstances caused by my blind religious zeal. I am being transparent to all that read this because I became a victim of my blind religious zeal. I knew I had a calling on my life. I know why so many bad experiences had to happen to me to get my attention. I found out that the devil knows who has a spiritual mark on them that prevents him from destroying you when God has a purpose for your life.

All I ever wanted to do was be a good servant as a confessing Christian but sought it through the eyes of men that cause me to move ahead of God. Only God could have rescued me to find my answer to the peace and rest spiritually I needed. Now that I was all alone, God open a spiritual door while in that broken state of mind in a motel room in a bad section of town; there alone, I met Satan in the spirit. This was orchestrated by God for my benefit so later I would know the depth of the enemy of our soul has on us from with-in. One evening while lying in a fetal position in bed, so depressed to where I felt knots in my stomach that took my appetite. This evil spirit came into the room so strong, I felt I was dying; I instinctively knew it was Satan.

He began telling me what people was saying about me in my hometown and how God had no more use for me, he tried to get me to commit suicide. I had no strength to resist his evil powers and just when I thought I would die, he would leave. Not knowing when he would return to tormenting me, during the course of three weeks, he visited me three times. I would always lie in a fetal position to hold on to my sanity. I tried to take my life after his taunting visits but could not get the nerve to follow through. He convinced me that God no longer had any use for me. Beloved, I do not want anyone to have this type of encounter for God to get your attention, but only God knows what he is doing to get the results needed to become a soldier of his cross.

I know I am not alone in this experience; this is to give some of you hope that have not made wise decisions in your life that cause you to suffer the loss of all things and family at the hand of your own ignorance. Satan is real and if you ever meet him like this with-out God in it, you are going to die. I found out how the spirit of suicide is activated if your number is up? That' when Satan sends the sickle angels from hell to take you there. My first impression was a false doctrine that nearly got me literally killed. I was a chosen vessel to the point that I did not get to live the easy comfortable life that many are deceived into thinking is the way of Christ. He used these experiences to show me who He really is beyond a shadow of doubt. My zeal to tell it like it is with no understanding of what kind of reaction I would receive as a young minister during that time, not being born from above but as a zealous person under man's teaching. **"I had a zeal for God but not according to knowledge". (Rom. 10:2)**

My impact provoked the whole Christian community in my hometown at that time. I did not know then what I come to know later that the hand of God was working all things out to my good to give me an experience that would seal the depth of my present convictions in faith to speak truth that cause me to suffer many rejections along the way. *2 Timothy 3:12 "(KJV)* *12 Yea, and all that will live godly in Christ Jesus shall suffer persecution."* I was not that godly at the time and suffered for my ignorance. I have not reached that comfort zone here on earth that most seem to have found in this new gospel that God said 98 percent are living in a false sense of security not knowing in these last days what is about to come upon them. In retrospect, I can say; I suffered the loss of all things to find God.

It took a tragic divorce to get my attention to save me from myself to serve God in his sovereign will. With no hope of regaining reconciliation with my first wife, God's patience waited another fifth-teen years into my second marriage. God used her to seal me with strong convictions. Through her He was going to use her to bring me to this present state spiritually. It took seven years to restore me in my spirit after that encounter with the devil. Through this second marriage, I was being preserved and taught to become an **end-time messenger**. She had not only become my means of stability in my flesh but gave me a new a focus to do what I did not do in my first marriage. When I inquired about this second marriage, He just told me to walk upright and be faithful and everything he had planned for me, I would walk into it.

She was not that religious but a good person. It would be after my visitation in my basement office I would begin to get bits and pieces of this revelation. I had not attended an assembly of any kind until she asked me that morning. I was gifted by God with the knowledge of the human body's functions and construction that led me to become a qualified professional as a Registered Medical Technologist & chief Pathologist Assistant to a forensic pathology group. God sent me to a local medical institute like the one I trained in that hired me on the bassist of what I told them and never asked me for my credentials.

I lost my qualification certificates too. That was his first act of favor in blinding the system that caused me to walk into that position of restoration to do what I had been trained and gifted to do. When He baptized me in the Holy Spirit and told me that I would walk into everything he had for me, my present wife is the second of these blessings I walked into. She is a unique woman, I found that God knows how to put a person in your life to serve His purpose in all things in His sovereign will. My background experiences that only God could have rescued me from are the bassist of my present deep convictions.

We were married in December of 1988. I have not had an easy life because

I was not blessed with the wisdom that some of you have in my early years … I made many mistakes along the way … outside of the Holy Spirit, my only comfort has been my wife, mother, my biological sister, a stepdaughter by marriage and a dear missionary brother are my close friend circle in the lord that help bring me this far. He said I would see the glory of his fullness and in the end as a son, that's the day I'm waiting to experience before I get to go home.

Never assume that you are good enough to go to heaven. *Mark 10:18 "(KJV)* *18 And Jesus said unto him, why callest thou me good? there is none good but one, that is, God."* When I came into the knowledge of the truth, I began to examine what pastor's say that keeps you paying tithes to support their kingdom buildings on earth instead of delivering souls into the kingdom of heaven. These here-say teachings that incorporate filler knowledge bordering on imagination, I no longer contribute too. *2 Corinthians 10:5 "(KJV) 5 Casting down imaginations, and every high thing that exalteth itself against the knowledge of God, and bringing into captivity every thought to the obedience of Christ;"* Each one of us as a confessing Christian are responsible for your own conversion in saving your soul first and only the real gospel can do that; although God sees our hearts along with those that are poor in spirit, he chooses his vessels through whom he will.

Now brother, when you say real gospel, what do you mean? … isn't all preaching out of the bible the gospel? When Jesus said, **"by the fruit ye shall know them"** I can now see, Satan has some of the best and most gifted seminary trained preachers and teachers I have ever seen behind a pulpit. I'm all for education but just like Jesus said … *1 Corinthians 1:26 "(KJV) 26 For ye see your calling, brethren, how that not many wise men after the flesh, not many mighty, not many noble, are called:"* What he was saying, when he shows up, people get healed delivered and set free without asking for and offering to get what God has freely given us all just by asking in faith. I say this because I have attended some tent revivals in my past where men who had some of these gifts, you had to get in a line to buy these blessings. That is why the unwise virgin's oil ran out. There are some of these men I have learned a great deal from because of their literary knowledge help me with various insights into the word. Despite some of their errors, God still use them for his purposes to gather souls. When Christ shows up, you do not return the way you came, at least I didn't.

Now if that is not happening in your assembly, this is what's happening … *Hebrews 4:2 "(KJV) 2 For unto us was the gospel preached, as well as unto them: but the word preached did not profit them, not being mixed with faith in them that heard it."* When Jesus is lifted in his power, purity and beauty of holiness, that's what will happen. **We all!** … have fallen from the holiness of Christ by not being the examples as he gave us in his apostles on the day of Pentecost. What transpired through them to bring us the doctrine of Jesus Christ, was completed beyond a shadow of a doubt, in those born from above.

This is the prophecy that has come to pass … *Isaiah 53:6 "(KJV) 6 All we like sheep have gone astray; we have turned everyone to his own way; and the LORD hath laid on him the iniquity of us all."* If he is the only God whose unity is in one body that shows no division, how did we ever get to be what we have become denominations and separate kingdoms, teaching in part. Many seminary train pastors and teachers are men educated in the fall-a-way of the doctrine; therefore, a great majority practice the principals taught under Jesuits professors from a literal logical theology standpoint. It sounds good, preaches well, makes you look smart and will elevate your status in the ministry with credibility among your peers. This is the broad road entry that does not require an ensample to gain knowledge of the word. It injects the thoughts of men and his opinions. This is when hirelings were brought into the church to compete as leaders for the flock. *Job 7:2 "(KJV) 2 As a servant earnestly desireth the shadow, and as an <u>hireling</u> looketh for the reward of his work:"* This layer of scripture applies also to educated pastors who are in the ministry for gain of wealth. They are seduced by Satan to take the easy way out. *John 10:12 "(KJV) 12 But he that is an hireling, and not the shepherd, whose own the sheep are not,* (These are pastors that claim you as members of their body and take possession of you as their sheep's and because of your lack of knowledge become your idols in the flesh.) *seeth the wolf coming, and leaveth the sheep, and fleeth: and the wolf catcheth them, and scattereth the sheep."* When you must purchase your education, it comes with the mentality of seeking to gain from it the prestige that comes with your sacrifice. The teachings of men brought division into the body; therefore, men begin to interpret God's word with a degree of imaginations by adding his own thoughts, he changed the context to interpret what he thought it meant; therefore, usurping authority over the Holy Spirit.

Isaiah 55:8 "(KJV) [8] *For my thoughts are not your thoughts, neither are your ways my ways, saith the LORD.* There are two kinds of Christians, those **born from above** and those **born from below."** The two categories can only be distinguished by the fruit of the spirit. Those **born from above** will seek your welfare and not their own. The word through them will be taught and preached with a demonstration of faith, power and with compassion that brings healing and deliverance from these spirits you know not of. Those **born from below** will come in the name of the lord as hirelings that demonstrate lack of convictions by not having the right spirit. They can have faith in the name and still not know what spirit they are of. I found out when it comes to spiritual things, pastors are imparting the spirit **error** or the spirit of **truth**; therefore, the people in your assembly are receiving what' in their pastor. You do not go to the assembly with a closed spirit; therefore, you are open to receive. That's why you are to search behind anyone who say they come in the name of the lord. *John 5:39 "(KJV)* [39] *Search the scriptures; for in them ye think ye have eternal life: and they are they which testify of me."*

That' what they did at a church in Berea when Paul preached to them out of the scriptures things hard to be understood. They search behind him. **(Acts 17:11)** To started ministry without the leading of the lord will not produce fruit that remain. I tried twice to start a work and God did not let it come to pass. I later found out that He had not finished with my conversion as to his perfect will for me as a chosen vessel. My second marriage was my wilderness experience to prepare me as a messenger; therefore, it became the means of my preparation. I was not qualified to be a pastor with two living wives at that time. This brought to light how you can be deceived by operating in his permissive will. **I was called to be a messenger, and a teacher, not a pastor.** I claim no office because He can speak for himself. He uses me to reveal what you are now reading in a clear voice He gave me ears to hear. I have learned that if you must explain what office you serve, you probably went ahead of God because he speaks for himself in the office He represents.

I have two living wives and therefore, I do not qualify to represent one of these positions in title or else I would become a stumbling block and a reproach to those that know truth. He refers to me as his prayer worrier and messenger and uses me as his mouthpiece. Although I have certain liberties in him, I minister as I am led. I never asked for an offering because He told me that all I need would be there when the need arise. That's when I learned to be content because he in me has no needs that have not been provided for. I lost everything to find God. He not only restored all things double in this life to me, being debt free, apart from a mortgage that the government pays through my SS, I now am content to live from day to day. Everything I need was given to me including cars. I have no needs that are not supplied because Christ in me has no needs. In most cases, the few churches that invited me to teach was so small, I left them an offering. God did not call me to start a ministry, I mostly give away what I don't need monetarily like the apostles did. I do not have a bank savings account.

I do not give just to be giving; I give as I am led to give and bless people for their good works and deeds when I encounter them without regards whether they are saved or sinner. This, my wife and I do in secret towards God. Many of us without knowing are strengthening the hands of the devil by lack of knowledge in our giving. My faith is in Christ and him being in me, I can witness he' more than able to supply his own needs. I am content at what state I am in. I am only just here for a few days in the flesh compared to eternity. I have more that I need as his child by doing things his way. You see my beloved; I am living in the last of my days on this Earth. When I found out, I had sins of omission in my life on my day of visitation, I began to work on what I needed to do to save myself if I wanted to live for eternity with him. What I have done up until this point was under grace and mercy until the appointed time for him to take over the vessel in the fullness of himself.

That visitation put me onto the straight path. I had been a confessing Christian for thirty years from 1972 to 2002 on my way to hell living in a way that seemed right but did not know it. That was my wake-up call to the sins of omission. When I came into this revelation knowledge of sins of omission, I understood that figure of the 98 percent state of the church. We, in this last generation are at the end of two parallels; we are going to have to suffer what the early church went through to bring back the gospel and 98 percent of confessing Christians are not ready to leave this world yet. They are like the people in the days of Noah, buying, selling, getting and gaining, marrying, giving in marriage, and looking to gain more stuff.

Don't let this word become a witness against you? I ask God to give me a detailed word to speak and write so there will be no misunderstanding of what I have been trying to communicate to you.

This is my personal testimony of a man that stumbled through most of his life as a fool, the least among men and to have been privileged to be given this opportunity to serve him in his perfect will at this late stage in my life that I have found worth dying for. I have a form of dyslexia that caused me to read at a third-grade level. God gave me something so unique as a gift, despite this mental handicap, I was gifted with the knowledge of the human body and how it works. I knew where every organ was located and how to remove it surgically from an autopsy point of view. That was a gift that walked me into becoming a certified medical lab technician and subsequent training to become a proficient autopsy assistant. God helped me pass my board exams to get my credentials.

I know now what it's like to have real joy that the world didn't give me, peace that surpass my understanding, love that I would lay down my life to give you the same opportunity to know the "GREAT I AM" as I have come to know him. He is **"The Same God Yesterday Today and Forever."** So be blessed my beloved, Dr. Martin Luther King said this before he was taken out by evil men as a messenger to this nation, I too have been privileged to look over the mountain top and what I saw leaves me no hope for this world in its present state. Now you know why I am looking forward to the day to be absent from this body and be present with the lord for eternity.

This epitaph chronical version of all my works, yet to be published, is to share with you to consider as to who is going to be your judge in the end and tell you what he is going to be requiring of all. We all are going to have to repent that have not heard or received this vision of our times. Fall on your knees and do what I did after many years in error, I had no choice but to repent. I am criticized for not belonging to an assembly because I found out that when God open my eyes, I also saw the state of the church. It was then, I began to activate the Holy Spirit to teach me how to deliver myself. Nothing I do in self will prosper with fruit that remain; that I knew from my past. The New Testament Church is in you, led by the Holy Spirit, will give God all the glory. You are the two in the earth that agrees with the father and the son in heaven as touching this gospel where he leads is when we all agree in **"one lord, one faith and one baptism,"** this is His church body that these signs shall follow them that believe. We are now living in part truths as touching the gospel, operating in separate kingdoms until Christ returns to restore our fallen state back to one body and take us home.

All during this time after the fall into denominational divisions, the elects are what's holding back the judgment. That is our state whether you believe it or not ... *Matthew 24:22 "(KJV)* [22] *And except those days should be shortened, there should no flesh be saved: but for the elect's sake those days shall be shortened."* The reason why we judge one-another, our different doctrines have caused these divisions among us as confessing Christians. Now it has infected the whole country right on up to division in the governing of this nation. This is the work of the Jesuit order of the Catholic Church. They built the seminaries that infiltrated and re-indoctrinated Christianity. It started with Constantine's introduction of pagan gods to Christianity. Given generations of these doctrines, men without knowing, became the masters of their own kingdoms just by one error, injected into the doctrine of Jesus Christ, man's intellect along with keeping pagan practices that shows he still does not know what spirit he is of.

Beloved, you may not have to go through what I did as God deals with your heart. God cause me to give up all to get to this place, so I would have the convictions and faith to speak the word reserved for this generation. I cannot fully comprehend the full scope of what he has given me to know. I only know that my past no longer occupies my thoughts. Now I know what Paul meant when he said he was **"forgetting those things behind and reaching forth for those things above"**. We are all going to die at the appointed time; the question is **what state are you in at that time.** We do not want to think about this reality fact of life.

Sadly, I have met some that do not believe there is a God. We all have an inborn mentality to want to live forever. That's what came when God brought life to Adam and when he sinned, we are all born in that state. This shadow of darkness has us under a grand delusion until we are born from above again. It' unfortunate that some of us are still living in that state of delusion as confessing Christians. This I did not know   until he brought me to life with a choice to live with Him for eternity or die in my sins. Now I am in waiting to come out of this wilderness as a John the

Baptist messenger of these last days. The lord is going about the earth choosing who he will use, so be careful not to defile yourself by speaking evil and judging others. Show the love that looks beyond each other's faults and as much as possible, learn to follow peace among yourselves. AMEN

Now on the national front

Our government has been infiltrated by spies in the camp that was manifested in the Trump administration as these men with nefarious business dealings with foreign enemies of the state, God exposed in his administration. These are the men that have international ties that connect them with this New World Order. We see disclosed in these investigations to the point that they cannot disclose the full scope of this covert national security breach to the public that Wikileaks and Edward Snowden brought to light. This is a new supercomputer shared by the NSA and the CIA and Interpol that went online after "911". It was designed not only to keeps tabs on suspected terrorist but private citizens also. It is linked to all, smart phones that use OS system as Apple, Microsoft and android. All other' must have a smart chip built into their software to be able to market their systems. They are gold sim cards, chips that are removable or built into the latest above devises that the government requires to link them to this supercomputer. Hacker's now have these sim card codes. The upgrade to this system has already been implemented that cannot be hacked and will fully be implemented in the cashless system.

That's why President Trump without knowing has become an agent for these conspiracy theorist, coins the phrase, **"Fake News."** The New World Order people are some of these billionaires appointed by President Trump. Therefore, has left Washington in a leadership gap in these non-political appointments to essential departments of Government. Russia and China are taking advantage of this corrupt government by their covert spies planted in place to leak our security secrets through government private contractors with high level security clearances to get covert code information to these foreign hackers. These sensitive documents will compromise our national security. Donald Trump's presidency tapped into this vacuum of discontentment of the people and became their spokesman. All of this was in God's prophetic plan. He will represent the return of the spirit of King Cyrus. His followers along with a dead church will gather around him as sheep following a false Sheppard. His captivating influence will cause the return of the Barabbas patriot spirit. His pride will provoke God to cut short his reign as a lying spirit that will show the state of the church.

The people of this nation are under judgment for legalizing sodomy. Donald Trump will become the last piece of the puzzle to bring an end to this nation as King #45. The high-level corruption as a nonpolitical leader with international ties in business, his behavior will contribute to government obstructionism. He will become their instrument of our final destruction economically; being a cymbal of business corruption and immorality as our president. He became the voice of blind evangelical patriot Christians. God has given the people through him a king Saul like spirit that feeds off the favor of the people that will be under his influence. What we fail to see is president #44 put the curse of Sodom on this nation by legalizing homosexuality. What this now represents, our moral, social and political priorities will become legally reversed by overturning laws that will corrupt our legal system as to what's good will now become evil.

The majority states with the help of the Electoral College put him in office, not the popular vote, all at the hand of God. He will become the catalyst that will bring the subsequent fall at the hands of his bold ignorance of not knowing the type of people he is dealing with, will be our downfall. He poses no threat to them as being the perfect man in office at the wrong time in history as their patsy. That's what presidents have become to them that are in control. That is why he was in campaign mode when he spoke to the people. This is his application of the art of the deal in his business dealings. He is just part of this grand delusion plan to fulfill bible prophecy. AMEN (updated for release 3/2020)

ADAM AND EVE, THE FIGHT FOR GENDER SUPREMACY

"The mystery of the beast with-in"

Most of us take evil for granted because we are born into it by nature with no knowledge of the degree of control it has over us. Men and women who get to read this chronicle, I desire that you give it much thought as using it to examine yourselves. Eve was the second of God's creation to disobey God and the first in man's timeline on Earth. Now I want you to keep this in mind because both male and female genders will be given equal time in this exposé of these evils with-in as to how they will be used against each other after the fall.

First, they were joined by God; **second,** Eve was of Adam as one created in the natural to become spiritual beings. They were angels in their natural spiritual state with no knowledge of sexual differences. Angels are sexless as spiritual beings. God in his foreknowledge of all things created and breathe his life in these two parts of himself, set the stage for what would be the fall of all species created as male and female including His image mates, Adam and Eve. The question is why did he create them male and female? *Isaiah 46:10 "(KJV)* [10] *Declaring the end from the beginning, and from ancient times the things that are not yet done, saying, my counsel shall stand, and I will do all my pleasure:"* God in his foreknowledge, set the stage for sin to run its course when they exercise their free will to choose the course of their life. Eve being of Adam made her a co-companion as his comforter being one in spirit. She will be to him what the Holy Spirit will become to those born again from heaven. She is the other part of himself that will be able to reproduce his and her images by his seeds from God's DNA in Adam. Her place is as the weaker vessel will not become known until she wonders off from her covering and listens to another voice other than God or her husband. *1 Peter 3:7 "(KJV)* [7] *Likewise, ye husbands, dwell with them according to knowledge, giving honour unto the wife, as unto the weaker vessel, and as being heirs together of the grace of life; that your prayers be not hindered."*

There are many mysteries that are not meant to be known to man after the creation because it would lead to further speculation to make man think he is his own god. This is how Satan will use forbitten knowledge to try to overthrow God's plan for man, created in his image using unsubstantiated scientific speculation. This will come through the unexplained artifacts found or discovered after the flood that will show evidence of things unknown to our level of comprehension. These are my Enoch moments to explain the historical significance surrounding these events in dispensational history, as revealed by the Holy Spirit. This part of her nature, having a free will, shows we are not created to be robots. You see, God's love and ways are beyond our level of knowledge to comprehend. Eden was a testing environment to see how they were going to use something in them they were not aware of; freedom to choose who to serve.

Women don't take this offensively, your curiosity is that weaker part of your nature that is the reason why God made them male and female; for them to live in harmony as one, they must walk as one in God's love that will give them the ability look beyond their faults while in this body of flesh. Only God knows who your rib mate is. Adam is the image of God; therefore, he has the greater responsibility as the Godhead, that is why he carries the seed that creates and duplicates them both through Eve. Their DNA when joined will carry the difference in the genders. That's why he is answerable to his creator as an earthly priest. They were equals as one in the garden as the two that became one that lacked no natural needs.

They were free to roam and do whatever God told them and eat whatever they wanted in the garden with one exception; this would be their test. *Genesis 2:9 "(KJV)* [9] *And out of the ground made the LORD God to grow every tree that is pleasant to the sight, and good for food; the tree of life also in the midst of the garden, and the tree of knowledge of good and evil. Genesis*

2:17 (KJV) [17] *But of the <u>tree of the knowledge of good and evil</u>, thou shalt not eat of it: for in the day that thou eatest thereof <u>thou shalt surely die</u>."* Now let's see what they had at their disposal that caused them not to have to work or have any lack or need. **First** God was in them, He has no needs. God in them at that time as His man-child had all they needed to sustain them forever, at that time did not require faith because all their provisions were provided for in their natural state because God had no needs. They were the first to be born from above as fully created adult children when he breathes upon them. They became His man-child children.

I want you to catch a vision at this point; after the fall, you would need faith in God to get those provisions from the enemy who now will take possession of them and become the enemy of your soul from with-in. Everything from that time on will be defiled as time continues; what had been meant for good, will become evil as man's wickedness becomes worst. Through-out time man will destroy himself at the hands of an enemy with-in. His purpose in you is manifested in this statement ... *John 10:10 (KJV)* [10] *The thief cometh not, but for to steal, and to kill, and to destroy: I am come that they might have life, and that they might have it more abundantly.* God made man to be the dominant leader with dominion authority as his priestly image, represented His presents in the earth. Therefore, Eve was to follow him as her lord in the earth together as one wherever they went in the garden because each knew their place as being of one spirit. She was of him as his counterpart and comforter. That's what God set in motion before the foundation of the world that cannot be changed. He alone can make you one that takes you both to heaven. *Matthew 19:6 "(ASV)* [6] *So that they are no more two, but one flesh. What therefore God hath joined together, let not man put asunder."*

This is what changed the course of all creation that would cause them to turn on each other. One evening, Eve decided to leave her husband's side and go on a curiosity mission right to the tree of forbidden fruit in the midst of the tree of the knowledge of good and evil that stood beside the tree of life, now of all the trees, why did she decide to go to that particular tree? Guess who was waiting for this moment to get back into the earth; Satan, disguised as a serpent.

You see, in Satan's case, this was the only tree that had a curse on it; that's why he was there. Here is a holy woman about to have a conversation with an unholy being and be deceived by her own curiosity, giving place to his lies. He is exceptionally smooth with an appealing enticing conversation. Satan knew she would not be there if not for that reason. This will be a pattern that will run its course through-out history. Now what we are going to see throughout history is the use of her appeal as the opposite sex to entice the male image of God to bring him down to the point of ruling over him. This is the dialogue that led to her being violated in the spirit that would result in the rejection of their off springs.

The next phase, she will be violated in defiling herself in the flesh by acting on his words. *Genesis 3:1-6 "(KJV)* [1] *Now the serpent was more subtil than any beast of the field which the LORD God had made. And he said unto the woman, Yea, hath God said, Ye shall not eat of every tree of the garden?* (He used the truth to get her attention.) [2] *And the woman said unto the serpent, We may eat of the fruit of the trees of the garden:* [3] But of the fruit of the tree which is in the midst of the garden, God hath said, Ye shall not eat of it, neither shall ye touch it, lest ye die.

Now that Satan has her attention, the truth will now be twisted into a lie in a way that would pique her curiosity into acting on his words. She has now been seduced to deceive her husband, giving place to this evil, planted in her heart.) [4] *And the serpent said unto the woman, Ye shall not surely die,* [5] *For God doth know that in the day ye eat thereof, then your eyes shall be opened, and ye shall be as gods,* (This is the first lie. Notice the small "g" … after this act is completed in her, Satan enters her soul to speak through her to entice her husband to do the same thing, act on his lying words. Adam with-out knowing, will be giving up all that God gave him to rule over when he acts on the word of this condemned angel speaking with Eve's voice. You see, Adam knew the voice of God and his co-companion Eve. That's how Satan used her voice to deceive him.) *knowing good and evil.* [6] *And when the woman saw that the tree was good for food, and that it was pleasant to the eyes, and a tree to be desired to make one wise, she took of the fruit thereof, and did eat,* (Satan represents sin and by her talking to him, his sin nature is appealing to her free will thoughts, activating her natural nature that's attracted to sin. The lust of the eye the lust of the flesh and the prides of life and when she yields to act, this is her sin.) **and gave also unto her husband with her; and he did eat."** Adam had the responsibility not to hear anyone but God's voice, Satan enters Eve as the evil now with-in without her even knowing what she had done. Now in Eve's body, he speaks to Adam. Disobedience has consequences, when he partook of the forbidden fruit at her request, they saw each other naked for the first time and hid themselves in shame and fear. These two spirits of Satan are now manifested in them both. Now God comes down in the cool of the evening to have his daily talk with Adam and he does not greet him as usual. This is that voice that was distinguished as the one he knew from the time he was created. **Genesis 3:10-13 "(KJV)** ¹⁰ *And he said, I heard thy voice in the garden, and I was afraid, because I was naked; and I hid myself.* Adam knew that voice.

(Now for the first time, he experienced fear.) ¹¹ *And he said, who told thee that thou wast naked? Hast thou eaten of the tree, whereof I commanded thee that thou shouldest not eat?* ¹² *And the man said, the woman whom thou gavest to be with me, she gave me of the tree, and I did eat.* (This was man's first manifestation of evil with-in, He did not except responsibility for his actions but rather, blamed God for giving him that woman. That's the lying spirit in him.)¹³ *And the LORD God said unto the woman, what is this that thou hast done? And the woman said, the serpent beguiled me, and I did eat."* (In that spirit, he put the blame on God and his other half when the responsibility was his fault by not taking heed to the warning not to touch that forbidden fruit. From that time on, he will have two voices in his mind.)

This is that naive nature in a time of innocence with no knowledge of the ramifications of your actions as being evil, exercising their free will to willfully commit the first act of a sin of omission. Adam partook of what God told him not to do, therefore, Satan's plan is now complete. This is the sin of omission that God told him not to commit. Satan not only took possession of the two of them, but now can procreate his own children using their corrupt DNA seeds with evil strands of his own DNA that will be used to produce men with megalomania minds with a god like superiority complexes that will know no bounds when it comes to evil.

Eve was the first act of disobedience as the weaker vessel in the Earth. After the resurrection of Christ, another woman representing her fall into immorality, will witness the new Adam's resurrection that not only restored her, but she will also carry the first message of her redemption to his disciples. Mary Magdalene and except for Peter, the others will reject her witness. I have heard women pastors use this phrase to justify their position as pastors. What God has allowed in his permissive will represents the fall of man. There's no change in the doctrine to justify this as what Jesus reminded them of when they tried to justify divorce under the law by telling Him what Moses said. **(Matthew 19:8)** When Adam sinned, he set in motion things that throughout times, ages, and dispensations that would after six thousand years, result in what we see as a church out of order. The time in between will be sin running its course to bring the world back to the first millennium conditions before the fall.

All biblical history from Noah to this present day is prerecorded in the mystery of the prophet's visions of time, ages and dispensations to be interpreted by revelation knowledge to man and persuade him to return to his creator. Throughout this time ... *2 Timothy 3:13 "(KJV)* [13] *But evil men and seducers shall wax worse and worse, deceiving, and being deceived."* There are doctrines that teach all are going to heaven by just being a good person because we can't live perfect in this world because of sin. That's because they have left Jesus the deliverer out of their doctrine. God moves in the spirit in the earth selecting souls he as predestined in the book of life to live with him for eternity. He reveals himself through his elects and those who receive them make their calling and election sure.

The traditions of the Christian church have put the Holy Ghost in the pew to contain him, so they can have some structure and order in their assemblies as to help God win souls the way man thinks it should be done. Therefore, History in the gentile age will be repeated. **Mark 7:9 "(KJV)** [9] *And he said unto them, Full well ye reject the commandment of God, that ye may keep your own tradition."* What man released without knowing is an unholy Ghost that will fill the house with all seven of these religious spirits in one body in Revelation two and three that will give place to the sins of omission by not knowing what spirit you are of or have become. He will be ... *2 Timothy 3:7 "(ASV)* [7] *ever learning, and never able to come to the knowledge of the truth."*

This will become a carnal assembly, worshipping flesh. This is where gender competition will now compete for authority over each other by exploiting each other's weaknesses. Seminary trained leaders will introduce logical theology that will appeal to our intellect that will transform their assemblies into forms of godliness by denying the standard of holiness in their assemblies. The rising of the Jezebel spirits is what happens in the book of Revelation at the church in the spirit of **Thyatira.** The female gender took advantage of men leaders who were becoming weak to the point of allowing their wives to have a voice in the male stead in the assembly. This is where they begin to teach the men and throughout time as they gained followers, appointed themselves as pastors; therefore, violating God's rule of order in the assembly. They will operate in the permissive will of God as representing the fall away from the apostle's doctrine.

This has put the church the apostles set up in a position for rebuke as Paul instructed Timothy not to deviate from. *Revelation 2:20 "(KJV)* [20] *Notwithstanding I have a few things against thee, because thou sufferest that woman Jezebel, which calleth herself a prophetess,* (In this context a pastor.) *to teach and to seduce my servants to commit fornication, and to* **eat things sacrificed unto idols."** (This is what caused Solomon to fall from God's favor by letting his wives seduce him to compromise God's commandments by serving other gods. This will be the test of your true convictions as the male image of God.) *1 Timothy 2:12 "(KJV)* [12] *But I suffer not a woman to teach, nor to usurp authority over the man, but to be in silence."* I must interject at this point; it was twenty-five years into my second marriage when she began to tell others I was her Abraham. Charity begins at home, If the God I serve is real, then I set out to prove that there's nothing too hard that he cannot change. For her to become my Eve, I had to become her Adam as the God man in her life. He proved His word to me that took twenty-five years to fulfill.

This is what got me put out of my hometown churches when I said I could not find a scripture context to justify God took Adam's head and put it on Eve when he failed from his position. Women may be used to prophesy, not as a pastor, but her primary calling is to teach women to women ministry just as I see a few holy women is doing in this time. I have learned to see the good being done in the right where sincerity of heart is concern. It is not my place to judge another man's servant.

As women, you are to be the holy version of Eve restored. The married women are to teach the younger married and single women how to conduct themselves among the male gender as to not tempt them. They play an especially important role in a man's life when they are joined as one; then they are equals that know their place in the order of God's kingdom. I like to see the transparency in Joyce's ministry regarding her husband; she tells it like it is with respect to her husband in her public ministry. We all have fallen short by not having a Godly example with convictions that point you to the father, not man. I have seen too many confessing Christian women whose children have gone astray by neglecting to train them by example the way they should go as a confessing Christian mother. Some have seen their children buried before them by not maintaining your place in the home. She is a helpmate to the man to build him up and not to speak evil of him in public.

Now tell me, is there anyone in your life as a fellow confessing brother or sister with convictions that would sacrifice their friendship with you before they would compromise standing on the truth? We need some Proverb thirty-one women. This is what I was shown in my re-teaching by the Holy Ghost to show how far we all have fallen, including me. This is where I concluded; we all have missed it except for those he elected to keep his presence in the earth to make our calling and election sure. Therefore, pastors do not deal with the third layer in these books of Romans, Peter, Ephesians, Timothy and the Corinthian letters as to the deep truth that will keep the devil's jezebel spirits from taking over their assemblies, be it male or female. This spirit use gender to its own advantage. I was told years ago before I was divorced that you cannot build a church teaching truth like this. Many have departed from me since I came into my divine calling as a messenger. All I wanted to do is show God how I love him, and this is what he gave me in return.

This teaching will test your marriage if you were not joined by God. If I had been taught this in my first encounter with salvation, I would have had the knowledge to save my marriage. When the Holy Spirit taught me this, I put God to the test by faith in his word because I did not want to lose a second time. *1 Corinthians 7:16 "(KJV)* [16] *For what knowest thou, O wife, whether thou shalt save thy husband? or how knowest thou, O man, whether thou shalt save thy wife? 1 Corinthians 7:15 (ASV)* [15] *Yet if the unbelieving departeth, let him depart: the brother or the sister is not under bondage in such cases: but God hath called us in peace."* That's why I had to become my second wife's Abraham to win her the right way. Your Judas might be lying beside you in bed. It has come to my attention that those that are called with these convictions are having to make some hard decisions that are costing some relationships in marriage to be in jeopardy as many are being tried as to their loyalties by their choices. I found out that my priority first is my home where I am to become a priest and her Abraham as a man of faith. This I did in my second marriage that came with four mature daughters and one son.

I have two sons of my first marriage. In my second marriage, I presented myself as a man that not only loved their mother but respected them as young women. When my biological son from my first marriage met them, they treated him as their brother in love. Now you know why I speak with such convictions. Although they think I am one of a kind, there are more; we are the few that walk like this. This is how I got to know God through his word. My life has always been one trial after another. I used God's fruits to help me die by judging my action according to his fruit. If the way I acted did not match His fruit, I just repented when I saw myself wrong. God will teach you how to love and live-in peace under the most difficult circumstances if you can humble yourself. That's what happens when you seek first his kingdom, he will work all things out to your good. This is what the Holy Ghost spoke through Peter on the day of Pentecost about saving yourself first. **(Acts 2:39)**

In our present state of apostasy, pastors and spiritual leaders in darkness and with their own agendas have caused us to lack faith in the doctrine the apostles preached, send us to hospitals and mental institution for not having the conviction to pay the price to let Christ do what he said he would do if we believed him. The first church in one accord was the hospital and mental institutions where sickness, diseases and demons were cast out. That's why I keep telling you that we all are going to have to repent for being so divided that caused this unbelief where the world cannot see Jesus in the assemblies that name his name.

It took the Holy Spirit to get to this win-win state of mind to keep the devil off me; as to say, to live is to be in the lord, to die is to gain eternal life. I strive to live with-in this hope; that's why I had to let everything go in my past and deny myself things I desired but had to let go to keep peace and see my future in heaven. When the fruit remains in you, God will use you to produce that fruit in others as an ensample of himself that it may remain in them. Then and only then he is seen to this degree in you. I must admit; I find myself always living on the edge of gain and lost in my determination to stand on the convictions the Holy Spirit has taught me.

It is the responsibility of every believer to have this type of relationship with Christ. You see, I am dyslexic and read at a third-grade level with a good memory. This work is of the Holy Ghost in me. All throughout grade school, I was often humiliated when I had to read. It put me in the position of being one of the class dummies, God help me pass my MT board's exam after four years of training at a well-known accredited research institution in New York City that qualified me for what he had gifted me to do. I walked into my profession. If God can use me like he did those disciples and some were ignorant unlearn men; well, I am in good company. I could not get anyone to take the time to edit my writings and I wondered why. The king James Bible is an unedited version of in-correct English; **"the people that read what I give to you to say will already have ears to hear it."** As an intercessor, I am warring in the spirit daily for souls I have never seen but God knows them and that's all that matters.

It cost me all to find God and if I must pay that cost to keep him again, to him be the glory. I am waiting for my day to give him the glory he so richly deserves for all he has done for an unworthy nobody like me. I do not grieve over the losses along the way … he has given me great comfort in taking the hurts away. Though in my striving, I came short so many times and so have many of you when I tried to help him by not understanding. I want to be as transparent as I can to show you what deliverance look like when you can only see what God has done and not you. Do not let pride be your sin of omission that get you judged as the devil's child. I am testifying of him. All I have left is his strength; I look forward to my day of redemption. I requested one last thing of him to let me experience him in the fullness of his glory before my departure time like Deacon Stephen whose name I bare. I want to be able to give him the same glory in my death. AMEN

Inquiry explanations expanded

Recently, I was asked to explain further about the beast in connection with the internet. I revealed in time past how the mysteries of the bible speak in **twos** and **threes**. The bible is written to the Jew and the Gentile believers under grace and truth; that's the **twos**. The **threes** are the layers of the word that reveal the full mystery revelations that when you seek ask and knock will be unlocked according to the times, age and the dispensation as to what applies in that time to be revealed.

Isaiah 28:13 "(KJV) [13] *But the word of the LORD was unto them precept upon precept, precept upon precept; line upon line, line upon line; here a little, and there a little; that they might go, and fall backward, and be broken, and snared, and taken."* God knew man down through time would fall victim of things unknown to him by his own willing ignorance that trust in his carnal environment of the senses.

The whole council of the word is in the complete three layers which is the revelation of Jesus Christ as revealed in the one new man coming out of the volume of the books of the bible. This mystery is found in this verse ... *2 Thessalonians 2:7 "(KJV)* [7] *For the mystery of iniquity doth already work: only he who now letteth will let, until he be taken out of the way."* This now is the work of the angel Michael, restraining the activity of the devil throughout these dispensations to control the activity of demon spirits from infringing upon God's timetable. God created Satan; therefore, he is the only one that can contain him. This scripture is the manifestation of the third layer of this mystery revelation. ... *Ephesians 2:2 "(KJV)* [2] *Wherein in time past ye walked according to the course of this world, according to the <u>prince of the power of the air</u>, the spirit that now worketh in the <u>children of disobedience</u>:"*

When Nebuchadnezzar saw the stature of the beast man, it was both literal and spiritual that held the mystery of the times that would be revealed in the stages of kingdoms and governments that would become wickedly evil throughout time as Daniel's interpretation of the dream. The **first** layer is Satan as a spirit operating in the earth in kingdoms. The **second** layer is him operating in man. The **third layer** is him operating as an AI (Artificial Intelligence) the beast system as the ten toes in the last days coming through the airwaves representing a mixture of all generations to take total control of man's mind. You see, in the time of grace, everything is spiritual; therefore, this beast of our time will be a spiritual manifestation of mind control by way of the airwaves that will be literally in a nonhuman existence but exercise authority over your mind with the ability to speak.

Satan had to be restrained. When the watcher angels came to the daughters of men, **(Genesis 6:2)** this was the mixing of heavenly DNA with man's earthly DNA; when manifested, would become the forbidden zone of knowledge that will infringe upon God's timeline by carrying the presence of this superior strand of heavenly DNA in the earth. We are now about to enter the ten toes of Nebuchadnezzar's dream when our economy collapses. This will be Satan's last stand to manifest in man what caused the flood. The use of this forbidden angelic DNA to control the world will be introduced through the airwaves we will come to know as the internet. America, the Modern Babylon, will introduce to the world the ability to communicate with each other in their own native language; in real time, this is Babylon of old returned through the technology that will bring the revelation of this third layer of the **"prince of the power of the air." (Ephesians 2:2)** Steve Jobs will be the carrier of this forbidden DNA knowledge that will bring Apple to the forefront of dominance with this technology.

It is no accident but by design a demonic manifestation that will be a sign to God's prophets and messengers when this appears. He will use this cymbal of an apple as his trademark. **(A bite out of the Forbidden fruit)** This is going to be the sign to the elects that he is going to be the one that become the major player among these megalomaniacs illuminated ones to be instrumental in causing the crossover into the new time continuum when he introduces **Seri** in his smart i-phone as the beast that speaks. What we are now experiencing in the world at this present time is the disruption of time brought on by using this forbidden knowledge. Steve Jobs knew he was special by having this superior Gene that gave him this ability. He and Bill Gates will become the techno giants of this time but separate because of their genius abilities.

Satan came through the airwaves in the introduction of the internet as a spiritual **Matrix** to captivate the minds of the whole world. When we realize this, it will appear to be spiritual ... *Revelation 12:9 "(KJV)* [9] *And the great dragon was cast out, that old serpent, called <u>the Devil, and Satan, which deceiveth the whole world</u>: he was cast out into the earth, and his angels were cast out with him."* This is what linked his DNA to the host of heaven. Once this was accomplished, now all he had to do is deliver the means to control each mind individually; in comes Satan's agent of that will decode your brainwave using this forbidden knowledge, Steve Jobs. He, with this strand of DNA, use this advance forbidden technology not only to discover and decode the wavelength to your brain but write the algorisms code that will decode your brain's fingerprint individually; therefore, hacking your brain's capability to resist this spirit that will seduce you to the mark. This will give them the ability to control masses of people.

Once this is in place, fear of the unknown will cause you to conform to the times. All civilizations or tribes who infringed upon the use of this knowledge in time past were destroyed. This was the work of Ark angel Michael restraining them. Steve Jobs, with all his billions, died of an incurable cancer when he introduced it. He transferred this technology to his head counterpart that introduced it in i-phones to enhance your inability to resist it. If you use an Apple product, it has been automatically upgraded. They brought back a modern revamped version of the Pokémon game to test it; that's when you saw all these people converging in public places without knowing why they were there.

They were post hypnotically sent there by this app when they opened it on their phone. This is evidence of how you will be marked in the spirit. That's why people with Apple i-phones can't live without them. They will send smart codes updates that cause you to upgrade each time a new product is introduced. When people were complaining of the phones being slow, this is a program to get you to purchase a new one. This type of mind manipulation is built in to sustain this company's edge in the use of this technology a sign of how you will be marked by the beast without even knowing what spirit possessed you to become its prisoner. They will eventually become the largest tech company in the world using this technology. AMEN Upgraded for release 5/2018)

NOW ON THE NATIONAL FRONT, OUR COUNTRY' STATE

(Observations as of 4/2017)

Recently, the events that led up to the election of President Donald Trump as I watched the activities of this President as they unfold in biblical history to avoid making statements regarding my own opinion. It is my desire to see what God sees. As a watcher of **"God's news behind the news,"** it is evident that spiritual forces of international origin are at work to deceive our government.

When God gave Israel over to her enemies for turning against him, it came in the form a delusion to blind their decision making. I see the same scenarios at work in the spirit world that delivered Israel into the hands of her enemies has now returned in our time as history repeating itself. To understand what I'm about to reveal to you, you must see things as history repeating itself biblically. In that last chronicle, I wrote about how I discovered the bible speaking in twos and threes. The twos represent the two nations chosen by God to deal with throughout times, ages and dispensations: Israel, his chosen and the Gentiles, Christ's body under grace and truth. The events we see literally are the transition signs to the tribulation of the Earth's second stage of restoration. God set all these things in motion before the world begin. **(Isaiah 46:10)**

Therefore, we are about to experience what has already happened before, just in another dispensation of time. It is the gentile's time to suffer that same fate as did their predecessor Israel. The new time continuum is about to be set to transcend into the last millennium. This period is known as the tribulation of man and the Earth which will be over a seven-year period. My chronicle, **"Revelation; The final layer revealed"** explains the transition of the events leading up to the new millennium. The last three- and one-half years during that seven will be cut short and complete the Messiah's ministry and remove his church in the rapture.

I am providing you with a background to help you not only see but understand the dilemma we as a gentile free born nation of people find ourselves that we are not prepared mentally to except. We have chosen to be willingly ignorant of our current position in world affairs; as its policeman, have now rendered ourselves helpless with no dignified way out but by war. Under the new administration, our national pride will now be the means of our downfall. The reason, God said … *Proverbs 16:18 "(ASV)* [18] *Pride goeth before destruction, And a haughty spirit before a fall."* It is the way the devil will deceive you into making you think you are right and lead you into his trap that guarantees you will fall in his hands. Those that are under the influence of this delusion will believe what they are doing is right … **Proverbs 16:25 "(ASV)** [25] **There is a way which seemeth right unto a man, But the end thereof are the ways of death."** That's why Paul prayed for every believer to have discernment. The actions of this president are certainly questionable as to our direction as a nation. The President #45 is going to try to change what has been set in motion for the past seventy years by the powers behind this N.W.O. It will result in re- energizing hidden prejudices of social injustice by producing riots and chaos. His spirit will be used to captivate and dominate our political agendas.

About the stock market

Our economy is about to collapse because of fighting two wars and hear we are about to create the conditions for the third and final one. A repeat of the 08-housing market is in the works. We are in a false bubble for housing demands as the interest rates are at an historic low. This time, God will take all these crooked banks down at the hand of their own greed and ignorance to think they can defy biblical history. The rise of the stock market will be a false bubble to catch many in its sudden fall over a short period of time. This time, we will not recover because those behind the

New World Order have planned it that way. Some of the most respected stock advisors are telling you to buy, anticipating this bubble and think that they are smart enough to predict at what point to sale when great profits can be gained in this bubble. This time, without knowing, God will catch them all in His break and prove them wrong. We are a nation under a delusion with the curse of Sodom and Gomorrah upon us as decreed under the Obama administration. This blindness not to see that we are a nation about to default and will show what it is to be the victim of a false sense of security. With all this corruption within-in, think we have the means to pull this off and recover.

The outcome of the campaign that led to Donald Trump's election. Is how God intervened to fulfill biblical prophetic history. Donald Trump reflects the choice that represents our mindset of a nation in delusion that has become a habitation of every foul spirit. These are spirits loosed to captivate the minds of people whose brainwaves are linked into this **matrix** of a non-realistic view of reality of the condition we find ourselves. This includes all religions that have departed from the apostle's doctrine in favor of patriotism to country and practice the inclusion of these pagan gods.

We are drunk with power and staggering into and abyss we created. We are now ruled by a hand-held device that controls how we interact with each other. Our love has turned cold with the use of these non-personal interactions by these AI devices. We can ruin each other's lives just by tapping a few keys on a computer. Godless people do godless things with no regard for human life because we have become blind to our own humanity by giving place to spirits in in our pets that are causing them to create organizations to protect them from us. That's that inward part of you that cause Cain, possessed with a murdering demon to literally kill his own brother Abel. That's what we can do when we are provoked to the point to expose the manifestation of these hidden evils from within. These seeds carried through many generations are now being manifested in confessing Christians not delivered from these hidden demons massed in a religious spirit. Psychiatrists call them crimes of passion.

This is a form of momentary insanity where this spirit that is capable of murder is activated by certain degrees of extreme inward anger that create this condition within some of us, activate this dark spirit that caused you not to know what made you do it. These demons are now being released from the pit. They have one mind set as not to break their ranks; to kill and destroy. If your spirit is still open to these by being under false teachings, you can be a candidate to receive these demons. I know that's a hard statement; just watch and pray and you will see them begin to manifest as things get worst.

That's why we need to be delivered completely from these spirits we know not of. Beware of the spirit of unforgiveness in your heart. Satan had to get deliverance out of the church that cause all these spirits to be cast out at the word spoken at the command of the Holy Spirit. America, being a nation founded in a Christian heritage, is targeted by Satan just as Israel; God's chosen. This is the battle in your mind for those who stand to inherit these blessings of divine authority and protection.

I strive to condense these messages to the point as the ministry of the Holy Spirit to bring you a well-informed background of how we got to be like this and why we all need to repent. I am not a seminary train teacher; therefore, I can keep it simple to understand without speaking Greek. If Jesus came to his own and they did not recognize him as their Messiah, having been given the law direct from God to study along with the prophets to inform them of the consequences of their actions and they fail to keep it. They had a history of what God had done to defend them and still chose to kill him. Do you think He is going to wink on our willing ignorance? Here we are as gentiles trying to impose the law on us that Jews could not keep by trying to mix law and grace together and think people are going to see Christ in the spirit?

Here we are at the end of the gentile's time, being judged as confessing Christians, not being able to recognize His voice because we have been made to think we are spiritual while yet carnal in our actions. Imposing the law in error in the time of grace and truth. If the Jews could not keep it in their time of the law, what is it that made you think that we are better than they and they had a long history to get it right. Speaking this kind of truth is what got the prophet kill by their own people they were sent to save. No doubt, this may come as an offence to some of you who practice a form of the law as a doctrine without mercy or love as judging others. Now do you see how history is repeated in the bible for this reason ... *Ecclesiastes 1:9 "(ASV)* [9] *That which hath been is that which shall be; and that which hath been done is that which shall be done: and there is no new thing under the sun. John 15:20 (ASV)* [20] *Remember the word that I said unto you, A servant is not greater than his lord. If they persecuted me, <u>they will also persecute you;</u> if they kept my word, they will keep yours also."*

I have provided this background to help you see the delusional state of our leadership from church divisions to government divisions; now can you see the parallels? We now have a president that shows signs of being doubleminded and unstable with a pattern of narcissistic tendencies in his decision making by not following national and international protocols. He has been allowed to get away with breaking constitutional laws by having a corrupt politically appointed Supreme Court and a legislative body that acts along party lines with no regards for what's good for the Republic but stands as a corrupt Republic in political derision.

Leaders in the House and Senate legislating, changing the laws as needed to suit their political agendas of this hidden government. What we have here is a failure to communicate among government agencies. We are about to witness a major fall from within. The corruption from the president all the way down to our local government's actions will guide us right into the hands of our enemies through blind pride. His dictator personality may have good intentions but at the wrong time in history. The only thing that will restrain him are the prayers of the saints. His personality, borders on a dictator mentality, personifies the spirit of our enemies as defending their actions will lead us right into their trap.

To demonstrate this religious madness, The Catholic church as a form of religion will use the seminary system they set-up to penetrate all the world's religions will corrupt Christianity by introducing pagan gods. The Middle Eastern tribes are motivated by the teachings of various forms of their Koran just as many Christian churches are motivated by their patriot Christian beliefs contrary to biblical teachings. The Catholic Church is the revived Roman Empire operating in the form of a religion that will use its wealth to captivate the whole world, the Klue Klux Klan are confessing Christians that killed people of color by hanging them in the name of white supremacy. Extreme factions of Muslim teaching told them to behead all who do not believe in their way of life. Jehovah's witnesses will banish members of their own family by ex-communication if they leave after being baptized as a convert while yet continuing to live worldly lives. certain sects of the Mormon's faith use the law of separatism to justify segregation and having multiple wives and creating the Masonic brotherhood of Satan. This is religious madness; taking advantage of innocent minds at a time of vulnerability, being captivated under these false teaching demons possessed men to produce religious fools that will turn him against his own brothers to do what Cain did to Abel; kill you all in the name of their god. This is what you can do by being under the influence of these powerful principality religious demons.

They are Satan's agents that take advantage of your lack of knowledge. *Hosea 4:7 "As they were increased, so they sinned against me: therefore, will I change their glory into shame."* What we see today is a result of what Eve used to influence her husband to sin against God, so did Sarah with her husband, produced a bastard child that has returned in great numbers and the most extreme are fighting among themselves and killing anyone who gets in their way to claim an illegitimate birth-rite. The white Anglos are trying to take back the nation through President Trump because they see that they are becoming the minority. When Dr Martin Luther King began to reveal this kind of truth, this nation killed him as all do to the real prophets. These things were written for our learning but only those born from above will have the convictions to reveal to you these truths in this short time you have here on Earth to hear them and be saved from the inevitable; sudden destruction from within.

When President Trump ordered that strike as a retaliatory act to an incident that did not happen on our soil, he overstepped the NATO alliance. This is the pride of being a self-appointed policeman of the world. Without knowing, we are being set up by forces of evil that got us into these wars by false intelligence will be the catalyst to start the third world war. One thing in my analysis of these last two presidents, Obama considered the consequences of the first gassings that happen on Syrian soil and used a diplomatic approach. Assad realized at that time from the response of the world and NATO, willingly gave up the weapons of mass destruction or be the target of his own demise. Let me provide you with spiritual insight behind this incident. These war hungry politicians in our Congress open the door for this deception that is leading up into another Middle East war trap. Do you not think that Isis could not get their hands on this gas and a plane to deliver it on Syrian soil?

They used us to take out that base for them. They know by us using what they know about our own spy technology in the sky. They learned that from drone attacks. Our satellites saw where the plane came from, they already know about the rational behavior of our current president, he played right into their hands. He did not even have to get the approval of the Congress because the mood in Washington was to give this president some political points to improve his image. No one brought charges to show how he violated the Constitutional War Powers Act by it not consulting congress. These acts of aggression were not committed on our soil or against us as a nation. God knew in these last days these people would destroy themselves along with any nation that gets in their way.

Those given over to Satan are born with an inbred killing instinct against the Jews for four thousand years; they will kill each other to see who can claim the birth rite tribe all the way to the battle of Amour getting. Russia and the United States destabilized their territories when we committed acts of aggression on their homeland soil. We are being manipulated by people who have studied war strategies and given the present technology we invented, are using this president to draw us into war traps. Russia and China are not at all bothered by our actions. They are going to use their offspring North Korea to manipulate this president into a war trap. God has them on the sideline watching to come in and burry us once we put the nails in our own coifing.

Obama did the right thing diplomatically. Although he was criticized by these war hungry politicians, President Trump's actions are dictated by the sentiment of the people and a blind House of Representatives who have lost their sense of scruples. He came into to office on his terms and will captivate the sentiments of the people already set-up to respond to his bold misguided action of a war weary nation. we will be taken out by his defiant ego by not going by established international protocols. May God have mercy on all that call upon his name. AMEN

THE WRATH OF GOD; THE MYSTERY OF THE SEVEN THUNDERS

Background Scriptures:

Revelation 10:4 "(KJV) ⁴ And when the seven thunders had uttered their voices, I was about to write: and I heard a voice from heaven saying unto me, Seal up those things which the seven thunders uttered, and write them not. Daniel 12:4 (KJV) ⁴ But thou, O Daniel, shut up the words, and seal the book, even to the time of the end: many shall run to and fro, and knowledge shall be increased. Daniel 12:9 (KJV) ⁹ And he said, go thy way, Daniel: for the words are closed up and sealed till the time of the end."

In the book of Revelation, there is no mention of the events of the seven thunders before or after the rapture that we can readily comprehend; there is no mention of the details of the seven thunders as outline in the seals, trumpets and vials; however, it is in the bible. All that is written to the Jews and the Gentiles are contained in the word through the prophets as God's method of warning his chosen under law and grace. When the church is removed in **Rev. 14:15-17**, the works of the Holy Spirit is finished, all the saints will rise in the rapture of the second resurrection, just as those who rose with Jesus in the first.

At that time, the church's final warning from the prophets and messengers, just as were in the days of Noah when he carried it, and the prophets when to the Jews would be in a state of apostasy. In that state, the church at that time will reject their warnings also, just as Israel did and therefore, history will be repeated. Just as the book of Revelation contain visions John saw in no particular order; it is not written in a discernable order on purpose to conceal its mystery to a church that would be taught to see only one side of God from a loving tiptoe through the tulips point of view.

They will be unprepared to receive the other side of God in his wrath state. The reason why there's no mention of the thunder details is because the teachers will be seduced to teach another doctrine that will reject the true prophets. This revelation was to be taught among the churches through those that remained in the apostle's doctrine where the whole council of the word is given through the five-fold ministry in **(Ephesians 4:11-12)** to set you free from all the oppression of the devil including lack of knowledge. Whether you believe this statement or not, it is a fact: we, as Christians in our divided state, only know in part until that we missed is returned in the outpouring of the latter rain; the perfect word.

Only God is the judge of who he has received up until that time. *1 Corinthians "13:12 (NASB77)* [12] *For now we see in a mirror dimly, but then face to face; now I know in part, but then I shall know fully just as I also have been fully known."* When the true church is removed, it was to escape the wrath that no one would survive because we will be entering another time continuum, only those chosen to repopulate the millennium will survive. The wrath is reserve for the wicked; that's why the tribulation will precede wrath a short time to purify the saints to make them whole in the image of Christ to His glory and be cut short. Now let me remind you of some mysteries the Holy Spirit revealed to me in time past.

First, Who or where is the mystery Babylon?

Revelation "17:5 (NASB77) [5] *and upon her forehead a name was written, a mystery, "BABYLON THE GREAT, THE MOTHER OF HARLOTS AND OF THE ABOMINATIONS OF THE EARTH."* America is the modern spiritual Mystery Babylon. **Explanation:** under grace and truth, everything takes on a spiritual meaning. We will invent the internet. It will give the world the capacity to communicate all over the world in real time and be understood in your own languages. This is the Modern Babylon;

returned through the **"prince of the power of the air;"** (Ephesians 2:2) Satan coming riding the air waves that will be represented in a non-human entity, **the beast**. America will confirm her fate when she goes to war by setting her troops on the soil of the Babylon of old, Iraq. She will be setting the stage that will cause history to repeat itself as you begin to see this mystery unfold to the end of the gentile age.

I wrote three sequences of this mystery in the book of **"Revelation"** as the third layer. released in two thousand eighteen. I published two previous versions; however, the covert nature of some of this information revealed to me is in this third and final layer, which is completed as the rest of the story to be release at this time. Now let's look at the witness the prophet Jeremiah shows of us in the third layer as a witness that reveal what's happening during the silent thunder judgment of the wrath of God as revealed through the eyes of Jeremiah. This prophecy will unfold in two parts; the Jews first and the Gentiles in the last days or **"in that day."** What he sees will be Israel's siege under Babylonian captivity of old that will be repeated in the last generation of the Gentiles under grace and truth in the modern Babylon. Only this time, Iraq (The descendants of Babylon of old) will join the army of the North, Russia. Yes, the Iraqites (Babylon of old) are coming back with a vengeance against the Jews as allies of the North. They are the ones that's rejoicing while others are lamenting over the downfall of America. **(Rev. 18)**

This is what Jeremiah lamented over in the siege of the Jews; this is what our prophets will lament over in our siege when they get this vision of the thunder judgment as explained in ... *Jeremiah 50:1-46 "(NASB77)* [1] *The word which the LORD spoke concerning Babylon, the land of the Chaldeans, through Jeremiah the prophet (This land is now modern Iraq and Iran.)* [2] *"Declare and proclaim among the nations. Proclaim it and lift up a standard. Do not conceal it but say, ' Babylon has been captured, Bel has been put to shame,* (Their idols in pride) *Marduk has been shattered; Her images have been put to shame, her idols have been shattered.* (When American troops went to Iraq, one of the first things they did is to remove the modern-day statures of the Saddam Husain.) [3] *"For a nation has come up against her out of the north;* (This is their northern invasion by America.) **it will make her land an object of horror,** (This will be the destabilization state we will leave them in that will contribute to tribal in-fighting for control).

and there will be no inhabitant in it. Both man and beast have wandered off, they have gone away! (This will be the effect when we are invaded by the armies of the north as did Babylon of Old as Russia, China and the Middle Eastern nation will do to modern Babylon.) [4] ***"In those days and at that time,"*** *declares the LORD, "the sons of Israel will come, both they and the sons of Judah as well; they will go along weeping as they go, and it will be the LORD their God they will seek.* [5] *"They will ask for the way to Zion, turning their faces in its direction; they will come that they may join themselves to the LORD in an everlasting covenant that will not be forgotten.* (When Israel's time of travail comes in the second half of the tribulation, they will repent as a nation in travail.) [6] *"My people have become lost sheep; Their shepherds have led them astray. They have made them turn aside on the mountains; They have gone along from mountain to hill and have forgotten their resting place.* (This will be their state in their day of visitation.) [7] *"All who came upon them have devoured them; And their adversaries have said, ' We are not guilty, Inasmuch as they have sinned against the LORD who is the habitation of righteousness, Even the LORD, the hope of their fathers.'* [8] *"Wander away from the midst of Babylon, And go forth from the land of the Chaldeans; Be also like male goats at the head of the flock.* (God will cause Israel to not participate in these wars we are fighting that they may prepare for their final war of wars that are designed to bring us into judgment during the first half of the tribulation. Israel' primary task is getting ready for their assault in the end.) [9] **"For behold, I am going to arouse and bring up against Babylon A horde of great nations from the land of the north, and they will draw up their battle lines against her; From there she will be taken captive. Their arrows will be like an expert warrior Who does not return empty-handed.** (Their weapons will hit their targets.) [10] *"And Chaldea will become plunder;* (When we invaded Iraq, the destabilization caused nearby tribes to plunder and destroy all the great artifacts of Babylon of old; therefore, these armies of the north will plunder the new Mystery Babylon, America when we are invaded.) *All who plunder her will have enough,"* *declares the LORD.* [11] *"Because you are glad, because you are jubilant, O you who pillage My heritage, because you skip about like a threshing heifer and neigh like stallions,* (Our enemies will rejoice at our downfall at the cost of their own stability. (Rev.18) *12 Your mother will be greatly ashamed, she who gave you birth will be humiliated.* (Great Britain has always regarded us as their offspring, as our mother, she will be sore grieved at to see the destruction of her daughter as the great whore.) *Behold, she will be the least of the nations, A wilderness, a parched land, and a desert.* [13] *"Because of the indignation of the LORD she will not be inhabited, but she will be completely desolate; Everyone who passes by Babylon will be horrified and will hiss because of all her wounds.* [14] *"Draw up your battle lines against Babylon on every side, all you who bend the bow; Shoot at her, do not be sparing with your arrows, for she has sinned against the LORD.* (When the invasion is complete, 70% of all Americans will have been destroyed.) [15] *"Raise your battle cry against her on every side! She has given herself up, her pillars have fallen, her walls have been torn down. For this is the vengeance of the LORD: Take vengeance on her; As she has done to others, so do to her.* [16] *"Cut off the sower from Babylon, And the one who wields the sickle at the time of harvest; From before the sword of the oppressor They will each turn back to his own people, and they will each flee to his own land.* (When the wars begin to target America, many will attempt to return to their home countries.) [17] *"Israel is a scattered flock, the lions have driven them away. The first one who devoured him was the king of Assyria, and this last one who has broken his bones is Nebuchadnezzar king of Babylon.* (Our president asking of Modern Babylon will desert Israel; therefore, all nations will turn against her to take her down because we no longer can defend her as the third **"Mystery Babylon"** in the book of revelation.) [18] *"Therefore thus says the LORD of hosts, the God of Israel: 'Behold, I am going to punish the king of Babylon and his land,* (This now will become the second wave of God's wrath on Modern Mystery Babylon for deserting Israel.) *just as I punished the king of Assyria.* [19] *'And I shall bring Israel back to his pasture, and he will graze on Carmel and Bashan, and his desire will be satisfied in the hill country of Ephraim and Gilead.* [20] *'In those days* (This has reference to Israel's restoration of Israel before and after the tribulation.) *and at that time,' declares the LORD, 'search will be made for the iniquity of Israel, but there will be none; and for the sins of Judah, but they will not be found;* (The tribe of Judah will rise and defend Israel in her travail just as they did by the help of angels in the 1967 war). *for I shall pardon those whom I leave as a remnant.'* (They are the remnant to repopulate the millennium.) [21] *"Against the land of Merathaim, go up against it, And against the inhabitants of Pekod. Slay and utterly destroy them," declares the LORD, "And do according to all that I have commanded you.* [22] *"The noise of battle is in the land, And great destruction.* (This is what's described in the book of Revelation as the battle of Amour Getting now coming against Israel.) [23] *"How the* *hammer of the whole earth Has been cut off as the third Mystery Babylon and broken! How Babylon has become an object of horror among the nations!* (We are destroyed in the first half of tribulation during the third world war.) [24] *"I set a snare for you, and you were also caught, O Babylon, while you yourself were not aware;* (Our pride that made us the policeman of the world, turned our allies into our enemies when we departed when we could no longer defend them and Israel.) *You have been found and also seized Because you have engaged in conflict with the LORD."* [25] *The LORD has opened His Armory and has brought forth the weapons of His indignation, for it is a work of the Lord GOD of hosts in the land of the Chaldeans.* (Our war with Iraq destabilized that area of the Middle East and cause the remnant tribe of the Chaldeans in Iran to rise and band with the army of the north; Russia.) [26] *Come to her from the farthest border; Open her barns, Pile her up like heaps and utterly destroy her, let nothing be left to her.* [27] Put all her young bulls to the sword; (They will plunder this nation; the slaughter of our young innocent soldiers during these wars as blood for blood.) *Let them go down to the slaughter! Woe be upon them, for their day has come, The time of their punishment.* [28] *There is a sound of fugitives and refugees from the land of Babylon,* (These are the few that escape America's judgment by rapture) ... *To declare in Zion the vengeance of the LORD our God, Vengeance for His temple.* (Those that were martyred for the gospel are referred to as his temples.) [29] *"Summon many against Babylon, all those who bend the bow: Encamp against her on every side, let there be no escape. Repay her according to her work; According to all that she has done, so do to her; For she has become arrogant against the LORD, Against the Holy One of Israel.* (We as a nation and a people are being punished for turning against Israel. Our only purpose as gentiles were to protect Israel until he returns.) [30] *"Therefore her young men will fall in her streets, and all her men of war will be silenced in that day,"* (This statement means, many young men will die in battle.) ... *declares the LORD.* [31] *"Behold, I am against you, O arrogant one," Declares the Lord GOD of hosts, "For your day has come, the time when I shall punish you.* [32] *"And the arrogant one* (The president in office at that time will become arrogant toward our allies and in their retaliation, we ... will stumble and fall With no one to raise him up; And I shall set fire to his cities, and it will devour all his environs."* (This is what will happen during the siege of America, The Modern Babylon.) [33] *Thus says the LORD of hosts, "The sons of Israel are oppressed, And the sons of Judah as well; And all who took them captive have held them fast, they have* *refused to let them go.* (Israel in her former siege was held captive for seventy years.) [34] *"Their Redeemer is strong, the LORD of hosts is His name; He will vigorously plead their case, so that He may bring rest to the earth,* (Christ, the lamb will plead for them and God will once again have to come to the aid of his people to save them and we will be punished for abandoning them.) *But turmoil to the inhabitants of Babylon.* [35] *"A sword against the Chaldeans," declares the LORD, "And against the inhabitants of Babylon, And against her officials and her wise men!* [36] *"A sword against the oracle priests,* (This has reference to the churches that became part of this last pope's movement to bring all religions together.) *... and they will become fools! A sword against her mighty men, and they will be shattered!* (When the rapture is delayed.) [37] *"A sword against their horses and against their chariots, and against all the foreigners who are in the midst of her, and they will become women!* (This is when you will see men displayed as weak vessels.) *A sword against her treasures, and they will be plundered!* [38] *"A drought on her waters, and they will be dried up! For it is a land of idols, and they are mad over fearsome idols.* [39] *"Therefore, the desert creatures will live there along with the jackals; The ostriches also will live in it, and it will never again be inhabited or dwelt in from generation to generation.* This happened in Babylon of old and now the modern Babylon, as described in the seventeenth as the whore and eighteen as a nation.) [40] *"As when God overthrew Sodom And Gomorrah with its neighbors," declares the LORD, "No man will live there, nor will any son of man reside in it.* (This curse is upon our land for legalizing sodomy.) [41] *"Behold, a people is coming from the north, and a great nation and many kings Will be aroused from the remote parts of the earth.* [42] *"They seize their bow and javelin; They are cruel and have no mercy.* (This is Russia and China and all our allies that joined with them when we abandoned them under the last president; now are coming to take some spoils in their Garden of Eden.) *Their voice roars like the sea, and they ride on horses, Marshalled like a man for the battle Against you, O daughter of Babylon.* [43] *"The king of Babylon has heard the report about them, and his hands hang limp; Distress has gripped him, Agony like a woman in childbirth.* (When our leaders see our doom coming, they will begin to whale in agony in anticipation of our destruction. (Rev. 18) [44] *"Behold, one will come up like a lion from the thicket of the Jordan to a perennially watered pasture; for in an instant I shall make them run away from it, and whoever is chosen I shall appoint over it. For who is like Me, and who will summon Me into court? And who then is the shepherd who can* *stand before Me?"* [45] *Therefore <u>hear the plan of the LORD which He has</u> <u>planned against Babylon,</u> and His purposes which He has purposed against the land of the Chaldeans: surely they will drag them off, even the little ones of the flock;* (This has reference to your young daughter taken by the invading armies will be raped and slaudered.) *surely He will make their pasture desolate because of them.* [46] *At the shout, <u>"Babylon has been seized!"</u> <u>the earth is shaken,</u> and an outcry is heard among the nations. Revelation 18:18-19 (NASB77)* [18] *and were crying out as they saw the smoke of her burning, saying, 'What city is like the great city?'* [19] *"And they threw dust on their heads and were crying out, weeping and mourning, saying, 'Woe, woe, the great city, in which all who had ships at sea became rich by her wealth, for in one hour she has been laid waste!'"*

The above passages are a description in parallel the thunder judgments on America and Israel that will be cut short for the preservation of the church at the last trumpet. The demonic spiritual forces at war for the souls of men would destroy the Earth if God did not intervene. God himself oversees the activity that will limit the degree of destruction they can do as restoring the Earth back to the conditions that existed in the first millennium. When all is complete during the seven years of these apocalyptic changes. This is the judgment that represents the vials or in Revelation, the re-alignment of the Earth's geography.

When Jesus told John not to write what he saw in Rev. 10:4; at that time, this mystery was withheld to be revealed to the last generation. All victims of false doctrines would lose hope having been marked in the spirit, given over to the beast by not knowing this side of God as being luke-warm confessing Christian assemblies. All other organizations as previously described will see this reality and many will repent; others' will be rejected by God spitting them out of His mouth. AMEN (Updated 4/2017)

THE RELEASING OF
THE SPIRIT OF FEAR

Background scripture:

Acts 5:8-11 "(KJV) [8] *And Peter answered unto her, tell me whether ye sold the land for so much? And she said, Yea, for so much.* [9] *Then Peter said unto her, How is it that ye have agreed together to tempt the Spirit of the Lord? behold, the feet of them which have buried thy husband are at the door and shall carry thee out.* [10] *Then fell she down straightway at his feet and yielded up the ghost: and the young men came in, and found her dead, and, carrying her forth, buried her by her husband.* [11] <u>*And great fear came upon all the church, and upon as many as heard these things."*</u> When I was given this passage of scripture as an opening, it seemed strange until the revelation came.

Recently in a previous chronicle, I also mentioned a spirit of fear has been released from the pit. The state of the people on a large scale are being controlled by media psychology, electronically induced mind control through smart media devices as the **"prince of the power of the air"** rides the airwaves into your minds. The evidence is all around us as not being able to live without this beast that speaks, held in your right hand. This has caused our attention span to be reduced to critical levels of tolerance that's leading to these increased numbers of road rage and mass suicide killings.

Our willing ignorance tend to ignore all these bad news reports until it reaches home. We are in the third phase of the troubling of the waters leading up to the tribulation. As confessing Christians, our level of knowledge in traditional church settings does not go into the layered deep spiritual revelations that are the mysteries the Holy Spirit wants to reveal to every one of us. Our limitation in knowledge is based in standards set by man's academia, limited to only what his father, (the devil) lead you to believe to ensure our destruction by keeping us ever learning but never coming to the knowledge of the truth.

Now to examine the background scriptures ... the story of Ananias and his wife Sapphira is another layered revelation story. **(Acts 5:1-3)** When God's spirit returns in the latter rain, you will instantly be given over to Satan for destruction as a luke-warm Christian for unrepented sins of omission when your state is revealed as living a lie. That's the curse of fear that comes with living a lie. That's why, if he can get you to deny God through fear of men, he knows he has you under his control. What God has given man for his good, in an evil environment will be used to destroy him by not knowing who is in possession of his vessel. Only the bible truth can give you the knowledge to examine this type of fruit, whether it be of God or of the devil because of Satan's many disguises. *Matthew 7:14 (KJV)* [14] *Because strait is the gate, and narrow is the way, which leadeth unto life, and few there be that find it. Matthew 12:33 "(KJV)* [33] *Either make the tree good, and his fruit good; or else make the tree corrupt, and his fruit corrupt: for the tree is known by his fruit. Matthew 7:16 (KJV)* [16] *Ye shall know them by their fruits"* ... This is the third layer to the background scriptures. What we chose to be ignorant of, God destroyed a whole civilization by bringing waters of destruction out of the ground and from the sky to end the first dispensation of man.

We cannot see our ignorance until we become the victim as in the days of Noah. Therefore, at the end of the sixth millenniums, God will release the enemy to send natural disasters as a sign, fires in and around your cities and waters to flood your towns. This sign is the mixture of fire and water, kept separated to serve its purpose as the coming signs of destruction. Fire and water are the two most devastating forces of major destruction. Water destroyed the Earth in the beginning, the **Alpha**. Man will produce the means of his own destruction by fire in the end, the **Omega**. These signs represent the beginning and the end. *Revelation 18:6 "(KJV)* [6] *Reward her even as she rewarded you, and double unto <u>her double according</u> to her* *works: in the cup which she hath filled fill to her double. Jeremiah 50:32 (KJV) ³² And the most proud shall stumble and fall, and none shall raise him up: and <u>I will kindle a fire in his cities,</u> and it shall devour all round about him."* (Just when we think we have arrived at peace and safety.) *1 Thessalonians 5:3 "(KJV) ³ For when they shall say, Peace and safety; then sudden destruction cometh upon them, as travail upon a woman with child; and they shall not escape."* Ask the citizens of California who will be victims of these sudden disasters.

When I hear the replies of those victims of natural disasters as well as those done by human intervention, I am some-what grieved that we still cannot see the scope of these disasters as being signs of bible prophecy of diverse occurrences. These natural disasters around the country are judgements that are going to intensify to the point of generating fears we have never had to face in this country before. Satan has gone before God to justify the destruction we see happening as evil men possessed with his spirit get worse and worse. Once again on the timeline of God, man has reached the point of no return as for prophecy being fulfilled. This is the vision that is only given through the spirit of prophecy for all with ears to hear and eyes to see what **"Thus Say the lord."**

I do not like being the barer of such bad news but there's hope, you are being warned before the worst comes to set your house in order because none shall escape. Everyone living that name his name must prove your love for God in the fires of tribulation. I have said many … many times in these writings, there is no new things in God's sight; all history he set in motion is just repeated throughout times, ages and dispensations. **(Ecclesiastes 1:9)** Christ cannot return until the church he set up as one body be restored as he established it in the beginning with the devil defeated under her feet. In other words, we must take back the Earth from the devil as the Adam restored to his dominion by force. There are too many religions in the world that have 98 percent of the world in a state of confusion. Only God himself must put an end to this religious madness by tribulation. That's when all the world will see who the real God is when He comes.

Only tribulation can clean up this mass of confusion we have made in the name of God. He is now walking in the earth by his spirit selecting souls as he did that established his first church that will have to go through what the early apostles did and spill their blood once again for the last time to justify his death, burial and resurrection before He can return. Many confessing Christians will be replaced at the marriage supper with the souls of some of their children and of those wounded at the hands of a sick divided church world. God will have mercy on some of your children and save them to replace you, just as he did those in the wilderness. They were too hard-hearted and therefore, left behind to die. The devil invaded the assembly and turned it into and entertainment center. In my observations of these times, I see the same willing ignorance that was present in the days of Noah.

There were scoffers who mocked him for building a boat when it had never rained. This mocking lasted for one hundred and twenty years before the judgment came with a drop of rain that came seven days after the door was closed to the Ark. That same spirit will be returned to judge man again at the end of his time to subdue the earth. Remember, **"911"** was a distress call marked by a major sign of the fall of the twin towers in America (the mystery modern Babylon) Though we are not mentioned by name in the bible, this will be the confirming sign. **Ezekiel 26:9 "(KJV)** [9] *And he shall set engines* (Airplanes hitting the World Trade Towers) **of war against thy walls, and with his axes he shall break down thy towers."** The place where this sign will be given is described in ... *Isaiah 30:25 "(KJV)* [25] *And there shall be upon every high mountain, and upon every high hill, rivers and streams of waters <u>in the day of the great slaughter, when the towers fall</u>."* This is a description of the World Trade Towers surrounded by water on the lower end of Manhattan Island in New York. I want you to see how detailed our future history is repeated by the interpretation of the signs Jesus told us to watch in our time as revealed through the spirit of prophecy.

God has delayed our judgment day to give his elects in the wilderness time to get ready to revive his church out of great tribulation to enter his kingdom. *Acts 14:22 "(KJV)* [22] Confirming the souls of the disciples, and exhorting them to continue in the faith, and that we must through *__much tribulation__ enter into the kingdom of God."*

If you want to be able to see in the spirit on this level, you must forsake your own thoughts and deny yourself of your desires. Everything has been judged by the word. In conclusions about what we see, the kingdom of God does not come by observation in the natural order; observations are the result of the signs. That's why those who try to predict by observations will always get it wrong. That's how Satan has deceived many that prove to be false prophets through false dreams and visions. *Luke 17:20 "(KJV)* *20 And when he was demanded of the Pharisees, when the kingdom of God should come, he answered them and said, the kingdom of God cometh not with observation":* One of the reasons I see pastors and so-called prophets in burn-out mode today is lack of vision in their messages by trying to help the Holy Spirit do what only God can, speak for himself. In their own strength, they are trying to keep their members from sleeping through the service. Jesus said ... *John 12:32 "(KJV) 32 And I, if I be lifted up from the earth, will draw all men unto me."* Self-denial is where we see Jesus feeding his church the true spiritual bread that delivers the soul.

The few times I have had the privilege to give a message in an assembly, I did not see anyone sleeping. Most of them were astonished at the depth of the message. In the end, their leader rejected it by having no vision of these times. I learned in my profession; death is inevitable and can be sudden; it will come to us all and some without notice. I have found that dying to yourself first is how you will literally overcome the fear of dying from this life. I strive to think as though I am living in the fullness in order that he may find the faith in me he expects to see as trusting him, this time in my body. This mind-set has help me overcome many attacks of the devil in my body and circumstances beyond my control.

I still have faults that cause me to make mistakes and miss the mark sometimes in judgments because of fleshly distractions I encounter in my daily walk. Thank God for grace and mercy. If you can be honest with God, you will be honest with others. Never forget that you came from sin to salvation, it's God you should fear, not man. Since God open my mind to the things as in ... *Jeremiah 33:3 "(KJV) 3 Call unto me, and I will answer thee, and shew thee great and mighty things, which thou knowest not"* ... I have never been the same nor have many understood me to a certain degree. The reason I am speaking in such a way is because I wish all could see beyond your fleshy existence with a deeper understanding of God's concepts of life in this world.

Not that I have arrived, I now know what Paul saw while in this state of mind and this is without literally seeing dreams or vision as some others. I have learned as to what God is doing in all things is to wait for the fruit as to the heart of the source. You may be saying, " we don't hear of you if you are having this type of relationship with the lord as seeing people getting healed and delivered?" What I am being taught is not to be manifested until the people are in a condition where they are ready to hear what they have willingly ignored, the truth. God is not going to waste this word on those who have had all this time to hear his voice, just to reject Him. Many without knowing have had their day of visitation and had they known his voice, would be prepared for what's coming.

When our economy collapses and all you depend on is gone, that will be the time I have been informing you to prepare for. Many have been deceived to think they have arrived and therefore, they are not ready to hear this message until God take their idols away. Although I have been brought to understand revelations beyond my level of comprehension, God is ready to have this kind of relationship with anyone that gives him your mind and quit trusting in yourself. This unconditional love to surrender as in ... *Matthew 6:33 "(KJV)* [33] *But seek ye first the kingdom of God, and his righteousness; and all these things shall be added unto you."* If you are continually having trouble in your spirit, soul and body, it is a sign that you are holding on to something you need to let go. This is the healing part of the mind of God when you are loosed from the entanglements of this world that transform and transport you into the kingdom of heaven. What grieves me is to know the persons problem and God said they are not ready to hear you; so, you must just follow peace because you are on God's timing as to when to speak. This you can do when you exercise the fruit of temperance. Quite people in the spirit are good listeners, that's why you are surprised at what they say when they speak. AMEN

Now on the national front

The Obama Affordable Health Care Act was written in such a way that it cannot be change; therefore, what you see the Republicans trying to do will only add a burden or take away the benefits to the people it was designed to help. This type of legislation should have been written shortly after the Social Security act; we as Americans would have perfected the health care system and contained the cost by having one of the best delivery systems supported by withholding both taxes at that time that would have insured equal opportunity quality-controlled healthcare. That's a Christian nation taking care of all its citizens equally.

This bill, written at this late stage in time, has come when the system of health care is too corrupt with fraudulent means of delivery without specific oversight guidelines in place for providers that have taken advantage by overbilling for services they have not provided. The "Obama Care" bill was passed fifty years too late at a cost that is far too high to sustain; once implemented, the twenty million people that benefited at that time in the first year is what the Republicans will have trouble within their attempts to make changes.

The economy cannot sustain itself with this belated added expense of the Obama bill that was crafted in such a way that does not leave any wiggle room without upsetting those that got insured when it was first implemented. This bill made your health care affordable by adding supplements from the government. Now the House and Senate are in a dilemma that is beyond party lines. They are trying to change what was done at the expense of not counting the cost at the time Obama Care was introduced. We are fighting two wars; they are appropriating money that has not been collected in taxes and this new tax bill being pushed by the rich will further deplete the treasury and speed up our collapse. That's the delusion they can't see that will cause them to be caught in God's break. They are robbing themselves of their own future.

Now we are in the third year when that cost is now realized but those on it don't want to give it up and they can't come up with a workable alternative. That is the quagmire that will cause a national crisis that they have found themselves in in the Houses of Representatives. This is amazingly simple to correct but their party loyalty comes before our national priority. Instead of improving on what's good for all regardless of party, they used the wrong term "repeal and replace" instead of improving; here, you see where the return of prejudice spirits against people of color, just because a man of color, President Obama, got it passed on his watch. The Republicans, using that term "repeal" after it was put into law and implemented, the problem they have created by trying to reverse Obama's legacy that reveals their hidden prejudices. The public has no idea of what the government is doing that is causing all these divisions in the two parties that is contributing to our internal collapse by inflating the real-estate market to a bubble that will once again burst as in 2008. Here in 2020, I see it is about to repeat again; this time, we will not recover.

The banks are back with a hidden agenda as being controlled by the powers that are currently controlling Washington, DC. The federal reserve is inflating the economy with worthless paper money that's contributing to high manufacturing cost as being made in America. These companies had to correct their financial instability by outsourcing. This all happened behind closed doors. In their secrete chambers, cause that one percent to get richer to the point of controlling 99 percent of the nation's wealth. The people that are behind this economic change in the transfer of wealth is what took out the middle class are the members of The Bilderberger's think tank, The New World Order. Donald Trump has been compromised through our number one enemy, Russia. Isn't it strange that his administration will not say anything against Russia with all the evidence we have on their hacking activity? All the spy agencies are supporting these allegations but not his administration. He called it **"fake News,"** That's because he is a conspiracy theorist believer. In the spirit of truth, a lot of news is reported along political lines. These revelations will be known of him soon. His spirit will control the republican party while not in office.

Just like I never thought I would see a President of the free world endorse Sodomy and the very next one come into to this office on his own terms in the history of Presidential elections. Never in our history had any President dictated his own terns in a campaign and succeed in getting elected by his own rules. God allowed that to show us how corrupt our justice system will become as we will see during his term in office as President #45. That's why he stays in touch with his supporters as still in campaign mode.

These multimillionaires in his cabinet are the people put there to begin implementing our downfall to bring in the N.W.O. The people got what they wanted, and they have their patsy in place for their final assault on this nation. He is the Saul that will betray God and resurrect the spirit of King Cyrus of Babylon of old, all in one as a nonpolitical leader. His control of the Republican party is a form of a pre-antichrist spirit, using him to further captivate and control this nation.

This has been sixty years in the making, they both are victims of the times to complete bible prophecy. The Obama Presidency is the fulfillment of Dr. King's prophecy dream of a man of color would come in this office on the bassist of the content of his character not the color of his skin. He will bring the Sodomy curse by legalizing homosexuality. Trump, chosen by people in a state of delusion did not command the office by popular vote but once again, a majority Republican Electoral College, voting in their favor in a close call to the point that God gave the people what they ask for, not by popular vote but by an election default. Through him we will see what patriotic pride will cost this nation in its blind state to become the victims of destruction at the hand of a foolish president not knowing he's being used to repeat history. If you have been reading and studying these chronicles, you have enough visional information to read and discern these signs. Yes, he will do some good things but ultimately, he will take the fall on his watch. Pray for him that God will give us time to reach more souls. AMEN (7/2017 Reprinted)

THE THIRD LAYER
OF SALVATION

Background scripture:

2 Thessalonians 2:7 "(KJV) [7] For the mystery of iniquity doth already work: only he who now letteth will let, until he be taken out of the way."

The depth of these chronicles is design to make you think about the seriousness of our salvation as to have no doubt of what God has given us and made available as we receive Christ as our savior. Many have said, this is too deep for them because they have not been taught this in their assemblies.

Living in the reality of the new birth; I, in my earlier years as a confessing Christian, went for more than thirty years operating in the first stage of my salvation. It was not until I was drawn in by the Holy Spirit as to my calling as a messenger, I begin to search into the total deliverance aspect that came with my salvation. I learned why some confessing Christians will have to be allowed to suffer sickness unto death; **for some, this is the only way they will continue to serve the lord.** God knows you better than you know yourself and allows certain things to remain in your life to keep you save until death. We tend to boast in our faith that will be tested by unexpected trials. Our convictions and faith in the word is what will get you delivered. Your body is your worst enemy because it was born in a sin state. It can only be contained through obedience to the word.

Once I asked a person this question? If you were completely healed, what would you do ... their reply, all the things I never could do before. That statement did not represent a real love for God, so I ask God to do according to His faith. When Jesus said, it is was according to your faith, I have never been sick with and illness that I didn't get delivered from. That is not to say that I cannot get sick because I have had some serious sickness in my life. When I learned what can justify what Satan can put on you, I begin to study what being converted to deliverance really means, and what gives you authority over the devil that when Jesus said ... ***Matthew 18:19 "(KJV)*** [19] ***Again I say unto you, That if two of you shall agree on earth as touching anything that they shall ask, it shall be done for them of my Father which is in heaven."***

During the seven years of my re-teaching by the Holy Spirit, I wanted to know what I HAD TO DO TO NOT BE A WORRIER ABOUT ANYTHING THAT GOD HAD DELIVERED ME FROM. ***Matthew 13:15 "(KJV)*** [15] ***For this people's heart is waxed gross, and their ears are dull of hearing, and their eyes they have closed; lest at any time they should see with their eyes, and hear with their ears, and should understand with their heart, and should be converted, and I should heal them."*** This scripture by lack of understanding kept me bound in a traditional church environment where this knowledge was not taught in the kind of faith to get you healed and stay healed. When the Holy Spirit got my attention, I started to look at the life of Jesus as he lived and walked while on this earth for that short span of three and one-half years, demonstrated what the father would do in them that followed his example.

I had been taught that we could not be as holy as Jesus. In the first stage of salvation, this makes sense because we are baby Christians when we first encounter truth. Now there is the second layer to study and learn why I am called a new creature and what do we have that we didn't have before. This is all up to you to seek out the answer to these questions and ask God to increase your faith to believe what he is telling you through his word. **Matthew 6:33 "(KJV)** [33] **But seek ye first the kingdom of God, and his righteousness; and all these things shall be added unto you."** His work to defeat the devil is finished. In that love he has given us, we must maintain that ability to look beyond other's faults while we are still in this body of flesh. ***1 Corinthians 2:2 "(KJV)*** [2] ***For I determined not to*** *know anything among you, save Jesus Christ, and him crucified."* When you realize that we all came from sin to salvation, that's why you can't judge another with-out condemning yourself. Instead of judging, you are to become what they are not by letting the Holy Spirit lift Jesus. The key is to surrender with a child-like faith.

This I found out was the reason for my short comings that seem to ware me out by asking God to forgive me many times for things I should have overcome by knowledge. It was because I did not act on that knowledge that kept me bound. After a while, I soon learned it was my environment I was entertaining that was causing my problem. I was trying to convince myself, what I was doing was not all that wrong by not surrendering fully. When you are around people that are continuing to sin; you will also. Now this was the hard part that we all have trouble with if you are honest with yourself ... *Ephesians 5:11 "(KJV)* [11] *And have no fellowship with the unfruitful works of darkness, but rather reprove them. 2 Corinthians 6:17 (KJV)* [17] *Wherefore come out from among them, and be ye separate, saith the Lord, and touch not the unclean thing; and I will receive you, John 15:18 (KJV)* [18] *If the world hate you, ye know that it hated me before it hated you. John 7:7 (KJV)* [7] *The world cannot hate you; but me it hateth, because I testify of it, that the works thereof are evil. Amos 3:3 (KJV)* [3] *Can two walk together, except they be agreed?"* If you continue to keep company with a person or people that is sinning ... *2 John 1:11 "(KJV)* [11] *For he that biddeth him God speed is partaker of his evil deeds."* God considers you as condoning the works of the devil. The only way that person will know whether you believe what you confess to be is by not keeping company with them in their sinful state. **1 Thessalonians 4:7 "(KJV)** [7] **For God hath not called us unto uncleanness, but unto holiness."**

Fact one:

You do not have anything to offer God that he did not give you; that is, your life. Our wickedness is what convicted us when we saw it presented to us by the Holy Spirit. Therefore ... *Isaiah 55:7-8 "(KJV)* [7] *Let the wicked forsake his way, (we were born that way) and the unrighteous man his thoughts:* (This is where your conviction causes you to surrender because you will see you are a victim of your own thinking.) *and let him return unto the LORD, and he will have mercy upon him; and to our God, for he will abundantly pardon.* (This is the first stage to becoming a new creature?) [8]

For my thoughts are not your thoughts, neither are your ways my ways, saith the LORD." (As you see, this was required in the old covenant to follow the commandments of God to be accepted. Now this is where the sacrifice of yourself will transform the whole man back to that new creature and take him out of the natural temple as Christ enters you as his new temple dwelling place, now as walking by faith.

1 John 4:4 (KJV) [4] *Ye are of God, little children, and have overcome them: because greater is he that is in you, than he that is in the world. 1 Corinthians 6:19 "(KJV)* [19] *What? know ye not that your body is the temple of the Holy Ghost which is in you, which ye have of God, and ye are not your own? Romans 12:1-2 (KJV)* [1] *I beseech you therefore, brethren, by the mercies of God, that ye present your bodies a living sacrifice, holy, acceptable unto God, which is your reasonable service.* [2] *And be not conformed to this world: but be ye transformed by the renewing of your mind, that ye may prove what is that good, and acceptable, and perfect, will of God."* The law did not make men sin free because he remained natural and had to use an animal's blood to atone for his sins in the old covenant. Jesus gave up his will, sacrificed his life-giving blood so the father could receive all men created in his image again. Therefore, Jesus is our only example to us in our body that this can be done, only in the same way Jesus did; surrender your will. This is what you will have to learn and act upon in his word as the beginning stages to walk as a new creature. This is stage two.

Fact two:

It took faith to get saved, now you must … *Hebrews 11:6 "(KJV)* [6] *But without faith it is impossible to please him: for he that cometh to God must believe that he is, and that he is a rewarder of them that diligently seek him."* The faith that God has made available to those that name his name is found in the whole council of the truth applied in all arrears of your life. The whole man walks the privilege of the new creature in the authority as the Adam restored. This is where we will begin to demonstrate the pure love of God in Christ to the world that can only be seen in the purity of a dying vessel being made meat for the master's consumption. This is what will bring separations from the world as he receives you into the family of God. You are now walking on that … *Matthew 7:14 "(KJV)* [14] *Because strait is the gate, and narrow is the way, which leadeth unto life, and few there be that find it."* All my shortcomings can be measured in unlearning the hear-say teachings through men that meant well but lacked revelation knowledge by not paying the price for the lord to show up in the assembly as he did in the early church established through the apostles. All who refuse to except God's invitation … *John 8:24 "(KJV)* [24] *I said therefore unto you, that ye shall die in your sins: for if ye believe not that I am he, ye shall die in your sins."* If you fail to continue in him, you will die spiritually by committing the sins of omission, which is a life of compromise and politically correct statements. Dying to self is what brings you to this third layer of complete deliverance that will cause rejections as you enter on that narrow road of the few.

The third and final layer of complete deliverance:

This is where you overcome the fear of death and dying. We don't like to think of literally dying but the reality is, it's the destiny of us all. We are born a child whose destiny is hell if we never claim our birth-rite to live for eternity when called by the Holy Spirit the day we hear the gospel. We were born under the curse of the law of sin and death as a child of the devil. I, after having heard of the miracles that evangelist was seeing in third world countries, it is representative of how far we are removed from the anointed presence of the Holy Spirit in our assemblies. It is hard to get people to believe in miracles when they don't see them as in the early church. Here in America, our blessings have overtaken us and become our idols.

The person that has unwavering faith in the full council of the word can keep the devil off him in every area of your life just by believing and acting on the word without doubt in his heart. This is the heritage that came when Jesus said, **"It is finish;"** now all we must do is stand on his word and watch him perform it according to your faith in every area of your life. *Jeremiah 1:12 "(KJV)* [12] *Then said the LORD unto me, thou hast well seen: for I will hasten my word to perform it."* In my inquiry of why we do not see the miracles in the assembly like this anymore, this was my reply … *Mark 11:17 "(KJV)* [17] *And he taught, saying unto them, is it not written, my house shall be called of all nations the house of prayer? but ye have made it a den of thieves."* The Holy Spirit' presence in the purity and power of holiness is what brings the healing virtue from heaven. We, in my observation are a long way from being a holy assembly.

When I was growing up in church as a young boy, I recalled every Wednesday night the people would come together and pray for an hour in the church. They called it prayer meeting night. The minister will give a short lessen; after, they would anoint with oil, anyone who was sick. The women were more faithful at doing this than the men and some got delivered from sickness. I recall as a young child, the early saints were poor in spirit, but they were faithful to the lord in their prayer life. That's the experience I had in my early exposure what God was going to take be back to. When I learn this was the key that was taken from Satan that loosed me from his bondage, I have been praying for souls every sense.

Matthew 5:3 "(KJV) [3] *Blessed are the poor in spirit: for theirs is the kingdom of heaven."* I personally have been working on my own faith in this area to remove all doubt. I am beginning to see some results in those I have taught how to deliver yourself just by standing on the word with no conditions, just putting God to the test. If you ever want to get to this third layer in your salvation, this is the faith He seeks to find when He returns. *Luke 18:8 (NKJV)* [8] **I tell you that He will avenge them speedily. Nevertheless, when the Son of Man comes, will He really find faith on the earth?»** You must learn to trust in Him without doubting. That is when you are a converted new creation, Christ can lift himself in you and draw those he has purposed to save using your vessel.

The point I want to leave you with is not to doubt your salvation because this can be a little strong for some of you; I want you to know the truth that will set you free are the benefits that came with your salvation. Now it is up to you to take back what the devil stole from you by having the faith to act and stand on his word. If you act on that word and remain faithful until death, you are in a win-win situation by resting in his word. You are going to die; why not die trusting him by standing on his word in the faith he expects to find in you that will give him the glory exercising his fruits in the spirit. This is our goal in the spirit while in this world but as he said, only a few will find it to this degree. That is why the church must go through a portion of tribulation to purify it back to a second Pentecost experience of the latter rain, so the world can see the real God of Abraham, Isaac and Jacob as the lord our God as one and once again to see ordinary men in His image do extraordinary exploits in the fullness. AMEN (Reprint from 6/2014)

THE GATHERING OF SOULS

Background scriptures:

Revelation 14:15-20 (Explained) "(KJV) [15] And another angel came out of the temple, crying with a loud voice to him that sat on the cloud, Thrust in thy sickle, and reap: for the time is come for thee to reap; for the harvest of the earth is ripe.(*1 Thessalonians 4:16-17 (KJV)* [16] For the Lord himself shall descend from heaven with a shout, with the voice of the archangel, and with the trump of God: and the dead in Christ shall rise first:" *1 Corinthians 15:52 "(KJV)* [52] In a moment, in the twinkling of an eye, at the <u>*last trump: for the trumpet shall sound, and the dead shall*</u> *be raised incorruptible, and we shall be changed." Ezekiel 37:12 (KJV)* [12] *Therefore prophesy and say unto them, thus saith the Lord GOD; Behold, O my people, I will open your graves, and cause you to come up out of your graves, and bring you into the land of Israel.")* Continue [17] *Then we which are alive and remain shall be caught up together with them in the clouds, to meet the Lord in the air: and so shall we ever be with the Lord.* Rev. [16] *And he that sat on the cloud thrust in his sickle on the earth; and the earth was reaped.* Revelation 7:9 (NKJV) [9] After these things I looked, and behold, a great multitude which no one could number, of all nations, tribes, peoples, and tongues, standing before the throne and before the Lamb, clothed with white robes, with palm branches in their hands. Revelation 14:17-20 (NKJV) [17] Then another angel came out of the temple which is in heaven, he also having a sharp sickle. [18] And another angel came out from the altar, who had power over fire, and he cried with a loud cry to him who had the sharp sickle, saying, "**Thrust in your sharp sickle and gather <u>the clusters</u> of the vine of the earth, for her grapes are fully ripe.**" This is the unwise virgins being punished as having to suffer the destruction of their flesh for their disobedience, aided by the prayers of the righteous on their behalf. [19] **So the angel thrust his sickle into the earth and gathered the vine of the earth and threw it into the great winepress of the wrath of God.** This is the first thunder judgment. This ends the gathering of all the saints. [20] **And the winepress was trampled outside the city, and blood came out of the winepress, up to the horses' bridles, for one thousand six hundred furlongs.** This is what the church had to be saved from that cut short their tribulation.

This mystery of the gathering of souls from Adam to those that died in Christ unto this very day is now in the third heaven being judged by Christ and the twenty-four elders. This is the destiny of all the saints that died after the first resurrection that took them out of paradise to the third heaven where Paul was when he was stoned. The second resurrection or rapture will be the last gathering as explained in above scriptures that will restore the glory of the former rain with a latter before the closing of the doors of all that will be saved at the end of the sixth millennium. This will be the new time continuum. What I have been made to see is what will determine your status in the judgment.

This was for my benefit in answer to one of my inquiries of the judgment of the saints that I can now reveal to those with ears to hear. **The Third layer of Salvation** is where Christ died to make you a completely restored version of Adam. When you fall in love with him to the point of total surrender. At that time, you will be walking in heavenly places in Christ Jesus. Sin separated Adams's present from God. That is why Adam hid from God in the garden. We who are born in sin as a result will hide from God too until he calls you unto himself. Until that time, you hid from the gospel as being a child of the devil. *2 Corinthians 4:3 (KJV)* [3] *But if our gospel be hid, it is hid to them that are lost:*

Your fears came from the devil; that's why Adam hid in fear when he heard the voice of God. *John 6:44 "(KJV)* [44] *No man can come to me, except the Father which hath sent me draw him: and I will raise him up at the last day."* You will never in your flesh state comprehend the reality of your sins and their consequences until God revealed them through his word in your heart. *John 6:40 "(KJV)* [40] *And this is the will of him that sent me, that everyone which seeth the Son, and believeth on him, may have everlasting life: and I will raise him up at the last day."* This is the work of the Holy Spirit sent to gather souls for the kingdom of God. If you ever deny your salvation by your actions against words by continuing to commit the sins of omission and die in that state, the law of sins and death will claim you for hell. **(Galatians 5:19-21)** They will send you to the Great **White Throne Judgment** seat of the wicked dead.

I was given a greater understanding of these two scriptures ... *Matthew 19:30 "(KJV)* [30] *But many that are first shall be last; and the last shall be first. Matthew 20:16 (KJV)* [16] *So the last shall be first, and the first last: for many are called, but few chosen."* This is what I saw through the spirit of God ... not many well-known men, given this privilege to build God's kingdom endured when the blessings came and over-took them for the glory of men and in the sight of God, they became the least. Many of them sought God for what he gave them without counting the cost of temptations and the blessings overtook them by claiming God's heritage for themselves. This is why ... *1 Corinthians 1:26 "(KJV)* [26] *For ye see your calling, brethren, how that not many wise men after the flesh, not many mighty, not many noble, are called." Matthew 19:24 "(KJV)* [24] *And again I say unto you, It is easier for a camel to go through the eye of a needle, than for a rich man to enter into the kingdom of God."*

This is the temptation that has befallen many of them, they exchange the glory of God for the glory of men. Only those that repented when God revealed the state of their heart are received in heaven before they died; there, they will become the least in the judgment for taking God's glory. Outside of the four and twenty elders, many of the thrones of glory are still empty and reserved for those who endure the testimony of Jesus Christ in tribulation where many will not well known in this life that walked Godly on this earth. *2 Timothy 3:12 "(KJV)* [12] *Yea, and all that will live godly in Christ Jesus shall suffer persecution." Luke 6:26 (KJV)* [26] *Woe unto you, when all men shall speak well of you! for so did their fathers to the false prophets."* I am not saying that I have reached that stage of Godly living in the fullness but in striving to arrive, there have been many separations and outright rejections along the way when you choose to go the way of the cross to obtain that crown of glory.

It was revealed to me that many women will sit on those thrones. This is where I learned that men of renowned status will react like the Pharisees to them that carry this unadulterated truth when they do not want to be rebuked by God because they are in love with the glory of men and the blessings of this world. Many have closed their doors to the prophet's vision and when God sends the least of men to warn them, many souls will perish under them that refused to repent. *Proverbs29:18 (KJV)* [18] *Where there is no vision, the people perish: but he that keepeth the law, happy is he.*

All those with ears to hear will receive that word and become as the wise virgins with gladness at their day of redemption. This is the pride that God hates that many spiritual leaders are infected with in these last days. When God extends his grace to call them to repent, many will become the least in heaven for their efforts in trying to help him; had they not repented when God gave them another chance, they would have come up in the Great White Throne Judgment. *Jude 1:11 "(KJV)* [11] *Woe unto them! for they have gone in the way of Cain and ran greedily after the error of Balaam for reward and perished in the gainsaying of Core."* Having faith is what got us saved but using it to gain all the world's goods is where we were persuaded to turn and worship the golden calf. The fullness of his glory is available to all men but only a few as elects will receive it. *Matthew 16:26 "(KJV)* [26] *For what is a man profited, if he shall gain the whole world, and lose his own soul? or what shall a man give in exchange for his soul?"*

The few that are given a throne room experience will carry the mantle of Jesus in humility. A great many of people in heaven that will occupy these thrones will not be well known in this world, yet this is where they earned that privileged by not taking God's glory as they were being used in their calling. They suffered along with Christ; this time in their bodies to get the reward. This is where I saw that many faithful women in this area that remained obedient in their place as God used them. They resisted the temptation to usurp authority over the male image as jezebels. They are the prayer warriors that keep God's house in order. I have read some of the testimonies of men who said they have visited with Christ in heaven. They think that that experience gave them favor with God with-out knowing, this can be a point of your deception when you think of yourself more highly than you should by having that experience. That is why I quick thinking so the Holy Spirit can keep my ability to discern through his mind what's of God.

These on those thrones, died to their flesh to show God how much they loved Him by letting Jesus be seen and not them. These are in the numberless multitude of saints that are looking down on this last generation to see the glory that they did not get to see because of their error in ministering while on Earth. God had given them a pure word that would have caused many more souls to be brought in with fruit that remained under their ministries had they not been tempted to compromise or take the glory of men.

Their status is that of the foolish virgins that lost their oil and only redeemed enough to obtain grace to be saved from the error of their ways. Those who sowed discord that caused divisions among the body are the ones that brought diseases upon themselves and to their assemblies that drank the cup of bitterness that Satan justified before God to take them down. *Isaiah 9:16 "(KJV)* [16] *For the leaders of this people cause them to err;* (Many of God's innocent souls were led into the hands of the devil by the error of their ways and teachings that caused them to be destroyed before their time.) *And they that are led of them are destroyed." Isaiah 3:12 (KJV)* [12] *As for my people, children are their oppressors, and women rule over them. O my people, they which lead thee cause thee to err, and destroy the way of thy paths."*

God allowed Satan to take them out by letting a disease come upon them to destroy them for not repenting in their day of visitation; those that do will receive grace but will be the least in heaven. Never appoint yourself an authority on what God is doing while ministering in your flesh. That is a form of claiming His glory. No man on earth has all the answers in the word but only the Holy Ghost. He only lifts Jesus, not flesh because we did not come from heaven. That's why God gave the gifts in a diverse manner to make us interdependent on each other as a body united in Him. No one will gain eternal life standing in his own spirit contrary to truth as naming the name of God. If you allow Satan to set yourself up as a spokesman in the flesh for God when he can speak for himself, you have taken the place of the Holy Spirit in your flesh and will be confounded in the end when this happens to you.

Satan will give you a false sense of humility. All who remain humble will see Christ as their head and remain that way until death. *Isaiah 50:7 "(KJV)* [7] *For the Lord GOD will help me; therefore, shall I not be confounded: therefore, have I set my face like a flint, and I know that I shall not be ashamed. Psalm 25:20 (KJV)* [20] *O keep my soul and deliver me: let me not be ashamed; for I put my trust in thee."* We are in no position to judge another since none of us came from heaven. Only those God chose for Him to manifest himself in will let him speak and demonstrate this love that looks beyond our faults to show us what we need that only he can give. None of us can hide from truth when we are exposed. Since my encounter with the truth as taught by the Holy Spirit, I am thoroughly convinced that I am but dust in the image of my creator to be used by God and if I remain in the background for him to get the glory he so richly deserves for this privilege; I get the reward to be with him for eternity. Now that's what saving yourself is!

"Love your enemies" as a new creature, representing good. You are looking at your old self in them before God called you out to be a light to them that are now without. There is no little sin. *1 John 5:17 "(KJV)* [17] *All unrighteousness is sin: and there is a sin not unto death."* I heard and old hard line holiness preacher say, the man that stole a straight pin and the other a million dollars, both went to the same place in hell, one made it worth-while but neither escape with-out repenting.

The way God taught me to win the favor of my extended family is by my actions that followed my words. I had to learn when to act and when to speak. I learn to let my actions follow my words; that is, if you really have the love of God in you. Do not beat yourself up when you make a mistake or even fail; if they are not forgiving, this is how you find out who really has God's love in them. Many of those that followed Jesus were not there for the word but for what they could get that only he had to give. When he allowed himself to be humiliated on the cross, those with pride turned away and they will do the same to you when you become as humble as Christ; then you will experience what real strength is because he will be the only one there with you in the end. Remember, it is the least among men that will let the glory of God be seen and they will be the ones to sit on those thrones if you eat his flesh and drink his blood all the way to your cross.

This is how Jesus replied to the women that ask to let her son sit with him on his throne … *Matthew 20:20-23 "(JKV)[20] Then came to him the mother of Zebedee's children with her sons, worshipping him, and desiring a certain thing of him. [21] And he said unto her, what wilt thou? She saith unto him, Grant that these my two sons may sit, the one on thy right hand, and the other on the left, in thy kingdom. [22] But Jesus answered and said, Ye know not what ye ask. Are ye able to drink of the cup that I shall drink of, and to be baptized with the baptism that I am baptized with? They say unto him, we are able. [23] And he saith unto them, Ye shall drink indeed of my cup, and be baptized with the baptism that I am baptized with: but to sit on my right hand, and on my left, is not mine to give, but it shall be given to them for whom it is prepared of my Father."* When he revealed to me about those who are in heaven that were great men here, it was not by open vision of a dream but by a revelation in my mind speaking to me. By having this kind of relationship of direct conversation revelation, I see many have been deceived through false visions and dreams. These things the devil would not reveal to you as his child. The error that caused them to become the least there, he also was giving me a choice to be one to sit on one of those thrones and what it would cost me that only he could give me the grace to endure. **"Maranatha" AMEN** (Reprint from7/2017)

THE ORIGIN OF THE DEEP STATE (PART I)

(The Real Warren Report Behind the Kennedy Assassination)

The Deep State New World Religion (Part II)

This information was given to me by a reliable source of which I cannot release. Now that all who participated in this disclosure are dead, I can print the full details.

I am reprinting this chronicle to help you who read these chronicles, have a clear understanding of what we are preparing to do spiritual battle within the earth-bound principalities operating in man.

This is an extension of the chronical titled **"How Satan Deceived the Whole World"** as revealed in the coming chronicle. We are now living in an age of knowledge with a massive information flow beyond our ability to comprehend. What I have observed spiritually has led to much deception, confusion and conspiracy theories, founded in the disclosures as a result of this knowledge explosion. To get to the point of this origin, that will later be known as the **"Deep State,"** we must go back to the present wholly Roman Empire. As they revived to become a religious state that will have the ability to penetrate all nations of the world as a religious entity. Having the plunder of early Rome to carry out this master plan, with the anointing of Satan, they will have the means to dominate the world, disguised in a religious state legally operating in each country they occupy with certain immunities. The order of Jesuits is a military company that will infiltrate the world governments they occupy as a religious state, will have the perfect cover. Under the inspiration of Satan ... *2 Corinthians 4:4 (NKJV)* [4] *whose minds the god of this age has blinded, who do not believe, lest the light of the gospel of the glory of Christ, who is the image of God, should shine on them.* They will represent the god of this world, as agents of Satan. These **Deep State** principality operatives will be known as **"Vatican Assassins."** Once their master plan has been put into place.

 The Jesuits are the military head of this secret world of a well-organized assassin agent. Their plan was discovered as leaked documents got into the hands of people who would be the informers of their master plan in this nation that was discovered in 1963 that led to the Kennedy assassination. The ruling Jesuit at that time was **Jean-Baptiste Janssens,** as their general, He under orders of from Pope Paul VI conspired along with **Francis Cardinal Spellman,** Archbishop of New York, as head of the American division of the "Vatican Assassins" as their Military Vicar. He, along with **J Peter Grace,** head of the Council of Foreign Affairs or Relations was also head of the US branch **"Knights of Malta."** He oversaw an operation known as **"Operation Paper Clip"** which is the military arm of their industrial complex. **John McCone,** a fellow Malta member would be head of the CIA which is the become an arm of their administrative and industrial complex. In communication with their worldwide legs in operation, Their German Malta agent **Reinhard Gehlen**, a Nazi Malta member, will use the CIA's operation to train what will become the Israeli version of MASSAD to become the operational complex in Israel to gain a foothold to monitor their intelligence activity. **James Jesus Angleton,** a Malta member, as an OSS counterintelligence officer in Rome NKVD/ KGB agent is head of the CIA desk in Rome and Israel agencies, together will devise the plan to implicate Oswald as the pond to link the blame to Castro in their plot to have President Kennedy assassinated who also is a member of the Knights of Malta also as a confessing Catholic. They will consult with the British agent **Kim Philby,** an SIS member of the Jesuit Maly Cambridge spy ring to further link Oswald to CIA/KGB associations as a false directive to label him as a potential defector. The next leg of the operation will be handed down to **William F Buckley, Jr.** a fellow Malta member and CFR/CIA officer also a **"Skull and Bones"** member, will be responsible for media control to see that the public blames Oswald. **Clay Shaw**, a Malta and CIA operative will be tried by **Jim Garrison** in 1969 who they suspected might have leaked this secret information. They will bring all these legs together to the head of **Time/Life' Henry Luce,** a Malta and Shull and Bones member to ensure Oswald and Castro will be the prime operatives behind the death of President Kennedy. Oswald is the patsy murdered by Jack Ruby, later imprisoned and murdered himself.

Gerald Ford Commission the Warren report as a free Mason, **Cartha D. Deloach,** a Malta, aids **Gerald Ford** in presenting this great Jesuit cover up of the century of the **death of President Kennedy** along with **E. Howard Hunt.** Their plan was to get America into a position as policemen of the world, then begin her downfall through de facto war games to draw us into undeclared wars that will weaken our economy. Ford, as President, issued a directive to reverse the decision to de-escalate the war in Vietnam that Kennedy apposed that would start the fall of America's economy. We will be used to police the world by our status economically, be led into undeclared wars for that purpose. This would lead to Johnson's resignation when he sees the truth of what was being done. They purchased the Zapruder film for 150,000 to insure the cover-up.

 In conclusion, here in America, **Cardinal Francis Spellman** presided over this directive as the world's most powerful American Jesuits to command the execution of President Kennedy, (a Malta also), as head of the **"Society of Jesus"** as a masquerade to penetrate Christianity, Cardinal Spellman was its leader from 1946 to 1964.They needed to prolong the cold war between the two most powerful countries, Russia and the United States which Kennedy objected. To gain a power hold in Russia, they would lead them into Afghanistan as a military exercise in a land of unchartered territory that would deplete their economic resources and cause their collapse from with-in. The objective of this order is to regain world influence status, over governments and put them under the Popes. They would finance both sides in these wars and manipulate the outcomes to gain control.

Pius XII was Hitler's Pope of his time in office, Pope **John XXIII** (Khrushchev's pope), **Pope Paul VI (**President Johnson's Pope). Any President that violated their agenda as members of the **knights of Malta** are removed by their deep cover Vatican assassins. They have a zero tolerance for those who violate the rules of the order. They subdivided to penetrate and organize the following secret societies known as **The Sovereign Military order of Malta, Freemasons, The Skull and bones society, Scottish-Rites & Shriner freemasonry, The order of the Illuminated Ones (Illuminati'), Knights of Columbus, The Knights of the Ku Klux Klan, B"nai B"rith, The nation of Islam, The private army of the seeds of Islam.** (A terrorist clan.) **Italian Mafia, Opus Dei and many other organizations that will fit into to helping arrive to their status of world domination.** They are the societies coming together to bring about the NWO. The **Massad's** general, an arm of the Jesuit international intelligence gathering agency, carried out the assassination of Israel' Prime minister **Yitzak Rabin** for opposing Rome's policy against Israel's sovereignty. They built and finance institutions of higher learning like, **Harvard, Cambridge, Oxford, MIT** and **Yale** to locate the finest minds and create secret societies that will cause them to serve their cause, once indoctrinated, all in the name of a false religion known as Catholicism. That's where the heart of this Cabal of megalomaniacs concentrates their source of power. They have by being a religious front as a separate nation state, is free to penetrate all nations to carry out their agenda. Now you can see how they chose to birth their worldwide administration of control by having the plunder of the world's greatest empire. This is the epic view of the **false prophet**'s master plan coming to a head as depicted in the book of Revelation. What we are seeing today is how they have infiltrated every aspect of our society and government as an arm of the **Freemason Society** in the American church. If your pastor is a member of any of these societies, under their origin, they are Satan worshipers in disguise. Many of which are unaware of this tie to them. This is the truth of not knowing what spirit you are under the influence of.

The infiltration of the Protestants and Baptist

We, as American Protestants and Baptist, were infiltrated through the seminary system that would produce the worship of man with academic credentials, introduce hirelings into their churches after they brought it under the control of the state as a 501c-3 religious corporation. This is what replaced the apostles' doctrine and changed it to a form of godliness as they become **popes in the pulpits**, ruling their corporate family ministry assemblies under a 501c-3 as religious corporations. This revelation will become apparent in these last days when they close your assembly doors captivated under the 501c-3 charter that bound the church under the state. Their plan employed the use of the **Society of Free Masons** arm that runs the **Beast System** of control of governments. Their agenda is to reduce the world's population with this forbidden technology received through those possessed with this fallen angelic DNA. Our minds have been hacked by this technology. One thing the Vatican has are books on forbidden knowledge of ancient ages that were confiscated in the archives of the Roman plunder. They now have this technology available to them that tell them how these angelic beings plan to return at the end as in the days as in Noah's time in the form of ETs. We are at the end of days. They operate under a 501c-8 as an independent state religion that gives them freedom to operate in any country, free from that government's oppression as an independent state religion. When this became known among the French and English, they were expelled from their countries. This scripture will be fulfilled when the truth become known ... *Revelation 12:9 (NKJV)* [9] *So the great dragon was cast out, that serpent of old, called the Devil and Satan, <u>who deceives the whole world;</u> he was cast to the earth, and his angels were cast out with him.* This was Satan's master plan in the earth to take down the church of the lord Jesus Christ. They, without knowing, will be the antichrist assemblies, seduced through Jesuit seminary professors, trained in religious theology to become great speakers and renown religious authorities among their peers. Once they have indoctrinated those who attended these seminaries, without their knowledge, will use them to build their own theology seminaries of all denominations. Those, as members of the **Freemason Society** as a confessing Christian, will gain the favor of government agencies with the same affiliation. They are the very people in our present CIA agency as operatives to recruit mercenaries to carry out mass destruction by inciting riots and chaos in the countries they seek to control. Under the Pope's orders, their objective is to maintain absolute power by using our CIA mercenaries in times like these. This is what's known as the **Deep State's** master cover; the Pope represent the revived Roman Caesar disguised in Catholicism.

Our current sitting president #45 is a seed link to neo-nazi Klan sympathizers as well seen by his action during these riots. God anoints every president as **"king of the free world"** to carry out his will at the appointed time in his predestined sovereign will during their time. Therefore, President Trump will be used by God for his purposes to bring this nation back to God and into judgement through his followers that will remain loyal when his time is up. His time in office is the end of our reign of kings. In the beginning, he will be seen as the savior during a divided nation.

His actions will bring political unrest. The #45 represent the end of parallels in kings for the two nations. What we see in his character will cause this nation's revival when we see what we have done, come together and pray. President Obama's motto was **hope** and **change**. His action changed the order of male and female by law to become one in the same, therefore putting a curse on the nation that cannot be reversed. The Arab seed in his bloodline, caused him to turn against Israel. In President #45, we are about to see worldwide surprises and change on a confounding scale as never seen before. Unlike Daniel and John, I can now reveal the mystery surrounding this election that many of these notable prophets fail to see in their zeal to be known as a prophet.

God's hand is in control of the world as we have reached the end of our time given man to subdue the earth, the sixth millennium. His time in office at the end of his term will begin the chaos that will lead to the third world war. We have been warned by messengers and prophets you have rejected as in the days of Noah. I am aware of these times of uncertainties where God's hand is confounding the norm. All who refused to heed these warnings, will be caught in God's break. We, as a churched nation, have now reached the point where tribulation is imminent or else if God tarried any longer, no flesh will be saved. ***Revelation 18:23 (KJV)*** [23] ***And the light of a candle shall shine no more at all in thee; and the voice of the <u>bridegroom and of the bride</u> shall be heard no more at all in thee:*** (The church will be raptured out of her to save the saints.) ***for thy merchants were the great men of the earth; for by thy sorceries were all nations deceived. Matthew 3:10 (KJV)*** [10] ***And now also the axe is laid unto the root of the trees: therefore, every tree which bringeth not forth good fruit is hewn down and cast into the fire. Matthew 24:22 (KJV)*** [22] ***And except those days should be shortened, there should no flesh be saved: but for the elect's sake those days shall be shortened.***

"Time is no more" for this nation that has legalized sodomy. ***Isaiah 59:12 (KJV)*** [12] ***For our transgressions are multiplied before thee, and our sins testify against us: for our transgressions are with us; and as for our iniquities, we know them;"*** What we are now seeing on a worldwide scale are all these judgements coming at once. This Covid-19 window has been given to Satan to take as many souls as he can through fear because his time on earth is coming to an end. We are at the end of God's mercy as a nation; remember, we have legalized sodomy as a Christian nation. That act alone has given Satan the right to release disasters of destruction in his sin strongholds where there is no prayer, knowing he has but a short time, you see, he's reaping chaos on all the world.

There is a battle in the spirit world for souls as now seen in the actions taking place in the world through this pandemic. One thing I do not see reported is the psychological tole of this national predicament is having on our domestic relations in our homes. What was supposed to bring us together at the same time, the enemy of our soul is taking our lives as the prince of the air, (Eph.2:2) riding in the spirit of fear through the airway. Many that survived the ICU treatments are suffering some form of ill effects in their bodies. Once this virus attacks a weak immune system, the damage can only be reversed through a miracle healing. Because of the Sodomy curse, we will only have two choices during this chaos, heaven or hell. Satan is riding this wave of fear as the ... *Ephesians 2:2 (KJV)* [2] *Wherein in time past ye walked according to the course of this world, according to the prince of the power of the air, the spirit that now worketh in the children of disobedience:* **(The Deep State)** All who live in fear are potential targets to be taken out. The **False** prophet has captured the church in division. They, without knowing, rejected the true prophet's vision. Therefore, all who remain in these false teachings, will perish. These principalities are represented in this deep cover known as the "**Deep State.**" The **Beast** is now getting ready to implement his plan to rule the world ... *Revelation 13:2-4 (KJV)* [2] *And the beast which I saw was like unto a leopard, (China) and his feet were as the feet of a bear, (Russia) and his mouth as the mouth of a lion: America) and the dragon gave him his power, and his seat, and great authority.* [3] **And I saw one of his heads as it were wounded to death; and his deadly wound was healed: and all the world wondered after the beast.** [4] *And they worshipped the dragon (Satan) which gave power unto the beast: and they worshipped the beast, saying, who is like unto the beast? who is able to make war with him?* To interpret the above scripture, the **Leopard** represent the godless nature of the Chinese, the **Bear**, Russia the evil tyrant waiting to tear us apart. They both will join forces and devour the **lion**, America.

This is the great grand delusion throughout time that describes our state that would deceive the very elect if they did not have his unction anointing on them. As you see, they have closed your assembly doors, controlled your gatherings, imprisoned you in your homes and through this fear pandemic are preparing to bring you under their absolute control; all in the name of religion. My calling as a messenger is to reveal the details of the most horrible things that God has reserved to be told to this last generation that is about to see biblical history repeated for the last time. The earth is being prepared to go through its second stage of a seven-year restoration geographically.

My beloved, I am no scholar of biblical history, just a simple messenger. I try to keep these revelations on the level to be understood by the simple minded. When God separated me from the church-world, I was given these revelations to write down just as John and the rest of the apostles, neither of these offices I claim as a title because he can speak for himself. All he need is a prepared temple to use, that's all I am. As you see, outside of God, we are already dumb sheep, waiting to be led to the slaughter. They employed their secret Islamic army to start the "911" calamity. They will use their seeds to begin dismantling our constitutional rights. God put President Trump in this position that will be the beginning of a national crisis such as this election will bring. Listen to his words when he speaks. One thing the evangelical Christians did when he was inaugurated, they told him that God was going to use him in a mighty way.

Many, representing evangelical denominations, took terms prophesying over him. *Ezekiel 14:9 (KJV)* *⁹ And if the prophet be deceived when he hath spoken a thing, I the LORD have deceived that prophet, and I will stretch out my hand upon him, and will destroy him from the midst of my people Israel.* He has a link to the past biblical history to Cyrus, a non-political King of Babylon of old. That's why he was confident that he will remain in office. Our pride is the epidemic, we as a nation is infected with that will cause our downfall ... *Proverbs 16:18 (KJV)* ¹⁸ **Pride goeth before destruction, and an haughty spirit before a fall.** That's why his followers are so defiant and loyal to him as their leader. In their patriotic delusion, do not know they are working against God's will as Barabbas to think they can take this country back and go on living as we always have. They are worldly Christian patriots in a state of delusion, led by a false prophecy

God gave them to destroy them at the end of this gentile age. **Donald Trump** is king #45 over **Modern Babylon** that will now experience the fate of Israel's past as history is repeated for the last time. Both #44 & #45 spirits will remain as a sign of their influence will direct the action of those that follow as time is extended that will lead to our demise and downfall. *Isaiah 29:6 (KJV)* [6] **Thou shalt be visited of the *LORD* of hosts with thunder, and with earthquake, and great noise, with storm and tempest, and the flame of devouring fire.**

In summary, our current president represents all our evils as manifested in his actions that can only be changed through repentance and prayer. We, as a Christian nation, allowed ourselves to come to this state of delusion. Do not pray for America to return to her old state that has now brought her to this judgement. God put Trump in the presidency to show us what we look like in his sight by his character as a nonpolitical leader, full of narcissistic pride. *Jeremiah 21:10 (KJV)* [10] *For I have set my face against this city for evil, and not for good, saith the LORD: it shall be given into the hand of the <u>king of Babylon</u>, and he shall burn it with fire.*

President #46, the judgement of America

The #45 as the last parallel to the Jews forty-five kings that ruled over them before they were turned over to their enemies that brought them into captivity. In #46 both #44 & #45, spirits have brought this nation into judgement. Number 46 will now become the fall guy.

We are at that #45. America can no longer be saved because the 44th President as king under his watch, legalized the curse of Sodom on this nation. Our fate as a nation cannot be reversed or else, he would have to apologize to Sodom and Gomorrah for destroying them without a warning. We were to pray for President Donald Trump to change his heart. He is compromised, and poses no threat to our chief enemy, Russia. God will use his actions to bring America back to their knees to pray for revival. He now will become the last President in our judgement as #45, as the end of the Gentile's time to serve our purpose to restore Israel back to national status in the 1967 Middle Eastern war; Forty years later, will end the last generation of the gentile's time to rule. Remember what happen to Barabbas when he took up arms in attempt to take back the nation as patriots, that's his spirit we see in the Trump movement. They will all be killed without mercy. When our enemies declare war on the United States, *Matthew 24:31 (KJV)* [31] *And he shall send his angels with a great sound of a trumpet, and they shall gather together his elect from the four winds, from one end of heaven to the other ...* we will be raptured before the nuclear disasters begin. *Matthew 24:22 (KJV)* [22] *And except those days should be shortened, there should no flesh be saved: but for the elect's sake those days shall be shortened.* Seventy percent of all Americans will be killed and those that remain will be killed by a fragmented asteroid impact on the western hemisphere as the Sodomy curse is fulfilled. *Matthew 24:34 (KJV)* [34] *Verily I say unto you, this generation shall not pass, till all these things be fulfilled.* That's why we are being warned through all these diversities of natural disasters and political as well as social unrest as Satan is loosed to begin the battle for souls.

We who know God's plan, are being prepared to come out of this wilderness in the spirit of Elijah and Moses to bring down all these wicked principalities in this final revival battle for souls and be taken to our heavenly home as this millennium comes to an end. *Matthew 11:12 (KJV)* [12] *And from the days of John the Baptist until now the kingdom of heaven suffereth violence, and the violent take it by force.* Through all this division and corruption, God will allow Satan to deliver us into the hands of our enemies as he did Israel when they departed from him. Ninety-eight percent of the church world have departed from God, many of their children will replace them in the coming revival by their hearts being deceived to become Christian patriots, more loyal to country than to God. Biblical history is about to be repeated; this time, heaven is the promise land. The world is not prepared for what it's about to see, the reality of our state of delusion to think that we can defy God's sovereign will, set in motion before the world began. We all must repent when we see all we have done in the name of God have brought us to this point of deception as were the Pharisees and the Sadducees that could not recognize their own Messiah standing before them and killed him in the name of God. Now we will repeat history by not being able to recognize his voice, telling us to Repent! For the Kingdom of Heaven is at hand. May God have mercy on all that call upon his name. AMEN (Updated for release 8/2020)

THE DEEP STATE' NEW WORLD RELIGION (PART II)

This is a further response to those of you that inquired about the events surrounding the Covid-19 Virus. This virus got its beginning through a research team in labs at NC State and Duke University in North Carolina. Due to the nature of this strain that was going to be linked to human DNA using gene splicing technology. The potential deadliness of this type of research, funded by our government, it was move to China for further development. The accident that infected all that was in that environment is suspected to have died from the exposure shortly after or with-in a two-month period before the final stages were to be completed.

Therefore, being a top-secret operation designed for military use as a new type of biological, specifically targeted to attack your immune system through the lungs. What they have now found out by this outbreak, it is mutating in people with previous vaccinations. The public at large affected are becoming the studies as human trials. This data is being used to track the reactions of its mutating stages. This outbreak primarily is most deadly among the elderly vulnerable population. This is a message to all confessing Christians as a last dramatic warning to get our attention before all chaos comes in the next planned crash of the economy by this **Deep State**. We as confessing Christians, are now being called to repent and return to the true temple that represent where we left our first love; that is, when we first got saved.

We all had a personal experience with God that changed our mind to become the temple with-in, not in a building with-out. What caused us to error is where we went to learn what we were supposed to be like from a spiritual point of view. The **Deep State** had control of our assemblies under the 501c-3 government mark that required pastors to have seminary credentials from a Jesuit school to qualify as pulpit CEO's (Pastors) to run a religious corporation. This put the present assembly's system out of will with God's order as having the Holy Spirit in charge of the assembly as often as we come together as new doctrines will be taught.

These divisions over generations will put those who attend these assemblies back into a law mentality as they mix law with grace without having the revelation of Christ, become demonstrations of gospels not taught by Christ and the apostles. This application will lead to the rise of new doctrines by this error of putting more emphasis on the natural temple rather than the spiritual one in you when you became born again. This is what we were told in the Book of Revelation would lead to the Nicolaitan doctrine (Rev.2:6) as noted under the 501c-3 corporate run church assembly that represent the assemblies that lost their first love. After generations of these in-part teachings, seduced by their own willing ignorance, will establish their denominational kingdoms in their own names as organized religious corporate bodies. Now under state control, they will be governed by **Deep State** operatives in control of this 501c-3 charter.

Those who become members of these assemblies will have to sign on as corporate contributors so the government can monitor your financial transactions you will be obligated to pay as a tithe. Where we went wrong in this area that led to them robbing you in the name of God, is to see what they did with your tithe offering sacrifices. There is no mention of tithing obligation in giving in the New Testament. That's the error they will capitalize on that only applied under the Jewish law. They will use this out of context to build their mega assemblies. They, as hirelings are standing in the pulpits as your CEO indoctrinating you in what will make them wealthy; all in the name of God. With-out knowing, you have strengthened the hand of the enemy to further their causes of religious deception. They gave you a tax credit for their support when you signed on under the 501c-3 government charter. Now you pose no threat to them because they now can control your activities and shut you down.

I am giving you who have eyes to see and ears to hear a background insight into how we got to this state where we are more controlled by what the world's agenda is than the God we supposed to represent. Now this brings us to the present state of why we are reacting with the world because the organized church assembly is snared by the 501c-3 mark by mixing law with grace. We were born again to worship God in spirit and in truth. Therefore, what you are to do from that time on is to be led by the spirit, not by the rules of a religious corporation. Now you are beginning to see why many of us have the same fears and doubt as the world as God use this pandemic to get our attention.

We all that have attended these assemblies under a corporate denomination name, have a part of a spiritual truth. However, you have not been equipped to deal with these deep spiritual things we are now encountering on a world-wide scale. That's because ... *1 Corinthians 13:9 (KJV)* [9] **For we know in part, and we prophesy in part.** God is sending messengers to warn you of what we all have missed to help those that hear them see our state, that **Repentance** is in order. *Isaiah 53:6 (KJV)* [6] **All we like sheep have gone astray; we have turned everyone to his own way; and the *LORD* hath laid on him the iniquity of us all. 1 Corinthians 13:12 (KJV)** [12] **For now we see through a glass, darkly; but then face to face: now I know in part; but then shall I know even as also I am known.** When God let me see what we have missed and you receive it, then you will be restored to the fullness of what you have missed through the word of these messengers. We are the few. This is part of that quick work of mercy. *2 Peter 3:9 (KJV)* [9] **The Lord is not slack concerning his promise, as some men count slackness; but is longsuffering to us-ward, not willing that any should perish, but that all should come to repentance. 1 Corinthians 13:10 (KJV)** [10] **But when that which is perfect is come, then that which is in part shall be done away.** That is why God had them to close your assembly buildings to get your attention. **Covid-19** is only one of the first world-wide earth events to shake our spiritual foundation. This is the is the footman stage of Revelation six. The next phase is when the horsemen arrive to begin a full-blown tribulation that none will escape but the children of God.

My answer and view on Covid-19

Now we have reached the point where they will use this pandemic to their advantage. This demonstrates to them how you can control the world through fear. This pandemic is all part of the next phase of total control of the world. *Ephesians 2:2 (KJV)* [2] **Wherein in time past ye walked according to the course of this world, according to the** *prince of the power of the air, the spirit that now worketh in the children of disobedience:* In the book of Revelation, It states this fact … *Revelation 12:9 (KJV)* [9] **And the great dragon was cast out, that old serpent, called the Devil, and Satan,** *which deceiveth the whole world: he was cast out into the earth, and his angels were cast out with him.* What this pandemic is showing to us all is how much control and power Satan has over the world by showing us what fear can do when we all are on one accord, the effect it will have on the whole world. The devil in man will only do what he said he would do, kill him before he comes to the knowledge of the truth. Mankind under the influence of his father the devil, cannot contain this evil within himself, that is why he must repent; only God can give you that power not to destroy yourself. Mankind has always gone beyond himself to enter the forbidden zone of knowledge he cannot contain that ends in self-destruction. In manipulating the human genes in our DNA, he has entered the forbidden zone that carries a curse that will lead once again, to his extinction.

The rapid mutation of Covid-19 is due to an already present activator in our system. If you have had a flu shot or any other vaccines or Soars. Then you are a potential candidate to become a victim of this strain that reacts with the previously injected vaccines. Most of the elderly are full of these vaccines by being injected once a year as they tell you what to do to prevent you from catching what they injected you with. Most confessing Christian's faith is not that strong to withstand these influences currently medical institutions are pushing as cures to all these sicknesses we are bombarded with daily in a mentally and physically sick society. All this is the sum tole of our daily fears. You see, we have been set up to receive what God said you were delivered from. **1 John 4:4 (KJV)** [4] **Ye are of God, little children, and have overcome them: because greater is he that is in you, than he that is in the world.** Now if you do not believe this as a confessing Christian, that fear has the potential to become your fate.

We have been taught faith positive principles in succeeding and getting wealth, only to die of a disease you hoped you would never get because your spiritual leaders were teaching you to be godly is to be wealthy. *Matthew 16:26 (KJV)* ²⁶ *For what is a man profited, if he shall gain the whole world, and lose his own soul? or what shall a man give in exchange for his soul?* God gave us the ability not only to be restored as the recreated Adam man, but to live in dominion of all the evils of this world and die a natural death in this body or his temple, as it decays back to the dust. You are going to die; the question **is**, who is in possession of your soul that will determine where you spend eternity. He proved this through apostle John as he dies on the island of Patmos as an old man that left his testimony of how the greater one in him kept him from all that the devil tried to do to kill him. *Luke 18:8 (KJV)* ⁸ *I tell you that he will avenge them speedily. Nevertheless, when the Son of man cometh, shall he find faith on the earth?* My beloved, I now know why God said … *Matthew 7:14 (KJV)* ¹⁴ *Because strait is the gate, and narrow is the way, which leadeth unto life, and few there be that find it.* Many of us know him as our savior but not as our deliverer. Now that's where the assembly of hireling have kept the whole council of the word from us so we can suffer sickness and disease along with the rest of the world by lack of knowledge. *Hosea 4:6 (KJV)* ⁶ *My people are destroyed for lack of knowledge: because thou hast rejected knowledge, I will also reject thee, that thou shalt be no priest to me: seeing thou hast forgotten the law of thy God, I will also forget thy children.* Christ sacrificed himself to make us the new Adam to have dominion over the devil. That's his standard of our being made perfect. (Matt.5:48)

I have people as me? Are you going to take the shot? My answer, If God is the greater one in me, he is to decide the answer to that question, not me. If he sent his own son to die for me to be delivered from all the oppression of the devil. When he revealed to me that it is up to me as to what attacks me, it's according to your faith what you decide to keep but none of this came from him. Your faith must see him as the possessor of your temple. When I got that revelation, from that time on, I learned it would be according to my faith. He said I was made whole as Adam when I was born from above, I became the new Adam. Therefore, he had no disease in him. This is the whole council of the word we have not seem demonstrated as it was in the days of the apostles.

God has not lost his power; we just fail to keep his word so he can perform it. *Jeremiah 1:12 (KJV)* [12] *Then said the LORD unto me, thou hast well seen: for I will hasten my word to perform it.* That's when I knew what he meant when he said … *"live by every word the proceeded out of my mouth."* If we really believe he is in us to this degree, then our only protection to living this privilege is to stay with-in the confines of his word so the devil cannot overtake you by your unbelief. I have been exposed to many diseases throughout my profession but never caught any sickness from these deadly diseases I have been exposed to. I see doctors as instruments of mercy until we acquire the faith to trust him unto death. I worked with some of the world's best doctors in my profession, I learned to put God in remembrance of his word and was delivered each time. Doctors are not the gods we look to them to be, just men trained in the art of servicing the human body. I limit my **you tube** searches not to contain too much negative media. This, I see is what's contributing to our present state of fear. As you can see, we are a long way from what God intended us to be. Now we are being tried for our confession of faith not to give place to what the world is pedaling through fear. We are going to have to prove not only that we know him but to let this love preserve us like it did John. *1 John 4:18 (KJV)* [18] *There is no fear in love; but perfect love casteth out fear: because fear hath torment. He that feareth is not made perfect in love.*

Now on the national front.

I mentioned in time past what it is to be in a state of delusion. Now to explain that further, God showed us how he hates pride by removing president #45 after he served his purpose in one term. I also told you how he was there to show us our state as an evangelical Christian church world, where our priorities were at this time in history. These are the facts that will determine our irreversible downfall.

1. After entering undeclared wars, beginning with Vietnam, our nation has racked up a thirty-two trillion-dollar deficit by spending more than we collect in taxes.

2. God has delayed our economic collapse to give his people time to get prepared for the eminent spiritual battle with the principalities.

3. This stimulus hand-out of worthless paper money will widen the sink hole that will aid in the sudden overnight crash.

4. We have created a welfare state that has consumed us with debts we can no longer pay.

5. This attempt to save this economy will fail by our houses of representatives being in division, will not see what they have done until the system collapses.

6. God is preparing his angels to hold back the spirit of suicide when this country comes face to face with this reality of an eminent crash.

7. Gas prices will rise, food shortages, water will be horded and eventually neighbors will turn on each other and begin to kill in search of food.

8. We will be seized by our enemies from within, then will come the destruction of this nation.

Only God can protect his temple when you agree to let him oversee your wellbeing by being content at what state you are in. We all as citizens, lived in a privileged country that has let these blessing overtake us to become our desires and aspirations. Some have created their own symbols of idolatry that has contributed to our present state in the sight of God. God is more than able to keep you from the evils of the world while he occupies it, in you. AMEN (updated for release 3/2021)

HOW SATAN DECEIVED
THE CHURCH WORLD

<u>Background Scriptures:</u>

Jeremiah 14:14 "(KJV) [14] *Then the LORD said unto me, the prophets prophesy lies in my name: I sent them not, neither have I commanded them, neither spake unto them: they prophesy unto you a false vision and divination, and a thing of nought, and the deceit of their heart. 1 Kings 22:22-23 (KJV)* [22] *And the LORD said unto him, Wherewith? And he said, I will go forth, <u>and I will be a lying spirit in the mouth of all his prophets.</u> And he said, thou shalt persuade him, and prevail also: go forth, and do so.* [23] *Now therefore, behold, the LORD hath put a <u>lying spirit in the mouth of all these thy prophets,</u> and the LORD hath spoken evil concerning thee. Jeremiah 16:19 (KJV)* [19] *O LORD, my strength, and my fortress, and my refuge in the day of affliction, the Gentiles shall come unto thee from the ends of the earth, and shall say, <u>surely our fathers have inherited lies,</u> <u>vanity, and things wherein there is no profit.</u> Revelation 12:9 (KJV)* [9] *And the great dragon was cast out, that old serpent, called the Devil, and Satan, which <u>deceiveth the whole world:</u> he was cast out <u>into the earth,</u> and his angels were cast out with him. Daniel 7:25 (KJV)* [25] *And he shall speak great words against the most High and shall wear out the saints of the most High, and think to change times and laws: and they shall be given into his hand until a time and times and the dividing of time."*

The world's fate is already determined for the children of the devil; however, the focus in this chronicle will be on what the church has failed to see as how it has been seduced to what it has become today. Recently, I was doing a study on the order of the Jesuits Priesthood and the influence it has on the Christian church. I was fascinated about Jesuit's and their history as the military company of the Pope. They in a way are the replacement of the Knights Templar's. What caught my attention is to see how this organization with tentacles' all over the world is able to carry out such a mission. I will attempt to share with you what I found in this revelation of how Satan has anointed them to carry out their master plan that is manifested in the above topic and supporting scriptures in these thirty-three agenda's.

The Jesuits are the ruling order of the Catholic Church. Its members start as Cardinals before they can qualify as a Jesuits. Their founder is St. Ignatius of Loyola. Their objective after the fall of Rome became the religious form that would be the military company to their Pope as a religious government that seeks to control and influence on world Governments and religions including Christianity. They are an independent national religious government power as a self-governing body; as a separate state, the Vatican has achieved international immunity as a sovereign state within the nations they occupy. Rome's fall from within as victims of their own greed, corruption, immorality and over taxation. Having inherited the wealth of the plunders of the knights Templar's, they emerged as a separate state operating under a religious charter. They are a highly disciplined organization with absolute devotion to their Pope. They have a ruling general that answers only to the pope. Each ruling general hold the highest rank in the order, some are selected to be the pope. Their origin and power dates to early Rome which confiscated the wealth plundered by the Knights Templar's of the nations they raided and stored in a secret place where to this day is not known to the world. They are privy to rare ancient manuscripts of information not known to the world incorporated the knowledge of many nations cultural treasures they plundered.

Because of their vast wealth and resources, they can establish and support their mission around the world, build institutions of higher learning, make investments in the nations they occupy to promote their agenda of world domination in the name of religion. The Jesuits are the army, sent out into all the nations they occupy to penetrate all societies and create new ones to further indoctrinate men to serve their causes. Their ordination as a Cardinal makes them part of the ruling council, answerable only to the pope. He is now the revived Emperor of Rome, ruling in the form of a religious organization. This path to become a Jesuit priest takes fifteen years. At that time, he takes a vow to the pope to become a Jesuit priest of the highest order as a member of the general counsel to the order answerable only to the pope.

Their constitution governing their body is secret, known only to the Jesuit's; however, the central focus of their doctrine is that **"The ends justify the means."** The absolute vow of discipline requires their members to obey their superiors even when it involves grievous sins committed among a member of the order of Jesuits. They are the hidden power behind the papacy that is ushering in a new Revived Roman Empire. Keep this in mind and in the above scriptures you will see how this anointing on them by Satan has brought down the church world. Through a systematic replacing of the apostle's doctrine, published and introduced new bible versions. This method of mind control by seducing spirits employs all the resources of this world at their disposal that when seduced, is so subtle, you will not even know it unless God reveals it to you. Remember, this sprit would deceive the elects if it were not for the presents of the unction anointing. As a form of a false religion, who worship in their cathedral like assemblies are putting their pope up as Jesus in the flesh. That's blasphemy in God's sight. Those who worship under their doctrine has blasphemed God by giving man the power to forgive men of their sins without a cross. *Matthew 23:9 "(KJV)* ⁹ *And call no man your father upon the earth: for one is your Father, which is in heaven."* This is by observation in comparison to the doctrine of the apostles given them by Christ.

In keeping with my charge as an instrument of the Lord to reveal these end time revelations to those that have ears to hear, through this inspiration of the Holy Spirit, I can now see him filling in the hidden mysteries behind the scriptural context of the knowledge to those that have been given ears to hear. I know these chronicles may provoke some of you because I have no regard for being politically correct in telling truth. Those who may be puffed up in your own knowledge, I challenge you to search the scriptures for yourself and try the spirit of truth, I must warn you to surrender your will first or you will be further deceived by your own thinking.

These are the (33) agendas of these lying spirits as Free-Masons in our society

1. We will penetrate and establish institutions of higher learning to seduce them into our doctrine of self-empowerment through principal bible teachings in our seminaries. We must print many unauthorized versions of the bible to cause doubt and confusion. **Revelation 22:18 (KJV) "[18] For I testify unto every man that heareth the words of the prophecy of this book, if any man shall add unto these things, God shall add unto him the plagues that are written in this book:"**

2. We must distort the truth to cause doubt so when they hear truth, they will not receive it. **Hosea 4:6 (KJV) "[6] My people are destroyed for lack of knowledge: because thou hast rejected knowledge, I will also reject thee, that thou shalt be no priest to me: seeing thou hast forgotten the law of thy God, I will also forget thy children."**

3. We must keep them from being born again from above so they will continue to fear man by not knowing God. **1 John 4:18 (KJV) "[18] There is no fear in love; but perfect love casteth out fear: because fear hath torment. He that feareth is not made perfect in love.**

4. Our prophets will demonstrate lying signs and wonders to further deceive the people by using his name. **Matthew 24:24 (KJV) "[24] For there shall arise false Christs, and false prophets, and shall shew great signs and wonders; insomuch that, if it were possible, they shall deceive the very elect."**

5. We must teach them the principals of faith on a carnal level to deceive them to think that they are spiritual by enabling them to prosper in their own way. **Proverb 16:25 "There is a way that seemeth right unto a man, but the end thereof are the ways of death."**

6. We must cause them to pray ritualistic prayers so the circumstances that require faith and patience will defeat them. **1 Timothy 2:8 (KJV) "⁸ I will therefore that men pray everywhere, lifting up holy hands, without wrath and doubting.**

7. We must convince them that they can never be perfect; by this they will deny God's ability to be perfect in them. **Romans 8:1 (KJV) "¹ There is therefore now no condemnation to them which are in Christ Jesus, who walk not after the flesh, but after the Spirit. Matthew 5:48 (KJV) ⁴⁸ Be ye therefore perfect, even as your Father which is in heaven is perfect."**

8. We must keep them in the carnal realm to be controlled by the circumstances of life that will make them unstable. **John 14:27 (KJV) "27 Peace I leave with you, my peace I give unto you: not as the world giveth, give I unto you. Let not your heart be troubled, neither let it be afraid. Isaiah 26:3 (KJV) "³ Thou wilt keep him in perfect peace, whose mind is stayed on thee: because he trusteth in thee."**

9. We must empower their thought process to draw their own conclusions about what the bible says. **Isaiah 55:7-8 (KJV) "⁷ Let the wicked forsake his way, and the unrighteous man his thoughts: and let him return unto the LORD, and he will have mercy upon him; and to our God, for he will abundantly pardon. ⁸ For my thoughts are not your thoughts, neither are your ways my ways, saith the LORD."**

10. We must deceive them to think that they are operating under grace, but their assemblies will operate under the law to keep them in bondage not knowing that they are the temple of God. **2 Corinthians 6:16 (KJV) "¹⁶ And what agreement hath the temple of God with idols? for ye are the temple of the living God; as God hath said, I will dwell in them, and walk in them; and I will be their God, and they shall be my people."**

11. We must teach them to see their pastors in the flesh as their holy fathers to reverence them and not God. **Hebrews 12:28 (KJV) ²⁸ Wherefore we receiving a kingdom which cannot**

be moved, let us have grace, whereby we may serve God acceptably with reverence and godly fear:

12. We must teach them to pervert the gospel by causing the world and the church to mix. **1 John 2:15 (KJV) "[15] Love not the world, neither the things that are in the world. If any man love the world, the love of the Father is not in him."**

13. We must teach them to preach messages that do not deliver to fill their assemblies. **2 Timothy 3:5 (KJV) "[5] Having a form of godliness but denying the power thereof: from such turn away."**

14. We must use secular entertainment to turn their assemblies into entertainment centers. **1 Timothy 4:1 (KJV) [1] Now the Spirit speaketh expressly, that in the latter times some shall depart from the faith, giving heed to seducing spirits, and doctrines of devils.**

15. We must seduce the church with secular teachings to break down family values to empower women to under-mind the priesthood of man and destroy marriages so their children will revolt against their parents. **Isaiah 3:12 (KJV) "[12] As for my people, children are their oppressors, and women rule over them. O my people, they which lead thee cause thee to err, and destroy the way of thy paths."**

16. We must teach them to have a false sense of security by their love of idol possessions. **Exodus 20:3 (KJV) [3] Thou shalt have no other gods before me. 1 John 2:15 (KJV)** [15] *Love not the world, neither the things that are in the world. If any man love the world, the love of the Father is not in him.*

17. We must seduce churches to become entertainment centers that promote the pre-eminence of self-worship. **Luke 6:26 (KJV) "[26] Woe unto you, when all men shall speak well of you! for so did their fathers to the false prophets."**

18. We must give them a spirit to build their individual kingdoms, therefore bringing about division among their established

assemblies to promote separate new doctrines. **Ephesians 4:5 "(KJV) ⁵ One Lord, one faith, one baptism, Luke 11:17 (KJV) ¹⁷ But he, knowing their thoughts, said unto them, every kingdom divided against itself is brought to desolation; and a house divided against a house falleth."**

19. Our seminaries will teach them the art of begging to further their own agendas as hirelings. **Philippians 4:19 (KJV) "¹⁹ But my God shall supply all your need according to his riches in glory by Christ Jesus."**

20. We must keep them divided against each other so they will become offended and confused by the truth. **Matthew 24:10 (KJV) "¹⁰ And then shall many be offended, and shall betray one another, and shall hate one another."**

21. We must entice them to judge each other by not knowing what spirit they are of. **Matthew 7:1-3 (KJV) "¹ Judge not, that ye be not judged. ² For with what judgment ye judge, ye shall be judged: and with what measure ye mete, it shall be measured to you again. ³ And why beholdest thou the mote that is in thy brother's eye, but considerest not the beam that is in thine own eye?"**

22. We must blind their leaders with false teachings so they will never know the truth. **John 12:40 (KJV) "⁴⁰ He hath blinded their eyes and hardened their heart; that they should not see with their eyes, nor understand with their heart, and be converted, and I should heal them. John 8:32 (KJV) ³² And ye shall know the truth, and the truth shall make you free."**

23. We must empower women to seduce their men and rule over them by changing the order in their assemblies. **1 Corinthians 11:3 (KJV) "³ But I would have you know, that the head of every man is Christ; and the head of the woman is the man; and the head of Christ is God. 1 Timothy 2:12 (KJV) ¹² But I suffer not a woman to teach, nor to usurp authority over the man, but to be in silence. Titus 2:4 (KJV) ⁴ That they may teach the young women to be sober, to love their husbands, to love their children,"**

24. We will infiltrate their seminaries to change their doctrines to mix with the world. **1 Timothy 6:3-4 (KJV) "³ If any man teach otherwise, and consent not to wholesome words, even the words of our Lord Jesus Christ, and to the doctrine which is according to godliness; ⁴ He is proud, knowing nothing, but doting about questions and strifes of words, whereof cometh envy, strife, railings, evil surmising's."**

25. We must gradually infiltrate our doctrine into their assemblies. Their pastors must become an idol to lord over them from the pulpit. **Psalm 146:3 (KJV) "³ Put not your trust in princes, nor in the son of man, in whom there is no help."**

26. We must deceive them with religious spirits and keep them in sin and think they are acceptable to God. **Proverbs 14:12 (KJV) ¹² There is a way which seemeth right unto a man, but the end thereof are the ways of death. 2 Timothy 3:7 (KJV) ⁷ Ever learning, and never able to come to the knowledge of the truth."**

27. We must convince them not to believe in New Testament prophets so they will not receive the warnings of their times. **Amos 3:7 (KJV) Surely the Lord GOD will do nothing, but he revealeth his secret unto his servants the prophets. Ephesians 3:5 (KJV) ⁵ Which in other ages was not made known unto the sons of men, as it is now revealed unto his holy apostles and prophets by the Spirit;"**

28. We must transform their religions into ritual, programs and traditions of man; teach them bible principles to deceived them into thinking they are saved. **Mark 7:9 (KJV) "⁹ And he said unto them, Full well ye reject the commandment of God, that ye may keep your own tradition. Hosea 4:6 (KJV) ⁶ My people are destroyed for lack of knowledge: because thou hast rejected knowledge, I will also reject thee, that thou shalt be no priest to me: seeing thou hast forgotten the law of thy God, I will also forget thy children."**

29. We will set up nonprofit corporations that will cause them to be subject to the state. **(501-C-3)** (The Catholic Church

operates under 501-C-8 as a separate state). **Acts 5:29 (KJV)** **²⁹ 'Then Peter and the other apostles answered and said, we ought to obey God rather than men."**

30. We must produce renowned authoritative heads of these Christian corporations to promote their secular material so the people will not read their bible. **Exodus 19:5 (KJV)** **"⁵ Now therefore, if ye will obey my voice indeed, and keep my covenant, then ye shall be a peculiar treasure unto me above all people: for all the earth is mine: 2 Timothy 2:15 (KJV) ¹⁵ Study to shew thyself approved unto God, a workman that needeth not to be ashamed, rightly dividing the word of truth."**

31. We must seduce them into immorality to replace the midwifes with male doctors to discover their secret parts and defile their women by aborting children God gave them. **Exodus 1:19-21 (KJV) "¹⁹ And the midwives said unto Pharaoh, Because the Hebrew women are not as the Egyptian women; for they are lively and are delivered ere the midwives come in unto them. ²⁰ Therefore <u>God dealt well with the midwives:</u> and the people multiplied and waxed very mighty. ²¹ And it came to pass, because the midwives feared God, that he made them houses. Isaiah 3:17 (ASV) ¹⁷ therefore the Lord will smite with a scab the crown of the head of the daughters of Zion, and Jehovah will lay bare their <u>secret parts."</u>** (Men delivering babies) **Ezekiel 16:36 (KJV) ³⁶ Thus saith the Lord GOD; Because thy filthiness was poured out, and thy <u>nakedness discovered</u> through thy whoredoms with thy lovers, and with all the idols of thy abominations, and by the blood of thy children,** (Abortions) **which thou didst give unto them;"**

32. We must create an immoral environment in their assemblies with the introduction of secular music to promote sensuality, fornication and adultery. **2 Timothy 3:6 (KJV) "⁶ For of this sort are they which creep into houses, and lead captive silly women laden with sins, led away with divers lusts,"**

33. In the end, we will succeed in bringing all religions under

one world rule. **Revelation 12:9 (NASB77)** [9] **And the great dragon was thrown down, the serpent of old who is called the devil and Satan, who deceives the whole world; he was thrown down to the earth, and his angels were thrown down with him.**

My fellow believers, these are the (33) agendas God has allowed Satan to use to deceive religious men, defiled the Church of Christ and seduced many assemblies to fulfill the great apostasy of this end time. This religion is a form of godliness of Jesuit priest in order to build institutions of higher learning to reduce the church to where we are today, victims of logical theology. Now to link them to all these agendas, let's go back to the opening background scriptures. God uses these principalities under satanic influence to carry out the word spoken by the prophets that all may be fulfilled in the timeline of man. **1 Kings 22:22-23 "(KJV) "**[22]**And the LORD said unto him, wherewith? And he said, I will go forth, and I will be a lying spirit in the mouth of all his prophets."** Knowing the end from the beginning. **(Isaiah 46:10)**

These will be the false prophets that will bring the lies to seduce the church. **And he said, thou shalt persuade him, and prevail also: go forth, and do so.** [23] **Now therefore, behold, the LORD hath put a lying spirit in the mouth of all these thy prophets, and the LORD hath spoken evil concerning thee."** This is where you see the sovereignty of God at work controlling all things. **Jeremiah 14:14 (KJV) "**[14]**Then the LORD said unto me, the prophets prophesy lies in my name: I sent them not, neither have I commanded them, neither spake unto them: they prophesy unto you a false vision and divination, and a thing of nought, and the deceit of their heart. 2 Thessalonians 2:9 (KJV)** [9] **Even him, whose coming is after the working of Satan with all power and signs and lying wonders, Jeremiah 16:19 (KJV)** [19] **O LORD, my strength, and my fortress, and my refuge in the day of affliction, the Gentiles shall come unto thee from the ends of the earth, and shall say, surely our fathers …** The pastors that were seduced to believe these lies and led their congregations into idol worship. **have inherited lies, vanity, and things wherein there is no profit**. This declaration describes the state of the Church when the prophet brings the message of the last days. The vanity of their state allowed Satan to deceive the whole world. **Revelation 12:9 (KJV) "**[9]

And the great dragon was cast out, that old serpent, called the Devil, and Satan, which <u>deceiveth the whole world:</u>" Because this is a form of religion, their priest will minister in their flesh; therefore, without Christ doctrine, will become an avenue to attract the spirit of homosexuality and pedophilia by not being allowed to marry.

He did this while performing God's sovereign will so none would escape the judgment. **He was cast out into the earth, and his angels were cast out with him.** The fall of man invoked God's plan of redemption while in the presents of these fallen beings in the form of demonic seducing spirits. **Revelation 16:14 (KJV) "[14] For they are the spirits of devils, working miracles, which go forth unto the kings of the earth and of the whole world, to gather them to the battle of that great day of God Almighty.** Now you see how God allowed the Jesuit order to spread lies that would change the order of service. This one organization alone will be responsible for the rise of the false prophet in the form of a new world religion. "**The ends justify the means**" of which they, under the inspiration of Satan's false vision are the architects of this New World Religion, the revived Roman Empire. Many of our pastors that attended their seminaries have become Popes in the pulpits. The false prophet will join with the beast in the battle to conquer the world.

<u>These are some observations of the Jesuit's in the doctrine of Catholicism?</u>

1. They do not ordain women as priest. We, as a Christian church, ordain Women as pastors. There is no scriptural justification for this type of ordination.

2. They do not promote abortions. Today, some churches now condoned this practice.

3. Although recent revelations exposed the immorality and sodomy within their order, it is not an open admission in the papacy. Today, the church openly condones homosexuality even to the point of ordaining gay pastors and bishops. This is the new seeker friendly politically correct change incorporated in Christian assemblies. **(Daniel 9:25)** This is their influence manifested in the church today; the Pope is worshiped as the Holy Father; **(Matthew 23:9)** Christians worship their pastors

as their holy fathers. This is the form of godliness we have been reduced too that came when we embrace the inclusiveness of other's doctrines. This is noted by the **renowned** status we have elevated pastors today.

4. Many seminary trained leaders will become hirelings to pilfer the people, using **Malachi 3:10** to further their own kingdom building agendas; <u>**the ends justify the means to build their kingdoms**</u>. The tithe system under the law will be the means to justify the building of their separate kingdoms. The earthly kingdom is cut off from the heavenly kingdom by not understanding the difference between law and grace. Under this separation, we now are in part truths as a body in division. Mixing law with grace put us in the same state of the Pharisees Jesus condemned; they had become a house of thieves. Under grace, the kingdom of heaven is in you, and as often as we assemble together in the faith that Jesus demonstrated and expect to find in your leader that are to impart it to you; these signs will follow them that believe … **the sick would be healed, the lame walk and demons cast out.** This is Pentecost continued when the whole council of the five ministerial graces can operate.

This gospel that was delivered in faith with a demonstration is what Jesus expects to fine when he returns. Because we are a divided body; therefore, there must be a second outpouring as in the latter rain. Your deliverance will now depend on your level of faith. … **Matthew 23:39 "(KJV)** [39] **For I say unto you, Ye shall not see me henceforth, till ye shall say, blessed is he that cometh in the name of the Lord.** Until that time, this is where we are as gentiles, let into the kingdom until he returns to his chosen people, by mixing law with grace will be the error that contribute to these divisions. This is a Jesuit teaching in their seminaries, placed their Jesuit trained professors to cast this snare into Christian doctrine that furthers their agendas. The principals agree.

Last, whether the Church believes it or not, the Jesuits have studied the prophets. As an organized sovereign religious state, God <u>gave them a lying spirit to think they can change history</u> and the course of events. They have been instrumental in fulfilling **(Daniel 7:25)** Today, the Church do not believe in prophets as in the Old Testament, the manifestation of this false teaching that rejects them is the doctrine of rapture and prosperity. They do not believe we have prophets like the Old Testament anymore, they have been taught under this new doctrine, they are going to fly out of here before trouble starts.

My fellow beloved, it has been my assignment as one of the messengers of God to reveal some of the mysteries that will have horrible consequences in these end time. It is to open our minds to the deeper things of God that have been kept being revealed at this time. We are the least known because the confessing Christian assemblies no longer recognize his voice as the least chosen to confound the so-called wise. Now may the grace of God be with you all until we meet in heaven. AMEN (Updated 12/2021)

THE BEAST THAT CAPTURED THE WHOLE WORLD

Background scripture:

Revelation 16:13 "(KJV) [13] *And I saw three unclean spirits like frogs come out of the mouth of the dragon, and out of the mouth of the beast, and out of the mouth of the false prophet. Revelation 19:20 (KJV)* [20] And the beast was taken, and with him the false prophet that wrought miracles before him, with which he deceived them that had received the mark of the beast, and them that worshipped his image. These both were cast alive into a lake of fire burning with brimstone. *Revelation 20:10 (KJV)* [10] And the devil that deceived them was cast into the lake of fire and brimstone, where the beast and the false prophet are, and shall be tormented day and night for ever and ever."

After being led to re-visit these earlier chronicle editions, the Holy Spirit is now adding more insight to the final layers to these messages as a continuous flow to put the pieces of this end-time mystery puzzle together. They had to be timed for release. We as a people are in a state of such confusion, I was led to hold back these mysteries prior to them happening so some of you might believe and seek salvation. Check the message dates as to the time of this release.

First: Who or What is this beast?

Regarding bible prophecy, in my studies as now being led by the Holy Spirit, I have found that virtually, everything has happened before. We are now in the last dispensation. The Holy Spirit must be our teacher and guide into all truth that has been kept hidden from man. Our thoughts have added imaginations where no biblical discernment is given spiritually. His purpose is to help us see into the spiritual side of our purpose here on earth during our short life span. He is the inspiration to write what God has given through man to know and save him from eternal separation. Therefore, he is the only one that can interpret accurately what all these mysteries mean in the right context for understanding since he originally led men to write the scriptures that would be our guide to eternal life.

Second: Let us begin where it all originated in the Old Testament dispensation under law. In the book of Daniel, chapter two, King Nebuchadnezzar has a disturbing dream; in that dream, he saw a large statue whose image troubled him. He calls all his magicians and subjects and advisors in to tell him the meaning of the dream. When they could not render the satisfaction of what it meant, he threatens them all with death. One of his subjects remembered Daniel and he enters in verse twenty-four to interpret his dream that will save their lives.

The dream depicted a statue of all the kingdoms that would follow from the king's time to rule. In the third chapter, he begins to build a stature as a memorial to his vision. When all is completed, he assembles all to come and worship at its feet by bowing down to it during the musical ceremonies of the dedication. The three Hebrew boys refused. The king was infuriated with them for refusing to obey and ordered them to be thrown into a fiery furnace heated seven-times hotter. This is going to be their tribulation to prove whose god is their God. As you read the account of the interpretation, we are now at the time of the mixture of iron and clay of the ten toes. This is literal under the law. After the death of Jesus, we will enter new covenant known as grace and truth, where our lives will take on a spiritual form of worship as being the restored version of Adam, born from above as new creatures, whose dominion has been restored. We will now worship God in spirit and truth by faith. Our lives as believers, will be lived by faith in the spoken word. All things will now take on a spiritual meaning after the advent of Pentecost.

The last book of the New Testament will contain the hidden mysteries to be revealed at the end of the last generation of the time man was given to subdue the earth. The book of Revelation will contain bits and pieces of the entire Major and Minor Prophets that will hold this mystery. At the appointed time, God will raise up prophets and messengers to interpret these mysteries. They will have the visions to the word for that time and those that receive them will be saved by making their calling and election sure. Throughout times, ages and dispensations, what God has given man for good. The presents of the devil will bring him under bondage through these earthly flesh temptations.

When all is revealed, our captivity will be apparent that he has taken over the whole world including the church of Christ. ***Revelation 12:9 "(KJV)*** *⁹ **And the great dragon was cast out, that old serpent, called the Devil, and Satan, <u>which deceiveth the whole world</u>: he was cast out into the earth, and his angels were cast out with him.***" This deception will come through men in high places ... ***Daniel 7:25 "(KJV)*** *²⁵ **And he shall speak great words against the most High and <u>shall wear out the saints</u> of the most High, and think to change times and laws: and they shall be given into his hand until a time and times and the dividing of time.***" False teachings and new doctrines will be introduced. We all are born children of the devil as per **John 8:44**. The day we hear the voice of God calling us to come and claim our birthright to continue to live for eternity is when we become His children. **Romans 8:16;** All who refuse to receive Christ awaits the destiny to spend an eternity with their father the devil in hell with him where embers are heated seven times hotter than any fire on earth. They will spend it there for eternity in the lake of fire. Your life came from God and God cannot be killed; therefore, hell was created for the devil and his angels, all sinners (his children claimed by him) will be there with him. ***Psalm 14:1 (ASV)*** *¹ **The fool hath said in his heart, there is no God. They are corrupt, they have done abominable works; There is none that doeth good.***" Unfortunately, many will only see this reality the day when they breathe their last breath of life.

What we will become in the future, will take place in our minds. This will be a war for the mind of mankind. Our transformation will come throughout these dispensations of time as God lead man to his end. When you study the scripture under the guidance of the Holy Spirit, this verse will become apparent … *Ecclesiastes 1:9 "(ASV)* [9] *That which hath been is that which shall be; and that which hath been done is that which shall be done: and there is no new thing under the sun."* However, under grace and truth, we have mixed law with grace. This will become the means that will cause us to live in error and not know what spirit we are of. How we will evolve into a human being controlled by a non-human entity will be one of the greatest mysteries of how over time, we evolve to this state.

This mystery image that will cause all to be subject to it, is described in … *Revelation 13:1-13 "(NLT)* [1] *Then I saw a beast rising up out of the sea. It had seven heads and ten horns, with ten crowns on its horns. And written on each head were names that blasphemed God."* At this stage in the end times, Satan will have succeeded in dividing the church into body parts as separate kingdom building religions that will begin to worship in assemblies that will reflect the spirit of **Laodicea,** ruled by the spirit of the Nicolaitan's.

This deception will represent a fall away from the apostle's doctrine. These new religions and teachings will all have one thing in common; they will claim to serve the same god without knowing what spirit they are of, therefore … *Mark 13:20 "(NLT)* [20] *"In fact, unless the Lord shortens that time of calamity, not a single person will survive. But for the sake of his chosen ones, he has shortened those days." …(Continue to) NLT* [2] *This beast looked like a leopard, but it had the feet of a bear and the mouth of a lion and the dragon gave the beast his own power and throne and great authority.* This will be manifested in the form of a New World Order, the birth of the UN. … **NLT** [3] **I saw that one of the heads of the beast seemed wounded beyond recovery—but the fatal wound was healed!"** This part has more than one layer, in this context, Great Britain, our mother country, nearly fell to ruins by the first of the beast system attempts to take over the world as a form of a pre-antichrist out of Germany.

When Russia was invaded, we became allies and combined forces to take Germany down by the Americans invading from the **West** while Russia took the **East** segment of the country. This is what saved Great Britain from being destroyed but left her gravely wounded; helped by her daughter, America. … **NLT the whole world marveled at this miracle and gave allegiance to the beast.** The newly formed UN will represent the parallel to the eighth invisible kingdom, that will begin to set up a system that would eventually bring all nations into a one world common market. ... **NLT** [4] **They worshiped the dragon for giving the beast such power** (America, Russia and China will become the three major powers in the world in the last days.) **and they also worshiped the beast. "Who is as great as the beast?"**

All the nations that joined this newly formed New World Order to prevent any one nation from ever dominating the world again through tyranny. This one organization will have a secrete army and charter that will set an agenda where their end game will justify the means by which they will benefit from this new future technology that will potentially control the people all over the world ... **NLT exclaimed. "Who is able to fight against him?"** Once this system is in place, it will become the eighth kingdom. They will declare the age of a New World Order when George H. Bush senior as head of the western division, is elected at that time. **NLT** [5] **Then the beast was allowed to speak great blasphemies against God. And he was given authority to do whatever he wanted for forty-two months.** Under their charter, they will pursue authority over the affairs of the world during the tribulation as in ... **Daniel 7:25 (ASV)** [25] **"And he shall speak words against the Most High and shall wear out the saints of the Most High; and he shall think to change the times and the law; and they shall be given into his hand until a time and times and half a time."** (This is the second stage during the tribulation period where they will gather their armies.) ... **NLT** [6] **and he spoke terrible words of blasphemy against God, slandering his name and his temple—that is, those who live in heaven.** The last president elected by the people, Obama #44, will speak and declare the first blasphemy against this nation; enacting new laws against the nature of God by legalizing Sodomy under his watch. Because he was elected by the popular vote to office by the people, his decrees will judge this whole nation as the modern-day Sodom. The Trump presidency in office by default will be the work of this covert government to fulfill prophecy and therefore, they will use him to start chaos in the nation by having the right views but at the wrong time in history. That is what they will do on his watch. The republican party stand as a party is against abortion, the democrats is the party of extreme liberalism that will bring this curse upon us as a nation.

The Christian church divided into many denominations that resulted in releasing lying spirits that will mix the world with the church as stated in ... **2 Chronicles 18:21 (ASV)** **²¹ "And he said, I will go forth, and will be a lying spirit in the mouth of all his prophets. And he said, thou shalt entice him, and shalt prevail also: go forth, and do so." ... NLT 7 And the beast was allowed to wage war against God's holy people and to conquer them. And he was given authority to rule over every tribe and people and language and nation. ⁸ And all the people who belong to this world worshiped the beast."** This is where this advanced technology that invented the internet, set the stage for the future will use the media platform that will dumb us down to a delusional state. The people in this grand puzzle, carrying strands of this DNA will have a megalomania personality. We will know by the impact they will have on societies and governments ... **(NLT) They are the ones whose names <u>were not</u> written in the Book of Life <u>before the world was made</u> —the Book that belongs to the Lamb who was slaughtered.** They are the people martyred by them for the testimony of Jesus Christ during the tribulation ... **NLT** ⁹ *Anyone with ears to hear* **should listen and understand. ¹⁰ Anyone who is destined for prison will be taken to prison. Anyone destined to die by the sword will die by the sword.** This is where the Barabbas type Christians will take up arms and be killed by the same means they chose to defend themselves.

As Christians, your choice will determine your fate at that time. ... (Continue) **This means that God's holy people must endure persecution patiently and remain faithful. ¹¹ Then I saw another beast come up out of the earth. He had two horns like those of a lamb. but he spoke with the voice of a dragon. ¹² He exercised all the authority of the first beast.** (The UN) **And he required all the earth and its people to worship the first beast, whose fatal wound had been healed.** Great Britain and the America will become the last two kingdoms to be conquered to bring in the eighth. **Ezekiel 16:44 "(KJV) Behold, everyone that useth proverbs shall use this proverb against thee, saying, as is the mother, so is her daughter."**

Residues of this DNA resided in Great Britain that was present when Hitler attacked them. The internet was invented in that country but was launched world-wide by American technology. This is when we become the mystery Modern Babylon (her daughter) is revealed. She gave the world the ability to communicate all over the world and be understood in your own language in real-time. This in biblical mystery that reveals the Mystery Modern Babylon of today spiritually. Now you remember why God confounded Babylon of old to keep them from advancing outside of his sovereign will of man's timeline to subdue the earth. Here again, we have reached a historical impasse to the point that if God tarried, we would become a Godless society rule by AI technology.

We have entered the forbidden knowledge that caused the flood. We are coming to the end of another dispensation of time continuum, the last millennium. This new Modern-Day Babylon (America) will introduce the spiritual form of a non-human entity in form of the **beast** over the airwaves that will be known as the internet … **NLT** [13] **He did astounding miracles, even making fire flash down to earth from the sky while everyone was watching.** The internet will be the means of his arrival that will bring everything right into your home through smart media devices. WOW! WHAT A REVELATION.

This technology in the hands of evil men will be instrumental in captivating the whole world. They will be able to produce holographic images on a large scale in the sky, bordering on introducing the world to angelic beings in the form of E T's. The Roman Catholic Church will be responsible means to introduce the **false prophet.** I revealed how they will use the seminary system taught by their Jesuit priest professors to re-educate the pastors that will be sent to the Christian churches in the chronicle, **"How Satan Deceived the Christian World."** They are indeed the **deep state.** This new technology in the sky will enable them to mesmerize the population of the world by having angels in the form of E T's to transform themselves spiritually through those linked with their DNA. They are linked to those with this strand of megalomania. They are already here operating in the bodies of men. Now it is not my intention to frighten you in any way. That is why I introduced you to the knowledge of the spirit world. This is what Ephesian 6:12 is speaking about. This energy will be generated by those in great numbers, looking for this great event. Imagination is a very powerful force that by faith in a false vision can produce these kinds of false miracle on this scale, that will set up the masses to receive this grand illusion … **Acts 7:42 "(ASV)** [42] **But God turned and gave them up to serve <u>the host of heaven</u>:"** (Angelic beings disguised as E T's in human form.) **Colossians 2:18 "(ASV)** [18] **Let no man rob you of your** prize by a voluntary humility and <u>worshipping of the angels</u>, dwelling in the things which he hath seen, vainly puffed up by his fleshly mind, *2 Corinthians 10:5 (KJV)* ⁵ *Casting down imaginations, and every high thing that exalteth itself <u>against the knowledge of God</u>, and bringing into captivity every thought to the obedience of Christ;"* The world, looking for something of this magnitude, in their imaginations, generated the energy to produce these kinds of miracles. *Revelation 13:14-18 "(NLT)* ¹⁴ *And with all the miracles he was allowed to perform on behalf of the first beast,* (The pre-antichrist man of sin.) **he deceived all the people who belong to this world. He ordered the people to make a great statue of the first beast, who was fatally wounded and then came back to life."** Now here is the next layered revelation to that verse … we know now that the internet is the spiritual beast system, Satan operating in the airwaves as **"the prince of the power of the air."** *Ephesians 2:2 "(KJV)* ²*Wherein in time past ye walked according to the course of this world, according to <u>the prince of the power of the air</u>, the spirit that now worketh in the children of disobedience:"* This is the "X" generation, (millennials) that will bring about their own destruction with this for-bidden technology that caused the flood. This "X" identifies this generation as in the time of their own **extinction**. As in past civilizations that introduced this forbidden knowledge.

When the world-wide crash comes, the present internet system will be replaced with a new system that will be cashless when it goes online. This transition will be gradual over time because this technology will come in the form of mind control. You will be linked by biological ID. This system cannot be hacked. The people of the world will be already spiritually marked as to their addiction to the internet smart phone system in their foreheads; however, the smart phone will be the device that will cause all under its power to take the mark through this device held in your right hand. This is the spiritual beast, brought to life. ¹⁵ **He was then permitted to give life to this statue so that it could speak.** Seri is our Hal as in 2001 movie. All you have read is symbolic of the hidden mystery in which the book of Revelation was written that was kept from being revealed until this time in our history. Here's where Steve Jobs will introduce the forbidden knowledge in his strand of Nephilim DNA that caused the extinction of past tribes and tongues in ancient history. Men of this caliber have cold personalities. They are marked for death which is a characteristic of this gene in their DNA.

This knowledge will once again infringe upon the technology that has the capability to change humanity into an in-humane existence, controlled by an AI technology. Steve Jobs discovered a way to link the **matrix** of our brainwaves to enter your mind as a control signal, wrote an encrypted algorism in the form of an app, incorporated into his smart i-phone that will become a hand-held computer that will interact individually with your own brain's wavelength. He built an encrypted wall with codes that only his company can enter. Just like **Hal** in the movie **"2001," Seri** will now become the new upgraded reality version of **Hal's** voice you will respond too when she speaks. They will bring back an updated version of the **Pokémon** game to test the level of its control on the minds of those who respond to this app's instructions. …" **(NLT) Then the statue of the beast commanded that anyone refusing to worship it must die. 16 He required everyone—small and great, rich and poor, free and slaves—to be given a mark on the right hand or on the forehead."** This AI technology will be introduced in new smart home technologies. This is where another tech giant will introduce a home monitoring system called **Alexa**. All that was captivated by this subtle seduction through the internet and smart phone will become the stage of receiving the mark, brought under control through Steve Jobs technology to a level that crossed into the forbidden knowledge zone. … **"NLT 17 And no one could buy or sell anything without that mark, which was either the name of the beast or the number representing his name. 18 Wisdom is needed here. Let the one with understanding solve the meaning of the number of the beast, for it is the number of a man. His number is 666."** This is the mystery of how you will receive the mark without your knowledge. This is another mystery I discovered in the spirit of truth. Satan, as the **"prince of the power of the air,"** will enter the minds of the people through this unseen spirit masquerading in the form of the internet, taking control of the world's population.

The Pope in office at that time will be the one to introduce the world to this new leader of the world as described in the book of Revelation revealed in the numerology of the symbols on his crown, representing the number **666,** which is the natural order of all things controlled by Satan. All the pieces of the puzzle will come together during the tribulation when the stock market takes its final dive when God will have them pull the final plug after they have the world set to take control after they have generated fear on a mass scale. This will be the rise of the eighth kingdom of the

New World Order. These new highs are designed to milk all the wealth from the financial system from those who are well connected as power become their idol and gods that are not connected to their bloodline. They will be taken down in their greed by their own willing ignorance as they manipulate the market. They will have great financial gains by the stocks they offer to seduce them to buy. They represent the ten toes of Nebuchadnezzar's dream that will be a mixture of different tribes, kindreds and tongues that will rule the world as the ten toes representing the ten different regional divisions in their new world at that time.

The beast revelation continued

This advance technology will be used by the gentiles in the first half of the tribulation to judge them for infringing into this forbidden knowledge zone. Just as those tribal nations were extinguished in the past, so will America be found no more at all in the end as the Modern Babylon. **(Rev.18:22)** The real church will rise out of the ashes of the dry bones of Ezekiel thirty-seven to reform this new body representing Christ in the fullness.

It will unfold in two parts; the **first** will be spiritual. This will be the church in judgment in the first half; the **second** literal. When Israel rejected their Messiah under the law, a veil of darkness came between them. They are waiting for the literal return of the two witnesses in the spirit of Moses and Elijah that will be their sign to look for their Messiah's coming. They will repent and prepare to receive Him. When Satan is cast out of heaven, he will resurrect himself in the pre-antichrist man of sin when he is cut down and rise again, he will gather the armies of the north as described in Ezekiel thirty-eight to attack Jerusalem.

That's why they can't give up any land regained in the 1967 war. They know that for the Messiah to return, they must have possession of the capital city, Jerusalem. As I have said before in my studies under this anointing, all things were happening in **twos** and **threes** as these mysteries are revealed. Many confessing Christians in my experience have not been able to receive these revelations because of long standing deep denominational beliefs that go back generations of false teachings. This I can understand; I was once in that state. The current spiritual state of darkness has many assemblies blind to this third layer of the book of Revelation that will judge all that are living in this time. These revelations will require enduring the test of faith to restore the apostle's doctrine before we can be translated out of this present world; thus, ending this dispensation of grace. AMEN

Now on the national front

There is a great mystery surrounding the election of Donald Trump that is yet to be revealed. This is still a point of doubt for many who have no knowledge of how to read the signs of bible prophecy. Therefore, many will be caught in God's break and destroyed for lack of knowledge and unbelief. This is evident of the apostate evangelical Christian church; in their blindness, God gave them a representative of what they have become. Now this has past, I can begin to reveal the signs surrounding his administration's time in office. He will need prayer to restrain his actions as a false representative of the Republic with a link that will cause him to be controlled by our arch enemy Russia. He was compromised long before he ran for office during his business dealings that will give them this advantage, now he is in office.

1 Peter 4:17 "(ASV) [17] For the time is come for judgment to begin at the house of God: and if it begins first at us, what shall be the end of them that obey not the gospel of God?" We are entering a season of national judgment. This is our spiritual state that justifies why we must go through a tribulation period to restore divine order in the world as in the beginning of time. The church is divided into many splits of the apostle's doctrine that has it in a deformed state. We all are divided in part truths and therefore, only know in part. Our tribulation is to restore the true doctrine of the apostles as in the beginning back to one body. Our state is judged under this scripture ... **1 Corinthians 13:9-10 "(ASV) [9] For we know in part, and we prophesy in part; 10 but when that which is perfect is come, that which is in part shall be done away."** These ministries are building their own separate kingdoms.

What will happen in the first half of the tribulation of the gentiles, will be the battlefield in the spirit of the mind of every believer in the body of Christ. All these denominational kingdoms that have operated under man's doctrines of separatist movements are a direct result of our leaders that were seduced by the seminary system under Jesuit professors. This is how the Catholic Church used their wealth to penetrate Christianity and got to their leaders through the seminary system. Our hypocrisy is now being exposed on all levels as a church, as a nation and as a government for the entire world to see. Our sins have found us out. That' why things are happening at such a rapid a pace as evil men get worse and worse. The increase in natural disasters are signs of God's anger being carried out by Satan. Those in the Barabbas Christian patriot spirit, Trump will be the man they will put their trust in to **"Take America back and make her great again."**

We are on the verge of becoming an extinct nation by a church that is blind to reality and deaf to the voice of God. All these revelations that were given to me are mysteries that were held back to be revealed now. The church divided would not give place to hear the true prophet's vision to speak in their assemblies. It would expose to their supporters how they have been deceived. This is what I discovered on my missionary trip around the state of Arizona as I visited one hundred and fifty-three churches of all denominations; they are not ready to receive you if you are not well known or a media figure with credentials in the Christian community. They were trained to reject these prophets. It is a sad time to experience spiritual leaders that can't recognize the voice of God's visitation. Many under their leader's delusions will be caught with them in God's break when they are rejected.

Therefore, **Proverbs 29:18 "(KJV)** [18] *Where there is no vision, the people perish: but he that keepeth the law, happy is he."* Now how many confessing Christians are happy to the point, they are ready to go home. You will find that answer in those born from above. Too often in a conversation with fellow confessing believers, they answer as having hopes for some future dreams in this world. That is evident of the deep-rooted false teachings that have blocked their minds to hear this level of truth. What's about to happen on the horizon, God must let the devil do what he has already justified; that is, to fulfill what the prophets have already predicted in time past. Satan's agents in the earth carrying strands of this megalomania DNA are about to be allowed to carry out their master plan as the self-appointed illuminated ones **(Illuminati's)** as Satan guardians of evil in the earth that the ark angel Michael was given the authority to restrain until such a time as this.

Time for us is no more. **Daniel 12:1 "(KJV)**[1] *And at that time shall Michael stand up, the great prince which standeth for the children of thy people: and* *there shall be a time of trouble, such as never was since there was a nation <u>even to that same time:</u> and at that time thy people shall be delivered, <u>every</u> <u>one that shall be found written in the book.</u>*"The horrors these foreigners in our government have planned for us as spies will be exposed with-out their knowing their own end will be double for double for trying to defy God's prophets. These illuminated ones behind the scenes that are in control our Congress, Senate and the presidency would not let any laws be passed concerning gun control; even during all these mass murders committed by the suicide demons released from the pit that was restrained up until this point. This is what Edward Snowden discovered in that back door of the NSA's AI system. It is no accident that he was given sanctuary in Russia. These are the seeds of generations past that were planted to reveal these secrets and return to their mother countries.

They want let our law maker pass any laws on gun control. They want the general population to have as many guns in your possession as you can buy so when they pull the plug, the chaos will pit neighbor against neighbor for survival and you will kill off each other in great numbers before they let the armies of Russia and China come to take their spoils. Among the communist sisters, they will adopt North Korea as their baby by making her an offer she cannot refuse that will cause her to play a major part in the future. They will become the three communist sisters as a bruit beast force that will manipulate the last president in office not elected by the people, Donald Trump. God will allow them to kill off 70% of the American population before he takes them out for attempting to take their Garden of Eden. *Joel 2:3 "(KJV) ³ A fire devoureth before them; and behind them a flame burneth: the land is as the <u>garden of Eden</u> before them, and behind them a desolate wilderness; yea, and nothing shall escape them.*"This awaits us as a nation given over to our enemies for destruction. This is our tribulation as gentiles. This nation, at the hand of the final president, will be destroyed by meteor showers as was in the days of Sodom and Gomorrah by his predecessor permitting the legalization of Sodomy.

There' is an asteroid fragment that will follow the larger one that has past as a sign warning, the smaller fragment is on the way that will hit the western hemisphere and split it into three parts. *Revelation 18:21 "(KJV) ²¹ And a mighty angel took up a stone like a great millstone, and cast it into the sea, saying, thus with violence shall that great city Babylon be thrown down, and shall be found no more at all."* There' a new series on TV called **"SALVATION"** it's not just entertainment, it's a warning. God is using Hollywood to show you your future.

Biblical Historical background

Israel's fate began when the people wanted to be like the rest of the world; they wanted a king they could see. God warned them by putting their life in the hands of a king in the flesh, they choose to rule over them will judge their nation's fate by the words and actions of that king. They chose Saul. He was handsome, well spoken, and therefore became the people's choice. Because they had been warned, in the end, as king he blasphemed the God by having that anointing on him, consulting a medium of the devil; therefore, went down in defeat. There are some that are saying Obama will return to replace Trump when he goes down; I reserve any comment on this because some of these prophetic messages have credibility and I do not go beyond what I have been given. We are in this last generation with Trump as king of the free world, he will commit an act of abomination against God as being arrogantly prideful. With the curse of Sodomy under Obama's watch, this will be our sign to the prophets of the end of the gentile age. This man that's working behind the scenes is devising a plan to captivate the attention of the whole world at the right timing.

Now let's fast forward to the end of times and see how those that refuse to take heed to study biblical history under the anointing of the Holy Spirit are doomed to repeat it. Obama was elected by the people as a symbol of hope and change. As head of this nation, he will be a symbol of a history making event. Historically, he is about to fulfill bible prophecy that will end this nation's reign as the gentile nation chosen to protect Israel. Dr. Martin Luther King became a symbol of reformation raised up by God to be a prophet to bring a warning to this nation as in the Old Testament tradition but under grace and truth.

Before he was taken out by this shadow government, he was raised up to warn, he spoke this prophecy of a dream of hope knowing that he would become a martyr. He told us what to look for when **in that day,** this man raised up would be judge by the content of his character not the color of his skin. Obama was that man that would lead us into the legalization of sodomy. Now to link this to King Saul and what he did in the beginning under the law is literal, the **Alpha** of the line of kings, Obama and Trump's actions represented the **Omega** of the line of gentile kings that committed this abominable act of legalizing Sodomy and the pride that cut this nation off while kings of the free world. God is judging his two nations that was given (45) kings to rule over them, whose time to reign is coming to an end.

Obama committed an unforgivable act of blasphemy on this nation by changing the truth order concerning God's creation of male and female to a lie when he endorsed the homosexual agenda by legalizing the union of the same sex marriage on his watch. Now what's evil will become good and what's good will become evil. When the Supreme Court did not reverse this degree, it became a law that spread to other states as king of the free world. Obama and Trump became the **(Omega)** the wicked leaders that will cause this nation as gentiles to be brought to a sudden and abrupt end as did Saul the **Alpha,** whose act condemned him. Israel was the beginning who put themselves under the rulership of a king they could see. Obama decreed that **"America is no longer a Christian nation";** therefore, breaking the covenant of protection from our enemies; Trump's pride became the ultimate insult as the leader of this nation; therefore, provoke God to cut him off. They will represent the end of the reign of these two chosen nations; the **Alpha** & the **Omega** coming to an end, as I have said before, Satan has justified what God must let him do through the spiritual laws of sin and death.

We are the last generation of gentiles and Jews on earth as nations. Both, as nations, are doomed to repeat history. The Pharisees and the Sadducees rejected Jesus as their Messiah because they had reached the point of apostasy where they could not recognize him as their Messiah literally in the flesh. They also entered a form of religion by exchanging the law in favor of their own traditions. *Mark 7:9 "(KJV) ⁹ And he said unto them, Full well ye reject the commandment of God, that ye may keep your own tradition. Hosea 4:6 (KJV) ⁶ My people are destroyed for lack of knowledge: because thou hast rejected knowledge, I will also reject thee, that thou shalt be no priest to me: seeing thou hast forgotten the law of thy God, I will also forget thy children."* This applied to the descendants of those that killed Jesus. Of the twelve brothers, Judah did not participate in what his brother's did to Joseph. His tribe' seeds blood was innocent though-out God's dealing with them through time. Their Messiah would come through his linage as the lion of that tribe of Judah, only to come out of hiding to save them from being destroyed as a nation when threaten in times of tyranny. He is their savior in that tribe.

This same word is to the church; we have evolved to where we have become, forms of religions, we do not recognize his voice when he speaks in the spirit as fallen from the apostle's doctrine. We, as a nation, inherited what the Jews rejected ... *Galatians 3:14 "(KJV)* [14] *That the blessing of Abraham might come on the Gentiles through Jesus Christ; that we might receive the promise of the Spirit through faith.* In 1776, that promise was fulfilled; we became that nation raised up to be responsible for the restoration of the nation of Israel as her protector from tyranny. Donald Trump, our current president #45, in his pride and arrogant doubleminded state, will not be allowed to complete his agenda; that is, to wake up the Barabbas patriots to try to change without knowing, what God has set in motion for these last days. **Proverbs 16:18 "(KJV)** [18] **Pride goeth before destruction and a haughty spirit before a fall."**

These blessings that came with this covenant have overtaken us as a nation and as a confessing Christian church. Thus, this has now become our destiny as a once great society and nation that shall soon be no more. Let us all examine what we believe and repent. May God have mercy on all that call upon his name with a brokenness and a contrite heart. This is what I did when he revealed the state of my heart. AMEN

LIVING A CHRIST LIKE LIFE

Background scripture:

2 Corinthians 5:17 "(KJV) [17] *Therefore if any man be in Christ, he is a new creature: old things are passed away; behold, all things are become new. Matthew 7:14-15 (KJV)* [14] *Because strait is the gate, and narrow is the way, which leadeth unto life, and few there be that find it. John 1:12 (KJV)* [12] *But as many as received him, to them gave the power to become the sons of God, even to them that believe on his name:"*

Often in unpredictable circumstances, I experience the Holy Spirit revealing things God wants all his children to know about your unlimited capabilities He has made available to all confessing believers. Everyone born from above owns everything in the Earth. You don't have to have it in your possession. All things belong to the children of God not the devil. All that is taught in the New Testament by the Holy Spirit is for you to enjoy these blessings and not be possessed to the point that these things bring sorrows. Your priorities are set first on the kingdom of heaven because now, that's your final destiny at the end of your life. Being free indeed is not being entangled with the cares of this life that adds sorrows. Satan cannot touch you when you are in control of all you possess in this life. Beware of being free as owning all you possess; for some, I see they have a false sense of security and humility coupled with hidden pride.

Adam's position when God put him in charge of all he created was unaware of the tempter until he became a victim. That's why everything in the New

Testament points to you as the new creation; Adam restored. All is now written is for your learning. The hidden things will be revealed in those born from above as elects. If we use the wisdom that is found in exercising the fruits of the spirit as a surrendered vessel, you will represent the new Adam restored in full ownership of the Earth. You see, in Christ, his thoughts are higher than these meagerly elements of this world. This is Christ as the second Adam giving you the privilege through him to walk as the first Adam again. What I have learned, God has given us back the Earth and everywhere you put your feet is yours because you live in the reality that He now is the greater one walking in you on Earth that owns it.

He is calling those things as needed daily by faith to come into your possession in your daily walk as needed. We all have an appointment with death. God has given us a time span on this Earth to accomplish what He has in His perfect will for you and He knows our departure date. All those have died before the final resurrection in Christ, that was their day of rapture for their soul. That's why He told us to be ready at any time. Only those that are alive and remain on the day of the rapture of all saints will get to see the glory we have never seen demonstrated in those saints that get to put the devil under their feet through great exploits. I cannot explain what is beyond our level of comprehension that will be done during the tribulation. Although through spiritual illumination, I'm aware that this is the time of the end of our dispensation on Earth.

While watching a news clip, meditating on what I saw, this came to my mind? Now before I explain this revelation, let me remind you that I do not think on what I see because my thoughts have already been condemned if not of God. I wait for the Holy Spirit to speak. While meditating, this is what the Holy Spirit begin to speak to my mind ... *"I have made you whole ... your mind has been synced to my mind ... if you can believe this, no weapon formed against you will prosper ... "I AM," your creator is in you and no weapons on earth can defeat me in you ... speak my word according to my will as you are led in faith, and I will perform it."*

I have been trying to live up to that word since that day. It was a bit overwhelming at that time. When I made up my mind to always reply with an understanding of what the word said, I noticed it has become an offense to some and a form of intimidation to others. Not being well known, most confessing Christians are not accustomed to seeing a fellow believer with such convictions living outside of the present church assembly, act on the word in this way. This is where you will hear some of the same words said to you as was said about Jesus. I am not that perfect yet, but I refuse to entertain doubtful thoughts God has said about this covering being in his word. All I have done is what God told all that come to him to do; believe without doubt and that did not come for me overnight. I can only say, in practice, I endured much rejection to do things His way. If I am going to experience what He said, I must be focused on His words and His words only. Though my faults are ever before me, my convictions caused many to depart from me.

I also realize why my understanding is becoming greater; He keeps adding pieces of His mind. My peace comes from keeping my mind stayed on the word in every situation. I had to learn how to discipline myself to come to this level of consciousness in my daily walk. Now to explain these background scriptures that tell you how He (the Holy Spirit) gets our attention to walk into the perfect will of God. *Matthew 7:14 "(KJV)* [14] *Because strait is the gate,* (When the Holy Spirit addresses your heart, you will become a doer of the word as walking down that road that leads to the strait gate.) *and narrow is the way, which leadeth unto life,* (When you enter that crossroad of making this decision, there will be no one there but **you, God** and the **devil.) and few there be that find it."** (The only way you will cross that intersection is to follow his directions in the word as you would your GPS.) *Mark 6:56 "(KJV)* [56] *And whithersoever he entered, into villages, or cities, or country, they laid the sick in the streets, and besought him that they might touch if it were but the border of his garment: and as many as touched him were made whole."* (This is the road that' connected to a direct flow from the throne room through Jesus Christ to keep you perfectly whole while on this Earth as you would be in heaven and that's a promise. That's why it is your faith that keeps that flow, even when you just believe in the name.

In **John 1:12,** the power of the Holy Spirit makes the connection that brings authority not seen with the necked eye out of the spirit world where you can see what the word spoken in faith created. This is the glory of His presence on the Earth through his testimony; now in you. That's why everyone that received Jesus as the son was made whole as you would be in heaven. Now if you can believe that rather than what he, she, it or they say, or the circumstances you find yourself in, this will be your test to see whose report you are going to receive. Personally, I do not want to live outside of his word. I am experiencing him perform it to my benefit and others that agree in faith. Your choices will determine your fate which is already spoken in His word. You see my beloved, that's the decision I had to make at that crossroad as to which way to turn. When I discerned who was speaking, he made known what was behind each choice, the good and the bad. Satan will not tell you the truth about where you are going or about yourself because he knows you don't want to face it, only God tells you that truth. You must learn how to discern his voice as in being born from above to receive His love. The mistakes you make along the way will be corrected as you repent and obey the leading of the Holy Spirit. That's what grace is to us in our unworthy state.

This thin line of deception that will cause you not to recognize his voice, comes through willful disobedience. This is how Satan gets to justify deceiving you by giving place to him as Eve did when she acted on what he said, she didn't know she was deceived until God told her what she did. Adam and Eve knew the voice of God as the first voice they heard as new creatures created in the Earth as spirit beings in the natural. Only God can open your mind to receive his words. *John 6:44 "(KJV)* [44] *No man can come to me, except the Father which hath sent me draw him: and I will raise him up at the last day."*

If we are tempted to wonder away from His presence as your covering, Satan will cloud your mind and counterfeit God's voice because you willingly gave place to him. This is what Eve did. We are warned to … *Ephesians 4:27 "(KJV)* [27] *Neither give place to the devil."* You have heard me speak about the sins of omission in **Galatians 5:19-21,** that's what Satan is trying to get you to do, accumulate these sins against you to justify taking you to hell before you come to the knowledge of the truth to repent. If you die in that state … *Daniel 5:27 "(KJV)* [27] *Thou art weighed in the balances, and art found wanting."* This is why everybody talking about heaven ain't going there. This will happen at the judgment; hell is being enlarged to receive a great number of deceived Christians. *Isaiah 5:14 (KJV) "Therefore hell hath enlarged herself and opened her mouth without measure: and their glory, and their multitude, and their pomp, and he that rejoiceth, shall descend into it."* Among these are many confessing Christians that will be deceived by not knowing His voice when they are called to repent. That's why those in your immediate surroundings many times will reject you if you can't prove who is in you by this new life that only can be known by the fruit as who is in the vessel.

Don't be surprised if your family members don't receive you; remember, we only read about four in Jesus's own family; Joseph & Mary, Jude and James. It is human nature to demonstrate this individuality to choose who you will follow or believe in. What I'm experiencing, many are having their day of visitation even when they have learned to recognize his voice. It will be your love relationship that will enable you to recognize His voice to the point of acting on it.

The test may come through someone you least expect that you may be taking for granted. Do not be in that crowd of 98 percent of false witnesses as were the Pharisees and Sadducees to repeat history by not knowing what spirit you are of; like the leaders in His day that couldn't recognize their own Messiah, after they were told what He would look like in **Isaiah 53** and what he would do in **Isaiah 61,** yet despite the evidence, they chose to reject him. Under grace and truth, those that are doers will be known by their fruit as being born from above.

Often, I hear fellow Christians say to me, I am not there yet; I say this not to offend you, but what you are saying is, I am not ready to give up what it takes to go to heaven. My beloved brothers and sisters, God has made it plain in His word the standards we will be judged by and it will not be by your church membership and what you did to please your leaders. Just keep this in mind; God is judging what is in our hearts that is well pleasing to Him. In my conclusion, what I see about myself, God used all my experiences, good and bad, to bring me to this present state of mind to prepare me for His calling in my life that was predestined before the foundation of the world as He … ***Romans 8:28 "(KJV)*** [28]***And we know that <u>all things work together for good to them that love God</u>, to them who are the called according to his purpose."*** You may think I am special but if I entertain that thought, it will put me on the broad road to hell. I have found out that to whom much is given, much will be required.

He is speaking to all of us the same way. If you are not hearing like this, loose yourself from the entanglements and surround yourself with people who are doer's of the word as a confessing Christian. I experience as much joy as I do sorrow and grief because of what I have been given to know and made to see. If you are being taught this in your assemblies, then we are as John said, we have this unction and will know each other when we meet, and the Holy Spirit will be our witness as was in Mary and Elizabeth when they met with anointed babies in their wombs. In my observations of the present-day church world, the traditions that Jesus rebuked the Pharisee's of, are still present in today's assemblies. Any time you know what is going to happen before you get there, that's a structured order that came out of seminary train pastors. This is the form of religion, as taught by Jesuit professors. It has nothing to do with the Holy Spirit which is unpredictable when it comes to the leading of the Lord. The church environment that contains all seven spirits in Revelation two & three, has contributed to the present divisions that have resulted in this separate kingdom building mentality. The Holy Spirit's only purpose is to lift Jesus and point you to the father, not man. We who are born from above worship God in spirit and in truth; therefore, where the spirit of God is liberated, he will heal, deliver and set souls free from sin and the oppression of demon spirits. This is where you will find those born of him from above. Those touched by them will show this sign of his testimony.

That teaching from the Holy Spirit opened my eyes as to who really believes the word as pastors and leaders by not liberating the Holy Spirit to take control of the assembly to have that experience each time we come together. The difference now is easily discernable, when you are a surrendered vessel coming out of the volumes of the books. A converted vessel of Christ gives the Holy Spirit the liberty to do what the father sent him to do in Jesus; this time in you. If I am willing to let him do this in me as being a converted believer that cause pastors and leaders to become offended when they see that they are misrepresenting the truth; this is what I too often will experience … **Acts 28:27 "(NLT)** [27] *For the hearts of these people are hardened, and their ears cannot hear, and they have closed their eyes— so their eyes cannot see, and their ears cannot hear, and their hearts cannot understand, and they cannot turn to me and let me heal them."* That' why I cannot fellowship in an assembly who is not willing to teach with convictions, the whole council of the word that shows the true love for a soul that needs to be delivered. *Amos 3:3 "(KJV)* [3] *Can two walk together, except they be agreed?"* Many of us are bound by lack of knowledge by keeping the traditions of men that can lead to Satan justifying putting sickness and diseases upon us. Paul tells us in the eleventh chapter of 1 Corinthians. In the administration of the sacrament. I have found it is hard to get people in the traditional church to receive this kind of deeper truth. I also see that there are even fewer that have ears to hear it unless God open their ears to it. There is an underground move back to the home church environment that is growing out of a hunger for the truth. God is leading them to come together in these last days in preparation for another Pentecost. AMEN

On the national front

Our nation is in a crisis condition. Biblical historians will see it being repeated as all eyes are on Israel. Her land is where God centers the activity in the world around. The reason you see so much war and rumors of wars represent God is being provoked once again to come to the aid of his people. Every nation that's against Israel in the Middle East is being destroyed by wars and the others are waiting to join the winners during the tribulation. Sense Obama pulled back on our support of Israel; this is what's causing us to experience these divisions and devastating natural disasters. When we drew back on protecting Israel, Satan justified reaping havoc on our nation. In the end, all nations that came against Israel will be destroyed along with their capital cities. When Joshua entered the Promised Land, God told him everywhere he put his foot would become the Abraham land grant to His children. Under grace and truth, this was magnified in giving the world back to every believer as the restored Adam but only by force will the devil give it up. **(Matthew 11:12)** In the war of 1967, they recovered their Capital city of David, Jerusalem. Now in these last days as history get ready to be repeated, all eyes will be on Jerusalem again as Satan attempts to destroy her once Modern Babylon (America) is destroyed for not protecting her.

Hurricane Harvey was a revelation of church and state in times of national crisis; Houston is a hub for some of the largest mega churches in America. What we see is God revealing to his people where they must put their trust and priorities. As you see by how much they came to the aid of the needy. Many prove to be self-help principal teaching assembly halls that demonstrated just where their priorities were in times of great perils and trial for his people.

Now you see what they are supporting that showed no love when the test came. The world had to expose them; therefore, we are being judged as Christians because the world is outdoing the church in taking care of their own. To show you just how much compassion the world has ... they even generate Go-Fund-Me pages to take care of their own. It grieved me to see the world criticize the church and be justified in their accusations. While pastors travel in opulent luxury at the expense of robbing their members to support their corporate family own kingdom assemblies, shows no love for the poor as in self-denial. By the action of these mega assemblies who must be pressured to open their doors and share the wealth. I told you that things were going to get worst. God is going to expose them for all to see soon. I'm sorrowing to have to bring such news but my calling in this area is in the spirit of Jeremiah. He was thrown in a hole for telling his own people the truth about their future; there is worst yet to come. AMEN

GET READY TO HEAR
THE FINAL CALL

Background scripture:

Isaiah 55:6 (KJV) "Seek ye the LORD while he may be found, call ye upon him while he is near: Psalm 46:10 (KJV) [10] *Be still and know that I am God: I will be exalted among the heathen, I will be exalted in the ,." 1 Corinthians 11:28 (KJV)* [28] *But let a man examine himself, and so let him eat of that bread, and drink of that cup. Acts 2:40 (KJV)* [40] *And with many other words did he testify and exhort, saying, Save yourselves from this untoward generation. 1 Thessalonians 5:2-3 (KJV)* [2] *For yourselves know perfectly that the day of the Lord so cometh as a thief in the night.* [3] *For when they shall say, Peace and safety; then sudden destruction cometh upon them, as travail upon a woman with child; and they shall not escape."*

I do not promote myself in any way because there are Major Prophets speaking under the influence of the Holy Ghost that will confirm some of these messages over the internet. In my calling, I fill in the mystery details of what these politically correct 501-c3 assemblies want preach or teach that's against building a mega assembly. We really don't want to face this type of truth is revealed. My place in this wilderness is as a John the Baptist type messenger being prepared to preach for a short time and martyred during the tribulation as one of a few to re-introduce the Christ to a backslidden church. When America's economy collapses during the chaotic riots brought on by the new president's actions, the people will come to the place to see that God is their only hope. Then they will cry-out to him when they see their state with no hope left and for the first time will see what God has been trying to tell them. These are the **Barabbas** type patriot Christians who had their hopes in taking back America in their attempts to make her great again will die by the sword.

When they take up arms, God will give them over to our enemies for letting the devil deceive you to think that the battle was theirs and not the lords. All we were asked to do as a church after the **"911"** warning was return to the God of Abraham, Isaac and Jacob as one nation under God. He would have healed our land and exposed our enemies within. The elects in the wilderness are being prepared to carry the everlasting gospel of the Kingdom to be preached for the last time. Many of us will be martyred during the time of Jacob's trouble in the tribulation that many still don't believe the church will suffer. This mystery hidden in the book of Revelation will be revealed at that time to the end-time church age. We are in the pre-tribulation phase of this nation as praying for peace and safety. Sudden destructions will come by not reading the signs of the times. These signs are to tell those with ears to hear and eyes to see, get ready for we are now **"in that day"** of Judgment.

When scientist can predict a date of an event in the cosmos, it is because God has calculated everything by a numbers system of universal changes that will return in cycles. Mankind has decoded those numbers that determine a time frame of events in these cycles of the cosmos. How are these dates significant to bible prophecy? These dates will become signs of events that will come in your life cycle time frame. The work of the prophets and messengers will tell you what to look for specifically and at that appointed time, God will reveal the mysteries held to be revealed at that time and in that dispensation but not the dates. Those who give specific dates are overtaken by their zeal to go ahead of God, will be confounded.

The dates are on God's biblical calendar in heaven is not revealed to mankind in his natural state; only God knows those dates of a specific time of an event foretold by his prophets. It will become a test of your faith to live as though you are ready to depart at your appointed time. Let me give you some human logic about time. If you knew the exact date you were going to die, you would have your bucket list of all you wanted to do in this world before that date and in your nature, would only repent on that day because of the evil desires within, would prevent you from coming before.

We are told to be always ready as having an appointment with our divine destiny, death. That is your individual day of rapture from this earth. When we go by observation as trying to predict what only God knows, this is what has contributed to the increase of scoffers by those who say they are prophets, in their zeal, giving specific dates of things that did not come to pass. Now the delayed signs are here manifesting in these natural disasters; here again, I see we are being set up by pre-mature sign from demonic forces to captivate the world's attention in a time of this vacuum of confusion that doctrinal divisions brought about. The true prophet's words are being overshadowed by all these false predictions that Satan is using to capitalize on their blind zeal and people's lack of knowledge.

Mankind has been led by Satan to enter the forbidden knowledge zone, now operating among us. Man has decoded the genetic gene-splicing technology, giving him the capability to reproduce himself as a perfect natural human being, with genetically altered DNA. These genetic engineers are working on designing him to be a perfect physical human being to be programmed to do what his masters command. This was the secret work that came with those German scientists we brought to this country after WWII. Their use of this forbidden knowledge through fallen angelic DNA was to help them become the master race people.

We as a Christian free born nation will suffer the curse as previous societies and will suffer double judgement for departing from God's covenant of divine protection. This judgment is the Sodomy curse coupled with the gene-splicing DNA technology. This spirit drove them to their own destruction as God had to intervene to prevent a pre-mature apocalypse. Given the fact that the world is coming to the end of another time continuum is an indication that what they have succeeded in doing, is already among us.

Steve Job's DNA knowledge gifted him to link your brain to the internet through his smart i-phone when he wrote the algorism app that decodes your brain's wavelength. That gave them access to areas of your brain that will control your actions. Gene splicing the DNA will give them the ability to create genetically altered human beings. This is what caused previous civilizations to become extinct. This is being done through a deep cover black operation unknown to some sitting presidents. They are a handpicked group assembly of the best of the best in all scientific fields answerable to the higher order of these illuminati's that are about to implement these advance technologies to drastically decreased the world's population to numbers that are to sustain this new society as their master plan.

They will use a form of a worldwide fear pandemic. This is what it would lead to if God allowed time to be extended. All these things are working simultaneously in these end time as Satan's master plan to take full control of the Earth. Now on the spiritual side, God is in control of time since He created all things. What his prophets have said take precedence over man in his deceived state, being used by these principalities is what those with spiritual eyes to see will tell the people with ears to hear, these mysteries by revelation from God as you are now reading in these chronicles.

All that receive the mark through a post hypnotic seduction except for the elects, will become the rejects given over to receive the fate of their father the devil as being used to carry out his master plan. These in-coded apps will alter a certain section of your brain's functions to follow the instructions of this beastly AI. This is the mind control they were seeking to gain over the population for mass seduction and control. Your brain can be programmed through this electronic wavelength that's unique as your fingerprint. Apple's apps are used to make alterations to your brain wave. Microsoft created the **X-Box** to captivate your children's minds to take the place of the time we should be spending with our children; instead, sent the mother out to help pursue the American dream of gaining the prides of this life. The home Gaming "X" Box took her place; therefore, this last generation will show this sign ... *Matthew 24: 12 "Because iniquity shall abound, the love of many shall wax cold."* There again, we see these two tech giants megalo-mind's effects on this last generation through this technology introduced by Bill Gates and Steve Jobs. Although Gate's foundation, fund a great deal of the research being done to create certain strains of these deadly viruses, his foundation shows a false sense of compassion for the people most affected by these diseases designed to reduce the world's population. Many public statements made by these men in their wealthy positions, tell you where their true agenda is.

Apple products cause you not to be able to function without it. It's what caused you to buy each upgrade regardless of the cost. That is the danger of this forbidden technology. If I seem to repeat this as in other chronicles, is to drive this point home to this generation on a grand scale, addicted to your AI device before you are given over to a state of delusion to be marked for hell. Most are looking for a physical mark but what will precede it will be the hacking of your mind that will cause you to be marked in your present state of mine to cause you to take a physical mark thinking this is only to be able to buy and sale. That's why I don't depend on my thoughts to guide me in life as a confessing Christian anymore. In disclosing such controversial information about what is happening behind the scenes in this vision of the covert activities with-in this **"Deep State"** government's operation. Just like we are in a state that cause us to reject biblical truth. Many of these revelations I cannot write just as John and Daniel about the covert activities of our government, that if you knew the full scope of what they have planned for this world, it would cause a pre-mature chaos. Just take heed to what you are now being told.

This is! the mystery of how Satan will finally deceive the whole world by coming in the form of **"The prince of the power of the air,"** This is the third layer of **"The Mystery of Iniquity,"** held to be revealed now. *Ephesians 2:2 "(KJV)* [2] *Where-in, in time past ye walked according to the course of this world,* (As a cursed child under Satan's control,) *according to the prince of the power of the air,* (Those under his influence are being used to further the cause of angelic beings using our altered DNA and our minds through electronic post hypnotic brain signals.) **the spirit that now worketh in the children of disobedience:"** Their main means to captivate the population is through fear that will test what degree of influence these devises have on the population through the use of the media. These are the children collected by the people behind the N. W. O. which carry this gene of angelic illumination DNA. They are referred to in their circles as **"Illuminati's.** This is the last generation. They are gathered in various secret scientific black opts projects we know as computer geeks and genetic science engineering and those with high intellect administration skills. They have these special abilities to set this grand scale plan in place, they used the controlled media to take advantage of our short attention spans to cause panic in the world. Only Presidents elected with this link will know of these operations that are among those that reach this 33rd degree of Masonic megalomania controlling our government. They are now ready to carry out their final assault on mankind to create this new world society that only need five hundred million people in the world to run. They are there to set certain things in place unknown to some past sitting presidents, using this forbidden technology that came to us through those German scientists. God warned Saul about taking spoils he condemned, now we will see we have brought upon ourselves from the enemy within.

Their seeds are cursed, that spirit is returning in these hate groups that carry these **swastika** and **Confederate flags,** financed through deep cover CIA operations. Let us not be fools by trying to deal with these fallen angelic spirits that was created in heaven, and you are from the dust of the Earth. The present church world poses no threat to these principalities. By having the 501c-3 mark, you will be no match for these principalities. If you are one of these few chosen by God to perform these exploits that will bring His glory back to one church, then you are blessed to be living in the reality of the greater one inside of your temple.

Satan is before the lord justifying taking a great deal of this last generation as confessing Christians that fail to keep his word to contain his activities in check by prayer. We are at the point of no return for this nation and God will cause many of our children to take our place as they did in the wilderness crossing. Satan has many of them marked with body art and piercings. 98 percent of the church world will reject the call by not knowing the voice of God. He will have mercy on our children for your hypocrisy and they will take your place.

As you see, we as a church world, fail to keep him under our feet; knowing his time is short, he asks for the children of this last generation that would release curses that would have been reversed had we remained faithful to his word as a nation. These signs would appear as literal physical marks on their bodies as tattoos and piercing as a sign of his influence over them. These signs will show just how strong this wave of evil spirits have over this last generation to the point of appealing to the previous generation to do the same to their bodies.

Those with skull tattoos are spirits that must return to the pit. Just look around at how many you see getting tattoos and piercings. If you find you have been a victim of these spirits, just repent but you will have to surrender all to get delivered and overcome their hold on you by these marks. This media technology, designed to reach the masses on a large scale will deceive you through the airwaves as Satan comes through the air as the prince of fear to cause all who are overtaken to receive what's behind his fear epidemic.

Remember what Job said … *Job 3:25 "(NKJV)* [25] **For the thing I greatly feared has come upon me,** *and what I dreaded has happened to me."* It was Satan that got permission to inflict diseases on him, not God. Therefore, what disease he has in the air with him in the form of fear, you can get without being exposed to something this contagious. Since Satan took possession of the Earth, the only way you will be able to live the privilege given us through Christ is to let Him be in control of us. This is that unction John spoke about in *1 John 2:20 (KJV)* [20] *But ye have an unction from the Holy One, and ye know all things.* That's your Job hedge that he must get permission to penetrate if you are walking by faith, keeping his words.

We are at the stage now where if God tarried any longer, we would become godless human beings controlled by A I's, using this forbidden technology that caused the flood. The present-day church except for a few anointed pastors was conquered through the seminary system. They taught them how to use principals that cause you to escape the suffering that only reveal God's good side. These events we see are not just something that is going to go away in time and let our lives be the same or better; that's what the world see as their hope. Church blindness put Trump in office which is the return of the spirit of King Cyrus of Babylon of old; he is their king Cyrus as a form of king Saul, catering to the people, raised up as a non-political leader to lead this conservative evangelical church, possessed by a pre-antichrist spirit (Rev. 13:3) to further give his followers this false hope to think that they can **"take back America and make her great again."** Yes, God put him in office as he did all the other kings of the free world this nation represent.

Many are under a state of delusion that caused them to believe in his lies without mentioning as **"the king of the free world,"** we must return to God as a nation through national repentance. Their favor of him is evidence of the mind-set of this nation. God will now begin to expose all hidden sins of people in high places. The day is on the horizon when all alive will come face to face with these faith teachings. The hidden pride behind these teachings that caused them not to receive this revelation.

It's against everything they have been told to strive for in this world as the prides of this life. The cultural divide of races put Obama in office. He is the delayed prayer cries of slaves who died in hope for change. He, as President and **"king of the free world,"** brought the curse of Sodom and Gomorrah on the nation by endorsing same sex marriage that was upheld by the Supreme Court on his watch. He was also elected by a people of color majority vote. President Clinton was, elected by the people as the first baby boomer to defile the office in an act of sodomy and under President Obama's term, legalized it; now we have the **curse of Sodom and Gomorrah on us**. This opened a portal in hell that released demons kept restrained by Michael. These fires around our cities are representative of the fiery anger of God that will in the end cause us to burn into extinction.

I do not want to miss the mark by having un-confessed sins of omission; therefore, I now find myself repenting randomly and at the end of each day for things unknown to me that Satan might use to attack me by justification. This is the warfare in the mind, fault by knowledge and revelation of what's going on in the unseen spirit world. We are his spiritual intercessory worriers to hold back judgment on many innocent souls that will ultimately replace many in that 98 percent of confessing Christians that are not ready. The 2 percent are the elect that will bring in this harvest of souls. Without them because of our state of apostasy, there would be none to save.

I no longer assume that I am going to heaven, it is acting on the knowledge of truth by revelation to be sure. Sins of omission are accumulated by taking what God said are his condition for granted. Unlike no other generation before us, what we are about to face as saints and sinners alike as trouble comes on the just as well as the unjust; we are not prepared spiritually to deal with without the spirit of God. We are that last generation that will by circumstances beyond our control, be tested for the depth of our convictions. These trials we are going to face will be God exposing everything evil for all to see that will show where your heart is.

I strive to let the Holy Spirit bring you a soul-searching truth that will cause us all to examine ourselves while the blood is running warm in our veins. Unless pastors and leaders let the whole council of the word be declared to the people that attend your assemblies, the loss of innocent souls will be the blood on their hands. I'm not speaking to you as one who has arrived but as a fellow believer sharing with you what He is telling me out of love. We are in a race to endure to the end, though we may be saved, none of us are walking in the full image of Jesus Christ.

It is by His grace and mercy that he grants us this privilege to come to the knowledge of his truth to walk in His perfect sovereign will for you. He will always address the matter of your heart as God sees you in His efforts to bring you to conviction and repentance. God does not want anyone to miss heaven without him reminding you how he loves you by not letting you die without knowing what he really required of you. I know how blinding tradition can be; I served under it for over twenty years. It is not an easy spirit to break from when you realize you were wrongly taught. It takes a love beyond your natural feelings and emotions that only come from God to help you break from these generations of cursed attachments.

They have caused us to come short by not knowing these sins of omission by serving God on the bassist of our thoughts, feeling and emotions and not being in control of our actions when provoked by acting contrary to what we confess to be. I too kept God in a box until he rebuked me with a condemning word. It is not my intensions to overwhelm you or cause doubt, but this is what we should be prepared to see at this time. Many of us have been attending an assembly long enough to know these things. Our spiritual leaders have not allowed their assembly goers to be exposed to the whole council of the truth through the Holy Spirit's perfection of believers that have this hope. We are all going to be tried for what we believe in. One of my book reviewers said in his summary, I had no regard for being politically correct in my direct statements in the interpretation of truth. He also added that they could not be rebuffed as being backed up by biblically sound scriptures.

All the good and fond memories of innocents, good times and joys we have had the privilege to experience in this country will suddenly be gone very soon. We are entering a state of sudden change seemly out of control. All who are walking in the faith of God will get to see Him do these exploits. They will be your only hope to endure to the end. My circle of church associations is limited because of my lack of credibility as not having seminary train credentials as some of you have been accustomed to hearing in your assemblies. I am one of those least that have found, many do not know the voice of God when He speaks. I am just a messenger;

therefore, I became familiar with rejection at an early age in grade school as having a form of undiagnosed dyslexia; I read at a third-grade level. Those, given ears to hear will receive this message.

They will recognize the voice of God speaking. To further explain this from the third layer context of the mysteries found in the scriptures, the Holy Spirit is revealing what we all fail to see as to what is happening now. Our judgment began on Sept. 11, 2001, when The World Trade Towels were brought down. *Ezekiel 26:9 "(KJV) 9 And he shall set engines (Airplanes) of war against thy walls, and with his axes he shall break down thy towers. Isaiah 30:25 (KJV) 25 And there shall be upon every high mountain, and upon every high hill, rivers and streams of waters in the day of the great slaughter, when the towers fall."* This describes the World Trade Towers on the lower end of the Manhattan River in the modern city of the mystery Babylon.

All prophecy will originate from Israel; the nation at the center of the world where all things begin with his chosen people. All gentile nations will be judged by Israel when they come against her in the final battle of amour-getting. Therefore, this is where we are now **"in that day"** being judged along with all the other nations as the nation raised up to protect her. Our fall will have a domino effect on all the world powers. As the Mystery Babylon **(America),** the third layer of this revelation in ... *Revelation 17:5 "(KJV) 5 And upon her forehead was a name written, MYSTERY, BABYLON THE GREAT, THE MOTHER OF HARLOTS AND ABOMINATIONS OF THE EARTH."* God set her up to be the stability of the world, when she falls, so will all the world's economies. The Catholic Church through the seminary system, infiltrated and changed the doctrine of Jesus Christ to where in these last days, we will become the spiritual harlot, an abomination in God's sight as becoming a nation to legalize sodomy. Now the stench of our sins has reached his nostrils. This will only be known when she appears in that state more wicked than the one that seduced her, The Roman Catholic Church.

Rome's association with Babylon refers to her as a melting pot of all nations, tribes, tongues and religions. She will become the stronghold of wicked spirits to fulfill their agenda. She invented a system that will identify her with Babylon of old. We developed the internet; that technology gave all nations, kindred's and tongues the ability to communicate in all languages and be understood in real time worldwide. That's the mystery

Babylon returned in the spirit through **"the prince of the power of the air." (Ephesians 2:2)** That's why the word **mystery** is there. You cannot associate Rome with Babylon other than being in a great nation birth with God's favor to bring her down spiritually. These are the capitalist link to their history that caused their downfall to open the door to captivate this nation of Christians in the form of a false religion. That is what Jesus warned in ... *Matthew 24:24 (KJV)* [24] *For there shall arise false Christs, and false prophets, and shall shew great signs and wonders; insomuch that, if it were possible, they shall deceive the very elect.*

According to the Jesuit's charter, **"the ends justified the means"** when President Obama endorsed the legalization of Sodomy. We became the modern-day outward harlot that released the spirit of **Sodom and Gomorrah** and will suffer double in our judgment for legalizing this sin as a nation. The church embraced this spirit by many of them holding leadership roles as closet Homosexual males and Lesbian women pastors at the time these laws were passed. The church, luke-worm in bondage under the state as 501c-3 religious corporations, not knowing what spirit they are of, now must exercise political correctness in their message to the world. Under the 501C-3 charter, they now control you and will close your assemblies if you take a stand against the state. This is to prepare those with ears to hear and repent, to get ready for the Elijah showdown.

We who are born from above were told to come out from among her so as not to receive her plaques. They will be in the form of sickness, pandemics, natural disasters and great divisions in high places of government. *Revelation 18:4-7 "(KJV)* [4] *And I heard another voice from heaven, saying, come out of her, my people, that ye be not partakers of her sins, and that ye receive not of her plagues.* [5] *For her sins have reached unto heaven, and God hath remembered her iniquities.* [6] *Reward her even as she rewarded you, and double unto her double according to her works: in the cup which she hath filled, fill to her double.* [7] *How much she hath glorified herself, and lived deliciously, so much torment and sorrow give her: for she saith in her heart, I sit a queen, and am no widow, and shall see no sorrow."* Our pride will be our downfall by denouncing God as a chosen nation. All will be revealed in our judgment. Here is the lamentation that applies to **America** and the rest of the world that are against Israel. This is the destiny of the **spiritual Mystery Babylon, America.**

Ezekiel 7:1-19 "(NASB77) [1] "Moreover, the word of the LORD came to me saying, [2] "And you, son of man, thus says the Lord GOD to the land of Israel, 'An end! The end is coming on the four corners of the land. [3] 'Now the end is upon you, and I shall send My anger against you; I shall judge you according to your ways, and I shall bring all your abominations upon you. [4] 'For My eye will have no pity on you, nor shall I spare you, but I shall bring your ways upon you, and your abominations will be among you; then you will know that I am the LORD!' [5] *Thus says the Lord* GOD, 'A disaster, unique disaster, behold it is coming! [6] 'An end is coming; the end has come! It has awakened against you; behold, it has come! [7] 'Your doom has come to you, O inhabitant of the land. The time has come, the day is near-- tumult rather than joyful shouting on the mountains. [8] 'Now I will shortly pour out My wrath on you, and spend My anger against you, judge you according to your ways, and bring on you all your abominations. [9] 'And My eye will show no pity, nor will I spare. I will repay you according to your ways, while your abominations are in your midst; then you will know that I, the LORD, do the smiting. [10] 'Behold, the day! Behold, it is coming! Your doom has gone forth; the rod has budded, arrogance has blossomed. [11] 'Violence has grown into a rod of wickedness. None of them shall remain, none of their multitude, none of their wealth, nor anything eminent among them. [12] 'The time has come; the day has arrived. Let not the buyer rejoice nor the seller mourn; for wrath is against all their multitude. [13] 'Indeed, the seller will not regain what he sold as long as they both live; for the vision regarding all their multitude will not be averted, nor will any of them maintain his life by his iniquity. (No one will escape this judgment.) [14] 'They have blown the trumpet and made everything ready, but no one is going to the battle; for My wrath is against all their multitude. [15] 'The sword is outside, and the plaques (This is the warning from the prophets and messengers.) and the famine are within. He who is in the field will die by the sword; famine and the plague will also consume those in the city. [16] 'Even when their survivors escape, they will be on the mountains like doves of the valleys, all of them mourning, each over his own iniquity. [17] 'All hands will hang limp, and all knees will become like water. [18] 'And they will gird themselves with sackcloth, and shuddering will overwhelm them; and shame will be on all faces, and baldness on all their heads. [19] 'They shall fling their silver into the streets, and their gold shall become an abhorrent thing; their silver and their gold shall

not be able to deliver them in the day of the wrath of the LORD. They cannot satisfy their appetite, nor can they fill their stomachs, for their iniquity has become an occasion of stumbling." "This Is! the Thunder judgment."

This is the destiny of America, The Modern Babylon that has me in morning of our coming state. Israel and America's judgments are also described in Jeremiah fifty and in Lamentation. This is a time of national morning for those of us that have to carry this message before the coming great revival that will bring in many souls that the church false messengers rejected. As for me of whom I have been privileged to mentor ... **1 Corinthians 2:2 (NKJV)** [2] **For I determined not to know anything among you except Jesus Christ and Him crucified.** Repent for the Kingdom of Heaven is at hand. **"Maranatha"** Come now lord Jesus lest we all perish. AMEN

SIGNS OF THE TIMES, PAST, PRESENT, AND FUTURE

My messages are only a witness to the present-day church of its state. My ministry will be to those that have been reserved to replace the many that shall reject the first call to repent. It is to them I have been prepared all these years to be a harvest messenger. Those of you who read my latest book should be well informed of our spiritual state as a church as well as on the national front. If you think we have seen the worst of things to come, you have chosen to be willingly ignorant of the signs of our times. This is the last generation of confessing believers that will have to restore what was lost in the former rain on the day of Pentecost that was delivered to the saints of the gospel of Jesus Christ. This will be history repeated to bring back the gospel.

Those chosen to do these exploits will come face up in the fullness of Christ to ... *Acts 14:22 "(KJV)* [22] *Confirming the souls of the disciples, and exhorting them to continue in the faith, and that we must through much tribulation enter into the kingdom of God."* This is what I see that many are not prepared to endure. I have set grievously in hours of prayer and meditation as Jesus let me feel a little of what he had to suffer in pain and sorrow as he saw the people turn in rejection of His message. Their choices demonstrated they favor their own traditional teachings brought down on the level of man's interpretation. My heart was too heavy to do any writing after that which seems to duplicate what his people did over time, fall away from God as a New Testament church. I have mentioned in time past, there are going to be many Judases revealed as being offended with those who are doers of the word in the real test. This is the time you will see the reality of ... *Matthew 10:36 "(KJV)* [36] *And a man's foes shall be they of his own household."* God reminded me of how deep-rooted hatred can be manifested in blood lines sibling to the point of murdering your own blood as in Cain and Abel; that was the beginning.

As kingdoms rose thereafter, this is literally what siblings did to gain power as being infected with murdering demons. *Mark 13:13 "(KJV)* [13] *And ye shall be hated of all men for my name's sake: but he that shall endure unto the end, the same shall be saved."* The devil hates his own because they are in the image of God and will use them to kill all that have been given over to him. We, in America have lived a privilege that accords us conveniences that kings did not have in time past. We are like none other; we can choose our idols, pursue them and once we obtain them, then we bow down to them in worship. Many confessing Christians are in denial as to idol worship until they must give them up. This will reveal what's in your heart. A spoil child being led by a false spirit will also have a false sense of reality and security.

You will be a danger to yourself as well as to those around you when all he or she has lived for is suddenly gone. These sudden changes will activate these demons of suicide. Now Satan is using them to commit mass murder. The brute beast nature of the man in sin will show the hidden evils in his heart of a spirit he or she knows not that is with-in until it manifests.

Jeremiah 17:9 "(KJV) [9] *The heart is deceitful above all things, and desperately wicked: who can know it? Matthew 13:13 15(KJV)*[13]*Therefore speak I to them in parables: because they seeing see not; and hearing they hear not, neither do they understand.* [14] *And in them is fulfilled the prophecy of Esaias, which saith, by hearing ye shall hear, and shall not understand; and seeing ye shall see, and shall not perceive:* [15] *For this people's heart is waxed gross, and their ears are dull of hearing, and their eyes they have closed; lest at any time they should see with their eyes, and hear with their ears, and should understand with their heart, and should be converted, and I should heal them."* When Jesus was speaking these words, they were to His own people who knew the law from memory as being taught each day in the Synagogues. They had fallen to this state ... *2 Timothy 3:7 (KJV)* [7] *Ever learning, and never able to come to the knowledge of the truth."* It is in this fall; many generational curse sins are revived that can kill by life threatening spiritual diseases that can hurt and maim; hidden with-in, they are release under duress of extreme anger that cause crimes of passion.

I once asked why I encountered hidden anger when telling the truth; why are we seen as mean spirited or mad when we stand on our convictions of truth. His reply … *"They are holding on to something in the world they are attached too, when my spirit exposes it, this is what you see".* These are the crimes we commit when we lose our sense of compassion and love in a moment of uncontrolled anger. This is what we need to be delivered from that Jesus died to take that power over you back from the devil. There are many confessing Christian's bound in spiritual prisons as victims of blind guides whose deliverance was not complete by not hearing the full council of the truth with a demonstration of the power when the Holy Spirit is released to reveal what is in your heart.

Many with these anointings are operating in part and not in full. They have a manifestation from the Holy Spirit but what happens; we fail to continue in the truth. Having over thirty years of exposure as a confessing Christian is where I now draw my conclusions and observations by once living in error of truth, having been a victim of some of these evils from with-in me that God himself without man delivered me from for my calling. This brought me to a mature spiritual reality of things we know not about the spirit world. What convicted me, you cannot defend yourself against the truth. I was guilty of hidden pride, and I did not even know it.

That's why I speak from a transparent standpoint of my own personal deliverance experiences God open my eyes to see to enable to be used to help others see why we must first be delivered from ourselves to conversion. I have found out by these experiences, you will have to be willing to be misunderstood, humiliated, lied on, borated and buffeted for your faults and not hold any of this in your heart against the people you are trying to help … who may be doing this to you.

It is easy to say what the word said but many forget that it is God that's judging you by your actions   contrary to His word that come out of your heart. A few years ago, I was asked why I do not take the sacrament as those in the traditional church do. My answer: This is not a ritual to me, when I came into the knowledge of who Christ is in me, I learned I was a work in progress. I found out through the teaching of the Holy Spirit, if you are born from above, you are committed to him unto death never to turn back. Taking the sacrament under these traditional teachings can result in the transference of spirits that open you up for what Paul said about these things that will bring sickness, diseases and premature death by partaking of this in fear, doubt and unbelief.

1 Corinthians 11:24-32 (KJV) [24] *And when he had given thanks, he brake it, and said, Take, eat:* <u>*this is my body, which is broken for you:*</u> *this do in remembrance of me.* *(What is He asking you to remember? The last time I took the sacrament, I knew what I was doing. Therefore, it was at that time, I made up my mind to be faithful until death.)*[25] After the same manner also he took the cup, when he had supped, saying, this cup is the New Testament in my blood: this do ye, as oft as ye drink it, in remembrance of me.* [26] *For as often as ye eat this bread, and drink this cup,* **<u>ye do shew the Lord's death till he come.</u>* (In my convictions, I want to be available to Him until death. When you take this and mix with the world, Satan is justified in attacking you by defiling the holiness God represents.) *1 Thessalonians 4:7 "(KJV)* [7] *For God hath not called us unto uncleanness, but unto holiness."* **(KJV)* [27] *Wherefore whosoever shall eat this bread, and drink this cup of the Lord, unworthily, shall be guilty of the body and blood of the Lord.* [28] *But let a man examine himself, and so let him eat of that bread, and drink of that cup.*

When Jesus gave the sacrament to His disciples and wash their feet, they all died at the hands of well-meaning antichrist fellow brethren to keep that oath, sealed in His blood by this act. Not one of the eleven chosen, died with any of these diseases Christ delivered them from; even Job in the old covenant was delivered before he died. It will be your love and faith in Him that will give him this glory until the end. [29] *For he that eateth and drinketh unworthily,* <u>*eateth and drinketh damnation to himself,*</u> *not discerning the Lord's body.* (I don't want him to find me in unbelief, fear and doubt after drinking his blood and eating his flesh.) [30] *For this cause many are weak and sickly among you, and many sleep.* (Satan gets to destroy your temple by your lack of knowledge and disobedience.) [31] *For if we would judge ourselves, we should not be judged.* (When we humble ourselves to do things His way, we are walking by faith as fruit inspectors.) [32] *But when we are judged, we are chastened of the Lord, that we should not be condemned with the world."* All those the lord loves as His sons and daughters will be corrected through the Holy Spirit. It will be up to those that hear Him speaking through His elect to make your calling and election sure at that time.

I have said these things before and just to remind you again in God's love. I'm speaking at the liberty of the Holy Spirit in this appeal to all that might not be prepared spiritually before the real trouble comes. One thing that is a constant reminder to keep me on the straight and narrow, every time I'm tempted, the Holy Spirit is a bit like bridle in my mouth. That moment always keeps me broken and humbled to want to be more like him as unworthy and wretched as some of us can be, he still loves us. Let us be honest, we are among all these temptations and only your love for God keeps you from being led astray. I ask for this to be my sign when I am being tempted or oppressed by the devil as we all will be every day until we depart this natural body. That's why we are in a race to endure to the end. AMEN!

Now, on the National Front

Our nation is under judgment for her past sins against her citizens and to Israel. All these evils we as a people in a once Christian nation, are now being exposed on all levels in our time. This is our spiritual atomic mushroom cloud, exposing all the evils of mankind at once. Satan has been given this time through this window of the absence of prayer that restrains him in the assemblies because of this command … *Mark 11:17 (KJV)* [17] *And he taught, saying unto them, Is it not written, My house shall be called of all nations the house of prayer? but ye have made it a den of thieves. Psalm 89:47 "(KJV)* [47] *Remember how short my time is: wherefore hast thou made all men in vain?"* (It is that vanity in our insensitivity to these realities to his window of opportunity, being taken for granted.) *Revelation 12:12 (KJV)* [12] *Therefore rejoice, ye heavens, and ye that dwell in them. Woe to the inhabiters of the earth and of the sea! For the devil is come down unto you, having great wrath, because he knoweth that <u>he hath but a short time.</u>"*

We are that nation given this blessing to be the protector of Israel; therefore, have now violated that covenant and this is what we must face. The bible identify man created in God's image as tribes, kindreds and tongues; that's what they would be referred too after the split at the Tower of Babel.

Therefore, if you are seeing yourself through eyes of race or ethnic pride, you are already in the wrong spirit. The situation in this country is going to get worst to where riots are going to demonstrate these inhumanities against each other because of the evils that have contributed to this manifesting degree of enmity against each other. This will cause the crash. Our enemies will rejoice when we crumble at the hands of the communist sisters.

Our sins of omission as a nation

1. The opioid epidemic is the curse for legalizing mind-altering drugs in a mentally unstable society. Satan is coming to take his spoils. *John 10:10 "(KJV)* [10] *The thief cometh not, but for to steal, and to kill, and to destroy ...* (We have let these blessings overtake us to the point that they have become our gods.) ... *I am come that they might have life, and that they might have it more abundantly."* This is our heritage we have been privileged to live, had we continued to keep Israel safe from her enemies. The kind of society we live in has become a breeding ground for all these evils. The corruption in government is going to be so obvious in our passivity, we as a people are going to go along with it; therefore, speeding up natural disasters and our internal judgments collapse. *Jeremiah 50:32 "(KJV)* [32] *And the most proud shall stumble and fall, and none shall raise him up: and I will kindle a fire in his cities, and it shall devour all round about him."* These fires you see burning in California and other places are evil strong hold of Satan's Sodomy spirits and a sign of God's anger. All these natural disasters will happen first on a large scale in these strongholds of evils. Another greater event of evil is in the works for a major city.

2. Because of the failure of the church to keep the standards of God's order of holiness in the assemblies from a biblical perspective; we are in a fight for gender supremacy. Jezebel's spirit has returned with a vengeance, now being exposed through the media. *Isaiah 3:12 "(KJV)* [12] *As for my people, children are their oppressors, and women rule over them. O my people, they which lead thee cause thee to err, and destroy the way of thy paths."* Our parental hypocrisy; have our children rising in rebellion against our authorities. Our sins against our abuse of women and people of color by unequal justice and treating the socially oppressed by degrading the disadvantaged is returning upon us as our sins have found us out.

3. **On tax cuts;** the nation is under a spirit of delusion. We are already

bankrupt. This tax cut for the rich is evident of that. God is allowing the economy to project all these false signs to catch those behind the financial institutions contributing to this in his break.

It is evident of a declining economy when the government starts printing more money that will speed up our internal collapse. We all will suffer horribly in this nation if we do not wake up and repent. We will face our worst fear and see the full scope of man's inhumanity against himself. Fear of circumstances beyond our control will cause many to lose their minds and become zombie like cannibals when all food is gone. *Micah 3:3 "(KJV)* [3] *Who also eat the flesh of my people and flay their skin from off them; and they break their bones, and chop them in pieces, as for the pot, and as flesh within the caldron."* If they are going to be eating the flesh of God's people literally, these are the children of disobedience being punished in the **first thunder**. The circumstances that will cause this are explained in the chronicle, **"What will Happen During the Tribulation siege"**. This will happen to the children of disobedience who will suffer the **first thunder.** When we are attacked from the East and West coast by the two communist sisters, they are coming to take the spoils after the crash. *Revelation 18:19-24 "(KJV)* [19] *And they cast dust on their heads, and cried, weeping and wailing, saying, Alas, alas, that great city, wherein were made rich all that had ships in the sea by reason of her costliness! for in one hour is she made desolate.* (We, the **Modern Babylon** was doomed to repeat history when we set foot on the soil of Babylon of old; Iraq.) [20] *Rejoice over her, thou heaven, and ye holy apostles and prophets; for God hath avenged you on her.* [21] *And a mighty angel took up a stone like a great millstone, and cast it into the sea, saying, thus with violence shall that great city Babylon be thrown down, and shall be found no more at all.* (A fragmented asteroid on a collision course has been detected by scientist, it will create a situation like that scene in the movie **"Deep Impact."** Another TV series that caught my attention is **"SALVATION;"** This is another way God uses current media to give visual messages to his prophets and messengers that don't have dreams or visions as a reminder that it's near. The general population will not know it until it's too late. It will split this country in half as part of the Sodomy curse and will restore the original latitude of the first millennium.) [Vs. 23] *And the light of a candle shall shine no more at all in thee; and the voice of the bridegroom and of the bride shall be heard no more at all in thee:* (This will happen after the church is raptured out of her.) … **for thy merchants were the great men of the earth; for by thy sorceries were all nations deceived.** (This has reference to our CIA used to police the world's activity by deceiving our allies until we were exposed as to what we were doing that God could no longer protect us in our evil state.) [24] *And in her was found the blood of prophets, and of saints, and of all that were slain upon the earth."*

Just like the Babylon of old did not exist after her fall any more by name; neither will we anymore as a nation after the tribulation. There will be nowhere to run or hide outside those who are under divine protection to repopulate the millennium and those used to glorify God during this time will demonstrate great exploits against the antichrist. Ninety-eight percent is going to reject the call among the confessing church-world just as the Jews rejected Jesus as their Messiah; the church will repeat history by not knowing his voice of warning through his messengers. They will be replaced by some of their children as in the wilderness and others will come out of the highways and byways better known as the homeless, pimps, prostitutes and the scum of the earth.

They will take their place at the marriage supper of the lamb. That was a parable when he spoke it to his people as a prophecy to be fulfilled during the great revival in the last generation. *Luke 14:21 "(KJV)* [21] *So that servant came and shewed his lord these things. Then the master of the house being angry said to his servant, go out quickly into the streets and lanes of the city, and bring in hither the poor, and the maimed, and the halt, and the blind."* God will open their hearts to receive this everlasting gospel and be saved. It is evident that hell is being enlarged during these natural disasters as seen when many volcanos begin to erupt. *Isaiah 5:14 "(KJV)* [14] *Therefore, hell hath enlarged herself and opened her mouth without measure: and their glory, and their multitude, and their pomp, and he that rejoiceth, shall descend into it."* *Dearly beloved*, what the Holy Spirit has revealed to me by way of these media modern visual revelations are the bassist of many of my writings. This is that new thing he said he will do that those who know his ways will see this vision. **Isaiah 43:19 (NKJV)** [19] **Behold, I will do a new thing, now it shall spring forth; Shall you not know it? I will even make a road in the wilderness and rivers in the desert.**

This is one of the ways he is using that has many people confounded as to His ways in our time. Those with ears to hear and eyes to see to save yourself from what is inevitably on the horizon any day now. Therefore, all these sayings will be tested by the spirit of prophecy in the days ahead as to truth to see who the real prophets and messengers of God are. **"Maranatha"** My prayer in faith is that none of you that got to read this vision being demonstrated in the media for all to see, God is using the media to warn those with eyes to see that these are judgments signs. Whether you believe it or not, we are approaching **the end of the gentile age.** AMEN (Updated (5/2018)

THE REALITY OF THE
SPIRIT WORLD

Background scripture:

1 Chronicles 10:13 (NKJV) [13] **So Saul died for his unfaithfulness which he had committed against the LORD, because he did not keep the word of the LORD, and because he consulted a medium for guidance.**

In rightly dividing the word, one must have a revelational understanding of the spirit world and **"the law of the spirit of life and liberty and the law of sin and death."** In this scripture, I will use King Saul as an example to make this point. Consulting with a medium under the law was forbidden by God's chosen people. The consequence is sudden death because the Holy One (God) is blasphemed as being the supreme creator of all things seen and unseen, then seek out Satan to get answers from God. Communicating with the dead is forbidden. This is a pagan worship of dead saints in the underworld that originated in the Catholic doctrine, more common among Latino cultures. It is forbidden in the sight of God. Such practices are among those who worship dead saints. This is the forbidden zone between Paradise and hell. Saul violated the law of sin and death with this anointing of God on him when he sought to consult with Samuel's spirit through a medium in the underworld. Samuel was not in hell but in paradise; therefore, God intervene by bringing up Samuel's spirit which judged and condemned him for breaking the law of sin and death by consulting a medium of Satan as an anointed vessel. Therefore, sealing his fate in hell.

Many present-day churches without knowing, are under the influence of familiar spirits. These are the fruits in those knowing only in part. The fullness of Christ is where all things are made known. These are the third layer revelations not many confessing Christians are not aware of. Case in point, I once was in a meeting with some fellow saints, one of the brothers confessed he had permitted his girlfriend as a sinner to have an abortion. The next thing I hear and see is one of the spiritual women telling him that his aborted daughter was standing there beside him as a young girl. This church was well known for following the apostle's doctrine. Even I did not understand it until later one of the brothers said the Lord had revealed to him that this was a form of witchcraft among those who believed in the apostle's doctrine. If you are not living to die from this world, it will be evident by lack of knowledge, you may be entertaining these spirits operating among the people. That's why He said ... *1 John 2:15 (KJV)* *"15 Love not the world, neither the things that are in the world. If any man love the world, the love of the Father is not in him. Matthew 7:21 (ASV) 21 Not everyone that saith unto me, Lord, Lord, shall enter into the kingdom of heaven; but he that doeth the will of my Father who is in heaven. 1 Timothy 4:1 (ASV) 1 But the Spirit saith expressly, that in later times some shall fall away from the faith, giving heed to seducing spirits and doctrines of demons, Ephesians 5:11 (KJV) 11 And have no fellowship with the unfruitful works of darkness, but rather reprove them. 1 John 4:1 Beloved, believe not every spirit but try the spirits whether they be of God. because many false prophets that are gone out into the world."*

This is Satan in disguised as an angel of light as a religious spirit in those who follow these under the influence of these demons by having a false standard of holiness. That is why we cannot seem to get along as confessing Christians; these spirits have their own personality and agendas by only knowing in part until that which is perfect returns. **(1 Cor.13:9,13:12)** One brother told me after reading my notes before they went to print, how would you know who is right? My answer, Only the word of God is right and if you live in it, you will know who is in the wrong spirit.

No oneness in spirit is that unction John spoke about is why we cannot recognize these spirits until they become dominant among you, represents fruit contrary to **Galatians 5:22-23.** I have been around long enough to see the fall of some of these men being seduced by these spirits, who said they have had a visitation in heaven. This I learned from the Holy Spirit; that is no guarantee that you have the favor of God unless you are an elect. The temptation I see after a while is the tendency to become a little prideful and puffed-up by thinking that experience gave you some special favor with God. People who do not know God ways are vulnerable to people with these testimonies. Even I myself being used to tell you these deep truths as having this type of relationship with God must endure to the end to get the reward. When one is truly born from above, he will show a sign of his conversion. Their spiritual DNA is linked to the host in heaven. They will not compromise and there-in is why they are persecuted.

 I have learned that these visitations are not all from God by the fruit that did not remain. When your mind is set on heavenly things, that's when you are a convert; you will not compromise under any circumstances because you live in the reality of Christ in you. *John 3:12 (ASV) "*[12] *If I told you earthly things and ye believe not, how shall ye believe if I tell you heavenly things?"* Only God knows himself in the spirit. This is that unction John spoke about as in all who are converted when he told Peter ... **Luke 22:31-32 (ASV) "**[31] **Simon, Simon, behold, Satan asked to have you, that he might sift you as wheat.** [32] **But I have prayed for thee, that thy faith fail not: and when thou art converted, strengthen thy brethren."** One reason Jesus said you will know them by their fruit; the devil can give you a false vision and make you think it is of God because he knows what heaven looks like; therefore, he can disguise himself as Jesus. I have no doubt that some may have seem Christ. That's why I ask for his mind to speak to me out of the volume of his word because of what I have seen happen from those who teach on the bassist of their dreams and visions, their lives do not always match up with the fruit of the spirit.

This is the work of Christ at the right hand of the father, selecting souls to be added to the kingdom. A remnant has been taken from each tribe, kindred and tongue from each time, ages and dispensations; therefore, no one can pluck them out of God's hand. (John 6:44) Satan's mediums can only operate in the realm of the souls appointed to hell. Remember, the medium Saul consulted was in great fear when she saw in her spirit the hand of God crossed over into the forbidden zone to Paradise to bring up Samuel. People with strong soul ties to worldly things, curiosities like Eve's in the Garden are candidates for these seducing spirits. That's how Eve was seduced. Jesus tells us ... *2 Corinthians 6:17 (KJV)* *"17 Wherefore come out from among them, and be ye separate, saith the Lord, and touch not the unclean thing; and I will receive you,"*

There are religions of cults that have people bound under these laws by unbelief and lack of knowledge in false teachings. If you are born from above, you will not keep company with those who may practice such things as consulting with mediums and say they are in touch with angels and tell you hidden secretes about your life as a sinner. This is what you do when you consult with such mediums. You open the seal to your soul, Satan enters in, reveals all your past sins you were forgiven of that was thrown in the lake of remembrance no more, because you open that seal to your soul, he then takes possession of your soul. That is the curse that sends you to hell with him that you cannot return from.

On cremation

I was asked about cremation for Christians; Let me give you some sound revelation on this subject. Your body came from dirt, the only reason we can see each other, is because we live in a natural body made from dirt. When one dies, the manner or the conditions that took them out could mean, there's no body to be resurrected if it were consumed by some beast or burned in a tragedy, so what is being resurrected? The sole of your existence is what's being resurrected by God; that's what's being judged. It is the spiritual knowledge you received from him into your revived spirit man while alive until death that He is resurrecting, not your body you lived in while here on earth. Your soul is what you must give an account of as your existence, not your natural body. When the scripture say you are being raised from the dead, that's your spirit man, not your natural body. The grave is a metaphor to help you understand what's happening at that time. Your body was that earthly house that decayed back to dust. It was only the house that time would pass away or return to the dust of which it was formed so we could see each other while in the natural state.

Soul bonds ties are evident when the person cannot let go biological or spiritual bonds that have him or her in bondage to a spirit. That's why those who hold to the pass that live between realities of old and new, can't seem to get deliverance by not letting go. Holding on to these things will blind your state of conscious reasoning. That's what causes you to not be able to let go when you are being abused against your will. These are mostly things that have life in them that will dominate your weakness that led you to idol worship. When one meditates on what dominates their thoughts, if these thoughts are evil, Satan will turn your thoughts into imaginations and a desire to have that person or thing. They can be so strong to the point of opening portals to the spirit world where you will see what you imagined. These are the counterfeit visions under Satan's power.

That's why the scripture say ... *2 Corinthians 10:5 (KJV) Casting down imaginations, and every high thing that exalteth itself against the knowledge of God, and bringing into captivity every thought to the obedience of Christ; Proverbs 23:7 (KJV) ⁷ For as a man thinketh in his heart, so is he: Eat and drink, saith he to thee; but his heart is not with thee."* Because of your past life as a sinner, this will be your war in the mind and the fruit will show who has the greatest influence. When one gives his heart to another, he or she will live for that person in a soul bond tie that can make them inseparable, even in death. That's why the bible speaks of divorcing as a sin because the fleshly memories of the past may be too strong to overcome while that person still lives. Your flesh has already been compromised in this area. These are the realities you will have to face in your second marriage.

As I have said before, Satan duplicates what God does because he knows nothing new. When we become new creatures, we have a soul tie to the Father and the son. His spirit has taken over our souls. Now that you are in the world, you are no longer of it. These spirits are among you in your un-regenerated family members and friends. That's why Jesus said ... *Luke 12:53 (KJV) "⁵³ The father shall be divided against the son, and the son against the father; the mother against the daughter, and the daughter against the mother; the mother in law against her daughter in law, and the daughter in law against her mother in law.* **Matthew 10:36 (NKJV)** ³⁶ **and 'a man's enemies will be those of his own household. Luke 14:26 (NLT2)** 26 If you want to be my disciple, you must hate everyone else by comparison—your father and mother, wife and children, brothers and sisters—yes, even your own life. Otherwise, you cannot be my disciple."

I must admit, this is a strong statement, so I ask God to explain this to give me understanding of its application. Only God in you can convert your family members. This passage of scripture above underlined, I must explain; the word **hate** in this context has reference to people in your immediate family that continue in sin as trying to persuade you to continue with them. Your friends are included in this also who may be of your past life in the world. You do not hate them but the sin nature that seeks to entice you in them. There are differences between holy and unholy. When one is converted, God can add all in that person's life what they need to keep them in his perfect will because they have surrendered their own will. This is an area I have found many are not ready to humble themselves because of pride, gender enmity and family ties.

When God takes over your life, He will transform your life to His perfect will. Now, this brings us to see the two parallels in the spirit world. As I have said, Satan duplicates everything God does; the difference, if you are carnal, you will never know you are deceived until God opens your eyes and ears to truth. Most of us as Christian converts are raised in some form of spiritual error as evident when we cannot agree in matters of truth. *Amos 3:3 "(KJV)* [3] *Can two walk together, except they be agreed?"* Remember, the Pharisees and Sadducees did not know what spirit they were of when Jesus told them they were of their father the devil. *John 8:44 (KJV)* *"*[44] *Ye are of your father the devil, and the lusts of your father ye will do. He was a murderer from the beginning, and abode not in the truth, because there is no truth in him. When he speaketh a lie, he speaketh of his own: for he is a liar, and the father of it. Luke 9:55 (KJV)* [55] *But he turned, and rebuked them, and said, Ye know not what manner of spirit ye are of."*

It is not my intentions to cause you to doubt your salvation; these are the spiritual truths we missed by lack of revelation knowledge by our spiritual leaders operating in part truth, mix with the principals that lead to selfish motives when the devil separated the fivefold ministry out of the assembly and replaced it with logical theology that caused divisions and led to separate kingdom builders under the 501C-3 government charter. Those who worship God in spirit and in truth know the destiny of all who die in him will live for eternity. The Holy Spirit of God does not seek to bring back spirits from heaven once you cross over in the sheading of the fleshly body from this world. The clinical death experience is an act of mercy from God to reverse the decision of Satan to continue that person's life for God's purposes, not the devils. Satan will try to take you out before your time. There is no communication in the afterlife for those in Paradise or the third heaven. Even there, we are as angels and will not relate to each other as we did here in the flesh; so, do not think you are going to be like you were here in the Earth in heaven. That's false teaching that comes out of adding to the word that does not match the description of heavenly things. You will not know what Jesus prepared for you until you get there. What's there is beyond your level of comprehension in the flesh.

On the other hand, if Satan has seduced you to serve another god while being a confessing Christian, this will be the void you seek to fill when your idol is gone, remember, **"Thou shall have no other gods before me."** We don't see them as other gods because we think what we are doing is alright. You are in the realm of the carnal that deals in feelings and emotions. This type of deception gets us condemned for eternal separation by committing sins of omission. If we die in that state. **Proverbs 16:25 (ASV) "²⁵ There is a way which seemeth right unto a man, But the end thereof are the ways of death. Hosea 4:6 (ASV) ⁶ My people are destroyed for lack of knowledge: because thou hast rejected knowledge, I will also reject thee, that thou shalt be no priest to me: seeing thou hast forgotten the law of thy God, I also will forget thy children." Matthew 7:21 (KJV) Not everyone that saith unto me lord, lord shall enter the kingdom but he that do the will of my father in heaven" Luke 6:46 why cal me lord, lord and do not the things I say"**

If you have been taught wrong, you will cause that spirit to be in your children. Therefore, some of our children will be judged under that same curse. There are seventeen sins in **Galatians 5:19-21 in the KJV,** if you die in unforgiveness of any one of these sins as a confessing Christian, you will not enter heaven. That's when I understood that 98 percent rejection that need to be prayed for. When Christ told his disciples what it would take to get to heaven, they were astonished to where peter replied, "who then can be saved" *Mark 10:26 (KJV) ²⁶ And they were astonished out of measure, saying among themselves, who then can be saved?* The cause of most of our grief is due to too many worldly attachments. As confessing Christians, if we do not obey the word of God, and choose to compromise the truth, we spread these spirits to our children who in return will rebel against us later when they discover that you are living in a form of hypocrisy. Speaking this kind of truth is what got the early saints killed. All that God brought into my life up until this day has served its purpose to get me to this place.

You cannot love the world and God too. *Matthew 6:24 (KJV) "No man can serve two masters: for either he will hate the one and love the other; or else he will hold to the one and despise the other. Ye cannot serve God and mammon. 2 Timothy 2:4 (ASV)" ⁴ No soldier on service entangleth himself in the affairs of this life; that he may please him who enrolled him as a soldier." 2 Corinthians 6:14 (KJV) ¹⁴ Be ye not unequally yoked together with unbelievers: for what fellowship hath righteousness with unrighteousness? and what communion hath light with darkness?"* These are the convictions that cause separations from the world. You are the property of God; in his army, your rewards will not only be the spoils of this life in the victories over the devil, but even greater in heaven. When someone close to us in the flesh dies in sin ... yes, it's grievous because you know that person will be separated from God for eternity. These new doctrines that teach us that we are all God's children and will be forgiven after you die in sin, is where Satan tells us that he or she is in heaven because we were convicted under a religious spirit that tell us what we want to hear. Remember, Satan is the spirit of religion not salvation. This spirit makes you feel comfortable keeping company with your worldly friends.

Some of these have created a cult like following that have separated themselves from all else to practice a form of the law of the word. Where there's no Jesus, it becomes a religious form of under the law. This is a carryover from the Pharisee's teaching under the law of separatism. They rejected Jesus and expelled anyone who followed him. That's when it then becomes a cult with-out the love of Jesus.

Satan will have you manifesting a counterfeit love. They only saw Jesus as a prophet like Elijah, not the son of God. We see this demonstrated in religious movements such as Jehovah's Witnesses, Mormons, and followers of Islam religions. Others will keep the Sabbath and judge you for not keeping it when the Jews could not keep it. This in part is due to extreme factions that causes these doctrinal splits that practices these errors in interpretation of scripture by mixing law with grace, usurping law over grace that makes the people you convert into two individuals ... *Matthew 23:15 "(NKJV) ¹⁵ Woe to you, scribes and Pharisees, hypocrites! For you travel land and sea to win one proselyte, and when he is won, you make him twice as much a son of hell as yourselves.*" ... They are denying that Jesus came not in flesh while keeping the law which will make them become a self-righteous judge of others that shows no Jesus like compassion, mercy or love like a Pharisee. These hireling pastors will send you out to save souls without being led by the Holy Spirit to fill their assemblies in the name of God.

These spirits will cause you to disown your own children through some of these extreme practices of separatism. I refused to be politically correct where the truth is concern. Men have died to keep God's gospel from being compromised. Now as the lord's free man, I can think of no grater honor in Christ than to die as a martyr in Him. This teaching that tells you no one can live perfect in this world and continue to say we are just sinners, and God will have mercy on us while we continue to sin without repenting is a lie. Another observation I see, those who mix law with grace tend to judge others. I learned in the teachings of Paul that through Jesus being lifted, His action speaks for Himself like Moses before Pharaoh.

Let none of you be judged under the law by what the Pharisees and Sadducees could not do that got them judged by God. I pray that God will open your eyes to the understanding of grace. *Colossians 2:16 (KJV)* [16] *Let no man therefore judge you in meat, or in drink, or in respect of an holyday, or of the new moon, or of the sabbath days: Whish are shadows of thins to come.* We see in the gospels, when Christ went before the sinners, it was not to participate in their sins but to show them the father and call those out the father has chosen.

A religious person confessing to be a Christian may not know their soul ties until that person or thing is severed from your life. Some of these are people that have deceived and hurt you that caused you to be in the state you are; if you have never renounced this tie, its effects will become apparent at the time of the lost. You are responsible for your own salvation, so learn to forgive those that have hurt you. Nobody in this world is worth losing your soul over.

This is what we see when a sudden change, brought on through circumstance that triggered you to react to this degree to change in character. This becomes the void you seek to fill in that lingering state; seeking answers to things you refuse to accept. This is what leads you to consult a psychological medium for mental help. We who are Christians indeed are not ignorant of these circumstances of life. We see things as they **are,** not what we imagined them to be. If the loss of someone closer to you than Christ and that person's spirit is constantly calling to you, this is evident that you are entertaining a soul tie. It is the worldly that seeks mediums, not a Christian. You can live that close to God that he will reveal the manner of your departure, but this will never happen until your die to this world and your mind is in heavenly places in Christ. You need to renounce that spirit and ask God to forgive you for letting that loss take his place.

Christ has redeemed us from the curse of the law of sin and death. When we know this is our destiny; **Hebrews 9:27 (KJV) "²⁷ And as it is appointed unto men once to die, but after this the judgment:"** Death in Christ becomes a joyous home coming to the saints to see a fellow brother or sister leave the troubles of this world. Jesus wept for a moment when Lazarus died. The cross of Christ gave us the right to claim our birth right after having committed the most heinous of sins, just by confessing them and repenting, we receive forgiveness. Now forgive yourself and go and sin no more.

Many of us have been divorce and married more than one time as Christians, this under grace and truth is permitted until one comes to the knowledge of the truth. The woman at the well was not convicted until she asks for that living water; that's when she came face to face with the truth, Jesus. Up until that time, she was an outcast among her own because of her sins. *John 4:11 "(KJV) ¹¹ The woman saith unto him, Sir, thou hast nothing to draw with, and the well is deep: from whence then hast thou that living water?"* When Jesus offered her that living water, she had to confess her sin of adultery; that's when she came to the knowledge of truth. Until you come to the knowledge of truth, sin will reign in your mortal body until you are convicted of it. If you are partially subject to the word of God, you will be partially subject to each other in marriage and friendships. As a confessing Christian, no matter what you speak in truth, the substance of what you do will always speak louder than your words. God has not changed his qualification for leadership under the ministerial graces; **(Ephesians 4:11-12)** therefore, you can work as an obedient servant and be as effective as one with the Godly qualification because God is no respecter of persons because he said these signs will follow them that believe.

Having a second living wife or husband would be a reproach under grace and truth as a bishop or a pastor. You will no longer qualify as a leader without reproach. This will not keep you out of heaven because under grace and truth God's use of you will speak for himself. You do not need a title to be used of God; however, the qualification to hold a position of leadership has not been compromised by God, only by man.

The lack of convictions to truth has caused us to operate in the permissive will of God. Therefore, these reproaches will follow you. There is no greater sin than letting someone or something become your god. Many of us will never see the truth until the real gospel is preached again in the purity and power of the Holy Ghost with signs, wonders and miracles following as having Christ returned to perform the greater works in the latter rain. That's why there must be a period of tribulation to clear up this mess we have made in divisions to see who the real God of Abraham, Isaack and Jacob is. I have learned this from the teaching of the Holy Spirit, our state under grace is mercy indeed. Just as I had to be told to quick thinking and surrender my will to activate the Holy Spirit; this is when I saw myself as becoming a little man child with a teachable spirit, then I begin to see what God sees. We will be judged by what His word has said and not one word will be compromised. Who can say who is in heaven or hell when God is the only one that know the secrets in your heart at death?

All He has said in His word is what we will be judged by as what He required. *Matthew 4:4 (KJV)* *"' But he answered and said, it is written, Man shall not live by bread alone, but by every word that proceedeth out of the mouth of God."* That means whatever we have learned that we must do. The way to Christ is through the draw of the Holy Spirit; he is your master teacher. I have come to see that the heart of man is wicked and only God can tame it. We came from sin to salvation. The reason why we fall short, the flesh has a will and desire of its own; even as Christians, we war with this daily. When we give place to seducing spirits that bring parts of our flesh to life, they will take control of our thoughts that reveal what spirit we are of when we are provoked. The real gospel, preached under the anointing of the Holy Spirit, searches out these deep-rooted spirits and expose them to your conscious state; then the hidden man of the heart that was there when God breathe into Adam, now can convict you of your state before God.

He represents the mind of God that has judge your state as a sinner, shows you the only way you will be able to get back in right standing with God is to repent. *Luke 6:46 "(KJV)* [46] *And why call ye me, Lord, Lord, and do not the things which I say?"* (**Romans 10:9-10**) This will be the sign of those chosen by God unto election that will preach and teach the real gospel. They will do what God say because they were given ears to hear and be convicted. *John 15:16 "(KJV)*[16] *Ye have not chosen me, but I have chosen you, and ordained you, that ye should go and bring forth fruit, and that your fruit should remain: that whatsoever ye shall ask of the Father in my name, he may give it you. Matthew 7:21 (KJV)* [21] *Not everyone that saith unto me, Lord, Lord, shall enter into the kingdom of heaven; but he that doeth the will of my Father which is in heaven"*. The uncompromised walk is by election because flesh and blood cannot serve God ... *John 4:24 "(KJV)* [24] *God is a Spirit: and they that worship him must worship him in spirit and in truth. John 4:23 (KJV)* [23] *But the hour cometh, and now is, when the true worshippers shall worship the Father in spirit and in truth: for the Father seeketh such to worship him. 1 Corinthians 15:50 (KJV)* [50] *Now this I say, brethren, that flesh and blood cannot inherit the kingdom of God; neither doth corruption inherit incorruption."*

It is a religious person that serves God out of a carnal mind which represents a lack of convictions to truth. They are not ready to fully obey so they serve God on the bassist of their feelings and emotions. This will also be manifested in our walk as a lack of knowledge of truth by not understanding what God requires. *John 6:44 "(KJV)* [44] *No man can come to me, except the Father which hath sent me draw him: and I will raise him up at the last day."* All of us will be given the right to claim our birth right through those chosen by election as were the original apostles. Those with ears to hear will receive them and make their calling and election sure. In the type and shadow of the old covenant, those that heard and obeyed God through Moses went into the promise land which in the end were only their children, Joshua, and Caleb. Their parents were left to die in the wilderness for falling away from the God that showed them who He really is. *Matthew 24:13 "(KJV)* [13] *But he that shall endure unto the end, the same shall be saved."*

The great fall away is due to there are not many Godly ensamples to keep God's presents before the body confessing to be of Christ. The time God takes to get you here, you may find you are among the few. That's why in our time of the end, this gospel that has been lost will be preached to them that are lost that the church fails to reach. We in the confessing Christian church-world have had two thousand years to get it right. Now we are in a state … ***Isaiah 53:6-7 "(KJV)*** [6] ***All we like sheep have gone astray; we have turned everyone to his own way; and the Lord hath laid on him the iniquity of us all. 2 Corinthians 4:3 (KJV)*** [3] ***But if our gospel be hid, it is hid to them that are lost:"*** that is given over to the devil for their disobedience as they did in the wilderness. This is the degree of deception that has resulted in this time of willing ignorance which has been the grief of God, **(the father of all creation)** to have to suffer many souls to be delivered unto their father they chose, when they were warned. They will meet his fate as children of the devil. **(John 8:44)** May God open your eyes to see the times you are living as this being a warning to us all, for some it will be our last. May God have mercy on all that call upon His name. AMEN (Updated for reprint 2/2021)

THE UNSEEN WORLD
OF THE SPIRIT

(Updated 6/2018)

Background Scripture:

1 John 4:1 (NASB) [1] **"Beloved, do not believe every spirit, but test the spirits to see whether they are from God, because many false prophets have gone out into the world. Matthew 24:5 (NASB)** [5] **"For many will come in My name, saying, 'I am the Christ,' and will mislead many. 1 Timothy 4:1 (NASB)** [1] **But the Spirit explicitly says that in later times some will fall away from the faith, paying attention to deceitful spirits and doctrines of demons, Ephesians 5:11 (NASB)** [11] **Do not participate in the unfruitful deeds of darkness, but instead even expose them;"**

The unseen world of the heavenly host is not visible to the natural man. Adam's creation was natural in the body form but spiritual in his existence. He had no concept of his natural state of his physical being until he sinned. He walked in the spirit daily and commune with God as one in spiritual accord. It was not until he sinned that he left his spiritual state, now a veil will separate the spiritual part of him from God.

This veil severed their spiritual communion and put all that came from his seeds under a curse as a child of the devil. He could no longer see or walk in the spirit as before he sinned. Mankind was reduced to a natural brute beast as were all the other animals in God's creation. The harmony became enmity. Satan dethroned in heaven now had succeeded in gaining access to this world again through the fallen state of man. He had no access to manifest himself in because he must have something with life from God to transfer his spirits. This access will provide bodies to these fallen disembodied angelic spirits.

When Adam sinned, this gave them access to enter man and all created things through their seeds being defiled that will be manifested down through times, ages, and dispensations including the cosmos and the universal things. All those born after Adam's sin will be under a curse as the children of the devil. **(John 8:44)** God's plan of redemption is in his sovereign will, ordained before the foundation of the world, set in motion before the presents of established evil. God foreknew all things and set them to run their course throughout time from the end back to the beginning. *Isaiah 46:10 "(KJV)* [10] *Declaring the end from the beginning, and from ancient times the things that are not yet done, saying, my counsel shall stand, and I will do all my pleasure:"*Throughout time, He will select his remnant during man's time on earth that will comprise the heavenly host of saints redeemed to live for eternity.

The first stage of God's mercy on man is stated in the law of the old covenant as conditions under which his chosen people are acceptable in his sight. The mystery of iniquity will be the revelation to man of the unseen powers in the spirit world that will be at war with-in his mind daily for his soul. The knowledge of good and evil by that choice made in the garden when he yielded to partake of the forbidden fruit; now he will war in his mind with the two wills, being free to choose. Man's obedience to the law in the old covenant and by faith in the spoken word after the resurrection of Jesus Christ will be contained in these two covenants. Until the advent of Jesus Christ, the sin nature, even under the law did not keep him from the sinning in the flesh. Satan's power over mankind will be in rejecting the Commandments of God.

Man's ignorance of the spirit world will cause him to live beneath his privilege as a confessing child of God. The revelation of the spirit world after the resurrection of Christ will give men the ability under this new covenant to live a sinless life in Christ. The re-created God man is Christ in you to restore the glory of the father in the regenerated souls of man, the new Adam. The revelation of Jesus Christ will give all who received him the power to become the sons of God. This warfare will border on the knowledge of good and evil which we now must deal with two thoughts, the knowledge of good and evil; the ramifications of your choices will dictate the consequences of our life circumstances.

God will use these circumstances to perfect our faith; lack of this knowledge will cause many to live beneath the privilege Christ died to give while others may lose their birth right by sins of omission. *Hosea 4:6 "(KJV)* [6] *My people are destroyed for lack of knowledge: because thou hast rejected knowledge, I will also reject thee, that thou shalt be no priest to me: seeing thou hast forgotten the law of thy God, I will also forget thy children."* The fall of man put him in a double minded state unstable at his best by not knowing what spirit he is of. Apostle Paul came to the knowledge of these two natures that's at war against the will of God in us all. **Romans 7:15-25 "(KJV/NLT)** [15] **I don't understand myself at all, for I really want to do what is right, but I don't do it. Instead, I do the very thing I hate.** [16] **I know perfectly well that what I am doing is wrong, and my bad conscience shows that I agree that the law is good.** [17] **But I can't help myself, because it is sin inside me that makes me do these evil things.** [18] **I know I am rotten through and through so far as my old sinful nature is concerned. No matter which way I turn, I can't make myself do right. I want to, but I can't.** [19] **When I want to do good, I don't. And when I try not to do wrong, I do it anyway.** [20] **But if I am doing what I don't want to do, I am not really the one doing it; the sin within me is doing it.** [21] **It seems to be a fact of life that when I want to do what is right, I inevitably do what is wrong.** [22] **I love God's law with all my heart.** [23] **But there is another law at work within me that is at war with my mind. This law wins the fight and makes me a slave to the sin that is still within me.** [24] **Oh, what a miserable person I am! Who will free me from this life that is dominated by sin?** [25] **Thank God! The answer is in Jesus Christ our Lord. So, you see how it is: In my mind I really want to obey God's law, but because of my sinful nature I am a slave to sin."**

These scriptures above by interpretation, Paul is acknowledging the ramification of his actions and ours that tend to act contrary to the will of God. This is where Paul received a revelation of who is with-in you that keeps you under conviction through knowledge of your sin nature that gives you the ability not to willfully commit sin. Without a revelation of the above Scriptures, we will continue to confess our infirmities; we cannot live perfect when the Scripture say to the contrary in... *Matthew 5:48 "(NLT)* [48] *But you are to be perfect, even as your Father in heaven is perfect."*

What Paul was describing is the nature of the old man of sin under which curse we were all born. The power to live perfect will require a revelation of who will in able you to live perfect by and through perfect obedience to God's spoken word. The Holy Spirit will give you this power to continue to live in this world and no longer be of it. *2 Corinthians 5:17 "(KJV)* [17] *Therefore, if any man be in Christ, he is a new creature: old things are passed away; behold, all things are become new."*

Our love for Christ will determine our degree of perfection. What this mystery will reveal, you must surrender totally to the will of God. Under grace and truth, we can now live perfect. The reason we cannot see how this is possible, we have not been convicted by Godly in-samples when the gospel is preached in the purity and power of true holiness through the inspiration of the Holy Spirit that brings deliverance to them that receive him. The Holy Spirit gives this power to as many as received Christ the ability to live perfect in spirit, soul, and body. Personally, I do not confess I can't live perfect because I have learned, this is His standard we should strive to achieve. It is he that will bring all things to your remembrance by receiving the engrafted word of God. Do not try to do this in your own strength; you must have that child-like faith that does not question Him. The word teaches us to die daily from that old sin nature to be replaced by the God nature. This process in our salvation is the transition period which will be according to your obedience to walk the straight and narrow road to perfection. **(Matthew 7)**

When Adam and Eve sinned, the knowledge of good and evil cause them to be in a state of confusion. This was because they were infected with a sin virus, the knowledge of evil. The evil nature they discovered for the first time, cause them to fear. They violated the law of sin and death and will now be given over to seducing spirits and demonic influence released through them and will infect all created beings. This is the great mystery of iniquity; Satan now has the power to enter God's creation by reasons of Adam's fallen state through his seeds. These fallen angelic beings now have at their disposal the bodies of all living creatures.

Colossians 1:16 "(KJV/NLT) [16] **Christ is the one through whom God**

created everything in heaven and earth. He made the things we can see and the things we can't see—kings, kingdoms, rulers, and authorities. Everything has been created through him and for him." The great mystery of iniquity will be manifested in all living creatures; therefore, defiling all God's creation. These demonic spirits will be seen in everything that God has created far good will now be used for evil. This is where we need that revelation of the spirit world and who is at war in your members, causing you to do good and evil at the same time while striving to serve God through a sincere conviction of sin.

This unseen spirit world will be ... *Ephesians "(KJV)* [12] *For we wrestle not against flesh and blood, but against principalities, against powers, against the rulers of the darkness of this world, against spiritual wickedness in high places."* Why does man have to have something to serve, it is his inherent nature to serve something other than himself. Now the gods of this world will be the things he will seek to serve through the lust of the eye, the lust of the flesh, and the prides of this life. This is the nature of the evil man controlled by his father the devil whose soul is now in his possession by birth under the curse pronounced on Adam and Eve. He will have the ability to gain the whole world and still end up in the lake of fire with his father, the devil. Now what I am about to reveal to you may cause many to be offended given the revelation of whom or what some of us are now in servitude too. *Exodus 20:3 "(KJV)* [3] *Thou shalt have no other gods before me."*

All of God's creation is at Satan's disposal. As natural brute beast, we will be victims of seduction through our five senses. Our choices will be influenced by our emotions dictated by the circumstances of life. We, as his child under that curse, will be shown the kingdoms of this world under his possessions to choose from as his servant; including the false churches he will establish in the name of religion. He will offer you what he offered Jesus in ... *Matthew 4:9 "(KJV)* [9] *And saith unto him, all these things will I give thee, if thou wilt fall down and worship me."* He will offer you the desires of one's heart through the lust of the eye, lust of the flesh, and the prides of this life.

The prosperity doctrine rose out of the fall from our first love. His kingdom is now earthly and ruled through the hearts and minds of un-regenerated souls of men motivated by seducing spirits, teaching positive self-help principles in the name of God from the bible. The diverse manifestation of these seducing spirits will show the inherent beastly nature of the fallen man that will cause him to embrace a lust for the prides of this world. There sole purpose is to reduce man to become servants of creatures and things in the Earth rather than his creator. We are born children of Satan; therefore, he will parade you before God as dehumanized degraded images of Himself, blind and left with a servant mentality never knowing what spirit we are of until God brings us out of that darkness.

Satan has been given the title deed to the Earth by Adam. *Matthew 4:7 "(KJV)* [8] *Again, the devil taketh him up into an exceeding high mountain, and showed him all the kingdoms of the world, and the glory of them;"* Jesus did not dispute with the devil about these earthly kingdoms because he knew how he got them. Now in God's image, man will serve the gods of this world by not knowing what spirit possesses him. The world and all its goods; without God, he has no way to resist these temptations. Through seminary seduction, he separated the Christian church leaders into building their earthly kingdom in the name of God.

Man; The Brute Beast. (Another Enoch moment)

This will become the nature of man in his fallen state; remember, Satan will have all creation available to his seducing spirits. We get a picture of this in his encounter with the Gergesenes man... *Matthew 8:28-32 "(KJV)* [28] *And when he was come to the other side into the country of the Gergesenes, there met him two possessed with devils, coming out of the tombs, exceeding fierce, so that no man might pass by that way.* [29] *And, behold, they cried out, saying, what have we to do with thee, Jesus, thou Son of God? art thou come hither to torment us before the time?* [30] *And there was a good way off from them an herd of many swine feeding.* [31] *So the devils besought him, saying, If thou cast us out, suffer us to go away into the herd of swine.* [32] *And he said unto them, And when they were come out, they went into the herd of swine: and, behold, the whole herd of swine ran violently down a steep place into the sea, and perished in the waters".*

These spirits had a right to be in the world and manifest themselves in any living creature, such as the swine. However, these manifested as legions in that man were the type that create multiple personalities that can be destructive to your flesh. It is not uncommon to be possessed with more than one personality as human beings through the transfer of generational curses. These spirits in animals of lesser degree than humans will change the nature of the beast it occupies and without you knowing, begin to control you, change your loyalties, and transform your mindset to their priorities and cause you to serve them. These are the spirits that create these organizations to protect themselves from humans by establishing animal rights organizations. All they need is someone in human form whose spirit agrees with theirs, then you will be used to do their bidding for their cause. All they need is something with life from God in it. The form or species does not matter; they just work around it by using each other in the right body form.

This mindset is devoid of humans as being superior to them because these spirits will now rule over you through these creatures. Human beings are the only species by nature, created in the image of God. In his condemned state, Satan will use the lesser creatures to rule him without his knowledge to mock God. We walk with our heads towards heaven, we stand up-right as a beast with superior intellect and abilities that will in-able him to lord over all creation in image of God. He then, without knowing will be at war with other spirits in this realm with different natures than his own. Because of his beastly nature, his flesh will become the means of his downfall. When Adam and Eve saw each other naked for the first time, their brain chemistry control by Satan brought their flesh alive with a desire unknown to them before.

Being opposites, sex wise, now we will see why God in his foreknowledge created he them male and female. This is what will lead to him being ruled by these lesser creatures such as those he willingly gave place that bonds him to a soul tie. This inherent weakness account for the bestiality in co-habitation with lower species in sexual acts due to a propensity of having common likeminded spirits, that by normal standards, represent a confusion in mind. This is the type of loyalty people have to their pet animals that go beyond human reasoning and borders on becoming subject to seducing spirits in your environment.

These influences they have over you can change your priorities. I have been known to not take too kindly to spirits in animals having influences over my spirit as pets. They in my assessment of my life are hindrances because of the attention they require; like all things in this world, it is a matter of choice. We as fellow human beings, allow ourselves to be controlled by things less than human while being created in the image of God. This is manifested without your knowledge of knowing that your flesh has a mind of its own that feeds off this weakness that cause you to subject yourself to this degree. Many of us are not well treated by fellow human beings. This inherent weakness in our flesh becomes the avenue of our vulnerabilities; therefore, these creatures have a six sense, this and cause you to become attached them. They were created to serve mankind.

This is a form of a soul tie because they will feed on that weakness of longing for attention, they will fill that void; even to the point of causing you to commit the sin of bestiality, mating with animals. *Leviticus 20:15 "(KJV)* [15] *And if a man lie with a beast, he shall surely be put to death: and ye shall slay the beast.* This is that line you cross that represents brut beast confusion in mind that cause them mix with other species unlike their own. *Ephesians 6:12 "KJV)* [12] *For we wrestle not against flesh and blood, but against principalities, against powers, against the <u>rulers of the darkness of this world,</u> against spiritual wickedness in high places."* Lack of knowledge of these evil spirits can manifest a double-minded personality in our actions that will cause us to lack stability in our lives.

Like Solomon observed in his time in the wisdom of God and my Enoch withheld secrets forbidden for us to know as being born in sin; this has been some of my experiences while waiting in this wilderness.

I observe one part is ruled by Satan, the other part is a subconscious knowledge of what is right but lack the will to do it such as what Paul explained in **Romans 7:15-25.** The rulers of darkness are manifested in flesh beings of God's creation, be it man or beast; the mystery of iniquity is revealed to those that seek Him for this revelation as Jesus reveals himself to you.

Our entanglements in the cares and affairs of this life are the reasons for our shortcomings by our willing attachments to things that have no spiritual value in our relationship to the Father and His son. *Luke 8:14 "(KJV)* [14] *And that which fell among thorns are they, which, when they have heard, go forth, and are choked with cares and riches and pleasures of this life, and bring no fruit to perfection. Luke 21:34 (KJV)* [34] *And take heed to yourselves, lest at any time your hearts be overcharged with surfeiting, and drunkenness, and cares of this life, and so that day come upon you unawares.*

Galatians 5:1 (KJV) [1] *Stand fast therefore in the liberty wherewith Christ hath made us free and be not entangled again with the yoke of bondage."* Anything that keeps you from performing the perfect will of God is considered an entanglement.

Hebrews 5:12-13 "(KJV) [12] *For when for the time ye ought to be teachers, ye have need that one teach you again which be the first principles of the oracles of God; and are become such as have need of milk, and not of strong meat. 1 Peter 3:18-20 (KJV)* [18] *For Christ also hath once suffered for sins, the just for the unjust, that he might bring us to God, being put to death in the flesh, but quickened by the Spirit:* [19] *By which also he went and preached unto the spirits in prison;* [20] *Which sometime were disobedient, when once the longsuffering of God waited in the days of Noah, while the ark was a preparing, wherein few, that is, eight souls were saved by water."* Not to discern the times you are living can cause many of us who are caught in the cares and the affairs of this life to miss God's Day of visitation. All of God's creation of living things and human beings are potentials to become idols and gods through the deception of satanic seducing spirits. They can attach themselves to things you desire that can become an idol in living things. If our affections are not on the things above, they are on things in the earth.

This is a constant temptation and warfare that trouble our minds daily of which without the power of the Holy Spirit, you will yield. That is the nature of our continuing in sin. *Matthew 24:13 (KJV)* [13] *But he that shall endure unto the end, the same shall be saved."* There are not many that will endure the temptations of this world without the love of Christ. IF WE CAN REMAIN HUMBLE, WE WILL KEEP OUR SIN CONCIOUSNESS TO ALWAYS BE READY TO REPENT. This is the state of those whose mind is on heavenly things awaiting our redemption. After having been given these mysteries, it grieves me to know these things about the unseen world and now see what we are dealing with requires the greater one in you to keep them from overtaking you. It is my love for God that keeps me with a sound mind through all this to the end. Some of these thoughts I am forbidden to pen down. I'm just a scribe bring used like the men He used to write the bible. You can judge this by the depth of insight to what you are reading. I did not have open dreams or vision to write these books. When I had my visitation in the spirit, He asked me what I wanted from him; I said, your mind. This is when He begins to walk me through the second and third stage of salvation through the teachings of the Holy Spirit. This is what's reflected in what you are reading. AMEN

Now on the national front

Historically, President trump's place in Biblical history is a mixture of Saul & Cyrus of our times as a non-political leader, put in office by an act of God through the Electoral College as **"king of the free world"** when there is a presidential election too close to call by popular vote. His personal ego will make him a perfect candidate for our enemies to manipulate; particularly, the three Communist sisters, Russia, China and North Korea. He shows signs of being possessed with a dictator spirit; therefore, look for him to be more favorable to foreign dictators by his actions. The Electoral College is the Republic's designee in each state to oversee that the election is just when all the votes are counted, they come together to confirm the winner by voting accordingly. Down through the years it has evolved into a political organization that now vote along district party lines. Therefore, when there is an election too close to call, they now have become the means to ensure their party gets their man in office as now representing a Republican majority.

They put George W Bush (the son) in office this way and now Donald Trump under the same conditions. This is their way of circumventing or over-ruling a close popular vote in a National Presidential Election. I said that President Obama would be the last president elected by the popular vote; some of you thought it was a false prediction when Trump was elected. Hillary commanded the popular vote under these same conditions. I also said that I did not see her as a world leader in these last days biblically. Her husband's presidency would be the end of their rise to power on the national scene. She became the cymbal of the rise of the Jezebel spirit we have seen recently that is leading a womens movement we as men have brought upon ourselves as our sins of abuse of them, returned upon us now in this fight for gender supremacy.

Everything done covertly is being brought to light as those in the public eye as idols in their positions are being exposed. All these crooked TV evangelists are going to be brought down in their boasted pride to let the people see just what they have done to rob their supporters to live extravagant lifestyles in the name of religion. The principality we let overtake the church, took the ten commandments out of the halls of justice and prayer out of the schools. Now in this last generation, the schools will become the killing grounds when these suicide demons are released to fulfill a curse on this last generation. God is going to bring many of them to salvation as his mercy on them as innocent children for our hypocrisy that led them to this slaughter. They, as the last generation, were claimed with a cursed on them for our hypocrisy as a Christian nation. The sign upon them is revealed in the chronicle of **"Observations of a messenger."**

Many are reserved to take their parents' place in the coming great revival during the tribulation period. Seducing spirits have used the media to reduce our attention span to moment by moment and hour by hour; therefore, most of you will forget this or reject it altogether because you have been trained to only listen to men of renowned credibility you have put your trust with-out knowing that … *1 Corinthians 1:27 (KJV)* [27] But God hath chosen the foolish things of the world to confound the wise; and God hath chosen the weak things of the world to confound the things which are mighty; *Philippians 3:3 (KJV)* [3] *For we are the circumcision, which worship God in the spirit, and rejoice in Christ Jesus, and have no confidence in the flesh."* We are to follow men as being examples in Christ as elects born from above. AMEN (Updated for release 8/2019)

PREPARATION FOR GLORY

"The Wilderness Experience"

God's instructions for those who are led into a wilderness experience, consisting of You, God and the Devil just as Christ.

I am currently in this wilderness waiting to carry this everlasting gospel to redeem this last harvest of souls out of this generation. Not discerning the times you are in, those leaders with a kingdom building mentality will be left out of this call. We have had over two thousand years to get it right and this is where we are now in division and separate kingdom building. This is where the elects are at this time being prepared to come out to save mankind and the remnant in tribulation; without which, no flesh will be saved in our present state. *Matthew 24:22 "(KJV) And except those days should be shortened, there should no flesh be saved: but for the elect's sake those days shall be shortened."*

This is what we are being prepared to do?

1. Because of the perils of the times, your footsteps must be orderd by the lord. *Psalm 37:23 (KJV) "23 The steps of a good man are ordered by the LORD: and he delighteth in his way. Isaiah 55:8 (KJV)* [8] *For my thoughts are not your thoughts, neither are your ways my ways, saith the LORD."* This is where you will be fully converted to save yourself from the wrath to come in glory by making your calling and election sure. **2 Peter 1:10 (KJV)** [10] **Wherefore the rather, brethren, give diligence to**

make your calling and election sure: for if ye do these things, ye shall never fall:

2. Every one that endures the wilderness will know Christ for them self. *Isaiah 53:1 (KJV) "1 Who hath believed our report? and to whom is the arm of the LORD revealed? Daniel 11:22 (KJV)* [22] *And with the arms of a flood shall they be overflown from before him, and shall be broken, yea, also the prince of the covenant. Romans 8:27 (KJV)* [27] *And he that searcheth the hearts knoweth what is the mind of the Spirit, because he maketh intercession for the saints according to the will of God."* We will have the mind of Christ.

3. All who entertain fear, doubt and unbelief will be cut off in this wilderness and shall not see God as in the days of Moses. *Matthew 10:28 (KJV) "28 And fear not them which kill the body but are not able to kill the soul: but rather fear him which is able to destroy both soul and body in hell. 2 Thessalonians 2:10 (KJV)* [10] *And with all deceivableness of unrighteousness in them that perish; because they received not the love of the truth, that they might be saved."*

4. All who will endure the wilderness will have the same spirit and will know one another. *1 John 4:6 (KJV) "6 We are of God: he that knoweth God heareth us; he that is not of God heareth not us. Hereby know we the spirit of truth, and the spirit of error. 1 John 2:20 (KJV)* [20] *But ye have an unction from the Holy One, and ye know all things."*

5. You will be led by fasting, prayer and the study of the word. *2 Timothy 2:15 (KJV) "15 Study to shew thyself approved unto God, a workman that needeth not to be ashamed, rightly dividing the word of truth. Zechariah 7:5 (KJV)* [5] *Speak unto all the people of the land, and to the priests, saying, when ye fasted and mourned in the fifth and seventh month, even those seventy years, did ye at all fast unto me, even to me?"* Before the natural temple was destroyed, none of his people sought him for a vision of time of his return. "Only my chosen elect will be given this vision at the appointed time."

Satan's Role While You are in the Wilderness

1. Satan will try to deceive you to go down the broad road. *Matthew 7:14-15 (KJV) "14 Because strait is the gate, and narrow is the way, which leadeth unto life, and few there be that find it.* He will contend with you to keep you from separating from all the Holy Spirit is leading you to do. Some of those close to you will be used to perfect you. [15] *Beware of false prophets, which come to you in sheep's clothing, but inwardly they are ravening wolves. Isaiah 50:7 (KJV)* [7] *For the Lord GOD will help me; therefore, shall I not be confounded: therefore, have I set my face like a flint, and I know that I shall not be ashamed."*

2. Satan will try to tempt you to compromise, many will turn against you by refusing his offer to do things his way. *Matthew 4:9 (KJV) "9 And saith unto him, all these things will I give thee, if thou wilt fall down and worship me."* Your knowledge of the word will be tested. *Matthew 4:4 (KJV)* [4] *But he answered and said, It is written, Man shall not live by bread alone, but by every word that proceedeth out of the mouth of God. Matthew 4:10 (KJV)* [10] *Then saith Jesus unto him, get thee hence, Satan: for it is written, thou shalt worship the Lord thy God, and him only shalt thou serve."*

3. When you are led into the wilderness, do not be anxious but try every spirit whether it be of God. *2 Chronicles 34:27 (KJV)* [27] *Because thine heart was tender, and thou didst humble thyself before God, when thou heardest his words against this place, and against the inhabitants thereof, and humbledst thyself* before me, and didst rend thy clothes, and weep before me; I have even heard thee also, saith the LORD." Romans 12:1-2 (NLT) [1] And so, dear brothers and sisters, I plead with you to give your bodies to God. Let them be a living and holy sacrifice—the kind he will accept. When you think of what he has done for you, is this too much to ask? [2] Don't copy the behavior and customs of this world, but let God transform you into a new person by changing the way you think. Then

you will know what God wants you to do, and you will know how good and pleasing and perfect his will really is."

4. God will let Satan try you for a season to purify you as his temple. *1 Peter 4:12 (KJV) "12 Beloved, think it not strange concerning the fiery trial which is to try you, as though some strange thing happened unto you: 1 Peter 5:10 (KJV)* [10] *But the God of all grace, who hath called us unto his eternal glory by Christ Jesus, after that ye have suffered a while, make you perfect, stablish, strengthen, settle you."* All end time saints chosen by election are in waiting to receive the spirit of Elijah and Moses and come out of this wilderness as John the Baptist to carry the message to revive this dead apostate church world that have become the dry bones.

5. Those that endure the wilderness experience will walk in the fullness of the "Kingly, Priestly and the Prophetic anointing of Christ. *Hebrews 1:9 (KJV) "9 Thou hast loved righteousness, and hated iniquity; therefore God, even thy God, hath anointed thee with the oil of gladness above thy fellows. 2 Corinthians 1:21 (KJV)* [21] *Now he which stablisheth us with you in Christ, and hath anointed us, is God;"*

What will be the difference the world will see in all those who endure their wilderness experience?

1. Your appearance will be like as unto Moses when you come out in the fullness. *2 Corinthians 5:17 (KJV) "17 Therefore if any man be in Christ, he is a new creature: old things are passed away; behold, all things are become new."*

2. You will represent the fullness of the God head bodily which we have never achieved to this day. *Mark 13:20 (KJV) "[20] And except that the Lord had shortened those days, no flesh should be saved: <u>but for the elect's sake</u>, whom he hath chosen, he hath shortened the days."* Whether you believe it are not, this is our state … *Isaiah 53:6* [6] *All we like sheep have gone astray; we have turned everyone to his own way; and the LORD hath laid on him the iniquity of us all."* In time past, our wilderness

experience was cut short by the teachings and the traditions of man's theological interpretations of the gospel that has led us down this broad road to the state of apostacy.

3. We will be prepared to make war with the principalities and powers of darkness as in ... ***Ephesians 6:12 (KJV)*** [12] ***For we wrestle not against flesh and blood, but against principalities, against powers, against the rulers of the darkness of this world, against spiritual wickedness in high places. Ephesians 4:12 (KJV)*** [12] ***for the perfecting of the saints, for the work of the ministry, for the edifying of the body of Christ:"***

4. He will begin to judge our state of wickedness through your vessel. ***1 Corinthians 6:2- (KJV)*** ["2] ***Do ye not know that the saints shall judge the world? and if the world shall be judged by you, are ye unworthy to judge the smallest matters?*** [3] ***Know ye not that we shall judge angels? how much more things that pertain to this life?"*** *(In time of tribulation ...* ***Proverbs 29:16 (KJV)*** [16] ***When the wicked are multiplied, transgression increaseth: but the righteous shall see their fall. 2Tim. 3:13 (KJV)*** [13] ***But evil men and seducers shall wax worse and worse, deceiving, and being deceived."***

5. The whole world will see the perfect man in this generation ... ***Matthew 5:48 (KJV)*** ***"48 Be ye therefore perfect, even as your Father which is in heaven is perfect."***

6. The fear of God will return to the assembly. ***Psalm 66:16 (KJV)*** ***"16 Come and hear, all ye that fear God, and I will declare what he hath done for my soul. Ecclesiastes 12:13 (KJV)*** [13] ***Let us hear the conclusion of the whole matter: Fear God and keep his commandments: for this is the whole duty of man."*** The return of the gospel of Jesus Christ will once again arrest the attention of the world and present to the world the only God.

A call to perfect love

Matthew 22:36-39 (KJV) ***"36 Master, which is the great commandment in the law?*** [37] ***Jesus said unto him, thou shalt love the Lord thy God with all thy heart, and with all thy soul, and with all thy mind.*** [38] ***This is the first***

and great commandment. [39] *And the second is like unto it, thou shalt love thy neighbour as thyself. 1 John 4:18 (KJV)* [18] *There is no fear in love; but perfect love casteth out fear: because fear hath torment. He that feareth is not made perfect in love."* Our separation into the wilderness is a repeat of the same wilderness as his people but in these last days as a type and shadow of those chosen to crucify your flesh to become meat for the master's use. *2 Corinthians 6:17 (KJV)* "[17] *Wherefore come out from among them, and be ye separate, saith the Lord, and touch not the unclean thing; and I will receive you, Matthew 4:1 (KJV)* [1] *Then was Jesus led up of the Spirit into the wilderness to be tempted of the devil."*

We are going through many changes as being tested to be brought into perfection. Those that endure this wilderness will walk in the fullness of Christ as he did when he came out of his wilderness. This time he will walk you through this wilderness in your temple to do the greater works. *John 14:30 (KJV* "[30] *Hereafter I will not talk much with you: for the prince of this world cometh, and hath nothing in me. Luke 4:14 (KJV)* [14] *And Jesus returned in the power of the Spirit into Galilee: and there went out a fame of him through all the region round about."*

The world will once again see what this present apostasy has failed to produce. Ninety-eight percent of the church world is not in a place spiritually to heed to the call to repent on their day of visitation as the true prophets bring this message.

Our affections are being set on heaven and going home. *Colossians 3:2 (KJV)* "[2] *Set your affection on things above, not on things on the earth. Luke 21:34 (KJV)* [34] *And take heed to yourselves, lest at any time your hearts be overcharged with surfeiting, and drunkenness, and cares of this life, and so that day come upon you unawares. James 1:12 (KJV)* [12] *Blessed is the man that endureth temptation: for when he is tried, he shall receive the crown of life, which the Lord hath promised to them that love him.* You cannot be led into this wilderness until you are fully ready to surrender your will to the leading of the Holy Spirit. This is to those that live in the reality of the greater one in you. *John 16:13 (KJV)* [13] *Howbeit when he, the Spirit of truth, is come, he will guide you into all truth: for he shall not speak of himself; but whatsoever he shall hear, that shall he speak: and he will shew you things to come. 1 John 4:4 (ASV)* [4] **Ye are of God, my little children, and have overcome them: because greater is he that is in you than he that**

is in the world. *Matthew 10:16 (KJV)* [16] *Behold, I send you forth as sheep in the midst of wolves: be ye therefore wise as serpents, and harmless as doves."*

Those of you being prepared as vessels for this last day move of God, the glory is beyond your comprehension. You will possess the fullness of the mind of Christ. **1 "Corinthians 2:16** [16] **For who hath known the mind of the Lord, that he may instruct him? But we have the mind of Christ."** This wilderness will bring the death of your flesh as the returned Adam. *1 Corinthians 7:29 (KJV)* [29] *But this I say, brethren, the time is short: it remaineth, that both they that have wives be as though they had none; 2 Corinthians 5:17 (KJV)* [17] *Therefore if any man be in Christ, he is a new creature: old things are passed away; behold, all things are become new."*

All that is a part of this last day move will suffer as the apostles to return the glory back to his body. *1 Peter 4:1 (KJV) "1 Forasmuch then as Christ hath suffered for us in the flesh, arm yourselves likewise with the same mind: for he that hath suffered in the flesh hath ceased from sin;"* All who are called will walk in the unity of the faith. *Ephesians 4:13 (KJV) "13 Till we all come in the unity of the faith, and of the knowledge of the Son of God, unto a perfect man, unto the measure of the stature of the fulness of Christ:"* All who are a part of this move, will rest from their labor. *Hebrews 4:9 (KJV) "9 There remaineth therefore a rest to the people of God. Colossians 2:9 (KJV)* [9] *For in him dwelleth all the fulness of the Godhead bodily"* This is the rest that allows Christ to have complete control of your vessel. *1 Thessalonians 5:23 (KJV)* [23] *And the very God of peace sanctify you wholly; and I pray God your whole spirit and soul and body be preserved blameless unto the coming of our Lord Jesus Christ.* This last day move will be the return of the second Pentecost, known as the latter rain.

This is what will be seen in those that endure the wilderness

1. God is walking in the earth selecting his people to be used; he will not tolerate disobedience.

2. Keep your eyes on God and not on the circumstances.

3. Remember Akin and Eli's judgment that cause their whole household to be lost because of their disobedience.

4. We are called to a total sacrifice of our will. Except you are willing to forsake all, you will not lead his people.

5. Let your words be few and seasoned with grace. Avoid idle chatter and worldly conversations that leads to babblings and judging.

6. You must learn to resist Satan's seducing spirits that will try to deceive you.

7. You will face many trials and circumstances that will try to prevent you from coming out the wilderness in Christ. These trials are to purify you.

8. All these trials are designed to bring you into full submission to perform his perfect will.

9. When you have fully surrendered, do not look back to those things you left behind. Remember lot's wife.

10. Cast all your cares upon him completely and put him first.

11. Waite for his instructions in ever thing by prayer.

12. Live in a conscious state that you are not your own.

13. All your sacrifices are not that important to God, only your obedience.

14. Subject yourselves to one another and your leaders.

15. When you feel a burden, seek the lord for the answer before you move.

16. Always be sensitive to the spirit.

Romans 14:13 "(KJV) [13] Let us not therefore judge one another anymore: but judge this rather, that no man put a stumbling block or an occasion to fall in his brother's way. 2 Corinthians 13:11 (KJV) [11] Finally, brethren, farewell. Be perfect, be of good comfort, be of one mind, live in peace; and the God of love and peace shall be with you." In my personal testimony, my first wilderness experience brought me to Phoenix, Arizona where I have been for these last thirty years. This has been my training ground all these years to perfect my fruit. These experiences cause me much grief and many separations an in my pass, the loss of all things to find God. The lord revealed to me that my life's parallels will be like that of Moses. When all is completed, I will have gone through two wilderness experiences and the loss of all things again to keep him. The first was to prepare me for the second as a deliverer of his people. The above revelations and instructions are for those elected to enter the wilderness experience. All these instructions are for those given ears to hear what the spirit is saying to the church through his elects of the last day move of God that will arrest the attention of the world. He that hear them will make their calling and election sure. AMEN

OBSERVATIONS OF A MESSENGER

Some have said, my writings are a hard read; but convincingly truth not taught to this degree in the churches. It has been my greatest revelations out of this experience to hear the **"Great I Am"** speak to me in a clear voice through the Holy Spirit to write these unedited revelations down as were done in those used to write the books that bare record of God's visitation to man. Since we are the lease known, this word will be for those who have been given ears to hear.

Romans 1:13 "(KJV) [13] *Now I would not have you ignorant, brethren, that oftentimes I purposed to come unto you, (but was let hitherto,) that I might have some fruit among you also, even as among other Gentiles."* When you read under the anointing of the Holy Spirit, he shows you the deeper layered revelations within the verses of scriptures. God uses whomever he will. Paul in the above verse speaks with a deeper interpretive meaning as follows. "When you live in the reality of God in you, you will not be ignorant of the right context meaning of the word for your times. the Holy Spirit speaks the deeper layer … "God desired to have full possession of you; however, your thoughts and ways hindered him from demonstrating the full capabilities of your newfound potential as to walk in the fullness of faith; therefore, he could not fully represent the father as he did in Christ. Now that's the third layer representing our shortcomings by being entangled in the cares of this life.

Many are being led to go down the broad road of destruction and be found guilty of the sins of omission. False teachings from well-meaning pastors and teachers, trained in seminary schools will cause this error that down through time will change the apostle's doctrine to become a form. That's the road whose fruits are identified in **Galatians 5:19-21**. These are your luke-warm confessing Christians, living in spiritual compromised conditions that bring no glory to God but to flesh as men seek the glory of men and themselves. They are not on sound biblical standards of true holiness. When the Holy Spirit oversees the assembly, the people are taught by God himself. This is Jesus returned in the spirit that confirms his presents ... people are healed, delivered and set free from demon spirits. I am very skeptical as not keeping company with people I'm not led to be with that does not have ears to hear the truth as it is demonstrated in the power of true holiness. That's because, I want to see these miracles done through me when I come out of this wilderness. Therefore, I must die.

Not that I am a judge, I just don't want the devil to justify destroying my flesh for lack of knowledge for keeping company with spiritual leaders that won't declare the whole council of the truth. *Ephesians 5:11 "(KJV)* [11] *And have no fellowship with the unfruitful works of darkness, but rather reprove them. Amos 3:3 (KJV)* [3] *Can two walk together, except they be agreed?"* The fruit of many of these organized religions are leaders influenced through seminary trained pastors. What I have observed in these new doctrines of rapture and prosperity, too many are making provisions for the flesh in a show of Godliness as to gain material possessions only. There is no mention of self-denial and seeking the welfare of others. *1 Corinthians 15:31 "(KJV)* [31] *I protest by your rejoicing which I have in Christ Jesus our Lord, I die daily."* Now if Jesus is our example that Paul followed as having his mind on heavenly things, then we should have this mind-set also ... *Colossians 3:1 (KJV)* [1] *If ye then be risen with Christ, seek those things which are above, where Christ sitteth on the right hand of God.* We who are born from above have the mind of Christ as ... *1 Corinthians 2:2 "(KJV)* [2] *For I determined not to know anything among you, save Jesus Christ, and him crucified."* Jesus strives to never comment about the obvious among people born in sin; they cannot help what they do under the influence of the devil. You are looking at your old self. That's why Jesus went about doing good.

He was looking beyond their obvious sins that must run its course to show them what they needed to help them overcome. When God told me what kind of faith he seeks to find in every believer, which should be our goal. I knew then that he was asking me not to doubt his word but rest in it to see him perform it. *Jeremiah 1:12 "(KJV)* [12] *Then said the LORD unto me, thou hast well seen: for I will hasten my word to perform it."* I readily saw that what he was requiring of me, meant total surrender in spirit, soul and body. God is not into earthly kingdom building; that's why he said … **Colossians 3:2 "(KJV)** [2] **Set your affection on things above, not on things on the earth."** The persecution and rejection that the early Christians faced was for not compromising this truth unto death. *2 Timothy 3:12 "(KJV)* [12] *Yea, and all that will live godly in Christ Jesus shall suffer persecution."* Therefore, if I believe he **is,** then everything that is happening to me is him taking the abuse in my body knowing already I have the victory. Now that's the faith he seeks to find.

The thought that boarders on pride is to think we are something in God's sight, we are but a mass of dirt mold in his image, breathing his breath and living in the life he gave us. That's all he has asked for is that body with his spirit and life to put his soul, intellect (knowledge) in those he chose to live for eternity is to just do whatever he has told us to do and be faithful until your time of your departure. Doing good is a matter of conscious convictions as a sinner; we all have a sense of right and wrong until you are provoked, then, the degree of restraint will show at that time, who is in control. That's why we must be tested so we can see the need of God's power in our new-found ability not to yield. During the learning process of time … *Romans 8:28 "(KJV)* [28] *And we know that all things work together for good to them that love God, to them who are the called according to his purpose."* This is what I have found out by observation from truth; Do not be surprised when you take this stand to find yourself among the few.

His called-out ones as his elects, born from above are preserved for his use before the foundation of the world for a time such as this. He has set all things in motions as knowing the end from the beginning. *Isaiah 46:10 "(KJV)* [10] *Declaring the end from the beginning, and from ancient times the things that are not yet done, saying, my counsel shall stand, and I will do all my pleasure:"* My beloved brothers and sisters, you will not know what deliverance is until you can be transparent to the point of humble humility where there's no pride left in you. I have also observed that the worst of sinners make the best Christians. They will only follow those that stand in truth without compromise. They, in many cases were condemned while in the world. They know the real thing.

We are all going to die. *Hebrews 9:27 "(KJV)* [27] *And as it is appointed unto men once to die, but after this the judgment:"* Whether you are a believer or not, you are going to meet him that gave you this life in the judgment. You will be rewarded for how you chose to live it in this short span here on earth. So, for the benefit of those who get to read these chronicles as a skeptic, none will escape these realities. Those who the devil caused to believe there is no God; in your judgment, you will see what it is to be a fool indeed. Having been given these revelations, I have no choice but to die to self, so He can get the glory out of this body of death. *Luke 12:48 "(KJV)* [48] *But he that knew not, and did commit things worthy of stripes, shall be beaten with few stripes. For unto whomsoever much is given, of him shall be much required: and to whom men have committed much, of him they will ask the more."1 Thessalonians 4:7 "(KJV)* [7] *For God hath not called us unto uncleanness, but unto holiness."* AMEN

Now on the National Front

I was asked about what I see in this last generation that seem to be caught up in an epidemic of body art, such as tattoos and piercings all over their entire body. They are now holding conventions for the sole purpose of exposing their body art and piercings. God forbids his people from marking their bodies in this manner as stated in … *Leviticus 19:28-29 "(KJV)* [28] *Ye shall not make any cuttings in your flesh for the dead,* (These type spirits will mark you according to your extent of evil.) **nor print any marks upon you:** (The type of tattoo can be a claim mark on your flesh such as skulls in the spirit world represents those spirits will return to hell in a violent death of the person they possess.) *I am the LORD.* [29] *Do not prostitute thy daughter,* (God foreknew that Satan put a curse on this last generation that can only come to pass if we break our national covenant as a nation.) *to cause her to be a whore;* (The curse of sodomy on our land will give him the right to take our young daughters as payment for all the aborted babies. The evidence will be seen in the manner of their scantily clad clothing to show the degree of their seduction.) *lest the land fall to whoredom, and the land become full of wickedness."* Now that we have the curse of Sodom and Gomorrah on us as a once Christian nation, many are being abducted and sold as sex slaves, raped and killed. I recall being in a meeting in 1998, hearing a prayer walking prophet whom God sent all over the world to break curses on lands. I recall him saying, he was walking on a Native American reservation that had descended from a Mexican Aztec Indian tribe. As soon as he put foot on that land, he fell terribly ill and inquired to the lord as to the reason he could not speak over that tribal land? He was told that they were a powerful war tribe that was wiped out during the resettlement of America. They put a curse over this nation on the last generation.

This was their appearance; they had tattoos all over their bodies and piercings on their body parts and were scantily clothes. They beat loud drums that can be heard all around the area. This curse would come in the form of a sign that would indicate the last generation where-in their spirit would enter them through the sodomy curse. I was quickened in my spirit when I began to see an increase in a spirit that was causing this epidemic of tattoos and body piercings on all parts of their bodies. I noticed it started in the poor neighborhoods with loud boom box music. This was after the year two thousand, when derogatory rap was accompanied with loud heavy bass music that caught my attention.

I noticed from that time to 2017 over this period, 60 percent of the American population have some form of a tattoo along with piercings on their body parts. I inquired about the validity of this sign. The curse could only be manifested if we as a nation departed from our Christian roots. The fall of the church into divisions and sodomy is how these spirits gained the momentum we see today that has produced this sign. *2 Thessalonians 2:3 "(KJV)* [3] *Let no man deceive you by any means: for that day shall not come, except there come a falling away first, and that man of sin be revealed, the son of perdition;"* Now the evidence of this sign being fulfilled, coupled with the Sodomy spirit is a sign of the release of this curse. Now on our beaches and in public gatherings, you see this being demonstrated when they take off their clothes and parade in their colored under-ware to show off their body art. An epidemic of abductions unreported of young girls are being sold in the underground sex trade. These are the same demons that pimp these young girls without any regard to their humanity. Primarily, these are young blond Anglos, Asian and Hispanic and girls from India to sale as putting in orders like livestock. This market in the selection of young Hispanic girls is fueled among those trying to cross the border. They have become easy prey for those in this type of trafficking in human flesh.

Look around at your daughters and granddaughters how they are scantily dressed that make them easy targets for these men possessed with these demons of pedophilia. What we have not been taught about the spirit world is where we see them taking the lives of the young school children which has become the killing grounds for these suicide demons for taking prayer out of the schools. They are mass-murdering demons in legions to possess those given over to Satan for destruction. When they have completed their task, they then cause the host to be killed. Much of this generation have been raised without a sense of reality or responsibility; therefore, they are naive and raised up as an accident waiting to happen.

The mercy of God is upon many of them that will take their parents place for being luke-warm in their practice of Christianity that delivered them into the hands of these cold-hearted merciless demon possessed mediums rising in this generation. They, without knowing, sacrificed their children to the devil for the prides of this life. Our government in its corrupt state, mortgage their future by putting a burden on them too heavy to carry; all in the name of pursuing a dream no longer obtainable by the present economic standards.

They are suffering this curse upon them for our hypocrisy. These final updated chronicles are the completed third layer revelations of this last generation. I know these are some hard words. I with-held this version to be released when all this is evident to convince you of these realities. Even I myself as the scribe view this as a last day epistle that is relevant of our state at the time of my visitation. Now let all these messages be judged by the spirit of prophecy as to true or false in the days ahead. *2 Timothy 3:12 "(KJV)* [12] *Yea, and all that will live godly in Christ Jesus shall suffer persecution. John 15:18 (KJV)* [18] *If the world hate you, ye know that it hated me before it hated you."* I cannot express in words what I feel for those who reject these words of warning, knowing what awaits them at death. I ask God to speak these words out of my wife's mouth when I became her Abraham. When my late wife saw what she had as a husband, God in her held me to the word where I had to walk that straight line. It took twenty-five years for that to come to pass. That day she said to me, I prove to be her modern-day Abraham before she left this world to be with the lord. God used her to perfect my fruit while in this wilderness. To him be the glory. AMEN

ARTIFICIAL INTELLIGENCE (AI) & UFO'S, IS IT REAL OR MYTH?

Background Scripture:

Hebrews 13:2 (KJV) [2] *Be not forgetful to entertain strangers: for thereby some have entertained angels unawares. Luke 7:27 (KJV)* [27] *This is he, of whom it is written, Behold, I send my messenger before thy face, which shall prepare thy way before thee. Jeremiah 33:3 (KJV)* [3] *Call unto me, and I will answer thee, and shew thee great and mighty things, which thou knowest not. Ephesians 3:5 (KJV)* [5] *Which in other ages was not made known unto the sons of men, as it is now revealed unto his holy apostles and prophets by the Spirit;* Deut. *28:14 (KJV)* [14] *And thou shalt not go aside from any of the words which I command thee this day, to the right hand, or to the left, to go after other gods to serve them. Colossians 2:18 (NKJV)* [18] **Let no one cheat you of your reward, taking delight in false humility and** _worship of angels_**, intruding into those things which he has not seen, vainly puffed up by his fleshly mind. Deuteronomy 11:28 (KJV)** [28] *And a curse, if ye will not obey the commandments of the LORD your God but* _turn aside out of the way which I command you this day, to go after other gods, which ye have not known._ *Revelation 22:18-20 (KJV)* [18] For I testify unto every man that heareth the words of the prophecy of this book, If any man shall add unto these things, God shall add unto him the plagues that are written in this book: ¹⁹ And if any man shall take away from the words of the book of this prophecy, God shall take away his part out of the book of life, and out of the holy city, and from the things which are written in this book. ²⁰ He which testifieth these things saith, Surely I come quickly. Amen. Even so, come, Lord Jesus.

In my constant efforts to stay focused on what God said out of His word, I learned you can't be entangled with the cares of this life or let your mind be captivated on other thoughts than the word. The mind of Christ is not that easy to keep; it takes perfect peace. *Isaiah 26:3 "(KJV) ³ Thou wilt keep him in perfect peace, whose mind is stayed on thee: because he trusteth in thee."* The temptations we encounter in our daily circumstances of this life are the distractions. This is where I learn why Paul taught about dying to the things of this world. As born-again Christians in Christ, we are the new Adam's or new creatures' rebirth back to our first created state. Being cursed at birth, we must be led back to our creator, God. This is where God's predestination has been set in motion to redeem souls, created in His image, to be use throughout the course of man's time given to subdue the Earth. This is where I found why this is such a straight and narrow way that few find unless you are and elect. This is how you get to this place ... *John 6:44 "(KJV) ⁴⁴ No man can come to me, except the Father which hath sent me draw him: and I will raise him up at the last day."* I also saw why I must forsake my thoughts and put absolute trust in what He (God) said alone.

The power for him to be manifested in the ability to speak in faith, what He said without doubt to see the results. God created all thing by and through His spoken word, as the greater one now in you, He's just using your body to continue to do what He has already set in motion. When you surrender your will to His, you get to see Him do all these exploits by faith in His spoken word. Now when it comes to the higher level of intellect in the realm of the spirit world, dealing with the principalities. There are two sets of angels, but many are on different assignments. These two classes are the ones sent from heaven by God to protect those he has chosen in the flesh in the Earth and those in the second heaven assign to occupy the bodies of all born under Adam's curse.

Now the third class are the residue of the DNA from the fallen angelic beings that left their first estate. Hell is the resting place for all condemned souls waiting to be judge along with Satan's angels and sent to the lake of fire. *(Genesis 6:2 "(KJV) ² That the sons of God saw the daughters of men that they were fair; and they took them wives of all which they chose.")* These are the angels that came from around the throne with special powers. They were sent to record the deeds of those in the book of life before the law was given. They are the ones that impregnated the daughters of Cain that gave birth to a more advanced form of a human being that will be linked to heavenly knowledge by their DNA now mixed with humans in the earth. Just one strand of their DNA when manifested will attempt to change earthly things to heavenly things. One of the characteristics of their nature, they will have a personality that boarders on megalomania, a larger-than-life influence.

This is what Michael (the ark angel) was given the task to restrain along with numerous other evil wicked spirits in the second heaven. Traces of Michael's work will be evidenced in unexplained natural phenomenon found on earth but no trace of the civilization or tribes that left them. In my observations, our greatest weaknesses are tested by withstanding the daily temptation not to use our free will to do evil. The only hedge you have against these spirits is the word of God; keeping your mind on what His word said in every situation is where the Holy Spirit will discern and give you what to say. Therein is where no weapon formed against you will prevail and you will not be overtaken with evil.

This state of the church will cause this scripture to be fulfilled … *1 Timothy 4:1-"2 (KJV)* ¹ Now the Spirit speaketh expressly, that in the latter times some shall depart from the faith, giving heed to seducing spirits, and doctrines of devils; ² Speaking lies in hypocrisy; having their conscience seared with a hot iron;" People in that state of mind will be the perfect candidate for these grand illusions that are on the way. This, in these last days, are the mysteries withheld to be revealed to a church whose is largely in a state of apostasy. This spirit that will link them to the deep dark underworld that has combined their forces of wicked demons to begin their assault in the earth. This manifestation will result in … *2 Timothy 3:13 (KJV)* ¹³ *But evil men and seducers shall wax worse and worse, deceiving, and being deceived.* What we are about to see come to pass is what our free will willingly refused to believe; a Cabal of global proportions masterminded through a think tank of megalomaniacs known as Bilderbergers to institute what we have come to know as the N.W.O. This is the result of over a seventy-year plan to ultimately rule the world. They are being assisted by some of the most sophisticated technology given those linked to heavenly angelic DNA.

They were in those German Scientist transferred to this country after WWII to continue their black operations, using this forbidden knowledge. The bible is written in a way to keep fallen man from pre-mature destruction by lack of this knowledge in his fallen state. God has all these affairs under his control. They are operating under a delusion that God gave them to affect His master plan to destroy these principalities linked to those described in **Jude 1:6**. We will see evidence revealed that we are among extraterrestrial beings in the form of angels disguised as friendly humans. This is what Jesus said to watch for in the last days … *Matthew 24:24 "(KJV)* [24] *For there shall arise false Christs, and false prophets, and shall shew great signs and wonders; insomuch that, if it were possible, they shall deceive the very elect."*

This is that very thin line of deception that the elects born from above will discern and likewise, warn others to prepare to die in the flesh to do battle with these principalities for the last time. They have planned every event that is happening in the world, using this forbidden technology that caused the flood. God gave them this delusion to carry out as part of his sovereign will in the earth. This is the scripture they will operate under … *Jeremiah 14:14 "(KJV)* [14] *Then the LORD said unto me, The prophets prophesy lies in my name: I sent them not, neither have I commanded them, neither spake unto them: they prophesy unto you a false vision and divination, and a thing of nought, and the deceit of their heart. 1 Kings 22:22-23 (KJV)* [22] *And the LORD said unto him, Wherewith? And he said, I will go forth, and I will be a lying spirit in the mouth of all his prophets. And he said, thou shalt persuade him, and prevail also: go forth, and do so.* [23] *Now therefore, behold, the LORD hath put a lying spirit in the mouth of all these thy prophets, and the LORD hath spoken evil concerning thee. Revelation 12:9 (KJV)* [9] *And the great dragon was cast out, that old serpent, called the Devil, and Satan, which deceiveth the whole world: he was cast out into the earth, and his angels were cast out with him. Daniel 7:25 (KJV)* [25] *And he shall speak great words against the most High and shall wear out the saints of the most High, and think to change times and laws: and they shall be given into his hand until a time and times and the dividing of time."* (The church will be given a mark that will put them under this grand delusion, (501c-3). It will be followed by an AI technology that will be done through mind controlling media to further divide the church body of confessing Christians.) *Revelation 13:15 -17 "(KJV)* [15] *And he had power to give life unto the image of the beast, that the image of the beast should both speak, and cause that as many as would not worship the image of the beast should be killed.* [16] *And he causeth all, both small and great, rich and poor, free and bond, to receive a mark in their* right hand, *or in* their foreheads: [17] *And that no man might buy or sell, save he that had the mark, or the name of the beast, or the number of his name."*

The internet will introduce you to this AI medium to control your mind (the fore-head) and the smart phone in your right hand will cause you to take the seal of the mark seen in the spirit world. I know why I never watched You-Tube during those seven years of meditation; I would have been corrupted by men using this channel at that time to deceive many before this revelation is revealed. Because I live in the reality of the creator in me, I fear no man on Earth. I strive to live in the faith He expects to see as Himself walking in me; therefore, who can defy God.

I have been rejected most of my life by those close to me, I know what it's like to have a Judas among you. The only thing these beings fear is those that don't fear them that have the seal of God on their foreheads. This is that mountain moving faith the size of a mustard seed that can stop them. All this is taking place in the unseen spirit world now being manifested in man. We are preparing to go to war with these wicked principalities in high places. The reason we are coming to the end of another time continuum, this is the forbidden knowledge zone that will cause the destruction of mankind if God was not in control. Those chosen to be saved … *Romans 9:28 "(KJV)* [28] *For he will finish the work and cut it short in righteousness:* This is when he will revisit His people for the last time the rapture or translation take place in Jerusalem in the second half of the tribulation when the two witnesses are literally killed there. **Rev,11:3, & 11:11-12)** This is the final rapture of New Testament souls.

About the building of the third temple:

When Donald Trump was elected president, The Jewish seeds of those Pharisees and Sadducees that rejected their Messiah as Jesus have received the spirit of a false vision that will cause them to attempt to rebuild the temple of Solomon which in the sight of God will be an abomination. They, without knowing will be seduced by an antichrist spirit in President Trump to attempt to crucify Jesus afresh when he makes the decree to build the temple in Jerusalem in the spirit of King Cyrus of the second Babylon. When Jesus rose from the dead, all things became spiritual; therefore, without a revelation of the spirit world, the cross-over will cause an error in teaching by mixing law with grace. Because the Gentiles are linked to the Jews through Jesus, many of the gentile believers will be taught to continue to practice the law under grace. Paul saw this happening among the gentiles who were taught by some of those who still adhered to the practice of the law. God chose to carry this message to the Gentiles as the new covenant. Therefore, *Colossians 2:16-17 "(KJV)* [16] *Let no man therefore judge you in <u>meat</u>, or in <u>drink</u>, or in respect of an <u>holyday</u>, or of the <u>new moon</u>, or of the <u>sabbath days</u>:* [17] *Which <u>are a shadow of things to come; but the body is of Christ.</u>"* That's why in these last days, they, under this false vision, will attempt to rebuild the temple as their sign to prepare this temple for their Messiah's return to be their king in the new millennium, thinking he would re-institute the sacrifices. Solomon's temple was condemned and nothing on earth is pure enough to replace it but those born from above.

This will be the delusion that will cause the Gentile Christians under false teaching to embrace this vision in these last days. This is the vision of the true prophets that will be sent from heaven, Christ Temple will not be built by the hand of men with a false antichrist vision. *Revelation 3:12 "(KJV)* [12] *Him that overcometh will <u>I make a pillar in the temple of my God</u>,* (We are his temple under grace that this foundation will now be built*.) and he shall go no more out: and I will write upon him the name of my God, and the name of the city of my God, <u>which is new Jerusalem, which cometh down out of heaven</u> from my God: and I will write upon him my new name.* (John, now in a vision, sees this as coming down with Christ out of heaven.) *Revelation 21:2 (KJV)* [2] *And I John <u>saw the holy city, new Jerusalem, coming down from God out of heaven, prepared as a bride adorned for her husband</u>."* They are attempting to build a temple as under the law that will cause all them to be destroyed except for a remnant. *Romans 9:27 "(KJV)* [27] *Esaias also crieth concerning Israel, Though the number of the children of Israel be as the sand of the sea, a remnant shall be saved: (These are the chosen in the old and new covenant.) *Romans 11:5 (KJV)* [5] *Even so then at* *this present time also there is a remnant according to the election of grace."* These are the chosen under grace and truth. This was the result of David's disobedience by numbering the people. *2 Samuel 24:2 (KJV)* ² *For the king said to Joab the captain of the host, which was with him, go now through all the tribes of Israel, from Dan even to Beersheba, and number ye the people, that I may know the number of the people. 2 Samuel 24:9 (KJV)* ⁹ *And Joab gave up the sum of the number of the people unto the king: and there were in Israel eight hundred thousand valiant men that drew the sword; and the men of Judah were five hundred thousand men."* Notice, only the tribe of Judah was named because all the other tribes were cursed for consenting to sale Joseph and lying to their father; that was the curse on their bloodline. Jesus will be linked to this tribe as their savior to come to their rescue through-out time when their enemies threaten to destroy them.

Now what about the UFO's

The last generation that will end the timeline God gave man to subdue the Earth, will end with a flurry of natural disasters and some by using AI technology. The church in its diluted state will pose no threat to the powers that are in operation at that time. All religious organizations brought under their control and given their mark number 501c-3. This is where you will find 98 percent of the confessing religious world in this nation, at that time, will be cut off by being subject to state control as having a physical building church mentality. That's the curse of keeping the literal temple law under grace. The first thing the Romans did when they came to destroy the nation of Israel is the destruction of their temple in 70 AD.

Now they will begin the implementation stage through fear, close your church buildings by being under the 501C-3 government charter. They will begin to create these grand delusions that will produce illusions through fear that will cause you to take the mark without knowing it. It will be done through your smart phone apps that have you now under their control. This AI technology will control you through media mind controlling apps. This is where they will receive the power to show up on a grand scale by reducing your attention span to do what they want you to do. Your imagination is one of the most powerful forces in the spirit world. Your faith in anything other than God will show up in what you have imagined in that form to be. It is a form of energy that empowers these spiritual forces to produce lying signs and wonders. They control all the media outlets; therefore, Hollywood will begin to produce entertainment to set you up to prepare for these grand illusions at the height of what they have generated in your mind to receive.

Among these movies, God will be showing His elect a message interpretation in these movies to his people to keep them from being deceived. They became my literal visions when I felt led to watch some of these movies. Too many false visions have people following those who are teaching from their dreams. I told people in my books that I did not receive one vision or a dream from God to write these books. I got to see a side of God the apostles saw that reflects how he will use his servants in the last days to keep them from being confused and misled by false visions. These movies will depict gross violence as in the Roman Colosseum times. I'm not that bothered by seeing gross violence as many are. This stems from my professional background. I worked in forensic pathology and got to be exposed to the worst of human carnage. I got to see the face of the fear of death without God.

The sudden changes in their lifestyles will cause great fear and much sorrow; others in great fear will lose their minds and become the **"Walking Dead."** Just when you think you have your life set; sudden disasters will cause you to lose everything. In these last days, there is no safe place anywhere but in Christ. You may not be on the grid, but you can't escape God's wrath. These horrors of God's wrath will be seen in the tribulation. God will send his prophets with this word to warn them before time, but they will be mocked by scoffers as Noah in the days before the flood. This is what cause my personal lamentation to see people reject what none will be able to escape except the people of God. After generations of false teachings, we just cannot see this happening to us, that's the strong delusion.

Jeremiah 35:15 "(KJV) [15] I have sent also unto you all my servants the prophets, rising up early and sending them, saying, Return ye now every man from his evil way, and amend your doings, and go not after other gods to serve them, and ye shall dwell in the land which I have given to you and to your fathers: but ye have not inclined your ear, nor hearkened unto me."

A vast majority of the church world will be caught up in this delusion and will reject this message because they no longer know the voice of God. This is that time Satan has been given to deceive the whole world and God will allow them to carry out their evil plans. God will lead them into their own trap to destroy them all at the end of the tribulation period. These false prophets will rise with a new age message that the true prophets of God will have forewarned them not to receive … *Jeremiah 25:6 (KJV)* [6] And go not after other gods to serve them, and to worship them, and provoke me not to anger with the works of your hands; *and I will do you no hurt.* *(That's God's hidden anger we are about to suffer.)* *Colossian 2:18 (KJV)* [18] *Let no man beguile you of your reward in a voluntary humility and worshipping of angels, intruding into those things which he hath not seen, vainly puffed up by his fleshly mind,"*

Now we will see the other side of God as Satan has justified letting him carry out this dubious plan, he thinks is going to take back control of the Earth. By the whole world being captivated in this wicked plan, their corporate imagination will generate the energy that will literally bring these ET angels right out of the sky; that's when you will see the world say … *Revelation 13:4 "(KJV)* [4] *And they worshipped the dragon which gave power unto the beast: and they worshipped the beast, saying, Who is like unto the beast? who is able to make war with him?"* This is what will happen when Satan is cast out of heaven when all the saints are sealed for the translation; his work as the accuser of the brethren will be finished. These angels will be in the form of E T's, and all will worship them as the savior of the world.

Their deception will be the end result of all these media influences that laid the groundwork to enter your mind to deceive you on this level … *Deuteronomy 11:28 "(KJV)* [28] *And a curse, if ye will not obey the commandments of the LORD your God, but turn aside out of the way which I command you this day, to go after other gods, which ye have not known."*

In my research on the internet, these are some of the people that are being used in a that state of delusion as being overwhelmed with the knowledge of these discoveries are being overtaken with a knowledge of the bible, many will become confused, Satan will take that word and do what he did to Eve; turn it into a lie. They will bring in this new age doctrine to lead you to believe we are going to overcome all this and be a better society. Even President Obama will speak these words that will renounce our Christian heritage as to say, **"America is no longer a Christian nation"** and Organizations like "Third Phase of the Moon."

There are many others that have been swept up in the UFO frenzy because of these black opt disclosures, tied to the doctrines of this New Age movement. Without them knowing what spirit possesses them, they have become instruments of Illuminati seduction, they, knowing the people in those audiences they are speaking too, are being given false hopes. The others, speaking the truth in this area, are not pointing the people to God, and that's their point of deception of not knowing who is giving them this inspiration that seem sound and right by using false biblical interpretations to further confuse these who sit and hear them. ***Proverbs 14:12 "(KJV)*** [12] ***There is a way which seemeth right unto a man, but the end thereof are the ways of death."*** Most people caught in this new age spirit, see themselves as the god of their own destiny. Remember what Satan told Eve in the garden; you will be as gods … ***Genesis 3:5 "(KJV)*** [5] ***For God doth know that in the <u>day ye eat thereof</u>, then your eyes shall be opened, and ye shall be as gods, knowing good and evil."*** Now relate that to the cymbal of the bite out of the apple on your i-phone. Their strong hold will be in the Sodomy movement. If there's one thing I have learn about the spirit world through the teachings of the Holy Spirit, man exposed to the paranormal activity in his natural state of mind becomes an open channel of demonic medium deception. You, without knowing, will become an extension of the source. That's why I don't entertain such thoughts. When God told me to quit thinking, now I know why I must decrease, so He can increase, it's the Holy Spirit's job to tell me these things so I just try not to block his thoughts from getting through to me. I am contently comfortable just being a free vessel. You see, I found out that without Him, I am just a piece of dirt, molded in His image with a soul that I will have to give an account of this life as recorded in the book of life. Study your bible with convictions, take time to meditate in your alone time with him, He is waiting to talk to you and give you a Jeremiah 33:3 experience. AMEN

LAW & GRACE EXPLAINED

Introduction:

When one gets delivered from self as becoming converted, it is then your eyes will become open to see the extent of the spiritual need of those to come to where you are, that is to really see truth. This is where you will begin to come out of the volume of the books as letting Christ be seen and not you. The more you open yourself up to the truth as becoming a doer of the word, the more is required of you as in ... *Luke 12:48 "(KJV) But he that knew not, and did commit things worthy of stripes, shall be beaten with few stripes. For unto whomsoever much is given, of him shall be much required: and to whom men have committed much, of him they will ask the more."* Given the fact that there are so many different versions of man's interpretation of the bible, it is no wonder we are so confused when it comes to what we really believe. That's why I do not depend on my thinking anymore, I have learned to lean on the master teacher, the Holy Spirit. When it comes to law and grace, I understand the difference in the two as to their application under grace and truth. In the spirit of discernment, the obvious needs no comment when you understand the nature of sin, this is where you learn to follow peace and wait for God's timing to demonstrate or speak truth. You will learn in the spirit; God's ways are not always what you see in the natural that should cause you to react. Being subject to the Holy Spirit's leadership, by employing the fruit of patience and temperance. Wait for Him to lead as being subject to God the father to follow his perfect and sovereign will to be done through you at that time. Many of us are not fully aware of who we really are.

Galatians 2:14 "(KJV) But when I saw that they walked not uprightly according to the truth of the gospel, I said unto Peter before them all, If thou, being a Jew, livest after the manner of Gentiles, and not as do the Jews, why compellest thou the Gentiles to live as do the Jews?" What Paul was demonstrating to Peter as well as all who handle the word of life is understanding law and grace. What Paul was telling peter ... you, being born a Jew and under the law, fail to do the whole law that pleased the God of our fathers, why are you trying to make Gentiles do what we could not do.

Real faith is in doing the word with an understanding of the right application. Instead, under grace and truth, lack of understanding will cause those you teach to ... *Romans 9:32 "(KJV) Wherefore? Because they sought it not by faith, but as it were by the works of the law. For they stumbled at that stumbling stone; Hebrews 4:2 (KJV) For unto us was the gospel preached, as well as unto them: but the word preached did not profit them, not being mixed with faith in them that heard it. Romans 3:27 (KJV) Where is boasting then? It is excluded. By what law? of works? Nay: but by the law of faith."* This is where I see many seminaries that trained teachers and leaders show this lack of understanding without first being born from above. All it takes is one major error injected into the apostle's doctrine to cause an error of this magnitude to be taught in the assembly after generations to make those under you become a judge of others; there-in is the birth of divisions among us. In these tainted applications, have men ... *2 Timothy 3:7 "(KJV) Ever learning, and never able to come to the knowledge of the truth. Galatians 2:16 (KJV) Knowing that a <u>man is not justified</u> <u>by the works of the law</u>, but by the <u>faith of Jesus Christ</u>, even we have believed in Jesus Christ, that we might be justified by the faith of Christ, and not by the works of the law: <u>for by the works of the law shall no flesh be justified</u>."*

This also accounts for our shortcomings in the applications of the word that leads to confusion and cause many to fall away over time. That explains why we are in a war spiritually, against the powers of darkness as in a fight that we must endure to the end. When Paul taught the Gentiles the truth, he did not want them to remain in bondage by lack of understanding. *Galatians 3:2-5 '(KJV) "This only would I learn of you, Received ye the*

Spirit by the works of the law, or by the hearing of faith? [3] *Are ye so foolish? <u>having begun in the Spirit, are ye now made perfect by the flesh?</u>* [4] *Have ye suffered so many things in vain? if it be yet in vain.* [5] *He therefore that minister to you the Spirit, and worketh miracles among you, doeth he it by the works of the law, or by the hearing of faith? Galatians 3:10 (KJV) For as many as are of the works of the law <u>are under the curse:</u> for it is written, <u>cursed</u> is everyone that continue not in all things which are written in the book of the law to do them."* Many teachers, by lack of understanding, used the above verse to mix law with grace.

Therefore, we must be born from above in the right spirit. *Matthew 7:14 (KJV) Because strait is the gate, and narrow is the way, which leadeth unto life, and few there be that find it.* This has resulted in gentiles keeping the Sabbath under grace that cause those who worship in this manner to become a potential judge of others who do not. *John 4:24 (KJV) "God is a Spirit: and they that worship him must worship him in spirit and in truth. Colossians 2:16 (KJV) Let no man therefore judge you in <u>meat,</u> or in <u>drink,</u> or in <u>respect of an holyday,</u> or of the <u>new moon,</u> or of the <u>sabbath days:</u> Colossians 2:17 (KJV) Which are a <u>shadow of things to come;</u> but the body is of Christ. Hebrews 9:10 (KJV) "Which stood only in meats and drinks, and divers washings, and carnal ordinances, imposed on them until the time of reformation."* We are in that last generation that the reformation of the true doctrine of Jesus Christ will be in true holiness and set all that has caused this division to come to an end and show the world that there **is** only … *Ephesians 4:5 (KJV) "One Lord, one faith, one baptism."* True worshippers demonstrate the application in fruits of the Holy Spirit.

Much of the church-world has been seduced into operating in parts of the doctrine but not in full. *1 Corinthians 13:9 (KJV) "For we know in part, and we prophesy in part. 1 Corinthians 13:12 (KJV) For now we see through a glass, darkly; but then face to face: now I know in part; but then shall I know even as also I am known."* The miracles you will see done will be according to the degree of faith of the individual that attends these assemblies. Only the full council of the Holy Spirit will produce the fruit from above that will remain in all that are called and anointed by God will be performed through Him in the earth, the Holy Spirit. This will be apparent in those born from above. You see, under grace and truth, as of the resurrection of Christ, the law is now alive in all those that have received Christ. Therefore, these two feasts are to be manifested in the gentile believers; the **feast of the tabernacle** which is, Christ in you twenty-four seven keeping you holy always under grace at the mercy seat, waiting to be taken out at the **last trumpet.**

He, through the power of the Holy Spirit will give all that continue in him the ability to be kept or endure unto death after your purpose has been served in His perfect will. They will be raised up at the last trumpet sounding. We are all waiting for our day of rapture, as in your appointment with death. All the laws in the new covenant is manifested in these commandments. *Matthew 22:37–40 (KJV)* [37] *"Jesus said unto him, thou shalt love the Lord thy God with all thy heart, and with all thy soul, and with all thy mind.* [38] *This is the first and great commandment.* [39] *And the second is like unto it, thou shalt love thy neighbour as thyself.* [40] *On these two commandments hang all the law and the prophets."*

Just remember, as you study under the leading of the Holy Spirit, He and He alone will guide you into all truth that will be in the acceptable perfect will of God. Another word for the meaning of conversion is to be set free from the teachings and the traditions of men. **John 8:36 (KJV) "If the Son therefore shall make you free, ye shall be free indeed."** When you come to the knowledge of the truth … *Romans 8:1 (KJV) "There is therefore now no condemnation to them which are in Christ Jesus, who walk not after the flesh, but after the Spirit."* Just remember, the restored Adam only is moved by the voice of God as a new creature that will know his creator's voice and do what he tells him to do. AMEN.

Now on the national front

It grieves me to see the extent of corruption openly displayed in our government for all the world to see. I said in time past that the Supreme Court will become politically divided. What we saw in the last nomination and selection of judges to sit on the Supreme Court is that reality fact. There's not much that I can say that's not already obvious in the daily actions of our government. We do not have to guess anymore to see how divided this nation has become politically. All is happening on the biblical schedule, and we are headed right over a hill down into the abyss. Living with this vision, and being rejected as those were before me, it is hard not to lament in grief over the state of humanity in the hands of and angry

God. The world is in turmoil with one disaster after another and yet the people are not seeing on a spiritual level the magnitude of the effect until it hits your home turf.

The reason we do not hear of the disasters happening in places like Russia and China on this scale, they also suppress and control their media as given over to be used by the devil. That is why they are waiting to take the spoils of a nation that supposed to have been a representation of truth and justice is now being judged for her wicked hypocrisy. Satan only goes after those with God's favor upon them not those he already has. The two nations with a covenant made with God in perils are America and Israel.

They are the last two nations that will mark the signs of the time as these events both having a "911" event begins the judgement of these two nations. Set your affection on going home as confessing Christians, all your hope for this nation and the world is about to end abruptly as in the days of Noah. May God have mercy on you all my beloved. AMEN

HOW TO JUDGE YOURSELF BY THE FRUIT OF THE SPIRIT

Background scripture:

1 Corinthians 11:31 (KJV) [31] **For if we would judge ourselves, we should not be judged. Luke 6:37 (KJV)** [37] **Judge not, and ye shall not be judged: condemn not, and ye shall not be condemned: forgive, and ye shall be forgiven: Matthew 7:16 (KJV) "Ye shall know them by their fruits. Do men gather grapes of thorns, or figs of thistles? Matthew 7:20 (KJV) Wherefore by their fruits ye shall know them. Galatians 5:22-23 (KJV) But the fruit of the Spirit is <u>love</u>, <u>joy</u>, <u>peace</u>, <u>longsuffering</u>, <u>gentleness</u>, <u>goodness</u>, <u>faith</u>,** [23] **<u>Meekness</u>, <u>temperance</u>: against such there is no law."**

It took God a while to get my attention to answer a simple question. That is why we should not get entangled with too many of the cares of this life. Now that he has my attention, this is the simple answer to what I thought was a difficult question. You see, we are to only follow Christ example to learn the perfect will of God. His character is found in the demonstration of the fruits of the spirit. Since I have come into the knowledge of this truth, I do not have a problem with judging myself anymore.

You see, all I must do when I find myself out of character, I compare what I am doing to the fruits of the Holy Spirit, if the way I'm acting is not one of these fruits, I know I must repent. We always hear sinners say, no one can live perfect. I hear a lot of Christians say the same thing. Now let me explain something I had to come to an understanding of; if God said be perfect, **(Matthew 5:48)** then I must find out how this is done in my flesh. When we confess salvation, that is just the beginning, from that time on, if we continue in Him, He will be teaching us through the study of the word by the Holy Spirit how to live by every word of God. This is the simple answer to this question; everything He tells you out of his word to do is His perfect will. Therefore, if you obey Him, you are perfect.

That is His perfect will for every believer. When you say we cannot live perfect it is by lack of knowledge or willful disobedience. Now as a Christian, this is where grace and mercy protect you from committing the sins of omission as in Galatians 5:19-21, that will send you to hell if unconfessed. When we act on the word, by trials of being in a world full of evil, the only protective hedge is found in keeping his word, you must believe He is … *Hebrews 11:6 (KJV) "But without faith it is impossible to please him: for he that cometh to God must believe that he is, and that he is a rewarder of them that diligently seek him. 2 Corinthians 5:7 (KJV) (For we walk by faith, not by sight:"* When I found out why I had to lose from all the entanglements that kept me constantly distracted from applying the word, that's when I saw why I had to deny myself to completely surrender. This is where I begin to set my mind on heavenly things if I wanted to have the power in my new-found life to endure to the end and inherit eternal life.

You see, in Christ as a new creature you already own the world, all you need is what it takes to get through each day. You live in the reality that this is temporary, you are only here for a short time to claim your birth-rite to continue living that life for eternity. All the instructions are written in the word and the Holy Spirit is your teacher and guide into all the mysteries of the truth. We are used to gather others he must call, using your body. *1 Corinthians 6:19 (KJV) What? know ye not that your body is the temple of the Holy Ghost which is in you, which ye have of God, and ye are not your own?* I have often been in awe when the answers He gives me are so simple, I can see how I became a tool of the devil by lack of understanding. Do not be in a hurry with God, use patience. You will get understanding as you act upon the word. You are to examine yourself by the fruits of the spirit to see where you stand with God as in surrendering. Any characters manifested contrary to His fruit is considered evil. That's how I found out what will keep us out of heaven if I can't do what he is telling you. We must do what He said, not by what we feel or think. Every day you will be challenged to stay faithful to your calling. It is the spirit of the world that will wear you down to compromise if you keep entertaining these temptations. I Learn to wait on God to keep my peace, do not be anxious to go ahead of him. You are already blessed with peace when you got saved, now to keep it, you will have to keep your mind on him in every situation.

Isaiah 26:3(KJV) "Thou wilt keep him in perfect peace, whose mind is stayed on thee: because he trusteth in thee." For many years and countless losses, I thought being a Christian was hard only to find out the reason my trial seemed so hard, I did not have the love nor the faith I thought I had. He showed me His goodness despite my sins of omission all those years in error and that is what brought me to the knowledge of a love I never knew that I wanted to have and fell to my knees in a broken state when He revealed what was in my heart and I have never been the same since.

I can hear the clear voice of the Holy Spirit speak to me when I am not distracted. That's how I got to be a scribe to write these teachings down to share with you in this book, so we can all grow together. Now my beloved, you can have a relationship with him too like this when you fall in love with Him. You will fall in love with others to the point that this love for them will not see their fault as in sin in hopes that they might be saved by you letting Christ example be seen in you that may draw them. *John 15:13 (KJV) Greater love hath no man than this, that a man lay down his life for his friends.* This is what I let the Holy Spirit teach me that persuaded me to stay in the right way striving for perfection in Him. I do not have many of likeminded spirit as I desire to share this with, other than those God give ears to hear it. Now may God richly bless you likewise my beloved. AMEN

LOVE: THE EPISTLES OF JOHN

John's life has been a great insight to me that showed me the power of the kind of love that lets you see God and not man. In John's epistles, is where we will find the truth about the loss of our first love.

Through the inspiration of the Holy Spirit

What you are about to experience in these selected teachings, are what the apostles taught in the beginning of the Gospel of Jesus Christ. It is my prayer that God has given you all ears to hear what the present church has fail to see, their state of apostasy from this doctrine.

You who receive these words have been chosen to enter the third and final stage of becoming a new creature. Many things you will read in these chronicles will shake your foundation as to the truth that can set you free from yourself and the world. Our state spiritually is a result of hearing in part because of the fall away. Many are living in part due to failure to adhere to the doctrine as taught by the apostles. *Matthew 7:14 "(NKJV)* *14 Because narrow is the gate and difficult is the way which leads to life, and there are few who find it."* The church God established, is run by the Holy Spirit. **John 6:44" (NKJV) 44 No one can come to Me unless the Father who sent Me draws him; and I will raise him up at the last day."** Salvation is not just something you inherit after confessing to be a Christian, you must know who you are spiritually as a believer daily. *Matthew 6:34 (KJV)* *34 Take therefore no thought for the morrow: for the morrow shall take thought for the things of itself. Sufficient unto the day is the evil thereof.* Therefore, this relationship becomes personal, and *it's between you, God and the devil.* Those born from above will teach and bring you the understanding of the full council of the word. The devil is defeated; therefore, you deal with him by knowledge of the word that proceed from God that created him by speaking in faith without fear, doubt and unbelief; that's your Job hedge. God does not seek to condemn you, but this is His mission in the New Testament is … **Luke 19:10 "(NKJV)** [10] **for the Son of Man has come to seek and to save that which was lost."** It's for this reason that we cannot take the word for granted because … **Matthew 22:14 (NKJV)** [14] **For many are called, but few are chosen." Matthew 7:21 (NKJV)** [21] **"Not everyone who says to Me, 'Lord, Lord,' shall enter the kingdom of heaven, but he who does the will of My Father in heaven. Ecclesiastes 9:11 (NKJV)** [11] **I returned and saw under the sun that-- The race is not to the swift, Nor the battle to the strong, Nor bread to the wise, Nor riches to men of understanding, Nor favor to men of skill; But time and chance happen to them all."** *Matthew 7:22 (KJV)* [22] *Many will say to me in that day, Lord, Lord, have we not prophesied in thy name? and in thy name have cast out devils? and in thy name done many wonderful works?* **2 Then I will say unto him, depart from me, I never knew you, you worker of iniquity."** (All will have the same equal opportunity to seek the lord on **His** terms to be saved.) **1 Corinthians 9:14 "(NKJV)** [14] *Even so the Lord has commanded that those who preach the gospel should live from the gospel. Hebrews 12:1 (NKJV)* [1] **Therefore we also, since we are surrounded by so great a cloud of witnesses,** (as presented in the historical accounts of what God did in man.) **let us lay aside every weight, and the sin which so easily ensnares us, and let us run with endurance the race that is set before us,"**

Lesson one:

The power of love, as taught by Apostle John

2 John 1:10 (KJV) [10] *If there come any unto you, and bring not this doctrine, receive him not into your house, neither bid him God speed:*

1 John 1:1-5:21 (NKJV) [1] **That which was from the beginning, which we have heard, which we have seen with our eyes, which we have looked upon, and our hands have handled, concerning the Word of life—** (John is testifying from a personal experience of what it was like to be an eyewitness.) [2] **the life was manifested, and we have seen, and bear** witness, and declare to you that eternal life which was with the Father and was manifested to us-- ³ that which we have seen and heard we declare to you, that you also may have fellowship with us; and truly our fellowship is with the Father and with His Son Jesus Christ. (Your personal relationship with him will become your testimony. God desires you to loved him just the way John did.) ⁴ *And these things we write to you that your joy may be full.* (All born from above will carry this same message as being of one spirit.)

Walking in the light

⁵ **This is the message which we have heard from Him** (The Holy Spirit) **and declare to you, that God is light and in Him is no darkness at all.** (How do we avoid being in darkness?)

(Isaiah 55:7-8 "(NKJV) ⁷ Let the wicked forsake his way, And the unrighteous man his thoughts; Let him return to the LORD, And He will have mercy on him; And to our God, For He will abundantly pardon. ⁸ "For My thoughts are not your thoughts, nor are your ways My ways," says the LORD.") ⁶ **If we say that we have fellowship with Him, and walk in darkness, we lie and do not practice the truth.** (How do you know you are living a lie?) ⁷ **But if we walk in the light as He is in the light,** (The same spirit from above) **we have fellowship with one another, and the blood of Jesus Christ His Son cleanses us from all sin.** (This is how we know we are one.) ⁸ **If we say that we have no sin, we deceive ourselves, and the truth is not in us.** (We all came from sin to salvation.) ⁹ **If we confess our sins, He is faithful and just to forgive us our sins and to cleanse us from all unrighteousness. "Ecclesiastes 1:11 (NKJV) ¹¹ There is no remembrance of former things, nor will there be any remembrance of things that are to come by those who will come after.** (The new man is spiritual and does not entertain his past or cater to the flesh.) **Isaiah 43:25 (NKJV) ²⁵ I, even I, am He who blots out your transgressions for My own sake; And I will not remember your sins."** (This is where you will begin to worship Him in spirit and truth; forsake self-condemnation of your past sins that Satan will not let you forget.) ¹⁰ **If we say that we have not sinned, we make Him a liar, and His word is not in us.**

Chapter two

[1] *My little children, these things I write to you, so that you may not sin. And if anyone sins, we have an Advocate with the Father, Jesus Christ the righteous.* (He prayed to keep you in right standing with God and the Holy Spirit will convict you to repentance of that sin, once committed.) [2] **And He Himself is the propitiation for our sins, and not for ours only but also for the whole world.** [3] **Now by this we know that we know Him, if we keep His commandments.** (Whatever the word says ... do it, which shows you love him. This is where you are walking by faith. This is how easy it is to lie.) [4] **He who says, "I know Him," and does not keep His commandments, is a liar, and the truth is not in him.** (This type of unbelief will bring divisions among you.) [5] **But whoever keeps His word, truly the love of God is perfected in him. By this we know that we are in Him.** [6] **He who says he abides in Him ought himself also to walk just as He walked.** (This is where the fruit of the spirit of Christ is seen.) **Love your brother** [7] **Brethren, I write no new commandment to you, but an old commandment which you have had from the beginning. The old commandment is the word which you heard from the beginning.** (This has reference to hearing the word over until you are persuaded to act on it.) [8] **Again, a new commandment I write to you, which thing is true in Him and in you, because the darkness is passing away, and the true light is already shining.** [9] **He who says he is in the light, and hates his brother, is in darkness until now.** [10] **He who loves his brother abides in the light, and there is no cause for stumbling in him.** (This is where the love of God is seen, when you can look beyond each other's faults by not criticizing each other for your dislikes in them. This form of buffeting can lead to becoming a judge.) [11] **But he who hates his brother is in darkness and walks in darkness, and does not know where he is going, because the darkness has blinded his eyes.** (If you were convicted that what you are doing is not of God, you would not do it. That is why many will be destroyed for lack of knowledge.) [12] **I write to you, little children, because your sins are forgiven you for His name's sake.** [13] **I write to you, fathers, because you have known Him who is from the beginning.** (This has reference to being taught the truth by those born from above.) **I write to you, young men, because you have overcome the wicked one. I write to you, little children, because you have known the Father.** [14] **I have written to you, fathers, because you have known Him who is from the**

beginning. I have written to you, young men, because you are strong, and the word of God abides in you, and you have overcome the wicked one.

Love not the world

¹⁵ **Do not love the world or the things in the world. If anyone loves the world, the love of the Father is not in him.** ¹⁶ **For all that is in the world--the lust of the <u>flesh</u>, the lust of the <u>eyes</u>, and the <u>pride of life</u> is not of the Father but is of the world.** ¹⁷ *And the world is passing away, and the lust of it; but he who does the will of God abides forever. (*How to know you have eternal life) ¹⁸ **Little children, <u>it is the last hour;</u>** (This has reference to not knowing your day of departure. {Revelation 3:3 (KJV) ³ Remember therefore how thou hast received and heard, and hold fast, and repent. If therefore thou shalt not watch, I will come on thee as a thief, <u>and thou shalt not know what hour I will come upon thee}</u> ... **and as you have heard that the Antichrist is coming, even now <u>many antichrists</u> have come, by which we know that it is the last hour.** ¹⁹ **They went out from us, but they were not of us; for if they had been of us, they would have continued with us; but they went out that they might be made manifest, that none of them were of us.** ²⁰ **But you have an anointing from the Holy One, and you know all things.** ²¹ **I have not written to you because you do not know the truth, but because you know it, and that no lie is of the truth.** ²² *Who is a liar but he who denies that Jesus is the Christ? He is antichrist who denies the Father and the Son.* (What does this statement mean?) ²³ **Whoever denies the Son does not have the Father either; he who acknowledges the Son has the Father also.** ²⁴ **Therefore let that abide in you which you heard from the beginning. If what you heard from the beginning abides in you, you also will abide in the Son and in the Father.** ²⁵ **And this is the promise that He has promised us--eternal life.** ²⁶ **These things I have written to you concerning those who try to deceive you.** (What are they trying you for?) ²⁷ **But the anointing which you have received from Him abides in you, and you do not need that anyone teach you;** (Those born from above, carry an anointing of knowing the father.) **but as the same anointing teaches you concerning all things, and is true, and is not a lie, and just as it has taught you, you will abide in Him.** (These are they that are elected to teach you the whole council of the truth through the Holy Spirit from above. They that hear them, make their calling and election sure.) ²⁸ **And now, little children,**

abide in Him, that when He appears, we may have confidence and not be ashamed before Him at His coming. [29] If you know that He is righteous, you know that everyone who practices righteousness is born of Him.

<u>Chapter three</u>

The evidence of a true believer

[1] Behold what manner of love the Father has bestowed on us, that we should be called children of God! Therefore<u>, the world does not know us</u>, because it did not know Him. [2] Beloved, now we are children of God; and it has not yet been revealed what we shall be, but we know that when He is revealed, we shall be like Him, for we shall see Him as He is. (It is our faith in him that causes us to obey his words that make us look and act like him.)[3] And everyone who has this hope in Him purifies himself, just as He is pure. [4] Whoever commits sin also commits lawlessness, and sin is lawlessness. [5] And you know that He was manifested to take away our sins, and in Him there is no sin. [6] Whoever abides in Him does not sin. Whoever sins has neither seen Him nor known Him. [7] Little children <u>let no one deceive you</u>. He who practices righteousness is righteous, just as He is righteous. [8] He who sins is of the devil, for the devil has sinned from the beginning. For this purpose the Son of God was manifested, that He might destroy the works of the devil. [9] Whoever has been born of God does not sin, for His seed remains in him; and he cannot sin, because he has been born of God. [10] In this the children of God and the children of the devil are manifest: Whoever does not practice righteousness is not of God, nor is he who does not love his brother. Love indeed and in truth [11] For this is the message that you heard from the beginning, that we should love one another,[12] not as Cain who was of the wicked one and murdered his brother. And why did he murder him? Because his works were evil and his brother's righteous. [13] Do not marvel, my brethren, if the world hates you. [14] We know that we have passed from death to life, because we love the brethren. He who does not love his brother abides in death. [15] Whoever hates his brother is a murderer, and you know that no murderer has eternal life abiding in him. (Now we must ask the question, who is my brother?) {Mark 3:34-35 (NKJV) [34] And He looked around in a circle at those who sat about Him, and said, "Here are My mother and My brothers! [35] For whoever does the will of God is My brother and My sister and mother.} [16] By this

we know love, because He laid down His life for us. <u>And we also ought to lay down our lives for the brethren.</u> ¹⁷ But whoever has this world's goods, and sees his brother in need, and shuts up his heart from him, how does the love of God abide in him? (We live in a very wicked time, how do you know when a person is really telling you the truth or just taking advantage of your generosity?) ¹⁸ My little children, let us not love in word or in tongue, but in deed and in truth. ¹⁹ And by this we know that we are of the truth and shall assure our hearts before Him. ²⁰ <u>For if our heart condemns us</u>, God is greater than our heart, and knows all things. (The world has organizations designed to take care of its own, beware you are not strengthening the hand of the devil.) ²¹ Beloved, if our heart does not condemn us, we have confidence toward God. ²² And whatever we ask we receive from Him, because we keep His commandments and do those things that are pleasing in His sight. (This is what will keep the devil from afflicting you through sickness or circumstances you can control by resisting him.) ²³ *And this is His commandment: that we should believe on the name of His Son Jesus Christ and love one another, as He gave us commandment.* ²⁴ Now he who keeps His commandments abides in Him, and He in him. And by this we know that He abides in us, by the Spirit whom He has given us.

<u>Chapter four</u>

Try the spirits

¹ Beloved do not believe every spirit, but test the spirits, whether they are of God; because many false prophets have gone out into the world. (How do we test or try the spirit. This is how … ² By this you know the Spirit of God<u>: Every spirit that confesses that Jesus Christ has come in the flesh is of God,</u> ³ and every spirit that does not confess that Jesus Christ has come in the flesh <u>is not of God</u>. (Jesus identifies with us as being in the flesh like us; He demonstrates how we are now able to walk perfect in the spirit while in your flesh body. He becomes your perfection by your obedience.) And this is the spirit of the Antichrist, which you have heard was coming, and is now already in the world. 4 <u>You are of God, little children, and have overcome them, because He who is in you is greater than he who is in the world.</u> ⁵ They are of the world. Therefore, they speak as of the world, and the world hears them. ⁶ <u>We are of God. He who knows God hears us;</u> (This is the test of those who

know his voice.) **he who is not of God does not hear us. By this we know the spirit of truth and the spirit of error.** (Those that resist hearing truth have been exposed to those born from below and live in error of a wrong life application of the word.)

The love that is of God

[7] **Beloved let us love one another, for love is of God; and everyone who loves is born of God and knows God.** [8] **He who does not love does not know God, for God is love.** [9] **In this the love of God was manifested toward us, that God has sent His only begotten Son into the world, that we might live through Him.** (Those living by his word, their names are in the lamb's book of life.) [10] **In this is love, not that we loved God, but that He loved us and sent His Son to be the propitiation for our sins.** [11] **Beloved, if God so loved us, we also ought to love one another.** [12] **No one has seen God at any time. If we love one another, God abides in us, and His love has been perfected in us.** [13] **By this we know that we abide in Him, and He in us, because He has given us of His Spirit.** [14] **And we have seen and testify that the Father has sent the Son as Savior of the world.** [15] **Whoever confesses that Jesus is the Son of God, God abides in him, and he in God.** [16] **And we have known and believed the love that God has for us. God is love, and he who abides in love abides in God, and God in him.** [17] **Love has been perfected among us in this: that we may have boldness in the day of judgment; because as He is, so are we in this world.** 18 <u>**There is no fear in love; but perfect love casts out fear,**</u> (Most of our fears come from teachings that does not come through example in those you put your trust in what they are saying is truth; if they are not seeing a demonstration of deliverance, it is because Jesus is not being lifted in love to demonstrate what we saw in the early church.) **because fear involves torment.** (Ask for prayer to get delivered from those you are persuaded that know God by these signs and their testimonies.) **But he who fears has not been made perfect in love.** [19] **We love Him because He first loved us.** [20] **If someone says, "I love God," and hates his brother, he is a liar; for he who does not love his brother whom he has seen, how can he love God whom he has not seen?** [21] **And this commandment we have from Him: that he who loves God must love his brother also.**

Chapter five

The victory of the believers

[1] Whoever believes that Jesus is the Christ is born of God, and everyone who loves Him who begot also loves him who is begotten of Him. [2] By this we know that we love the children of God, when we love God and keep His commandments. [3] For this is the love of God, that we keep His commandments. And His commandments are not burdensome. [4] For whatever is born of God overcomes the world. And this is the victory that has overcome the world--our faith. [5] Who is he who overcomes the world, but he who believes that Jesus is the Son of God? [6] This is He who came by water and blood--Jesus Christ, not only by water, but by water and blood. And it is the Spirit who bears witness, because the Spirit is truth. [7] For there are three that bear witness in heaven: The Father, the Word, and the Holy Spirit; and these three are one. [8] And there are three that bear witness on earth: The Spirit, the water, and the blood; and these three agree as one. [9] If we receive <u>the witness of men</u>, the witness of God is greater; for this is the witness of God which He has testified of His Son. [10] He who believes in the Son of God has the witness in himself; he who does not believe God has made Him a liar, because he has not believed the testimony that God has given of His Son. [11] And this is the testimony: that God has given us eternal life, and this life is in His Son. [12] He who has the Son have life; he who does not have the Son of God does not have life.

God answers prayers

[13] These things I have written to you who believe in the name of the Son of God, that you may know that you have eternal life, and that you may continue to believe in the name of the Son of God. [14] Now this is the confidence that we have in Him, that if we ask anything <u>according to His will</u>, He hears us. [15] And if we know that He hears us, whatever we ask, we know that we have the petitions that we have asked of Him. [16] If anyone sees his brother sinning a sin which does not lead to death, <u>he will ask, and He will give him life for those who commit sin not leading to death</u>. There is sin leading to death. I do not say that he should pray about that. [17] All unrighteousness is sin, and there is sin not leading to death. [18] We know that whoever is born of God does not sin; but he

who has been born of God keeps himself, and the wicked one does not touch him. [19] We know that we are of God, and the whole world lies under the sway of the wicked one. [20] And we know that the Son of God has come and has given us an understanding, that we may know Him who is true; and we are in Him who is true, in His Son Jesus Christ. This is the true God and eternal life. [21] Little children keep yourselves from idols. Amen.

The second Epistle of John

Part Two

Honoring those walking in truth:

2 John 1:1-13 (NKJV) [1] *The Elder, To the elect lady and her children, whom I love in truth, and not only I, but also all those who have known the truth,* [2] *because of the truth which abides in us and will be with us forever:* [3] *Grace, mercy, and peace will be with you from God the Father and from the Lord Jesus Christ, the Son of the Father, in truth and love.* [4] *I rejoiced greatly that I have found some of your children walking in truth, as we received commandment from the Father.* [5] *And now I plead with you, lady, not as though I wrote a new commandment to you, but that which we have had from the beginning: that we love one another.* [6] <u>This is love</u> that we walk according to His commandments. This is the commandment, that as you have heard from the beginning, you should walk in it. [7] For many deceivers have gone out into the world who do not confess Jesus Christ as coming in the flesh. This is a deceiver and an antichrist. (Who is the antichrist? (Explain) Those born from above are as John said are one with Christ and no one-another. Those born from below are followers of the doctrines of man in his traditional assembly teachings. Those born from above are the doers of the word, those born from below are hearers only; both are confessing Christians but one sect doesn't know what spirit they are of.) [8] Look to yourselves, that we do not lose those things we worked for, but that we may receive a full reward. (John 16:13 (NKJV) [13] However, when He, the Spirit of truth, has come, He will guide you into all truth; for He will not speak on His own authority, but whatever He hears He will speak; and He will tell you things to come.) [9] *Whoever transgresses and does not abide in the doctrine of Christ does not have God. He who abides in the doctrine of Christ has both the Father and the Son.*

(These are the doers of the word.) [10] *If anyone comes to you and does not bring this doctrine, do not receive him into your house nor greet him;* [11] **for he who greets him shares in his evil deeds.** Those who may have been seduced to compromise as pastors and teachers by not declaring the whole council of the truth as inspired by the Holy Spirit which includes the prophet's vision.) [12] *Having many things to write to you, I did not wish to do so with paper and ink; but I hope to come to you and speak face to face, that our joy may be full.* [13] **The children of your elect sister greet you. Amen.**

Part Three

Knowing those who labor among you

3 John 1:1-14 (NKJV) [1] *The Elder, To the beloved Gaius, whom I love in truth:* [2] *Beloved, I pray that you may prosper in all things and be in health, just as your soul prospers.* [3] **For I rejoiced greatly when brethren came and testified of the truth that is in you, just as you walk in the truth.** [4] *I have no greater joy than to hear that my children walk in truth.* [5] **Beloved, you do faithfully whatever you do for the brethren and for strangers,** [6] **who have borne witness of your love before the church. If you send them forward on their journey in a manner worthy of God, you will do well,** (Those who have been a blessing to you spiritually, support them with whatever the lord provides ... for this reason, they came giving freely in faith asking nothing of you.) [7] **because they went forth for His name's sake, taking nothing from the Gentiles.** [8] *We therefore ought to receive such, which we may become fellow workers for the truth.* (The words they speak are from God.) [9] *I wrote to the church, but Diotrephes, who loves to have the preeminence among them, does not receive us.* (These are men in the ministry for selfish reasons for gain.) [10] **Therefore, if I come, I will call to mind his deeds which he does, prating against us with malicious words. And not content with that, he himself does not receive the brethren, and forbids those who wish to, putting them out of the church.** (These are men into self-kingdom building.) [11] *Beloved, do not imitate what is evil, but what is good. He who does good is of God, but he who does evil has not seen God.* [12] *Demetrius has a good testimony from all, and from the truth itself. And we also bear witness, and you know that our testimony is true.* [13] *I had many things to write, but I do not wish to write to you with pen and ink;* [14] *but I hope to see you shortly, and we shall speak face to face. Peace to you. Our friends greet you. Greet the friends by name.* What we see in the life of John is the power of the love of Christ in you that we must be willing to demonstrate by faith to have the same testimony as to go through your life and be delivered from all the works of the devil and die a natural death in old age. Now that's the power of his love, living by faith. **AMEN**

WHERE IS THE
TEMPLE OF GOD?

As one who has been re-taught by the Holy Spirit, I have learned that he is my source of all we need to know that reflects the mind and will of God for every believer. This is an individual journey that one must seek to know the destiny and purpose you were born to serve. We all have some form of a gift from God whether saved or sinner; however, the enemy of our soul will keep you entangled in the cares of this life that keep you from achieving your full potential. He does not care about who or what you are as born his child, if you remain in this state, *2 Timothy 3:7 "(KJV) [7] Ever learning, and never able to come to the knowledge of the truth."* (That's the state we were all born in. Now anyone that brings the gospel from above under the anointing of the Holy Spirit will have this understanding as to what will enable you to walk in the perfect will of God.) *Romans 12:1-2 "(KJV) [1] I beseech you therefore, brethren, by the mercies of God, that ye present your bodies a living sacrifice, holy, acceptable unto God, which is your reasonable service. [2] And be not conformed to this world: but be ye transformed by the renewing of your mind, that ye may prove what is that good, and acceptable, and perfect, will of God. 2 Corinthians 5:17 (KJV) [17] Therefore, if any man be in Christ, he is a new creature: old things are passed away; behold, all things are become new."* This is how you will be taught by the Holy Spirit if you continue in him. *Isaiah 28:10-13 (KJV) [10] For precept must be upon precept, precept upon precept; line upon line, line upon line; here a little, and there a little: [11] For with stammering lips and another tongue will he speak* to this people. *12 To whom he said, this is the rest wherewith ye may cause the weary to rest; and this is the refreshing: yet they would not hear. 13 But the word of the LORD was unto them precept upon precept, precept upon precept; line upon line, line upon line; here a little, and there a little; that they might go, and fall backward, and be broken, and snared, and taken".* This is what I found to be the reason for my shortcomings; my thinking did not allow me to completely yield to His teaching. Our priority is to learn how to believe God is who He said He is by … *Matthew 6:33 "(KJV) 33 But seek ye first the kingdom of God, and his righteousness; and all these things shall be added unto you. Hebrews 11:6 (KJV) 6* But without faith it is impossible to please him: for he that cometh to God must believe that he is, and that he is a rewarder of them that diligently seek him. He is found standing at the end of that straight and narrow road the Holy Spirit pointed to. He is calling you to come to Him to receive total deliverance from the devil. Therefore, you must … *Matthew 7:14-15 "(KJV) 14 Because strait is the gate, and narrow is the way, which leadeth unto life, and few there be that find it. 15 Beware of false prophets, which come to you in sheep's clothing, but inwardly they are ravening wolves."* To keep from being deceived, you must … *Isaiah 50:7 "(KJV) 7 For the Lord GOD will help me; therefore, shall I not be confounded: therefore, have I set my face like a flint, and I know that I shall not be ashamed." Proverbs 4:27 "(KJV) 27 Turn not to the right hand nor to the left: remove thy foot from evil."* Those who seek God like this will find Him in the fullness; they are the few. Your love for Him coupled with faith will cause you to live in the reality that He is the greater one now in you. Now you are His new temple … *1 Corinthians 6:19 "(KJV) 19 What? know ye not that your body is the temple of the Holy Ghost which is in you, which ye have of God, and ye are not your own?"* This is where you will fulfill your full potential in the perfect will of God in Christ. One of the things I had to be delivered from are teachings from a denominational standpoint, men that meant well but were victims of lack of knowledge and convictions also. You will not be able to blame your leader for your short comings before God in the judgment. We, as confessing Christians are responsible for … *Acts 2:39-40 (KJV) 39 For the promise is unto you, and to your children, and to all that are afar with many other words did he testify and exhort, saying, <u>Save yourselves from this untoward generation.</u>"* We have failed to produce the kind of fruit that is acceptable by it not remaining in us to the degree that Jesus is seen as in the days of the apostles. Many have fallen away from our first love.

Now he that hath an ear, let him hear?

Many of us take the sacrament on religious bases as taught in our assemblies; however, this sacrament act, carries serious consequences. *1 Corinthians 11:26-28 "(KJV)* [26] *For as often as ye eat this bread, and drink this cup, ye do shew the Lord's death till he come.* [27] *Wherefore whosoever shall eat this bread, and drink this cup of the Lord, unworthily, shall be guilty of the body and blood of the Lord.* [28] *But let a man examine himself, and so let him eat of that bread, and drink of that cup."* When the lord opened my eyes to many traditional practices, we take for granted, have become ritualistic in our assemblies where the devil gets to justify putting on us, things God has delivered us from by deceiving us into a way that seem right. It has been my experience to see many well-meaning fellow believers seeking the return of God's acts without returning to doing things that represents his ways will be caught being judged under the sins of omission by lack of knowledge and convictions. Our short coming show we need to do some repenting.

If God did not have this calling on my life, I would still be a victim of lack of knowledge by ever learning but not coming to the knowledge about the truth of my own state in His sight. This is that area of the sins of omission as found in … *Galatians 5:19-21" (KJV)* [19] Now the works of the flesh are manifest, which are these; *Adultery, fornication, uncleanness, lasciviousness,* [20] Idolatry, *witchcraft, hatred, variance, emulations, wrath, strife, seditions, heresies,* [21] *Envyings, murders, drunkenness, revellings, and such like: of the which I tell you before, as I have also told you in time past, that they which do such things shall not inherit the kingdom of God."* These are unconfessed sins confessing Christian's are guilty of by being in traditional teachings that have led to divisions in our Christian Walk. I have written to you as fellow Christians to help us all examine ourselves. Unfortunately, many of us have been taught in a way that seems right and will refuse this call to repent. I asked God as to how can I judge myself and be sure that I am living in your perfect will? The answer: *"Every time you act contrary to the fruits of my spirit, you need to repent."* Now I repent as often as need too, to keep myself in right standing with God and His son. There is no such doctrine as once saved always saved in the bible. Why would he say … *Luke 6:46 "(KJV)* [46] *And why call ye me, Lord, Lord, and do not the things which I say. Matthew 7:21-23 (KJV)* [21] Not everyone that saith unto me, Lord, Lord, shall enter into the kingdom of heaven; but he that doeth the will of my Father which is in heaven. [22] *Many will say to me in that day, Lord, Lord, have we not prophesied in thy name? and in thy name have cast out devils? and in thy name done many wonderful works?* [23] *And then will I profess unto them, I never knew you: depart from me, ye that work iniquity."* Until you come to the knowledge that you are the temple God dwells in, there's no division in that body. They will know one-another by having the right spirit. Those who are like minded will fellowship in unity, as on the day of Pentecost. This is when you will see signs of the fruit that has remained. They have the potential to perform signs, wonders and miracles as in the days of the apostles as often as you come together. I have written two books that reveals the mysteries of our times as titled: **"Everybody Talking about heaven Ain't Going There"** and **"Life is a Terrible Thing to Waste."** They are available on Amazon under my name as the author of these books. When God told me not to pray for my wife's deliverance but that she remains faithful unto death. This was his mercy to save her from what is coming; I was greatly comforted in hearing those words. God had all five of her children with me for one week and gave us all an experience that rivals any funeral, we got to spend that quality time in her final days and though she could not speak or move, God did something that only he could do; she would always give you a thumbs up when she was pleased at something done for her. He raised her right hand with her thumb in an upright position two days before she passed to let us know, all is well. I have a photo of that moment on my phone.

We as a nation are entering the stage of a tragic downfall from which there is no recover. Look at the diverse natural disasters God is allowing to get our attention. We are coming to the end of a new time continuum as in the days of Noah. My fellow brothers and sisters, as confessing Christian believers, I am always pleading in these messages as from what I have been made to see as the other side of God's anger. We now have allowed the curse of Sodom to be legalized in this nation. God would have to apologize to Sodom and Gomorrah if we were to escape. Our judgment as a nation is now set in the stone tablets of heaven, is about to be carried out on us as our punishment by our enemies we deceived as self-appointed policemen of the world. According to Revelation 18, in the end, we will be found no more as the Modern Mystery Babylon at all.

God has raised up prophets and messengers with the vision of our times with a warning; those who reject their call to repent will lose your soul. We, in this nation, have become complacent to the point that many will be taken by being overcome by fears of that we thought we would never suffer. We are at the mercy of evils we helped produced by departing from our covenant **"In God We Trust."** A-I technologies have taken over many of our minds as a set up to be marked through a co-vert media of seduction. The internet and smart phone mind altering apps are the means to carry this forbidden technology that caused the flood, once again, introduced by fallen angel DNA incorporated in human DNA. Whether saved or sinner, we all are going to be tested as to whose report you choose to believe, so let us all do our repenting now and prepare for the worst to come. May God have mercy on all that call upon His name. AMEN

THE MYSTERY OF THE MARK OF THE BEAST

It is unfortunate that many in the traditional assemblies setting of religious rituals are unaware of the visions of the prophet's and messengers of our times. *Proverbs 29:18 "(KJV)* [18] *Where there is no vision, the people perish: but he that keepeth the law, happy is he."* This mass seduction has taken place in my observation through renowned seminary trained pastors and teachers under Jesuit professors. No man can teach only what the Holy Spirit was sent to do; reveal these mysteries to those that have ears to hear. The reality is, we are dirt, created in the image of God. We are born under a curse with the mind of the devil. The Holy Spirit was sent to those chosen to receive him to reveal your state in the sight of God.

Those that have been given ears to hear him will repent; they will become the children of God by election. They are adopted as sons and will be treated as such in the spirit. Those who are born again under these elected saints, will receive the same power as making their calling and election sure by remaining in the truth as taught by those born from above. They are the few that carry the vision of your times that God use to tell you what to look for during the time you are given to live before you die. God has a universal word for the world that this vision must reach as those chosen for salvation to hear in each time, age and dispensation. This is that number that no one knows but God. God set these things in motion from the beginning of time that cannot be changed. Arch Angel Michael has been given the power to restrain Satan's activity to preserve all events as Satan is release back into the world by Adam's sin. This is the mystery of iniquity that many deceived will not believe unless you have been given ears to hear.

What I am telling you are third layer revelation truths that are not taught by seminary trained men of renowned in religious circles. This is not for hirelings. Many, in their renowned state, usurp their thoughts to interpret only what the Holy Spirit knows. Given generations of man's kingdom building, these divisions have led to the establishment of all these different denominations that represent our present state of religious doctrinal confusions. We have had over two thousand years to be captivated under some of these divisions that have put us in this state of the final **"end of days;"** Adam, in his fallen state, was given to subdue the Earth after the fall. The end time church will become victims of these deceptive religious teachings that will compromise the doctrine and cause a fall away from the doctrine the apostle's taught. Therefore, will incorporate all the spirits of the seven churches of Revelation two and three that will bring about these divisions that will reject those who come speaking truth that exposes the errors of their ways. Those worshipping God in spirit and truth are manifesting a character as coming out of the volume of the books that refuse to compromise.

He is calling and separating out those he will use for His glory. All things predestine by God will work to the end as He has ordained before the foundation as in ... *Isaiah 46:10 "(NASB77)* [10] Declaring the end from the beginning and from ancient times things which have not been done, Saying, ‹ My purpose will be established, And I will accomplish all My good pleasure›; *Romans 8:28 (KJV)* [28] **And we know that all things work together for good to them that love God, to them who are the called according to his purpose."** Now we are at the end of those days; once again, man has reached a place of evil continually as in the days of Noah. Since the end of the final seven years of calm that followed **"9/11/01,"** that ended in the year of 08. The end time of the gentiles and Jews under grace, will be the time He will reveal the revelations hidden from previous dispensations. They will become the chronicles of this last generation in Daniel chapter twelve which is the 70th week or final seven years of mysteries to be revealed by Jesus to those that have ears to hear in the opening of the seals in the book of Revelation.

The increase in knowledge that Daniel said would come. (Dan.12:4) What the church has fail to see is this hidden knowledge that will become the forbidden zone for mankind that will become the means of his self-imposed bondage through a spiritual entity of Satan, traveling through the airwaves in the form of an Artificial Intelligence, (A-I) that will transform himself into the prince that will travel through the airways in his children linked to angelic DNA. *Ephesians 2:2 "(NASB77)* ² *in which you formerly walked according to the course of this world, according to the prince of the power of the air, of the spirit that is now working in the sons of disobedience."* These are the children of the devil, carrying strands of fallen angel DNA. They will introduce this forbidden technology that will change man's state of mind to be controlled by A-I technology that will become the **beast** that speaks, introduced through the airwaves. This will be done over a timed period through a media known as the internet, that will be used to captivate the whole world.

Revelation 12:9 "(NASB77) ⁹ **And the great dragon was thrown down, the serpent of old who is called the devil and Satan, who deceives the whole world; he was thrown down to the earth, and his angels were thrown down with him. Revelation 16:14 (NASB77)** ¹⁴ **for they are spirits of demons, performing signs, which go out to the kings of the whole world, to gather them together for the war of the great day of God, the Almighty."** These signs will precede the great day of the wrath in the form of great diverse natural disasters all over the world, even some of its great wonders of the earth will fall.

Human interactions will become evil toward each other as these spirits are released by the church being overtaken in a delusional state. A reverse of circumstances as you see the world will begin to take care of its own during this period. Great ministries will fall as the evils of those dens of thieves as false doctrine churches are exposed. This great fallaway will be the greatest sign of church delusion of this age. This is what will cause many to be marked in that delusional state of willing ignorance. Satan's spirit, traveling through this A-I technology in the **first** stage in the introduction of the internet **Matrix,** designed to open a portal into your mind to duplicate it's operation without emotion that will steal your soul. Hollywood has given us a pictorial view of this through the movie **"Matrix."** This movie depicts the warfare in the mind of those seduced into serving this medium designed to control your mind. It will contain all the knowledge of this known world we live in and speculate the possibility of new worlds to come.

There will be an increase in paranormal activity and UFO sightings. These will be the distractions to lead you into skepticism that will lead to your captivity. This will be the means to reduce your attention span by having this information at your fingertips. Once your mind has been made a dependent on this convenience, this first stage will be complete. Biblically, **we are entering the ten toes of the stature in Nebuchadnezzar's dream** as they plan the set-up of the NWO. The mixture of iron and clay. This is when these fallen angel DNA will once again mix with humans. *Daniel 2:43 "(KJV)* [43] *And whereas thou sawest iron mixed with miry clay,* <u>*they shall mingle themselves with the seed of men:*</u> *but they shall not cleave one to another, even as iron is not mixed with clay."* If God would allow, these beings will attempt to rule the universe with this from of heavenly DNA. Once man is conquered, outer space would be their next frontier. Under Grace and Truth, this is the spiritual phase of the manifestation of the spirit world to people, blind to the reality of what will cause their own destruction. This is the vision the prophets and messengers will be revealing to this generation of the end time that will be explaining the signs of that time to those that have been given ears to hear them and eyes to see. Now that the internet has captivated the world's mind, the next stage is to flood the media outlets with too much information for your mind to process daily. This will ultimately bring short attention spans, confusion and divisions as the self-appointed authorities begin to spew news rhetoric to the general populations of the world. The love of many will wax cold due to the impersonal nature of these A-I devices that will let you talk with your finger to people you will never meet and take your attention away from personal contact. This **first phase** of the A-I system will have linked the **Matrix** of the masses to this **internet** system. This is the mark in the **forehead.** *Revelation 13:16 "(KJV)* [16] *And he causeth all, both small and great, rich and poor, free and bond, to receive a mark in their* <u>*right hand, or in their foreheads:*</u> *Revelation 14:9 (KJV)* [9] And the third angel followed them, saying with a loud voice, If any man worship the beast and his image, and receive <u>*his mark in his forehead,*</u> or <u>*in his hand,"*</u>

The **second phase** will be the means of how you will receive the mark through a device held in your **right hand**.

This revelation blew me away when it was revealed to me the first time as I wrote it in my books. This is a more detailed version. These children given over to the devil linked by DNA, are the ones to be used to transport the DNA of fallen angels through these condemned angels in the second heaven who now possess the souls of all born under the curse of Adam, will be the means to transfer a residue remnant of this DNA into human bodies, when revealed, be known as the illuminated one's in the earth or, **illuminati's.** They will have a form of superior intellect knowledge of the forbidden world that cause past civilizations and tribes to become extinct when introduced into those dispensations of time to prevent any changes to God's predestined timeline. **Steve Jobs** will be one of these illuminati humans to introduce this forbidden technology that will cause his own destruction in the flesh. All will worship this AI beast. It will propel his company to become the largest tech giant in the world.

The revelation signs to the prophets and messengers will be the cymbal he will use as a trademark to the company that will bring the world to your fingertips; **"a bite out of an apple;"** that will be our sign as watchman's. This is the end of our dispensation. They are now beginning to implement their plan. Now you can see this hidden cymbal with a mystery tie to Eden, without this vision of your times, you will become a victim. He will introduce this through what will become known as a smart i-phone computer system of communication. It will be the hallmark of this technology.

Those with these encrypted i-phones, have been **Matrix** mind linked through the internet. Through this forbidden A-I technology, he will write the algorism to decode the link to your brainwaves DNA fingerprint that will take control of your mind to receive post hypnotic suggestions, generated through this built-in technology in the form of apps. Each of these apps written by his company will connect your brain's function when opened. When they, through previous stages of this phone's introduction, the i-10 model will complete his role in this grand scale of mind control to dumb down the general population without them ever knowing until they wake-up marked. This is the work of those gathered as the illuminated ones. This mind control, through these apps will cause him to become the riches tech giants in the world. Their final test will be a revamped version of the Pokémon game; when the app is open by mostly those into gaming, they will be given a post hypnotic suggestion to go to a certain place. Most of you became aware of this phenomenon when it made national news. Now the reason you saw them congregating in various places such as parks and open spaces, they were pre-programed by that app that told them where to go. It can send you anywhere with built-in GPS co-ordinances. All i-phones are now automatically upgraded with encrypted codes that can be sent at any time because the users attention span is controlled by this link it has in your mind. This accounts for the increase in rage among the populated cities. That's the mystery of how you will be marked in the spirit without ever knowing how it happens. Here again, we see why the bible tells us why? *Proverbs 29:18 "(KJV)* [18] *Where there is no vision, the people perish: but he that keepeth the law, happy is he." It is for this reason ...* *Hosea 4:6 "(KJV)* [6] *My people are destroyed for lack of knowledge: because thou hast rejected knowledge, I will also reject thee, that thou shalt be no priest to me: seeing thou hast forgotten the law of thy God, I will also forget thy children."*

Now let us go back to the beginning of this chronicle; this is where I had a difficult time receiving this statement in 1988 when God told another Prophet that 98 percent of the church in the last days will not be in a place spiritually to survive what's coming because of false teachings. They will live with a false sense of reality and security. Many are in mass confusion about the end times. I did not have this revelation at that time. When Inquired about the children of the last generation that are victims of their parent's hypocrisy, this was what I was made to see? *"History has always been repeated in cycles, that's why I raise up prophets and messengers to warn the people when one is about to be repeated. Many of their children will replace them at the marriage supper of the lamb. They will be part of the first sickle harvest in the rapture in Rev. 14:15-17. I will have mercy on them as I did when I gave my people over to Satan for their hard hearts in the wilderness experience. Those who remain in the Laodicean church spirit will be cut off in their luke-warm state as I spew them out of my mouth. I will cause those assemblies that failed to be a light of refuge in salvation and deliverance that lead my people astray, I will cause those whose hearts were right to return to me in the great harvest."*

My beloved brothers and sisters, we are in the cycle of another historical time continuance. These are the repeat of the days of Noah. All the doctrinal confusions have led to produce more skeptics in the world as well as in the church that are the mockers in our time this message is being made known to the people of the world, just as in the days of NOAH. As I have revealed the mystery of the mark of the beast, coming through the airways, now you can examine yourself as to the extent of control these A-I devices in your possession may have a certain degree of control over you. God will take the least among you to confound the wise. *1 Corinthians 1:27 "(KJV)* [27] *But God hath chosen the foolish things of the world to confound the wise; and God hath chosen the weak things of the world to confound the things which are mighty;"*

It has been my experience to be the least accepted in religious circles as not being well known among religious peers. I learn that the spirit of Elijah in John the Baptist will return to warn the people to prepare for the great showdown as to who is the real God, this time, in His wrath. I am just one of the voices in this wilderness where many that do not know the voice of God will reject the call to repent. Many of you can remember how bold you were to tell the people of your new-found salvation, have let Satan put out your fire that cause you to lose that first love you once had for God. While those convicted under false pastors or teachers have a zeal for God but may be lacking in the knowledge of the full council of the truth as to who is to do the speaking in our vessel. After over twenty years in that state, God had mercy on me and open my eyes to my state; though I meant well as a confessing Christian, all that time, I was on my way to hell. We have been judging ourselves on the premise of what people think of us instead of the one who is going to judge you and say where you are going to go. *Luke 6:26 (KJV)* [26] *Woe unto you, when all men shall speak well of you! for so did their fathers to the false prophets.* Let us all examine ourselves while His mercy is upon us and do our repenting while the blood is still running warm in our veins. May the grace of our lord Jesus Christ be with all that call upon his name. AMEN (Updated 12/2018)

TRUMP; THE END OF THE GENTILE CYCLE OF KINGS

Ezra 1:2-3 (KJV) [2] *Thus saith Cyrus king of Persia, The LORD God of heaven hath given me all the kingdoms of the earth; and he hath charged me to build him an house at Jerusalem, which is in Judah.* [3] *Who is there among you of all his people? his God be with him, and let him go up to Jerusalem, which is in Judah, and build the house of the LORD God of Israel, (he is the God,) which is in Jerusalem. Isaiah 44:28 (KJV)* [28] *That saith of Cyrus, He is my shepherd, and shall perform all my pleasure: even saying to Jerusalem, thou shalt be built; and to the temple, thy foundation shall be laid.*"I have always said that the word of prophecy is layered to be interpreted in divisions of the time it is to apply. President Trump's place in biblical history can be found in the numerology of biblical mathematics as king of the gentile nation that will be judged as the return of modern Babylon, #45. He is the return of the last parallel of the gentile king to fulfill the same number of the kings of Israel,45. The mystery of his reign in this end times is another revelation hidden that takes on a spiritual meaning in this time of grace. Therefore, all things now must be related from a spiritual perspective since we now worship God in spirit and in truth. The Holy Spirit in man 24/7 will reveal the next layer to this end time mystery to repeat history.

Since I do not depend on dreams or visions by having a direct revelation relationship with the Holy Spirit as Enoch experienced, verified by biblical scripture, I have had to wait for more revelations about his reign in this present time in history. His spirit's return will represent the end of the reign of the gentiles as the church of Christ that will be taken out at the last **trump**. By being a non-political version as the former king Cyrus when he was put in office as the **"King of the Gentile nation, America; the Modern Babylon,"** the nation raised up to be the protector of Israel. When he declared to Israel that Jerusalem is their capital openly, that was their sign the Orthodox Jews was looking for. This to them was their sign to the Jewish historians, who are the descendants of the **Pharisees** and **Sadducees** that crucified Jesus; to them, he is the modern-day Cyrus. To the gentiles, he will represent a form of a pre-antichrist spirit to galvanize and captivate this nation for its final judgement. They have been waiting for this endorsement in preparation to rebuild the third temple in these last days.

America and Israel are connected spiritually as being the revived Mystery spiritual Babylon. Now here come the connection of the Cyrus decree in the prophecy of the Old Testament to President Trump. *Ezra 5:13 "(KJV)* [13] *But in the first year of "<u>Cyrus the king of Babylon</u>"* (Now he will be the mystery, Cyrus.) **the same king Cyrus made a decree to build this house of God."** The background history for the reign of king Cyrus ... *Ezra 1:7-8 (KJV)* [7] *Also Cyrus the king brought forth the vessels of the house of the LORD, which Nebuchadnezzar had brought forth out of Jerusalem, and had put them in the house of his gods;* "(This is the spiritual interpretation; America will use her wealth to aid Israel not only in their restoration as a nation, but provide the means to help them in this endeavor to rebuild a third temple in these last days). **treasurer, and numbered them unto Sheshbazzar, the prince of Judah.** Those in charge of these Jewish artifacts will invite him to see their plan because he is the Gentile king that is identified with the Cyrus of old biblically by his decree as their sign to them as his approval. His household will be connected to their lineage by marriage. *Ezra 3:7 (KJV)* [7] *They gave money also unto the masons, and to the carpenters; and meat, and drink, and oil, unto them of Zidon, and to them of Tyre, to bring cedar trees from Lebanon to the sea of Joppa, according to the grant that they had of Cyrus king of Persia.* Our grants to Israel will help them gather the best craftsmen to undertake this endeavor.

President Trump, operating in the spirit of Cyrus of old in these last days as king of America; the Modern Babylon, will be their sign. *Ezra 5:13-14*

(KJV) ¹³ *But in the first year of <u>Cyrus the king of Babylon</u> (Donald Trump) the same king Cyrus made a decree to build this house of God.* ¹⁴ And the vessels also of gold and silver of the house of God, which Nebuchadnezzar took out of the temple that was in Jerusalem, and brought them into the temple of Babylon, those did Cyrus the king take out of the temple of Babylon, and they were delivered unto one, whose name was Sheshbazzar, whom he had made governor; These will be the administrators that will be in charge of overseeing the treasures that will go into this temple. *Ezra 5:17 (KJV)* ¹⁷ *Now therefore, if it seem good to the king, let there be search made in the king's treasure house, which is there at Babylon, whether it be so, that a decree was made of Cyrus the king to build this house of God at Jerusalem, and let the king send his pleasure to us concerning this matter.* This is where you will see Trump's son-in law, being a Jew, become the mediator during his time in office. *Ezra 6:3 "(KJV)* ³ *In the first year of Cyrus the king the same Cyrus the king made a decree concerning the house of God at Jerusalem,* (We as Gentiles will show our allegiance to them in this approval.) *Let the house be builded, the place where they offered sacrifices, and let the foundations thereof be strongly laid; the height thereof threescore cubits, and the breadth thereof threescore cubits;"*

This is another mystery I can reveal now. God had the Arab descendants to build on that site the **Temple Mount** we see today to prevent this abominable attempt. When they proceed to build this modern-day temple, this act will become an abomination to God for attempting to crucify Jesus a fresh. This along with David's curse that limit their numbers will cause a great majority of Israel to be destroyed during the tribulation. These are the seeds of the Pharisees and Sadducees that crucified him as the messiah. They are attempting to restore the veil in this act. These same seeds are being awakened in this nation that is causing a return of racial divide as sins of this nation, operating under a sodomy curse decreed by former president Obama. Every president in office will have to give an account of his term in office in the judgment because God put them there to serve his purposes until the end of the gentile's time continuum of this dispensations of truth, comes to an end. *Isaiah 44:26-28 (KJV)* ²⁶ **That confirmeth the word of his servant, and performeth the counsel of his messengers; that saith to Jerusalem, Thou shalt be inhabited; and to the cities of Judah, Ye shall be built, and I will raise up the decayed places thereof:** ²⁷ **That saith to the deep, Be dry, and I will dry up thy rivers:**

[28] ***That saith of Cyrus, He is my shepherd***, (God will repeat history as the spirit of Cyrus returns as the last non-political leader as king of the free gentile nation in President Trump. When God blinds a nation, a spirit of delusion will be sent out to take over all that chose to be willingly ignorant to think that they can change what God has set in motion to happen on his timeline. Their action in the sight the righteous, shows what spirit possesses them; because they chose to run the course of sin, their blindness will lead them into the hand of their enemies that will be used to destroy them.) ***and shall perform all my pleasure: even saying to Jerusalem, Thou shalt be built; and to the temple***, ***thy foundation shall be laid***. This is a prophecy of Israel's future restoration. This underlined statement will be the point of deception to the evangelical patriot Christians and the Jews. His actions, as king of the free world, America) ***and shall perform all my pleasure: even saying to Jerusalem, thou shalt be built; and to the temple, thy foundation shall be laid.***"The historical side of his reign is God's sovereign will, explained in this chapter as to his place in prophecy being fulfilled when Jesus returns. His spirit will overtake the evangelical patriots and rule them as their Sheppard.

Isaiah 46:9-12 (KJV) [9] **Remember the former things of old: for I am God, and there is none else; I am God, and there is none like me,** [10] **Declaring the end from the beginning, and from ancient times the things that are not yet done, saying, My counsel shall stand, and I will do all my pleasure:** [11] **Calling a ravenous bird from the east, the man that executeth my counsel from a far country: yea, I have spoken it, I will also bring it to pass; I have purposed it, I will also do it.** [12] *Hearken unto me, ye stouthearted, that are far from righteousness:* This is the mystery that will be a surprise to those that do not see this in the vision of our times prophetically. All this will be done in a short period of time during #46 reign; set in motion by #44 & #45. Our state of apostasy will cause many deceived Christians to miss this revelation. God cannot ignore the vanities of this generation as a nation which has **legalized sodomy** under Obama's time to reign. He would have to apologize to Sodom and Gomorrah for destroying them without notice if we were to escape. *In Isaiah "46:10 (KJV)* [10] *Declaring the end from the beginning, and from ancient times the things that are not yet done, saying, my counsel shall stand, and I will do all my pleasure:"* Donald Trump is the spiritual version of Cyrus whose reign will open with a mystery as a sign of how he was put into office by

God. His followers represent the return of the Barabbas patriot spirit in Christian evangelical supporters. He will be used to bring out all the evils in the world as these mysteries begin to unfold that will confound all the world by his actions as led by God. His spirit will be in the form of the pre-antichrist to captivate this nation for their final judgement. When the truth is revealed as a result of his action ... *Isaiah 45:16–17 "(KJV)* [16] *They shall be ashamed, and also confounded, all of them: they shall go to confusion together that are makers of idols.* [17] <u>*But Israel shall be saved in the LORD with an everlasting salvation:*</u>"Most of his supporters are beginning to see what they have done, yet their delusional state is of such, they can't speak against his actions because of political party loyalty is more important than what's good for the preservation of the state of our democracy. This will be the time when God will prepare the world for the great harvest revival. Satan has justified this by bringing us to this state of division levels, where you see every evil performed in this divided state makes us ripe for our enemy to come and take us as his spoils. God will open his people; the Jews eyes a nation, and they will return to him.) *ye shall not be ashamed nor confounded world without end."*Now what happens in between these times in the above verses is the mystery that will lead up to the end of Donald Trump's reign as a nonpolitical leader. Remember, we are a Christian nation under a curse for legalizing sodomy. That is the mystery revelation I was led to write about in unveiling the book titled; **America, Judgement of the Republic for which it Stands"** (One Nation Under God). This is all I can reveal about this mystery currently. It's evident of that 98 percent, God is going to catch many in his break for following the wrong vision as to think we are going to be forgiven as a nation and return to our old ways. That is when you heard President Trump say in the oval office ... **"This is the calm before the storm."** That word was prophetic.

That was a message to God's elects to confirm this mystery. God is allowing some of these recognized modern-day prophets connected to the **Laodicean** church spirit under the 501c-3 curse to operate in error by false visions of literal observation with no discernment of the signs of the times and miss this mystery spiritual revelations that is connected to his reign in our time, manifested in Donald Trump. In chapter forty-seven we, the Modern Babylon will begin to be judged under his reign. In these last days, President Trump as the spiritual Cyrus *Isaiah 47:10 (KJV)* [10] *For thou hast trusted in thy wickedness: thou hast said, none seeth me.* (His early character will be manifested in arrogance; his heart will be hardened as he is confounded in his pride by not being re-elected.) *Thy wisdom and thy knowledge, it hath perverted thee; and thou hast said in thine heart, I am, and none else beside me.* (This is the action you see him demonstrate as the result of the election). *Revelation 18:7 (KJV)* [7] *How much she hath glorified herself, and lived deliciously, so much torment and sorrow give her: for she saith in her heart, I sit a queen, and am no widow, and shall see no sorrow."* Trump, in his narcissistic pride will attempt to defy God, lead this nation into attempting to defy the will of God as to take this nation under a curse back from God. This is what will bring this nation to the point of civil war when he sees he has failed. The return of the Barabbas patriot spirit in Christians captivated in these false visions will utter this term, **"We will take back America and make it great again," or else there will be a national blood bath."** This will be the self-fulfilling prophecy as a result of this last election. Watch the spirit of pride as it comes to a head before we fall. *Proverbs 16:18 "(KJV)* [18] *Pride goeth before destruction, and an haughty spirit before a fall."* **Isaiah 5:14 (ASV)** [14] **Therefore, Sheol** (hell) **hath enlarged its desire, and opened its mouth without measure; and their glory, and their multitude, and their pomp, and he that rejoiceth among them, descend** *into it.* **Isaiah 49:3 "(KJV)** [3] **And said unto me, thou art my servant, O Israel, in whom I will be glorified."**

Israel will come out of this in glory as we go down in defeat. All eyes will be on Israel in the end after we as a nation is destroyed after serving God's purpose as Gentiles. He will return to His people to preserve them till the end. *Isaiah 49:5-6 (KJV)* [5] *And now, saith the LORD that formed me from the womb to be his servant, to bring Jacob again to him,* (This is the mystery Cyrus spirit in this time that will bring Israel also into judgment by his action that will lead them to attempt to rebuild a third temple.) *though Israel be not gathered, (That's during the tribulation.) yet shall I be glorious in the eyes of the LORD, and my God shall be my strength.* [6] *And he said, it is a light thing that thou shouldest be my servant to raise up the tribes of Jacob, and to restore the preserved of Israel: I will also give thee for a light to the Gentiles, that thou mayest be my salvation unto the end of the earth."*

One of the signs of our obvious delusions as evangelicals, we have lost our ability to discern good from evil by standing up in support of his obvious lies. Although some of his statements will come true, it is evident we need to get on our knees and pray for God's people during this transition when he has served his purpose in his term. God is not going to let this ultra-liberal administration carry out their agenda. Trump's actions will awaken the Gentile church to a great revival of the spiritual dry bone in Ezekiel Thirty-seven when they see they have been deceived. God will use Trump to show the evangelical's how them, they are more patriotic to country, than God. They that follow him will ignore the evils manifested through him that will cause more suffering. Remember, all liars will have their part in the lake of fire. Pray for him, he has a soul that needs to be saved. AMEN (updated 02/2021)

THE CONFOUNDING
WORD OF PROPHECY

Background scripture:

Isaiah 55:7-10 (KJV) [7] *Let the wicked forsake his way, and the unrighteous man his thoughts: and let him return unto the LORD, and he will have mercy upon him; and to our God, for he will abundantly pardon.* [8] *For my thoughts are not your thoughts, neither are your ways my ways, saith the LORD.* [9] *For as the heavens are higher than the earth, so are my ways higher than your ways, and my thoughts than your thoughts.*

Recently, I was reminded that I alluded to president # 45 would be the last president. What I see that has always been what cause many like me to be rejected is in that 98 percent of the confessing church that does not know what spirit they are of by lack of spiritual insight, result to their outside carnal influences. When I published my last two books depicting the Obama, Trump administrations as presidents #44 & #45, I knew at the time what I was disclosing, many would not catch the vision. Now there's no #46 in biblical history. To elaborate to a greater spiritual degree of understanding, there are those that said that Obama would return. Legally, that cannot happen because he has served his two terms, he would have to be in another capacity. First, let's deal with the # 44 Obama, brought the curse of Sodomy on his watch and legalized it. That curse as a once declared Christian nation cannot be reversed. Therefore, historically, he has served his purpose God preordained for his time to serve as king of the free world.

Now comes #45 Trump, His time in office will be to attempt to change from a none-political view, the norm. His actions will confound the political structure at a time in our history to speed up our end as a nation. He will become their right leader at the wrong time in history. He will attract the evangelical church world by promoting what they have been waiting to hear a leader in the office of the president say. By being blind to the sodomy curse, they will attempt to change what they have allowed to become our judgment of doom. This is what the church fails to see.

1. Where was the voice of the church when prayer was taken out of schools.

2. Where were they when the ten commandments were removed from the halls of justice.

3. Where were they when abortions were permitted to become legal by the Supreme Court.

This is the blindness under the 501C-3 Government charter. Now by their actions, God is showing them their state by sending the resurrection spirit of King Cyrus who was a non-political leader in Babylon of old when Israel went into captivity and lost their nation. His is a Saul as a people pleaser and Nebuchadnezzar when it comes to his level of pride. Russia, China and all the middle eastern nations will bring our destruction as a nation as The Roman's did to destroy all places of worship as did the Jewish temple. Although it looked like he would serve out two terms as others, he was put there to show the evangelical church world their state of delusion. He had the right intensions but at the wrong time in history. What the church failed to do to prevent this judgment was already set in place by their passive inaction.

Why did God cut his time off as to only serve one term? His purpose had been served during that first four years. God is confounding all the world by unpredicted sudden changes. Only those with His mind will know these things and they are the few. This is what the church failed to see as their state; their traditions have reached the point of not knowing the biblical history that is going to befall them by being in a divided state of spiritual blindness. It has cause chaos in the Republican party to the point of damage control for this president. They will be blind to the reality of what we have as a confessing Christian nation, let the government we were to oversee, put us into bondage in our divided state, under a 501c-3 government charter. That's the mark on the buildings when we as a body, went back to the natural temples, that gave them the power to close them. We as a Christian nation, has entered a state of delusion. That state of blindness will be what caused us to be ignorant of what we have already let the enemy of our soul do.

Now let's explain president #46. Obama #44 brought the curse on his watch. The Biden administration will become the delayed continuance of Obama's spirit to further impose these ultra-liberal changes against the laws of nature and immorality by endorsing the release of the LGBT to give them legal standing. That will embolden our enemies to begin their assault on this nation as they take a stand against this type of immoral behavior now endorsed as legal in a so-called Christian nation. Now that's Obama's spirit returned to complete this evil that will bring the judgment of Sodom on us as a nation that cannot be reversed once it has been legalized. Therefore, it will end on their return that will provoke God's anger to release his wrath on this nation. *Jeremiah 25:6 (KJV)* [6] *And go not after other gods to serve them, and to worship them, and provoke me not to anger with the works of your hands; and I will do you no hurt.* Now that same crowd is trying to bring back Trump #45, His spirit is also still ruling a sector of influence in the government. I see now why many of us have miss this revelation because these were only meant to be known at the end so God can catch many in his break. Get ready for the parable of the marriage supper of the lamb. God is giving us all a chance to examine ourselves; the choices you make now will determine where you will spend eternity. (Updated for released 1/2021)

A WORD FOR OUR TIMES

Many of you will not hear of me in the church world circuit because of my calling as a messenger to those that have been given ears to hear. I have been prepared all these years to be an end time harvest messenger. As of 2011, I have written five books. My latest two releases titled; **"Everybody Talking About Heaven Ain't Going There"**

And **"Life is a Terrible thing to Waste."** They are to remind us of what we all have fail to see as confessing Christians, what the Holy Spirit has revealed in the fullness of these two books. Spiritually, if you think we have seen the worst of things to come, you have chosen to be willingly ignorant of the signs of our times. This is the last generation of confessing Christians that the real prophetic vision of this third and final layer, must be told to the church that will not escape tribulation. Our divisions are the reason there must be a tribulation. *Acts 14:22 "(KJV)* [22] *Confirming the souls of the disciples, and exhorting them to continue in the faith, and that we must through much tribulation enter into the kingdom of God."* This is what I see that many are not prepared to endure. I have set grievously in prayer and meditation as Jesus let me feel a little of what he had to suffer in pain and sorrow as he saw the people turn in rejection of His message. Like the Pharisees and Sadducees, they continue to favor their own traditional teachings, brought down on the level of man's interpretation.

My heart was too heavy to do any writing after that experience that seem to duplicate what we have become as a New Testament church. I have mentioned in time past, there are going to be many Judases revealed as being offended with those who will become doers of the word. This is the time you will see the reality of ... *Matthew 10:36 "(KJV)* [36] *And a man's foes shall be they of his own household."* God reminded me of how deep-rooted hatred can be manifested in blood lines sibling to the point of murdering your own blood as in Cain and Abel; that was in the beginning. We as a nation, are being invaded with murdering demons. *Mark 13:13 "(KJV)* [13] *And ye shall be hated of all men for my name's sake: but he that shall endure unto the end, the same shall be saved."* The devil hates his own because they are in the image of God and will use them to kill all that have been given over to him. We, in America, have lived a privilege that accords us conveniences that kings did not have in time past. We are like none other; we can choose our idols, pursue them and once we obtain them, bow down to them in worship.

Many confessing Christians are in denial as to idol worship until they are forced to give them up, there-in is revealed where your heart is. The blessing of living in this nation has given us a false sense of reality and security. These sudden changes are what's activating these demons of suicide in those who can't face reality. Now Satan is using them to commit mass murder. The brute beast nature of the man in sin will show the hidden evils in his heart of a spirit he or she knows not is with-in until it manifests. *Matthew 13:13-15 "(KJV)* [13]*Therefore speak I to them in parables: because they seeing see not; and hearing they hear not, neither do they understand.* [14] *And in them is fulfilled the prophecy of Esaias, which saith, by hearing ye shall hear, and shall not understand; and seeing ye shall see, and shall not perceive:* [15] *For this people's heart is waxed gross, and their ears are dull of hearing, and their eyes they have closed; lest at any time they should see with their eyes, and hear with their ears, and should understand with their heart, and should be converted, and I should heal them.* (When Jesus was speaking these words, they were to His own people who knew the law from memory as being taught each day in the Synagogues. They had fallen to this state ... *2 Timothy 3:7 (KJV)* [7] *Ever learning, and never able to come to the knowledge of the truth."* When you do not act on the word you know, you enter a form of ritualistic routines that lead you to being religious without convictions.

It is in this fall away, many generational curse sins are revived that can kill, hurt and maim; are hidden with-in. They are release under duress of extreme anger that cause crimes of passion. I once asked why I encountered hidden anger when telling the truth; why we are seen as extreme when we stand in our convictions of truth. His reply, *"They are holding on to something in the world they are attached too, when my spirit exposes it, this is what you see."* These are the crimes we commit when we allow ourselves to be provoked to lose our sense of compassion in a moment of uncontrolled anger. This is what we need to be delivered from that Jesus died to take that power over you back from the devil. There are many confessing Christians' bound in spiritual prisons as victims of being led by blind guides whose deliverance was not complete as not hearing the full council of the truth with a demonstration of the power of the Holy Spirit. Many faith teachers are not declaring the gospel in full but in part; therefore, the principals are true but does not fully prepare those who support these ministries, are not getting the whole council of the truth. These are the ones that teach the doctrine, to be Godly is to gain wealth.

Many with these anointings are operating in parts of this truth but not in full. They have a manifestation from the Holy Spirit but what happens; we fail to continue in the truth. Having over thirty years of exposure as a confessing Christian is where I now draw my conclusions and observations by once living in error of truth; having been a victim of some of these evils from within me that God himself without man delivered me from for my calling. This brought me to a mature spiritual reality of things we know not about the spirit world. What I found within myself was hidden pride, and I did not even know it.

That's why I speak from a transparent standpoint of my own personal deliverance experiences in my life to be able to be used to help others see why we must first be delivered from ourselves to conversion. I found by these experiences, you will have to be willing to be misunderstood, humiliated, lied on, borated and buffeted for your faults and not hold any of this in your heart against the people you are trying to help … who may be doing this to you. It is easy to say what the word said but trials will determine the depth of your conviction. You will act on what comes out of your heart. A few years ago, I was asked why I do not take the sacrament as those in the traditional church do. My answer: This is not a ritual to me, when I came into the knowledge of who Christ is in me, I learned I was a work in progress. I found out through the teaching of the Holy Spirit, if you are born from above, you are committed to him unto death never to turn back. Taking the sacrament under these traditional teachings can result in the transference of spirits that's why we should not let anyone lay hands upon you that is not in the right spirit open you up for what Paul said about these things that will bring afflictions such as sickness, diseases and premature death by partaken of this fear, doubt and unbelief.

This lack of knowledge will cause your premature destruction. *1 Corinthians 11:24-32 (KJV)* [24] *And when he had given thanks, he brake it, and said, Take, eat: this is my body, which is broken for you: this do in remembrance of me.* (The last time I took the sacrament, I knew what I was doing. Therefore, I made up my mind to be faithful until death.) [25] *After the same manner also he took the cup, when he had supped, saying, this cup is the new testament in my blood: this do ye, as oft as ye drink it, in remembrance of me.* [26] *For as often as ye eat this bread, and drink this cup, ye do shew the Lord's death till he come.* (In my convictions, I want to be available to Him until death. When you take this and mix with the world, Satan is justified in attacking you by defiling the holiness of God in you. *1 Thessalonians 4:7 "(KJV)* [7] *For God hath not called us unto uncleanness, but unto holiness." (KJV)* [27] *Wherefore whosoever shall eat this bread, and drink this cup of the Lord, unworthily, shall be guilty of the body and blood of the Lord.* [28] *But let a man examine himself, and so let him eat of that bread, and drink of that cup.*

When Jesus gave the sacrament to His disciples and wash their feet, they all died at the hands of well-meaning antichrist fellow brethren to keep that saccate oath, sealed in His blood by this act. Not one of the eleven chosen, died with any of these diseases Christ delivered them from. It will be your love for Him that will give him this glory.) [29] *For he that eateth and drinketh unworthily, eateth and drinketh damnation to himself, not discerning the Lord's body.* (Now that I know what I'm doing, I don't want him to find me in unbelief, fear and doubt after partaking of this blood covenant.) [30] *For this cause many are weak and sickly among you, and many sleep.* (Satan gets to do this by lack of knowledge.) [31] *For if we would judge ourselves, we should not be judged.* (When we humble ourselves to do things His way, we will walk by faith.) [32] **But when we are judged, we are chastened of the Lord, that we should not be condemned with the world."** All those the lord loves as His sons and daughters will be corrected through the Holy

Spirit. It will be up to those that hear Him speaking through His elect to make your calling and election sure at that time.

I have said these things before and just to remind you again in God's love. I am speaking at the liberty of the Holy Spirit in this appeal to all that might not be prepared spiritually before the real trouble comes. One thing that is a constant reminder to keep me on the straight and narrow is every time I tend to stray, I look up in my spirit and see Jesus hanging on that cross, looking straight in my eyes as to show just how much he loves me. That moment always keeps me broken and humbled to want to be more like him as unworthy and wretched some of us can be when we lose our first love; yet he still loves us. Let us be honest, we are amid all these temptations and only your love for God keeps you from being led astray. That's why we are in a race to endure to the end. AMEN!

Now, on the National Front

Our nation is under judgment for her past sins against her citizens and to Israel. All these evils we as a people in a once Christian nation, are now being exposed on all levels in our society. This is our spiritual atomic mushroom cloud exposing all the evils of mankind at once. Satan has been given this time through this window of denominational divisions, by this absence of God's vision in the assemblies that name his name ... *Psalm 89:47 "(KJV)* [47] *Remember how short my time is: wherefore hast thou made all men in vain?* (It is that vanity of our natural state we give place to that is his window of opportunity.) *Revelation 12:12 (KJV)* [12] *Therefore rejoice, ye heavens, and ye that dwell in them. Woe to the inhabiters of the earth and of the sea! For the devil is come down unto you, having great wrath, because he knoweth that <u>he hath but a short time.</u>"*

We are that nation given this blessing to be the protector of Israel; therefore, having now violated that covenant, this is what we must face? The bible identify man created in God's image as tribes, kindreds and tongues; that' what they would be referred too after the split at the Tower of Babel. Therefore, if you are seeing yourself as a confessing Christian through eyes of racial superiority or minorities, you are already in the wrong spirit. We as his creations, all have an equal opportunity to come as you are. We all were sinners when we were called. The situation in this country is going to get worse, as social injustices cause riots that will demonstrate these inhumanities against each other. These evils that have contributed to this, are the enmities we hold against each other; unfortunately, some of us are confessing evangelical Christians.

Our sins of omission as a nation

The opioid epidemic is the curse for legalizing mind-altering drugs in a mentally unstable society. Satan is coming to take his spoils through this pharmacology door and using this pandemic to show us the degree of our fears. We have let these blessings overtake us to the point, they have become our gods. **John 10:10 (ASV)** [10] **The thief cometh not, but that he may steal, and kill, and destroy: I came that they may have life and may have it abundantly.** This is our heritage we have been privileged to live, had we continued to keep Israel safe from her enemies.

The kind of society we live in has become a breeding ground for every foul spirit for legalizing homosexuality. The corruption in government is going to be so obvious along party lines, and we as a people are going to be divided along with them; therefore, speeding up our internal judgments and collapse. *Jeremiah 50:32 "(KJV)* [32] *And the most proud shall stumble and fall, and none shall raise him up: and I will kindle a fire in his cities, and it shall devour all round about him."* These fires you see burning in California and other places are evil strong hold of Satan' Sodomy spirits. All these natural disasters will happen first on a large scale in these strongholds. Because of the failure of the church to keep the standards of God's order of holiness in obedience from a biblical perspective, we are in a fight for gender supremacy. Jezebel' spirit has returned as exposed through the media, with a vengeance. *Isaiah 3:12 "(KJV)* [12] *As for my people, children are their oppressors, and women rule over them. O my people, they which lead thee cause thee to err, and destroy the way of thy paths."* Our parental hypocrisy has our children rising in rebellion. Our sins against the abuse of women and people of color by unequal justice and socially, degrading fellow humans in the image of God by advantage, is returning upon us.

On tax cuts

The nation is under a spirit of delusion. We are already bankrupt. God is allowing the economy to project all these false signs to catch us in his break overnight. This tax cut to the wealthy, took out the middle class. We all will suffer horribly in this nation if we do not repent. We will face our worst fear and see the full scope of man's inhumanity against himself. Fear of circumstances beyond our control will stress many to lose their minds and become zombie like cannibals when this reality becomes a fact, and all food is gone. *Micah 3:3 "(KJV)* [3] *Who also eat the flesh of my people and flay their skin from off them; and they break their bones, and chop them in pieces, as for the pot, and as flesh within the caldron."* I know this may be an extremely hard saying, but my dear beloved, **we are out of time.** They mocked Noah for one hundred and twenty years for telling them it was going to rain. I am no stranger to mocking either for revealing these horrible truths to a nation that has never been invaded by a foreign country. If they are going to be eating the flesh of God's people, we must be in tribulation.

The circumstances that will cause this are explained in my latest book; **"Biblical Prophetical Chronicles of the Last Generation (Revelation, the final layer revealed")** available on Amazon. This is what will happen to the children of disobedience who will suffer the **first thunder.** When we are attacked the from East and West coast by our enemies, they are coming to take the spoils after the crash. *Revelation 18:19-24 "(KJV)* [19] *And they cast dust on their heads, and cried, weeping and wailing, saying, Alas, alas, that great city, wherein were made rich all that had ships in the sea by reason of her costliness! for in one hour is she made desolate.* (America, the Modern Babylon, will repeat the history of Babylon of old. We have the curse of Sodom and Gomorrah on this nation as decreed under President Obama time to rule. Our ultimate end will be that of Sodom and Gomorrah). [20] *Rejoice over her, thou heaven, and ye holy apostles and prophets; for God hath avenged you on her.* [21] *And a mighty angel took up a stone like a great millstone, and cast it into the sea, saying, thus with violence shall that great city Babylon be thrown down, and shall be found no more at all.* The asteroid fragment on its way has been detected by scientists.

It is on a collision course to create a situation like that scene in the movie **"Deep Impact"** none of you will know about it until it's too late. It will split this country in half as the Sodomy curse.) [Vs. 23] *And the light of a candle shall shine no more at all in thee; and the voice of the bridegroom and of the bride shall be heard no more at all in thee:* (This will happen after the church is raptured out of her.) ... **for thy merchants were the great men of the earth;** When our CIA started to police the world's activity by deceiving our allies until we were exposed as to what we were doing, God could no longer protect us in our evil state.*)* [24] *And in her was found the blood of prophets, and of saints, and of all that were slain upon the earth."* We, as a nation, killed Dr. Martin Luther King who brought the attention of our racial injustices. Just like the Babylon of old did not exist after her fall any more by name; neither will we after the tribulation. There will be nowhere to run or hide outside those who are under divine protection ... *Isaiah 26:20 "(NKJV)* [20] *Come, my people, enter your chambers, And shut your doors behind you; Hide yourself, as it were, for a little moment, Until the indignation is past."* They are the ones to chosen to repopulate the millennium.

Because of false teaching, 98 percent will reject the call among the confessing church-world just as the Jews rejected Jesus as their Messiah; the church will repeat history by not knowing his voice of warning through his messengers. Many will be replaced by their children as God have mercy on them for the hypocrisy of their parents, along with those in the highways and by-ways known as the <u>homeless</u> and <u>scum of the earth the</u>, the <u>pimps</u>, <u>prostitutes</u>, <u>dope addicts</u> and <u>extortioners</u>. God will have mercy on them as they see him as their only hope and repent and save themselves as he did the Paneth thief. This is the mystery taking place at the marriage supper of the lamb. Just as we (the gentiles) replaced the Jews when they rejected their Messiah whom they got to literally see, once again, the church will reject his unknown messengers by not knowing his voice in the call to repent. This is God's mercy to the lost by the churches failure to be a beacon of light and deliverance. **Luke 14:21 "(NASB77)** [21] **"And the slave came back and reported this to his master. Then the head of the household became angry and said to his slave, 'Go out at once into the streets and lanes of the city and bring in here the poor and crippled and blind and lame.'** That's why it is evident that hell is being enlarged during these natural disasters. *Isaiah 5:14 (KJV)* [14]*Therefore, hell hath enlarged herself and opened her mouth without measure: and their glory, and their multitude, and their pomp, and he that rejoiceth, shall descend into it.*

Dearly beloved, what the Holy Spirit has revealed to me by way of these media revelations are the bassist of all my writings to this end-time generation as an unknown scribe to pin down this vision to those with eyes to see and ears to hear. Save yourself from what is inevitably on the horizon any day now. Therefore, all these sayings will be tested by the spirit of prophecy in the days ahead. We are amid a mass religious confusion as to who are the real prophets and messengers of God. My prayer in faith is that none of you that got to read this vision, be lost. Whether you believe it or not, we are approaching **the end of the gentile age.** Many are unaware of the times as caught up in religious separatist movements as pastors build their legacy family kingdoms through a tithe system that overtook the Jews by the wealth it produced in the name of God at the expense your own willing ignorance not to search behind them for the truth that applies under grace. The whole council of this short chronicle is graphically explained in detail in the two books written under the inspiration of the Holy Spirit to verify what we all need to know. Seek the Lord while He may be found. Since 2011 God has kept me out of the limelight of the media by self-publishing these chronicles at various stages in these end times. AMEN (5/2019)

TRIBES, TONGUES
AND KINDREDS

Jeremiah 33:3 (NKJV) ³ 'Call to Me, and I will answer you, and show you great and mighty things, which you do not know.' Ephesians 3:5 (NKJV) ⁵ which in other ages was not made known to the sons of men, as it has now been revealed by the Spirit to His holy apostles and prophets: When God spoke those words to me in 2004, I had no idea of what I would experience when it comes to spiritual things unknown to man. Some of which are just between him and I. All I know, out of this experience, I see who and what I am in his sight as just what he made me to be for his use, a vessel, that's all. I have seen through my mind being illuminated with his thoughts, the end of the destiny of mankind in the coming tribulation of the Earth's second phase as returning to its original origin. If I am to obtain the privilege to live with him for eternity, I must die to this world.

Romans 8:29 (NKJV) ²⁹ For whom He foreknew, He also predestined to be conformed to the image of His Son, that He might be <u>the firstborn among many brethren</u>. God used two women to get me to this place. One was to let me experience rejection that was going to be the course of my life; the other, what is to win a soul who was used to perfect me in him within your own household and see her reap the benefit of eternal life. Truly, truly, God ways I found are pass finding out. Just do what he said without question is the key to entering the throne room of knowledge.

If you do not stop on that straight and narrow road, all your mistakes and sins will be covered under grace and mercy by the blood, treated as a son. All the early saints died at the hands of well-meaning blind brethren who were not born from above, that is why Jesus forgave them for not knowing the enemy of their soul and still sacrificed himself for them. When you become one with him, you will do the same for others. **John 15:13 (NKJV)** [13] **Greater love has no one than this, than to lay down one's life for his friends.** AMEN

Another Enoch moment

The following revelation is for those with ears to hear. When God called me, he later told me that my seed was of Moses linage of from his <u>first born of his two sons</u> of his Ethiopian wife when he was banished in the wilderness. I am the <u>first born</u> from that linage in my families dispensational timeline, now in my wilderness, waiting to be sent to preach the everlasting gospel to this last generation to replace that 98 percent of those who have rejected the first call to repentance from our state of apostasy as this new thing as stated in … **Isaiah 43:19 (NKJV)** [19] **Behold, I will do a new thing, now it shall spring forth; Shall you not know it? I will even make a road in the wilderness and rivers in the desert.** All this is still beyond me from the day I heard it.

The one language of the world at that time before the flood, was the language Adam Spoke. After the flood, all would descend from the children of Noah. Here we will see the only selected seed to be of God's DNA would be Shem, the **first born** will began the bloodline of the new spiritual world order to transfer God's chosen seeds through-out times, ages and dispensations. Now to get an understanding, Lets go to … **Genesis 11:1-9 (NKJV)** [1] **Now the <u>whole earth</u> had one language and <u>one speech</u>.** [2] *And it came to pass, as they journeyed from the east, that they found a plain in the land of Shinar, and they dwelt there.* [3] **Then they said to one another, "Come, let us make bricks and bake them thoroughly." They had brick for stone, and they had asphalt for mortar.** [4] **And they said, "Come, let us build ourselves a city, and a tower whose top is in the heavens; let us make a name for ourselves,** (Now at this point, I want you to see where man's origin will always be the point of his beginning to establish his background of origin.) **lest we be scattered abroad over the face of the whole earth."** [5] *But the* **LORD came down to see the city** and the tower which the sons of men had built. ⁶ And the LORD said, "Indeed the people are one and they all have one language, and this is what they begin to do; now nothing that they propose to do will be withheld from them. ⁷ Come, let Us go down and there confuse their language, that they may not understand one another's speech." (This is where we will encounter a language barrier among the tribes and nations that will come out this split.) ⁸ So the LORD scattered them abroad from there over the face of all the earth, and they ceased building the city. ⁹ *Therefore its name is called Babel, because there the* LORD confused the language of all the earth; and from there the <u>LORD scattered them abroad over the face of all the earth.</u> Notice! that covered all the known land masses that appeared after the flood. This is what will become the nations of these tribes that came out of Babylon of old that will now speak different languages.

God selects his people from a tribe of the fall of Babylon of old

Genesis 11:10-26 (NKJV) ¹⁰ **This is the genealogy of Shem: Shem was one hundred years old, and begot Arphaxad two years after the flood.** ¹¹ **After he begot Arphaxad, Shem lived five hundred years, and begot sons and daughters.** (Here I want you to see that selection as the **first born.** The rest of the genealogy will be given over to repopulate the world.)

¹² *Arphaxad lived thirty-five years, and begot Salah.*
¹⁴ **Salah lived thirty years, and begot Eber.**
¹⁶ **Eber lived thirty-four years, and begot Peleg.**
¹⁸ **Peleg lived thirty years, and begot Reu.**
²⁰ **Reu lived thirty-two years, and begot Serug.**
²² **Serug lived thirty years, and begot Nahor.**
²⁴ **Nahor lived twenty-nine years, and begot Terah.**
²⁶ **Now Terah lived seventy years, and begot Abram, Nahor, and Haran.**

From these three seeds, God will lay the foundation to select from them a tribe of people as a nation to rule the Earth. In this order we see the genealogy of God coming down to the selection of Abram (or as we know him as Abraham.) These people that Abraham would meet are from the tribes of the split that have now settled as nations in these regions of the world. Their differences in physical appearance will be the mixing of genes coupled with the geography of the area that will determine the intensity of their skin color. The farther they are from the Equator, the lighter their skin until after many generations, will evolve with no color and will differ with outside physical features. Our connection with God is that we will all be as Adam and Eve underneath the outer-skin shades. The seed of enemy of his soul will cause the geographics of the world as knowledge in these arears of people of no color to from a superiority complex.

The spirit of enmity released when Adam sin against God, will be what will cause a repeat of Cain and Abel, men conceived under this curse will begin to kill his own kind, not knowing who is in possession of his soul. Being a natural bruit beast, his conscious will be his only means of restraint in the choice of evils he will be forced to do being disconnected from his creator. He is now an instrument of the god of this natural world, controlled by an ET spirit being from another time dimension whose intent is to destroy all that represent the image of his creator who now has become his arch enemy in this natural world. These two seeds will be at war for the next six thousand years. God will intervene throughout time to prevent these fallen angel DNA from destroying his creation before he returns to redeem his selected seeds to live with him for eternity in what we know as the rapture.

All mankind will have tribulation periods in our lives is to bring us all to the reality of the God of this universe that we will all have to give an account of our life's origin in the judgment of these two seeds. Regardless of who or what you have become or gained in this world, if the enemy of your soul can get you to renounce the God that gave you his life before he requires your soul, you will spend it in eternity with Satan and his host of servants like him, cast out of heaven, your soul align to become his servant till your end. Therefore, with him, you will spend eternity in the lake of fire, heated with brimstones, seven times hotter than any known fire on Earth tormented forever. Your only hope to reverse this curse is to REPENT BEFORE YOUR DAY AND BE REDEEMED FROM THE ENEMY OF YOUR SOUL. LET US ALL EXAMINE OURSELVES WHILE THE BLOOD IS STILL RUNNING WARM IN OUR VEINS. AMEN (4/2021)

GET READY FOR MORE CATASTROPHIC NATIONAL EVENTS

Recent earthquakes in California, is a sign that state is about to have another major catastrophic event of epic proportions … *1 Thessalonians 5:3 "(NKJV)* **³ For when they say, «Peace and safety!» then sudden destruction comes upon them, as labor pains upon a pregnant woman. And they shall not escape."** This is a sign given by Chuck Youngbrandt back in May of 2017 before he died. Now when I am given a word in part, I don't put dates on things that's on God's calendar; I just write it as a warning. We are living in a time where people have become scoffers because of the failure of the church to let the real prophets in to give the people the vision of the lord for our times.

California is a major stronghold of demonic spirits, with an open portal in Hollywood that is about to bring about its final judgments by fire. This is a sign of God centered anger. They are in for a major shaking Higher than a 10.5 magnitude quake. God always give his prophets and messengers a sign that will precede a major event of this magnitude that will leave portions of that state under water. This was our sign that the major one is on the way. Now as I said, I don't give dates because we are on God's timeline of events of this magnitude regarding all these newsworthy national and international events. *Matthew 13:15 "(NKJV)* **¹⁵ For the** *hearts of this people have grown dull. Their ears are hard of hearing, and their eyes they have closed, lest they should see with their eyes and hear with their ears, Lest they should understand with their hearts and turn, So that I should heal them."* That's the state of most of the confessing Christian church that 98 percent are not prepared to suffer without this word. The great delusion is apparent as we see how oblivious people are to the events of the times that are warnings of their impending destruction.

Those of us that God has tucked away to carry this last message of the everlasting gospel to the people that shall take the place of many confessing Christians at the final call to the marriage supper of the lamb are in for a great shock when they see they are the ones left behind. **Luke 14:16-24 "(NKJV) [16] Then He said to him, "A certain man gave a great supper and invited many, [17] and sent his servant at supper time to say to those who were invited, 'Come, for all things are now ready.' [18] But they all with one accord began to make excuses. The first said to him, 'I have bought a piece of ground, and I must go and see it. I ask you to have me excused.' [19] And another said, 'I have bought five yokes of oxen, and I am going to test them. I ask you to have me excused.' [20] Still another said, 'I have married a wife, and therefore I cannot come.' [21] So that servant came and reported these things to his master. Then the master of the house, being angry, said to his servant, <u>'Go out quickly into the streets and lanes of the city, and bring in here the poor and the maimed and the lame and the blind.'</u> [22] And the servant said, 'Master, it is done as you commanded, and still there is room.' [23] Then the master said to the servant, <u>'Go out into the highways and hedges, and compel them to come in, that my house may be filled.</u> [24] For I say to you that none of those men who were invited shall taste my supper.'** I hear these same excuses as history is repeated. At that time this was spoken, it was a parable because they didn't have ears to hear; it will be a prophecy fulfilled in these last days before the rapture. If you have some relatives in California, you might want to tell them to get ready for the big one because it's on the way. When I wrote about the asteroid that passed with-in two hundred thousand miles as a sign of the final one that will obliterate the western hemisphere to destroy America as God did Sodom and Gomorrah during their tribulation period.

This also is a sign that, that region of the guff will be completely under water along with the lower half of Florida also when all these natural disasters are complete. This final earthquake will leave a great portion of the California coastline under water. It is sad to see people are in this state of mind, until it hits their home. They are not concerned about all these signs. That's the peace and safety delusion that will catch many that are already marked in the spirit for hell as lukewarm Christians, being spit out of God's mouth at that time because of hidden fear, generated by the present pandemic that will be overtaken by these circumstances.

Major Prophets are dying off that have been for the most ignored. I have never claimed the office of a prophet; I'm just a messenger that interprets what the prophets have said to be revealed in our times. I don't even have dreams or vision about these things. In this area, I'm just a scribe. What God has given me to see is by direct revelation, leaves me no other hope for this world that's about to see the end of another time continuum. I know that all these revelations paint a dim view of our eminent future. I don't claim to be a prophet, but I know how they felt, carrying this type of message and being rejected. I too, like Jeremiah lament over this nation's eminent judgment. My dear brothers and sisters, I plead with you who get to read this, not to take it passively; the worst is yet to come. AMEN (Updated for release 9/2019)

Now on the national front

I am a conservative for the republic this country was founded on as **"One Nation Under God,"** in my observations, many are more patriotic to country than to God. That's the snare that has the church blind under the 501-c3 curse now under state control. I have always told people to wait for the fruit when it comes to leadership; however, if you are not in the right spirit, you also will be deceived by seducing spirits to go along with the world. That's what I see that happen to many evangelical confessing Christians, caught up in this patriotism of Country. God had to give them a president with a link to Old Testament history that will deceive a willingly blind church along with the Jews by giving them a false sign; in their blindness, will not see this false truth are calling bad fruit good and we both are about to become the worms of this rotten fruit they are presently eating.

This is that strong delusion that came in this great fall-away. The revival is already happening in the third world countries when it gets here, we will be as they; without nothing to look to but God. What I see that get many with good intentions caught up in the details of the times, they are caught up in the circumstances by only knowing in part and speaking in part. **1 Corinthians 13:9-10 "(NKJV)** *⁹ For we know in part and we prophesy in part.* **¹⁰ But when that which is perfect has come, then that which is in part will be done away."** (What I see is the whole picture, these people and administrations are just bits and pieces of the grand puzzle. This is what it's like without this vision. If you want true peace in times like these, this is where you must be in the spirit.) **John 14:27 "(NKJV)** ²⁷ **Peace I leave with you, my peace I give to you; not as the world gives do I give to you. Let not your heart be troubled, neither let it be afraid. 1 John 4:4 "(NKJV)** ⁴ **You are of God, little children, and have overcome them, because He who is in you is greater than he who is in the world. 2 Corinthians 11:14 (NKJV)** ¹⁴ **And no wonder! For Satan himself transforms himself into an angel of light."**

This is where most of the church-world is currently. These religious assemblies that produce these patriots, now in the name of religion, have facilitated the return of the Barabbas zeal, worshipping in a religious nation in his name only to think that they are going to **"take back America and make her great again,"** without knowing, this nation was cursed on the previous president's watch, Obama. Now can you see my beloved what it's like to be under a delusional spirit and not even know it. The Jews couldn't recognize their own Messiah, standing before them in the flesh; now, we can't recognize the voice of the God we say we serve when he speaks. May God have mercy on all that call upon his name. AMEN (Updated for Release 3/2020)

THE TWO PARALLELS OF THE GOSPEL; THE JEWS AND THE GENTILES

To the Jews … ***Deuteronomy 6:4 "(KJV)*** *⁴ **Hear, O Israel: The LORD our God is one LORD:*** (To the Gentiles …) **John 1:12 (KJV)** ¹² **But as many as received him, to them gave he power to become the sons of God, even to them that believe on his name:"** This session with the Holy Spirit, enlightened me to understand grace and mercy under this new covenant. The Jews were never required to be spiritual because the only thing the law would be given them to do is make them righteous in the sight of God that chose them as his own. Since they were going to be in a natural carnal environment, they were going to be judged by the keeping of these laws as a matter of self-government, answerable only to God. These laws would be given to Moses during the exodus as outline in the book of Deuteronomy & Leviticus.

They would govern the civil, ceremonial, and moral actions as his nation of chosen people. However, under the new covenant, it would be by revelation of who now is the new man in you that will abide with you forever by your willing free will. They, as Jews, will have three thousand years to come to know their God as through their ancestor Abraham in the historical accounts of all he will do to prove he is the one and only God. They were to administer the law with justice, mercy in righteousness as God directed them through his prophet to keep them in remembrance of their covenant with him.

Under the dispensation of law, God instituted the tithe system of self-support to keep the wealth among themselves as a nation. This system down through the years will cause them to become wealthy and rich as a nation and a people. Since they were carnal and not spiritual; this will prove to be a temptation that in the end, cause them to become ritualistic to the point of institution of their own tradition that will put them out of will with God. This delusion will continue for four hundred years before Jesus comes as their Messiah. They would be reminded time and time again by their prophets of the error of their ways; in the end, God would send their Messiah to correct them in the flesh as noted in the parable of the vineyard. **(Luke 20:13)** This will be their last chance to turn back to the God they left without ever knowing this had happen to them. This is where they were when Jesus came as their Messiah.

(Compare to KJV) Matthew 23:2-13 "(NLT2) [2] **"The teachers of religious law and the Pharisees are the official interpreters of the law of Moses.** [3] **So practice and obey whatever they tell you, but don't follow their example. For they don't practice what they teach.** [4] **They crush people with impossible religious demands and never lift a finger to ease the burden.** [5] **"Everything they do is for show. On their arms they wear extra wide prayer boxes with Scripture verses inside, and they wear robes with extra-long tassels.** (We see these stripes on the robes of those who are doctors in the religions world.) [6] *And they love to sit at the head table at banquets and in the seats of honor in the synagogues.* [7] *They love to receive respectful greetings as they walk in the marketplaces, and to be called 'Rabbi.'* [8] *"Don't let anyone call you 'Rabbi, (or reverend)'* (It is for this reason Jesus said, they will become your masters you look up to instead of Jesus.) *for you have only one teacher, and all of you are equal as brothers and sisters.* [9] *And don't address anyone here on earth as 'Father,' for only God in heaven is your spiritual Father.* [10] *And don't let anyone call you 'Teacher,' for you have only one teacher, the Messiah.* [11] *The greatest among you must be a servant.* [12] *But those who exalt themselves will be humbled, and those who humble themselves will be exalted.* [13] *"What sorrow awaits you teachers of religious law and you Pharisees. Hypocrites! For you shut the door of the Kingdom of Heaven in people's faces. You won't go in yourselves, and you don't let others enter either.* (This has reference to those who handle the word with deceitful motives as hirelings who work in the assemblies in the name of God for a fee.) **Matthew 23:15-39 (NLT2)** [15] **"What sorrow awaits you**

teachers of religious law and you Pharisees. Hypocrites! For you cross land and sea to make one convert, and then you turn that person into twice the child of hell you yourselves are! (Most assembly organization send out members to save souls that are not aware of the sins they are not yet converted in the truth, therefore, they are as …) ¹⁶ **Blind guides! What sorrow awaits you! For you say that it means nothing to swear 'by God's Temple,' but that it is binding to swear 'by the gold in the Temple.'** ¹⁷**Blind fools! Which is more important—the gold or the Temple that makes the gold sacred?** ¹⁸ *And you say that to swear 'by the altar' is not binding, but to swear 'by the gifts on the altar' is binding.* ¹⁹ **How blind! For which is more important—the gift on the altar or the altar that makes the gift sacred?** ²⁰ **When you swear 'by the altar,' you are swearing by it and by everything on it.** ²¹ **And when you swear 'by the Temple,' you are swearing by it and by God, who lives in it.** ²² **And when you swear 'by heaven,' you are swearing by the throne of God and by God, who sits on the throne.** ²³ *"What sorrow awaits you teachers of religious law and you Pharisees. Hypocrites*<u>. **For you are careful to tithe even the tiniest income**</u> **from your herb gardens, but you ignore the more important aspects of the law—justice, mercy, and faith.** <u>**You should tithe, yes,**</u> (This underlined was spoken under the law that will be no longer the requirements under grace and truth after his resurrection.) **but do not neglect the more important things.** ²⁴ **Blind guides! You strain your water so you won't accidentally swallow a gnat, but you swallow a camel!** ²⁵ **"What sorrow awaits you teachers of religious law and you Pharisees. Hypocrites! For you are so careful to clean the outside of the cup and the dish, but inside you are filthy—full of greed and self-indulgence!** (These are they that teach to be godly is to gain.) ²⁶ **You blind Pharisee! First wash the inside of the cup and the dish, and then the outside will become clean, too.** ²⁷ **"What sorrow awaits you teachers of religious law and you Pharisees. Hypocrites! For you are like whitewashed tombs—beautiful on the outside but filled on the inside with dead people's bones and all sorts of impurity.** ²⁸ **Outwardly you look like righteous people, but inwardly your hearts are filled with hypocrisy and lawlessness.** ²⁹ **"What sorrow awaits you teachers of religious law and you Pharisees. Hypocrites! For you build tombs for the prophets your ancestors killed, and you decorate the monuments of the godly people your ancestors destroyed.** (We kill the people that was sent to save us and speak well of them after they are gone, build monuments to their efforts.) ²⁰ **Then you say, 'If we had lived** in the days of our ancestors, we would never have joined them in killing the prophets.' ³¹ "But in saying that, you testify against yourselves that you are indeed the descendants of those who murdered the prophets. ³² Go ahead and finish what your ancestors started. ³³ Snakes! Sons of vipers! How will you escape the judgment of hell? ³⁴ "Therefore, I am sending you prophets and wise men and teachers of religious law. But you will kill some by crucifixion, and you will flog others with whips in your synagogues, chasing them from city to city. (He is telling them what they will do to him and those that follow his teachings after the resurrection.) ³⁵ As a result, you will be held responsible for the murder of all godly people of all time—from the murder of righteous Abel to the murder of Zechariah son of Barachiah, whom you killed in the Temple between the sanctuary and the altar. ³⁶ I tell you the truth, this judgment will fall on this very generation. ³⁷ "O Jerusalem, Jerusalem, <u>the city that kills the prophets and stones God's messengers!</u> How often I have wanted to gather your children together as a hen protects her chicks beneath her wings, <u>but you wouldn't let me</u>. ³⁸ *And now, look, your house is abandoned and desolate.* (This is going to be their state after they reject him. The church will repeat history in division in the last days by not knowing the voice of God when they are warned.) ³⁹ *For I tell you this, you will never see me again until you say, 'Blessings on the one who comes in the name of the* LORD!'" (They were in that state for four Hundred years and didn't even know it until Jesus told them of their state in) ... Mark 7:9 "(NLT2) ⁹ Then he said, "You skillfully sidestep God's law in order to hold on to your own tradition. (We, under grace and truth have put the Holy Spirit out and replaced him with structured order under well-meaning seminary trained theologians so you can expect a certain pattern to be repeated each time you assemble.) **Hosea 4:6 (NLT2)** ⁶ **My people are being destroyed because they don't know me. Since you priests refuse to know me, I refuse to recognize you as my priests. Since you have forgotten the laws of your God, I will forget to bless your children."** *Luke 9:55 (KJV)* ⁵⁵ *But he turned, and rebuked them, and said, Ye know not what manner of spirit ye are of.*

When they rejected their Messiah, that put them in a state of being unacceptable to God, their father. All these seeds that rejected Jesus as their Messiah was condemned to not enter the kingdom until he opens the door for them to come in after the second resurrection. This was the state of the Gentiles at that time. *Ephesians 2:12 "(NLT2)* ¹² *In those days you were living apart from Christ. You were excluded from citizenship among the people of Israel, and you did not know the covenant promises God had made to them. You lived in this world without God and without hope."* Paul would be chosen to introduce us to the one true God of Abraham, Isaac and Jacob: the God of Israel. This will open the door to the age of grace where ... *John 7:37 "(KJV)* ³⁷ **In the last day, that great day of the feast, Jesus stood and cried, saying,** *If any man thirst, let him come unto me, and drink."* Now we, the Gentiles can now claim our birthright to serve the one and only living God. One of the historical facts about the scriptures, time always seem to be repeated in cycles that bring an end to a dispensation as I have found expressed in the scriptures. Israel had (45) kings before they were given over to their enemies. The Gentiles will also parallel with (45) presidents who will serve as kings in this nation before we are given over to our enemies. Truly this verse became apparent ... *Ecclesiastes 1:9 "(KJV)* ⁹ *The thing that hath been, it is that which shall be; and that which is done is that which shall be done: and there is no new thing under the sun."*

Here we are some two thousand plus years later, about to see history repeated spiritually in an apparent great fall away from the original gospel, preached on the day of Pentecost. When Jesus came literally to the Jews in the flesh, they did not receive him after having a record of the works he would do to prove the fulfillment of the scriptures before they delivered him over to the Roman government for crucifixion. When one is seduced by another spirit, you will never know it until God opens your eyes as he did the Jews of their state when they refused to receive him. Jesus told them in a parable what they would do to him, but they never understood because they were given over to the devil to fulfill the scriptures ... *Mark 12:9* **9 What shall therefore the lord of the vineyard do? he will come and destroy the husbandmen and will give the vineyard unto others.** ¹⁰ **And have ye not read this scripture; The stone which the builders rejected is become the head of the corner:"**

This was what literally happen to them under the law that showed how far removed from the original laws God gave Moses to them. In my study of the scriptures by the leading of the Holy Spirit, I found that if God didn't have an elect, none of us would survive the evils of this world not knowing who possess you. Even now in the gentile age, living under the

New Covenant, we still have trouble believing to the point of acting on the word that would show the world who is the real God.

We too, have fallen away from the reality of demonstrating the fruit of the right spirit we confess to be of. Could it be that many of us know not what spirit we are of? Here we are some two thousand years later, only to find ourselves in the same state that Jesus found his people in when he came; unable to recognize his voice in the spirit when he speaks. Yes, by revelation I see this is what many assemblies have become in this great fall-away … **Matthew 23:25 "(NLT2)** [25]**"What sorrow awaits you teachers of religious law and you Pharisees. Hypocrites! For you are so careful to clean the outside of the cup and the dish, but inside you are filthy—full of greed and self-indulgence!"**

Just as the Pharisees and Sadducees represented two different beliefs under the law, we in the Christian world have evolved into new doctrines that represents a split; <u>one believes in rapture before tribulation</u>; the <u>others are teaching that to be godly is to gain</u>. These two parallels are the same state of the Sanhedrin split in their administration of the law when Jesus confronted them about their state. <u>The Sadducees believed in no resurrection</u>, while <u>the Pharisees believed there is</u>. Now you can see how history is always repeated. Time is your worst enemy in a world where evil continually becomes a way of life with each passing generation. I have learned why Jesus said … **Matthew 6:25 "(NLT2)** [25] **"That is why I tell you not to worry about everyday life—whether you have enough food and drink, or enough clothes to wear. Isn't life more than food, and your body more than clothing? Matthew 6:34 (NLT2)** [34]**"So don't worry about tomorrow, for tomorrow will bring its own worries. Today's trouble is enough for today."** *1 John 4:4 (KJV)* [4] *Ye are of God, little children, and have overcome them: because greater is he that is in you, than he that is in the world. Philippians 4:19 (KJV)* [19] **But my God shall supply all your need according to his riches in glory by Christ Jesus.**

Most of us are not delivered to the point of total transparency about our own personal struggles that would help others see that only God and your love for him is what will enable you to endure until the end; out-side of him, there's no hope. In all we do as being obedient to his word … *1 Peter 4:18" (KJV)* [18] *And if the righteous scarcely be saved, where shall the ungodly and the sinner appear?* **Isaiah 64:6 (NKJV)** [6] **But we are all like** an unclean thing, and all our righteousness are like filthy rags; We all fade as a leaf, and our iniquities, like the wind, Have taken us away." Once again, I remind you, we have Jesus inside of us and many still can't believe he can do all his word said he watches over to perform. We live beneath what Jesus died to give us all, perfect deliverance.

After having been told these revelations, I asked, how do I judge myself that I may know that I'm right? The answer: *"whatever you do, if your character does not match my fruit, then you need to repent. So, whatever I do that's contrary to the fruits of your spirit, I must repent for that deed daily; yes, that's how you remain in right standing with me. Your enemy, the devil, don't get to keep that in his book to condemn you in the judgment by having too many unconfessed sins of omission."* These are the sins of omission ... **Galatians 5:19-21 "(KJV)** [19] **Now the works of the flesh are manifest, which are these; *Adultery, fornication, uncleanness, lasciviousness,* 20 Idolatry, *witchcraft, hatred, variance, emulations, wrath, strife, seditions, heresies,* 21 Envyings, *murders, drunkenness, revellings, and such like: of the which I tell you before, as I have also told you in time past, that they which do such things shall not inherit the kingdom of God."* What makes this new covenant a better one, you can by knowledge of the word, judge your own self before you leave here and know where you will be; that's why we will be without an excuse in the judgment.

The world is under-going many natural diverse changes in hope that God will get our attention of his eminent coming in our time by the signs as foretold in Matthew 24 and Luke 21. There is not much I can add that you don't already see; the trouble is, are you ready to believe the world's version of the times, or God's. God is preparing all he has given ears to hear and eyes to see, to get ready to come home to your eternity with Him. Time as you know and see is about to pass away as predicted by His prophets in His word. We have all these signs, weather you believe it or not, you are at that end this time continuum as in the days of Noah. I am grateful for the support of you who have shared some of your blessings with me that have been enough to publish these books over these years. I have prayed for your needs to be supplied through the faith of these words of warning that God may grant you the strength to endure the trouble that's soon to come on us all. May he be glorified in your mortal body. AMEN

THE TRUTH ABOUT WOMEN
IN PASTORAL POSITIONS
AS CHURCH LEADERS

When I preached my first sermon in Sept. of 1977, at that time, I did not know it would become one of the most controversial topics of discussion down through the years that would cause so many divided opinions. Here again, this is becoming another topic of discussion to the point of provoking confrontations that has led to further confusion in terms of spiritual clarity in the application as we presently see in the church world. The foundation must be laid to bring you an understanding from a biblical perspective; I held an opinion that reflected the doctrine taught in the epistles, regarding a woman's place in the church. *1 Corinthians 11:3 "(KJV)* ³ *But I would have you know, that the head of every man is Christ; and the head of the woman is the man; and the head of Christ is God."* That's the genesis of the order of things received in heaven, set in motion by God. The sins of Adam and Eve will begin the fight for gender supremacy.

We all know from the Old Testament; Women, even as prophetess never exercised any authority over the men when they were used if you study the context of their actions. The New Testament doctrine of the apostles confirms this in Paul's letter to Timothy as saying … *1 Timothy 2:12 "(KJV)* ¹² *But I suffer not a woman to teach, nor to usurp authority over the man, but to be in silence." 1 Corinthians 11:8 "(KJV)* ⁸ *For the man is not of the woman; but the woman of the man."* In creation, the woman became his comforter in the natural and helpmate as a part of him as we are now a part of God through the Holy Spirit, He now becomes our comforter. In the New Testament, we are now restored back to become the new created spirit being as the man Adam and the woman Eve, through the resurrection of Jesus Christ. *Galatians 3:28 "(KJV)* [28] *There is neither Jew nor Greek, there is neither bond nor free, there is neither male nor female: for ye are all one in Christ Jesus."* Does this mean that Christ compromised his order regarding the genders? *1 Corinthians 14:40 "(KJV)* [40] *Let all things be done decently and in order."* Now we must ask the question; where did women get this authority to be over the male gender and be accepted? To answer this question with an understanding of how this came into being, let's go to *Revelation 2:18-21 (KJV)* [18] *And unto the angel of the church in Thyatira write; These things saith the Son of God, who hath his eyes like unto a flame of fire, and his feet are like fine brass;* [19] *I know thy works, and charity, and service, and faith, and thy patience, and thy works; and the last to be more than the first.* [20] *Notwithstanding I have a few things against thee, because thou sufferest that woman Jezebel, which calleth herself a prophetess,* (The word prophetess is referring to a woman usurping her position as a leader over the male image.*) to teach and to seduce my servants to commit fornication,* (Fornication in this context, the husbandman as head of the house of God, representing the image of Christ, has allowed the jezebel spirit to seduce him to take his place as head of his own house and the house of God.) *and to eat things sacrificed unto idols.* [21] *And I gave her space to repent of her fornication; and she repented not."* In this context, this is a warning, as leaders, you would have to suffer this to be so. This has put the church in a position that only God now can do the separating to set his house in order. He will set His house back in order as separating the wheat from the tares when he returns to his house just as de did in Jerusalem, this time in the latter rain.

This is the reality of what has happened over the past two thousand years; our disobedience has caused much division and confusion. She will become the new image in the house. Now because God is a spirit and moves in the spirit, He is going to have to use whoever is available to Him to carry out his will according to the predestination of man's time to rule on Earth. God foreknew this when he set all things in motion that in the end of man's time to rule, all would be as he ordained in the beginning. That's why Paul taught so strong to Timothy about upholding the doctrine. *Colossians 2:5 "(KJV)* [5] *For though I be absent in the flesh, yet am I with you in the spirit, joying and <u>beholding your order,</u> and the steadfastness of your faith in Christ."* What God has allowed and permitted under grace, where there is neither male of female but His order from Heaven has never changed in their operations. Those born from above will be persecuted for upholding this doctrine as taught by Paul. Just like the people pressed Moses to wear him down to permit them to divorce their wives, He didn't change the law. This is what Jesus said about that … *Matthew 19:7-8 "(KJV)* [7] *They say unto him, why did Moses then command to give a writing of divorcement, and to put her away?* [8] *He <u>saith unto them,</u> Moses because of the hardness of your hearts suffered you to put away your wives: <u>but from the beginning it was not so</u>.*

Daniel prophesied that Satan would ware out the saints that will reflect where we are today. **(Dan.7:25)** What God has permitted because of the failure of the male image of His person to keep the order, has allowed in the spirit, the female gender to usurp authority over him through a seducing spirit of enmity between the genders that resulted in her gaining her position of lordship, but this was not so in the beginning. **(Matthew 19:1-8, 1 Tim. 2:12)** Throughout the bible we see that women are more loyal when they were under the right convictions, will carry out the will of God more faithful than some men. These are the sins of omission we are guilty of.

They were created to serve as helpmates if they remain faithful to Him, God will now use them to navigate your walk on the right path that will honor the male gender and stay in her place. Personally, if it were not for some good women in my spiritual walk like my mother, grandmother and after convicting my second wife, she kept me on the straight and narrow along with few others. Their lives are always before me as good examples. We are at the end-time in bible history where God Himself will have to come and set His house back to the order He ordained before the foundation of the world to take it back with Him. We are at a place where you need to know the voice of God with-out reference to gender as walking in the spirit. God has permitted women to exercise this position because of the failure of men to uphold His image in the assemblies. As men leaders, she now is a sign of our failures to keep the doctrine of the apostles. I can follow a woman that is following Christ in times like these when there are not many men, that holy in the sight of God.

We do our work in our prayer closets that helps Michael restrain the devil. I am an intercessory prayer warrior; we are not well known or understood by those around us because of our peculiarities. Sometimes I get up in a meditation daze unaware of my surroundings. I may have been at war for someone's soul that I'm assigned to uphold in prayer the devil is trying to claim. I have learned to be open always to the Holy Spirit to get the right answers for those that inquire of me. Many women will occupy those thrones in heaven but as sexless creatures as angels that served him in the earth. I myself fail in this area and had to be taught by God to see and understand by spiritual revelations according to the times. Over the years, standing on the apostle's doctrine has brought many separations in my life. I get my revelations by just saying and standing on what the word said and at the appointed time, God brought the revelations. I was being tested by my faith in the spoken word to stand on it and let Him prove who He is. My peace comes from learning to keep my mind on the word and live one day at a time.

 I strive to abstain from the things that would break my meditation to get through the day. To get my answers, I must exercise great patience and sometimes fast to keep my thoughts from interfering with His. The Holy Spirit has all the answers that will keep you of sound mind if we would learn to depend on him instead of letting the circumstances dictate our reactions. Don't be so easy to be provoked when you don't understand something; that's how God taught me patience to wait on Him. This I learned through many trials and errors before I got it. *Psalm 37:34 ("KJV)* *34 Wait on the LORD, and keep his way, and he shall exalt thee to inherit the land: when the wicked are cut off, thou shalt see it."* God is testing the fruit of all that will be a part of this last day move; beware of seducing spirits that are seeking to rob you of your birth-rite. AMEN

Now on the national front

We are facing a gender rebuke as males in recent media disclosures. The sins of the male genders are coming to the forefront of exposure as in … *Numbers 32:23 "(KJV)* *23 But if ye will not do so, behold, ye have sinned against the LORD: and be sure your sin will find you out."* We are in the last days and God is exposing the evils long neglected as the abuse of women as the weaker vessel comes to a head. The difference we see in the media, the world in its social interactions has come to a turning point as the spirit of Jezebel takes its position of advantage as now manifesting in the gender of oppression, the female. Satan is a spirit of timing; his intent is to take advantage of the circumstances that led up to this confrontation.

The male gender is being exposed with no credibility that will justify his sins that have brought him to this present state. Since we are the dominant species in this fight, all Satan had to do is wait for his window of opportunity to reveal our evil deeds against the opposite gender. The church-world is in for its biggest spiritual battle as he uses this credibility gap to wage war on the church in the days ahead. The great confrontation coming to the church will be the Jezebel spirits masquerading in dominant females in leadership; when provoked, become the strongholds of seduction of false religious doctrine of men that empowered them to fornicate the gospel. They will join the antichrist church. Given the spirit of sodomy's presents among these religious factions, in that state, they will be the true church persecutors. God used holy women in his permissive will to preserve his body by election as true leaders that helped guide his people; on the opposite end, the false worldly church that came out of **(Rev.2:18-20)** will be against the true church.

I see confessing Christian women being seduced to follow worldly women icon's; teachings and turning them against what was right. Many of them don't have their own house in order. The vanity of idol materialistic gains has infected the church assemblies by putting emphasis on the outer appearance is this kind of seduction. Yes, this worldly women movement is Satan taking advantage of the times. This will be the test of some of our marriages when you refuse to give in to these seducing spirits of the times. The Jezebel spirit must have something to rule over; be it male or female in this division. If you forget your place in God's kingdom, you could wound up cast out in the great separation of the wheat from the tares. May God have mercy on all that call upon His name. AMEN (Updated 6/2019)

WHO ARE THE CHILDREN OF DISOBEDIENCE?

Background scripture:

Ephesians 5:6 "(KJV) [6] *Let no man deceive you with vain words: for because of these things cometh the wrath of God upon the children of disobedience. Ephesians 2:2 (KJV)* [2] *Wherein in time past ye walked according to the course of this world, according to <u>the prince of the power of the air</u>, the spirit that now worketh in the children of disobedience:"* Throughout time, as being born in a sin and living in a sin filled environment; we, as confessing Christians are coming from sin to salvation. We are living in the hope of that day to be absent from this body and be present with the lord. However, many of us over time as confessing Christians, error as being forgetful hearers and faithful doers of the word we are to live by.

In the book of Revelation, some of us are described as being luke-warm. This carries a judgment that many caught in that state will not escape. *Revelation 3:15-16 "(KJV)* [15] *I know thy works, that thou art neither cold nor hot: I would thou wert cold or hot.* [16] *So then because thou art lukewarm, and neither cold nor hot, I will spue thee out of my mouth."* These are the class of Christians that are considered as lukewarm. They are under the doctrine and teachings of man that have many guilty of the sins of omission. Why are they in that state? They have been seduced to follow those on the broad road that represent the **Laodicean** spirit.

What did they do that put them out of the perfect will of God? They have not separated themselves from those who keep pagan traditions. What do they do in their Christian practices that have them in a way that seems right? They have a double-minded mentality in the application of what they confess to be in practice. We all are called to worship God in spirit and in truth; therefore, by the fruit of the spirit you will know what spirit you are of. This was my fault when God got my attention, I wasn't living a holy life as the word described. If we keep company with sinners, our lights are out. We are deceived if we think God approves of these associations. *2 Corinthians 6:17 "(KJV) ¹⁷ Wherefore come out from among them, and be ye separate, saith the Lord, and touch not the unclean thing; and I will receive you, 1 Peter 1:15 (KJV) ¹⁵ But as he which hath called you is holy, so be ye holy in all manner of conversation;"*

These are the characteristics of a lukewarm Christian that make you unacceptable to God.

1. You still love the world. *1 John 2:15 "(KJV) ¹⁵ Love not the world, neither the things that are in the world. If any man love the world, the love of the Father is not in him".*

2. He or she lusted after the prides of this world. *Galatians 5:16 "(KJV) ¹⁶ This I say then, walk in the Spirit, and ye shall not fulfil the lust of the flesh.*

3. They are more obedience to their doctrines of man, rather than God. *Acts 5:29 "(KJV) ²⁹ Then Peter and the other apostles answered and said, we ought to obey God rather than men."*

4. They will compromise what they know to be truth by not taking a stand. *Matthew 10:33 "(KJV) ³³ But whosoever shall deny me before men, him will I also deny before my Father which is in heaven."*

5. They tend to be more patriotic to country than to God. *1 John 3:13 "1 (KJV) ¹³ Marvel not, my brethren, if the world hate you. John 15:18 (KJV) ¹⁸ If the world hate you, ye know that it hated me before it hated you."*

6. This is a hard saying for most Christians, their biological family links seem more important than your heavenly family. *Matthew 12:48-50 "(KJV) ⁴⁸ But he answered and said unto him that told him, who is my mother? and who are my brethren? ⁴⁹ And he stretched forth his hand toward his*

disciples, and said, Behold my mother and my brethren! *50 For whosoever shall do the will of my Father which is in heaven, the same is my brother, and sister, and mother." Luke 14:33 (KJV) 33 So likewise, whosoever he be of you that forsaketh not all that he hath, he cannot be my disciple. Matthew 16:25 (KJV) 25 For whosoever will save his life shall lose it: and whosoever will lose his life for my sake shall find it. Matthew 19:29 (KJV) 29 And everyone that hath forsaken houses, or brethren, or sisters, or father, or mother, or wife, or children, or lands, for my name's sake, shall receive an hundredfold, and shall inherit everlasting life."*

7. They embrace these new politically correct changes to the laws of morality, as they have been seduced to follow these new doctrines that embrace immoral behavior as a sign of the great fall away will ... ***Romans 1:24 (KJV) 24 Wherefore God also gave them up to uncleanness through the lusts of their own hearts, to dishonour their own bodies between themselves:*** *Proverbs 16:25 (KJV) 25 There is a way that seemeth right unto a man, but the end thereof are the ways of death."*

8. They are reluctant to embrace certain biblical truths that cause them to change their ways. ***Job 34:27 "(KJV) 27 Because they turned back from him and would not consider any of his ways:*** *Isaiah 55:8 (KJV) 8 For my thoughts are not your thoughts, neither are your ways my ways, saith the LORD."*

What does the bible say about those who may be guilty of these reservations to submit? If you die before you repent, this is what may happen in the judgment? *Daniel 5:27"(KJV) 27 Thou art weighed in the balances, and art found wanting."*

Under the new covenant, these are sins of omission as found in **Galatians 5:19-21**. My beloved brothers and sisters, I have not heard men preach or teach these scriptures in the third layer of truth that let Jesus be the savior and not you. It takes being born from above to teach these truths that produce fruit that remain in you where your family member can see Jesus and not you. This I experience in the salvation of members of my extended family by marriage.

The doctrine of Jesus Christ was completed in the sheading of his blood and in the blood of his disciples that followed, it will take the sheading of blood to get it back. We all have fallen away from that demonstration of truth that set us free as it did in the days of the apostles. That's why there must be a latter rain before the rapture can take place in these last days; many will have to repent. *Isaiah 53:6-9 "(KJV)* ⁶ All we like sheep have gone astray; we have turned everyone to his own way; and the **LORD** *hath laid on him the iniquity of us all.* ⁷ He was oppressed, and he was afflicted, yet he opened not his mouth: he is brought as a lamb to the slaughter, and as a sheep before her shearers is dumb, so he openeth not his mouth. ⁸ *He was taken from prison and from judgment: and who shall declare his generation? for he was cut off out of the land of the living: for the transgression of my people was he stricken.* ⁹ *And he made his grave with the wicked, and with the rich in his death; because he had done no violence, neither was any deceit in his mouth."* The only children of disobedience that will escape will be those that someone laid down their life in prayer for. Their fate will be as Paul stated in ... *1 Corinthians 5:5 "(KJV)* ⁵ To deliver such an one unto Satan for the destruction of the flesh, that the spirit may be saved <u>*in the day of the Lord Jesus.*</u>" They will suffer with the wicked as stated in ... *Ephesians 5:6 "(KJV)* ⁶ *Let no man deceive you with vain words: for because of these things cometh the wrath of God upon the* <u>*children of disobedience*</u>." These are they that will come up in the second sickle reaping in **Rev. 14:17-20.** Beloved, every time I read these words, I see my short comings and weep for strength to carry my cross as Paul by dying daily. We, in America have lived a privilege in a nation that was blessed with the freedoms to pursue happiness and joys that came with living in a free country. Now we are about to see it all come to an end, unfortunately, we are not prepared. This what God is trying to get our attention to see. We are in the time when many will experience what it is to live with a false sense of security ... *1 Thessalonians 5:3 "(KJV)* ³ *For when they shall say, Peace and safety; then sudden destruction cometh upon them, as travail upon a woman with child; and they shall not escape."*

All these natural disasters, killings, divisions in churches, governments, national and worldwide unrest are signs of God trying to get our attention. Do not believe what the economists are saying, we are on the verge of an economic collapse to bring in the N.W.O. Another sign I see is the implementation of the national ID's, which is to become the new data base facial recognition technology that will precede the cashless society after the crash. One morning you will awake to the news that all banks are closed, there will be mayhem and chaos in the streets; neighbors will turn on each other and kill each other for food and water. There will be nowhere to run or hide because you are seeing the end of a time continuum, come to an end as days of Noah. The biblical details of this circumstance that no one will be able to escape are written in this biblical book of chronicles. Therefore, I was inspired to rewrite this updated testament to give you all a chance to examine ourselves as to what we believe and do our repenting before the real trouble come on that dreadful morning and overtake you in fear. No matter what god or doctrine you are now currently serving, if you are denying the doctrine of Jesus Christ, the son of God, you are doomed for a three by seven cell in hell with a bed of embers heated seven time hotter than any fire on earth waiting to take your last breath if you do not repent when warned. Take heed to these warnings, God's mercy is still among us. May God have mercy on all that call upon his name. AMEN (Completed for release 3/2018)

TITHES & OFFERINGS AS PRESENTED IN THE NEW TESTAMENT

Charitable giving:

Luke 11:41 (KJV) ⁴¹ But rather give alms of <u>such things as ye have;</u> and, behold, all things are clean unto you. **Luke 12:32-33 (NKJV)** ³² Do not fear, little flock, for it is your Father's good pleasure to give you the kingdom. ³³ Sell what you have and give alms; provide yourselves money bags which do not grow old, a treasure in the heavens that does not fail, where no thief approaches nor moth destroys." (This verse below will become the heart of the New Testament teachings in the lives of the preachers and teachers. *Malachi 3:10 (KJV)* ¹⁰ *Bring ye all the tithes into the storehouse, that there may be meat in mine house, and prove me now herewith, saith the LORD of hosts, if I will not open you the windows of heaven, and pour you out a blessing, that there shall not be room enough to receive it.*

What do we have in this new covenant under grace that replace tithing?

Acts 3:6 (NKJV) ⁶ *Then Peter said, «Silver and gold I do not have, but what I do have I give you: In the name of Jesus Christ of Nazareth, rise up and walk.»* (They had just come from a meeting where people sold their possessions to help the poor and free others from their debts. These men did not keep a dime for themselves. This is what they inherited that was more precious than worldly possessions?) **Acts 9:36-42 (NKJV)** ³⁶ *At Joppa there was a certain disciple named Tabitha, which is translated Dorcas. This woman was full of good works and charitable deeds which she did.* ³⁷ **But it happened in those days that she became sick and died. When they had washed her, they laid her in an upper room.** ³⁸ **And since Lydda was near Joppa, and the disciples had heard that Peter was there, they sent two men to him, imploring him not to delay in coming to them.** ³⁹ *Then Peter arose and went with them. When he had come, they brought him to the upper room. And all the widows* **stood by him weeping, showing the tunics and garments which Dorcas had made while she was with them.** ⁴⁰ *But Peter put them all out and knelt down and prayed. And turning to the body he said, «Tabitha, arise.» And she opened her eyes, and when she saw Peter she sat up.* ⁴¹ **Then he gave her his hand and lifted her up; and when he had called the saints and widows, he presented her alive.** ⁴² *And it became known throughout all Joppa, and many believed on the Lord.* (This is the church established as one united in the doctrine of Jesus Christ that continued to do what he did; this time, in them as His apostles. The gifts and offerings they brought to that meeting, went to help those who needed deliverance, not into the apostle's pockets.

This is that love manifested in them that are born from above. I have had much controversy in making this statement, **"born from above,"** these are the elects that demonstrate the perfect will of God; they are the few. They carry the vision that's holding back the judgments. They are the true prophets and messengers.) *Matthew 6:1-4 (KJV)* ¹ *Take heed that ye do not your alms before men, to be seen of them: otherwise <u>ye have no reward of your Father which is in heaven</u>.* ² *therefore, when thou doest thine alms, (or giving) do not sound a trumpet before thee, as the hypocrites do in the synagogues and in the streets, that they may have glory of men. Verily I say unto you, they have their reward.* ³ *But when thou doest alms, <u>let not thy left hand know what thy right hand doeth:</u>* ⁴ *That thine alms may be in secret<u>: and thy Father which seeth in secret himself shall reward thee openly.</u> Matthew 6:33 (KJV)* ³³ *But seek ye first the kingdom of God, and his righteousness; and all these things shall be added unto you."* (All the world belongs to you as the new man child, the restored Adam. This gospel that was preached was followed by these signs in those born from above by election, whom the lord walked in to show his presents in the earth. This is the faith God seeks to fine when he returns. *Luke 18:8 (KJV)* [8] *I tell you that he will avenge them speedily. Nevertheless, when the Son of man cometh, shall he find faith on the earth?* You will be given what you need at the time you need it because he in you **is** the reality of the new Adam taking dominion of the things he possesses, using your body. When it comes to giving, this is what Paul told the people do to support the things of God <u>after your needs are met.</u>) *1 Corinthians 16:2" (KJV)* [2] *Upon the first day of the week let every one of you lay by him in store, <u>as God hath prospered him,</u> that there be no gatherings when I come".* (He didn't tell them to pay a certain percentage. If Your pastor or leader is born from above, he will walk in the reality of the greater one inside; therefore, by faith, all his needs are met as being content to let Christ in him seek the welfare of others.) *2 Corinthians 8:11-14 (KJV)* [11] *Now therefore perform the doing of it; that as there was a readiness to will, so there may be a performance also out of that which ye have.* [12] *<u>For if there be first a willing mind, it is accepted <u>according to that a man hath, and not according to that he hath not."</u></u>* (God doesn't need what he already has; all the wealth of his world is available to you because he is in you. That's why he called us to self-denial. Our lack of wisdom to use the resources he has made available to us wisely is where we fall short into the bondages of this world. You see, the day you were born again, you inherited the wealth that came with your new father. You are wealthy as your father in heaven as his child; now you will be taught how to use it for the good of others to bring them into the kingdom of heaven, not build your kingdoms here on earth.

God is the cure for welfare, if you walk by faith in him, you will be content and fare well, having enough to meet your needs daily and give to others.*)* [13] *For I mean not that other men be eased, and ye burdened:* [14] *<u>But by an equality,</u> that now at this time your abundance may be a supply for their want, that their abundance also may be a supply for your want* (or need) *that there may be equality:"* (This is the revelation of what we have been freely given. God's way is to free yourself from all these entanglements so you can freely give of your substance without being in bondage. Wait on his leading as to how to navigate around the temptations of this world that will lead you into bondage. Self-denial is not taught in in these doctrines that tell you to be godly is to gain. God had me to give away all my saving and pensions funds to the needy during those seven years. I had to reframe from attending assemblies under the 501c-3 curse that gave them license to rob you in the name of God. After that experience, he told me not to ask for anything, I would have what I need when the time comes.

This world belongs already to you by inheritance. ***Psalm 50:10 "(KJV)*** [10] ***For every beast of the forest is mine, and the cattle upon a thousand hills. Matthew 6:33 (KJV)*** [33] ***But seek ye first the kingdom of God, and his righteousness; and all these things shall be added unto you. Luke 12:29 (KJV)*** [29] ***And seek not ye what ye shall eat, or what ye shall drink, neither be ye of doubtful mind."*** All you need during your short stay here in the flesh is what it takes to get through each day. Don't let any leader put you into a guilt bondage by insisting you pay their organization a tithes percentage of your earnings. The above scriptures make no mention of a tithe in your giving. It's according as to how the lord has blessed you. Your knowledge of truth will lead your giving according to what you have as from your heart ... ***2 Corinthians 9:7 (KJV)*** [7] ***Every man according as he purposeth in his heart, so let him give; not grudgingly, or of necessity: for God loveth a cheerful giver."*** If your assembly is bringing you guilt by insisting you pay a tithe and offering and begging each time you come together for one cause or another when there is no deliverance, you are into kingdom building as having a hireling in the pulpit. You have employed a thief in the pulpit. These men retire like those in the corporate world.

God will build the house he dwells in, and this is what you will see? Deliverance from the bondages of demon possession, sickness, physical disabilities and diseases; that's the saint's hospital. ***Acts 3:2 "(KJV)*** [2] ***And a certain man lame from his mother's womb was carried, whom they laid daily at the gate of the temple which is called Beautiful, to ask alms of them that entered into the temple; Acts 3:6 (KJV)*** [6] ***Then Peter said, Silver and gold have I none; but such as I have give I thee: In the name of Jesus Christ of Nazareth rise up and walk."*** When we look at the scriptures taken from the New Testament, there is no mention of a tithe when it comes to giving. Why was this not mentioned in the Old Testament? If you would meditate on everything you read in the bible, the Holy Spirit will tell you the revelation knowledge and understanding according to your times that word applies. We are now under grace and truth.

I must admit, I did not have a good understanding of what grace really was under the New Testament until the Holy Spirit re-taught me these truths. In the last days, the church world will have evolved into the spirit of **Laodicea**; teaching the doctrine of the **Nicolaitan's** which will represent man's re-interpretation of the scriptures out of context to apply to a new-found theology of a mixture of Law and Grace. This is the teachings of the Catholic Jesuits who built the seminary institutions to infiltrate Christianity that led to confusion when man began to interpret what only the Holy Spirit knows. The reason why the early church was so persecuted, they stayed in the accord of the oneness and did not regard the traditions of the Sanhedrin, as letting the Holy Spirit continue teaching this grace that would represent the new man; Adam restored with dominion over the devil. Did Christ destroy the law… no; then how was it fulfilled under grace and truth?

Sense we are talking about tithes and giving, let's see how this is applied and what has been added to keep us under bondage to law when God is now dealing with you from your heart by having mercy on you in your predicament. When you are free of the entanglements of this world, you will know that riches are not in having things of this world, all you receive will be free to give to others as being free yourself. You see, if you are free from all the entanglements of this world, everything you get is a blessing and you will have not only enough for yourself but be able to give to others in need. That's what the New Testament teaches. Christ in you has no need that has not already been supplied because he owns everything and now, he is in you. That is what being content really means.

Let's examine the scriptures above to see why tithes are not mentioned. There must be an error in the application of giving under the New Testament as to why it is not called a tithe. We all were raised under this teaching; therefore, I don't expect this to be well received as a return to what the apostle's taught; it' just to let you see how far we are from the truth in this Laodicean church age. I will use the NLT as a parallel to the KJV … **1 Corinthians 16:2 "(NLT) 2 On the first day of each week, you should each put aside a portion of the money you have earned. Don't wait until I get there and then try to collect it all at once."** Your leader must have an attitude of contentment as there to seek the welfare of others as a servant of God. His needs are already met as being content in Christ to properly minister with a sound balance, the biblical principles of giving as taught in the New Testament wisdom of God. God's love will not create an atmosphere of bondage when you come together to be set free. The real

Gospel as preached under the anointing of the Holy Ghost is convicting people in all kinds of circumstances and condition that only God can get them out of. That' the work of the Holy Spirit when he oversees the five-fold ministries.

That's how he calls us to repentance. He is calling the **poor,** the **rich,** those in bondage to **drugs, alcohol, sex, debt,** and **demon possession.** When Christ shows up, people are completely delivered from all these condition by showing love and compassion that can deliver them out of their circumstances to the place where they too can be productive in the kingdom of God to help others. That's why this Gospel must be demonstrated as Christ in you to let people see a demonstration of faith that will give them hope for their own deliverance. He does not seek to condemn you but deliver you.

The word of truth tells you of your state in sin that only God can deliver you from. That word reaches the heart of you that cause you to repent. The degree of the manifestation of the spirit is determined by the degree of love that brings you to the point to be set free. This will bring the revelation of the true riches more valuable that silver or gold. Christ, the pearl of great price. That is why they that had vast possessions sold them to help free those who came in financial bondage in an atmosphere of deliverance so those that receive this love would do the same for others. What I see in the application of parts of this doctrine are these cults that separate into communal living, employing the doctrine of separatism.

All brothers and sisters that get to grow up in the same house will have different abilities to the benefits of others in the kingdom of God. *2 Corinthians 8:12 "(NLT)* ¹² *Whatever you give is acceptable if you give it eagerly and give <u>according to what you have,</u>"* (You see, it's from the heart of what you have, not a percentage of what you don't have. Remember the widow's mite) ... *Luke 21:4 "(NLT)* ⁴ *For they have given a tiny part of their surplus, but she, poor as she is, has given everything she has."* Beloved, it cost me everything to get to this place to be able to tell you these revelations as coming out of the volume of his books. This is how God designed my experiences to get me here so he can speak through me as a freed vessel being made meat for the master's use. Having faith in God is acknowledging Him in all your ways. This is the new attitude of giving as taught by Christ. You are not to draw any attention to yourself. Did

Christ tell any that followed him to pay him a tithe? That' why he said I am here to serve, not to be served. If you are in debt bondage, you must be taught the principle of self-denial to get free to be able to give to others. Those who are financially free, God may cause them to bless you to help relieve that burden. This is that love they received on the day of Pentecost that caused them to realize they had something more precious than their possessions. They that were freed indeed, wanted others to be as free as they were and able to give to free others.

That's why Jesus said… *Luke 18:8 "(KJV)* [8] *I tell you that he will avenge them speedily. Nevertheless, when the Son of man cometh, shall he find faith on the earth?"* The reason why our giving in today's assemblies does not set you free is the lack of spiritual discernment of what is the truth in our giving. That's why God hates tradition, it operates in lack of knowledge of the truth. The Devil knows how to rob you in the name of God as a carnal Christian, that is why he seduced the church to put it under a worldly system mark number 501C-3. He then sent them to be schooled as hirelings to the church world to rob them by lack of knowledge to build their family kingdoms here on earth. This is where our feelings and emotions are played upon by hirelings in the pulpit handling the word deceitfully; even appointing themselves renown authorities by their degrees. The world has a system that takes care of its own and so do the church. It is the mixing of law with grace that the enemy preys on your ignorance for lack of knowledge to discern that will cause some of us to support earthly kingdom building causes. Let the one who's giving be fully persuaded in his own heart for God is more than able to replace any losses out of good intensions.

Now let's examine the Old Testament teaching on tithes *Malachi 3:10 (KJV)* [10] *Bring ye all the tithes into the storehouse, that there may be meat in mine house, and prove me now herewith, saith the LORD of hosts, if I will not open you the windows of heaven, and pour you out a blessing, that there shall not be room enough to receive it.* If you have been brought up under this teaching, this chapter tells you how you rob God by not giving to those who live in self-denial seeking your spiritual welfare and not their own. They will live in the reality of Christ in them has no needs that has not already been met. That's the faith he seeks to find when you are taught under the anointing of the Holy spirit.

This will become the revelation as previously described in the above teachings. The tithe commandment was given to support the Levitical priesthood under the law. It was a Jewish tax only to support them as an independent nation to have no ties to the world. This whole tribe linage was to minister in the temple as priest and servants of the temple in the sacrificial rites. The 10% God required them as a nation of his people, would make them independent of the world's system. Without going into all the history, the Holy Spirit likes to keep all things simple on the level where God gives the understanding. There is nothing wrong in tithing … **2 Corinthians 9:7 "(NLT)** [7] <u>**You must each decide in your heart how much to give.**</u> (He did not say anything about a percentage.) **And don't give reluctantly or <u>in response to pressure.</u>"** Most King James only Christians, tend to adhere to generations of this errors in spiritual interpretation of grace over the law. We are now under a spiritual law as a mixture of all tribes, kindreds and tongues. The tithes law does not apply under grace and truth because God is judging the heart of men in this new covenant when it comes to giving.

Now all who teach the law of tithing under grace and truth, if they are not following the apostles' example as their lifestyles will be guilty of robbing the people for selfish gain. Many leaders under traditional teachings on this subject will reject this view.) **"For God loves a person who gives cheerfully."** Keeping this law under grace as a tradition, is the error in practice; they will not be open to this revelation knowledge to be guided by sound scriptural interpretation that clarify the **KJV Bible**. These parallel interpretation bibles I quote from are used for that purpose to help clarify the understanding of God's intent as guided by the Holy Spirit. **Just be led by him.**

This is the way God accepts your giving under the New Testament. He is judging the attitude of your heart. He doesn't need what He already has. It is in your giving to help others, your needs are met in what he has called you to do because in you, he owns everything. Giving freely, set this principle in motion as … *Ecclesiastes 11:1 (KJV)* [1] *Cast thy bread upon the waters: for thou shalt find it after many days.* Now you must be free of any worldly entanglements as the lord's free servant so everything you get will be a blessing to you to understand what it is to be free indeed and you can pass it on to others. *Mark 4:19 "(NLT)* [19] *but all too quickly the message is crowded out by the worries of this life, the lure of wealth, and the desire for other things, so no fruit is produced."* That is the type of bondage we will be in by not waiting on God's divine directions. **Romans 8:32 "(NLT)** 32 **Since he did not spare even his own Son but gave him up for us all, won't he also give us everything else? Matthew 10:8 (NLT)** 8 **Heal the sick, raise the dead, cure those with leprosy, and cast out demons. Give as freely as you have received! Mark 16:17 (NLT)** 17 **These miraculous signs will accompany those who believe: They will cast out demons in my name, and they will speak in new languages."** What we have been given freely by God, money can't buy. To do all these things, you must be converted and set free by God. That's what he told Peter. **Luke 22:32 (KJV)** 32 **But I have prayed for thee, that thy faith fail not: and when thou art converted, strengthen thy brethren.** Be careful of your gifts in this area that you do not be overtaken in a fault. This you cannot do in yourself, or else Jesus gave himself for nothing. The fact that we have been given all things freely is why we no longer must beg or be required to pay a given percentage of your earnings. God is now judging your heart when it comes to giving.

Now all we must do as keepers of his word is ask according to his will and you will have what you need. The reason why you would not ask a miss, the Holy Spirit will give you what to ask for that God want you to have. The Holy Spirit in you knows the will of God and will not ask anything that is not to the benefit of others. If we were to follow Christ's example, we will see this new creature in Christ that does all these things that shows he owns the whole world. That is the Adam restored as having dominion over all your circumstances by being in control. In all our efforts to do right, it will just get you through one day at a time. Have you ever considered that if God were to give you all you ask for; you might leave him?

God knows you better than you know yourself and designs your trial to keep you in him. We all want to live forever and free from sickness and diseases while in the earth, that is why some will suffer unto death. This is a truth; **Matthew 6:25 "(NLT)** 25 **"That is why I tell you not to worry about everyday life—whether you have enough food and drink, or enough clothes to wear. Isn't life more than food, and your body more than clothing? James 4:14 (NLT)** 14 **How do you know what your life will be like tomorrow? Your life is like the morning fog—it's here a little while, then it's gone."** In our apostate state, many lack the faith to live the full privilege God gave us. Those in the early church lived as though nothing was theirs and share equally the blessing of God that adds no sorrow with others. We are in a divided state as a broken body, one must have keen discernment in this state. You may know not the day of your departure, that's your day of rapture or translation from this life.

We no longer teach or practice the apostle's doctrine as in the early church; therefore, we are being robbed in the name of God by corporate train theologians to build their family own kingdoms here on earth under the 501c-3 government mark as a tax-exempt nonprofit corporation. The curse of this is seen in the way they run their assemblies as a corporation run the same way as in the world's system. The deacons are your board of directors, administering a structured order in the name of God, operating in the Holy Spirit's stead. The leaders sent from God will have a humble spirit of self-denial as having the right spirit to sacrifice to those that are in need. The government supposed to be in fear of the church in Christ, they are carrying a sign of God's presents, and will have to answer to God for how they ministered in their office to protect our liberties under grace and truth, they will help him, and meet his need for what he doesn't have to give spiritually and materially. This in love and compassion in action. This is what must be done in the household of believers first ... so the world can see the love of God in action. We have something in our Godly family that the world doesn't have; the ability to love unselfishly and be totally delivered from the devil. The anointed teachings will not take care of those that don't want to work to keep the wealth equally distributed among the saints. Grace is freedom from the Law of bondage; if you mix the two together, you will fall short of the glory that let the world see God in you when it comes to compassion. I see the world taking care of their own without mentioning tithes by posting go-fund-me pages for those in dire need in the world. None of the apostles lived in this lavish luxury we see in the lives of many church leaders today. It cost them their lives and imprisonment to stan against the world's system. Now, as a leader, who do you represent?

That's why we must return to our first love to be reconciled in the doctrine that started the church on the day of Pentecost. That has been my revelation message as to why there must be a period of tribulation; a return to the first church of Pentecost. Now do you see why so few will find the Christ, manifested as in the early church. That's the straight and narrow path. **Matthew 7:14 (NLT)** [14] **But the gateway to life is very narrow and the road is difficult, and only a few ever find it. AMEN** (completed for release 8/2017)

FEAR – THE FINAL
BATTLE FOR SOULS

Background scriptures:

Revelation 14:7 (NKJV) [7] **saying with a loud voice, "Fear God and give glory to Him, for the hour of His judgment has come; and worship Him who made heaven and earth, the sea and springs of water." 1 John 4:18 (NKJV)** [18] **There is no fear in love; but perfect love casts out fear, because fear involves torment. But he who fears has not been made perfect in love. Psalm 53:5 (NKJV)** [5] **There they are in great fear** where no fear was, For God has scattered the bones of him who encamps against you; You have put them to shame, Because God has despised them.

These are my Solomon observations

Once I had a fellow brother to ask me … **What do you mean when you say, being caught in God's break?** Judgment has already been passed on the unrepentant sinner; therefore, who are the ones caught in his break? All who are luke-warm confessing Christians that have fallen away from their first love and do not know it; even after they hear the truth of their state, refuse to repent. How many years have many of us been associated with a religious assembly, under some form of a denomination's name, you know what will happen each time you come there? If you answered that question as having a foreknowledge of what was going to happen in the same routine, you are in a traditionally structured assembly order under the 501c-3 mark, set up by seminary train leaders that sold out the apostle's doctrine to politically correct influence to become a non-profit corporate assembly. This is the work of the Jesuit professors trained by the Catholic order to penetrate Protestant assemblies with Jesuit trained pastors. They built that seminary system to penetrate Christianity. All the word of God is good for mankind, but only those operating in the full council of the truth, will demonstrate the same fruit as did the w apostles.

That's the teaching of the New Testament new creature; the total Adam man being restored back to his power over the devil in this evil world. **John 17:15 (NKJV)** [15] **I do not pray that You should take them out of the world, but that You should keep them from the evil one. 2 Corinthians 5:17 (NKJV)** [17] **Therefore, if anyone is in Christ, he is a new creation; old things have passed away; behold, all things have become new.** What I see in this last generation that will experience the wrath of God, is a willing ignorance of what we as confessing Christians should know ... who we are and what we are as new creations with Christ inside of us. Now, that's what your enemy, (the devil) doesn't want you to know. What I want you to see, we are on his territory; as the enemy of our soul, what we do not realize, he has already been defeated. It will be by knowledge of truth that will keep you walking in victory as to say in faith ...*John 8:32 (KJV)* [32] *And ye shall know the truth, and the truth shall make you free.* **Matthew 4:4 "(NKJV)** [4] **But He answered and said, "It is written, 'Man shall not live by bread alone, but by every word that proceeds from the mouth of God.'" Matthew 4:10 (NKJV)** [10] **Then Jesus said to him, "Away with you, Satan! For it is written, 'You shall worship the LORD your God, and Him only you shall serve.' 1 John 4:4 (NKJV)** [4] **You are of God, little children, and have overcome them, because He who is in you is greater than he who is in the world."** As confessing Christians, God is our source of strength and power to keep Satan from touching him in you. Now you must be persuaded to give yourself totally to him so he can keep you whole as the restored Adam. If you cannot believe that the God of heaven is in you as the greater one, then you are already spiritually defeated by seducing spirit that caused you to doubt His ability to keep you from being overcome by the devil. What you should be entertaining in your mind is what the word said that cause you not to doubt.

What you **see, taste, touch, smell** and **hear.** These five gates are a direct channel to your mind, must be willingly closed by you from being influenced by the carnal world you are being delivered from. What you do thereafter will determine the depth of your beliefs and convictions to act on His word or be overtaken by the circumstances. When you become converted, (*that is*) to know the reality of Christ in you, you will have faith to act like the devil is defeated. We are taught to ... **James 4:7 (NKJV)** [7] **Therefore, submit to God. Resist the devil and he will flee from you.** The word in faith is your only weapon against his power that is manifested in our ignorance. **Another thing I observe;** there are many more sinners enjoying these benefits than the saints. **Why is that?**

We came from sin to salvation; therefore, we must unlearn all the negative things we were taught and that takes time. If your assembly is not teaching the whole council of the truth that sets you free, then you are being destroyed by lack of knowledge. The devil will single you out to keep you from performing God's sovereign will for your life. Paul gave us this revelation in ... *1 Corinthians 11:27 (KJV)* [27] *Wherefore whosoever shall eat this bread, and drink this cup of the Lord, unworthily, shall be guilty of the body and blood of the Lord.* What does this mean? If you do not act on what the word said about who you are in Christ, this act justifies Satan's right to attack you. **1 Corinthians 11:30 (NKJV)** [30] **For this reason many are weak and sick among you, and many sleep.** (*Die before you time*) Now I'm going to say something that will cause some of you to stumble at this statement. The sin of not being one with Christ is the cause of sickness and diseases that cause you to doubt what God said he will do. That's why Paul said ... **1 Corinthians 11:29 (NKJV)** [29] **For he who eats and drinks in an unworthy manner eats and drinks judgment to himself, not discerning the Lord's body.** It is Satan that brings sickness and diseases, not the lord.

Now this brings us to the power of positivity. This principle, taken from the context of truth, used by the world under the inspiration of the devil, keeps his children well, while under his influence, mock Christians as to show, we have power too. That's why Jesus said ... **Matthew 5:45 (NKJV)** [45] **that you may be sons of your Father in heaven; for He makes His sun rise on the evil and on the good and sends rain on the just and on the unjust.** God has put with-in man, the power to heal himself by aligning himself to be one with him in the universe. You don't have to be saved to experience this because he gave you that power by being in his image. These are the principals of truth, if practice in faith will do what his word said. As a child of the devil, he will cause you to use the principle that works without salvation and die and go to hell.

This knowledge was given to man for good, now Satan will seduce man to work the principals that does not glorify God but gives the credit to the devil in man; therefore, he will be deceived in this way ... **1 Corinthians 13:2-13 (NKJV)** [2] *And though I have the gift of prophecy, and understand all mysteries and all knowledge, and though I have all faith, so that I could remove mountains, but have not love, I am nothing.* [3] **And though I bestow all my goods to feed the poor, and though I give my body to be burned, but have not love, it profits me nothing.** [4] **Love suffers long and is kind; love does not envy; love does not parade itself, is not puffed up; Mark 8:36 (NKJV)** [36] **For what will it profit a man if he gains the whole world, and loses his own soul?** This knowledge of the truth will be used to cause men to get wealthy with these gifts, used in the name of God. **John 1:12 (NKJV)** [12] **But as many as received Him, to them He gave the right to become children of God, to those** <u>who believe in His name:</u> *Mark 8:36 (KJV)* [36] *For what shall it profit a man, if he shall gain the whole world, and lose his own soul?*

Another observation I see:

The media is being used to spread fear on a mass level by showing us extreme negativity of what we are exposed to in our daily life. This accounts for these phobias people have by being able to isolate themselves. As Americans, being able to afford some of the finer things in life, the human mind is nothing to play with; it will respond to what its exposed to in forms of extreme trauma that can create a mental block in your ability to function normally. What you are exposed to will determine how you are able to deal with life circumstances. I have met people who do not believe they are to give an account to your creator in the judgment for how you lived your life; whether good or bad.

We are possessed with hidden unknown spirits of fears and anger that can be provoked by sudden changes or circumstances when we are faced with them. Because of a false sense of reality and unbelief, many of us will not live the full privilege of being a Christian. **Mark 7:14-15 (NKJV)** [14] **When He had called all the multitude to Himself, He said to them, "Hear Me,**

everyone, and understand: [15] *Beware of false prophets, which come to you in sheep's clothing, but inwardly they are ravening wolves.*

These are Satan's ministers, sent before you to cause you to error using the word. Read the chronicle; **"First Impressions are not always the right ones."** Willing ignorance harbors hidden fears. It will become the enemy that will defeat many in the suffering that's yet to come in this last generation. You see the told this recent pandemic has over the world. That is a biblical sign to all confessing Christians, your faith is about to be tried. AMEN (Completed 3/2021)

"LIFE & DEATH" WHAT IS MAN

The origin of immortality

1 Timothy 6:15-16 (KJV) [15] **Which in his times he shall shew, *who is* the blessed and only Potentate, the King of kings, and Lord of lords;** [16] **Who only hath immortality, dwelling in the light which no man can approach unto; whom no man hath seen, nor can see: to whom *be* honour and power everlasting.** Amen.

Man is a mortal human being

Genesis 2:7 (KJV) [7] **And the LORD God formed man *of* the dust of the ground and breathed into his nostrils the breath of life; and man became a living soul.** (God's breath and life is the soul of your existence. Therefore, the body now will become the natural temple that will give us the ability to see God in the flesh in the form of Adam. Anyone who does not believe God's version of Man's origin will have to give and account of his life in the judgment.)

What will happen to the body

Ecclesiastes 12:7 (KJV) [7] **Then shall the dust return to the earth as it was: and the spirit shall return unto God who gave it.**

Our life is in the breath of God

Job 27:3 (KJV) [3] **All the while my breath *is* in me, and the spirit of God *is* in my nostrils.**

Death's Reality

Hebrews 9:27 (KJV) [27] **And as it is appointed unto men once to die, but after this the judgment: Job 7:9-10 (KJV)** [9] **As the cloud is consumed and vanisheth away: so he that goeth down to the grave shall come up no** *more*. [10] **He shall return no more to his house, neither shall his place know him anymore. Psalm 104:29 (KJV)** [29] **Thou hidest thy face, they are troubled: thou takest away their breath, they die, and return to their dust.** (You cease to exist until the lord return to recover your soul.) **Psalm 146:4 (KJV)** [4] **His breath goeth forth, he returneth to his earth; in that very day his thoughts perish. Ecclesiastes 9:5 (KJV)** [5] **For the living know that they shall die: but the dead know not anything, neither have they any more a reward; for the memory of them is forgotten. Psalm 115:17 (KJV)** [17] **The dead praise not the LORD, neither any that go down into silence.** (This is hell)

<u>Set time to be raised from the dead</u>

Job 14:12-13 (KJV) [12] **So man lieth down, and riseth not: till the heavens** *be* **no more, they shall not awake, nor be raised out of their sleep.** [13] **O that thou wouldest hide me in the grave, that thou wouldest keep me secret, <u>until thy wrath</u> be past, that thou wouldest appoint me a set time, and remember me!** This is a prophecy statement. Job's hope of being raised from the dead is what we in the last days will experience by resurrection during the tribulation. We will be saved from his wrath. **Job 15:5 (KJV)** [5] **For thy mouth uttereth thine iniquity, and thou choosest the tongue of the crafty. Acts 2:29-37 (KJV)** [29] **Men** *and* **brethren, let me freely speak unto you of the patriarch David, that he is both dead and buried, and his sepulchre is with us unto this day.** [30] **Therefore being a prophet and knowing that God had sworn with an oath to him, that of the fruit of his loins, according to the flesh, he would raise up Christ to sit on his throne;** [31] **He seeing this before spake of the resurrection of Christ, that his soul was not left in hell, neither his flesh did see corruption.** (What happen to Christ after three days in the Earth?) [32] **This Jesus hath God raised up, whereof we all are witnesses.** [33] **Therefore being by the right hand of God exalted and having received of the Father the promise of the Holy Ghost, he hath shed forth this, which ye now see and hear.** [34] **For David is not ascended into the heavens: but he saith himself, The LORD said unto my Lord, sit thou on my right hand,** [35] **Until I make**

thy foes thy footstool. (When did this happen?) ³⁶ **Therefore let all the house of Israel know assuredly, that God hath made that same Jesus, whom ye have crucified, <u>both Lord and Christ</u>.** Christ defeated the devil in the underworld, now you who receive him will experience what his presence really mean ... **1 John 4:4 (NKJV) ⁴ You are of God, little children, and have overcome them, because He who is in you is greater than he who is in the world.**

What happen when Christ rose from the dead?

Matthew 17:9 (KJV) ⁹ And as they came down from the mountain, Jesus charged them, saying, Tell the vision to no man, until the Son of man be risen again from the dead. Peter, James and John saw him transfigured on the mount of transfiguration but could not speak of this being truth until he literally raised himself from the dead. Therefore, those who receive him as being born from above, will have the right spirit.

What happen at the resurrection?

Matthew 27:52-53 (KJV) ⁵² And the graves were opened; and many bodies of the saints which slept arose, 53 And came out of the graves after his resurrection, and went into the holy city, and appeared unto many. This is the sole of the spirit they died in, not their literal bodies. Though we bury the natural body, the angel assigned to you mark the place your spirit departed as the point of your resurrection. All this at that time becomes spiritual. We come along and pick up the body remains and bury it. That's not going to be raised.

What was Jesus doing in paradise for three days?

Jesus said to the thief on his right ... **Luke 23:43 (KJV) ⁴³ And Jesus said unto him, Verily I say unto thee, To day shalt thou be with me in paradise. 1 Peter 3:19-20 (KJV) ¹⁹ By which also he went and preached unto the spirits in prison; 20 Which sometime were disobedient, when once the longsuffering of God waited in the days of Noah, while the ark was a preparing, wherein few, that is, eight souls were saved by water.** He paid the price to get all that died under the law dispensation freed from the sin so they can be received in heaven when he rose.

Where was paradise located? This is what Paul saw.

2 Corinthians 12:2-4 (KJV) [2] **I knew a man in Christ above fourteen years ago, (whether in the body, I cannot tell; or whether out of the body, I cannot tell: God knoweth;) such an one caught up to the** <u>third heaven.</u> [3] **And I knew such a man, (whether in the body, or out of the body, I cannot tell: God knoweth;)** [4] **How that he was** <u>caught up into paradise,</u> **and heard unspeakable words, which it is not lawful for a man to utter.** Paul was having an Enoch experience beyond his level of comprehension that cannot be explained to a natural man that he could understand and what he heard and saw could not be told on Earth at that time. **AMEN**

HELL, IT'S REALITY!

Biblical background:

Matthew 7:21 (NASB77) ²¹ "Not everyone who says to Me, 'Lord, Lord,' will enter the kingdom of heaven; but he who does the will of My Father who is in heaven. Luke 6:46 (NASB77) ⁴⁶ "And why do you call Me, 'Lord, Lord,' and do not do what I say? Matthew 7:22-23 (NASB77) ²² « Many will say to Me on that day, ‹Lord, Lord, did we not prophesy in Your name, and in Your name cast out demons, and in Your name perform many miracles? ²³ "**And then I will declare to them, 'I never knew you; DEPART FROM ME, YOU WHO PRACTICE LAWLESSNESS.' Psalm 18:5 (NASB77) ⁵ The cords of Sheol** (Hell) **surrounded me; The snares of death confronted me. Revelation 3:17 (NASB77) ¹⁷ 'Because you say, " I am rich, and have become wealthy, and have need of nothing," and you do not know that you are wretched and miserable and poor and blind and naked, Revelation 3:16 (NASB77)** ¹⁶ ‹So because **you are lukewarm**, and neither hot nor cold, I will spit you out of My mouth. Revelation 3:19 (NASB77) ¹⁹ 'Those whom I love, I reprove and discipline; be zealous therefore, and repent. 1 Peter 4:17 (NASB77) ¹⁷ For *it is* time for judgment to begin with the household of God; and if *it begins* with us first, what *will be* the outcome for those who do not obey the gospel of God? Isaiah 5:14 (NASB77) ¹⁴ Therefore, (Hell) Sheol has enlarged its throat and opened its mouth without measure; And Jerusalem's splendor, her multitude, her din *of revelry*, and the jubilant within her, descend *into it.***

As American's, under a covenant with God to be the protector of Israel, because of the pride of living in a nation that has accorded us with the ability to create idols to serve that has changed the way we live and serve God. In my observations, pride has created a state of delusion in heightened imaginations; we do not have a reality view of our state as a nation, a people and a sound view of Christianity as a nation that was supposed to be the light of all nations as dedicated to Christianity by evangelizing the world. Instead, we have become blinded by our prosperity teachers that have changed our mindset to materialism that have become our pursuits and our gods. Although many will not admit this, that's the delusion we choose to deny. The love of money and precious things have brought us to this state of luke-warmness. With all these new doctrines, it's evident we have not only lost our way but as confessing Christians, our first love. This is what God has to say to us now in this generation … **Revelation 2:4-5 (KJV) ⁴ Nevertheless I have *somewhat* against thee, because thou hast left thy first love. ⁵ Remember therefore from whence thou art fallen, and repent, and do the first works; or else I will come unto thee quickly, and will remove thy candlestick out of his place, except thou repent.**

We are in the times Daniel prophesied about in **Daniel 12:4 (NASB77) ⁴ "But as for you, Daniel, conceal these words and seal up the book until the end of time; many will go back and forth, and knowledge will increase."** This is how the devil used the seminary system to turn the pulpit assembly into a forum of knowledgeful speakers and entertainment, producing fruit contrary to that of the Holy Spirit. Knowledge is good only if you act on the truth of it that is inspired by the Holy Spirit to profit you eternal life. Lack of convictions will put you in that category of lukewarmness, **2 Timothy 3:7 (NASB77) ⁷ always learning and never able to come to the knowledge of the truth.** This new way of preaching the gospel seemly appeals to our intellect rather than our heart. The evidence of these new assembly teachings, there's no standard of holiness. **1 Thessalonians 4:7 (KJV) ⁷ For God hath not called us unto uncleanness, but unto holiness.**

I have had the liberty of these times to see how God's ways are not discernable if you are not in his state of mind. I have not had any dreams or visions as to these writings, therefore in him I have a sense of what he is doing by direct revelation. This experience has changed my whole view of scriptural biblical revelation by hearing his voice clearly as he speaks. That does not make me special, that's just the way he chose to deal with me according to the revelations of the times we are living. Many that teach on the bassist of dreams, it's evident that there is a point of deception, many are not scripturally sound. God is not saying anything he has not said in the prophets of old; He's just interpreting what they said about what to look for in our generational times.

In the Jeremiah 33:3 zone of knowledge, God chooses who he will share it with. That does not make you or me all that special because having this type of relationship, you can still end up in hell if I do not obey. **1 Corinthians 13:2-3 (KJV)** **² And though I have *the gift of* prophecy, and understand all mysteries, and all knowledge; and though I have all faith, so that I could remove mountains, and have not charity, I am nothing.** **³ And though I bestow all my goods to feed *the poor*, and though I give my body to be burned, and have not charity, (Love) it profiteth me nothing.** Just remember what Satan told Jesus in the wilderness … **Matthew 4:8-9 (NASB77)** **⁸ Again, the devil •took Him to a very high mountain, and •showed Him all the kingdoms of the world, and their glory; ⁹ and he said to Him, "All these things will I give You, if You fall down and worship me."** These are they in the judgement, boasting about their wonderful works in this scripture … **Matthew 7:22-23 (KJV)** **²² Many will say to me in that day, Lord, Lord, have we not prophesied in thy name? and in thy name have cast out devils? and in thy name done many wonderful works? ²³ And then will I profess unto them, I never knew you: depart from me, ye that work iniquity.** 'They did not recognize that man's reorganization of the assemblies under Satan's influence, sent them into the wilderness and they took the bait. That's how we got to bring in the hirelings in the corporate chartered assemblies under the 501C-3.

This is what I was made to see about HELL that confessing Christians that go there, guilty of the unconfessed sins of omission as in Galatians 5:19-21 will experience.

Warning, the content below may be overwhelming and fearful to the faint hearted.

As confessing Christians, based on your sins, Satan will create a special place in hell for those who find themselves in the second judgment. Those demons that enticed you will torment you as a reward of their victory over you in the world for eternity.

- The nature of the unconfessed sins that brought you there as a confessing Christian, will become a torment to horrible to describe, you will experience sevenfold throughout eternity.

- False preachers and teachers will have a special place of torment in Satan's hall of liars. A special sect of demons will torment you as a liar to horrible to describe.

- Those who fail to preach the whole council of truth in true holiness and compromised the truth in their assemblies, will experience hellfire and damnation along with the congregation of demons that sent you there to be tormented seven-fold in the lake of the flames of fire for eternity.

- In Galatians 5:19-21 of these sins, those guilty in the second judgement will be tormented by these demons while confined to a 3 by 7 cell, with a bed of embers heated seven times hotter than any fire known to man on earth and you will feel that pain for eternity. These demons suffer the torment of being in hell, but you, coming from flesh will fill the pain of the torment these demons will inflict upon you from eternity to eternity.

This is what awaits those in that luke-warm state. As for the sinners, their torment will be as their father the devil, sevenfold the torment of hellfire in their 3 by 7 cells on their bed of embers tormented by the demons they entertained that brought them there to spend eternity. I have watched some of the videos on You Tube of those who testified of a hell visitation. Many have different accounts of this experience. There is no comfort in having to write such horrible things to be told to this last generation. I have been made to see what grace and mercy is regarding us in God's sight. This is truly a time of self-examination for all of us that name his name. May God have mercy on all that call upon his name in repentance. AMEN (completed for print 8/2021)

A TIME OF NATIONAL CRISIS

"Words of warning series"

Scriptural background:

1 Thessalonians 5:3 (KJV) ³ *For when they shall say, Peace and safety; then sudden destruction cometh upon them, as travail upon a woman with child; and they shall not escape.*

Looking at the world through the eyes of God, I can see why men who walked in this office as a prophet or messenger of God, felt so much grief in what you are able to see from the spiritual perspective. What is happening in the exodus of **Afghanistan** by our actions, represent the reality of the curse of the sins of this nation returning to destroy us for attempting to police and control the world. That's not in the covenant we made in the founding of this nation as trusting in the one true God. Our problem that's returning in all these defeats at the hands of third world nations is the fact that we had no business being there medaling in their affairs. Especially the middle eastern nations.

They are nations that play a part in bible prophecy. Their linage goes back to Abraham; therefore, any gentile nation that set foot on their soil that is not in their linage prophecy, will go down in defeat. They have the mark of Cain on them to be used throughout time in God's predestination to carry out what he has set in motion before the world begin. This is what the Lord said to Cain when he was banished from his presence as a child of the devil? *Genesis 4:15 (KJV)* ¹⁵ *And the LORD said unto him, Therefore, whosoever slayeth Cain, vengeance shall be taken on him sevenfold. And the*

LORD set a mark upon Cain, lest any finding him should kill him. These are some of the hidden mysteries to be revealed by and through his prophets and messengers at the appointed time in bible history. This is where we have become a victim of history we choose to ignore. Every nation that has tried to take over nations in that area have fail because you will be trying to change history, set in motion by God. Those who inhabit that area of the world are being used to balance the powers of evils that will come out of these warring faction as a result of tribal end-fighting among themselves for sectors of territories they seek to control.

This is what God set in motion that those who fled from the split at the Towel of Babel will do as time progressed as separate tribes, tongues and kindreds. What God wanted us to know is revealed in the word by the Holy Spirit. He is our teacher, guide and link to heaven, if you choose to ignore him as your teacher, you will not go back with him because that's where he will return to and if you have obeyed his instruction here on earth that allowed him to use your vessel to do what God sent him to do in your temple, you get to go back with him.

The Holy Spirit was sent to this nation to show the world what a new nation as gentiles conceived in the liberty to release the Holy Spirit will have the same covenant on them as Israel in their conception to be favored by God. That's that Abraham blessing we have on us AS A GENTILE NATION RAISED TO AID GOD'S PEOPLE to return to national status as a nation. We voted for them to become a state in 1948 in the UN. Since this is an area where these tribes have been at war since the days of Abraham; naturally, they were going to attempt to change what God set in motion and go to war again in 1967 with his chosen and once again, Joshua's angels will be call upon again to aid the tribe of Judah in victory that would result in them regaining the Abraham land grant in what we know today as the Gaza strip, which included their capital city of Jerusalem. Biblically, they are now a recognized nation as a result of that war.

Any nation that has interfered with this end-fighting was never successful in taking land in these territories. England, Russia, and now America. God promised Hagar that He would bless her seed from Abraham as in Ismael and the subsequent seeds born after the deaf of Sarah. All these seed are what's the end-fighting is about for four thousand years. They are all trying to acquire a birth right they will never have because they are not the chosen. They just have the same father but different mothers. That land will produce a bounty that will fuel other countries' economies. That's that promised fulfilled. All outsiders have gone down in defeat that have attempted to take their land. God never intended for any nation to interfere with what he was doing in that area and what we now see is our pride and military strength go down in utter defeat for trying to defy what God set in motion. If we were conscious of this history as a Christian nation, we would have never entered in these wars. Our first warning came in **Vietnam**, we did not see the handwriting on the wall, so now we are being crushed so our enemies can see what we have become as an arrogant prideful nation. *Proverbs 16:18 (KJV)* [18] *Pride goeth before destruction, and an haughty spirit before a fall.* Now President # 46 will become the fall guy as a victim of bible history that has caused the blood of all these young soldiers to sacrifice their lives in vain.

These are the young men that has cause me to weep in prayer every time I hear of another batch of lives being lost on enemy soil that carried a curse when they put their boots where they should not be. In our Pride, we overstepped our bounds to become the world's policemen. Therefore, God blind our military leaders to ignore the war lessons learned in military schools like West Point that has confounded all military reasoning and logic as to why we let something like this happen to us. Ronald Regan said this during his time in office, **"If we as a nation choose to ignore our God, we will be a nation gone under."** Another Lincoln moment in history as a president. Now the time of judgement is upon us with no way to escape. All our war fighting military hardware is in the enemies' hands, left in their possession to where we cannot return even if we wanted too. After twenty years, our soldiers are war weary and broken.

We have created an economic burden as these veterans, maimed and wounded in these vain wars have become a burden too big for the government to properly administer. After twenty years in the last of these vein causes, we have exhausted our economic resource capabilities to rebuild our own infrastructure with multiple national disasters. Now the **"prince of the power of the air"** (the spirit of the antichrist is about to set up his assault) by cyber espionage will dismantle our infrastructure from with-in to take us over without a fight. The details of what they have planned is in the chronicle's titles… **"The Epic View of WWIII and During the Tribulation Siege."**

God has had me in this wilderness preparing me for the past thirty-two years to preach the everlasting gospel to gather the harvest to be reaped in this last coming revival. 98 percent of the church divided by denominations and cults, will be turned over to the world they refuse to let go as in the days of the exodus. Some of their children will take their places as their hearts, captured in traditional Christianity as parents, sacrificed them to the world for these creature comforts and put a burden on them to mortgage a future they will never see. God is not going to hold them responsible for our hypocrisy but have mercy on them as in the exodus.

God is calling their parents to repent before the door is closed. I have seen the face of many the church has failed to reach and pray daily for their preservation. They are ready to hear something that will give them some hope during all this chaos. God is preparing their hearts for that day he has planned to harvest this end time residue of souls to replace those that are rejecting this word to come and sit down at the table in their place at the marriage supper of the lamb. They are the pimps, prostitutes, murderers, dope addicts, prisoners, homeless, scums of this world, and the hopeless. Their hearts are ready to hear what God has prepared them to receive that will take their places along with your children.

Remember, the reason why sin seem so rampant is because of the Sodomy curse, and a church compromised by worldly programs that has contributed to this famine of the pure word. What we see is Satan being released in his strongholds in the form of selected diverse natural disasters, murder, mayhem and finally releasing a de-population pandemic on the world to collect all the souls he can through the spirit of fear in the world. Viruses such as this in modern times must be manufactured, using this forbidden technology as a military weapon, in the hands of evil megalomaniac's German scientist we were supposed to destroy after WWII, which had residues of the Nephilim DNA, contributing to the coming end of this time as in the days of Noah because what they have planned, if God did not intervene, we would become a godless society as in some of these science fiction movies.

The tribulation ahead that will take seven years to complete will bring us into a new time continuum of the last millennium. We are now entering a stage of the battle for your soul. As always, examine yourself and repent. God allowed our assembly doors to be closed to get our attention for the last time. If you want to know why God keeps us to himself, the state of our apostacy is of such, God knows that they are not worthy of our presence as we will become the martyrs of our time to preach the doctrine of Jesus Christ that will bring the latter rain to those who have been prepared to hear it. May God have mercy on all that call upon his name. AMEN (8/2021)

THE TRUTH ABOUT CHRISTMAS

Scriptural Background

Jeremiah 10:1-4 (KJV) [1] *Hear ye the word which the LORD speaketh unto you, O house of Israel:* [2] *Thus saith the LORD, <u>Learn not the way of the heathen</u>, and be not dismayed at the signs of heaven; for the heathen are dismayed at them.* [3] *For the customs of the people are vain: for one cutteth a tree out of the forest, the work of the hands of the workman, with the axe.* [4] *They deck it with silver and with gold; they fasten it with nails and with hammers, that it move not.*

I am beginning to see the numbers "11" on the clock right on the hour I look at the time. After many times, it began to get my attention that God was sending me another sign relating to the numbers that led to the year of my first release of the chronicled writing, the year 2011. Now to give you some background into generations of this long-standing heathen practice and the origin of its original roots that have the whole world under captivity, we must know the **Deep State's** agenda as described in my chronicles. This root of Roman Catholicism was a compromise under **Constantine** that allowed them to keep their pagan practices while claiming to accept Christianity. Since they were the dominant rulers during that time he embraced Christianity, naturally, he wanted to keep some of his long-standing pagan practices.

Now what I am about to explain to you in a very simple way is the reason men like me are mostly tolerated than believed. I have experienced much rejection in striving to speak truth from a biblical standpoint. We are the ones that were persecuted and killed under the old covenant. Since God does not change the way he does things, as in … *Malachi 3:6 (KJV)* [6] *For I am the LORD, I change not; therefore ye sons of Jacob are not consumed.*

We who are called in this latter time, will suffer the same fate. That's why in the end, our lives will be separated unto him to prepare to deliver the testimony of Jesus Christ. Receiving truths like this by direct revelation is very intimidating to those who get to know you by your convictions. Not that I have arrived at perfection, this is just by acting in faith on his spoken word.

Roman Catholicism as we know it came from the transformation of the old fallen state of an unconquered empire that revived itself by a vision from Satan to become a new religious state. It will be known as the Roman Catholic church and state in the form of a new world religion with-in its own nation. As a country, it will be administered by a puppet government at the behest of a well-organized **Deep State** form of religion that will embrace all religions of the world and be allowed to set up its roots in every nation and begin to implement its agenda of world domination. As a form that will become known as the **false prophet**; its mystery will be revealed in the book of revelation to the last generation in its captivity. *Revelation 12:9 (KJV)* [9] *And the great dragon was cast out, that old serpent, called the Devil, and Satan, which deceiveth the whole world: he was cast out into the earth, and his angels were cast out with him.* This is what I was raised up to reveal at this time that will cause me to suffer what it's like to bring a message to an apostate confessing Christian world. That 98 percent you read about in my chronicles.

Our Paganism in the practice of Christianity

The Romans had statues of all their pagan gods; therefore, what **Constantine** did, added all these pagan holiday practices into to the practice of his newfound Christian religion that is not recognized as bible truth that God accepts. Their new form of worship will transform these statues into saints in the bible that will take their place. Therefore, all who in the name of Christianity that keep such pagan holidays and bow down to these idol gods, are not accepted as true Christians in the sight of God. Now I know how hard it will be to change generations of these traditions of pagan practices. It took ten years to persuade my wife to forsake these traditions to complete her salvation from the world. That was a priority as her husband and priest of my home. I got out of the way and put God's word to the test and let patience run its course until the changed came. After that, I wanted to become her Abraham by having my faith increased. It took fifteen years later to hear her tell all that knew me, this is my Abraham.

I must be direct in declaring this truth as inspired by the Holy Spirit. All those who continue to practice paganism as confessing Christians are committing the sins of omission, if you do not repent, you are judging yourself unacceptable to enter the kingdom. *Galatians 5:19-21 (KJV)* [19] Now the works of the flesh are manifest, which are these; Adultery, fornication, uncleanness, lasciviousness, [20] ***Idolatry, witchcraft, hatred, variance, emulations, wrath, strife, seditions, heresies,*** [21] Envyings, murders, drunkenness, revellings, and such like: of the which I tell you before, as I have also told you in time past, that they which do such things ***shall not inherit the kingdom of God***. Those that are underlined cover the sins of omission that leads to idol worship that takes God's place in your application of truth.

The Real Meaning of Christmas

These national holidays that represent what the world has come to accept as their practices are to be compared to what is accepted by God as a confessing Christian. Santa is Satan spelled backwards which represents worldly materialism, the desires the lust of the eye, the flesh and the prides of this world he can give you if you worship him … *Matthew 4:9 (NKJV)* [9] *And he said to Him, "All these things I will give You if You will fall down and worship me."* He is the spirit of bondage that visits those in captivity at that time of the year to decorate the world as you see, during that time of year. It has nothing to do with Christ birth biblically. **Now get this**, *the true meaning of Christ birth is celebrated when he was resurrected in you the day you were born again from above.* That was the day you received all things freely from Christ and now commissioned to give to others that which money cannot buy. He then becomes someone you worship 24/7 not just on one day out of the year. That's why Jesus rebuked his own people for keeping traditions that took his place. *Mark 7:8-9 (NKJV)* [8] *"For laying aside the commandment of God, you hold the tradition of men--the washing of pitchers and cups, and many other such things you do."* [9] *He said to them, "All too well you reject the commandment of God, that you may keep your tradition. Hebrews 4:1 (NKJV)* [1] *Therefore, since a promise remains of entering His rest, let us fear lest any of you seem to have come short of it. Matthew 15:11-12 (NKJV)* [11] *Not what goes into the mouth defiles a man; but what comes out of the mouth, this defiles a man."* [12] *Then His disciples came and said to Him, "Do You know that the Pharisees were offended when they heard this saying?"* So have I with these teachings. That's what will happen when you tell the truth from the biblical standpoint of what God will require of all to enter heaven.

Now on the national front

The only comfort I get out of what I know as being re-taught by the Holy Spirit of God, is to know I am in his perfect will. It takes him in me to maintain my stability and sanity as to what I have been given to know about these coming events that can no longer be changed through prayer. What makes it so grievous to the point of lamentation, is to see the church and the world agreeing as one in their actions. Now, I am beginning to see the number "11" again, all hours of each day, that **one, one** represents the judgment of the Jews, and the Gentiles are at hand. In previous chronicles, I mention the number "46" as the president that would begin the judgment of this nation as the return of number "44," the spirit of Obama's presidency. This will be the second stage of the release of the Jezebel spirits to be recognized as in the LBGT movement now can come out of hiding and take their place as the laws are changed to include them under #46.

It will only add to the stench in God's nostrils to speed up the judgment and reveal a mystery that will cut short time, not only for this nation that has made it legal to give them a platform. This declaration has guaranteed our extinction as the Modern Babylon as did the Babylon of old but this time by fire and water as the curse of Sodom and Gomorrah in the coming meteorite asteroid. This will be in the from a splintered asteroid on its way to hit the western hemisphere as in the Movie, **"Deep Impact;"** with **Morgan Freeman** as **President.** They have been my visions from the Hollywood movie of what it will be like. There will be no escape as in the movie **"2012."** This will be the crossover at the end of the tribulation as in the days of Noah of a new time continuum. I am not a conspiracy theorist; I interpret what the lord will have us to know at this time. I write this out of God's love for you that have ears to hear what the Spirit of God is saying to the church; REPENT! Therefore, I was led to increase my daily prayers as an intercessor. There are too many souls being lost in this fear battle.

Those of you with some money in the bank, before the blackout, as God has blessed you, begin to remove hundreds in denomination of $5, 10, 20 and some 100's over the next two-month period. Store water, canned goods, beans, rise and carbohydrates. This will be used to help fellow Christians as in the days of the apostles. Your obedience is what will help save you from the chaos that will get you killed if you are on the streets. Daily prayer will bring your angels to protect you. There will be no place for safety but in the lord as you prepare to be taken out of this world.

Our lives are about to take a drastic change for the worse. All of you that have taken at least two doses of the Covid vaccine as a confessing Christian, have delivered your temple into the hands of the enemy of your soul through fear, will suffer a horrible death in this next linked mutation of this virus designed to have an Ebola affect that will begin the process of reducing the world's population in millions. The return of the fallen angel DNA that is controlling this Cabal of these megalomaniacs are at war in these men. There are two factions of angelic forces in the spirit at war in a power fight among themselves that's causing a rapid increase in the timeline. The DNA in the sect of angels that caused the flood, are warring with Satan and his angels for the control of the earth. The world is entertaining angels in the form of human beings. That's why we see evil becoming worse and worst. That's the hidden mystery of the **Seven Thunders** in Rev. 10:4 that John was told not to write in the book of Revelation that could not be revealed to mankind until he finds himself deceived to this degree.

Don't be frightened as a Christian, that's how many have lost their souls. I know these are hard words, but we are at the end of time. These angels in the earth in the form of men are what's causing this rapid increase in evil. These are some of the mysteries withheld from the church by not being taught the whole council of the truth that reveals the third layer revelations of the spirit world. To further increase the fear factor, their hackers will take down the power grid for an indefinite period. The Ma Gog division of angels control by Satan, will start the third world war operations through the antichrist communist armies of Russia and China. They will begin their assault on the world. When they have destroyed millions of the remaining world population, the asteroid on its way will impact in the western hemisphere. Seventy percent of all Americans will die or about one hundred and ninety million. Somewhere in between, the rapture will take place, or else no flesh will be saved. God' hand will destroy these two factions of warring angels or else they would destroy planet earth. (Received 12/26 2021 @ 7:20 AM)

A WORD FROM YOUR
END TIME MESSENGER

I am not a 501c-3 ministry. Therefore, I have asked no one for any support. I used my pensions and home equity to finance the publishing of these books and to give to them in need as did the apostles. Those who believed that these messages are from the lord in love are the ones I will receive an offering from. Some of you spiritually as to let you see what I was made to see when God opened my ears to hear and eyes to see what I am relaying to you. Any offering I receive goes to the benefit of helping the publishing of these books and newsletters. Most of you have given to religious corporations to help these hirelings seminary trained men build their family earthly kingdoms that have deceived you by not telling you the truth.

If you do not believe in what is being told to you is truth, I don't need your money. I live like the apostles from day to day and month to month, Praying and interceding for many souls I will never see that have been deceived by false teachers that have led the church to be in this state of apostasy, have led to the closing of your assembly doors by not knowing what spirit that assembly was under, when we went there to hear what we thought was truth. Truly our love for God is now being tested. *1 John 4:18 (NKJV)* [18] *There is no fear in love; but perfect love casts out fear, because fear involves torment. But he who fears has not been made perfect in love.*

I am not a conspiracy theorist, I was called and set apart to interpret the signs of the times. These are detailed insights to my existing chronicles, relevant to the times that over a seven year period, separated to God to write the end time hidden revelations to this last generation.

This message will reveal the coming catastrophic events surrounding the wars taking place in the spirit world that represent the third layer of the whole council of the word we all fail to see. There are many things I could not put in print because we do not have a spiritual foundation to receive knowledge as was told to Enoch in his time. The degree of spiritual darkness has put the church in this state for not taking a stand against these principalities when they begin to show themselves by changing the constitutional laws to legalize their actions, manifested in human beings linked to angelic DNA as the evil we will see in man.

What I have prepared and revealed in the coming chronicles will tell you the rest of the story. The fact that God is using these unknown nobodies like me to reveal these hidden mysteries, locked in the word of truth, is to judge yourself by these things we were not told in our assemblies to this degree that represent that third layer of the revelation of Jesus Christ; which is to guide you through the evils in this world that only he can keep at bey to preserve you by living in the reality of ... *1 John 4:4 (KJV)* *4 Ye are of God, little children, and have overcome them: because greater is he that is in you, than he that is in the world.*

The word Christmas

Now let's divide this word out and you will see why I said that this day we celebrate has nothing to do with Christ birth. Let's go back to the pagan practices of serving other gods. This pagan holiday incorporated Christ as the Christian's saint in their annual <u>mass</u> celebration. This was their festival of gift giving, blessings and good will and offerings to their gods; get the picture. **Constantine,** as a confessing Christian, incorporated Christ as the heavenly saint Christian's worshiped. That's when it became CHRIST-<u>MASS</u> DAY. It has no reference to the time or his date of birth. When you believe a lie, you will live a lie. *Revelation 21:8 (NKJV)* *8 But the cowardly, unbelieving, abominable, murderers, sexually immoral, sorcerers, idolaters, and <u>all liars</u> shall have their part in the lake which burns with fire and brimstone, which is the second death."* If we choose to ignore that fact which makes us a partaker of their evil deeds, all those who keep such pagan holidays, are judged with the world; no matter how good, we think we are ... *2 John 1:11 (KJV)* [11] *For he that biddeth him God speed is partaker of his evil deeds.*

Now about the spirit world: (Another Enoch moment)

Hebrews 13:2 (KJV) [2] *Be not forgetful to entertain strangers: for thereby some have entertained angels unawares.* I will use this verse again to open your mind to how God brought me into this revelation of angels in the form of human beings. Remember, in the spirit world, God created all things as the supreme ruler of all things seen and unseen. The angels he created to send in the world to be among humans, was here for only one purpose, to record the deeds of man before the law as their names were written in the book of life; we all will have to give an account of. That was a special class of angels, separate from the ones assign to Satan. They were to stand in the judgement as a witness for or against your conscious of righteousness before the law was given. They stand around the throne of God and had the knowledge of all things of God and heaven. That's God's spirit in Adam that gives you a sense of right and wrong.

Under Cain's linage, was some of the most beautiful women to walk the face of the earth. Remember, he is the first child of Satan born of his seed, Satan was the most beautiful angel in heaven. Now, through Cain, produce some of the most beautiful daughters in the natural to walk on the face of the earth. These women were as perfect as women can get in the natural body. They were as angels with the ability to procreate but were of Cain. Their beauty attracted these angels in the form of men to leave their first estate, **(Jude 1:6)** take on human form so they could marry them. What they were doing is what was going to become the great mystery that had to be withheld from the world until the last generation at the end of man's time (the sixth millennium) to rule the earth. This is the mystery withheld in the seven thunders of **Rev. 10:4.** God knew mankind as natural creations, born in his sin image, would not be spiritually prepared to receive such a revelation, in an apostate condition by divisions in our beliefs. This revelation, when revealed, would make science fiction a reality when we learn there are aliens living among as UFO as angelic beings when they become known as the return of the Nephilim DNA in man to us by the technology they introduce to the world.

As you can see, this revelation of two sects of angels is now at war at the end of days in the spirit world that is causing these things you see in the natural world to speeding up time. It is creating all this fear by the things they have developed through their evil nature. This return of fallen Nephilim angelic DNA is rising to take their last stand to gain the world and create a heavenly utopia on earth. When I received this revelation, it was like seeing myself in the middle of a science fiction movie, hidden mystery truth, revealed in the bible for us at this time that have ears to hear it and a mind to receive it. To generate more fear and chaos, they will shut down all power and communication for an indefinite period soon to bring in the cashless society. Great fear will cause many to commit suicide to where God will have to bind that spirit to punish them that contributed to killing Christians. All debts will be cancelled. When the system comes back up, if you have not been vaccinated, you will not be able to buy of sale anything. Many will be taken to camps for the unvaccinated to die after you have been given that final dose.

We gave our technology to China in our greed for more wealth, in exchange for cheap labor, we have given our enemy the means to shut our nation down without a fight through cyber warfare. God gave them this vision to take us down as delivering us into the hands of our enemies for forsaking him as in history of his people Israel when they departed as his nation. They engineered a back door in these smart chips that enabled them to shut down everything that has one of these chips at the push of a button through our GPS system. They can now shut down cars, trains, electrical grids, cell phones, etcetera. This is the work of the illuminated ones with fallen Nephilim DNA. One thing that is unknown about this technology, they can cause accidents that can kill in masses.

The technology and biological weapons created by these humans with angelic Nephilim DNA, known as the **illuminated** ones or **illuminati'** in human form, are in our military deep cover black opts secret divisions creating and funding the research to bring about the reduction of the world's population by inoculating them with these biological vaccines linked to your DNA that will bring a slow death over a short period of time. They are linked to breakdown the body in these ways through DNA linked attacks as they mutate through the body such as the first strain will attack the lungs with a severe form of inflammation, blood clots, myocarditis arrythmias, leukemia and multisystem failures that cause death. While new mutant strains will cause the weakening of your immune system. Many children after vaccination will get sick because of corrupt DNA. Expectant mothers vaccinated; their children may manifest developmental problems. The elites will make a public show of inoculating themselves with the cure shot to keep them immune, just as you saw what happen when President Trump was infected. People didn't notice how fast he recovered.

This was to generate an acceptance to get the general public to take the deadly strain that will begin to mutate when it is introduced unto your body and activated by DNA links to previous vaccinations. It cannot be stopped because the more boosters you get, is to ensure that those who have a strong immune system will be overtaken by these constant recommended injections that will have an effect at some point later. It takes up to ten years to formulate a vaccine that will work with your body chemistry to do good. These are the ones you were given when you were born that last up to fifty years. That's why those over fifty get Shingles because that's the life span of the vaccine. The antidote is usually formulated before the vaccine is released. This I learned while working in two world renowned medical research institutions. The **Deep State** controls the media.

Your assemblies will be operating at normal capacities. This is the word I was sent all over the state of Arizona to give to 153 churches in 2005 … *1 Peter 4:17 (KJV)* [17] *For the time is come that judgment must begin at the house of God: and if it first begin at us, what shall the end be of them that obey not the gospel of God?* In God's timing, was delayed fifteen years. Now let me distinguish these two sets of angels you see manifested in this natural world. The Ma Gog principalities are the angels that rebelled with Satan when he was cast out of heaven. Their spirits are dominant in countries with antichrist freemason administrations. Those of you who took the oath to become a Masons, your soul is under the captivity of the brotherhood of Satan. If you do not renounce this link, you will be sent to the lake of fire with him no matter how much good you have done.

Many of the organizations that fund private hospitals are run by some of these lodges as part of their well-organized non-profit programs. These are some of the continents they have a strong hold in that are preparing for the third world war … *Ezekiel 38:1-7 (NKJV)* [1] Now the word of the LORD came to me, saying, [2] «Son of man, set your face against Gog, of the land of Magog, the prince of Rosh, Meshech, and Tubal, and prophesy against him, [3] and say, ‹Thus says the Lord GOD: «Behold, I am against you, O Gog, the prince of Rosh, Meshech, and Tubal. [4] I will turn you around, put hooks into your jaws, and lead you out, with all your army, horses, and horsemen, all splendidly clothed, a great company with bucklers and shields, all of them handling swords. [5] *Persia, Ethiopia, and Libya are with them, all of them with shield and helmet;* [6] *Gomer and all its troops; the house of Togarmah from the <u>far north</u> and all its troops--many people are with you.* [7] *"Prepare yourself and be ready, you and all your companies that are gathered about you; and be a guard for them.* [8] *After many days you will be visited. <u>In the latter years</u>* (This is where we are now <u>in these latter times</u>. These battles in the spirit are being manifested in the earth at this time, is being waged by those sent to destroy mankind.) *you will come into the land of those brought back from the sword and gathered from many people on the mountains of Israel, which had long been desolate; they were brought out of the nations, and now all of them dwell safely.*

(God will shelter the people to be saved for the millennium before they are attacked. *Isaiah 26:20 (NKJV)* [20] *Come, my people, enter your chambers, And shut your doors behind you; Hide yourself, as it were, for a little moment, <u>Until the indignation is past.</u>* All the remaining middle eastern nations will join with Russia and China as stated in the verses below. The rapture will happen at some point or else the saints would not survive.

Ezekiel 39:1-7 (NKJV) [1] *"And you, son of man, prophesy against Gog, and say, 'Thus says the Lord GOD: "Behold, I am against you, O Gog, the prince <u>of Rosh,</u>* (Russia and China will be the ruling powers used by Satan at that time.) *Meshech, and Tubal;* [2] *and I will turn you around and lead you on, bringing you up <u>from the far north</u>, and bring you against the mountains of Israel.* [3] *Then I will knock the bow out of your left hand and cause the arrows to fall out of your right hand.* [4] *You shall fall upon the mountains of Israel, you and all your troops and the peoples who are with you; I will give you to birds of prey of every sort and to the beasts of the field to be devoured.* [5] *You shall fall on the open field; for I have spoken," says the Lord GOD.* [6] *And I will send fire on Magog and on those who live in security in the coastlands.* (These are the elites as seen in the **"2012"** movie, their sheltered places will become their graves.) *Then they shall know that I am the LORD.* [7] *So I will make My holy name known in the midst of My people Israel, and*

I will not let them profane My holy name anymore. Then the nations shall know that I am the LORD, the Holy One in Israel. Israel will repent and the city of David will be spared for Christ return.

When will World War three begin?

After they crash our economy, we will be reserved as their last battle of the war effort. They will start their assault in the European countries first, when they begin their assault on America, that's when the asteroid will hit the western hemisphere as the Sodomy curse is carried out with fire and water. The details are described in, **"What Will Happen During the Tribulation Siege."**

When the asteroid hit the western hemisphere, the force of that impact at 6,000 mph, volcanos will erupt all over the world, rising tides will take out the shoreline of every nation in the world and some the smaller nations below sea level, will be lost under water as overcome by these giant waves. It will be part of the reorganization of the earth's geography. This is our days of Noah. *1 Thessalonians 5:3 (NKJV)* [3] *For when they say, "Peace and safety!" then sudden destruction comes upon them, as labor pains upon a pregnant woman. And they shall not escape.* The above scripture is the next layer of the mystery of the false peace treaty. This peace treaty you hear about will be the last attempt to preserve the world for these Illuminati elites that are trying to take over the earth. We are going into a new time continuum. There is nowhere you can hide because this is God, rising out of his sabbath rest ... *Matthew 24:20-21 (NKJV)* [20] *And pray that your flight may not be in <u>winter or on the Sabbath</u>* 21 *For then there will be great tribulation, such as has not been since the beginning of the world until this time, no, nor ever shall be.* In his anger, will once again judge the evils of mankind as in the days of Noah. Now you see what it is to be caught in God's break, shaking without the power because of false teachings. Now do you see why no one chooses to carry a message like this. *John 6:44 (NKJV)* [44] *No one can come to Me unless the Father who sent Me draws him; and I will raise him up at the last day.* (Part II Received 12/28/2021 during my prayer time meditation)

NOW THE COMING EPIC VIEW OF WORLD WAR THREE

Introduction:

I wrote this version based on what I can see that is set in motion by the current administration's action that is contributing to this becoming an eminent possibility. I felt led to incorporate this into becoming a fitting ending to these chronicles that all who read this will have a full understanding of what's in store for all Americans. Many of us in the western world are unaware of the eminent circumstances we find ourselves in at this point in biblical history. The church world no longer believe God still raise up prophets and messengers as he did in the Old Testament. The evils in the world are turning nations against nation to war as stated in the scripture below. Treaties for peace are being broken, creating hostile international relationships. America is in the middle of a nuclear mushroom in the hands of our enemies, China and Russia. God holds the power when to let them pull the final trigger to bring about the collapse of this world and time as we know it. The Christian church, in division, for the most part, is under a grand delusion. This grand state of delusion will be the sudden destruction that will affect the whole world, except for His elect.

What will come as a result of this willing ignorance, will cause all that is described in biblical history to be fulfilled in this end time generation. Scripturally, here's how it will all go down. Nations will be pitted against one another to … **Mark 13:8 (NKJV)** [8] For nation will rise against nation, and kingdom against kingdom. And there will be earthquakes in various places, and there will be famines and troubles. These are the beginnings of sorrows. (The increases in natural disasters here and in other countries, are the signs we are willingly ignoring. America's economic crash … *Revelation 18:19 (KJV)* [19] *And they cast dust on their heads, and cried, weeping and wailing, saying, Alas, alas, that great city, wherein were made rich all that had ships in the sea by reason of her costliness! for in one hour is she made desolate.* (This is where our enemies will come to take the spoils.)

The invasion

Joel 2:4-7 (NKJV) [4] **Their appearance is like the appearance of horses; And like swift steeds, so they run.** [5] **With a noise like chariots Over mountaintops they leap, Like the noise of a flaming fire that devours the stubble, like a strong people set in battle array.** (These are the invading forces) [6] **Before them the people writhe in pain; All faces are drained of color.** (This will be the surprise when the people see them coming.) [7] **They run like mighty men, they climb the wall like men of war; Everyone marches in formation, And they do not break ranks.** This is the demonic army of Russia and China as the Gog & Magog curse coming from the north to fulfill this prophecy … **Ezekiel 38:15 (NKJV)** [15] **Then you will come from your place <u>out of the far north,</u> you and many peoples with you, all of them riding on horses,** (Tanks in our time) **a great company and a mighty army.** (All these middle eastern tribes will band together with the northern armies of Russia and China to begin their assault. Because we defied the word of the prophets and messengers by saying) … **Jeremiah 5:12 (NKJV)** [12] **They have lied about the LORD, and said, "It is not He. Neither will evil come upon us, nor shall we see sword or famine.** This is the pride in those that say, **"we are going to take back America and make her great again;"** great fear will be in the land. Man, in his brute beast nature to survive will turn on his own blood like Cain on his brother … **Matthew 24:10 (NKJV)** [10] **And then many will be offended, will betray one another, and will hate one another.** (America, beaten down by these long undeclared middle eastern wars, will put our military leaders in this state … **Jeremiah 51:30 (NKJV)** [30] **The mighty men of Babylon have ceased fighting, They have remained in their strongholds;**

Their might has failed, They became like women; They have burned her dwelling places, The bars of her gate are broken.

Now comes the Sodomy curse on this nation.

This curse under President Obama's watch, changed the laws that released demons from the pit that led to the legalization of homosexuality, was bound by the angel Michael, will begin their assault on this nation by empowering this formerly hidden spirit that reverse the laws of nature. **Isaiah 4:1-2 (NKJV)** [1] **And in that day seven women shall take hold of one man, saying, "We will eat our own food and wear our own apparel; Only let us be called by your name, To take away our reproach."** (These will become polygamist types of marriage agreements.. **Isaiah 3:12 (NKJV)** [12] As for My people, children are their oppressors, and women rule over them. O My people! Those who lead you cause you to err and destroy the way of your paths.» (This represents the reversal of the roles of the two genders, will mark the return of Jezebel's spirit. As a nation and a people, this curse will be twofold in its manifestation; **First,** in the siege ... **Nahum 3:10 (NKJV)** [10] **Yet she was carried away, she went into captivity;** (This is addressing America, being led into captivity.) **Her young children also were dashed to pieces at the head of every street; They cast lots for her honorable men, and all her great men were bound in chains.** (They will kill off all the men left; great fear will be in the land. Famine will be widespread that will cause people to result to cannibalism as you see in these disaster movies and this is what they will do ... **Jeremiah 19:9 (NKJV)** [9] And I will cause them to eat the flesh of their sons and the flesh of their daughters, and everyone shall eat the flesh of his friend in the siege and in the desperation with which their enemies and those who seek their lives shall drive them to despair.» ‹ Ezekiel 5:10 (NKJV) [10] Therefore, fathers shall eat their sons in your midst, and sons shall eat their fathers; and I will execute judgments among you, and all of you who remain I will scatter to all the winds.

The prideful and high-minded

This curse will be upon those, especially those prideful high minded in their earthly palaces to the point not being around anything filthy. Many will be overwhelmed to the point of losing their minds. The conditions will be so hard, like Job said ... *Job 3:25 "(KJV) For the thing which I greatly feared is come upon me, and that which I was afraid of is come unto me".* Women caught in the siege during the war in those days ... *Isaiah 3:24 (KJV) And it shall come to pass, that instead of sweet smell there shall be stink; and instead of a girdle a rent; and instead of well-set hair baldness; and instead of a stomacher a girding of sackcloth; and burning instead of beauty. Isaiah 4:1 (KJV) And in that day seven women shall take hold of one man, saying, we will eat our own bread, and wear our own apparel: only let us be called by thy name, to take away our reproach.*

There will be a shortage of men as a result of these wars. The invading armies will rape the young women left after that have killed off the men. Many, as Christians, caught up in the Barabbas patriot spirit that supported Trump in their delusion to think that they could **"take back America and make her great again,"** had forgotten we are under the sodomy curse that cannot be reversed, will band together to become part of the antichrist church and be killed in great numbers for taking up arms). *Deuteronomy 28:56 (KJV) The tender and delicate woman among you, which would not adventure to set the sole of her foot upon the ground for delicateness and tenderness, her eye shall be evil toward the husband of her bosom, and toward her son, and toward her daughter,* (This is what those who are finicky and proud as spoiled women with Jezebel spirits use to having their way, will be in a condition where you will wear your stinking garments until you die. AMEN

THE MYSTERY OF THE PYRAMIDS REVEALED

"Another Enoch moment"

Hebrews 13:2 (KJV) [2] *Be not forgetful to entertain strangers: for thereby some have entertained angels unawares.*

Historically, these natural unexplained phenomenal wonders of the world all have a story to tell. Their location has something to tell us about why they were constructed on that site. The stone wall with multifaceted shapes in Peru that are cut so precise and large, they didn't need mortar to keep them intact. There are many sites that will never be unearthed because of the tribes or civilization that constructed them had to be made extinct. They had knowledge that bordered on heavenly intellect. They all spoke one language which magnified their capabilities. Scientifically, those that choose to be willingly ignorant of the origin of their own existence are some of those that have become renown in their own arears as experts, deal with thing in the cosmos that can leave you hanging because it cannot be factually proved by today's standards of academia.

These are theories that boarder on the pre-historic existence of things he can't explain that go beyond his ability to comprehend. It has always amaze me when they come up with terms like billions and billions of years or even put a specific date like twenty billion on an origin of a find. The bible states ... *Genesis 1:1-2 (KJV)* [1] *In the beginning God created the heaven and the earth.* [2] *And the earth was without form, and void; and darkness was upon the face of the deep. And the Spirit of God moved upon the face of the waters.* This is the beginning of willing ignorance as being born a child of the devil. What God wanted man to know is written in his word, no thanks to Adam, his use of his free will to act against his creator, caused us all to be born ignorant and on the way to hell. That's because we refused to believe who created us or where our origin begins. God didn't put a number or a time on the creation of the earth; he just stated that he created it.

We are now mindless buffoons of the enemy that gained access to our soul through the first created man-child in the image of his creator, Adam. A child's mind must be developed into the image of what or who he is exposed to. Now if you are born as an evil seed of the devil, how is it that your thoughts can be no other than what he put in your mind to do, sense he now has possession of your soul. You were not created with a thought; therefore, you will have to give an account of who gave you your life, whether you believe it or not. When God brought man to life through his breath, that's when you became a living soul accountable to him as your source and means of existence. He gave you a free will to choose the course of your life. This was Adam before he listens to a condemned angel who once had the power to rule the earth. Though he blamed it on his counterpart Eve, he had the initial responsibility to only listen to his creator. The point I am trying to get the reader to see is, your life here on earth is one big adventure trip that takes you through the valley of the shadows of death with only one way back; that is, to return to the one that created you to give you the ability to navigate through this defiled world by following his instruction to live with him for eternity. That for some, will take a lifetime and yet many will refuse take the invitation to be led out of your worldly wilderness to save yourself from the destiny of the one that led you to go down that road to destruction, death and finally spend eternity in a 3 by 7 cell on a bed of embers heated seven time hotter than any known fire on earth, with the one that led you there. You see, he knew where he and all his co-harts were condemned to go, he just got to take you along as company because you thought you were smarter than the devil without the mind of God. Adam gave our mind to the devil; that's why we can't do right consistently enough to save our soul. He was created in heaven and now with his third of angels that rebelled with him, they get to use our bodies under Adam's curse.

Now let's get to the other sect of angels. ***Genesis 6:1-2 (KJV)*** [1] ***And it came to pass, when men began to multiply on the face of the earth, and daughters were born unto them,*** [2] ***That the sons of God saw the daughters of men that they were fair; and they took them wives of all which they chose.*** What made them so desirable, they were the daughters of Cain. Remember, Satan was the most beautiful angel in heaven before iniquity was found in him that got him cast out into the earth with a third of angels that followed him, they are bound in the second heaven. They are waiting to be cast in the lake of fire in the final judgement. They are the ones that are assigned a body every time a life is born in the earth because of Adam sin.

These daughters of Cain were so perfectly beautiful, they were like angels with the ability to procreate. Their beauty caused this special class of angels to transform themselves into humans that would give them the ability to procreate. This is what came out of the mixture of heavenly seeds with mankind. ***Genesis 6:4-5 (KJV)*** [4] ***There were <u>giants</u>*** (or Nephilim angelic DNA) ***in the earth in those days; and also after that, when the sons of God came in unto the daughters of men, and they bare children to them, the same <u>became mighty men which were of old, men of renown</u>.*** (That knowledge was of a forbidden time Enoch wrote about that could not be known to men in the cross over and neither can I reveal it.) [5] ***And GOD saw that the wickedness of man was great in the earth, and that every imagination of the thoughts of his heart was only evil continually.*** This is what was going to lead up to the flood and the crossover into a new time continuum, called the days of Noah.

When the bible said there were giants, these are some of the residue artifacts found after the flood. They lived in a separate area because of their size. Those that were ordinary human-like, mixed with the population. These illuminated ones changed the culture where they inhabited to the point of exhibiting a dominant presence over ordinary humans. Their intellect was far superior to ordinary men. Moses encountered a residue of them when he sent spies that brought back fruit too large for human consumption. When they began to build cities, speaking one language, they began duplicating things in heaven. Originally being sons of God by origin as created being, their heavenly DNA skills gave them the ability to invent musical instruments we have today, they did not sound like those made by them in their time. Because of their mathematical skills, in the knowledge of the cosmos, the preciseness of what they built was such that these monuments we see that have been left standing and unearth today in our time, have become the wonders of this world. It is this DNA incorporated in humans that has caused God to bring their strong holds where they dwelled to an abrupt end when they would begin to infringe on his timeline by attempting to duplicate what was in heaven.

That's why we see no trace of the tribes that became their stronghold. They are what we are up against in ... *Ephesians 2:2 (KJV)* [2] *Wherein in time past ye walked according to the course of this world, according to the prince of the power of the air, the spirit that now worketh in the children of disobedience:* In our time as having a stronghold of existence in Germany, they attempted to dominate the world by using the angels of Satan to form an army of war mongers to take over where Napoleon left off. This is where God had America and Russia to become allies to stop them that resulted in the division of east and west Germany. What happened after the capture of those involved in war crimes is where the evil nature of the two countries went wrong. They took those scientists back to their home countries and used their technology to develop our military might that pitted the two nations against each other. They were to be captured and destroyed by execution. That's what has contributed to our present state of wars and rumors of wars. They have been allowed to spread their DNA in both countries.

These strands are what we see employed in the various high-tech companies, run by these illuminated ones to gather them together for the final assault. This is where you see the love of many waxed cold. The AI devices they have invented are designed to rob you of your humanity. Their goal in the use of this forbidden technology is to bring all humans under control for the next phase of mass destruction by creating a condition of worldwide fear. The nature of their seed has no regard for human life. That's what was disclosed in the experiments they were conducting in Germany, discovered in the action towards the Jewish tribe. Anyone that comes to the knowledge of the truth of their activity before their final plans was set in place, was covertly eliminated by members of their elite murder squad. We will come to know them as the **Deep State.** These are the residues of their DNA spread around being used by their corporations designed to bring about the technology that has brought us to our present state of control by the devices they have invented, such as the internet, cell phone, sophisticated communication monitoring devices used in your home. Now all they must do is push buttons on their computer terminals to control all aspects of our lives.

Now about the construction of the Pyramids

The history is in the opening of this chronicle. These angels stood around the throne of God as witness judges in the earth. They had the knowledge of God in them as created being. The splendor of the throne room, they were in the presence of **"THE GREAT I AM."** Being sent to judge those born before the law was given was their purpose in the earth as angels among men. They had special powers. We know that under Cain's linage, they were master builders. In the beginning, by marrying and impregnating Cain's daughters, they, having power to **levitate** objects is how they were able to manipulate any element on earth to build what they already had knowledge of in heaven down on earth. **That was in these transformed sons of God**. Now what I am about to tell you is to end the mystery surrounding this great wonder. It was built by them known as Nephilim angels that left their first estate before the flood. When they unearth the Sphinx, buried under the sand, you can still see the receding water marks that are consistent with the water marks on the rocks in the Grand Canyon. The capstone at the top is evident of how long it took for the water to dissolve the outer polished limestone that created a mirror glow image that could be seen all over that area. It was built to stan as a sign of their beginning dominance in the earth.

The reason we can't find any evidence of how these stones were cut and lifted, they used their collective powers of their mind to **cut and levitate** these giant stones into place. This is the residue of their creative powers given to them as they stood around the throne. That's why God repented that he had made man when he saw what they were doing using the bodies of men he created to try to change what he had set in motion as knowing the end of all things ... *Isaiah 46:10 (KJV)* [10] Declaring the end from the beginning, and from ancient times the things that are not yet done, saying, My counsel shall stand, and I will do all my pleasure: This is the mystery Daniel and John could not reveal what they saw . Mankind performing these evils will become the victim of what he does not know that could only be seen when the technology has been developed to bring all these mysteries into reality. That's why all they attempted to build before the flood are some the wonders found by archeologist unearthing these artifacts. Many cities they constructed are buried deep in the earth that are not meant to be found. That's why God did not allow any of Enoch's account of the historical detailed facts that cause the flood to become part of the scripture. If mankind won't believe in God as his creator with God's written account of his origin as his roadmap to heaven, he need not be further corrupted with this knowledge. I am allowed to disclose this to let all read, just who or what we are dealing with that is now causing the end of another time continuum. This is what Daniel saw in his vision, as knowledge increased, (Daniel 12) what will happen through the ages, man in the presence of these evil angels would only succeed in destroying himself without the presence of God on earth in his elects. That's why we are at a stage where that is imminently about to come to pass that … *Matthew 24:22 (KJV)* *²² And except those days should be shortened, there should no flesh be saved: but for the elect's sake those days shall be shortened. Jude 1:6 (KJV) ⁶ And the angels which kept not their first estate, but left their own habitation, he hath reserved in everlasting chains under darkness unto the judgment of the great day.* In the book of Ezekiel chapter thirty-nine is where it all will end. As I have said in time past, it has been my experienced, men like me are tolerated rather than believed and for some without knowing the voice of God, it will be their day of visitation judgement for them. We carry no credentials of credibility by man, we are called and set apart to speak as in the days of the prophets. We are God's spokesmen to help as many as receive us, to make their calling and election sure. Now may the grace of our lord Jesus Christ be with you till the end. AMEN (Completed for release as final warning in these chronicles after 2/2022)

NOW ON THE NATIONAL NEWS FRONT

The state of the American government is now in the hands of God. Our time to reign as a nation is up. We have now come to the point where we have exhausted every resource to where our fall is imminent.

These are the critical points that have brought this present reality by not fulfilling the covenant we made with God as a nation freed to worship the God of Abraham, Isaac and Jacob.

1. We have for the past forty years policed the world's activities through covert CIA operatives.

2. We have overextended our military to ware it down by sending our men to fight in undeclared wars from Korea to Afghanistan that has depleted our economic resources and available manpower.

3. Being a capitalist nation, we have run our course to repeat history through over taxation, greed, corruption and immorality that runs rampant to the point of causing great division in the political divides that have pitted us against our own governments' function.

4. This present state of corruption that feeds on our capitalist greed has given our enemies an advantage by financing our overextended financially burdened economy. We are now the property of our enemy from within by invitation. They are now preparing to come and collect what they now own by our own

willing blindness to think that we were too big as a nation to be taken over by outside forces we invited in as allies.

Now from a Biblical Perspective

Now the numerology of biblical prophecy will become our downfall. These are the numbers I will explain in detail. "911", 3, 7 and 11.

As I mentioned in the outset, we have come to the end of our existence as a nation biblically, given our history which is described as the mystery Babylon of the last generation in our existence as a nation shrouded in biblical history. Now let's get into the numbers.

"911" When we experience this national event on our soil, it will captivate the attention of the world. This is where the Mystery Babylon will be revealed to the world as pointed out in this scripture ... Ezekiel 26:9 (NKJV) 9 He will direct his battering rams against your walls, and with his axes he will break down your towers. That's what happen on our soil September 11, 2001. On that day the towels of modern Mystery Babylon (America) fell. That's why America was never mentioned by name in the bible because we will become the third Babylon shrouded in this great mystery that will mark the end of Nebuchadnezzar's vision of world governments that will complete the time of the end. Now go study the history of Nebuchadnezzar's Babylon and you will see the mystery that will describe America at that time we are to be judged when God sends those Plaines into the world trade center. Those two towels represent the economic stability transaction that controls the world: Modern Babylon. Now that's what "911" represent from a biblical perspective.

The number "3" The next phase will be the activities of the last three presidents that will bring the judgement upon America, #44, 45 and 46. Now let's explain what these three Presidents will do that will effect the whole nation at that time. This number "3" will also represent the next stage of the Earth's transition as we are about to enter the second time continuum of Earth as the judgement signs will show in the natural elements as well as the evil activities performed through evil men.

President #44 Obama will legalize the curse of Sodomy on his watch as king of the free world. This will activate the signs of the times as depicted in Matthew twenty-four. By being the king of the free world, this curse cannot be reversed once legalized. Therefore, our fate is now sealed as that of Sodom of old. The next president #45 Trump will represent the return of the King Cyrus spirit as a nonpolitical leader that ruled Babylon when the Jews was led into captivity. He will be raised up as a sign to the Jews as well as lead this nation into its final judgment being possessed with a narcissistic form of the pride of Nebuchadnezzar that will captivate the minds of apostate evangelicals and patriots that will show their loyalty is to the nation and not to God. Not knowing we were judged under #44's curse, they will try to defy God by saying we will take back America to restore her greatness. His spirit will captivate all who follow him who will be saying all the right things at the wrong time in biblical history that is now gathering all under this grand delusion to be led into captivity as did the days of Barabbas as a Christian patriot and be killed. The Spirits controlling the New World Order, are being used to lead all that are caught-up in this sea of iniquity, currently ruling the world, will perish in the chaos that will cause America's economic fall out of this final election. #46 Biden, brought the second curse by releasing the spirits that were a stronghold in Gomorrah. He is the extension of the spirit in Obama to bring the double judgement on us as a nation. Rev. 18:6

Now the #"7" Biblically, time runs in lifecycles that are repeated so God can let man tract history he can't change. There is nothing new because God has set time in motion to run its course throughout history. (Ecclesiastes 1:9) Just as we had our "911" so will Israel's come on their calendar as November 7,2023. This will be the sign that both nations' judgement will start the beginning of wars. The number "7" currently represent the time cycle of the gentiles is complete. Israels war will be fault by having to take many casualties of souls. The nature of their war will cause all nations to turn against them including the United States for having to defend themselves by taking innocent lives. What the world is blind too will lead to our downfall by turning against Israel. God has no regard for people who try to take out his chosen people. Therefore, they will have to do what Josuah did, kill all that took up arms against them. Therefore, the families of these warring tribes against them will be destroyed along with the enemy soldiers. Now this is the reason why America will be destroyed without remedy; we only exist to protect Israel from her enemies. The day we cease to do this, we will no longer exist as a nation because that was our only purpose under the gentile age we were preserved to do. The world in a war state will be the condition that will lead to the third and final world war.

Now the #"11" This represents the Jews and the Gentiles have now had their wake-up judgement call. The two are as one now becomes "11-7". The Jews and the Christians now must get ready to be glorified as God's chosen by entering tribulation to prepare to be taken out in the rapture as the two becomes one as on the day of Pentecost. In Revelation 11:11 after Israel has completed their visitation of the two witnesses, all will be gathered by the sickle angel in Rev. 14:15-16 at that time. To read the details of the full account that will lead up to the rapture, read the chronicle "Revelation, The Final Layer Revealed"

A WORD FROM THE LORD

(Time is no more)

"Thus Say the Lord" *"<u>The time has come to judge the world</u>,* **1 Peter 4:17** *"(NKJV)* [17] *For the time has come for judgment to begin at the house of God; and if it begins with us first, what will be the end of those who do not obey the gospel of God?* I am walking in the earth, selecting those that will be used to do the exploits as I did before Pharaoh in Moses. Those who <u>dwell in my tabernacle,</u> are in prayer before me to examine yourselves, for all the vein things outside of my word. Those who worship me in spirit shall see my glory and my power within them for their obedience. <u>I am not interested in your sacrifices;</u> I'm judging the state of your heart. The enemy of your soul has come up before me to accuse you of your <u>sins of omission</u> to justify taking many souls. I have opened the door for all that love me to examine yourself and do your repenting before the time to deal with <u>man of whom I created</u> is cut off. Just as I had to sacrifice my chosen who left Egypt but was found not worthy to enter the promise land because they forgot all that I had done for them, so have many of you that name my name. I gave them space to repent but they continued to rebel against my servant Moses, so <u>I left them there to die</u> after I showed them who I AM. I am your God; besides me there is none other. These things were written in my word to let you know who "I AM;" the God of Moses who led them out of bondage and because of their hard hearts, left them to die in the wilderness and raised up Joshua to lead their children into the promise land. Take heed, <u>as I have warned you through my messengers,</u> less I find you in that same state and you also will be left to be judged with the wicked. You see by the signs in the earth, <u>Hell is being enlarged</u> as I shake this earth as I did in the days of Noah. <u>A great majority of you are not</u>

prepared spiritually for the judgment that cannot be changed; you have become the land of Sodomy. Once again, I must do battle with the enemy of your soul to preserve my earth. Take heed that none of you that name my name fall into the hand of the enemy as those in the wilderness that loved the pleasures of sin, were left to die in that state. These things were written for you that you might know that I am a just God, and I change not. I am patient and long suffering that all that have this hope will be given a chance to repent. So, as it was in the days of Noah, it shall soon be again. Thus say the Lord"

I expect to receive much controversy and outright rejections from these chronicles revealing what we all fail to see as a confessing Christian in a divided nation. God has reserved a few of these unknowns in the wilderness to use for his return in glory to be revealed in the exploits they will do in the latter rain. This mystery is as stated in … ***Isaiah 43:19-21 (KJV)*** [19] ***Behold, I will do a new thing; now it shall spring forth; shall ye not know it? I will even make a way in the wilderness, and rivers in the desert.*** [20] ***The beast of the field shall honour me, the dragons and the owls: because I give waters in the wilderness, and rivers in the desert, to give drink to my people, my chosen.*** [21] ***This people have I formed for myself; they shall shew forth my praise.***

I have outlived two wives to be in this place currently. I now understand why I had to have these experiences; the lord used them to teach me. I am now the lord's free servant. We are the messengers in the spirit of John the Baptist that will preach the everlasting gospel that will arrest the attention of the world in the Elijah showdown as Christ returns in the fullness to take his church and the residue of his people home to heaven. AMEN 5/2021)

Your End time messenger sent from God
Steven B Riddley

THE END

www.ingramcontent.com/pod-product-compliance
Lightning Source LLC
Chambersburg PA
CBHW020914140626
46545CB00015B/1